THE COLNE VALLEY & HALSTEAD RAILWAY

CV&HR carriage and wagon maintenance staff stand in front of 4-wheel passenger brake van No. 4 at Halstead. Courtauld's chimney rises high in the background.

M. Root collection

An Edwardian view at Halstead station with a family lined up for a group photograph in front of a 6-wheel coach, although the boy is more interested inspecting the carriage. CV&HR 0-4-2T No. 1 – with bell-top chimney, polished dome and auxiliary side tanks – waits to depart with the Up train to Chappel.   *M. Root collection*

THE COLNE VALLEY
& HALSTEAD RAILWAY

PETER PAYE

Lightmoor Press

© Peter Paye and Lightmoor Press 2022

Designed by Nigel Nicholson

British Library Cataloguing-in-Publication Data. A catalogue record for this book is available from the British Library

ISBN 9781 915069 06 1

LIGHTMOOR PRESS

Unit 144B, Lydney Trading Estate, Harbour Road, Lydney, Gloucestershire GL15 4EJ

www.lightmoor.co.uk

Lightmoor Press is an imprint of Black Dwarf Lightmoor Publications Ltd
Printed in Poland; www.lfbookservices.co.uk

ABOVE: LMR '2MT' 2-6-0 No. 46467 rounds the curve away from Chappel Junction with the 5.20pm Walton-on-the-Naze/5.27pm Clacton-on-Sea to Cambridge train on Sunday 7th July 1957.
G.R. Mortimer

FRONT COVER: A timeless and busy scene at Halstead as Hawthorn, Leslie & Company 2-4-2T No. 2 *Halstead* waits to depart with a Haverhill to Chappel service, although passenger seem in no hurry to join the carriages. The locomotive carries the large C V initials on the side tank each side of the nameplate, whilst the headcode depicts a stopping passenger train.
Painting by Malcolm Root

Contents

Introduction 7

1 Advent of the Railway 9

2 Opening to Traffic 19

3 Completion to Haverhill 29

4 Halcyon Years 43

5 World War One and After 59

6 Grouping Under the L&NER 73

7 Nationalisation and Closure 85

8 The Route Described 101

9 Permanent Way and Signalling 177

10 Officers and Railway Staff 203

11 Timetables and Traffic 209

12 Locomotives 241

13 Coaching Stock 269

14 Wagons 277

Appendices

1 Level Crossings 285

2 Bridges 287

3 L&NER Amended Bridge Mileages, 1939 290

4 L&NER Amended Level Crossing Mileages, 1939 . . 291

5 CV&HR Appendix to the Working Time Book, 1905 . . 292

Bibliography 310

Acknowledgements 310

Index 311

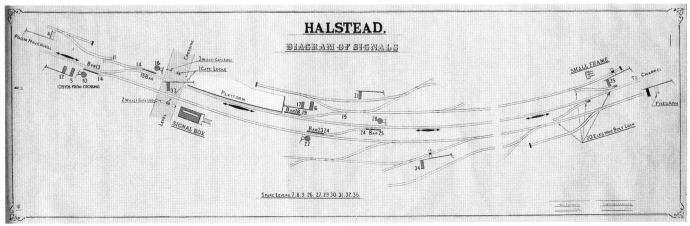

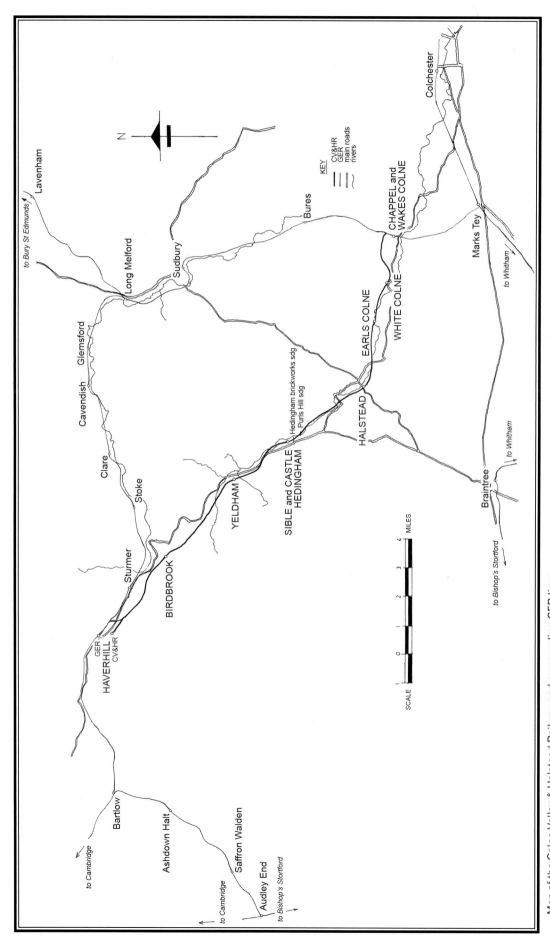

Map of the Colne Valley & Halstead Railway and surrounding GER lines.

Introduction

A SUMMER AFTERNOON IN THE EARLY 1950s at Marks Tey, the busy junction on the former Great Eastern main line from London to Ipswich and Norwich. A semi-fast train has just departed on the Down main line and two 3-coach trains stand at the curved bay platform providing connecting services to various destinations in rural Essex, Suffolk and Cambridgeshire. As the sound of the main line train recedes, platform staff bustle to get the first branch train away on its journey. A final look round, carriage doors are closed, the guard signals to the engine crew and after a short resounding whistle the train sets in motion. As the service disappears round the curve a slightly rotund and perspiring clergyman, complete with small case, appears on the platform gasping for breath, bemoaning the fact that he had wanted to catch the departing train in order to attend an important engagement at one of the Cambridge colleges that evening. The platform staff assured him that all was not lost and gently persuaded the minister to join the train standing at the platform. Slightly protesting and ill at ease, he entered the carriage on being reassured by the guard that all was well. However, learning the destination of the train was Haverhill his doubts returned. *'At least it's nearer Cambridge.'* The train thus departed with the worried priest, who settled down to enjoy the journey as best he could. After further questioning of the guard who reassured him not to worry, the next hour was whiled away contemplating the pleasant rolling Essex countryside, with its meandering river, in isolation for few passengers joined or departed from his train at the seven intermediate stations. After almost an hour's journey the train pulled into Haverhill with the cry of *'All change.'* Descending to the platform our clergyman was bemused when the engine and stock shunted into a siding, leaving him wondering what the next move would be. Within minutes an engine whistle was heard as another train approached the platform. The friendly guard reappeared ushering the puzzled reverend on the train. In the short time that followed the guard explained *'You can thank the Colne Valley for the rescue'*, and went on to say the train he had missed at Marks Tey was the train he was now joining for the continuation of the journey to Cambridge and his important engagement. The Stour Valley train had travelled the 28 miles via Sudbury and Long Melford whilst the Colne Valley train had cut across country the 22 miles via Halstead and reached Haverhill minutes before the other arrival. On the continuing journey to Cambridge the clergyman offered up a silent and grateful thanks for the Colne Valley train and its staff.

The Reverend Gentleman was not the only soul to benefit from the two railways crossing rural East Anglia in close proximity to one another, and indeed 'those in the know' often took the short cut on the Colne Valley train, instead of using the longer Great Eastern route, in order to spend the extra few minutes with friends and acquaintances or enjoy an extra half pint at the local hostelry. But why provide two railways in such a bucolic location, with few important towns and villages? The answer lay, as with many schemes, in the nineteenth-century dread of isolation from the developing and expanding railway system. The Colne Valley & Halstead Railway genesis came as a result of the silk weaving and manufacturing town of Halstead being ignored, despite being included in the grandiose titled Colchester, Stour Valley & Halstead Railway incorporated on 26th June 1846, to build a railway from a junction at Marks Tey, on the Eastern Counties Railway from Shoreditch to Colchester, to the market and silk weaving town of Sudbury at the head of the Stour Valley with a branch to Halstead. After a perilous infancy it was initially leased to the Ipswich & Bury St Edmunds Railway and in 1847 extensions to Clare and Bury St Edmunds were authorised. These were nullified when the Eastern Union Railway, which was constructing a line from Colchester to Ipswich, absorbed the Bury St Edmunds Company and pressed for a line from Stowmarket to Sudbury. The ECR management were concerned that by taking such action the EUR was invading its territory. The Sudbury line opened in July 1849 on a 999 years lease to the EUR and the proposed Halstead branch was abandoned. The ECR, however, took over the EUR commitments in 1854.

Halstead businessmen were distraught at the isolation and indeed from neighbouring Braintree, which had enjoyed railway status since 1848 being connected to the main line at Witham. Plans were prepared in 1855 to connect Halstead with Braintree but the CSV&HR, EUR and ECR objected. With such opposition the local dignitaries withdrew and proposed building their own railway along the valley of the Colne to connect with the Stour Valley line at Chappel some 3 miles north of Marks Tey. Little opposition was raised and the Colne Valley & Halstead Railway received the Royal Assent in 1856, authorising the building of a line from Chappel to Halstead. Construction duly commenced, and bolstered by success the 13¼-mile extension from Halstead to Haverhill was authorised 13th August 1859. The first section to Halstead, opened on 16th April 1860, initially met with severe opposition from the ECR, who resurrected plans for an extension of the Stour Valley route to both Bury St Edmunds and Cambridge via Long Melford. The CV&HR, undeterred, pressed on and the short distance from Halstead to Hedingham opened 1st July 1861. Encouraged with progress the directors sought to extend beyond Haverhill to Saffron Walden and Audley End and later to Cambridge, there to connect with the London & North Western Railway with the possibility of a takeover or, at the least, running powers. Progress on the authorised line continue with the opening to Yeldham on 26th May 1862 and finally to Haverhill Colne Valley station on 10th May 1863, from where the company established a horse-bus connection to the university city. Futile attempts were also made to extend to Colchester and to prevent progress of the competitive extension by building branches from Birdbrook to Clare and Wixoe.

In the meantime the ECR had merged with several other East Anglian companies to form the Great Eastern Railway, incorporated by Act of Parliament on 7th August 1862, which reiterated the ECR extensions to Bury St Edmunds and Cambridge. During the building of the line to Halstead the ECR treated the CV&HR with contempt but by clause 274 of the GER 1862 Act of incorporation the company was empowered to operate the Halstead Company if the CV&HR directors so desired. The GER reached Haverhill from Shelford, south of Cambridge, in June 1865, and a connecting spur was opened to the CV&HR by August. By now relationships between the two companies had vastly improved, the Cambridge horse-bus service was withdrawn, and thereafter the majority of CV&HR passenger trains ran to Haverhill GER station to provide connections with GER services and the Colne Valley station was used for goods traffic, except for early morning and late evening passenger services which continued to use the facilities.

The CV&HR directors had quickly realised their line was now almost entirely reliant on the GER with control of the junctions at both end of the railway. In early days the company was constantly short of finance and during 1865 the line was worked by Sir Daniel Gooch of Great Western Railway fame, while in the following years it was taken over by Charles Brogden Sperling for expenses only. A motley collection of motive power included locomotives from the ECR, London, Brighton & South Coast Railway and former Cornwall Minerals Railway. A Cornish entrepreneur kept alive the affairs of the concern whilst rolling stock was purchased and owned by individuals. The line never generated sufficient traffic to cover the capital debt and the inevitable bankruptcy followed in 1874, the company remaining in the hands of the receiver until it was rescued by an Act of Parliament in 1885 which was highly critical of mismanagement and dictated the future direction of the undertaking. Some semblance of order was restored, new locomotives were ordered and delivered and certainly after 1903 when Elyot Hawkins of the Cambrian Railways became General Manager the company became a respectable railway maintaining close liaison with the GER when through coach working to Marks Tey was established. The small locomotive workshop at Haverhill was transferred to Halstead in 1906 and thereafter day-to-day rolling stock repairs were effected in the minor workshops. Hawkins even obtained second-hand bogie coaching stock from the Metropolitan District Railway which became the pride of the line.

Many applications were made by the CV&HR directors to sell out but the GER constantly refused takeover as on several occasions inspections revealed the poor condition of the permanent way, and rolling stock left much to be desired. The GER continued to keep the CV&HR at arms length, citing clause 279 of the 1862 Act whereby in lieu of takeover the company afforded as much assistance as possible. Thus, over the years as well as offering through booking facilities and allowing running powers to Marks Tey, the major company also supplied permanent way and signalling material, and provided works and heavy maintenance on CV&HR locomotives, and carriages and wagons if required, as well as offering the benefit of engineering and commercial expertise. The CV&HR board, however, persisted in their attempt to have the GER absorb the company and as late as 1914 threatened to take the case to the High Court. World War One intervened and the CV&HR directors subsequently negotiated with the GER board regarding terms of takeover under the grouping in 1923.

Burgeoning traffic from the silk industry at Haverhill and Halstead, together with brick traffic from Hedingham and engineering commodities, kept receipts buoyant and in 1919 revenue was £36,656 – but passenger traffic was always moderate and suffered with the introduction of competitive bus services after 1914. Rising expenditure and increase in staff costs after World War One almost crippled the organisation, but a ten per cent reduction in wages in 1921 for a year and the withdrawal of winter Sunday services helped ease the situation. Grouping under the L&NER from July 1923 could not have come sooner for the company was experiencing insoluble problems and although the CV&HR had surrendered its identity to become another minor branch line, local staff were patriotic and to the end never yielded to becoming GER, L&NER or even BR personnel, but *'Colne Valley and proud of it'*.

The new regime made gradual changes: Haverhill CV&HR was closed to passenger traffic on 14th July 1924; motive power and coaching stock with a few exceptions was quickly replaced by GER engines and carriages; track was improved and a general tidying up completed. Halstead works and depot were closed although a locomotive and two sets of men were retained at Haverhill until the withdrawal of steam traction. Excursion traffic was maintained, as were the Sunday services, whilst World War Two brought heavy military and armaments traffic, especially to Earls Colne and Birdbrook to serve several United States Air Force bases. After the war, traffic declined as competitive bus services were increased and the motor lorry removed much of the light goods and parcels traffic. Nationalisation with British Railways from January 1948 initially brought few changes but Hedingham brick traffic was exhausted by the early 1950s and although the branch passenger trains had been extended to and from Marks Tey there was insufficient traffic to retain the Sudbury and Colne Valley lines serving the same tract of country. The cost-conscious BR management constantly investigated ways of reducing costs and with a view to economy, diesel multiple units and diesel railbuses took over passenger working from September 1958, operating in some cases through services to and from Cambridge. Steam traction was then eliminated from the freight workings and diesel locomotives hauled the dwindling traffic scheduled to run on weekdays only, but were often cancelled at short notice by lack of commodities. Traffic reductions continued and after the obligatory Transport Users Consultative Committee inquiry passenger services were subsequently withdrawn on and from 1st January 1962, when the line was also closed completely from Yeldham to Haverhill Colne Valley Junction. Freight continued mainly to cover the completion of existing contracts until facilities were withdrawn from Yeldham and Sible and Castle Hedingham on and from 1st December 1964. The truncated section between Chappel and Halstead retained traffic until 19th April 1965, when the line was closed completely bringing to an end 105 years of service to the public. A small section of preserved railway on the original track bed has been established by local enthusiasts near Sible and Castle Hedingham and several artefacts from the original line are on display. I have attempted to trace the fascinating and often tempestuous history of the CV&HR from conception to closure and details have been checked with available documents, but apologies are offered for any errors which might have occurred.

Peter Paye
Bishop's Stortford

Post Script: The Colne Valley & Halstead Railway was not always in the ecclesiastical good books, for when it commenced running trains on the Sabbath the local clergy complained bitterly the action would result in lost congregations and in consequence lost souls! The company later expiated the situation at the turn of the 19th and 20th centuries, when it proudly conveyed many wagons of bricks from Hedingham, which were used on the construction of upward of sixteen churches in north London!

1

Advent of the Railway

THE EASTERN COUNTIES RAILWAY was incorporated on 4th July 1836, with a share capital of £1,600,000 to build a 126 mile line from Shoreditch in East London to Norwich and Yarmouth via Colchester, Ipswich and Eye. All but £58,100 of shares had been sold by September and there was great concern that only a twelfth of the total share capital raised was of local origin. In late March 1837 construction commenced at the London end only, as incomplete negotiations with landowners prevented a concurrent start planned between Norwich and Yarmouth. The troubles continued as landowners along the route of the proposed railway demanded high compensation. By October 1838, forty per cent of the capital had been called but only nine miles of railway were under construction. With creditors pressing, only urgent action prevented total ruin, and in April 1839 Lancashire proprietors, who had taken a large stake in the undertaking, forced the decision to terminate the line at Colchester.

The first public trains ran from a temporary terminus at Mile End to Romford on 20th June 1839, with extensions each end to Shoreditch and Brentwood opening for traffic on 1st July 1840. In the meantime the ECR directors called in Robert Stephenson for engineering advice, but he could only confirm that a further £520,000 was required to complete the railway to Colchester. Mutinous shareholders were almost bludgeoned into meeting the call for shares whilst application to Parliament for further £350,000 share capital was made in 1840. With the combined assets and borrowing powers sanctioned by a further Act in 1840, construction of the final section was possible. Inclement weather in 1841 caused delay and damage to earthworks, but eventually the line was opened to Colchester for goods traffic on 7th March 1843 and for passengers on 29th March 1843. The 51-mile line had taken seven years to construct at a cost of nearly £2½ million and the works at £1,631,300 had exceeded the original estimate for the whole project from London to Yarmouth.

The decision of the ECR to terminate its project at Colchester was a matter of grave concern to the merchants of Ipswich and Norwich, who were fearful of isolation from the expanding railway network. A number of ECR shareholders in Suffolk and Norfolk, alarmed at the slow progress and decision of April 1839 obtained a decree nisi in the Bail Court to force the fulfilment of the company's contract with the public, but this was nullified in 1840 when Parliament refused to extend the ECR powers beyond July of that year. Undaunted local factions then planned a railway linking Norwich with Yarmouth, and this was enacted in 1842, to be followed the next year by a projected line from Norwich to Brandon. Such developments caused further consternation to Ipswich traders and businessmen, and these were aggravated by the ECR planning a possible extension to join up with the Norwich and Brandon line at Thetford, with the main line by-passing Ipswich altogether.

Representations against such proposals fell on deaf ears and so the merchants and tradesmen of Ipswich produced their own scheme for a line linking the town with the ECR at Colchester,

based on plans submitted by Peter Schuyler Bruff of 22 Charlotte Street, Bloomsbury, London, who had already worked on surveys for the initial ECR route. The leading advocate was John Chevallier Cobbold, from the wealthy Ipswich banking and brewing family, who was a member of the original ECR Board of Directors. As well as connecting Ipswich with Colchester the promoters of the scheme also intended to pursue the idea of a railway running north to Norwich and a new company entitled the Eastern Union Railway received the Royal Assent on 19th July 1844. The railway to Colchester, 17 miles in length was designed by Joseph Locke, with Peter Bruff, who had moved to Ipswich as Resident Engineer.

Meanwhile the ECR route to Thetford was abandoned but a group of businessmen in Bury St Edmunds were concerned their town would also be isolated from the expanding railway network and suffer further economic depression. In February a deputation met Directors of the ECR but found they were unwilling to extend their line beyond Colchester. The townsfolk were thus forced to promote their own line – the East & West Suffolk Railway – and were advised the EUR would not oppose such a venture, provided the route went from Bury St Edmunds to Ipswich via Hadleigh and did not interfere, with the direct line from Ipswich to Colchester. After the Railway Department of the Board of Trade had made a special study of the railways in Suffolk and Norfolk, the report published on 4th March 1845 gave full support to the EUR scheme to Ipswich and for the extension to Norwich.

North of Ipswich the tract of land towards Bury St Edmunds duly received the attention of railway developers and on 21st July 1845 the Act authorizing the Ipswich & Bury St Edmunds Railway received the Royal Assent. With an initial capital of £400,000 the new concern appeared nominally independent but was, however, an extension of the EUR, boasting no fewer than six EUR directors out of a total of fifteen board members. The Ipswich & Bury Railway also occupied the same head office at Ipswich and had the same Engineer, Secretary and contractor as the EUR.

On Monday 1st June 1846 the EUR had opened for goods traffic from Ipswich to Colchester pending the official Board of Trade inspection. General Pasley conducted this on Thursday 4th and the official opening took place on 11th June 1846. Passenger traffic commenced on and from 15th June, by which time £240,000 had been expended on the works between Ipswich and Colchester. The Bury St Edmunds to Ipswich line was constructed quite rapidly and the official opening took place on Monday 7th December 1846, with passenger services commencing on Christmas Eve.

The ECR, however, had not abandoned the goals of Norwich and Yarmouth, but had taken the first steps to reach Norfolk via an alternative route. On the same day the ECR was incorporated, a rival company – the Northern & Eastern Railway – received the Royal Assent to build a line over the 53 miles from Islington to Cambridge financed by a share capital of £1,200,000. The N&ER, like the ECR, soon encountered financial difficulties and it was 1839 before construction commenced, and even then only with the sanction of the ECR. To conserve finances the N&ER route was diverted from Tottenham via Stratford, where running powers were permitted into the ECR Shoreditch terminus. Like the ECR, the new line was built to a gauge of 5 feet and despite abandonment of the route north of Bishop's Stortford by Act of Parliament in 1840, had reached the Hertfordshire market town on 16th May 1842, at a cost of over £23,000 per mile. In 1843 the N&ER secured an extension Act for a line to Newport, some 10 miles nearer Cambridge, but on 22nd December of that year the ECR agreed terms on a 999 years lease for the company from 1st January 1844. Once the lease was in force the ECR lost no time obtaining powers linking Newport to the Norwich & Brandon Railway at Brandon via Cambridge and Ely on 4th July 1844. The N&ER line, along with the existing ECR line, was converted to standard gauge 4 feet 8½ inches in the late summer of the same year and, after a formal opening the previous day, the entire line from Bishop's Stortford to a temporary terminus at Norwich (Trowse) commenced public service on 30th July 1845.

In 1845 an ambitious scheme, the Chelmsford & Bury Railway, was proposed linking the two towns via Braintree, Bocking, Halstead, Sudbury and Lavenham. The 39-mile route was estimated to cost £750,000 and shares were mooted at £25 each but the venture failed to gain support and met its demise in March 1846. The Maldon, Witham & Braintree Railway obtained its Act of Parliament (9 Vict cap lii) to connect the two towns with a flat crossing of the ECR at Witham on 18th June 1846. Then an independent promoter gave notice in the Parliamentary session for 1846 of the intention to apply in the next session for powers to extend the Witham to Braintree branch to Halstead, but again the proposal was doomed with insufficient financial backing.

The area north of the ECR Colchester main line was not abandoned, for on 26th June 1846 the Colchester, Sudbury & Halstead Railway received the Royal Assent (9 &10 Vict cap lxxvi) authorising the building of a line commencing at Marks Tey station of the ECR in the County of Essex, five miles south west of Colchester, to Sudbury in the County of Suffolk, with a branch to Halstead together with a branch railway from the Eastern Union Railway in the Parish of St Michael, Mile End in the Borough of Colchester to The Hythe in the same Borough. The statute authorised the raising of £161,250 in £25 shares with £32,360 loans to finance the scheme. Intermediate stations on the Sudbury line were planned at Chappel and Bures. A triangular junction at Marks Tey was originally proposed but the spur joining the main line on the London side of Marks Tey was never built. The Engineer was Peter Bruff and the contract for construction awarded to George Wythes at a price of just under £100,000. Wythes divided the work into sub-contracts under his agent John Jackson. The ECR had initially opposed the scheme by promoting a rival line to Bures and the Stour Valley from Lexden, nearer their Colchester terminus, but this was withdrawn.

The Stour Valley Company approached the Ipswich & Bury Railway to work the railway and a 999 years lease at an annual rent of £9,500 was negotiated and subsequently authorised by the Act of Parliament (10 and 11 Vict cap xxi) dated 7th June 1847. Meanwhile, by the Act of Parliament (10 and 11 Vict cap xi) of 8th June 1847 the Stour Valley company obtained powers to build an extension from Sudbury to Long Melford and Clare, with a branch from Long Melford to Lavenham. A further Act on the same day (10 and 11 Vict cap xviii) authorised the company to build an extension from Lavenham to Bury St Edmunds. The Eastern Union Railway was ahead of the game and absorbed the Stour Valley Company by

the Act of Parliament (10 and 11 Vict cap clxxiv) dated 9th July 1847 and the terms were revised when the EUR paid a rent equal to the guaranteed minimum of 5 per cent on £83,000 together with a guaranteed minimum of 3 per cent on the running costs of the railway. Whenever the EUR paid its own 'B' and 'C' shareholders more than 5 per cent, an equal sum was to be paid on the £83,000 capital and whenever those shares received more than 3 per cent, then an equal rate was to be paid on the remainder expended on the line, but in no case more than 6 per cent. Thus by default the EUR had gained possible access to large swathes of Essex and Suffolk much to the chagrin of the ECR management.

The CSV&HR obtained running powers over the ECR between Marks Tey and Colchester, but the company under its contractor's agent Jackson succeeded in constructing only 12 miles of single track railway between Marks Tey and Sudbury, with intermediate stations provided at Chappel and Bures. The works included provision for a second line of rails if traffic developed. On 30th May 1849 a directors' special formed of two coaches ran to Sudbury to be greeted by a peal of church bells and the line opened to traffic on 2nd July 1849 with the first train operated by the EUR conveying the official party from Colchester, with the Mayor of Sudbury joining at Marks Tey. The journey rook less time than expected and although a great crowd of people were waiting at the yet unfinished station with bells pealing and flags flying, the passengers arriving at Sudbury by the directors' special train after a short round of speeches were left to meander round the town until lunch was ready. The day was not without incident for the triumphal arch erected for the occasion at Marks Tey was dislodged by the locomotive, which conveyed the laurels, woodwork and other decorations festooned round the chimney and dome throughout the journey to Sudbury!

The railway between Marks Tey and Sudbury crossed the valley of the River Colne by Chappel viaduct; originally a timber structure was planned but Peter Bruff in a paper to the Institution of Civil Engineers advocated the low cost of a brick viaduct at £21,000. The viaduct was subsequently built for double track and had a total length of 1,136 feet with a maximum height from foundations to rail level of 80 feet. There were, and still are, thirty-two semicircular arches of 30 feet span and the line is on a 1 in 120 rising gradient from south to north, each arch having a springing point 3½ inches above the previous arch with a total rise of 9 feet 6 inches. Eighteen of the piers are on mass-concrete foundations with the remainder on brick footings. George Wythes found adequate good brick earth clay locally; construction commenced in July 1847 and was completed by the spring of 1849. The final cost was £32,000 and 7 million bricks were used on the construction.

The short branch, 1½ miles in length, constructed from the Eastern Union Railway near Colchester to the Hythe – which was the limit of navigation on the River Colne, forming the harbour for Colchester – was opened as early as 31st March 1847. The first train ran the following day, when a *powerful engine* traversed the line conveying ten wagons with 200 quarters of malt and grain and about 30 tons of coke up to Colchester station.

By an indenture of lease dated 1st July 1852 between the Stour Valley Company and the Eastern Union Railway, made under or by virtue of the powers of the CSV&HR Lease Act 1847, and an Act to amalgamate the Eastern Union and Ipswich & Bury St Edmunds railways and of the EUR Railway Arrangement Act of 1852 (15 and 16 Vict cap cxlviii) of 1st July 1852, the undertaking and premises of the Stour Valley Company were demised to the EUR on a 999 years lease from at an annual rental of £9,500. The EUR workings

An Up train hauled by a 'J15' Class 0-6-0 crossing the Colne Valley viaduct en route to Marks Tey. As one railway guide reported: 'travellers arrived at the only feature of importance which this branch presents namely Chappel viaduct, an erection of which at the height of 80 feet crosses the valley of the River Colne by 32 arches each 30 feet in span and the whole admirable for the manner wherein great strength is combined with extreme simplicity of structure and considerable economy in the skilful disposition of materials.' Author's collection

were then taken over by the all-powerful ECR on and from 1st January 1854 under an agreement made on 19th December 1853 and retrospectively sanctioned by the Act of Parliament (17 and 18 Vict cap ccxx) of 7th August 1854, although the company was not officially liquidated until 1862.

By the early 1850s Braintree was benefiting as a major marketing centre because of its 1848 railway connection to the ECR main line. Disappointed with the failure to provide a railway to Halstead, local factions entertained the proposal to resurrect the scheme to connect the town with Braintree. On 23rd August 1855, however, the ECR directors notified their intention of opposing the building of a line from Halstead to Braintree, and later the Stour Valley Company added their objection. The promoters were left in no doubt as to the outcome if matters progressed and fortunately wiser counsels prevailed. The Halstead to Braintree plans were aborted in favour of a railway from Halstead to Chappel connecting with the Stour Valley line. On 18th October 1855 the ECR authorities promised to let this scheme advance. Notice of intention was placed in the *Chelmsford Chronicle* for three weeks and once in the *London Gazette* on 1st November. Copies of the plans and sections prepared by Messrs Bruff and Beardmore were duly deposited with the Clerk of the Peace for Essex at his Chelmsford office on 30th November. The bill was sent to the Parliamentary private bill office and to the parish clerks of the various parishes through which the proposed line was routed on the same day.

To counteract opposition, copies of plans were sent to two landowners, Robert Hills and H.H. Cowardine, who were unfavourable to the coming of the railway. Strangely Hills was a shareholder in the original CSV&H Railway proposal and had only sold his shares in 1855, whilst J.N. Brewster originally objected because of the impending damage to his estate but then withdrew his opposition. Notice of the intended railway was sent to relevant landowners, lessees and occupiers of property on the proposed route before 15th December 1855.

The initial meeting of the promoters was held on 14th December 1855 at the home of Edward Hornor, The Howe, Halstead. In attendance were John Hills, Robert Ellington Greenwood, Duncan Sinclair, James Brewster and the solicitor George I. Mayhew of Mayhew & Salmon, Halstead and 30 Great George Street, Westminster, London. The object of the gathering was to discuss and approve the plans produced for the proposed railway. All except Mayhew were willing to become provisional directors with Hornor and Brewster each promising to purchase fifty shares each and the remainder twenty-five shares each.

A week into the New Year, on 8th January 1856 the provisional directors met at Halstead to hear the solicitor present his plans for the advancement of the scheme. A total of £40,000 was required for building the line with an additional £3,000 for the Parliamentary plans in the Court of Chancery. The solicitor recommended the interested parties raise the deposit by means of a Parliamentary subscription. If little or no money was raised then the scheme would be aborted. The gathering then discussed ways of raising the deposit, either from monies provided by stockholders interested in the railway becoming shareholders or by bankers' loans. A contract had yet to be agreed for the construction of the railway and the solicitor observed that nobody was willing to part with the first shilling until the Act of Parliament was passed. The ECR had withdrawn their opposition raised in 1855 and now agreed to the Halstead to Chappel railway proposal. Landowners on the proposed route were not expected to raise any objections. Considerable difficulty had been experienced obtaining signatures to the subscription contract by 30th December 1855 but Mayhew advised that William Munro the contractor and friends had offered to purchase 571 £10 shares paying an initial £856 10s 0d, whilst local people had promised to purchase 1,329 £10 shares, initially paying a deposit of £1,993 10s 0d. As it was necessary to raise the subscription to three quarters of the estimated total of £27,000 the contractor had been approached on 31st December and with his friends had signed for a total of £23,210 on the understanding that no further money was to be obtained from that source. Subsequently an estimate was made for £36,000 and the contract estimate, petition and bill was duly deposited in the Parliamentary bill office on New Years Eve.

The prospectus published and circulated showed a map of the present line as planned and a proposed extension. The meeting then considered a deposit of £2,700 should be found and it was therefore necessary for the interested shareholders to pay in full, interest in turn to be paid in full. Unfortunately the required deposit could not be readily raised and at their meeting on 9th January 1856 the provisional directors agreed to seek a loan for the required £2,700 from the London & County Bank so that payment could be made to the Court of Chancery.

The next meeting of the provisional directors was held in the company offices at Halstead on 8th April 1856. In attendance were James Brewster, Duncan Sinclair and R.E. Greenwood, with Edward Hornor in the chair. Mayhew, the solicitor, gave details of the progress of the bill and reported on the petition against the railway from five local landowners, H.H. Cowardine, Robert Hills, Osgood Hanbery, Henry Skingley and James Beard, together with that from a tenant, Thomas Taylor. Mayhew explained he had negotiated terms with Cowardine and his tenant Taylor whereby the petition would be withdrawn on payment of £100 per acre and £400 compensation for damages to include the tenant's interest and £50 for manorial rights on the Parish of Earls Colne. In addition a station was to be built on the land owned by Cowardine, whilst no more than four acres was to be taken from the estate for the proposed

railway. The directors were opposed to the requested terms but were willing to pay ten per cent over the value of price per acre. They were also willing to pay Cowardine £150 per acre, a price which included severance and damage as well as the tenant's interest. The company was also willing to pay £50 for the enfranchisement of the manorial rights on the four acres of land at the same time paying the stewards bills. The directors remained adamant they would not pay Cowardice's opposition costs.

The directors then considered the petition of Robert Hills, which stipulated that no station was to be provided between Colneford Hill and Colne Park Lodge. A letter from Hills dated 7th April concerning the routing of a new road connecting the Bures Road with the suggested site of the station was also read. The directors directed Mayhew to respond advising Hills that it was deemed 'inexpedient' to site the station on the east side of the Sudbury Road and indeed the company had no plans to site the station immediately alongside the Sudbury Road but some way to the west with an access approach from the said road. Mayhew was told to reiterate to Hills the railway company had a duty to the public to provide convenient access to the station and he and his property would be given every protection.

The question of bridges was then debated and after some deliberation it was agreed if the Board of Trade deemed it necessary to provide bridges in lieu of level crossings the fair price for additional land in the Parish of Colne Engaine was £100 and £130 in the Parish of White Colne. Whatever transpired, not more than three acres of land was to be acquired. At the conclusion of the meeting Mayhew reminded the provisional directors that the petition of Osgood Hanbury had yet to be settled. The solicitor was instructed to offer Hanbury £100 per acre for land and severance on the same terms as Cowardine.

Nearly a month later, on 2nd May 1856, Mayhew reported back to the directors of his successful negotiations with the opponents of the railway on the undermentioned terms.

With Henry Holgate Cowardine of Colne Priory, Earls Colne:
1. No more land in the Parish of Colne Engaine owned by Cowardine to be taken than that wholly necessary for the railway.
2. The new railway not to be made nearer than 35 yards from his stockyard.
3. A footpath to be provided as required by the tenant Thomas Taylor.
4. The Sudbury Road to be crossed on the level but no station or any other erection, except a crossing keeper's lodge to be provided.
5. A sum of £150 per acre to be paid for land but the property acquired not to exceed four acres.
6. All timber and trees cut down during the course of construction of the railway to belong to Cowardine.
7. The Colne Valley Company to pay Cowardine £50 exclusive of steward's fees for the enfranchisement of all copyhold land in the Parish of Earls Colne.
8. The Colne Valley Company to pay £50 for costs and charges incurred by Cowardine and Thomas Taylor and pay all other costs of settlement.
9. If the preamble was passed clauses to be inserted in the Act of Parliament to cover the alterations required.
10. If all items agreed no further opposition to the railway to be raised by Cowardine or Taylor.

ANNO DECIMO NONQ & VICESIMO

VICTORIÆ REGINÆ.

****

Cap. lxi.

An Act for making a Railway from the *Chappel* Station of the *Colchester, Stour Valley, Sudbury, and Halstead* Railway to *Halstead* in the County of *Essex*, and for other Purposes.

[30th *June* 1856.]

WHEREAS the making of a Railway from or near the *Chappel* Station of the *Colchester, Stour Valley, Sudbury, and Halstead* Railway to *Halstead* in the County of *Essex* would be of great local and public Advantage: And whereas the Persons herein-after named, with others, are willing at their own Expense to carry such Undertaking into execution, if authorized by Parliament so to do: May it therefore please Your Majesty that it may be enacted; and be it enacted by the Queen's most Excellent Majesty, by and with the Advice and Consent of the Lords Spiritual and Temporal, and Commons, in this present Parliament assembled, and by the Authority of the same, as follows:

I. That the Provisions of "The Companies Clauses Consolidation Act, 1845," "The Lands Clauses Consolidation Act, 1845," and "The Railways Clauses Consolidation Act, 1845," except so far as the same are

8 & 9 Vict. cc. 16. 18. & 20. incorporated.

[*Local.*] 10 P

Colne Valley and Halstead Railway Act 30th June 1856 front page.

Agreement with Osgood Hanbury of Holfield Grange:

1. All culverts and watercourses built for the railway through the property owned by Hanbury to be built to the satisfaction of Hanbury's agent.
2. All timber and trees felled during the course of the construction of the railway to become the property of Hanbury.
3. The price of £100 per acre to be paid for land required for the railway but such land not to be acquired until the crops are harvested.
4. If the Colne Valley Company purchase land in excess to requirements, which was ultimately not required for the railway, such land to be returned to Hanbury's ownership with the railway company paying any costs incurred by Hanbury in selling or buying back the property.
5. All clauses within the agreement to be included in the Act of Parliament.
6. No further opposition to be made against the railway.

Agreement with Robert Hills:

1. No station building or section of any building, except a lodge be made on the Sudbury Road between Coleford Hill and Colne Park Lodge, in fields numbered 22 and 23 on the deposited plans in the Parish of White Colne, and fields numbered 2, 2a, 3 and 5 in the Parish of Colne Engaine. In the event of the company wishing to erect a station on the allotment fields marked 20 in the Parish of White Colne, the company was required to make a proper approach to the station from the Colchester Road.
2. If the Sudbury Road was crossed on the level, the site of the lodge and the design to be approved by Robert Hills with a total cost of £150.
3. In the event of the railway company not making the new road connection from the Sudbury Road to the Bures Road, a proper and permanent connection was to be made and maintained by the company, either over the line to the allotment fields or if the company make such a road it was to be adopted for carriages and to be located as close as possible to the railway fence.
4. The land lying between the fence dividing field numbered 14 in the Parish of Colne Engaine from the common meadow and the railway, was to be retained by Robert Hills and purchased by the company at his option.
5. All culverts and ditches to be constructed to the satisfaction of Hills' agent.
6. All timber and trees felled during the course of construction to be the property of Robert Hills.
7. The company to pay to Robert Hills the sum of £130 per acre for land purchased for the railway.

The Colne Valley and Halstead Railway Act 1856 subsequently received the Royal Assent on 30th June 1856 (19 and 20 Vic cap lxi). The statute authorised the making of a railway:

James Brewster,
CV&HR Chairman from 1856 to 1886.

commencing by a junction with the Colchester, Stour Valley, Sudbury & Halstead Railway at a point thirty seven yards north of the platform at Chappel station in the Parish of Wakes Colne and terminating in a meadow on the west side of the public road from Halstead to Stisted, south of and adjoining a bridge over the River Colne known as Parson's Bridge, at a point about fifty yards from the centre of the said public road, at a point at which the railway is intended to cross the same, and which said point is situate within and about forty yards south of the centre of the said bridge in the parish of Halstead, in the said county of Essex, and which said meadow is in the occupation of the Reverend Charles Burney and Gabriel Daking Green.

The railway was to pass through the parishes or extra-parochial places of Wakes Colne, White Colne, Colne Engaine, Earls Colne and Halstead, all in the County of Essex.

By clause xxi of the Act the junction with the CSVS&HR was to be built to the approval and satisfaction of the Engineer of the Eastern Counties Railway. The following clause directed that the company was not to interfere with the land or works of the CSVS&HR except by consent between the two parties. The railway was authorised by clause xxiii to cross the following public roads: No's 8 and 18 in the Parish of White Colne, No. 45 in the Parish of Colne Engaine and No. 10 in the Parish of Earls Colne, all by level crossing. Clause xxiv stipulated the company to provide lodges or stations adjacent to these crossings and failure to provide rendered the CV&HR liable to an initial penalty of £20 and £10 per day thereafter. Two years were allowed for the compulsory purchase of land and four years for the completion of works. The company could enter into agreement with the CSVS&HR and the EUR, and through them the ECR, subject to the approval of the BOT and a percentage of shareholders.

To finance the building of the railway the Act authorised the company to raise £40,000 in £10 shares, with powers to borrow £13,333 once the whole of the original capital was subscribed and half actually paid up. The initial directors of the CV&HR were Edward Horner, James Brewster, Robert Ellington Greenwood, Duncan Sinclair and John Hills.

At the first meeting of the promoters held in the Town Hall at Halstead on 25th July 1856 and chaired by Edward Horner the gathering stressed priority for the immediate construction of the line. The Engineer appointed was Nathaniel Beardmore with Mr Mayhew, Solicitor and A.E. Williams Secretary.

The first half yearly meeting of shareholders was held at the Halstead Town Hall on 29th September 1856 when Edward Horner relinquished his chairmanship of the company because of his intended absence from the neighbourhood for the ensuing year, and passed the reins to James Brewster. The gathering was advised the company had entered into conditional agreement for the compulsory purchase of land with five principal landowners at prices less than the Parliamentary estimate and little more than agricultural value. The amount of capital authorised by the Act was 4,000 shares at £10 each equaling £40,000 and borrowing powers to raise £13,333 6s 8d, making a total of £53,333 6s 8d. The directors had received an offer from a large contractor to take £25,000 of the capital in shares as part payment for the contracted work but had thought it inadvisable to accept the terms. The capital account on the basis of the contractor's offer could be stated as 3,015 shares subscribed for equaling £30,150 leaving 985 shares unappropriated at a total of £9,850. The Chairman continued reminding the proprietors that the railway was projected to accommodate the larger population of Halstead and as a commercial speculation the directors believed the cheap construction would ensure it being remunerative from existing local traffic only, but when regarding its position in reference to the proposed extension as being the nearest route from Harwich and Colchester to the North they were of the opinion it would be an important link in railway accommodation and as such prove a profitable investment of money. He then iterated the resolution passed at the influential public meeting on 25th July held at the Halstead Town Hall of the importance of extending the railway to Haverhill and possibly to Clare and through to Cambridge. Existing shareholders would have preference in purchasing shares in the new scheme. The meeting concluded with the news that Messrs Sperling & Harris had been appointed as solicitors in conjunction with the present solicitors Mayhew & Salmon.

No fewer than nine contractors tendered for the construction of the railway:

	£
Allcock	23,775
Wrigg	21,713
Munro	21,700
Furness	19,989
Treadwell	19,968
Murray	19,857
Baldwin	19,314
Cameron	19,050
Hale	18,424

An informal approach as to the operation of the future railway resulted in the ECR directors agreeing on 22nd July 1867 they would work the CV&HR on a cost basis and the Secretary duly informed the local board. They had initially offered to construct the railway but wiser counsels prevailed. And the offer was declined.

Realizing much activity would ensue with construction work, on 5th August the ECR authorities agreed to the provision of a horse to assist shunting in the goods yard at Chappel because of the expected growth in traffic but it was on the terms of occasional hire at 3s 6d per week.

On 16th February 1858 William Munro of Dornock, Scotland, 34 years of age, was awarded the contract to construct the section of line from Chappel to Halstead to coincide with the ceremonial cutting of the first sod. James Brewster performed the deed, in the presence of principal officers of the company and the contractor, at Elms (Over) Hall, near Langley Mill, Colne Engaine, the home of John Jeremiah Mayhew the Solicitor. Various speeches were made advocating the well-being of the railway before Brewster dug a spit of earth with a decorative ceremonial spade and turned it into an ornamental wheelbarrow constructed of mahogany with silver fittings. Dignitaries attending included William Munro, the contractor. Jeremiah Mayhew, the solicitor, and other directors then took their turn in turning a spit of earth and altogether fifty people attended the function. The local press reported, 'Enthusiasm was not

great'. After the ceremony the guests retired to the house to partake of a sumptuous meal.

William Munro was no stranger to the area for he constructed the first section of the nearby Tendring Hundred Railway between Hythe and Wivenhoe as well as the later Wivenhoe & Brightlingsea Railway. He was also involved with the abortive Mistley to Walton Railway. Munro employed George Wines as his resident contractor; Wines, 29 years of age in 1861, was living in Great Yeldham together with his wife and two daughters. He in turn was assisted by Robert Strong and Joseph B. Fryer, both managers, and foreman Henry Smith. Thomas Rayner acted as contractor's agent. Construction was expected to proceed apace.

Meanwhile all was not well on the neighbouring ECR for on 10th March 1858 the 3.00pm ex Sudbury goods train collided with a wagon of flour, which had run away on falling gradients from Chappel. Both the station master and porter-in-charge of the shunting were dismissed because of negligence of duty. The local residents were soon petitioning for the reinstatement of Station Master Brown but the Traffic Committee refused the application at their meeting on 28th April 1858. Then on 7th July 1858 the ECR General Manager complained the wagon turntable at Chappel required clearing of dirt and other debris, which was causing problems when turning. On 4th August 1858 Mr Moy was instructed to remove the heap of manure he had deposited at Chappel as the smell was offensive and obstructing the future development of the CV&HR.

At the CV&HR shareholders meeting held in August 1858 the gathering was told of the continuing satisfactory progress of works, with expected completion the following spring. The consensus of opinion when asked if the line should continue to Halstead or stop at Blue Bridge was for construction to continue to the town as quickly as possible.

At this stage James Brewster of Ashford Lodge, near Halstead was Chairman of the CV&HR, with fellow directors Robert Ellington Greenwood of Sloe House, near Halstead, John Jeremiah Mayhew of Over Hall, Colne Engaine, Duncan Sinclair of Halstead, George Richardson of 1 New Broad Street, London EC and The Wycke, Burnham, Essex, and Daniel Gurteen of Haverhill, Suffolk. The Secretary was Albert Edward Williams; Engineer Nathaniel Beardmore of 30 Great George Street, Westminster; Auditors W.O. Hustler and A.J. Brown, both of Halstead, and Solicitors Mayhew and Salmon, also of 30 Great George Street, Westminster.

Complaints were again received regarding the obstruction of the horse and cattle dock at Chappel with heaps of coal. On 1st September 1858 the ECR station master was instructed to order Mr Appleby, the coal merchant, to remove the offending coal with the added warning that works on the new railway would require better arrangements for storage of commodities in the goods yard.

On 29th September 1858 the ECR board directed Sinclair to cooperate with the CV&HR Engineer on the proposed junction at Chappel and the possible extension of the railway to Cambridge. Certain conditions were stipulated and the agreement was to be made provided the CV&HR opposed the proposed railway from Ilford to Great Dunmow. To adequately safeguard ECR interests, if the line was extended to Cambridge, Sinclair was to ensure the CV&HR was worked by the ECR as part of the conditions. On the same day authority was given to extend the electric telegraph route from Chappel on to Bures.

The proposal for the extension of the CV&HR was published on 8th November 1858 and advised the intention of the company to make application to Parliament for a railway commencing by a junction with the authorised line at or near Parsons Bridge, in the Parish of Halstead, in the County of Essex, and passing through or into the following parishes and places or some of them: Halstead, Gosfield, Great Maplestead, Little Maplestead, Sible Hedingham, Castle Hedingham, Toppesfield, Great Yeldham, Little Yeldham, Northey Wood, North Wood otherwise Belchamp North Wood, North End otherwise Belchamp Northend, Belchamp St Paul's, Tilbury otherwise Tilbury-juxta-Clare, Ovington, Ridgewell, Ashen, Stambourne, Birdbrook, Steeple Bumpstead, Helion's Bumpstead, Sturmer, Kedington Hamlet, Haverhill Hamlet, Haverhill in the County of Essex; Wixoe, Haverhill Hamlet, Haverhill, Little Wratting and Withersfield in the County of Suffolk; Shudy Camps, Castle Camps, Helion's Bumpstead and Ashdon in the County of Cambridge; Radwinter, Ashdon, Bartlow, Hempstead, Wimbish otherwise Wimbush, Saffron Walden, Sewers End, Little Walden, Audley End, Wendon, Newport and Little Bury (sic) in the County of Essex, and terminating in the said Parish of Wendon by a junction with the ECR at or near the Audley End station of that railway. Charles Brogden Sperling, the newly appointed Engineer, estimated the cost of construction at £150,000. The application for the bill included clauses to permit the ECR to subscribe to the undertaking and enter into arrangements for working and maintaining the railway. Copies of the Books of Reference and plans were deposited with the Clerk of the Peace for the County of Essex at Chelmsford, the Clerk of the Peace for the County of Suffolk at Bury St Edmunds and the Clerk of the Peace for the County of Cambridge at Cambridge on 30th November, together with copies to all parishes through which the railway was to pass. Copies of the document were also deposited in the private bill office of the House of Commons on 23rd December.

A special committee of the ECR met on 11th November 1858 to consider new railway projects and in particular the independent railway mooted from London to Dunmow, Clare and Bury St Edmunds, and the CV&HR proposed extension to Audley End. After much discussion the solicitor was instructed to contact his CV&HR counterpart to enquire if the extension to Audley End might counteract the Dunmow to Bury St Edmunds proposal.

In November 1858 a dispute arose regarding the rights and losses of ECR land to the CV&HR. In the former case the CV contractor had entered ECR property without permission, to lay rails for a locomotive to enter the CV&HR land. Sinclair had objected strongly to such action without due consultation and gave instructions for Munro's men to be evicted and for the works on ECR land to be removed. The CV&HR representative claimed the works were carried out to get a locomotive on to the line and the matter was duly passed to the ECR board on 24th November.

On 8th December 1858 the ECR board noted the scheme presented to Parliament for the extension of the CV&HR and the Bedford to Cambridge via Potton line, with which the Colne Valley hoped to connect. Another railway mooted and of concern to the ECR was the London, Dunmow, Clare and Bury St Edmunds line, and the solicitor was instructed to register the company's objection to both proposals. During the ensuing three months, construction continued and on 8th April 1859 the CV&HR application to make the physical junction at Chappel was passed to the ECR directors for approval. Although permission was granted, relations between the two companies soured over several minor points. Then, despite such grandiose proposals, the CV&HR withdrew the plans for extending to Audley End and on to Cambridge, realizing that such

schemes were beyond their restricted finances, and concentrate on reaching Haverhill.

The Colne Valley and Halstead Railway (Extension) Act 1859 received the Royal Assent on 13th August 1859 (22 and 23 Vic cap cxxii) and authorised the company to extend their line wholly in the County of Essex, commencing at an end on junction with the authorised line in the Parish of Halstead and passing through the Parishes and places or some of them: Halstead, Great Maplestead, Sible Hedingham, Castle Hedingham, Topesfield, Great Yeldham, Ridgewell, Stanbourne, Birdbrook, Steeple Bumpstead, Helion's Bumpstead, Sturmer and Haverhill to terminate in the Parish and hamlet of Haverhill, near the boundary between the counties of Essex and Suffolk.

By clause V the company or its agents were not to take or interfere with lands numbered in the plans 68, 69 and 77 in the Parish of Halstead without the consent in writing of the owner. Level crossings were authorised by clause VI across public highway No. 7 and turnpike road No. 61 in Parish of Halstead, whilst the following clause VII prohibited the company shunting trains to or from any siding near to the level crossings; to pass any trains over

ANNO VICESIMO SECUNDO & VICESIMO TERTIO

VICTORIÆ REGINÆ.

****

Cap. cxxii.

An Act to enable the *Colne Valley and Halstead* Railway Company to extend their Railway from *Halstead* to *Haverhill* in the County of *Essex*.
[13th *August* 1859.]

WHEREAS by an Act passed in the Year One thousand eight hundred and fifty-six the *Colne Valley and Halstead* Railway Company (in this Act referred to as "the Company") were incorporated, "for making a Railway from the *Chappel* Station of the *Colchester, Stour Valley, Sudbury,* and *Halstead* Railway to *Halstead* in the County of *Essex,* and for other Purposes," and the Company are proceeding with the Construction of the said Railway, and it will soon be completed: And whereas the Extension of the said Railway from *Halstead* to *Haverhill* would be attended with great local and public Advantage, and the Company are willing so to extend their Railway: And whereas Plans and Sections of the proposed Extension, showing the Line and Levels thereof, with a Book of Reference to the Plans, containing the Names of the Owners or reputed Owners, Lessees or reputed Lessees, and of the Occupiers of the Lands through which the Extension will pass, have been deposited with the respective Clerks of the Peace for the Counties of *Essex, Suffolk,* and *Cambridge*: And whereas the estimated Expense of constructing the said Extension is Ninety thousand Pounds: And whereas the before-mentioned Object cannot be accomplished without

19 & 20 Vict. c. lxi.

[*Local.*]   20 C   the

Colne Valley and Halstead Railway Extension Act 13th August 1859 front page.

such level crossings, or to allow trains to stand across the crossing when standing at a station. Under clause VIII, before the opening of the extension the company was required to construct and maintain a footbridge over the railway at level crossing No. 61. Three years were allowed for the purchase of the land required for the railway and five years for the completion of works. Clause IX required the company to erect a station or crossing keeper's lodge at or adjacent to the above level crossings whilst the BOT could demand for reasons of public safety the erection of bridges in place of any level crossing if so desired.

Capital for the new works was to be raised by the issue of £80,000 in £10 shares, although no dividend was to be declared until the extension was opened for six months. The company was also authorised to borrow £26,000 once half the original capital was raised and the full total subscribed.

The animosity between the ECR and CV&HR companies continued unabated and finally deteriorated to petty squabbles. Early in September 1859, the CV&HR contractor asked for a truck of lime standing on the ECR siding at Chappel to be shunted through the junction. The application was refused, the authorities stating that as the line was not yet open to traffic, the truck could not proceed. The omission to include the arrangements for constructing and providing a junction at Chappel now came to bear. The connection was obviously to be to the satisfaction of the ECR Engineer, and argument and counter argument ensued; Sinclair for the ECR and Beardmore for the Colne Valley had several abortive meetings until the matter was put to arbitration. The Colne Valley incurred considerable expense until it was agreed the company would pay a sum of £1,500 for the right to have access to Chappel station and for occupation of a small strip of land. Even then the solicitor pointed out to the Colne Valley board that the money should not be paid to the ECR who only leased Chappel station and the wisest course was to pay the sum awarded to the Court of Chancery and the board wisely followed the advice.

The proposed opening of the CV&HR between Chappel and Halstead was considered at the ECR board meeting on 14th September 1859. A committee formed of Sinclair, Robertson and Moseley was to report on the application for the ECR to work the new railway. The decision to pay the £1,500 to the Court of Chancery infuriated the ECR board and the company retaliated with a further period of inactivity until tiring of the impasse the CV&HR applied to the Court of Common Pleas for a writ of mandamus requiring the ECR to state whether they intended to make the physical junction or not. A sub-committee was appointed by the CV&HR board to negotiate with the ECR and if the access to Chappel station was still denied it was empowered to construct a platform on Colne Valley property as near to the ECR station as possible. Under the pressure the ECR yielded and announced it would open the junction and a series of meetings was held between the CV&HR Chairman and Horatio Love the ECR Chairman. Agreement was finally reached, one of the points being the annulment of the lease for the ECR working the line as the contract had been awarded to William Munro the contractor. At the conclusion of the meetings Love remarked that *'Boards were not to be hurried … and that they required time for consideration.'* At an earlier ECR shareholders meeting concerning branch lines independently owned, Love said:

The duty of your directors has been when a line has been opened and is ready for working, to offer all reasonable facilities and on no account to interfere with the wishes of the public as regards the transit of goods. We hold this rule sacred!

The double talk left the CV&HR directors bewildered. On a different note the CV&HR was party to the Railway Clearing House from 1859 to ensure the fair transactions on traffic moving to and from the railway and later became a member of the Railway Companies' Association.

On 31st December 1859, Munro wrote a letter of protest to the ECR stating that as a result of the renewed hostility, his engine and coach, standing at Chappel, were not being permitted on to the CV&HR line. He advised that because of the decision not to allow any vehicles to pass on to the new railway, the rolling stock would proceed to Halstead by road. As a consequence he would be charging the ECR for the cost of men, horses and waggons to carry out the operation. On receipt his letter was passed to the ECR solicitor on 4th January 1860. Munro also offered to lease the railway in 1859 once it opened to traffic but his application was dismissed. As work was nearing completion the Secretary was instructed to request the statutory inspection.

Colonel William Yolland conducted the official Board of Trade inspection of the Chappel to Halstead section of the CV&HR on 4th February 1860, with the ECR loaning two of their heaviest locomotives to assist in the testing of bridges and permanent way. He noted the section submitted for inspection was 6 miles 2 chains in length commencing at a junction with the Sudbury branch of the ECR at Chappel and terminating at Halstead. The line was single although land had been purchased and one of the overbridges constructed for double track. There were sidings at each of the two stations, Coleford Hill (*sic*) and Halstead, and also a short length at Chappel station, the spacing between the running line and the sidings being 6 feet. Two overbridges spanned the line, both constructed of brick with lime mortar, the greatest span being of 26 feet square and 29 feet 6 inches on the skew. Two underbridges had brick abutments and wrought iron girders, the largest span being 35 feet square. In addition to these bridges there were four viaducts constructed of lattice girders resting on wooden piles, the greatest having a span of 23 feet 6 inches. Yolland considered the bridges and viaducts well constructed and sufficiently strong. There were no unauthorised level crossings.

During the inspection the Colonel drew attention to several unsatisfactory items. The signal box at Chappel was not located opposite the junction with the ECR line but midway between the junction and a pair of facing points leading into the siding, which abutted upon and stopped short of the road crossing the railway at the north end of Chappel station platform. The inspector stipulated the provision of buffer stops at the end of the siding and observed that the natural place for the signal box was opposite the junction. No platform or station was erected at Chappel for the CV&HR services and Yolland was concerned that at the time of inspection no arrangements had been made with the ECR, either for working the line or for use of their station, or indeed the adoption of the junction signal erected for the use of both lines. The ECR line to Sudbury was single, with a short siding at Chappel, with their single platform station on the west side of the railway and the company only had a station signal to protect the station. The inspector was adamant that a clear understanding as to the method of working the new railway and the junction was to be agreed between the two companies. *'At present an engine cannot be moved from the front to the rear of the train without shunting and trespassing on to the ECR',*

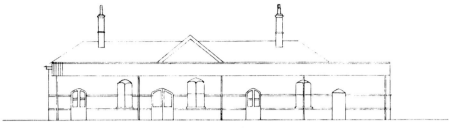

Halstead station platform elevation.

and to protect the station Yolland stipulated the provision of a distant signal on the Marks Tey side of Chappel station to provide a warning for drivers of approaching trains.

Along the line at Colneford Hill the inspector found no station buildings had been erected and on checking the signalling, found that the distant signal towards Halstead for Up trains could not be seen from the platform and therefore required repositioning. The gates at the authorised level crossings were in all cases placed too near to the running lines to allow adequate clearance, whilst the accommodation for crossing keepers was spartan, with wooden huts being provided instead of properly erected lodges. At Halstead station the corner of the waiting room and the coke loading platform for replenishing locomotive supplies were both placed too close to the line, whilst buffers were required at the end of the railway to prevent engines or vehicles running beyond the end of the rails and across the public highway. Clocks were also to be provided at both stations, positioned so they could be seen from the platform.

Two public level crossings bisecting the yard on the approach to Halstead station were considered by Yolland as *objectionable and dangerous*. The inspector recommended the provision of a single footbridge spanning the lines at the site of one of the paths and the rerouting of the other path to the bridge. The company officials attending the inspection stated they had the matter in hand and they were taking steps to provide the structure. Although the permanent way was much improved, Yolland required the rails next to the joints to be secured to the sleepers by fang bolts instead of dog spikes *as the latter could not be relied upon to preserve the gauge especially on curves*, although all appeared correct during the inspection. When details of the line had first been submitted to the BOT in November 1859, Yolland had objected to the weak construction of the bridge platforms but was gratified during the inspection to find that these had been strengthened by the insertion of longitudinal timbers under the rails. Despite these improvements much remedial work was required, and as the railway was in an incomplete state Yolland refused to sanction opening to traffic.

The lack of the footbridge at Halstead was soon rectified when the contract for a timber bridge was awarded to Rayner & Runacles for £160 provided it was completed within five weeks. The structure spanned the width of the yard and gave pedestrians access between King's Road, then known as Coat Road, to the west of the station and the junction of Factory Lane to the west and the Causeway to the east.

By February 1860 relationships between the ECR and CV&HR companies had improved and much to Munro's surprise on 15th of the month a truck of flints en route from Manningtree to Halstead was allowed across the junction at Chappel. Nathaniel Beardmore reported to the board on 24th February 1860 that Halstead station was nearly ready *for the purpose of any present opening of your line; the corrugated iron engine and goods sheds have been some time in hand, and will be completed within a month.*

On 29th February 1860 it was agreed the signal balance weights at Chappel would be altered and the bells placed in the signal box and the ECR booking office. In addition it was agreed that Sinclair would hold a meeting with Beardmore to agree the method to be adopted for the interchange of traffic at Chappel. By 14th March the CV&HR Company were reporting that no action had been taken regarding the signals and both men were instructed to convene a meeting as a matter of urgency. The ECR operating superintendent was still reticent regarding the interchange of traffic but just over a month later on 28th March, authority was given for two wagons conveying a traversing table to be allowed through the junction en route to Halstead. In the meantime Munro's men were attending to outstanding requirements.

Colonel Yolland returned to re-inspect the line on 31st March 1860 and was advised the directors of the CV&HR had reached an understanding with the ECR directors regarding the joint use of the station and rearranged signalling at Chappel. After travelling to Halstead and back, Yolland was still dissatisfied with what he found. The signalling at the junction was incomplete and an assurance was sought regarding the erection of station buildings and crossing keepers' lodges with a definite timescale, after the inspector had found little had been done since his previous visit. Fang bolts had not been provided to secure the rails to the sleepers next to the joints and from observation the visit was *considered a waste of valuable time*. In his report of 2nd April, the Colonel required written confirmation of the method of working to be adopted and whether engine turntables were to be erected at both ends of the line. If the remainder of the works had been satisfactory Yolland would have permitted the railway to open for traffic provided the line was worked by a tank locomotive or locomotives, pending the provision of turntables, but because of the incompleteness of works sanction was again refused.

Following the inspection, Mr Williams wrote to the BOT on the same day that Yolland compiled his report. The Engineer confirmed the signalling arrangements at the junction were completed and the CV&HR company would undertake to work all traffic over the completed line by tank engine. Arrangements would be made to erect turntables at the extremities of the railway once the line was extended. The installation of fang bolts and construction of lodges for crossing keepers was also promised. The correspondence was placed before Yolland, who agreed to the line opening for traffic without re-inspection.

On 11th April 1860 the ECR board noted the CV&HR would open for traffic on 16th April with costs for operating the Junction at Chappel to be arranged between Robertson and the CV&HR manager, Robert Johnson Watt. The formal opening of the line from Chappel Junction to Halstead took place on Monday 16th April 1860 and the occasion was celebrated by the running of an excursion train over the ECR to Colchester at the return fare of 1s 0d.

The 2-2-2 well tank locomotive purchased from the London, Brighton & South Coast Railway for the opening of the CV&HR. Driver Charles Taunton is standing by the cab, whilst the gentleman with the top hat is Halstead station master John Titman.
Author's collection

2

Opening to Traffic

On 25th April 1860 the ECR directors agreed to three important concessions to the CV&HR: the inclusion of CV trains in their timetable; the operation of through coaches from Halstead to Marks Tey and return to obviate passengers having to change trains at Chappel, thus easing the shunting requirements at the junction station; and through passenger bookings to and from the ECR stations. It was also necessary to notify the Railway Clearing House of the employment of a junctionman (sic) at Chappel to check the numbers of the wagons exchanged between the companies.

Satisfied with his previous work, on 21st May 1860 the CV&HR directors awarded the contract for the construction of the Halstead to Haverhill section of line to William Munro. Sir William Cubitt was retained in an advisory capacity in recognition of his work in securing the progress of the Parliamentary bills through the Commons and Lords; his son Joseph Cubitt, a respected civil engineer, was subsequently employed as a consultant engineer and was to remain as such until the railway was completed to Haverhill in 1863.

The cutting of the first sod for the new section was carried out on 19th June by Miss Gurteen of Haverhill, a member of a long established family in the town, in a field located two miles from the town and owned by a Mrs Walton. In contrast to the poor turnout at the ceremony on the Chappel to Halstead section, over 2,000 people attended the ceremony and *'great enthusiasm prevailed'*.

Despite the opening of the railway to Halstead, road competition continued when Mr Smith, the owner of livery stables in the town, ran a horse bus to Braintree on Wednesdays and Colchester on Tuesdays and Saturdays. The latter was soon suspended when excursion traffic commenced, initially with the Tuesday journey and finally the Saturday run. John Cook, a local carrier, also commenced conveying passengers to Colchester on Wednesdays and Saturdays in the winter and Mondays, Wednesdays and Saturdays in the summer months but the 3½-hour journey in each direction resulted in limited patronage.

On 18th July 1860 the ECR directors agreed to retain the £1 per ton cartage for meat consignments from Halstead to London for the markets, whilst a locomotive would be allowed transit to and from Stratford Works for repairs, although no discount would be allowed on the usual rates.

The Stour Valley company's failure to extend their railway north of Sudbury engendered local factions to attempt inroads into CV&HR territory and the first positive moves came with the passing of the Sudbury and Clare Railway Act (23 and 24 Vict cap clxiii) on 23rd July 1860. The statute authorised the making of a railway commencing in the Parishes of Sudbury St Gregory and of Great Cornard or in one of those parishes by a junction with the Colchester, Stour Valley, Sudbury and Halstead Railway at or near where the railway crossed Lady Lane, passing by way of Long Melford, Glemsford, Cavendish, Clare and Chilton in the County of Suffolk and Ballingdon, Bulmer, Brundon, Borley, Liston Fixearth and Pentlow in the County of Essex and terminating in the Parish of Clare at a field called or known as the Bailey. Three years were allowed for the compulsory purchase of land and four years for the completion of works. The company was authorised to raise the sum of £65,000 in £10 shares with borrowing powers for £21,000 once the whole authorised amount had been subscribed for and one half actually paid up. Scarcely had the ink dried on the paper than the local company was absorbed by the ECR.

At their meeting on 15th August 1860 the ECR directors were disturbed to find a shortfall on the 50 per cent receipts agreed on through traffic from and to the Halstead line. The committee agreed to demand the outstanding sum from the CV&HR or cease the through booking facilities. At the same meeting a fares revision was sanctioned between Chappel and Colchester with the road distance being a guide whilst Halstead to Sudbury would be treated in the same way. It was also agreed to place Halstead and Colne stations on the weekly excursion list for London and Harwich at the same fares as Sudbury and Bures.

On 22nd August James Brewster succeeded Edward Horner as Chairman of the Company whilst Joseph Cubitt became Engineer for the Haverhill section of line. Williams the Secretary resigned and was replaced by Edmund Harvey at a revised salary of £500 per annum but the meeting refused to sanction the excessive salary and after internal threats of resignations the directors limited the salary to £300. Then on 29th August the ECR directors were advised that Mr Cressal, who had previously taken his goods from Halstead to Braintree for onward transit to London via rail, was now taking his goods all the way by road. It was agreed Moseley should meet the CV&HR Manager to negotiate with Cressal to return his custom to the railway.

At the ninth half yearly meeting held in the Town Hall at Halstead on 28th August 1860 the directors advised the shareholders the line had been opened between Chappel and Halstead on 16th April and had since been worked regularly; arrangements had been made with the ECR for the interchange of traffic at Chappel and the relevant accounts were passing through the Railway Clearing House. On the new section of line the first sod of earth was turned on 19th June and the contractor was actively at work on the heavier sections. The company had acquired more than half of the required land and the railway would be open as far as Hedingham by Christmas. The remainder of the line would be *'pushed on with the greatest possible dispatch consistent with other calls upon shareholders, and the contract provided for completion of the whole line by November 1861'*. The directors were pleased to advise the last session of Parliament authorised completion of railway communication between Bedford and Cambridge and *'it appears to your directors desirable that the Colne Valley line should be extended from Haverhill to meet the Cambridge and Bedford line and thus secure direct communication with the Midland Counties and with the North and West of England'*. They also optimistically advised:

a short extension from Chappel junction to Colchester will complete the railway communication from the ports of Harwich and Colchester and thus connect with the central army barracks at Weedon and Cannock Chase and afford connections to Oxford, Birmingham, Manchester and Liverpool with 'these Eastern Ports.

Joseph Cubitt had reported from his office at 4 Great George Street in a letter dated 22nd August on the progress of the Haverhill extension, where working surveys had been conducted and several sections of the line were completed. Other sections had been marked out and a considerable portion of the required land had been obtained. A start had been made on the earthworks of a number of cuttings near Halstead and on the heaviest portion of the line near Haverhill.

After some months of operating it was apparent that difficulties were experienced in dealing with CV&HR and ECR trains at Chappel. The matter was investigated and on 10th October 1860 it was agreed to extend the station platform by 150 feet at the south end to accommodate trains and provide a crossover from the main line to the second line south of the junction. The CV&HR

siding was totally inadequate for the transfer of traffic and the ECR Secretary duly wrote to the CV&HR board giving details of the proposed alterations and costs.

By now relationships between the two companies had noticeably improved and on 7th November 1860 the ECR authorised a CV&HR locomotive to run light engine from Chappel to Colchester and back for turning to ensure the even wear on the tyres and flanges. Sinclair advised against the acceptance of any further repair work on the company locomotives. The ECR Traffic Committee, however, was concerned to hear a report from the General Manager that the CV&HR had made two surveys for an independent line to Colchester.

On 12th November 1860 a bill was placed in the Parliamentary private bill office seeking authority in the 1861 session for a railway commencing at a junction with the authorised extension of the CV&HR in the Parish of Haverhill in field No. 15 referred to in the CV&HR (Extension) Act 1859 to run via Ashdon and terminate at a junction with the Bedford & Cambridge Railway at Trumpington, south of the university city. Certain branches were also proposed, linking Birdbrook and Clare, and Wakes Colne to Colchester independent of ECR lines. The branch to join the Sudbury & Clare Railway at Clare commenced in the Parish of Birdbrook by a double junction in or near field No. 36 to a junction with the Sudbury & Clare Railway. The branch from Wakes Colne was to terminate in Colchester on the east side of Mill Street, ninety yards south of Butt windmill. The bill also sought to empower the London & North Western Railway to help finance the cost of construction, guarantee interest payments, offering in return the possibility of a working agreement. The ECR, registering their opposition to all schemes, gave notice of their intention to extend the Stour Valley route beyond Sudbury to Cambridge and Bury St Edmunds.

Receipts for the six miles of operational line between Chappel and Halstead for the period 16th April to 31st December 1860 was £1,691 compared with working expenses of £1,638 and at the tenth half yearly meeting held early in 1861 the directors reported the delay in completion of the contract for construction of the extension to Hedingham was *'no fault of their own'*. The Chairman blamed the bad weather just before Christmas 1860 with constant snow showers and bitterly cold winds but hoped Munro would complete the work by February. He also apportioned some blame on landowners who had not released their land and were demanding an increased price for their portion of property required for railway construction. Having established a regular parcel traffic the company thought they could exploit the market and on 2nd January 1861 the CV&HR Secretary wrote to the ECR requesting a charge of 2d in respect of terminal charges for each parcel but the parcels manager stipulated the Railway Clearing House charge of 1d per parcel would remain in force.

When the CV&HR bill for the extension to Cambridge appeared likely to fail under standing orders, support for the scheme was strengthened by petitions from the mayors, aldermen and burgesses of Cambridge and Colchester *'praying that it should not be set aside'*. This ensured the application complied with the standing orders and on 7th March 1861 the *Halstead Gazette* reported the bill had passed its second reading in the Commons and the standing orders in the Lords. Construction of the ECR line running almost parallel with the CV&HR proposal would effectively prevent it from taking any through traffic from points east of Chappel and west of Haverhill. The objectors to the ECR bill were the Stour Valley Railway, Norfolk

---

COLNE VALLEY AND HALSTEAD
RAILWAY COMPANY.

The Report of the Directors

To the NINTH HALF-YEARLY MEETING of the SHAREHOLDERS, to be held at the Town Hall, HALSTEAD, on TUESDAY, the 28th day of August, 1860.

"Your Directors have to report that the Line to Halstead was opened on the 16th of April last, and has since been regularly worked, and that the Traffic is steadily progressing. Arrangements were made with the Eastern Counties Company for the interchange of Traffic, and the Accounts pass through the Clearing House, but in consequence of the recent period at which the Line was opened, and of many matters of detail which have to be settled upon the first division of Traffic, the Balance Sheet from the Clearing House has not yet been received, and the Board is unable to append any statement of receipts.

As respects the New Line, the first sod was turned on the 19th day of June last, and the Contractor is now at work upon the heaviest portions. More than half the land along the Line has been put into his possession, and the Board are directing their attention to the earliest possible opening of that portion of the Line between Halstead and Castle Hedingham. They have urged the Contractor to complete this with the least possible delay, and he has promised, provided that no difficulty occurs in obtaining possession of the land, that it shall be open for traffic by Christmas next.

The remainder of the Line will be pushed on with the greatest possible despatch, consistently with the statutable limitation of the calls upon the Shareholders, and the Contract provides that the whole shall be completed by November in next year.

In the last Session of Parliament an Act passed authorising the completion of Railway communication between Bedford and Cambridge.

It appears to your Directors desirable that the Colne Valley Line should be extended from Haverhill to meet the Cambridge and Bedford Line, and thus secure direct communication with the Midland Counties, and with the North and West of England.

This communication will open a Market at Birmingham for Agricultural produce, and will afford facilities for procuring Coals from the Midland and Northern Counties at a most material saving in the cost.

A short Extension from the Chappel Junction to Colchester will complete the Railway communication from the Ports of Harwich and Colchester with the Central Barracks at Weedon and Cannock Chase, and afford ready intercourse to Oxford, Birmingham, Manchester and Liverpool, with these Eastern Ports.

A resolution will be proposed at the meeting enabling the Company to exercise the Borrowing Powers conferred by the Extension Act, and a vote will also be taken to fix the remuneration of the Directors.

(Signed)
JAMES BREWSTER, CHAIRMAN.
ALFRED EDWARD WILLIAMS, SECRETARY.

Halstead, August 21st, 1860.

The Report of the Engineer

To the DIRECTORS of the COLNE VALLEY and HALSTEAD RAILWAY COMPANY.

GENTLEMEN,—I have to report, with respect to progress on the Extension to Haverhill, that during the past half-year the Working Surveys and Sections of the Line have been completed and the Line set out. Most of the Notice Plans for purchase of the Land are prepared, and possession of a considerable portion of the Land obtained.

A commencement has been made with the Earthwork at two or three of the Cuttings at the Halstead end, and at the heaviest portion of the Line which is nearer Haverhill.

The Contractor reports materials for the permanent way in a forward state of preparation, and that deliveries may be daily expected.

It will be desirable to urge the works at the Halstead end so as to accomplish a further opening at the earliest possible period, at the same time taking care to push the works near Haverhill steadily forward.

I am, Gentlemen,
Your obedient Servant,
JOSEPH CUBITT.

*6, Great George Street,
22nd August, 1860.*

The Report of the Auditors

To the DIRECTORS of the COLNE VALLEY and HALSTEAD RAILWAY COMPANY.

Halstead, August 22nd, 1860.

"GENTLEMEN,—We beg to submit a Statement of the Company's Accounts from its commencement to the 30th of June, 1860, and from a careful examination of the Books can testify to their entire correctness.

We have the honour to be,
Gentlemen,
Your most obedient Servants,
W. O. HUSTLER, } AUDITORS.
A. J. BROWN, }

Report to the Directors 28th August 1860.

Railway, Eastern Union Railway and the CV&HR. The objectors to the Colne Valley bill were the ECR, which had absorbed the EUR, the Bedford & Cambridge (a subsidiary of the ECR), the Norfolk Railway and the Eastern Union Railway.

At the ECR board meeting on 24th April 1861 it was reported that Sinclair, Robertson and Moseley had visited the route of the proposed Mid Eastern Railway and also Castle Hedingham and Haverhill, including its connection with the CV&HR at Castle Hedingham during a tour of inspection on 18th, 19th and 20th April.

The respective Bills came up for consideration at the Parliamentary Committee stage on 13th May 1861 under the chairmanship of Mr Mowbray. Sargeant, Wrangham, Denison and J. Clark appeared for the CV&HR; Hope Scott, O. Merewether and Burke for the Eastern Counties, and Sir F. Slade, Wilkinson and Hayley for the Eastern Union and Norfolk railways, which were opposing both bills. The Colne Valley and Halstead Railway bill revealed that the company wished to extend their railway to Cambridge, Clare and Colchester and for other purposes. From the opening dialogue the 'other purposes' was to enable them to make connection with the London & North Western Railway at Cambridge and then lease the entire undertaking to that Company; in return the L&NWR were prepared to contribute to the capital cost. Thus the ECR was determined to stop this union at all costs to prevent the L&NWR entering and gaining a foothold in East Anglia. The learned counsel for the CV&HR advised the gathering that the line from Haverhill to Cambridge was 16 miles 6 furlongs in length, that from Chappel to Colchester 7 miles 3 furlongs in length and the branch from Birdbrook to Wixoe and Clare 4 miles 2 furlongs in length. He made great play emphasising the hostile attitude of the ECR toward the Colne Valley in the early years and then its opposition to the bill for the Colne Valley extension in 1859 and to the *delicate matter of detestation and the derision with which the ECR was regarded by local inhabitants*. The arguments failed to convince the members of the Committee and to the disappointment of the CV&HR contingent their bill was rejected in favour of the ECR bill.

Meanwhile, construction on the authorised line had advanced and on Monday 24th June 1861 Colonel Yolland returned to Essex to inspect the second portion of the CV&HR, the 3 miles 27 chains extension from Halstead to Hedingham. In attendance were R.E. Greenwood, a director, Munro, the contractor, R.J. Watt, Manager, and C.B. Sperling, Assistant Engineer. It was noted the line was single with sidings at the two stations, land had been purchased and overbridges built for double track with the formation 18 feet in width. During his inspection Yolland closely examined the three overbridges and two wooden viaducts and found one overbridge constructed entirely of brick, whilst the others had brick abutments and cast iron girders, with arched brickwork between the girders. One of these bridges was considered to have an *'ugly appearance'*, some of the girders being crooked either from poor casting or excessive weight on the superstructure. The Engineer informed Yolland the sections were crooked on receipt. The inspector was satisfied the brickwork showed no signs of weakness although he recommended an occasional check. The viaducts were considered to be sufficiently strong for the traffic but where the foundation of one structure was *'questionable'*, he required a regular local check. At Hedingham the extension works were noted and Yolland advised he had no objections to the second section of the line opening to traffic provided it was worked by a tank engine pending the provision of turntables at the extremities of the railway.

By 30th June 1861 the CV&HR receipts and expenditure were:

RECEIPTS	£	EXPENDITURE	£
Shares	24,650	Preliminary works	5,903
Shares extension line	50,782	Extension Act 1859	2,815
Debentures	37,559	Land and compensation	18,450
Suspense account	686	Works Contractor	77,511
Temporary issues	16,302	Engineer	6,559
		Permanent way	199
		Plant and rolling stock	6,527
		Interest on loans	3,688
		Chappel Junction award	1,509
		Direction and auditing	890
		Compensation	2,509
		Cost of 1861 Act	1,000
		General charges	2,419
	129,979		129,979

At this time the board of directors had welcomed Edward Horner JP of Howe Park, Halstead, and Major the Honorable Standish Prendergast Vereker of Warwick Square, Pimlico, in place of J.J. Mayhew and Duncan Sinclair. The General Manager was Robert J. Watt of Halstead, with Joseph Cubitt of 6 Great George Street, Westminster as Engineer. The Company Secretary was Edward Harvey and Auditors W.H. Wilson and A.J. Browner. For the six months ending 30th June 1861 receipts of £1,555 were largely offset by working expenses of £1,542.

The formal opening of the extension to Hedingham took place on Monday 1st July 1861, when a peal of church bells was rung, flags were flown and the band of the 12th Essex Rifles paraded. Evergreens straddled the level crossing at Halstead displaying 'Progress and Prosperity'. The *Halstead Gazette* enthused *people were roused from the even tenor of their ways by a merry peal from the church tower, a fluttering of flags and the inspiring strains of the brass band of the 12th Essex Rifles*. It continued:

the Colne Valley Railway was opened to the public as far as Castle Hedingham. The iron road has not only reached but shot beyond the town and as it carries in its wake the elements of opening out, beautifying and enriching a country, so it leaves in its train [sic] those advantages extended and consolidated and more – in proportion to the existence of feeder lines that rub right and left of the special locality. The shareholders have cause to congratulate themselves on the accomplishment of an effort that their children's children will boast of, and on the possession of a property that we doubt not will very shortly be remunerative.

The inhabitants of Hedingham remained aloof and only C. Hilton bothered to put up decorations, and that was on the railway bridge, whilst he also paid for the band. No additional services were run but the special return fare from Hedingham to Halstead of 4d and Chappel 6d encouraged a large gathering. One thousand seven hundred passengers travelled on the first day and overcrowding necessitated some passengers to ride in *'cattle trucks as there were not enough coaches to accommodate such numbers'*. One return journey from Chappel was almost an hour late owing to the difficulty of *'reassembling and reseating those who thought to avail themselves of a longer stay than had been prescribed.'* As a result of the opening the CV&HR manager requested the ECR if a through train could be operated via Chappel to Marks Tey at reasonable fares. Two days later on 3rd July the matter was discussed at the ECR board meeting but the subject was deferred although later a through Composite carriage working was authorised at a weekly charge of 9s 0d.

The railway soon claimed it first casualty, although indirectly. At the inquest into the death of 51-year-old Walter Ruggles it was reported the deceased had been sent to Wethersfield in charge of a couple of horses to collect a seed machine. On his journey home at about 4.30pm he was nearing the railway bridge in the vicinity of Blue Bridge when a train passed and startled the horses. The pair swerved to the near side of the road and two of the wheels of the seed machine mounted the embankment at the side of the road. Ruggles evidently lost his footing on the bank and was dragged underneath the machine for sixty yards. A witness, Ephraim Chambers, managed to stop the horses by shouting and running to get hold of the reins but by the time the animals were halted Ruggles was dead.

At this period the opportunity for local people to travel for the first time by rail was not popular with local churchmen who petitioned to bring excursions, and especially those operated on a Sunday, to an end. The exodus to the coast affected attendance at Sunday services and letters for and against the train services appeared regularly in the local Halstead papers.

ANNO VICESIMO QUARTO & VICESIMO QUINTO

VICTORIÆ REGINÆ.

****

Cap. ccxxxvii.

An Act to increase the Capital of the *Colne Valley and Halstead* Railway Company; and for other Purposes. [6th *August* 1861.]

WHEREAS the *Colne Valley and Halstead* Railway Company (in this Act referred to as the Company) were by "The *Colne Valley and Halstead* Railway Act, 1856," incorporated and authorized to make a Railway from the *Chappel* Station of the *Colchester, Stour Valley, Sudbury, and Halstead* Railway to *Halstead* in *Essex*; and by "The *Colne Valley and Halstead* Railway (Extension) Act, 1859," the Company were authorized to extend their Railway from *Halstead* to *Haverhill*: And whereas the Railway sanctioned by the Company's said Act of Incorporation has been made and opened to the Public, and the said Extension to *Haverhill* is being constructed: And whereas the Company have Powers by the said firstly-recited Act to raise Forty thousand Pounds by Shares and Thirteen thousand three hundred and thirty-three Pounds by borrowing, and by the secondly-recited Act Eighty thousand Pounds by Shares and Twenty-six thousand Pounds by borrowing: And whereas it is expedient that the Company should be empowered to raise further Sums of Money by Shares and by borrowing:

[*Local.*]   41 *A*   borrowing:

19 & 20 Vict. c. lxi.

22 & 23 Vict. c. cxxii.

Colne Valley and Halstead Railway Act 6th August 1861 front page.

Shortage of motive power was an early problem for the embryonic railway but, because of refusal by the ECR, on 5th August 1861 the CV&HR borrowed a locomotive from the London & North Western Railway through the good offices of Major Standish Prendergast Vereker. To further finance the Haverhill extension on 6th August 1861 the Colne Valley and Halstead Railway Amendment Act (24 and 25 Vict cap ccxxxvii) received the Royal Assent empowering the company to raise £30,000 by a new share issue to be initially issued to existing shareholders, together by clause 12 borrowing powers of £10,000 once the whole of the new shares had been subscribed for and half actually paid up.

The ECR Act for the extension beyond Sudbury to Cambridge and Bury St Edmunds also received the Royal Assent on 6th August 1861 (24 and 25 Vict cap ccxxxi) authorizing by Clause 7 several railways including Railway No. 2 commencing in the Parish of Sudbury, St Gregory and Great Cornard in the County of Suffolk and by a junction with the Stour Valley Railway in or near a field numbered 48 in that parish on the plans of the Sudbury and Clare Railway Act 1860 and terminating in the Parish of Long Melford; Railway No. 3 commencing out of the above railway and terminated in the Parish of Clare in the County of Suffolk in a field called 'The Bailey'; Railway No. 4 commencing out of railway No. 3 in the parish of Clare and terminating by a junction with the ECR in the Parish of Great Shelford in the County of Cambridge, and Railway No. 5 commencing out of railway No. 2 at Long Melford and terminating in the Parish of St James, Bury St Edmunds. Of specific interest was Railway No. 6 wholly in the parish of Haverhill in the county of Essex commencing out of the intended railway No. 4 and terminating by a junction with the said extension of the Colne Valley & Halstead Railway. Clause 19 required the junction with the Colne Valley & Halstead Railway to be made to the reasonable satisfaction of the Engineer of that Company. Clause 27 stated:

The company shall forthwith proceed to the construction of the line between Haverhill Junction and Cambridge and no part of the railway shall be opened until the said line from Haverhill Junction to Cambridge shall be opened to the public.

Two years were allowed for the compulsory purchase of land and three years for the completion of works. Clause 66 required the Sudbury & Clare Railway to abandon or relinquish construction of the whole of the works authorised by the 1860 Act. Clause 69 noted that if at any time any part of the Colne Valley company line from Chappel station to Haverhill was completed *'to the satisfaction of Mr John Fowler or in the case of his death to the satisfaction of an engineer to be appointed by the Board of Trade'*, the Colne Valley Company could under notice of their Common Seal require the ECR to take their plant and stores at valuation and work permanently those railways that were completed, whilst the following clause stipulated the terms of the takeover, the ECR paying the CV&HR 50 per cent of the gross receipts earned between Chappel and Haverhill and their mileage proportion on traffic from or destined to the CV&HR earned between Haverhill and Cambridge. If the company did not take over the working of the Colne Valley Company by clause 70 the company was to afford reasonable and proper facilities for through booking and the running of carriages and wagons. The ECR company was authorised to raise £600,000 to finance the new venture and borrow not exceeding £200,000 once the entire capital had been subscribed for and half actually paid up.

After the initial opening of the CV&HR, Mr Cressall, the principal carrier from Halstead, experienced the unfair competition provided by rail, especially to London. Not wishing to surrender his business altogether he agreed to act as a feeder to the CV&HR and transfer his London traffic to the railway. The transfer was welcomed by both the ECR and CV&HR and on 23rd October 1861 it was agreed traffic would be conveyed at the usual rates whilst Cressall would be issued with a Second Class pass for one day each week between Halstead and Bishopsgate to enable him to negotiate business at the London end. Unfortunately the service encountered early problems and early in December 1861, Cressall complained of serious delays to his traffic at Halstead awaiting wagons and at Chappel station where wagons were standing for days awaiting an engine to take them forward. The CV&HR authorities complained that the ECR was sabotaging the traffic whilst the ECR officers countered stating the carrier and the local company were detaining wagons unnecessarily and threatened to raise demurrage.

The unruly and unorthodox ways of rural railwaymen came to light on 6th November 1861 when CV&HR Signalman Goose of Chappel was accused of riding on the footplate of an ECR locomotive, with the full cognizance of the engine crew for the purpose of shooting a hare. The report was evidently fabricated on its journey to Bishopsgate and thence back to Halstead, for at the subsequent enquiry Signalman Goose was exonerated from blame but the ECR station master admitted to receiving a hare from the fireman and both men were duly cautioned as to their future conduct.

In December 1861 the subject of delays at Chappel and Marks Tey were again raised but the ECR operating authorities were adamant that only five minutes' waiting would be permitted at Chappel Junction and it was totally the responsibility of the CV Company to ensure their trains ran to time to maintain connections. Apparently the chaotic arrangements continued, further fuelled by a claim for £11 9s 0d from a Mr Jarman early in January 1862, in respect of a wagon lost in transit between London and Halstead. The local ECR staff reported its delivery to Chappel and transfer to the CV&HR and therefore the local company should settle the claim. After further enquiries the CV&HR staff were equally adamant the wagon had not been handed over and on 12th February refused to admit liability. In the meantime the ECR agreed for a Composite carriage to run through from Castle Hedingham to Marks Tey on payment of mileage charges on the ECR. The CV&HR complained and could not agree so the weekly charge of 9s 0d would remain.

Meanwhile, adverse weather delayed construction of the extension; heavy rain on Wednesday 8th and Thursday 9th January 1862 had left the terrain near Yeldham like a quagmire. When excavation of a cutting some ten feet in depth resumed on Friday 10th the navvies found it extremely difficulty at the workface and at about 11.00am the earth suddenly gave way and buried two labourers under several tons of earth. Immediately their colleagues struggled to release the men and it was only after half an hour of frantic digging that Henry Bunton of Stambourne and John Watkinson of Sible Hedingham were released. Unfortunately Bunton was already dead, and although Watkinson was found unconscious he succumbed fifteen minutes later. At the Coroner's inquest held at the White Hart Inn Great Yeldham on the following Monday, 13th January, Joseph Lady the ganger in charge of the thirty-seven men at the workface explained the embankment had not been undermined and the fall of earth

was, in his opinion, totally caused by the extremely wet surface. William Smith and John Smith, both navies who had witnessed the fall, supported the evidence and indeed the former praised Thomas Ruggles who had been injured for pushing him out of the way of the collapsing earth. William Codd, the Coroner, returned a verdict of Accidental Death and recommended that William Munro as contractor might exercise more caution in future.

The temporary buildings provided at Halstead for the opening of the line were a source of complaints and on 6th February 1862 tenders were invited for the construction of a permanent station to the design and specification of Cubitt. The specification revealed to the public two weeks later required the structure to be built of white stock bricks, facings to be of blue, red and terracotta patent bricks. The platform was to be covered in with a handsome awning of corrugated zinc and plate glass supported by six handsome iron columns. The contract was subsequently awarded to Rayner & Runnacles who tendered at £2,730.

In March 1862 severe flooding caused the swollen River Colne to destroy the railway fencing near Blue Bridge, allowing sheep to stray on to the line. An approaching train ran into the flock killing three animals belonging to Bridges Harvey, a major shareholder of the railway company, and adequate compensation was duly obtained.

By the end of March the construction of the extension was almost completed and the Secretary advised the BOT that the obligatory inspection was required. Colonel William Yolland duly inspected the 2 miles 42 chains extension from Hedingham to Great Yeldham on 29th April 1862. He found the width of the formation was again 18 feet, as land had been purchased and overbridges built for double line, although only single track was laid. A siding was installed at Great Yeldham and spacing between the main line and the siding was the correct 6 feet. In his detailed examination Yolland inspected three underbridges, one overbridge and two small timber viaducts on the section. The underbridges all had brick abutments, two had cast iron girders and the other wrought iron girders, the latter having the greatest span of 38 feet 9 inches on the skew. All had timber platforms on which the rails were spiked to longitudinal sleepers. The girders were considered to be sufficiently strong by calculation and gave moderate deflections to bear the weight of the locomotives working the line. The occupational overbridge was incomplete at the time of inspection, although the arch had been formed and the centre struck for some time. The inspector considered one of the small wooden viaducts could be improved by having the piles which supported the centre longitudinal timber carrying the rails diagonally braced, as on similar structures. A 12-foot-wide brick culvert had sunk under the weight but as the condition had shown no further deterioration an occasional check was the only requirement.

During the inspection Yolland noted several items requiring remedial attention and listed them in his subsequent report. An unauthorised level crossing carrying a private carriage road over the railway at Yeldham should have been an underbridge. The crossing was installed at deference to the wishes of the local inhabitants and the inspector could see no difficulty in providing a bridge. On the three underbridges, tie rods were required to connect the iron girders and provide necessary strengthening. A short distance of line near Yeldham station required straightening, lifting and packing, and attention to drainage, whilst the siding leading to a shed near Yeldham station in which the contractor's engine was stabled was either to be removed or properly protected by signals if extended use was likely. At Hedingham station the railings at the end of the platform were too close to the line and required setting back to a distance of 6 feet from the platform edge. Indicators were also required on the facing points on the main line.

The Engineer had informed Yolland that the contractor expected to finish the line to Haverhill within three to four weeks. The Colonel was adamant that if the railway was to remain independent of the ECR, engine turntables would be essential at Chappel and Haverhill if the line was to be worked by tender locomotives. Concluding his report, Yolland considered the line to be in fair order but regretted the chairs were only secured to the sleepers by trenails. If it was the intention for the CV&HR to be *worked as a through and fast line* the permanent way was insufficient to ensure public safety. Because of this and the incompleteness of the works, Yolland refused to sanction the opening of the section beyond Hedingham.

Disappointed by the decision, Munro was instructed to make good the deficiencies. Yolland then returned to re-inspect the line on 17th May 1862 and found the indicators to the facing points on the main line were on order. The points leading to the contractor's shed at Yeldham were still in place but the company officials assured the inspector they would be removed before the line opened to traffic. A clock was required at Great Yeldham station viewable from the platform. Cubitt, the CV&HR Engineer,

ANNO VICESIMO QUINTO & VICESIMO SEXTO

VICTORIÆ REGINÆ.

****

Cap. ccxxiii.

An Act to amalgamate the *Eastern Counties*, the *East Anglian*, the *Newmarket*, the *Eastern Union*, and the *Norfolk* Railway Companies; and for other Purposes.   [7th *August* 1862.]

WHEREAS by the Local Act Sixth and Seventh of *William* the Fourth, Chapter One hundred and six, relating to the *Eastern Counties* Railway Company, the *Eastern Counties* Railway Company were incorporated: And whereas by the Local Acts herein-after mentioned, relating to the *Eastern Counties* Railway Company, (that is to say,) First and Second of *Victoria*, Chapter Eighty-one; Fourth of *Victoria*, Chapter Fourteen; Seventh of *Victoria*, Chapter Nineteen; Seventh and Eighth of *Victoria*, Chapters Sixty-two and Seventy-one; Eighth and Ninth of *Victoria*, Chapters Eighty-five, One hundred and ten, and Two hundred and one; Ninth of *Victoria*, Chapter Fifty-two; Ninth and Tenth of *Victoria*, Chapters One hundred and seventy-two, Two hundred and five, Two hundred and fifty-eight, Three hundred and fifty-six, Three hundred and fifty-seven, and Three hundred and sixty seven; Tenth and Eleventh of *Victoria*, Chapters Ninety-two, One hundred and fifty-six, One hundred and fifty-seven, One hundred and fifty-eight, and Two hundred and thirty-five; Fifteenth of *Victoria*, Chapters Thirty,

[*Local.*]   42 *H*   Thirty-

6 & 7 W. 4.
c. cvi.
(Eastern
Counties
Railway.)

Recital of
Eastern
Counties
Railway
Acts.

Great Eastern Railway Amalgamation Act 7th August 1862 front page.

promised iron spikes would be inserted with the trenails fastening chairs to the sleepers at the rail joints. After a recent accident at Faversham on the London, Chatham & Dover Railway, Yolland did *not feel justified in passing any line on which chairs are fastened to the sleepers by trenails*. In his report the Colonel remarked he had *not received details of the method of working the line or action the company proposed to take regarding the unauthorised crossing*. Once these details were received and were to the satisfaction of Their Lordships, he had no objection to the section of line opening for traffic.

During his visit to the CV&HR the Colonel also inspected the portion of line where part of the turnpike road leading from Hedingham to Great Yeldham ran alongside the railway. The Trustees of the Essex Turnpike Road had approached the BOT for the erection of screens as they considered *horses would be frightened by railway engines and carriages, thus endangering travellers on horseback or in horse drawn vehicles*. Yolland was met on site by Mr Majendie and Mr May, local representatives of the Trustees. He found the road ran for a considerable distance at 14 to 16 feet away from the line. May thought the erection of a screen would be ineffective and considered the deviation of the road the only solution. Brewster, the CV&HR Chairman agreed to the diversion, paying a portion of the sum originally set aside for the screens for the work. In return it was agreed the Trustees would arrange and finance the cost of the order. It was also agreed to erect screens 300 yards south and 60 yards north of the bridge carrying the road over the turnpike on the south and west side of the railway, the screens being 8 feet in height and close boarded.

May 1862 was an unfortunate month for Munro, the CV&HR contractor, for he was apprehended on two occasions for travelling from a Colne Valley station to Witham ECR with outdated tickets. On 21st May the ECR directors agreed to prosecute. Undeterred, the following day Munro was advertising for one hundred men to assist with the construction of the line through the parish of Ridgewell, between Yeldham and Birdbrook, with the promise of high wages

The requisite details required by Yolland following his inspection having been forwarded to the BOT, the line from Hedingham to Yeldham opened to traffic on 26th May 1862 with only minor celebrations to mark the event. For unknown reasons a board meeting refers to the drawing up of a draft agreement for the line to be leased to a Mr Birkbeck, but such proposals came to nothing. For the opening, the local squire not only entertained some of the railway dignitaries but also provided a dinner for all the 400 navvies who had constructed the line, in lieu of the normal barrels of beer. To celebrate the occasion the company provided a special train service for the public with return fares of 6d from Colne and 4d from Halstead. The purchase of land for the new section of line had been expensive, for at the half yearly meeting for the period ending 30th June 1862 it was revealed that for the eleven and a half miles completed and open for traffic, land costs and compensation had cost £31,000.

The half yearly report for the period ending 30th June 1862, presented on 7th August, advised that Cubit as Engineer was of the opinion the line to Haverhill would be completed by the end of the year, *with fair exertion on the part of the contractor Mr Munro* who was employing between 300 and 400 men on the work; in fact earthworks proved more difficult than anticipated and a further 300 men were subsequently engaged in September. The balance sheet showed the standing of the capital account.

	£
Parliamentary Expenses (Original and Extension Acts)	15,798
Contractor	104,850
Engineer	10,160
Permanent Way	489
Rolling stock	10,784
Access to Chappel junction	1,500
Interest on loans	9,406
Station buildings	564
Auditors and directors	2,093
General charges and office expenses	2,931
Land and compensation claims	31,000
Total	189,575

Revenue account:

	£	s	d
Passenger duty and rates	41	4	5
Coal and coke for locomotives	225	11	11
Oil, tallow and other stores	59	7	7
Engine and wagon repairs	66	14	0
Clothing (overalls for enginemen)	4	10	0
Oil and gas for signals and carriages	5	6	3
Coal for station use	10	18	10
Uniforms for station staff	12	19	1
Horses (feed and other expenses)	30	0	11
Maintenance of permanent way	503	1	3
Advertising	18	5	4

For the six-month period a total of 1,811 passengers travelled First Class, 4,631 Second Class, 8,565 Third Class and 7,078 Parliamentary, with £819 5s 10d collected in fares. Goods receipts were £1,063 5s 10d in respect of the conveyance of 1,515 tons of coal and coke and 1,421 tons of mineral traffic The carriage of livestock, mail, parcel and demurrage payments amassed a further £169 18s 8d.

Having leased or taken over the workings of all major railways in East Anglia, the ECR was the principal party to a scheme being prepared for the amalgamation of the Eastern Counties, Eastern Union, East Anglian, Newmarket and Norfolk railways into a new undertaking to be known as the Great Eastern Railway. The Act sanctioning the amalgamation – the Great Eastern Railway Act 1862 (25 and 26 Vict cap ccxxiii) – received the Royal Assent on 7th August 1862 but took effect retrospectively from July of that year. The Act authorised anew those clauses granted in the 1861 Act for the extension from Sudbury to Cambridge and Bury St Edmunds, and several clauses in the lengthy statute involved relationships between the GER and the CV&HR.

Clause 201 authorised the GER line to Long Melford from the termination of the CSVHR line from Sudbury and on to Clare, Haverhill and Shelford, as well as Long Melford to Bury St Edmunds. Of specific interest was the Haverhill branch, being a railway wholly in the Parish of Haverhill in the County of Essex, commencing from and out of the said intended Clare and Shelford line and terminating by a junction with the Haverhill extension of the Colne Valley and Halstead Railway. By clause 213 the communication between the Haverhill branch and Haverhill extension of the CV&HR was to be made and maintained by the GER to the reasonable satisfaction of the CV&HR Engineer, and in case of dispute the matter was to be determined by a referee to be appointed on the application of either company by the Board of Trade.

Clause 274 instructed that:

if at any time and as often as any part of the Colne Valley and Halstead Railway Company from Chappel to Haverhill shall have been completed to the reasonable satisfaction of Mr John Fowler, Civil Engineer, or in the case of his death to the satisfaction of an engineer to be appointed by the Board of Trade and the officer appointed for that purpose shall have reported the same fit for public traffic, the Colne Valley and Halstead Company shall by notice under their common seal require the (GER) Company to take their plant and stores at a valuation, and to work permanently those railways or the part thereof which have been completed, and shall deliver up possession thereof, and of all stations, buildings, works, plant, stores and machinery appurtenant thereto the company shall within one month after delivery – pay the value of the plant and stores to be ascertained by valuation – and thereupon work and manage the said Railway.

The GER was then beholden to manage the line and work the traffic and supply all rolling stock and provide and pay all railway staff. Clause 275 stated that the sum to be appropriated and retained by the GER in respect of working and managing the system, unless otherwise agreed, was 50 per cent of the gross receipts per annum. After completion of the CV&HR between Chappel and Haverhill, and the opening of the GER route from Haverhill to Cambridge, the GER was to credit the CV&HR their full mileage proportion of receipts calculated upon the shortest route. One half of all traffic arising at Cambridge or Haverhill or at any intermediate station and passing to or destined for Chappel or Colchester or any intermediate station, and of one half of all traffic arising at Colchester or Chappel or any intermediate station and passing to or destined for Haverhill or Cambridge or any intermediate station, whether the traffic was carried by the GER over the CV&HR route or by any other route, the GER was required to keep separate accounts of all receipts and payments so the CV&HR Secretary or Auditor could at reasonable times giving 24 hours notice, examine the accounts. Clause 276 stipulated that any agreement made under the Act was to be approved by the Board of Trade, whilst the following clause stated that any modification could be negotiated and amended after a period of ten years, although clause 278 permitted the GER to give notice to the BOT if they required to terminate any agreement.

Clause 279, however, offered the GER an escape by stating that:

if and whenever the Company do not work the CV&HR then the Company was required from time-to-time to afford all reasonable and proper facilities, by through booking, the running of carriages and otherwise, for the transfer of traffic to and from each line, subject to necessary agreements between the two parties.

In the case of disagreement, clause 281 required the matter to be settled by arbitration as determined by The Railway Companies Arbitration Act 1859.

The early opening of the line beyond Yeldham was highly optimistic and almost impossible, for Munro had only started his recruitment drive for another three hundred workers when James Brewster, Chairman of the CV&HR, wrote to the Horatio Love, Chairman of the newly formed GER, on 2nd September 1862 advising that the CV&HR intended to open their line between Yeldham and Haverhill in the near future. He suggested the GER abandon their proposed line between Melford and Haverhill in favour of a short line from Clare to Yeldham in connection with the CV&HR, to which he alluded the residents of Clare approved. He reiterated that the CV&HR, when opening between Yeldham and Haverhill, would provide no intermediate stations, although one could be provided at a later date. Brewster considered that by using the CV&HR route from Clare to Haverhill the GER would benefit from considerable savings, which he suggested could be better used to take over the CV&HR. Failing that, he proposed the two companies could reach an amicable agreement for the GER to operate the CV&HR services.

Sinclair, the GE Engineer, was requested to investigate and on 30th September reported that Parliamentary approval would be required if the GER abandoned the Melford to Haverhill line, and a pledge had been made to construct the railway in its entirety. Brewster's suggestion was totally unacceptable and would result in a circuitous route from Haverhill and Clare to Bury St Edmunds. Sinclair was adamant the GER would not abandon the proposed parallel route near Haverhill unless Cubitt, the CV&HR Engineer confirmed the abandonment of the CV route. He considered the independent line in the middle of GER territory would cause *'considerable mischief'* and recommended the GER absorb the smaller company. J.B. Owen, the GER Secretary, replied to the CV&HR on 8th October stating his company had no intention of abandoning their proposed line from Long Melford to Haverhill, the GER Parliamentary obligation would not let the GER deviate or build a line from Clare to join up with the CV&HR. Owen added that the GER was willing to purchase the local company outright on suitable terms. The CV&HR Secretary was duly advised of the proposal and the company was asked to submit their terms for purchase so that the Bishopsgate directors could consider the matter. E. Harvey, the CV&HR Secretary, duly replied on 1st November 1862, reporting that his directors regretted the *'continuing persistence'* of the two lines running parallel for four miles near Haverhill. His directors still considered it practicable for the GER to deviate their line to run to the CV&HR route northward from Haverhill. The CV&HR directors would support the bill to construct the connecting line and would accept GER preference stock already credited to the

amount expended on the CV&HR line and transfer that to the GER Company. If the GER purchased the CV&HR Company it would be beneficial to the district and save the larger company £50,000. The GER directors considered the proposals but, with their own line in such an advanced state, saw little advantage in taking over the CV line. Owen duly replied to the CV&HR on 11th February 1863 declining to take over the company.

Matters between the two companies then deteriorated and, because of the poor service provided by the GER connections at Chappel, the CV&HR sent a deputation to Bishopsgate in November 1862 to seek improvements in the train service to Marks Tey. Their hostile approach met with little success.

The CV&HR full results for half year ending 31st December 1862, compared with the same period in 1861, showed an encouraging increase in passengers, freight tonnage and not the least in revenue.

	Six months ending	
	31st December 1861	31st December 1862
Passengers	27,887	31,425
Goods Tonnage	13,209	14,789
	£ s d	£ s d
Passenger receipts	886 3 1	1,156 18 10
Goods receipts	1,689 13 9	1,389 16 10
Parcels receipts	174 3 2	192 10 9
	2,150 0 0	2,689 6 5

The half yearly meeting of shareholders was held in the Town Hall, Halstead on Tuesday 24th February 1863. Although the line had been open to Yeldham for some months, completion of the section thence to Haverhill was not expected until late April despite the presence of an additional 300 workers. The unfinished works did not preclude one of Munro's engines with three coaches conveying shareholders from Haverhill to Halstead for the meeting, although all passengers were advised they travelled at their own risk! James Brewster chaired the meeting, which was attended by some sixty people, and after the initial introductions gave the directors report

LM 2MT 2-6-0 No. 46467 breasts the minor summit east of Chappel and Wakes Colne with a Marks Tey to Haverhill train via the Colne Valley on 1st April 1952.
G. Powell

on progress. The permanent way on the opened sections was in good order and additional chairs had been installed between Halstead and Chappel to consolidate the track. The locomotives and rolling stock were being efficiently maintained and additional carriages were being obtained. The gathering heard that the directors had been unable to make any definite agreement with the GER regarding the arrangements at Haverhill and despite correspondence from Owen, the GER Secretary, it was still thought advantageous to lodge a bill in Parliament for a line from Clare so that the GER could use the CV&HR to Haverhill, instead of building a separate route. The subject was to be laid before the GER board. Cubitt reported there were few problems with the earthworks on the way to Haverhill and completion of the line was expected within eight weeks. The revenue account for the half year ending 31st December 1862 was £2,689 6s 5d, which after deduction of working expenses amounted to £1,050 2s 8d.

Safety on the railway left much to be desired, for on 28th February 1863 at Halstead Petty Sessions John Everett, a labourer employed by Mr Metson of Great Maplestead, was charged with wilfully leaving the gates open at Metson's occupational level crossing. Giving evidence, William Stimpson, the permanent way inspector, reported the gates had been deliberately left open requiring a train to stop at the crossing to avoid running over animals. Everitt was found guilty and fined 10s 0d with 12s 0d costs.

Having almost completed the railway, Munro began disposal of all equipment in a sale that was conducted in Haverhill station yard by the auctioneers F.C. Fitch of Baythorne Grove near Halstead, and Samuel J. Surridge, also of Halstead. The auction was advertised in the *Halstead Gazette* in early February 1863 and the various lots included: locomotives, 200 wagons, barrows, tumbrels, carts, timber carriages, temporary rails and sleepers, complete with *'numerous other effects'*, forming *'first rate railway plant'*. The following month the next auction was advertised for 6th March at 11.00am as a *'clearance sale'*, and included fifty wagons, 100 barrows, a timber carriage van, two French cart tumbrels, a portable 6-horsepower engine, as well as twenty valuable and powerful young horses and numerous sets of harnesses and other effects. Twenty lots of building ground were also available.

Although on the surface problems appeared to be resolved, a long-standing argument had been fought between James Brewster, the CV&HR Chairman, and Ashurst Majendie, a prominent landowner at Castle Hedingham, who had complained the railway was built too close to the Turnpike Road at Castle Hedingham. Not meeting with any satisfaction, Majendie had taken his complaint to the 'Court of Trust' at Chelmsford. Brewster retaliated and wrote an open letter to the *Halstead Gazette* emphasizing Majendie's own land agent had asked for the line to be deviated. Brewster added:

the entire line through Castle Hedingham was altered to the very serious loss of the Company to meet Majendie's wishes and therefore he should not have made the complaint. He was of the opinion that he and Cubitt, the engineer had yielded far too much to such landowners in the neighbourhood.

The case was heard in April, after which William Munro added his voice, writing to the *Halstead Gazette* criticizing local people who did nor appreciate the improvements the railway would bring and for the fabricated stories that were aired at the Court of Trust hearing, where it was claimed horses were *'being frightened by engines'* because the rail was too near the Turnpike. He then slated

Majendie: *'Why fix on the poor little line a cost the wealthy can afford?'* Munro then threatened to take the case to the BOT regarding the *'origins of the diversion'* and precedents on other lines. A fortnight later a further letter made reference to the *'The Hedingham Squire and his regrettable behaviour against the railway'*, the writer adding it was the actions of *'a fussy old bachelor'*.

Other disputes came to the fore. On 19th June the case of Selby versus the Colne Valley and Halstead Railway was heard at the Vice Chancellor's Court in London concerning the progress of the railway through Hedingham and the effect of altering the junction of two roads thus enabling the company to build only one bridge instead of two structures. The Vice Chancellor, Sir J.P. Wood, ruled that the company was entitled to modify the plans as necessary and there was no way that inferred they had acted improperly. He also praised the testimony given by the Company Engineer Cubitt and dismissed the case with costs.

The CV&HR directors were still seething at losing the opportunity for extending the railway; they published a further Bill for the 1863 session proposing the construction of a line from the junction at Haverhill with the GER line already under construction to link up the Clare to Shelford line in the adjoining parish of Withersfield and a branch from Birdbrook to a junction with the Clare to Shelford line. It further proposed the GER should abandon their line between these two points and also to abandon their Haverhill branch. The appeal was more successful and the company was granted statutory authority to construct these lines. The proposal had its disadvantages, however, for it left the CV&HR totally dependent on the GER and thus gave it no independent access to either Colchester or Cambridge. The failure resulted in the L&NWR totally losing interest and the proposed financial support was withdrawn. With the withdrawal of such powerful backing the CV&HR found it impossible to raise the necessary funds and the powers were allowed to lapse.

On 13th April 1863 the CV&HR manager requested the through running of CV trains to Marks Tey. The GER traffic authorities considered the matter and, as they were seeking to promote additional traffic, replied stating they would accept such working on the payment of 50 per cent of the gross receipts for the section of journey between Chappel and Marks Tey and return. At this period three of the company directors fell into disagreement, resulting in the resignation of Brewster, with Major S.P. Veriker becoming Chairman although Brewster remained a director.

After what seemed an impossible length of time to the shareholders, the railway reached Haverhill. Captain H.W. Tyler inspected the final section of the CV&HR from Yeldham on 23rd April 1863. The route was just over 7 miles in length with the steepest gradient of 1 in 80 and sharpest curve of 44 chains radius. The line was single except for the addition of sidings at Haverhill. Tyler found the nine underbridges and two overbridges substantially constructed and standing well, although he recommended checks to be added by the side of the timber beams on one structure. The sleepers required packing at the end of some of the underbridges whilst clocks were to be seen from the platform at Yeldham and Haverhill. Several pairs of temporary points and sections of track used by the contractor, required removal. The Captain recommended the Train Staff and Ticket method of operation for the single line and the provision of a 40 feet diameter turntable at Haverhill. Steven's patent switches were also required at the facing points connecting with the main line at Yeldham and Haverhill. Because of the incompleteness of the works Tyler refused to sanction the opening of the line and also required a certificate from the CV&HR for the method of working. He also stipulated the installation of facing point switches was to be completed within a timescale of three months.

On 6th May 1863 Cubit advised the BOT that all the minor deficiencies had been rectified and provided a certificate confirming the company would work the single line by Train Staff only. He iterated that work was in hand to provide a 40 feet diameter turntable at Haverhill and switch indicators at Yeldham and Haverhill within three months. On receipt of the information Tyler agreed to the final section of line opening for traffic without further inspection. The turntable was never provided and Cubit, dissatisfied with the operation of the railway, made several approaches to lease the line.

ABOVE: CV&HR 2-4-2T No. 4 formerly *Hedingham* at Halstead. Built by Hawthorn, Leslie & Company to the specifications prepared by George Copus, the General Manager, it was delivered in 1894 (Maker's No. 2283). Like others of the class, the engine visited the GER Stratford Works in several occasions for general and intermediate repairs. The running number was allocated in 1902/3 but the name was not removed until 1911.

M. Root collection

LEFT: Earls Colne goods shed formed of corrugated iron and timber under construction for brickwork has yet to be installed at the base of the structure. The goods office is located at the far end of the building, which already bears evidence of smoke from locomotives using the entrance on shed road. *M. Root collection*

3

Completion to Haverhill

THE FIRST TRAIN TO HAVERHILL ran on Monday 10th May 1863, to the temporary station. Following this official opening the directors and others went to the home of Daniel Gurteen, a director and shareholder, and owner of a cloth manufacturing plant at Haverhill. Horner, Greenwood and Brewster attended, the latter with his daughters, and among the guests was Thomas Moy, who was developing his coal distribution business. A notable absentee was Major Veriker. In addition to the station, other facilities provided at Haverhill included a goods shed, a locomotive repair shop and engine shed. In the two days following the opening over 2,000 people took advantage to journey on the new line. Robert Johnson Watt was displaced as General Manager about this time and replaced by John B. Cooper, with Charles Brogden Sperling as Company Engineer. For the opening of the section from Yeldham to Haverhill the station at Birdbrook was not completed and trains called at a temporary halt at Ridgewell Wash, if required, until the structure was completed by mid-June.

Not all was harmony on the CV&HR, however, for on 18th May 1863 many people gathered to watch the arrival of Sangers Circus to Halstead. The procession, almost half a mile in length and including the gigantic elephant Ajax, was proceeding towards the town but on reaching Trinity Street level crossing found the way blocked by low strung telegraph lines which had been erected between Halstead and Yeldham the previous year. Proving too low for some of the vehicles to pass under, the procession was forced to turn round and find another way into town, much to the annoyance of several hundred observers eager to seen the animals.

Shortly after the opening of the railway to Haverhill, Halstead market was resurrected amid much rejoicing. The railway had played an important part in the decision to reopen the facility and prosperity was such that a public dinner was held at the town hall on the first anniversary of the event.

The shortage of finance and several outstanding operational problems were resolved when the Colne Valley and Halstead Railway Act (26 and 27 Vict cap clxxxvi) received the Royal Assent on 21st July 1863. The statute authorised the company to increase their capital and use part of the Great Eastern Railway at Haverhill (when completed). Clause 2 ratified that it was lawful to construct a level crossing over carriage road No. 59 in the Parish of Great Yeldham as deposited in plans attached to the CV&HR Extension Act 1859, either by single or double line of rails; but the following clause forbade the shunting of trains or allow any train, engine, carriage or truck to stand across the same, Clause 4 dictated that for the convenience and security of the public the company was to provide a lodge adjacent to the level crossing. Clause 6 empowered the Great Eastern Railway to allow the Colne Valley Company to use their railway between the Colne Valley Junction and the GER station at Haverhill, together with the use of assets. Of more importance to the local company were the powers included in clause 8, authorising the company to raise an additional £28,000 by the issue of new shares, whilst clause 13 permitted the borrowing

of £9,000 once the new shares had been wholly subscribed for and half actually paid up.

On 4th September 1863 the third and last clearance sale of railway equipment used by contractors, blacksmiths, brickmakers and others was held in the yard adjoining Haverhill station at 12.00 noon. The lots included two good engines – the *Cam* and *Colne* built by England & Company, a portable 4-horsepower steam engine, railway wagons, barrows and carts, timber and engine carriages and several useful cart horses, harnesses for horses and a *'handsome pony'*. Smaller items included blacksmiths' bellows and brickmaking requisites. The two locomotives were probably removed from the sale at an early stage for they were initially used

ANNO VICESIMO SEXTO & VICESIMO SEPTIMO

VICTORIÆ REGINÆ.

****

Cap. clxxxvi.

An Act to enable the *Colne Valley and Halstead* Railway Company to increase their Capital, to use Part of the *Great Eastern* Railway at *Haverhill*, and for other Purposes with respect to the same Company.　　[21st *July* 1863.]

WHEREAS by "The *Colne Valley and Halstead* Railway (Extension) Act, 1859," the *Colne Valley and Halstead* Railway Company were authorized to extend their Railway from *Halstead* in *Essex* to *Haverhill* in the same County: And whereas in the Year One thousand eight hundred and sixty-one an Act was passed enabling the *Eastern Counties* Railway Company to make a Railway from *Long Melford* in *Suffolk*, through *Clare* and *Haverhill*, to join the *Eastern Counties* Railway in the Parish of *Great Shelford* in the Neighbourhood of *Cambridge*: And whereas by an Act passed in the last Session of Parliament the *Eastern Counties* Railway Company was dissolved, and was merged in a Company incorporated by the same Act under the Style of " *Great Eastern* Railway Company," and by the same Act all the Railways in the Counties of *Norfolk*, *Suffolk*, and *Essex* are,

22 & 23 Vict. c. cxxii.

24 & 25 Vict. c. cxxxi.

25 & 26 Vict. c. ccxiii.

[*Local.*]　　　　　O　　　　　with

Colne Valley and Halstead Railway Act 21st July 1863 front page.

by Munro on the completion of the Wivenhoe to Brightlingsea line and then transferred to Ireland and re-gauged for use on the Athernry to Ennis contract.

At the end of September 1863 the CV&HR approached the GER with a request that two of their engines be conveyed from Chappel to Stratford for repairs. In a gesture of goodwill it was agreed on 30th September that the locomotives would be moved at half the normal charges.

The railway then settled to provide the local populace with a regular service although mishaps continued to occur. On New Year's Day 1864 the Up morning train which was not booked to stop at Colne demolished the level crossing gates. The crossing keeper who had totally overlooked the running of the train was later admonished for his error.

The possibility of a takeover was again mooted at the end of March 1864, when the CV&HR directors again approached the GER regarding the possibility of through running between Chappel and Marks Tey. The Bishopsgate directors discussed the matter on 31st March and asked the Superintendent to investigate. The officer duly reported to the Traffic Committee on 13th April stating that the GER were 'most anxious' to promote the through running for their convenience and also for the public. Whether voicing his own thoughts or passing on the general opinion of local railwaymen he added that the company was prepared to take up the working of the CV&HR for 50 per cent of the gross receipts in accordance with the Act of Parliament and such action would best serve the interests of both companies!

The through running between Chappel and Marks Tey never materialised, for at the end of April 1864 the CV&HR authorities complained to the GER that lack of Third Class accommodation on GER trains operating between Sudbury and Marks Tey was having a detrimental effect on passenger traffic and it was suggested the Braintree branch, where adequate Third Class accommodation was provided, was drawing patronage away from the CV&HR as the pro rata mileage fares paid were much higher via Chappel and Marks Tey than via Braintree and Witham. It was also stated the GER would delay a CV&HR train from entering Chappel station, thereby causing passengers to miss their connecting service. The GER authorities retaliated, stating the ban on allowing CV trains to run between Chappel and Marks Tey was because of the poor condition of the CV rolling stock. It was, however, agreed to make an effort to break the deadlock and ask for an independent assessment of the situation, after which the GER would possibly allow running powers.

The disappointment of the loss of possible backing from the L&NWR found the CV&HR directors seeking other ways of maintaining a connection to Cambridge; on 6th May 1864 the Company advertised in the Colchester Gazette (actual date of notice 2nd May) inviting tenders from Post Masters, Coach Proprietors and others to provide and work a daily omnibus service, Sundays excepted, between Haverhill and Cambridge. Parties tendering were requested to state terms per month until the following August or until such time as the GER extension to Cambridge was opened. So desperate was the company for such trade that a subsidy 'for the proper performance of the service' was offered. Tenders were to be forwarded to John B. Cooper at his office in Halstead.

Following the offer made in April, by 23rd June 1864 the CV&HR directors intimated their willingness to be absorbed by the GER and it was mutually agreed that a Mr Harrison of the North Eastern Railway would act as assessor for settlement of the terms of amalgamation. The GER board, however, remained aloof of such proposals and agreed on 21st July that Harrison remit his report determining the value of the CV&HR line to the GER.

The Essex & West Suffolk Gazette reported on 1st July 1864 that James Brewster's health had improved to the extent he had resumed his full duties as Chairman of the company. The Hon Major Vereker was Vice Chairman, whilst Robert J. Watt was reappointed as temporary General Manager in place of John B. Cooper who had resigned on 23rd June 1864.

The poor financial standing of the Halstead company continued despite the cash injection authorised by the Act of 21st July 1863, for the GER Traffic Committee made reference to the outstanding issue of the rental to be paid by the CV&HR Company for the use of Chappel station at their meeting on 19th July 1864. The Secretary was duly instructed to remind the Company of the overdue payments and the need to resolve the issue.

In 1864 the Halstead Local Board of Health advocated the building of a Corn Exchange on a site chosen adjacent to the railway station forecourt. The land was assumed to belong to Halstead United Charities and the Trustees of the Charities had donated a sum of £1,500 from the rates for the expected costs. The CV&HR directors, however, tactfully reminded the authority that by Act of Parliament they owned the required land but were prepared to transfer ownership provided it was for 'the purpose, which will promote traffic upon the railway.' In retaliation, the United Charities advised that the railway company had not paid for the purchase of the land and so the Local Board sought legal opinion and engaged a solicitor to investigate. The matter was dealt with by Robert Baxter of Baxter, Norman & Rose of Westminster and, after investigation, on 10th July 1865 he was of the opinion 'the railway company have powers to take the land and are in fact in possession of it'. He added no claim of creditors against the railway company can affect the power to deal with the land they possess. As the CV&HR was in agreement with the building of the Corn Exchange he suggested a deed be drawn up between the three parties. The corn exchange was subsequently completed in December 1865 at a cost of £1,130.

The importance of interchange at Chappel resulted in the GER Goods Manager requesting the provision of a stable to accommodate two horses. The necessary authority for construction, estimated at £50, was given on 17th August 1864. Work commenced on construction of the connecting line between the GER and CV&HR at Haverhill in 1864, thus enabling the smooth interchange of traffic under the direction of C.B. Sperling for the Colne Valley company and the GER Engineer.

At the half yearly meeting held in August 1864 the CV&HR shareholders were advised traffic earnings were much below what the district was capable of producing. The want of sufficient rolling stock, the difficulty experienced organizing an efficient traffic staff on such a short line, and the non-completion of the extension to Cambridge fully accounted for the state of the company, which was 'hemmed in on every side by the GE'. To ease matters, the rolling stock was sold to Robert Tweedy of Truro for £9,010 and leased back. At this period the Chairman was Major the Honorable S.P. Vereker of 10 Warwick Square, London, with fellow directors James Brewster of Ashford Lodge, Halstead, Robert Ellington Greenwood of Sloe Park, Halstead, Daniel Gurteen of Haverhill, Edward Horner JP of Howe Park, Halstead, and J.E. McConnell of 2 Dean's Yard Westminster, London SW. The temporary General Manager was Robert J. Watt of Halstead, with Edmund Harvey of 6 Victoria Street, Westminster, as Secretary and Joseph Cubitt of 6 Great

George Street, Westminster, as Consultant Engineer. The Auditors were W.H. Wilson of 6 Victoria Street, Westminster, and A.J. Browne of Halstead, whilst Baxter, Rose & Norton of 6 Victoria Street were Solicitors.

The struggle to find a suitable permanent general manager for railway operations found the directors searching far and wide, and they finally acquired the services of none other than Daniel Gooch who had recently resigned as Locomotive Superintendent of the Great Western Railway, As well as his involvement in the steamship *Great Eastern* and the laying of transatlantic cables he was related by marriage to the Tweedy family, wealthy Cornish bankers from Truro, who had a considerable financial interest in the minor Essex railway. He probably accepted the task to try to stem the financial losses his relations were incurring and on 31st December 1864 the company entered in agreement with Daniel Gooch for the operation of the railway. Clause 1 summed up the responsibilities:

The said Daniel Gooch will from the date thereof efficiently work and maintain the railway and works of the said company, and will find and provide the motive power, rolling stock, moveable plant, materials, and all consumerable [sic] articles necessary and incident to the working and maintenance of the said railway and works, and will support the permanent way and works in due repair and condition, and will also find and employ at his own expense all the officers and servants necessary for the due and efficient management and conduct of such workings, the receipts of the tolls and transaction of all business of whatever kind connected with the working and management of the said railway, and perform and discharge all obligations which by statute or otherwise are laid upon the said company with reference to the working and maintenance or the transit of traffic over the said railways.

Gooch officially took over the running of the line for 35 per cent of the gross receipts on and from 1st January 1865, but he kept an arms length interest in day-to-day affairs which were handled by his manager Robert Rogers; Watt departed for a lucrative appointment with the Ceylon Government Railways at the end of January 1865.

The net balance of revenue for the six months ending 31st December 1864 was £1,177. During the half-year, traffic earnings had increased by £39 per mile for the entire 19½ miles when compared to the corresponding six months of 1862, when only 11½ miles of line was open to traffic. Although the figures were encouraging the finances were still in a parlous state so the directors decided not to accept any increase in remuneration awarded by the shareholders, having already decided to lease the line in an effort to achieve some improvements. By the end of the year there were wholesale changes on the board, for James Brewster was Chairman and Vereker, Gurteen, Horner and McConnell were displaced. The new directors were Robert Charles Hanam of 1 Alderman's Walk, London EC, Edgar Corrie of 26 Lombard Street, London EC, Frederick Payne of Wixoe and George Gamble of Bedford Place, Russell Square, London.

During the early hours of Friday 6th January 1865, severe gale force winds blew across the Essex landscape uprooting small shrubs and damaging trees. At Hedingham station a wagon standing in the siding without any form of brake or scotch being applied was set in motion by the gusts. With no staff in attendance the movement went unnoticed and unhindered until the wagon picked up speed on the falling gradients towards Halstead. Aided by the tremendous gale the vehicle gathered momentum and progress was only arrested as it smashed through Trinity Street level crossing gates, which were open for the road and across the railway. Fortunately no persons were injured. On the same day part of Halstead goods shed was blown down by the wind.

On 18th January 1865, GER officers reported to the board that the CV&HR was in difficulties and it was suggested the Railway Clearing House be notified in case of future problems that might arise, whilst the following day the GER paid over the first instalment of £196 to contractors for the construction of the connection between the Colne Valley line and Haverhill Junction.

On the last day of February 1865 at Halstead Petty Sessions, John Everitt, a labourer employed by Mr Metson of Great Maplestead was again charged with wilfully leaving the gates open on Metson's level crossing. Giving evidence, William Stimpson, the CV&HR permanent way inspector, proved the gates were left open to the railway on a number of occasions; once an approaching train had to stop at the crossing to avoid running over animals which had strayed on to the line and another time a train had almost killed one of Metson's horses. Robert J. Watt had written to Metson on two occasions and Alfred Page, a sub-ganger, testified he had spoken to both Metson and the defendant who both refused to close the gates. Everitt, who had been found guilty back in February 1863, was again fined 10s 0d with added costs of 12s 0d for his misdemeanours but Metson escaped prosecution.

Despite being granted authority to raise £236,333 by four Acts of Parliament in 1856, 1859, 1861 and 1863, the company were desperate to acquire further capital to discharge outstanding liabilities which they had incurred. The directors therefore sought Parliamentary authority to raise the necessary funds and on 7th April 1865 The Colne Valley and Halstead Railway 1865 Act (28 Vict cap i) was passed authorizing the company to raise an additional £40,000 by ordinary and preference shares and borrow on Mortgage the sum of £13,300 once the original capital had been subscribed for and one half paid up.

As the work on the connection line from the GER Haverhill station progressed, so the contractor was paid a further £136 on 30th March and £531 on 13th April 1865 for completed works, followed by another £378 on 11th May 1865.

A BOT inspection had been requested and Colonel William Yolland subsequently examined the short connecting spur from the GER station to Colne Valley Junction, along with the section of GER line from Shelford to Haverhill, on 22nd May 1865. Of necessity, only remarks pertaining to the connecting spur are referred to in this volume. Of the 15 miles 78 chains submitted for inspection only 55 chains of single line concerned the CV&HR. Both underbridges were satisfactory, having brick arches, brick abutments and parapets. An engine turntable was provided at Haverhill GER station although signalling was incomplete. Sinclair, the GER Engineer, promised completion by 1st June when it was planned to open the line from Shelford to Haverhill. Yolland was concerned to find no arrangements had been made between the CV&HR and GER as to the method of working by either company over the single line from Haverhill station to the junction where the route joined the single line from the CV Haverhill station, and at which signalling was also incomplete. The inspector duly authorised the opening of the railway from Shelford to Haverhill but considered the route thence to the CV&HR was a danger to the public and refused to sanction opening. Yolland finally stipulated the GER was required to work trains to and from Cambridge because of the absence of a turntable at Shelford.

The GER opened their line between Haverhill and Shelford on the Cambridge main line on 1st June 1865, whereupon the CV&HR attempted to secure running powers between Chappel and Colchester and Haverhill and Cambridge. The Bishopsgate management immediately dismissed the proposal.

The subject of the new line from Haverhill to Shelford had been raised by the GER with the BOT; on 14th June 1865 the Traffic Committee read a report submitted by Moseley, the General Manager, on the arrangements made with the CV Company, pending the opening of the GER route to Sudbury:

1 Through goods trains should run daily between Cambridge and Colchester via Haverhill and Chappel.
2 All traffic to and from the Great Eastern station until further notice to be sent via Haverhill and Chappel whenever such route was shortest.

ANNO VICESIMO OCTAVO

VICTORIÆ REGINÆ.

****

Cap. i.

An Act to enable the *Colne Valley and Halstead* Railway Company to increase their Capital.

[7th *April* 1865.]

WHEREAS the Undertaking of the *Colne Valley and Halstead* Railway Company (who are herein referred to as "the Company") consists of a Railway from the *Colchester, Stour Valley, Sudbury, and Halstead* Railway (now leased to the *Great Eastern* Railway Company) at *Chapple* to *Haverhill*: And whereas the Company were authorized by the Acts hereinafter mentioned to raise by Shares and by Loan the Sums specified with relation to each Act, and they have exercised the said Powers; and they require further Capital for the Discharge of Liabilities which they have incurred, and for the general Purposes of their Undertaking,

Colne Valley and Halstead Railway Act, 1856	Shares	40,000
	Mortgage	13,333
Colne Valley and Halstead Railway (Extension) Act, 1859	Shares	80,000
	Mortgage	26,000
Colne Valley and Halstead Railway Amendment Act, 1861	Shares	30,000
	Mortgage	10,000
Colne Valley and Halstead Railway Act, 1863	Shares	28,000
	Mortgage	9,000
Total Capital		£236,333

And

Colne Valey and Hasltead Railway Additional Capital Act 7th April 1865 front page.

3 The Colne Valley Company to be allotted their mileage proportion of receipts from such traffic after allowing the Great Eastern 20% from its working expenses.

Moseley then reported on the rearrangement of facilities for the interchange of traffic at the Junction. The Colne Valley Company would have the free use of Haverhill station for all their passenger trains; that the goods traffic between the two lines would be worked by one or more trains, as might be required, from Haverhill to Chappel or Marks Tey, by a GER engine under such arrangements as to the payment for use of the engine on the Colne Valley line as may be agreed upon; and, last, in the case of a station for interchange of traffic at the Junction, should it be required at any time, it shall be jointly by the two companies. Despite completion of the connection the contractor continued to be paid, receiving £170 on 15th June.

By 20th June 1865 agreement as to the method of working the new single line was reached and Sinclair duly notified the BOT the intention of using the same Train Staff between Yeldham and Haverhill CV&HR and Haverhill GER stations, thus ensuring only one train was in section at any one time. On receipt of the correspondence Yolland agreed to the opening of the line on condition that both companies completed the signalling at the junction before services commenced. If no such agreement was reached the inspector required traffic to interchange at the junction and before such action was taken, accommodation, sidings and signalling were to be provided.

The working arrangement between the Company and Daniel Gooch Esq MP, the contractor working the Colne Valley line, was revised from 25th June 1865:

1 Colne Valley trains to run into the Great Eastern Haverhill station on the following terms.
2 The Great Eastern Company to afford accommodation for passenger traffic and use of the said station, sidings, turntables, signals, porters, and other usual servants without any charge on the understanding that the local as well as the through passenger traffic is worked in and out of the said station. The Great Eastern is to be allowed their mileage proportion of the fares as between Haverhill station and the junction between the Great Eastern and Colne Valley lines less 25 per cent to Mr Gooch for working expenses.
3 A good and efficient connection to be made if possible by mutual concession from each party between Colne Valley trains and Great Eastern trains at Haverhill, both Up and Down, so as to secure a through service on the Colne Valley line and Cambridge by one train each way daily. The present or an equally effective connection at Chappel and Marks Tey to be maintained.
4 Through booking facilities between Colne Valley stations and Great Eastern principal stations in the Cambridge District such as Shelford, Cambridge, Newmarket, Hitchin, Huntingdon, Ely and Peterborough.
5 A through Colne Valley carriage to be run between Marks Tey and Cambridge by one train each way daily upon the receipt by the Great Eastern Company of a requisition from Mr Gooch.
6 A through Great Eastern carriage to be run over the Colne Valley line by one train each way daily, if the carriage is run as mentioned in clause 5.

7 Equal fares to be charged between Haverhill and places on the Great Eastern line to which the Colne Valley forms a competitive route, except to places between Haverhill and Chappel via Sudbury.

8 Receipts on London and Haverhill goods traffic conveyed into or from the Great Eastern Haverhill station to be divided as follows, whether carried via Shelford, Sudbury or Halstead:

First   The Great Eastern Company to be credited with 50 per cent of the gross receipts.

Second   The apportionment of the remaining 50 per cent to be credited thus:

Terminal at Haverhill to be divided in the following manner:

A   Carted terminal 3s 0d per ton to the Great Eastern Company; 1s 0d to the Colne Valley Company.

B   Station to station traffic – the whole terminal to the Great Eastern Company.

Terminal at London Great Eastern Stations all to the Great Eastern Company.

The residue to be divided on the mileage by the two companies via the Great Eastern Brick Lane station to Chappel and the Colne Valley Chappel to Haverhill. This arrangement of the division of London and Haverhill traffic to date from the opening of the Shelford to Haverhill section of railway on 1st June 1865.

9 Referring to clause 8, the quantity of traffic sent over the Colne Valley line is not to be in a greater proportion to the whole traffic than the proportion of receipts allotted to the Colne Valley route bears to the whole of the receipts, but if an excess of such proportion be so sent, the Colne Valley to be credited with their mileage and terminal thereon.

10 All claims for damages to be dealt with according to the route carried and according to Railway Clearing House Regulations, i.e. Colne Valley not to be liable to contribute to any claim unless the goods have been actually carried over their line.

11 Equal facilities and accommodation to be given to Colne Valley passengers and traffic at Haverhill.

12 The Colne Valley to have the right to satisfy themselves by inspection of the Great Eastern Books as to the correctness of the accounts rendered to them.

13 This arrangement to be terminable on six months notice from either party.

14 The Great Eastern Railway Company to work the Haverhill Junction signals. Mr Gooch contributing £30 per annum towards the expenses.

At this time the company was notoriously bad for settling outstanding petty debts and at the company half-yearly meeting in February 1865 the Chairman James Brewster made reference to a number of persons who had begun actions against the CV&HR for outstanding payments and iterated to the gathering that these *'should be the last to be paid'*, adding that he had given orders for small tradesmen to receive initial payments: *'the first object was to keep the little dogs quiet'*. Several months later the payments were still outstanding, forcing solicitors Cardihall & Wright of Halstead to appeal to the Local Board of Health to intervene on behalf of their clients. Ultimately four creditors registered claims through the Court of the Queen's Bench on 11th July 1865, when the following judgments were obtained:

25th January	R.C. Hughes & Son of Halstead £24 17s 0d plus £5 19s 0d costs.
27th January	J. Sudbury & Son of Halstead £23 13s 0d plus £5 19s 0d costs.
27th January	E. Pudney & Sons of Cole Engaine £98 12s 3d plus £5 19s 0d costs.
6th July	Executors of John Rayner of Great Maplestead £100 16s 5d plus £8 6s 0d costs.

On 9th April another payment of £1,303 5s 0d was paid to the contractor for Haverhill spur. The balance of payment for the Haverhill connecting line of £1,303 5s 0d was not paid to the contractor until 11th February 1867. Having completed most of the remedial work required by Colonel Yolland, freight trains started using the new connection at Haverhill. However, on Tuesday 8th August 1865 a GER goods train consisting of a tender engine and sixteen wagons was crossing the embankment north-west of Birdbrook station when eight of the vehicles became derailed. A considerable amount of track was torn up as the wagons bounced along the ballast and one wagon plunged down the embankment. Fortunately nobody was injured but the line was blocked until the following day, 9th August, when the vehicles were cleared and repairs effected to the track by the combined gangs of GER and CV&HR permanent way staff. Luckily this coincided with the GER opening of the final section of their Stour Valley line between Haverhill and Sudbury for passenger traffic; thereafter, except for the first Up train in the morning and the last Down train at night, all CV&HR trains terminated and started back from Haverhill GER station.

The CV&HR directors reported on 2nd September 1865 that capital had increased by £307, whilst £800 had been advanced from revenue to pay outstanding claims for land and compensation. Daniel Gooch, the contractor working the line, advised total receipts for the year were £4,439, whilst 35 per cent of gross receipts totalling £1,654 were available to contribute towards interest payments for the current half year. In the corresponding half year in 1864 the earnings were only £3,890. The capital expended on the line was £262,636.

James Brewster had been re-elected CV&HR Chairman at the half yearly meeting in July 1865, whilst Major Veriker resigned as a director on 9th November. Weeks later, Robert Ellington Greenwood was dissatisfied with Brewster's leadership and also resigned. Problems were still being experienced on the apportionment of charges between the two companies and on 8th November 1865 the GER Manager recommended that as there were two routes for London to Haverhill goods traffic the gross receipts should be divided between the two companies as follows; 50% to the credit of the GER route via Shelford, all of which should be retained by the GER. The remaining 50% to be credited to the Colchester line, the GER taking their mileage proportion to Chappel, 49½ miles, the Colne Valley Railway taking their mileage proportion Chappel to Haverhill, 19 miles subject to the first deduction of terminals, viz 8s 6d per ton London and 4s 0d per ton to Haverhill – such arrangement to be made on condition that any vexed question between the two companies be adjusted.

The question of the outstanding debts owed by the CV&HR to the GER was raised on 20th December 1865. Sinclair reported that as soon as he could obtain information he would report on the counter claims the CV had made against the GER. Waddington, a director, also attending the meeting, reported of a claim for £1,244 2s 6d against the CV&HR constituted by:

	£	s	d
Rent for use of Chappel station			
to 30th June 1865 at £150 pa	781	5	0
Junction expenses at Chappel station			
to 30th June 1865	255	9	10
Repairs to engines	207	7	8
	1,244	2	6

In mid-January 1866 rain fell continuously for two days swelling rivers and streams. The ground was already waterlogged from earlier snow which had melted. The continuous precipitation found the River Colne rising and on Saturday 12th of the month, after the passage of a train, floods swept away a large portion of the railway embankment between Hedingham and Yeldham leaving the rails suspended in mid-air without support. Services were curtailed between the two stations until CV&HR engineers and permanent way staff, with the help of GER staff, rebuilt the embankment and consolidated the trackbed. To the credit of all repair staff, the line reopened the following Tuesday morning.

The GER Locomotive Superintendent reported to the Traffic Committee on 1st March 1866 that the GE Company had been performing necessary repairs to the CV&HR rolling stock, charging for materials and labour with a percentage for the use of the shops and tools. The CV&HR company were now asking that the engine *Colne* be sent to Stratford for repairs and Kitson, a local contractor, was asking if he was to continue. After considerable discussion the Secretary was instructed to advise the CV&HR Company that the GER would continue the programme of repairs to CV locomotives provided the company settled all outstanding payments for repairs carried out to date.

The GER Traffic Committee received a report on 9th May 1866 that the nearest route for traffic from Peterborough to stations on the Colchester main line between Chelmsford and Manningtree, including intermediate branches, was via Cambridge and the Colne Valley line to Chappel. It was pointed out that the GE route via Cambridge, Melford and Sudbury was only five miles longer and the question had now arisen between the GE and CV as to via which of the two the traffic should be routed. It was resolved that, subject to approval by both sets of directors, coal traffic would be routed by the Colne Valley, whilst goods and cattle would be sent via Melford and Sudbury.

On 23rd May 1866 the GER General Manager reported on the anomaly regarding the passenger traffic at Haverhill. To retain a connection between stations on the CV line and the GE at Haverhill would necessitate an outlay of £10,000 in provision of additional sidings. To avoid such expenditure he recommended the CV Company trains be allowed to use the GE Haverhill station without charge providing the CV&HR consented to close their own station. He also suggested the London to Haverhill goods traffic be divided into two equal portions as the mileage via both routes was almost the same. The CV Company would then retain their mileage portion of one half.

The appointment of Daniel Gooch as manager had improved operational efficiency but the amount of receipts apportioned to the CV&HR declined from £1,605 in the half year ending 30th June 1865 to £1,217 for the half year ending 30th June 1866 and the directors were concerned that unless remedial action was taken matters would deteriorate further.

GER train crews working the daily coal trains over the Colne Valley line complained of the rough riding and poor condition of the permanent way. The General Manager instructed his Engineer to examine the line and provide a detailed report to Brewster, the CVR Chairman, Mr Rogers the Traffic Manager and Daniel Gooch who was contracted to work the line. By 18th July 1866 the report had been handed over with the rider that the GER would hold the CV&HR responsible in the event of an accident.

On 10th September 1866 two tank engines hauled an excursion train to Chappel. They returned from the junction station at 7.00am, coupled together running chimney first; while travelling at a speed of approximately 25 to 30 mph, half a mile west of Colne station, the second engine became derailed. Eight days later, on 18th September another derailment occurred near the bottom of Colne bank when a coal truck on a GE goods train left the rails and then caused the following van to derail a quarter of a mile further along the line. The train was brought to a stand about three-quarters of a mile beyond the site of the wagon derailment. Fortunately in both instances no persons were injured. On learning of the derailment the GER board asked Samuel Swarbrick, the General Manager, to look into the working arrangement with the CV&HR; Captain F.H. Rich conducted the subsequent BOT enquiry into both accidents.

From his investigation into the first incident, Rich ascertained that the line at the point of derailment was straight and falling at 1 in 70. Both drivers had shut off steam at the top of the bank and they were coasting down the gradient. As soon as they became aware the second engine had derailed, they applied the brakes and both locomotives were brought to a stand about 66 yards from where the derailment occurred. The permanent way was damaged for a distance of about 60 yards. On closely examining the permanent way the Inspector found that the section of line had been opened to passenger traffic in 1860 and was formed of flat bottom rail weighing 65 lbs per yard. The rails were fished and fastened with dog spikes to the sleepers, laid transversely at intervals of 3 feet 3 inches, except near the rail joints where the spacing was 2 feet 6 inches. The rails on each side of the joints were fixed in cast iron chairs, with iron washers bolted down and the chairs were fastened to the sleepers with wrought iron spikes driven inside trenails. The sleepers appeared in good condition and the line was generally well ballasted. Rich, however, found places where the sleepers required boxing up and this appeared to be the case where the engine derailed. He was of the opinion that the permanent way was light and was not maintained correctly. It was therefore of no surprise that two tanks engines, each weighing 23 tons and travelling at the reported speed, should have split the road. He concluded the weight on each pair of wheels could not be ascertained as the company had no weighing machine capable of weighing the locomotives. The wheelbase of the engine that derailed was 14 feet 3 inches and it had been *'thoroughly repaired and the wheels turned up in the Great Eastern workshops, about a month previous to the accident'*.

Turning to the second incident, the Captain was informed the train in question was formed of a tender engine, fourteen to sixteen coal wagons and a brake van. He was unable to interview the crew of the GER train and could not therefore ascertain their report of the circumstances. The CV&HR Manager advised him that he found a broken axlebox from the coal truck a short distance from the site of the derailment and the official attributed the derailment to the breakage of the axlebox. Rich was not entirely convinced and thought the poor state of the permanent way might have contributed to the accident. In his report from Whitehall dated 14th December 1866, the inspector recommended the provision of two intermediate fang bolts inserted in each length of rail and the boxing up of sleepers with ballast. He also required more attention to the packing and regulating of track maintenance. Until the work was completed he recommended the reduction in speed of passenger trains and a restriction of 20 mph on tank engines running without trains. He also noted there were no turntables on the line.

The report was sent to the CV&HR for action on 18th December and was discussed by the board the following day. It was resolved a copy of the report be sent to Sir Daniel Gooch (he was knighted in 1866), who was responsible for the upkeep and operation of the railway, together with a copy of Article 1 of the agreement between the company and himself dated 31st December 1864, reminding him of his obligations and asking for necessary recommendations to be implemented.

As the CV&HR was in desperate financial straits, once again Brewster wrote to the GER directors suggesting the GER work the line for a period of five years and then have the option of absorbing the company. The matter was considered on Boxing Day 1866, when it was resolved the CV&HR Chairman and Secretary be invited to attend a meeting in early January 1867. On the last day of 1866 Sir Daniel Gooch terminated his agreement to work the CV&HR, and on 1st January 1867 Charles Brogden Sperling commenced operations under a similar contract, with the company taking the net receipts after working expenses, although the directors stipulated the new arrangement could be terminated at one month's notice. Sperling at the time lived at 'The Astles', Castle Hedingham, but eventually returned to his ancestral home at Dynes Hall, Great Maplestead. For the half year ending 31st December 1866 the revenue totalled £4,586, which after working expenses resulted in net earnings of £1,605, an acceptable 35 per cent profit. It was announced the money would help pay settlements on claims by landowners.

Swarbrick, the GER General Manager, reported on 16th January 1867 of his meeting with Colne Valley officials and had advised them that a tour of inspection would be made within the next week. On 17th January, Brewster and Harvey attended the gathering chaired by Charles Henry Turner, the GER Chairman. The CV&HR Chairman presented the arguments for amalgamation, citing that average weekly traffic for the year 1866 was £7 per mile exclusive of GE transfers, which equated to receipts of not less than £10,000 per annum. The GER authorities demurred, stating that the true receipts were only £7,280 with no likelihood of any increase and suggested renting the line. Brewster, ever keen to reduce the financial commitments suggested a rental of £5,000 per annum advising that £4,800 of that would enable the company to pay percentage allocations against debentures and preference shares. Turner, after deliberating with his colleagues, pressed for a reduction to £4,350, which Brewster said he would consider. At the same meeting it was announced agreement had been reached with Sir Daniel Gooch the previous December regarding the apportionment of goods traffic charges and receipts. The CV&HR was to receive fifty per cent of Haverhill traffic after terminal charges for traffic entering or departing to the GER via Shelford. For other traffic entering the line from the south, fifty per cent of charges were to be apportioned based on distance: London to Chappel 49 miles and Chappel to Haverhill 19 miles.

The promised tour of inspection was delayed and it was 23rd February 1867 before the GER Directors visited the CV&HR to view at first hand the railway they were being asked to absorb. Attending for the GER were Messrs Simpson, Gamble, Swarbrick, Moseley, Robertson, Birt and Hadfield, who met at Chappel with Brewster, the CV Chairman and fellow director Hanam. After the inspection the directors were far from satisfied with the condition of the line and were scathing in their report:

1   The station buildings at Colne, Halstead and Haverhill are substantially built. Yeldham and Birdbrook are temporary structures. The station yards are ample – sufficient for work – there being in most cases suitable goods sheds and sidings for coal with spare land for extensions if required later. The buildings, however, want painting and papering and otherwise furnishing. There are no Station Master's houses at the stations and none have been found by the company. The line is single and 19 miles in length.

2   Surplus land is not considerable and consists of 2¾ acres at Colne station, 1 acre near Colne and 1½ acres between Colne and Halstead. Large pieces of land on each side of Halstead station, a plot of land at Castle Hedingham, a strip of land on each side of Yeldham station, a field at Haverhill Junction, from which the ballast was taken, and also a large piece of land on each side of the old Haverhill station.

3   State of the Permanent Way – This is in a very indifferent state of repair. The sleepers, which are small, are exposed for the want of ballast, which is scanty. The road in many places is wet for want of drains, the rails are worn and insecurely fastened and little better than an ordinary tramway – the banks are slipping in all directions, fences dilapidated and in need of considerable attention, the side ditches are much filled up in consequence of insufficient drainage. Cuttings are in a deplorable condition and there are very serious slips, which will involve a considerable outlay of money before the slippage is entirely stopped. The rails weigh 60 lbs, 65 lbs and 70 lbs per yard. Sir Daniel Gooch has had 65% of receipts to work and keep the line and stations in a perfect state of repair but the line is in a very defective state. Gradients from Chappel are 1 in 100 and at other parts 1 in 70. There are eight level crossings, with either brick or wooden huts attached. Swarbick stated at considerable length his views regarding the position, which the CVR line occupied in the district.

The report was placed before the board on 27th February and was passed to the Law Clerk to report on his views as to the GE company objecting to working the line. He was also asked to investigate an outstanding claim for land compensation at Haverhill Junction.

Early in May 1867 the Manager of the CV&HR submitted a request to the GE to allow CV&HR trains to run over the GER between Chappel and Marks Tey, with a view to saving an engine in their daily working. On 22nd May the application was declined on the grounds of the poor condition of the rolling stock

On 15th June 1867 C.B. Sperling relinquished working the CV&HR, the experiment, in Brewster's terminology, 'being unsuccessful' and Robert J. Watt was again appointed General Manager, becoming the contractor responsible for working the services.

On 8th July 1867 the disputed claim in respect of traffic passing between London and Haverhill, damage to rolling stock and injury to the CV&HR permanent way, brought by the CV&HR against the GER, was referred for arbitration to Mr Dawson, the Secretary of the Railway Clearing House. He replied in early August that no London to Haverhill goods traffic carried since 31st May 1865 should be expected from the division of receipts, which the two companies agreed on 25th June 1856. Thereafter the receipts from London on goods which the Colne Valley Company had taken into their own Haverhill station, should be divided into the proportion stated in clause 8 of the agreement, except as to terminals at Haverhill – which in his opinion should be kept apart so as to give the CV Company a greater share than they received on traffic conveyed to and from the GE Haverhill station. With regard to the second and third claims, Dawson was of the opinion that each company pay for their own damage, i.e. the working company pay for all damage to the train whether such damage was to their own or other parties rolling stock and demurrage, whilst the CV&HR would pay for repairs to the railway infrastructure. The ruling was passed to both companies and at their meeting on 14th August 1867 the GER Traffic Committee authorised the payment of £1,180 10s 0d in full settlement of the claim.

The footbridge spanning the railway at Halstead was evidently not of the best quality, for by the summer of 1867 the structure was in urgent need of repair. It was used as a short cut by local residents, and especially by workers at Courtauld's factory, and on 15th August Robert J. Watt, the CV&HR general manager, advised George P. Arden, the Clerk to the Local Board of Health that the footbridge was undergoing repairs, adding that it was *customary for the parish authorities to take in hand, after the lapse of a year, the repairing of such bridges so far as the foot or roadway was concerned. He then required the authority to take whatever action was necessary* to keep the span in good order. The request was met with outright refusal and by 1868 the CV&HR gave instructions that repairs and remedial work was to cease.

In March 1868 Thomas MacKay, the station master at Colne and the only employee at the station, left the service after a disagreement with the management. He had been paid £5 per month but as a result of alleged misconduct was dismissed. He subsequently sued

for payment of £4 2s 10d, consisting of £3 2s 10d salary from 1st to 22nd March, plus fine of 10s 0d and 10d expended on postage.

The saga of the footbridge was resurrected when the Local Board of Health asked the Halstead United Charities for opinion and guidance. George William Harris, Clerk to the Charities, replied on 13th July 1868 that he was not prepared to give an opinion as to whether the railway company was responsible for repairs. He then added the United Charities repudiated any responsibility in the matter. The Local Board then approached the Secretary of the BOT Robert Herbert complaining and he in turn wrote to the CV&HR seeking an explanation. Edmund Harvey, the Secretary, replied on 30th June stating the Local Board had taken over the new road constructed by the company on the approach to the footbridge and therefore they were responsible for repairs and maintenance, as well as being responsible for upkeep of the footbridge. On receipt of the CV&HR letter the BOT Secretary advised the Local Board of Health that under the circumstances the railway company was not responsible for repairs and maintenance of the structure. He added a rider that any attempt at compulsion would be unlikely to succeed and therefore he advised the two parties reach a compromise. This was reached and took effect from 31st December 1869, whereby the Railway Company agreed to complete the *substantial repairs and repainting of the footbridge on the understanding future maintenance would be the responsibility of the local board*.

At the GER Traffic Committee meeting on 8th December 1868, the General Manager submitted correspondence and minutes of a meeting on the subject of outstanding accounts with the CV&HR. After discussion, the Committee authorised the General Manager to settle accounts directly.

On 4th February 1869 the GER Locomotive Superintendent reported to the board that a 6-wheel saddle tank locomotive was laying derelict in the Wagon Repair Shop at Stratford and was in

A general view of Halstead station in the late 1890s. To the left are the goods shed and front yard and back yard sidings. The partially completed Down-side platform which was not brought into use is occupied at the far end by Halstead signal box. A train hauled by 0-4-2T No. 1 enters the single platform on the Up side of the line. To the right are the well house and water storage tank, which supplied the water cranes at each end of the platform.   *Author's collection*

a condition that was only suitable for scrap. The engine was the property of either the CV&HR or the Waveney Valley Railway; he had written to both and awaited their reply. In the meantime it was agreed the locomotive should be valued and ultimately sold. The CV&HR denied any knowledge of the locomotive.

At the CV&HR half yearly meeting held at Halstead on Thursday 25th February 1869 the directors announced they intended to improve Yeldham and Birdbrook station buildings which were described as *'most miserable and little more than shepherd's huts'*. The work would commence as soon as funds were available. While the CV&HR was experiencing problems, the GER encountered troubles of their own when early in March 1869 the wall backing on to Haverhill station collapsed after heavy rainfall had caused water to undermine the foundations. On 24th of the month the Engineer was instructed to repair the wall as a matter of urgency.

On 31st March 1869 Samuel Johnson reported he had engaged William Adams, Locomotive Superintendent of the North London Railway, to value the derelict locomotive and he had priced the engine at £85. It was agreed to scrap the engine and retain Adams letter in case of dispute over ownership.

In mid-September 1869 Mr Scudamore of the General Post Office proposed to take advantage of two wires running alongside the railway between Colchester and Chappel, the property of the Electrical & International Telegraph Company, for the purpose of giving independent communication from Colchester Post Office to places in the Colne Valley. The GE Traffic Committee debated the proposal at their meeting on 29th September and deferred their decision.

Yet again the problems concerning the footbridge at Halstead were raised, for the Local Board of Health reneged on the agreement made on the last day of 1868 and the railway company decided to seek arbitration. Mr Rose subsequently awarded the CV&HR the full costs of the completed works and severely cautioned the Local Health Board as to their future conduct. Despite this action the Local Beard, stung by the decision, appealed to the Local Government Officer at Whitehall, who replied on 24th December 1869 highly critical of the further *'unjustifiable attempt to repudiate payment to the railway company and subsequent acceptance of liability for repairs and maintenance of the footbridge'.*

The following year the long-running dispute between the Colne Valley & Halstead Railway and the GER regarding the interpretation of Sections 274, 279, 280 and 281 of the GER Act of 1862 was resurrected and taken to the Court of Common Pleas for guidance, who in turn passed the case to none other than Henry Whatley Tyler of the BOT Railway Inspectorate to arbitrate. In the course of his deliberations Tyler noted that Clause 274 called upon the GER, if required to do so, to enter upon, work and manage the CV&HR, whilst clause 279 stipulated that if the GER did not work the CV&HR they would provide reasonable and proper facilities for through booking and the running of rolling stock on their system as well as conveyance of traffic to or from the ultimate starting point or destination. Section 280 dictated that all such facilities for the transmission of traffic should be afforded by the GER subject to the payment of fares and tolls not being greater than that charged by the GER to other companies. In the event of disagreement the matter was to be settled by arbitration. Section 281 ruled that differences between the GER and CV&HR regarding performance or non-performance of any of the provisions was to be determined by arbitration in the manner provided by the Railway Companies Arbitration Act 1859. Both parties agreed with

the appointment of Tyler as arbiter on 29th March 1870 and as no further evidence was required the inspector began his investigations. These were completed and published on 10th May and the report was witnessed by O.C. Woodward, Clerk to Messrs Wyatt & Hoskins, Solicitors of 28 Parliament Street, Westminster. The document was countersigned after examination by L.F. Semonin and Thomas Newman, Clerks to Messrs Baxter, Rose, Norton & Company, Solicitors of 6 Victoria Street, Westminster on 8th June 1870.

Tyler, after investigation, *'awarded, adjudged and determined'* the following:

1. The GER not to charge any higher mileage rate for the conveyance of CV&HR passengers over their line to or from their stations at Chappel and Haverhill than the lowest mileage rate charged for the conveyance of passengers of the same Class to or from their stations at Braintree or Kelvedon or to or from any of their stations between Chappel and Haverhill, regard being had in each case to the respective distances.

2. Through fares for passengers booked from any station on the CV&HR to any station on the GER or vice versa were in no way to exceed the sum of the local fares charged by each company for the portion of the line run over and neither company was entitled to a larger proportion of any through passenger fare than the amount of their own local fares. The GER was not under any obligation to carry through passengers from any station on the CV&HR by their express trains at less than express fares or to provide ordinary trains for the conveyance of CV&HR passengers. Subject to any arrangement between the two companies the CV&HR was entitled to receive from the GER out of all sums received by the latter company in respect of through passenger bookings, and the GER to be entitled to receive from the CV&HR out of all sums similarly received by the latter company; the respective sums determined to be the maximum amounts to which the said companies shall be entitled in respect of through bookings in the event of the through fares being fixed on the principle of equal mileage for both companies; each company would receive the proportion of such through fares corresponding to the distance on their respective lines over which the passengers were carried, subject always to the right of either company to charge express fares for such distances that passengers were carried by express train.

3. The GER to make traffic arrangements for the transmission of through passengers from the CV&HR to their trains from Chappel that the detention at Chappel or Marks Tey shall be no greater than can be avoided, and shall not exceed 10 minutes for any train by which a minimum of 100 passengers shall on a monthly average be tendered to them from the CV&HR line for any one direction, or in like manner 20 minutes for 50 passengers or 30 minutes for 25 passengers.

4. The GER to attach to their trains at Chappel or Haverhill junction as the case may be and carry forward to their line to the terminus or extreme point to which such trains may be proceeding any carriage of the CV&HR which shall contain at least one half of its complement of through passengers and shall make to the CV&HR Company such allowance in respect of the use of their carriages in manner aforesaid as may from time to time be prescribed by the regulations of the

Railway Clearing House and shall in all respects comply with such regulations.

5 The amounts of excursion fares, and the respective shares of the two companies in such fares to be arranged by special agreement between the Companies.

6 If and whenever and so long as the GER Company shall issue season tickets or market tickets at reduced rates from their Haverhill and Chappel stations or from any of their stations between Chappel and Haverhill to any other of their stations by their own line, they shall also issue for the Colne Valley district such tickets at mileage rates not higher than those charged from their own Haverhill and Chappel and intermediate stations respectively; and the CV&HR shall be at liberty to issue season tickets or market tickets from any of their stations and the GER shall take forward from Chappel or from Haverhill any passengers with such tickets from any CV&HR stations at the same rates as charged by themselves in respect of similar traffic from their Haverhill or Chappel and their intermediate stations between those places respectively. However, the GER is not bound to issue season tickets or market tickets from Haverhill or Chappel or from any of their intermediate stations between those places.

7 The rates for the through conveyance of goods and merchandise to and from the several stations on the CV&HR shall be determined as follows. The CV&HR Company's stations named in the first column of the undermentioned schedule will be considered an equivalent to the GER Company's station in the second column. The through rates for goods and merchandise between the CV&HR stations and any of the GER stations shall be the same as those charged from time to time by the GER for the equivalent stations in the second column. The GER Company shall afford to the traffic at the several CV&HR stations advantages as respects general or special rates, fares and tolls, and otherwise howsoever, at least equal to those afforded at the several equivalent GER stations. Provided always that no higher mileage rates shall be charged for goods between any CV&HR station and any GER station than shall for the time being be in force as between Kelvedon or Braintree station and the same GER stations. Provided also as regards inland coal traffic that so long as the local rate of the GER Company for conveyance of coal from Peterborough to Braintree, Sudbury, Bures and Chappel shall not be less than 5s 0d per ton, or from Peterborough to Hythe not less than 4s 6d per ton, so long shall the local rate from Peterborough to Haverhill not exceed 3s 6d per ton and so on in proportion. And provided also as regards sea-borne coal traffic that the local rates from any of the GER ports to Chappel shall not exceed in mileage proportion, and the charges for wagon hire shall not be proportionately greater than the rates and charges for wagon hire from the GER ports to Braintree or to the stations of the GER at or between Chappel and Haverhill.

The schedule:

Colne Valley Stations	Great Eastern Stations
Colne	Bures
Halstead	Sudbury
Hedingham	Sudbury
Yeldham	Melford
Birdbrook	Stoke
Haverhill	Haverhill

8 The charge of 1s 6d per ton now charged by the Victoria Dock Company on manure shall when carried over the GER and forwarded to any CV&HR station, be borne by the two companies in proportion to the gross traffic earnings of companies upon the manure so carried.

9 The CV&HR was not entitled to any alteration in the present rates for through conveyance of cattle to the CV&HR stations.

10 The costs of the arbitration process and the award to be borne and paid for equally by the CV&HR and GER.

On 11th May 1870 Wyatt & Hoskins wrote to the GE from their office at 28 Parliament Street, London stating that Captain Tyler's award was now available for collection from their office on payment of the arbiter's charge of £208.

In early July 1870 a Mr Mayd approached the GER to provide a footbridge to connect the platforms at Haverhill, as crossing the running lines was considered dangerous. The matter was discussed at the meeting of the Way and Works Committee on 20th of the month and passed to the Engineer for his comments and observations. Evidently there was local backing for the provision of the bridge and the subject was again raised at the meeting on 3rd August but again deferred.

For the half year ending 31st December 1870 the gross earnings of the CV&HR were £4,191, compared with £3,977 earned in the similar period ending 31st December 1869, whilst receipts for the half year ending 30th June 1871 were £3,761 compared with £3,400 earned in the six months ending 30th June 1870. The capital of the company to 30th June 1871 was £265,134, consisting of £62,918 ordinary shares, £65,580 preference shares, £57,714 debentures, £76,200 Lloyd's bonds and balance of £2,721. At this time Robert Johnson Watt was General Manager and Lessee of the company.

On 15th April 1871 two passenger trains approaching Colne Valley Junction signal box from opposite directions came into collision at an estimated speed of 6 to 7 mph. Four passengers complained of minor injuries and at the ensuing local enquiry it was established the collision would not have occurred had not the Train Staff regulations for single line working been ignored. It also became clear that the Train Staff regulations were habitually broken with indicators being manipulated to show 'line clear' when a train was in section. Both engine crews were severely cautioned for not keeping a watchful eye on the road ahead, for if they had paid full attention to the task the accident could have been avoided. On 21st June 1871 the company finally authorised Mr Mayd's bridgework at Haverhill to be done.

In December 1871 the CV&HR company auctioned land which was surplus to requirements, with a view to satisfying outstanding land claims. A proportion was sold outright and the directors were in treaty to sell the residue. Increasing interchange of freight traffic between the two railways at Chappel necessitated increased accommodation and on 12th March 1872 authority was given for an additional siding at a cost of £230.

On 22nd July 1873 the driver of the 7.40am Colne Valley passenger train from Haverhill to Chappel, on approaching Chappel station was aghast to see the road blocked by a GER goods train shunting some 145 yards from the signal box. The driver of the goods train was in the course of reversing his engine towards the station and pushing fifteen wagons into the goods yard siding. Fortunately the passenger train was also travelling slowly and the

CV&HR driver was able to shut off steam and apply the brakes. Despite this action the two locomotives collided at a slow speed, the GE engine was undamaged but the CV engine sustained a broken buffer. Only a few passengers were on the train, some were shaken but none injured. At the ensuing enquiry there was conflicting evidence from the driver of the passenger train and the junction signalman as to whether the Chappel Junction Up CV distant signal was clear or at caution. The GE signalman stated he had let out the junction auxiliary to protect the goods train whilst the CV&HR engine driver and guard asserted the signal arm displayed 'all right' when their train passed it. The BOT inspecting officer, Captain H.W. Tyler, decided the CV driver and fireman had failed to observe the junction distant signal at caution and had allowed the train to pass the junction home signal at danger. He also required both companies to provide additional accommodation and sidings at Chappel to ensure the safe passage of trains through the station, thereby obviating the blocking of the main single line for shunting purposes when a passenger train was due. The GER acted on the recommendations and on 22nd October 1873 plans were submitted for additional sidings costing £1,245, and improved and additional signalling costing £600.

Early in December 1873 William Birt, the GER General Manager, reported that *a good deal* of grain was transported from stations on the Colne Valley line to Mistley, whilst in the opposite direction there was a regular flow of coal traffic, offloaded on the quay and transported by rail to the same stations. Unfortunately the CV Company was objecting to the GER using CV wagons for the coal traffic on the grounds that their total stock was small. Birt stated that this method of working was unremunerative as CV wagons were worked back empty and GE wagons were utilised. After the Traffic Committee discussed the matter on 17th December 1873, the Goods Manager was instructed to inform the CV authorities that as long as they refused to allow CV trucks to be loaded with coal for stations on their line then the GE could not undertake to provide their own wagons for the traffic. On 22nd April 1874 a draft of a letter to Robert Watt, the CV&HR Manager, regarding the discontinuance of GER wagons on coal traffic from Mistley

to CV stations was passed to the Traffic Committee. It was agreed stronger representation was necessary and the Chairman of the Traffic Committee agreed to write to Brewster, the CV&HR Chairman, whilst the Secretary was instructed to write to Mr Watt.

Following the accident and BOT recommendation regarding the signalling at Chappel, on 24th March 1874 the Superintendent reported that the signals and points at both Chappel and Haverhill were not interlocked although the work at Chappel Junction and the connection with the CV&HR was in hand. By 22nd April, three tenders for the signalling work had been received: £803 10s 0d from Saxby & Farmer, £807 10s 0d from McKenzie Clune and £1,187 10s 0d from Stevens & Company; on 6th May the contract was awarded to Saxby & Farmer. To complement the signalling work at Chappel it was agreed on 5th August 1874 to extend the platform at the station from 234 feet to 318 feet in length. All work was completed by December 1874.

Although the CV&HR company had achieved a small working surplus from the late 1860s, there was insufficient to repay the capital debt; the parlous financial state of the company continued until 19th November 1874 when James Brewster, acting for himself and other bond-holders, successfully applied to the Court of Chancery for the appointment of a receiver to manage affairs and the Company Secretary, W.G. Bailey, was appointed to the post. The receivership was to span the next eleven years. It also became apparent that James Brewster's son, Charles Edward Brewster, owned most of the locomotives and rolling stock and was still owed approximately £5,000.

Captain H.W. Tyler carried out the official BOT inspection of the new signalling and signal box at Chappel Junction on 27th January 1875. He noted the revised arrangements were installed at the behest of his findings into the accident in 1873. Tyler inspected the new installations and noted that all points and signals were interlocked with one another and worked from a new signal box and, subject to minor adjustments in the locking, sanctioned the equipment for use.

On 24th February 1875 the price of gas to Haverhill GE station was 8s 4d per 1,000 cubic feet, whilst on 24th March 1875 minor

Halstead station circa 1878 with 0-4-2T locomotive No. 1 standing at the head of the 11.30am mixed train from Chappel with three goods wagons placed ahead of the passenger vehicles, a practice later banned by the Railway Inspectorate. The three vehicles behind the goods wagons are, a First/Second Class 4-wheel Composite, a 4-wheel full Third and 4-wheel Passenger Brake van. In the foreground are a miscellany of items including, small kegs, chicken crates and milk churns. To the right is the cart shed with horse whilst to the left three wagons stand at the loading dock. The fenced off access way in the foreground was then known as Coal Road as it led to the coal grounds in the railway goods yard but after development in 1904 it was known as Kings Road.

In 1879 John Crabtree, the CV&HR General Manager purchased an 0-6-0 tank locomotive formerly used on the Cornwall Minerals Railway and named it *Haverhill*. The engine survived on the Essex line until 1889 when it was sold to South Hetton Colliery.

Author's collection

alterations were authorised on the signalling interlocking at Chappel costing £65. On 7th April the Goods Manager requested the provision of a loading gauge at Haverhill GE, and on 20th October the application to prove a tar covering on the platform at Chappel was deferred. Then, on 2nd May 1876, sanction was given for the provision of stables to accommodate two horses at Haverhill GE station at a cost of £50.

In October 1875 the CV&HR directors had again made application to the GER for absorption of their line. The matter was raised at the board meeting at Bishopsgate on 3rd November when it was agreed the General Manager would meet with Mr Matthews of the CV&HR.

The continuing strained relationship between the CV&HR and the GER came to light in a dispute recorded in the *Halstead Gazette* for 1st June 1876. Robert Watt, the CV&HR Manager, was the chief witness for the prosecution of John Thomas Titman, the station master at Halstead, who was charged with embezzlement of the Company's funds. It soon became evident from questions by the defence and from the learned clerk, as well as comments from other witnesses, that Watt was regarded with extreme disfavour. Despite covert manoeuvres, Watt was unable to prevent illegal practices from being revealed. Excess fares from foreign companies were not being included in returns to the Railway Clearing House, the GER being the principal loser. Equally, money collected for these fares was not being accounted for in the CV&HR books. It also became clear there were incorrect procedures being perpetuated on a daily basis. GER wagons being loaded at Birdbrook were actually invoiced as being loaded at Halstead or Colne so that mileage was lost to the owning company, the cash being pocketed to the credit of the CV&HR. It also became clear that Birdbrook excursion ticket issues were being credited from Colne for the same illicit purpose. To cross

examination, Watt also admitted that monies received for the sale of old sleepers, ironwork, rails and other surplus material was not recorded in the Company's ledgers; timber chains from the GER were retained and then stamped CVR. It was of no surprise that the GER sent two detectives to watch the proceedings and report back. At the end of the proceedings all charges against Titmuss were dismissed. Watt's career appeared to be in tatters.

Further evidence against Watt's management came on Friday 22nd June 1876 when a deputation of Halstead traders attended the CV&HR directors meeting to air their grievances over the number of charges raised by the railway company for the collection and delivery of goods receipts from Brick Lane, the charges for booking and forwarding of small parcels, the delay in settlement of claims for loss or damage of goods, irregular charges for carriage of commodities and the lack of staff available to assist with the loading and unloading of goods at stations. The management promised to investigate and introduce improvements.

On 20th January 1877 a pair of horses owned by Francis Whitlock were being led across the railway at Yeldham when an oncoming train struck the animals. The carter jumped clear and escaped injury but the leading horse was killed. As a result of the accident the instruction was issued that the drivers of all trains had to sound the locomotive whistle on the approach to the crossing, which was on a curve partially obstructed the driver's view. With claim and counter claim regarding his poor management increasing day by day, Robert Watt took the only course available and resigned as General Manager, the vacant position being taken by John Crabtree.

As mentioned earlier, the company never owned the rolling stock running on the railway, when from 1864 the vehicles were sold to Robert Tweedy of Truro for the grand total of £9,010 and the later locomotives were hired from C.E. Brewster. On 9th April 1877 the stock was valued at £6,547 and a

C.E. Brewster, son of James Brewster, who purchased three new locomotives and rolling stock for the CV&HR, hiring them to the company.

court order subsequently decreed that from 4th May 1878 that sum was to be paid to C.E. Brewster at the rate of £1,200 per annum plus 5 per cent interest on the balance, the vehicles remaining his property until the debt was settled.

The *Halstead Gazette* for 27th September 1878, reported that a passenger waiting on an excursion train from Cambridge had overheard a heated exchange between two men, one of whom had earlier *'purchased'* a small girl for the princely sum of 2s 6d. Just before departure the second man argued with the purchaser but failed in his attempt to retrieve the child before the train departed leaving the excursionist to travel home with his new *'daughter'*.

As the decade was drawing to a close the GER cross-country route from Cambridge to Colchester was experiencing increased trade, bolstered by the news at a meeting on 23rd April 1879 that agreement had been reached for the installation of a new siding at Haverhill at a cost of £250, for the Essex Show to be held in the town. By 22nd August the price had been reduced to £225, whilst on 6th April the following year the GER Way and Works Committee authorised the paving of the cattle pens at Chappel station at a cost of £8 15s 0d. Progress was also being made on the CV&HR: plans had been prepared and construction commenced on a new station at Ford Gate between Colne and Halstead.

LEFT: In the 1880s a series of photographs were produced showing damage to the railway caused by wet weather and flooding. Here the aftermath of a bank slip at 8 miles 60 chains appears to have affected Alderford overbridge No. 13 at 8 miles 59 chains (later renumbered by the L&NER No. 14). Baulks of timber and replaced rails litter the scene
M. Root collection

BELOW: The section of line in the cutting on the approach to Sturmer Road overbridge, No. 32, between Birdbrook and Haverhill, later renumbered 33 by the L&NER. This circa 1880 view shows that relaying is required after a bank slip and flooding caused by the lack of side drainage. *M. Root collection*

Cutting; showing Slips and no side ditches at 17 m. 10 between Birdbrook & Haverhill.

A rather poor view of Halstead station from the south circa 1880 with 0-4-2T No. 1 in original condition pulling into the platform.

M. Root collection

Halstead station facing towards Chappel circa 1880 showing the original low platform and higher extension. Several passengers are waiting for a train in the open, declining the meagre protection of the canopy. The design of the building was attributed to Joseph Cubitt and constructed in white brick with quoins and dressings in red brick by Rayner & Runnacles at a cost of £2,730. The same firm provided the original footbridge spanning the running lines and goods yard at the much cheaper price of £160. A covered van stands by the goods shed. The abysmal condition of the permanent way with gravel and ballast covering the sleepers was one of the reasons the GER refused to take over the CV&HR.

M. Root collection

4

Halcyon Years

By mid-September 1880 the new station at Ford Gate was ready for inspection and on 23rd September Major F.A. Marindin duly examined the facilities. He found the new structure by the Ford Gate Road consisted of a short platform with a shelter shed and a booking office, whilst at the end of the platform was an authorised level crossing of a public road with gates closing across either the line or the roadway. The inspector ascertained the gates were visible from an Up train for a distance of about half a mile but from a Down train they were only visible from a distance of 250 yards because of the curvature of the line. A signal had therefore been placed at the end of the platform to protect the crossing and this was worked by the gateman. It was not the intention to provide any other signal as there were no siding connections. Marindin thought the accommodation, although small, was acceptable considering the small number of trains and nature of the traffic on the single line, but as the railway was worked by Train Staff and Ticket he considered it might also be possible by error in the block working, which was provided by telephone, for a train or engine to follow from Colne station before the preceding train had reached Halstead. He therefore recommended the use of the station could not be sanctioned until home and distant signals were provided in each direction to protect the line.

On 18th January 1881 severe snowstorms swept across the Home Counties and East Anglia. On the Colne Valley, the last Up train had a difficult run with snow blowing across the line and the locomotive often slipping on the wet rails. Having reached Chappel the engine and stock formed the last evening train away from the junction but after curving away from the Sudbury line almost immediately ran into a deep snowdrift. After several abortive attempts to batter its way through the drift the engine well and truly stuck and after a while the passengers were escorted back along the track in deep snow to Chappel where they sought shelter for the night. The train was finally dug out of the snow the following day after the blizzard abated.

In late February 1881 the CV&HR requested a further extension of the platform at Chappel and provision of a new waiting room for interchanging passengers. The GER agreed to the extension at a cost of £45 but held over the decision on the waiting room. At the end of March it was also realised no paving had been laid in the cattle pens at Chappel; on 5th April the directors required urgent action and authorised the work to proceed at a cost of £115. During the summer public complaints were on the increase, which resulted in the Halstead Local Board of Health complaining of the *evil smell emanating from fish wagons stored in the goods yards at various stations*. The chief culprit was a consignment of surplus sprats, which had not been offloaded as the cargo *was not worth the trouble*. As the problem stemmed from wagons stabled over the weekend the General Manager was instructed to arrange with the GER to place an embargo on any inward movements on Saturdays and Sundays. The complete embargo of movement of fish traffic

across the Colne Valley at weekends appears to have solved the problem, for no further complaints were made.

On 1st March 1881 the CV&HR signed an agreement with the Postmaster General for the maintenance of the electric telegraph route along the line. Then in July 1881 the GER directors were advised of a scheme for a railway linking Rayne on the Bishop's Stortford to Braintree line to Haverhill; on 2nd August it was suggested a meeting be arranged between the GER Chairman and Colonel Brise MP and a deputation, although the proposers were uncertain of the actual route of the line. It was announced the GER would be prepared to work the line, if built, for 60 per cent of the gross receipts. On 6th September the directors agreed to meet a deputation, but this time the line was shown as running

CV&HR hand lamp rests on a carpenter's bench at White Colne in March 1961. *J. Watling*

from Dunmow to Haverhill. The CV&HR directors appeared to be oblivious to the proposed railway cutting across their territory but the scheme failed to materialise.

As traffic was increasing, partly because of the interchange of traffic between the GER and CV&HR, on 17th January 1882 the GER Way and Works Committee authorised the construction of a new granary at Haverhill at an estimated cost of £425; on 4th April the contract was awarded to J. & A. Brown after the firm had tendered at £425, subject to completion within ten weeks of the contract date.

After nearly six years with the CV&HR, Crabtree departed in 1882 to take up his new appointment as General Manager of the Great Northern & Great Eastern Joint Railway; his replacement was George Copus. He found the motive power situation on the line was dire and purchased an ex-North London Railway 0-4-2 saddle tank locomotive to help meet the shortage. The improvements to the new station at Ford Gate, including the provision of goods accommodation and signalling, were nearing completion by mid-July 1882 and a BOT inspection was requested. Major General Hutchinson duly conducted the inspection on 4th August and noted the station was provided with a single platform, with the usual accommodation for passengers. The levers working the points of the goods loop line were concentrated in a new raised signal box and properly interlocked. A clock visible from the platform was the only requirement and subject to its early provision the inspector sanctioned the opening of the station to passenger traffic.

The finances of the company were a continuing problem and left much to be desired. Matters came to a head in July 1883 when a committee of bondholders was set up to investigate and seek improvements. Unfortunately the members of the committee could not agree with the directors as to the best way of handling the delicate negotiations and ultimately the impasse was referred to Parliament. In the meantime several board members pressed for the railway to be sold to the GER and an approach was made to Bishopsgate for an inspection, but the main line company was in no hurry to respond.

On 5th February 1884 Wilson, the GER Engineer, and Worsdell, the Locomotive Superintendent, reported to the directors on their examination of the CV&HR and its rolling stock and plant, and gave their estimate of the approximate value. The report was far from flattering for the pair had found most of the works were for single line and there were flaws in the permanent way and sleepers. The formation was waterlogged and the cuttings were wet, the level crossing gates and bridges in poor condition, signalling old and inefficient, the station buildings in a 'wretched' condition, and very little of the rolling stock and plant would be of any use to the GER. In view of the findings the Secretary was instructed to write to Brewster declining his proposition for takeover. Thus, with no alternative, later in the year the subject was passed to Parliament and The Colne Valley and Halstead Railway (Arrangements) Bill was prepared.

The CV&HR board of directors in 1884 consisted of William Clarke MICE of 45 Parliament Street, Westminster SW, Chairman, with fellow directors James Brewster of Ashford Lodge, Halstead, Henry John Tweedy of New Square, Lincoln's Inn, London WC, J.R. Vaizey of Attwoods, Halstead, George James Addison Richardson of the Manor House, Burnham, Maldon, Essex, and Robert Walker Childs of 5 Fetter Lane, Fleet Street, London EC. The Secretary and Receiver was William George Bailey of 3 Throgmorton Avenue EC, which was also the company's registered office. The Auditor,

R.B. Rose, also operated from the same address. The General Manager of the CV&HR was George Copus of Halstead, Essex, whilst the Solicitors were Baxter & Company of 6 Victoria Street, Westminster and Mayhew, Salmon & Whiting of 30 Great George Street, Westminster.

The gross receipts figure for the half year ending 30th June 1884 was £4,832, which was wholly overtaken by working expenses of £5,140, whilst the capital and expenses account at 30th June 1884 showed:

RECEIPTS	£	EXPENSES	£
Ordinary shares	61,200	Cost of Acts of Parliament	19,163
Preference shares	84,250	Land, works,	
Debentures	58,245	engineering,	
Lloyds Bonds	76,200	permanent way,	
Receipts on account of arrears	789	stations and plant	270,043
		Direction and expenses	6,240
Total	295,446	Total	295,446

The impasse between bond holders and directors requiring Parliamentary approval took some time before actual application was made to the Private Bill office for the necessary legislation. The Colne Valley and Halstead Railway (Arrangement) Act 1885 (48 and 49 Vict Cap cxciv) was passed on 14th August 1885 and established the way forward to straighten out the affairs of the ailing company. Before advising on the legislation agreed, the opening paragraphs made sorry reading, enumerating the succession of Acts of 1856, 1859, 1861, 1863 and 1865 which showed the total share capital as:

	AUTHORISED ORDINARY	ISSUED PREFERENCE	UNISSUED
£218,000	£61,200	£84,250	£72,550
Deduction of preference shares by this Act		£60,000	
New Total		£24,250	
LOAN CAPITAL	AUTHORISED	ISSUED	UNISSUED
	£71,633	£57,745 3s 8d	£13,887 16s 4d

The statute recorded the Company became financially embarrassed and borrowed at various times £50,000 and deposited with the lenders as collateral security 6,000 preference shares with the nominal value of £60,000 which were included in and formed part of the sum of £84,250 shown in the above table. The Company was subsequently sued for these advances and judgments were obtained against the Company for the sum of £40,612 5s 6d, being the balance of the moneys then due and owing, and the judgments so obtained were now included in the sum of £49,520 referred to as the amount owing to Judgment creditors.

One hundred and thirty four preference shares with the nominal value of £1,340, part of the £60,000 subsequently returned, were now in the hands of the Company, leaving 5,866 shares with the nominal value of £58,660 in the hands of the creditors, which with the passing of the Act were returned. Robert Tweedy of Truro, Cornwall, held 5,116 of the 5,866 shares and James Brewster of Halstead, Essex, held the other 750; it was expedient that these shares were cancelled, and Robert Tweedy and James Brewster had both agreed to surrender their shares to the Company by the passing of the Act.

The capital raised – both share and loan – was insufficient to pay the contractor for the construction of the line. The Company gave to the contractor before the passing of the Railway Companies Act 1887 certain certificates of indebtedness under their common seal, now known as construction bonds, amounting to £76,200 bearing an interest of 5 per cent per annum. The Company had also created certain rent charges as compensation to landowners for the purchase of their lands amounting to £96 per annum which had all been paid regularly, and there were outstanding against the Company certain claims for the purchase of lands totalling about £750 which they are entitled to and had regularly received interest at the rate of 5 per cent per annum.

Judgments had been obtained against the Company for certain simple contract debts totalling £49,520, some of which were entitled to an interest at 4 per cent per annum but the interest only had been paid since judgment was made; judgments for more than £40, 000 were obtained prior to the year 1887. Judgements had also been obtained against the Company in respect of statutory bonds and construction bonds.

As a result of the foregoing, on 19th November 1874 James Brewster on behalf of himself and all other holders of bonds and debentures of the Company issued under the Acts of 1856 and 1858, or either of them, had instituted in the High Court of Chancery before the Vice-Chancellor Sir Charles Hall a suit against the Company, seeking amongst other things the appointment of a receiver of tolls and other property and effects of the Company, and William George Bailey the Company Secretary was appointed receiver and had remained and still was in receipt of the Company's affairs. Whereas the greater portion of the engines and rolling stock and moveable effects used by the Company for the conveyance of their traffic was hired by the Company from Charles Edward Brewster, and it being deemed expedient for the Company to purchase the equipment, by an order of 9th April 1877 the stock was valued at £6,547 and subsequently Charles Edward Brewster having agreed to sell at that valuation, the Court by an order dated

4th May 1878 directed the receiver to purchase the stock at the rate of £1,200 per year out of the Company's surplus income after payment of working expenses and preferential claims, with interest on the unpaid balance at 5 per cent per annum. The rolling stock and engines were to remain the property of Charles Edward Brewster until full payment was made. It was noted £5,000 was still owed to Brewster but interest had been paid.

By an order dated 9th August 1884, Mr Justice Key in the same suit directed the receiver might be at liberty to purchase out of the funds of the Company two engines for a sum not exceeding £1,900, each with certain rolling stock, and these engines and rolling stock to be paid for by annual instalments not exceeding £700 per annum for seven years; the Company having to pay that amount annually to the Great Eastern Railway for the hire of two engines.

No dividend had been paid on ordinary or preference shares since 1864, nor had any interest been paid on the statutory bonds or construction bonds, and the aggregate of the several amounts entitled to interest but had not been paid was substantial:

	£	s	d
Statutory Bonds	57,745	3	8
Construction Bonds	76,200	0	0
Judgment Creditors	49,520	0	0
	183,465	3	8

To pay interest at 4 or 5 per cent per annum respectively on these amounts required a total annual payment of £8,678 1s 2d, which since 1864 had been accumulating year by year resulting in a large sum outstanding. The total gross income of the Company in 1870 was only £7,591, which since that date had been slowly but steadily increasing and by 1883 had reached £11, 353, but after paying the working expenses and satisfying the orders of the Court there was only a surplus of £2,500.

All the capital raised by the Company having been expended, the directors after paying the rent charges and interest on the outstanding land claims with instalments on the rolling stock as ordered by the Court of Chancery had been complied with for

In 1883 another second-hand locomotive was purchased from the Whitehaven Colliery Company receiving the number 2. The engine, an 0-4-2 saddle tank, was originally built in 1860 for the North London Railway and survived on the CV&HR until 1894. The locomotive and train of early coaching stock are standing at Haverhill GER circa 1895.
Author's collection

many years past to expend from time-to-time further large sums out of revenue for certain necessary capital purposes, which at the close of 1884 amounted to £28,747 7s 6d and left nothing for other purposes.

The Bill to enable the Colne Valley and Halstead Railway to raise further monies, to arrange with their creditors to regulate the capital and future management of the Company, *'and for other purposes'*, was introduced into Parliament in the 1884 session by a committee of bond holders elected in or about July 1883 to act on their behalf at a general meeting of the bond holders, and the Bill included many of the provisions of the current Act. However, in consequence of the committee of bond holders and the Company directors being unable to agree the terms of arrangement between the Company and its creditors the Bill was referred to a Committee of the House of Lords who reported it was expedient to proceed with it. The introduction and discussion of the Bill led to negotiations between the committee of bond holders and the Company directors which resulted in the present Act. The Company, the receiver and the bond holders had all incurred considerable expense in preparation of the Bill and it was expedient they should be repaid.

It was expedient the management of the Company be vested with all the necessary powers in a Board which holders of the statutory

Colne Valley and Halstead Railway (Arrangements) Act 14th August 1885 front page.

bonds and construction bonds of the Company, and the judgment creditors of the Company, or some class or classes of holders and creditors, as well as the preference and ordinary shareholders, should be represented.

It was expedient to discharge the existing receiver and to direct the appropriation of any moneys in his hands at the date of his discharge. The rights, liabilities, priorities, values and interests of various persons who are or claim to be bond holders, judgment or other creditors or shareholders of the Company were to be referred to arbitration. As the Company was unable to satisfy the legal claims of the bond holders, judgment and other creditors, and in order to render the revenues of the Company in some degree to all parties, it was expedient that such discretion be placed in the hands of an arbitrator or referee especially constitute for the purpose to determine not only the rights of the several parties but also the most equitable methods of rearranging, modifying and reconstituting the loan and share capital of the Company, and for the settlement of affairs of the Company as required by the Act of Parliament.

The arbitrator was to be appointed by the Board of Trade and, as it was expedient, to authorise the Company to raise further capital by borrowing on mortgage, and secure the repayments with interest by a special charge upon the Company's undertaking and revenues in priority to all existing charges except rent charges existing at the date of the passing if the Act. The trustees, executors, guardians and persons having a limited interest to consent to any arrangements made under the powers of the Act permitted to take and hold debentures and stocks or shares to be granted or created by order of the arbitrator in lieu of existing bonds, security, debt claims or shares.

Because of the embarrassed financial position of the Company many of the shareholders and bond holders considered their money to have been totally lost, having neglected to register any alteration of ownership or change of residence, and had ceased to be interested in the matter having not answered any communication and therefore the registers were totally imperfect. Many letters had been returned through the Dead Letter Office. The Bill was submitted by the directors to a meeting of ordinary and preference shareholders convened as required by the standing order of both Houses of Parliament. The directors had made application to the Judgment creditors and out of a total holding of £49,520 had received consents from those holding £46,559 16s 6d. Written applications explaining the objects of the Bill was made to holders of statutory and construction bonds requesting their agreement or not to the Bill with the following result:

	AMOUNT OF BONDS ISSUED			TOTAL AMOUNT OF BONDS CONSENTING			AMOUNT UNANSWERED		
	£	s	d	£	s	d	£	s	d
Statutory bonds	57,745	3	8	44,393	15	0	13,351	8	8
Construction bonds	76,200	0	0	66,200	0	0	10,000	0	0
Totals	113,945	3	8	110,593	15	0	23,351	8	8

None of the persons applied to, dissented.

Clause 4 of the statute stipulated the present board of directors would continue in office until a new board was elected, when all powers would be transferred; clause 6 provided powers to discharge the receiver appointed by the High Court of Chancery on 19th

November 1874, whilst the BOT was authorised to appoint an arbitrator in clause 7, his duties being enumerated in clause 9. Clause 27 empowered the Company to borrow on mortgage a sum not exceeding £36,000 to settle outstanding debts and purchase new engines, rolling stock and plant, as well as permanent way equipment.

Under the Act of 14th August 1885, whereby the directors were to refer the affairs of the company to arbitration, the Right Honorable Lord Bramwell was appointed arbiter. To resolve the dispute he made two awards: a preliminary on 21st November 1885 and a final award on 11th February 1886. By these awards his lordship authorised the raising by pre-preference debentures the sum of £50,000, to be called 'A' debenture stock, less administrative charges of £96 per annum. This sum was considered a mortgage with first priority to any of the company's borrowed or other capital for repayment. He further stipulated the conversion of existing statutory bonds, construction bonds and judgment debts, together with existing arrears amounting to the sum of £367,365, into 'B' debenture bonds. These bonds were not entitled to any dividend except out of the net earnings for the year ending, thereby rendering any subsequent arrears of that stock impossible. The arbiter then decreed that the net income of the CV&HR, after payment of rent charges and interest in 'A' debentures stock, was applied first in paying interest in 'B' debenture stock until a total of one per cent had been paid. If any other money was apportioned to dividends it was to be divided between 'B' debenture stock and preference and ordinary shares in such a ratio that 'B' debenture holders received not exceeding four per cent or twice the percentage of preference stock holders who in turn received twice the percentage of ordinary shareholders. Lord Bramwell also consolidated the two classes of preference stock, the second of which amounted to only £1,750, and limited the maximum preference dividend to five per cent. By 1885, out of a total authorised capital if £289,633 the company had raised £236,333 by the issue of £70,000 ordinary shares, £108,000 debentures and borrowed £58,333, a shortfall of £53,300.

Certain services on the CV&HR were operated as mixed trains conveying passengers and freight; one such service was the 11.30am service from Chappel to Halstead, which ran with passenger vehicles attached behind the goods wagons. On arrival at Halstead to allow the passengers to alight, the train pulled across Trinity Street level crossing, thereby blocking the road and in complete contravention of section 7 of the 1859 Act, which made it unlawful

---

COLNE VALLEY & HALSTEAD RAILWAY
(ARRANGEMENT) ACT, 1885.

Preliminary Award

AS TO THE

CONSTITUTION OF THE NEW BOARD OF DIRECTORS AND THE FUTURE GOVERNMENT OF THE COMPANY.

In pursuance of the power conferred on me by the COLNE VALLEY AND HALSTEAD RAILWAY (ARRANGEMENT) ACT, 1885, I, George Lord Bramwell the Arbitrator appointed under the said Act, do hereby make and publish this my separate Award for the purposes mentioned in Section 3 of the said Act, (that is to say).

I DO AWARD, ORDER AND DIRECT AS FOLLOWS :—

1. The Board of Directors for the future government of the Company shall consist of six—three to be appointed by the Statutory Bondholders, Construction Bondholders and Judgment Creditors (who are hereinafter called "the Creditors"), voting together without distinction of class, and three by the Preference and Ordinary Shareholders (who are hereinafter called "the Shareholders"), voting in the same way.

The Directors elected by the Creditors shall be called "Creditors' Directors," and those elected by the Shareholders shall be called "Shareholders' Directors."

2. The qualification of a Creditors' Director shall be his being a Creditor of the Company to the amount of £500, and the qualification of a Shareholders' Director shall be his holding shares in the said Company to the amount of £500.

[97982]

1885 Act – Preliminary Award front page.

COLNE VALLEY & HALSTEAD RAILWAY
(ARRANGEMENT) ACT, 1885.

Final Award.

To ALL TO WHOM THESE PRESENTS SHALL COME, I, GEORGE LORD BRAMWELL, the Arbitrator appointed under the Colne Valley and Halstead Railway (Arrangement) Act, 1885, SEND GREETING. In pursuance of the power conferred upon me by the said Act, I, the said Arbitrator, do make and publish this my further Award in writing, that is to say,

I DO HEREBY AWARD, ORDER, AND DETERMINE AS FOLLOWS :—

1. The Colne Valley and Halstead Railway Company (hereinafter called "the Company") may borrow on mortgage of their Undertaking the sum of £14,000 further than, and in addition to the sum of £36,000 in the said Act mentioned, making in the whole the sum of £50,000, and no more. such borrowing to be on and by Mortgage Debentures or Debenture Stock, which shall be called A Debentures or Debenture Stock.

2. Part III., relating to Debenture Stock, of the Companies Clauses Act, 1863, shall be included in and form part of this Award so far as relates to A Debenture Stock only, except in so far as the same may be, if at all, inconsistent with this my Award.

3. The Creditors on Statutory Bonds and on Construction Bonds, and the Judgment Creditors shall rank on an equality, and they shall receive Debenture Stock, to be called B Debenture Stock, in satisfaction and lieu of their present rights and claims.

4. The debts due to the several Creditors aforesaid shall be taken to be, and shall be, the various sums respectively mentioned in the Schedule hereto annexed ; the name in the Schedule mentioned being no adjudication of ownership, but only an identification of the debt.

5. The Company shall have power to and shall create B Debenture

A

1885 Act – Final Award front page.

to shunt trains to or from sidings near any level crossings or to allow trains to stand across the crossing when stopping at a station. The owner of Adams Brewery in Trinity Street, through his solicitor, on 10th August 1885 wrote to the local Board of Health requiring the company to take action to obviate the problem. The clerk Robert Rutherford Morton forwarded the complaint to George Copus and on 19th August the General Manager retorted that if the provisions of the Act were literally applied they would cause much greater inconvenience as the gates could remain closed to road traffic except when the occasion demanded they be opened to road users. Copus continued that no accident had happened to any pedestrian, notwithstanding the crossing gates were the *'resort of idlers and the playground of children of the locality'*. Adams, however, persisted and the directors subsequently insisted Copus take action. On 16th October Copus advised the Local Board that *'the passenger carriages now attached to the 11.30am goods train from Chappel will be taken off, and the present necessity for bringing that train to the platform and the consequent fouling of the crossing for two minutes will be removed'*. He then advised he had informed manufacturers and merchants *'interested in the traffic to and from the sidings contiguous with the crossing of the necessity for them to arrange the cartage hitherto entailed'*.

To all to whom these Presents shall come, I, HENRY WHATLEY TYLER, of High Elms, Hampton Court, in the County of Middlesex, late a Captain in Her Majesty's Royal Engineers, and now of the Railway Department of the Committee of Her Majesty's Privy Council for Trade and Foreign Plantations, send greeting.

Whereas by "The Great Eastern Railway Act, 1862," it was enacted (Section 274) that the Great Eastern Railway Company (hereinafter called the Great Eastern Company) should if required so to do by the Colne Valley and Halstead Railway Company (hereinafter called the Colne Valley Company) enter upon, work, and manage the railways of the last mentioned Company, as in the said Act provided. And (Sec. 279) that if and whenever the Great Eastern Company should not work the railways of the Colne Valley Company, then the Great Eastern Company should from time to time afford all reasonable and proper facilities by through booking and invoices, the running on of carriages and waggons, and otherwise for the transmission of, and should transmit on their railways, or any parts thereof, any traffic which having passed over the railways, or any part of the railways of the Colne Valley Company, should be from time to time tendered to the Great Eastern Company for transmission on their railways, and also all traffic which should be from time to time tendered to the Great Eastern Company for transmission on their railways, or any part thereof, for the purpose of being afterwards conveyed on the railways, or any part of the railways of the Colne Valley Company. And (Sec. 280) that all such facilities for the transmission of traffic should be afforded by the Great Eastern Company, subject to such rules and regulations, and on payment of such tolls, rates, fares and charges, (not being in any case greater than those for the time being made by the Great Eastern Company against other parties for the like traffic), as the Great Eastern Company and the Colne Valley Company should from time to time agree upon, or failing agreement, as should be settled by arbitration. (Section 281) That all matters in difference between the Great Eastern Company and the Colne Valley Company by the said Act directed to be settled by arbitration, or as to the construction or effect of the preceding enactments or the performance or observance or non-performance or non-observance of any of the provisions thereof should (except as far as related to complaints made to the Court of Common Pleas) as and when the same should arise, be referred to and determined by arbitration, in the manner provided for by "The Railway Companies Arbitration Act, 1859," and as if the two Companies had agreed to refer the same to arbitration in accordance with that Act. And whereas the Great Eastern Company do not work the railways of the Colne Valley Company, and the two Companies have failed to agree upon the facilities to be afforded by the Great Eastern Company for the transmission of traffic, and the rules and regulations subject to which, and the tolls, rates, fares, and charges on the payment of which, respectively, such facilities are to be afforded, as provided by the said Act. And whereas by an agreement dated the twenty-ninth day of March, One thousand eight hundred and seventy, and made between and duly executed by the Great Eastern Company of the one part and the Colne Valley Company of the other part, in pursuance of the directions in that behalf contained in the said Act, the Great Eastern Company and the Colne Valley Company agreed to refer, and thereby referred to arbitration, in accordance with the Railway Companies Arbitration Act, 1859, the differences, questions, and other matters thereinafter specified, and thereby agreed to refer, and referred, the same respectively to the arbitration of me, the said HENRY WHATLEY TYLER, as a single arbitrator; and the said two Companies thereby agreed and declared that the questions so agreed to be referred, and referred, to me as such arbitrator as aforesaid were the following (that was to say)—the facilities which ought to be afforded by the Great Eastern Company, in accordance with the 279th and 280th Sections of the Great Eastern Railway Act, 1862, to the Colne Valley Company for the transmission of traffic as provided by the same sections, and the rules and regulations subject to which, and the tolls, rates, fares, and charges upon payment of which, such facilities ought to be afforded, and all other matters and things collateral with, or incidental to, such questions, as were or ought to be done, observed, or performed by both or either of the said Companies for carrying into full effect the 279th and 280th Sections of the last mentioned Act; and it was further agreed that inasmuch as I, the said HENRY WHATLEY TYLER, was in full possession of all the facts relating to the several questions so referred to me as aforesaid, it should be lawful for me, the said HENRY WHATLEY TYLER (if I should think fit so to do), to make my award upon all or any of the questions thereby referred to my arbitration, as aforesaid, without requiring or hearing any further statements or evidence by or on behalf of the said two Companies, or either of them, and

1885 Act – Enquiry by H.W. Tyler front page.

Thus after 31st October 1885 the 11.30am Chappel to Halstead ran as a passenger train and was extended to Haverhill on Mondays and Saturdays, thereby upsetting many local businesses which relied on the delivery of goods by mid-day. Charles Portway, the owner of the 'Tortoise' works, was immediately put to considerable inconvenience by having to cart all his traffic to the station as his siding north of the level crossing was rendered unusable.

On 2nd February 1886 the GER board considered yet another letter received from the CV&HR, reminding them that under the GER Act of 1862 the GER company could be called upon to take the CV&HR stock at valuation and work the line for 50 per cent of gross receipts, and since the CV&HR had since put its affairs in order it invited the GER to take over the line. The GER General Manager reminded the gathering of the adverse report made by Wilson and Worsdell after their visit to the line in 1884. It was decided to defer any decision pending further investigation. By 6th April it was stated Sir Henry Tyler had reported on his visit and inspection of the line and the Engineer and Locomotive Superintendent were asked to furnish detailed reports on the CV&HR permanent way, works, locomotive and rolling stock, and the cost of putting it into efficient condition.

The matter was again raised at the GER board meeting on 6th July 1886, when the General Manager reported that the obligation for the GER to take over the CV&HR existed only at the completion of the line and did not exist at present, and was in any case conditional on the line being in good order. Wilson, the GER Engineer, had reported that it would cost £67,000 to put the line in reasonable condition, whilst Holden had reported that the three engines owned by the company and valued at £940 were in bad condition and of no use to the GER. The fourteen coaches were worn out and of no value, whilst of the sixty-seven wagons, valued at £1,195, many were of no use. Earnings for 1884 were £11,720 against expenses of £11,494, which were 98 per cent of the earnings. In 1885 the earnings of £11,294 was exceeded by working expenses of £13,582 after deducting exceptional expenses reduced to 85 per cent and 100 per cent respectively. The gathering decided that the CV&HR be advised the GER was under no legal obligation to purchase the railway; if the line was put in order the GER might be prepared to work it but would regard the 50 per cent as totally inadequate.

The GER board meeting held on 3rd August 1886 considered the letter from the CV&HR stating that they had no doubt the obligation for the GER to take over CV&HR was a continuing one, imposed by Parliament in allowing the GER extension to Cambridge rather than the Colne Valley extension, and in allowing the amalgamation of various companies to form the GER. The CV&HR directors were ensuring their line was put into suitable condition as rapidly as possible but in the meantime were putting the questions over the working of the line to the Railway Commissioners or other suitable arbiters. The company were seeking to send a deputation for an early meeting with the GER Board but since it had taken the GER six months to reply to a previous letter it was hoped an early reply would be furnished. The GER directors agreed to receive the deputation but offered 5th October as the earliest date in view of the holidays. They also agreed to take Counsel's opinion on the question of enforced amalgamation.

The Secretary of the CV&HR wrote from his office at 3 Throgmorton Street EC to the GER on 9th August 1886 acknowledging receipt of the letter of 4th August. He reiterated that because of additional and growing traffic it was necessary to provide additional rolling stock. Since his first letter of 25th January the

Circular to the Creditors and Shareholders.

COLNE VALLEY AND HALSTEAD RAILWAY

(ARRANGEMENT) ACT, 1885.

48TH & 49TH VIC., CAP. 194.

LONDON, 3, THROGMORTON AVENUE, E.C.,
27th November, 1885.

SIR,

The Board of Directors of this Company have instructed me to inform you that the application to Parliament made by the Company last Session for

"*An Act to enable the Colne Valley and Halstead Railway "Company to reconstitute the Board of Directors to refer the "affairs in that Company to Arbitration to raise additional Capital "and for other purposes,*"

received in due course the Royal Assent on the 14th August last, under the Title named above.

Under the said Act the Board of Trade are authorised to appoint an Arbitrator for the purposes aforesaid, and under Clause 3 of the said Act such Arbitrator is required to provide by a separate award, before proceeding with any other matter,

"*The number and proportion of Directors to be elected by "the Creditors and Shareholders respectively their respective "qualifications the mode of their election the order of their "retirement the appointment of the Chairman together with all "other provisions relating to the constitution of the Board and "the future government of the Company.*"

The Board of Trade having, in pursuance of the powers vested in them, appointed Lord Bramwell as Arbitrator, His Lordship has made an award in respect of these preliminary matters.

[97977]

2

A copy of this Award is sent herewith, and by this it is provided that the new Board shall consist of six members, three to be elected by the Statutory Bondholders, Construction Bondholders and Judgment Creditors as Creditors' Directors, and three by the Preference and Ordinary Shareholders as Shareholders' Directors, and that the said new Board shall be elected on the 15th December next. I am therefore further instructed to transmit to you a notice for convening separate General Meetings of the Creditors and Shareholders on the said 15th December for the purposes aforesaid.

This Act, amongst other things provides as follows, viz. :—

Cl. 10. "*That the Board shall prepare and submit to the "Arbitrator a scheme or schemes for the reconstitution and "future government of the Company the modification readjust- "ment and fusion of its borrowed and share capitals funds and "separate stocks respectively and the application of its revenue "and other property: Provided that any two or more Directors "who may dissent from the scheme or schemes of the said Board "and with leave of the Arbitrator any person or persons holding "any portion of the share capital of the Company or of the "Company's Bonds or any judgment or other creditor of the "Company to an amount not less than five thousand pounds "altogether may at any time submit such a scheme or schemes "as aforesaid.*"

Under this Clause the present Board of Directors have submitted a scheme to the Arbitrator, and the Arbitrator has appointed the 5th January next at 11 o'clock precisely, in Room 20, Westminster Palace Hotel to hear parties upon that or any other scheme which may be submitted to him by other parties consistently with this Clause.

The powers conferred upon the Arbitrator by the said Act are defined in Clause 11 as below, viz :—

Cl. 11. "*The Arbitrator may as between the Company their "creditors and all other persons settle and determine all matters "in question which may come before him under the provisions of "this Act upon such terms and in such manner in all respects as "he in his absolute and unfettered discretion may think most fit "equitable and expedient having regard to the amount of the "Company's indebtedness the value of the undertaking the various "classes of creditors and shareholders of the Company and the "circumstances under which and the manner in which loans were "made to the Company and the values and priorities of securities "and as fully and effectually as could be done by Act of Par- "liament.*"

(By order)   WM. GEORGE BAILEY,

ABOVE: 1885 Act – Statement dated 27th November 1885.

The CV&HR mobile crane at Halstead carriage shed lifts a 6-wheel 5-compartment coach to enable a wheel change. The crane was also used on bridge reconstruction work, but could not be used in the event of locomotive derailments, when the GER had to assist.

Author's collection

CV&HR Hawthorn, Leslie 2-4-2T *Colne*, built in 1887 (Maker's No. 2080) in original condition with stovepipe chimney and Naylor safety valve. *M. Root collection*

situation was critical and his company was asking the GER to take over their system as provided for in the GER 1862 Act. The Traffic Committee considered the matter on 17th August and agreed to receive a deputation on 5th October 1886. The deputation duly attended and after discussion it was agreed the GER General Manager would negotiate, without prejudice, the terms of a working agreement, to include the provision for the repair of the line to the satisfaction of GER engineers.

After meetings with the CV&HR directors, the GER General Manager reported to the board meeting on 1st February 1887 that it would cost an estimated £58,000 to put in order the Colne Valley company's bridges, interlocking, repairs and renewals to stations, goods sheds and yards, turntables, fencing, permanent way and other infrastructure. The CV&HR stated they were only prepared to spend £10,000. The General Manager then reported the average annual earnings of the CV&HR over the previous ten years was £10,324 and the average working expenses 104 per cent of revenue after excluding exceptional expenses of 86 per cent, which might be reduced to 75 per cent by the GER. If the CV&HR wanted to enforce the Amalgamation Act and make the GER work the line at 50 per cent the CV&HR would have to bring their line up to a standard set by an independent engineer appointed by the Board of Trade. After discussion the Secretary was asked to write to the CV&HR board declining to prolong the negotiations unless the company put their line in order. In the meantime the CV&HR were invited to joint discussions with a view to getting Counsel's opinion on the exact meaning of the 1885 Act. On 1st March 1887 the GER directors were advised the Colne Valley directors had replied stating the sum required by the GER far exceeded what could possibly be required for a single line and they therefore proposed to order rolling stock and continue working the line themselves. A portion of the new capital acquired as a result of the 1885 Act was utilised to purchase two new locomotives from Hawthorn, Leslie & Company in 1887, as well as a steam travelling crane.

Permanent way ganger Allen, walking the Hedingham section of line just after 1.00pm on 9th May 1887, found a man laying with his head on the rail in an attempted suicide. Fortunately the next train was not due to pass the spot for an hour and despite being told of this and other persuasion the man kept his head on the rail. Allen remained with the man until the time for the train was imminent when he walked along the track towards the approaching train and

signalled to Driver Samuel Plum to stop. Once the train had halted Allen returned to the man accompanied by Plum to persuade him to have a change of heart. The man still refused to budge but when the pair were joined by a Mr Slaughter, the three forcibly removed the man from the track and conveyed him on the train to Halstead where he was handed over to the local constabulary.

Meanwhile, the CV&HR Engineer had reported it was imperative that two bridges receive remedial repairs, and work was authorised as a matter of urgency. Major General C.S. Hutchinson inspected the two reconstructed bridges near Colne and Hedingham stations on 22nd June 1887. The bridge near Colne had a skew span of 22 feet, which the inspector found had been entirely renewed with brick abutments carrying cast iron main girders and Lindsay steel troughing floor upon which the longitudinal road was laid. The bridge near Hedingham was of 20 feet square span but here the old abutments were retained with alterations to the wing walls, the construction being otherwise similar to the bridge at Colne. The inspector found both structures appeared to be standing well, whilst the girders gave ample theoretical strength or moderate deflections under test.

By 1888 expansion of goods facilities at Ford Gate station enabled the directors to propose the complete closure of Colne station, which hitherto had insufficient capacity to handle the increasing amount of freight traffic. What was totally unexpected was the decision to withdraw passenger facilities as the platform had been recently raised in height, following complaints from passengers. A petition signed by local people generated some 1,500 signatures and was handed to the railway management on 7th November. A terse reply stated '*the directors express their regret that they cannot alter their decision to close the station*'. The reply was not received until after the petition was discussed at the Board of Directors meeting in February 1889 and the station was due to close on 31st March. A protest meeting was hastily arranged and was held in the Institute Earls Colne in early March when several nobilities and villagers were present. Reuben Hunt, the owner of the nearby Atlas Foundry, chaired the meeting and after extensive discussion which concentrated mainly on the inconvenience and dangers the public faced negotiating the mile-long walk from the village to Ford Gate station, which included overhanging trees and no pavements, with the '*prospect of being robbed and murdered in the course of their journey*' a formal resolution was passed:

That this meeting, being aware of the determination of the directors of the Colne Valley Railway to close the present station now in use, requests them, in their own interest, and in the interest of the inhabitants of the neighbourhood to reconsider the question. In the event of the station being closed another meeting will be called to consider what steps shall be taken to render us independent of the Company.

The CV&HR management chose to ignore the protest.

A further bridge was reconstructed near Hedingham early in 1889. The underbridge with brick abutments supporting wrought iron girders carried a flooring of Lindeaugh (*sic*) patent steel troughing longitudinally to which the rails were fastened. The span of the bridge was 30 feet 7 inches, replacing an old structure constructed of cast iron girders and timber flooring. Major General Hutchinson inspected the structure on 4th May 1889 and found the new bridge substantially constructed, the girders having sufficient theoretical strength giving moderate deflections under test.

On the same day Hutchinson also visited Ford Gate station to inspect the new arrangements. These comprised a new loop line, which the inspector understood was thereafter to be used for passenger traffic when a new platform had been constructed. There was also additional siding accommodation and a new goods shed. As the facilities were enhanced, the existing signal box – now containing a new 26-lever frame, with 23 working and 3 spare levers – was provided to operate the points and signals. The alterations were properly carried out except that No's 2 and 3 signals required interlocking. No. 2 signal was also required to lock No. 14 signal in position whilst No. 24 signal was to be relocated to the Up side of the level crossing. Subject to completion of the alterations the opening of the improvements at Ford Gate station were sanctioned. Hutchinson thought the passenger accommodation at the station was *'very limited'* and *'no unnecessary time should be lost in improving it by providing proper waiting rooms etc.'* The inspector also required the platform to be made a uniform height throughout and ramped at the end. He emphasised the improvements were all the more necessary as the station now dealt with traffic formerly handled at Colne station, which had been closed on 30th April 1889, officially the following day.

In July 1889 heavy delays were incurred by the failure of a GER freight train between Sudbury and Bures. The train provided a connecting service at Chappel for wagons from the CV&HR requiring onward transit to destinations. Due to shortage of engines no assistance was available and connections from Marks Tey were also lost. The CV&HR management suggested that in the event of a similar occurrence it would be advantageous for the Colne Valley engine to work both CV&HR and GER wagons through to Marks Tey so that connections could be kept. Such arrangements were not possible at present as the CV&HR drivers did not have route knowledge between Chappel and Marks Tey, and the GER General Manager was asked to investigate. At the board meeting held at Bishopsgate on 6th August the General Manager reported that if the engine of one company had to run unexpectedly over the line of another company it was necessary to provide a pilotman. None of the nine staff employed at Chappel were competent to act as pilotmen and therefore it was proposed to allow two or three CV&HR drivers to learn the road between Chappel and Marks Tey. Holden would arrange to grant certificates of fitness and inspect the Colne Valley engines before implementation of the arrangement.

The Regulation of Railways Act 1889, as well as requiring block working on most lines and the interlocking of points and signals, also stipulated the compulsory provision and use of continuous brakes on passenger trains, and the correct marshalling of mixed

Passengers and staff congregate under the awning fronting the station building at Halstead. Note the slightly sub-standard height of the platform, which was later raised.   *Author's collection*

trains. Increasing speeds and traffic growth, combined with ineffective braking systems, inevitably led to accidents and as a result the Railway Inspectorate had complained long and hard for passenger vehicles on mixed trains to be coupled to the locomotive with goods wagons marshalled behind the passenger stock with a goods brake van at the rear of the formation. The CV&HR, because of its precarious financial position, subsequently received a sum of £12,150 to improve equipment.

On 4th February 1890 the construction of four cottages at Chappel was authorised by the GER Way and Works Committee at an estimated cost of £900, but before the contract was awarded the cost had increased to £958 14s 5d and the decision to build was deferred. After investigation and examination of tenders on 15th April 1890, authority was given for the construction of the four railway cottages at Chappel at an estimated cost of £958 14s 5d. On the same day, sanction was also given for the interlocking of points and signals at the junction station at an estimated cost of £6,500, the contact being awarded to Saxby & Farmer. Along the line at Haverhill GE station, authority was given on 15th April 1890 for the provision of a parcels office at an estimated cost of £55. Tenders were also invited for interlocking and resignalling at Haverhill, estimated at £3,770. The General Manager reported the high cost at Chappel was because of the extensive traffic at the station, augmented by the junction with the CV&HR and the fact that the station and infrastructure dated from the 1850s.

On 6th May 1890 the GER directors heard that the CV&HR had again made approaches regarding the possible sale of their line and the General Manager was asked to investigate. He reported on his findings at the board meeting on 1st July 1890. The capital of the company was £499,155 and the average annual gross earnings were £13,116 with average net earnings £4,744 per annum. The CV&HR average working expenses were 64 per cent and gross receipts 2s 3d per train mile compared to the average GER working expenses of 52 per cent on gross receipts of 2s 3d per train mile. The price demanded by the Colne Valley company equalled £6,162 per annum so that if the GER took over the line the revenue would be reduced by £3,466 per annum, divided £1,641 interest on the sum required to bring the line up to standard, £1,350 loss on the division of coal earnings and £275 the effect of RCH rule 44 through earnings. Thus to meet the annual payments of £6,162 the GER would be left with £1,278 making a loss of £4,884 per annum. At the conclusion of the report it was decided to set up a committee to consider the proposals with remit to report at the next meeting. In the ensuing weeks, meetings were held between representatives of the two companies but the CV&HR delegation refused to accept the GER terms and would not agree to appoint an independent expert to assess the amount of money required to put the railway in order. The Chairman, Charles H. Parkes, duly informed the CV&HR representatives that the GER would only operate a working agreement on the basis of the 1862 Act of Parliament.

On 5th August 1890 the GER directors awarded the contract for the provision of a footbridge at Haverhill to J. Westwood at a cost of £265 4s 6d, and a footbridge to connect the platforms at Chappel to the same firm for £341 2s 6d. Then on 18th November 1890 the contract for the erection of the four cottages at Chappel was finally awarded to Alfred Coe of Ipswich, who also received the contract for the construction of new station buildings and goods shed after tendering at £2,990. On 2nd December it was reported the contractor was seeking an extension of time for work at Enfield Lock station and Chappel and permission was duly granted.

Aggrieved by the decision regarding the level crossing and siding at Halstead made in 1885, Portway instituted proceedings towards the railway company on Christmas Eve 1890. The matter was passed to the Railway Commissioners but before any action was taken the Local Board of Health agreed that the few wagons passing over the crossing did not constitute a danger and did not constitute a train as referred to by the Act and agreed for the siding to be reopened. The Railway Commissioners eventually agreed to the proceedings and suggested both parties pay their own costs and the siding was allowed to remain operational.

After a protracted delay, on 6th January 1891 the contract for the interlocking of points and signals at Chappel and Haverhill GER stations was awarded to Saxby & Farmer Limited and work started at both places in February.

The CV&HR receipts and expenditure to the 30th June 1891 were:

Receipts	£	Expenses	£
Ordinary shares	61,200	Costs of obtaining Acts	
Preference shares	25,590	of Parliament	19,163
'A' debentures	46,700	Land, works,	
'B' debentures	367,365	engineering	
Premium on issue of		permanent way,	
'A' debentures	3,040	stations	270,043
		Direction, audit etc	6,241
Balance	6,328	Additional capital	
		created in payment	
		of interest on	
		statutory and	
		construction bonds	
		and judgement debts	159,458
		Reconstruction	
		account	51,852
		Regulation of Railways	
		Act	3,465
	510,223		510,223

The officers of the company at this period were Chairman, W. Bailey Hawkins, of 32 Lombard Street, London EC and his fellow directors Stephenson Robert Clarke of 4 St Dunstan's Alley, St Dunstan's Hill, London EC, William John Denton of Crofton House, Kew, William Clarke MICE of 45 Parliament Street, London SW, John Robert Vaizey of Attwoods, Halstead, and Daniel Gurteen of The Duddery, Haverhill. The Secretary was William George Bailey of 3 Throgmorton Avenue, London EC, whose office was also the registered office of the company. General Manager was George Copus of Halstead, the Auditor James B. Laurie ACA of Gresham Buildings, London EC, and the Solicitors Wilkins, Blyth, Dutton & Hartley of 112 Gresham House, London EC.

On 29th September 1891 the GER Way and Works Committee authorised the installation of platform canopies on both Up and Down platforms at Haverhill at a cost of £535. By the beginning of October 1891 the alterations at Haverhill Junction were completed and available for inspection. The examination was conducted by Major General C.S. Hutchinson on 7th October and he found the alterations consisted of a change in position of the loop line points at each end of the station and a new double junction for the Colne Valley line, new and altered siding connections and a rearrangement of the signalling. The inspector noted the levers for working the points and signals were concentrated in two new raised signal boxes.

Haverhill Station signal box contained a 25-lever frame with 17 working and 8 spare levers, whilst Haverhill Junction signal box had a 42-lever frame with 36 working levers and 6 spares. After testing the interlocking in both signal boxes, extensive alterations were required in both structures:

Haverhill Station signal box:
   No. 4 lever to be released by No. 1 lever.
   No. 18 lever not to be released by No. 17 lever only.
   No. 14 lever not to be released by No. 10 lever only.
   No. 8 lever to be released by No's 10 and 13 levers.
   No. 15 lever to be released by No. 13 lever.
   No. 23 lever to lock No. 13 lever between the stroke.

Haverhill Junction signal box:
   No disc signal to be given for running along the wrong line unless for going into a siding or for crossing to the right line.
   The lettering on some levers also required attention and alterations.
   No. 24 lever to connect with No's 11 and 18 levers in either position.
   No. 31 lever to connect with No. 25 lever.

Hutchinson also tried an experiment to ascertain whether vehicles breaking loose from a train standing on the Down line on a 1 in 110 falling gradient would run back as far as Sturmer, the next station on the line to Long Melford, and found that it would do so. Hutchinson therefore required the GER authorities to provide arrangements to guard against such eventualities, and until such precautions were in place he refused to sanction the use of the new works.

By 21st December re-inspection at Haverhill was possible and Hutchinson returned to view the alterations. All outstanding work had been attended to including runaway catch points to prevent vehicles running back from Haverhill towards Sturmer.

The alterations at Chappel were completed in February 1892 and consisted of the provision of a loop line and second platform, general rearrangements of siding connections and renewal of the signalling. New sidings were provided as well as a footbridge connecting the platforms, which now had waiting rooms and other accommodation. Major General C.S. Hutchinson inspected the new facilities on 25th March 1892 and noted the points and signals were worked from a new signal box containing a 38-lever frame with 31 working and 7 spare levers, together with a 12-lever ground frame, having 10 working and 2 spare levers. The following minor adjustments were to be completed before 1st April when the GER wished to bring the new works into use:

1   Additional releasing number required to be shown on No. 21 lever.
2   No's 35 and 36 levers should precede lever No. 38 and lever No. 5 should precede levers No's 1 and 3.
3   The Up starting signal required to be moved nearer to the Up line.
4   The bolt lever on the ground frame required painting in a distinctive colour.
5   A facing point lock and bar required to be fixed at the Up end of the loop points.

Subject to completion, Hutchinson sanctioned the use of the new works although he returned on 5th July to confirm the authority.

Whilst alterations and improvements had been made on the GER, the CV&HR had been making great advances to infrastructure and signalling and Major General Hutchinson made a return visit to the line on 10th May 1892 to inspect the new facilities at Halstead and Birdbrook. At Halstead he found that alterations had been made to the siding connections and a new goods shed constructed. The object of the exercise was also, at a later stage, to provide a proper passing place and additional platform for passenger trains. The gates of the public road level crossing north of the station were now worked from a new signal box containing a 36-lever frame, with 27 working and 9 spare levers, one key for a ground frame and a gate wheel. The ground frame released by Annett's key in the signal box contained a 7-lever frame, with 5 working and 2 spare levers.

CV&HR 0-4-2T No. 1 fitted with an ugly stovepipe chimney after a visit for general overhaul at the GER Stratford Works in 1894, when the locomotive emerged painted raven black. It is standing at Haverhill GER station in 1895. Note the ornate water column to the right. *Author's collection*

Unfortunately not all the works were to the inspector's satisfaction and the undermentioned modifications were stipulated:

1 Disc signals to be provided for No's 11 and 24 points, that for the latter to be worked with No. 14 points.
2 No. 22 disc signal to apply to the straight line as well as the crossing through No. 24 points and required to be interlocked with the ground frame key.
3 No's 19 and 24 points not to be interlocked with the gate wheel, this being interlocked instead with disc signal No. 21 and one to be provided with No. 24 points.
4 No. 34 signal to release No. 36 distant signal.
5 Additional release numbers to be painted on No. 21 lever.
6 Repeaters required for No's 35 and 36 signals.
7 On the ground frame, levers No's 2 and 5 and 3 and 6 to be interlocked.

Hutchinson also observed that if and when providing a footbridge between the old and new platform, it was *'most desirable to render it available for foot passengers using the level crossing, which would obviate the use of the wicket gates'*. The second platform was, however, never provided.

Along the line at Birdbrook the inspector noted the signalling and point work was controlled from a new raised signal box containing an 11-lever frame with 10 working and 1 spare lever. The arrangements were satisfactory except that:

1 No. 8 lever was required to lock No. 5 lever in both positions.
2 Release numbers to be painted on the levers.
3 No. 4 lever, the spare, to be painted white and lever No. 7 painted blue.
4 A repeater was required for No. 11 distant signal.

Concluding his visit, Hutchinson stipulated the lengthening of the platform at the Haverhill end of the station and shortening at the Halstead end so that it terminated short of the siding. Handrails were required on the parapet of the underbridge close to the Haverhill end of the platform to prevent passengers from stepping out of the carriage doors and falling on to the roadway below. The works at both stations was sanctioned subject to the completion of outstanding requirements within a period of two months.

After a seemingly long period, the contract for erection of canopies over the platforms at Haverhill GE station was awarded to Collins, Barber & Company in August 1892 after they tendered at £415. No roof was provided on the footbridge connecting the platforms but this was provided later.

As finances permitted, so improvements continued to be made in the Colne Valley to bring the line up to the standards required by the Regulation of Railways Act 1889 and on 23rd November 1892 Major General C.S. Hutchinson inspected the improved arrangements at Hedingham. He noted that the alterations had been made to the siding connection, making it a passing place for passenger trains despite the absence of a second platform. The signals and points were controlled from a new raised signal box containing 25 levers, with 21 working and 4 spare levers, with an Annett's key locking a separate 9-lever ground frame where all levers were in use. The works were satisfactory and the interlocking correct, except that a repeater was required for No. 25 distant signal whilst No. 9 lever on the ground frame required locking. Hutchinson recommended sanctioning of the works subject to completion within two months.

Whilst visiting Hedingham, the inspector took the opportunity to reinspect the facilities at Halstead and Birdbrook, noting that all the requirements except one of his report of 10th May 1892 had been completed. With regard to the repeaters for the distant signals at both locations, Hutchinson was advised the electrical department

Halstead signal box in independent years, located on the Down side of the line adjacent to Trinity Street level crossing. The structure dating from 1892 was provided with a 36-lever Saxby & Farmer frame, initially with 27 working and 9 spare levers with an associated 7-lever ground frame, and later with 25 working and 11 spares plus a wheel to operate the crossing. In the background, a CV 5-plank open wagons stands by the buffer stops.

M. Root collection

Colne Valley 2-4-2T *Hedingham*, festooned with flags, bunting and evergreens for Queen Victoria's Jubilee celebrations in 1897.
M. Root collection

of the Post Office had the matter in hand. At Birdbrook no platform alterations had been made and the Major General stressed the importance of having this done as a matter of urgency and required the company to report to the BOT when work was completed.

Despite the many warnings issued to the general public of using the railway as an unofficial footpath or not heeding the presence of an approaching train, in 1892 Sarah Beard, aged 69 years, was killed by a train at Langley Mill crossing as she attempted to cross the railway to deliver a parish magazine to Langley Mill. The later inquest recorded a verdict of accidental death.

A deputation of the promoters of the proposed railway linking Takeley on the Bishop's Stortford to Braintree branch with Haverhill attended Bishopsgate at 12.30pm on 18th April 1893. Those attending included Lord Brooke, Marquis of Bristol and seven others including Mr Levey, the promoter, Teagle, the Engineer and Franklin, Hon Secretary to the committee. The gathering explained that the proposed railway from Takeley to Haverhill via Thaxted was 18½ miles in length and traversed land largely belonging to Lord Brooke. A paper was submitted giving details of the building programme and costs were estimated at between £145,000 and £155,000, including purchase of land and parliamentary expenses. The Chairman of the GER Traffic Committee explained the position of the company and that they were unable to assist in promotions of this kind, neither could they give any pledge that the company would work the line if it was authorised. The proposal was evidently amended, for in June 1893 the GER General Manager met the promoters and on 6th reported back to the directors. The line passing through purely agricultural district with a sparse and scattered population, and with a ruling gradient of 1 in 70, which could be reduced to 1 in 100, would not cover its working expenses. The promoters were subsequently advised the GER would work the line at 75 per cent of earnings up to £10 per mile and 70 per cent for earnings over £10 per mile. The scheme subsequently faded into oblivion.

On the CV&HR the directors were encouraged by the development of brickworks near Castle Hedingham with the promise of the conveyance of bricks and tiles by rail. The new siding connection between Halstead and Hedingham station to serve the Hedingham Brick Company Purls Hill Brickworks was completed in the spring of 1893 but it was 17th June before Major General C.S. Hutchinson made the official BOT inspection. He found the new connection was worked from a 5-lever ground frame enclosed in a lineside hut, the frame being locked by a key on the Train Staff for the single line section. The works were satisfactory and

Hutchinson sanctioned the use of the siding. Thereafter the brick traffic was a major source of revenue for the railway company.

Elsewhere improvements were made at Yeldham and the signalling was completed in December 1894, but it was 17th January 1895 before Major F.A. Marindin carried out the necessary inspection. He noted the station possessed a single platform with loop sidings on both sides of the line and a public road level crossing at the Up or Halstead end of the layout. The new signal box contained a 26-lever frame with 23 working and 3 spare levers, and a wheel for working the level crossing gates. There was also an outlying ground frame bolted by an Annett's key which when taken from the signal box locked all the necessary levers and No. 12 disc signal. At the conclusion of the inspection Marindin required the following alterations to the locking to be completed within two weeks of the visit:

1 No. 12 lever to be locked by the withdrawal of the Annett's key.
2 No. 16 lever to lock No. 20 lever in either position.
3 No. 12 lever not to lock No. 24 lever.
4 No. 8 lever not to lock No. 10 lever.

For almost two decades, Halstead Local Board made complaints regarding the condition of the pavements and approach to Halstead station and as the years had progressed the subject became a spat between Morton Clark, later also of the Urban District Council, and George Copus. The detritus was always blamed on the CV&HR and Copus replied to numerous allegations in 1896 that he:

wished to call attention to the obstruction of the entrances to the railway station by waggons and horses standing for hours at a time and in some cases left without horses attached to them, and to ask whose duty it was to remove such obstructions – whether that of the police or otherwise.

The UDC even complained of the state of footpaths along the railway. Morton was still at loggerheads with CV&HR management in 1910!

After years of leasing and working several small railways in East Anglia, each entailing its own problems, the GER directors resolved to tidy up the excessive costs of administration by purchasing the several leased and worked lines, including the Marks Tey to Sudbury line. On 6th May 1896 it was resolved to prepare a suitable Bill to the next session of Parliament. The process, which involved several other undertakings, took some time to come to fruition and it was not until 1st February 1898 that the GER proprietors approved unanimously of the bill for the company to acquire the CSV&HR. The takeover was completed with the passing of the Great Eastern Railway (General Powers) Act 1898 (61 and 62 Vict cap lxvi) on 1st July 1898. To finance the acquisition the GER was to raise £235,972 by new debenture stock bearing interest at the rate of 4 per cent from 1st July 1898, when registered proprietors of £100 preference stock of the Colchester company would receive £125 of new stock paying 4 per cent interest, with registered proprietors of Colchester consolidated stock receiving the balance pro rata according to their respective holdings. The sale of the CSV&HR was to be completed within three months of the passing of the Act. Within the financial structure, by powers conferred by the GER (General Powers) Act 1878, the GER held either in their own name or in the name of Lord Claud John Hamilton as trustees on their behalf the sum of £7,000 ordinary stock of the Stour Valley Company. On 5th April 1898 further improvements came with authorisation of Tablet working between Haverhill and Bartlow at a cost of £368 to replace Train Staff and Ticket operation of the single line.

As a result of the passing of the Light Railways Act, in 1896, a scheme for a line leaving the GER main line at Elsenham and running via Thaxted to connect with the CV&HR at Hedingham and Haverhill was mooted, and in the following year the Ongar, Dunmow & Yeldham Light Railway was suggested. In 1898 the CV&HR was more directly involved with the proposal for a Hedingham & Bardfield Light Railway as they were invited to work the line if and when completed, but the GER registered their objection. The same year saw further abortive schemes, with a light railway linking Kelvedon with Coggeshall and Halstead, and from Hedingham to Long Melford, and the Central Essex Light Railway with its route from Ongar to Dunmow and Sible Hedingham, to which the GER also objected. The Solicitor duly reported on 5th October 1898 that clauses were to be inserted to protect the GER interests in the Kelvedon, Coggeshall & Halstead Light Railway proposal, which was to join the CV&HR at Colne Engaine; the Central Essex (Ongar, Dunmow and Yeldham) enquiry was to be held on 13th October; the Hedingham and Melford on the same date; whilst the Bardfield and Sible Hedingham promoted in connection with the Elsenham, Thaxted & Bardfield Light Railway had already been passed by the Commissioners.

In 1898 and 1899 receipts on the CV&HR improved considerably with an upturn in freight traffic, and at the half yearly meeting for the six months ending 30th June 1899 W. Bailey Hawkins, the Chairman, stressed that brick traffic – largely from Sible and Castle Hedingham but also from the Hesworth Brick Company siding at Haverhill where the contract for the construction of the siding had been finalised on 22nd April 1899 – was producing increased returns. Passenger traffic was also increasing owing to a general improvement in wages allowing people to travel more regularly. However, prices of commodities used by the company had increased but nevertheless twenty new wagons had been purchased in the half year.

Yet another application for the GER to purchase the CV&HR came in early June 1899. The General Manager reported to the

CV&HR 0-4-2T No. 1 pollutes the countryside as she approaches Hepworth Hall bridge west of Halstead, with a 4-coach train formed from the engine: a 4-wheel Brake Third, a 6-wheel 5-compartment Composite, another 4-wheel Brake Third and one of the original 4-wheel coaches. The locomotive has lost its stovepipe chimney for a lipped variety and acquired additional side tanks. *Author's collection*

As a result of the Regulation of Railways Act 1889 the CV&HR was required to provide proper block signalling and interlocking of points and signals on the line. Over a short period of time the company complied and one of the signal boxes provided was at Yeldham in 1894, which contained at 26-lever Saxby & Farmer frame with 23 working and 3 spare levers. A view in independent days shows the signal box without nameboard on the Up side of the railway wedged between the end of the station platform and the level crossing. *M. Root collection*

GER board on 7th June, reminding them of the report he made on 1st July 1890 setting out the facts and recommending against purchase. He was now of the opinion the condition of the line had deteriorated, the earnings were less, the capital now at £513,161, with dividends paid on 'A' debentures only and none paid on 'B' debentures since 1892. Nothing was ever paid on preference or ordinary stock. He then explained the ambiguities of the 1861 ECR Act. The matter was referred to a special committee and the Locomotive Superintendent and Engineer were to report on the condition of the line and rolling stock, and the Goods Manager and Superintendent on any traffic requirements, if any.

To cater for the ever increasing goods traffic and the interchange of traffic between the CV&HR and GER, the GER Way and Works Committee authorised the extension of sidings at Haverhill at a cost of £330 on 19th September 1899. On the same day they also sanctioned the building of a retaining wall at the station at a cost of £200.

On 8th November 1899 the GER board were advised of the findings of their officers regarding the condition of the CV&HR. The Superintendent was of the opinion none of the stations except Halstead were adequate for the handling of traffic, which the Goods Manager reported the accommodation was up to the standard of GER country stations except there were no truck or cart weighbridges. The Locomotive Superintendent assessed the value

of the locomotives and rolling stock at £9,500 and the Engineer estimated the cost of bringing the line up to standard including work at stations was £61,500. The General Manager concluded the line was of no value to the GER except to prevent an incursion into GER territory. The board concluded that the CV&HR General Manger be asked to make an offer for the sale. Thus on 1st January 1900 George Copus wrote to the GER Secretary stating that his directors were now willing to sell the line to the GER for £190,000, but two days later their hopes were dashed when the GER board declined the offer.

In the meantime, on the evening of Friday 8th December 1899 Driver H. Bartholomew was in charge of the Up goods train hauled by 2-4-2T No. 3 *Colne*, which was standing in the Down loop at Halstead waiting to depart for Chappel. For some inexplicable reason Bartholomew started the locomotive and the train subsequently passed a signal at danger before continuing along the loop, which ran parallel to the main single line almost as far as Parsonage Street level crossing. Fireman J. Roope never questioned Bartholomew as to his actions, believing him to have received a signal from the guard Harry Turp. As the locomotive trundled on, neither man noticed the points at the end of the siding were set for the headshunt and not the main line. Henry Keeble, the gatekeeper at Parsonage Street, well aware the approaching train was not heading for the main line, in the darkness attempted to

A mixed train from Haverhill to Chappel passing Parsonage Lane crossing not long after a 2-4-2T locomotive demolished the signal box in 1899. The locomotive is a GER 'K9' Class 0-4-2T on loan to the CV&HR. The rolling stock included a 4-wheel full brake, a 6-wheel 5-compartment full Third and the two ancient 4-wheel coaches built by Wright & Sons of Birmingham for the opening of the line. At the tail of the formation is a rake of low-sided wagons. *Author's collection*

attract the driver's attention by swinging his red lamp but to no avail. As Keeble took avoiding action the engine ploughed through the buffer stops, then smashed through the gates before embedding itself in Parsonage Street signal box on the opposite side of the road. Driver Bartholomew and Fireman Roope suffered only minor injuries, whilst the locomotive sustained minor damage to buffer and bunker. Of the twelve wagons forming the train, four were damaged beyond repair, including one loaded with flour which was scattered liberally far and wide, whilst live chickens escaped from another smashed wagon. As a result of the incident the main single line was blocked and the GER breakdown train was

summoned from Ipswich to help clear the railway, arriving just after midnight. The passenger train service was operated to a point on each side of the accident and passengers walked between connecting trains until the line was cleared just after midday on Saturday 9th December.

On a brighter note, increasing passenger traffic was recorded at Halstead on Saturday 23rd December 1899 where in excess of 450 tickets were issued and the station handled over one thousand passengers. Station Master Blackmore also reported his staff had dealt with more than 3,000 parcels during the previous week, whilst the Post Office traffic had been *'exceptionally heavy'*.

The aftermath of the accident at Parsonage Lane crossing on Friday 8th December 1899 as staff survey the wreckage of the demolished signal box, buffer stops and the derailed 2-4-2T *Colne*. *Author's collection*

5

World War One and After

IN 1900 A DISPUTE AROSE between A.W. Kibble, Manager of the Tortoise Foundry at Halstead, and the CV&HR concerning the use of the private siding leading to the works located on the Up side of the main single line north of Trinity Street level crossing after an earlier disagreement was resurrected. The connection was used for the loading of heavy castings and other ironwork and required wagons to be propelled over the level crossing and into the siding to be loaded. The dispute, originally raised in 1885 and again in 1890, was brought about by a clause in the CV&HR Act which stipulated no shunting was to be performed over the level crossing and no train was allowed to stand foul of the crossing whilst trucks were shunted to and from the siding. George Copus interpreted this as barring all movements to the siding and forced the Tortoise Foundry to purchase a horse to pull the wagons between the foundry siding and the station yard. The dispute festered and was passed to the Railway Commissioners in 1901. Settlement was by compromise and both parties were ordered to pay their own costs. Copus took the partial defeat as a personal affront and attempted persecution of Kibble. He had constructed a high wall with a lean-to shed in front of Kibble's house in King's Road so that his front window overlooked a blank wall, which was later used for fly-posting at the rate of 10s 0d per annum. It became known in later years as the 'Spite Wall'. Hawkins stopped the fly-posting, and the wall and shed were later used by coal merchants. The Tortoise Foundry siding was closed for two years after Hawkins arrival but then reopened as it provided much trade to the company.

On 15th May 1900 the introduction of Train Tablet working between Chappel and Marks Tey was authorised by the GER board at a cost of £165, to eliminate Train Staff and Ticket working of the single line. Then on 19th June 1900, Wotner Smith were awarded the contract for repairs and painting of Haverhill GER station at a cost of £188, although on 17th July the contract was transferred to Vigor & Company at a cost of £210.

As already mentioned, the Light Railways Act of 1896 had been promoted to alleviate the distress of the agricultural depression by allowing inexpensive railways to be constructed in rural areas, with the proviso that those so constructed would be freed from the obligation to build to the high standards laid down by the Board of Trade for main lines. Section 5 of the Act stated that where the Board of Agriculture certified that the provision of a light railway would benefit agriculture, the Treasury might agree to the building of the line out of public money. One such scheme directly involving the CV&HR was for the Elsenham, Thaxted & Bardfield Light Railway, and application was submitted on 18th November 1896 for a line 10 miles 6 chains or thereabouts in length, commencing at Elsenham station on the GER Liverpool Street to Cambridge main line and passing by way of Thaxted to terminate in the Parish of Great Bardfield at a point at, or near, the western side of the High Road linking Great Bardfield and Finchingfield, about 12 chains from the entrance of Pake's Farm. Initially it was proposed to build the railway to a gauge of 2 feet 6 inches, thus keeping the costs down to an estimated £30,565. The GER was not happy with the construction of a narrow gauge railway and after protracted negotiations neither the promoters nor the GER had sufficient funds for immediate advancement. Then in 1900 the Braintree & Halstead Light Railway was proposed but the GER and CV&HR gave no

The former 'spite wall' at Halstead. A dispute between A.W. Kibble, Manager of the Tortoise Foundry, and George Copus, the CV&HR Manager, that originated in 1885 and continued again in 1890, concerned the interpretation of a clause in a CV&HR Act which precluded trucks destined for the factory siding from being shunted across Trinity Street level crossing. The matter was subsequently passed to the Railway Commissioners in 1901, resulting in a compromise with both parties paying their own costs. Copus, expecting victory, took the partial defeat as a personal affront and in retribution ordered the construction of a high wall with a lean to shed on railway land directly in front of Kibble's house in King's Road, which was later used for fly-posting at the rate of 10s 0d per annum. It thus assumed the title of the 'spite wall' but Hawkins stopped the fly-posting, and the wall and shed were later used by coal merchants. *M. Root collection*

support. On 18th November 1901, however, the Light Railway Commissioners authorised the Bardfield & Sible Hedingham Light Railway Order authorizing the construction of the Light Railway in the County of Essex, to join the proposed Elsenham, Thaxted & Bardfield scheme with the Colne Valley & Halstead Railway. The new line was to connect at Great Barfield with the Central Essex Light Railway authorizing the construction of a light railway from the GER station at Ongar with Great Bardfield.

The promoters included Issac Everson Winslow, Edmund Alfred Hopkins and Holman F. Stephens, the latter famous for his association with many light railway schemes. The proposed railway, constructed to a gauge of 4 feet 8½ inches, was 7 miles, 5 furlongs and 6 chains or thereabouts in length. Commencing in enclosure No. 206 in the Parish of Finchingfield by a junction with the proposed Elsenham, Thaxted & Bardfield Light Railway (when constructed), and passing eastwards across the main road from Finchingfield to Great Bardfield, keeping to the south of Daw Street Farm and on the north side of the village of Wethersfield, thence running in a north-easterly direction past the east side of Poor Park Wood and on the north side of Gray's Farm and of the site of Kennigale Hall, and traversing the centre of Thorley Grove and keeping on the north side of Tredgell's Wood, and crossing the north corner of Lowt's

Wood and the occupational road leading from Hostage Farm to the main road from Wethersfield to Hedingham, thence turning eastwards and across the road leading from Church Street, Sible Hedingham to Forry's Green, thence turning to the north-west and crossing the main road from Colchester to Haverhill at a point 20 yards or thereabouts measured along the said road northwards of the northern side of Sydney Villa, Swan Street, and turning to the north passing 100 yards or thereabouts to the east side of Brook Farm, and terminating in the Parish of Sible Hedingham by a junction with the Colne Valley & Halstead Railway at or near Sible and Castle Hedingham station. Three years were allowed for compulsory purchase of land and five years for completion of works.

The company was required to carry the railway on bridges over public roads at the undermentioned points:

ROAD NO. ON PLAN	PARISH	SPAN	HEIGHT	SPACE
38	Wethersfield	25 feet	15 feet	10 feet
45	Sible Hedingham	20 feet	15 feet	10 feet

The company, if required by the local authority, was to construct to a reasonable satisfaction and transfer to them a footpath from the point where the railway intersected the existing footpath from Swan Street Sible Hedingham to Church Street, the footpath immediately adjoining and outside the south fence of the railway. Gates were to be provided at the level crossing on public roads No. 2 in the Parish of Great Bardfield and No. 5 in the Parish of Wethersfield and No. 53 in the Parish of Sible Hedingham. Where gates were not required, open crossings were authorised protected by cattle guards at each end of the road to prevent cattle or horses entering on the railway, whilst white posts standing 300 yards on each rail approach to the crossing were erected to warn drivers of the necessary speed limit. A notice board was to be erected 50 yards distance on each road approach to the level crossing cautioning the public to 'Beware of the Trains'.

Clause 29 of the document stipulated the light railway company was not to enter upon the lands or works of the CV&HR except by permission, and then only for the purpose of construction. The junction between the two was to be effected within the deviation points shown on plans and during construction the company was not to interfere with the CV&HR works except by permission, nor cause delay to train services through obstruction or interference. The light railway company had to make good any loss or damage incurred by the CV&HR and at their own expense, and to provide on their own land all necessary sidings for the interchange of traffic and accommodation for light railway traffic. No engine or item of rolling stock was to have axle loading greater than 14 tons but the limit could be raised to 16 tons provided rails weighing 70 lbs per yard were used. The speed limit was restricted to 25 mph, reduced to 20 mph on gradients steeper than 1 in 50 and 10 mph approaching and over ungated road level crossings. The new company was authorised to enter into agreements with the Central Essex Light Railway and CV&HR, and was responsible for all costs of constructing any junction with the Central Essex Company. To finance the Bardfield & Sible Hedingham Light Railway the company was authorised to raise £39,000 in £10 shares with borrowing powers of £13,000 once all shares were allocated and half actually paid up.

On the CV&HR, the receipts for the half-year ending 31st December 1901 totalled £9,403, an increase of £465 compared with

LIGHT RAILWAYS ACT, 1896.

BARDFIELD AND SIBLE HEDINGHAM LIGHT RAILWAY ORDER, 1901.

ORDER

MADE BY THE

LIGHT RAILWAY COMMISSIONERS,

AND MODIFIED AND CONFIRMED BY THE

BOARD OF TRADE,

AUTHORISING THE CONSTRUCTION OF A

LIGHT RAILWAY IN THE COUNTY OF ESSEX, TO JOIN THE PROPOSED ELSENHAM, THAXTED AND BARDFIELD LIGHT RAILWAY WITH THE COLNE VALLEY AND HALSTEAD RAILWAY.

Presented to both Houses of Parliament by Command of His Majesty.

LONDON:
PRINTED FOR HIS MAJESTY'S STATIONERY OFFICE,
By DARLING & SON, LTD., 34-40, BACON STREET, E.

And to be purchased, either directly or through any Bookseller, from
EYRE & SPOTTISWOODE, EAST HARDING STREET, FLEET STREET, E.C.,
and 32, ABINGDON STREET, WESTMINSTER, S.W.;
or OLIVER & BOYD, EDINBURGH;
or E. PONSONBY, 116, GRAFTON STREET, DUBLIN.

Bardfield and Sible Hedingham Light Railway Order 1901 front page.

Earls Colne station facing Chappel with 0-4-2T No. 1 approaching on a Down train and the new brick-built station master's house and station buildings in the background. *Author's collection*

the same period in 1899. The total was formed of passenger £2,446, parcels £479, mails £32, goods £5,629 and miscellaneous £817. The capital of the company at the same date stood at £516,000, divided as follows:

	£
Ordinary shares	61,000
Preference shares	26,000
'A' debentures	60,000
'B' debentures	367,000
Balance	2,000

In January 1902 a new siding connection facing Up trains was provided on the Down side of the line at Halstead station leading from the single line. The points and signals were worked from a 16-lever ground frame with all levers in use; this was locked by an Annett's key which when removed from the Station signal box locked all the protecting signals to danger. Lieutenant P.G. Von Donop visited Halstead on 14th February and found the interlocking correct and the arrangements satisfactory. During his visit he mentioned a letter received by the BOT from the Colne Valley General Manager dated 8th February 1902 regarding a new underbridge and requested a copy of the drawing giving details, as required by BOT Requirement A6. The CV&HR management attending the inspection pleaded ignorance as to the existence of the document and Von Donop arranged for a copy to be sent to Halstead. On 15th April 1902 Vigor & Company were awarded the contract for repairs and painting of Chappel GER station at a cost of £234.

The financial standing of the CV&HR company for the half-year ending 30th June 1902 showed a reduction in income of £31 compared with the same period in 1901.

	30TH JUNE 1902			30TH JUNE 1901			REDUCTION		
	£	s	d	£	s	d	£	s	d
Passenger	1,880	1	3	1,884	19	0	+ 4	17	9
Parcels	433	9	5	515	8	9	+ 81	19	4
Mails	32	10	0	32	10	0			
Goods	5,276	4	3	5,321	0	6	+ 44	16	3
Miscellaneous	786	5	8	685	9	8	–100	11	1
	8,408	5	8	8,439	7	11	+ 31	2	3

Unfortunately the reduced receipts combined with a period of increase in working expenditure:

	30TH JUNE 1902	30TH JUNE 1901	INCREASE
	£	£	£
Station, way and works	1,507	1,373	+134
Carriage and wagon	1,021	853	+168
Rates and taxes	429	408	+ 21

Passengers carried in the six months ending 30th June 1902 totalled 1,380 First Class and 60,918 Third Class.

A strange occurrence befell Driver Salmon as he stood in the cab of his engine during a thunderstorm in August 1902. At the precise moment he had his hand on the regulator the locomotive was struck by lightning and Salmon was thrown across the cab. As well as bruising he received serious burns and was absent from work for several days.

On 30th December 1903, as the 6.20pm Up goods train from Haverhill was approaching Box Hill, a quarter of a mile from Halstead on a 1 in 475 falling gradient, the couplings parted between two wagons as the driver braked the train for the station stop. Initially the rear wagons halted before setting off down the gradient and colliding with the front portion derailing vehicles. Guard Turpin, suspecting only a snatch, realised too late that his portion of the train was running away and he failed to apply the handbrake in his van. In the resultant collision he was severely shaken but uninjured. When Hawkins was advised of the derailment he immediately rejected the call for the GER breakdown train. CV&HR permanent way staff and traffic staff were summoned to site with jacks and packing. On arrival they found only one Colne Valley wagon loaded with bricks was derailed whilst one pair of wheels on the following wagon was also off the line. By using the jacks the two wagons were quickly rerailed but further examination of the CV&HR vehicle found the axle guard out of alignment. Hawkins instructed the wagon to be unloaded and the bricks transferred to another vehicle. The damaged wagon was then turned over off the track and rolled down the embankment to be recovered the following day. The remaining wagons were recoupled and the train continued its journey. Unfortunately the permanent way was damaged as a result of the derailment and train services were suspended until the following morning when repairs could be effected.

In 1903, George Copus retired due to ill health and his successor was Elyot Stephen Hawkins. Copus had not had the best of relationships with the local populace, or indeed with the GER. In 1904 Bailey, the Secretary, retired and Hawkins also assumed that role. Bailey, however, continued in an advisory capacity for a further two years earning a salary of £50 per annum. Improvements came gradually but initially Hawkins had to take stock of the company's finances and cement a stable relationship with the management at Bishopsgate and indeed with his own staff.

The GER Directors were advised on 8th June 1904 an application had been made to extend the time for purchase of land for the Central Essex and Bardfield & Sible Heddingham light railway orders granted in 1901, whilst on 6th July the CV&HR renewed the agreement with the Postmaster General for the maintenance of the telegraph.

On 4th October 1904 it was announced gas prices at Haverhill GE station had been reduced by 5d per thousand cubic feet. Along the line at Earls Colne it came as a shock to the CV&HR management to learn that they had been under the misapprehension they had purchased outright the 484 square yards on which the station buildings and station master's house were erected from the executors of the late Reuben Hunt for £720. On being advised that the area covered by the goods yard was not part of the sale the CV&HR management hastily agreed to lease the land from Reuben Hunt's heirs and associates for 99 years at a rent of £6 per annum in an agreement dated 20th

Elyot Sidney Hawkins,
CV&HR General Manager from 1903 to 1923.

October 1904. A little over a month later, on 22nd November, having settled outstanding disputes and disagreements, a contract was signed regarding the working of Portway & Sons' siding at Halstead.

As no progress had been made constructing the light railway from Ongar to Bardfield and on to Sible Hedingham, both parties agreed to a merger and on 4th September 1905 the Central Essex Light Railway (Amendment) Order 1905 was passed granting an extension of time for the compulsory purchase of land to five years from the date of the order and seven years for the completion of works, and the winding up of the Bardfield Company

Halstead station presents a busy scene with 2-4-2T *Hedingham* at the head of a 2-coach Up train to Chappel with bearded driver by the cab. The locomotive is in near original condition with stovepipe chimney, sandbox on the front footplate and headlamp mounted on the bracket on the smokebox door. The Down starting signal appears above the station canopy to the right and to the left wagons are stabled by the loading dock. *M. Root collection*

with all powers transferred to the Central Essex Company. At the end of the year, on 21st December the CV&HR signed a contract with the Anglo American Oil Company to permit the storage of fuel at Halstead.

A new siding connection at the former Colne station between Chappel and Earls Colne stations, and facing Down trains, was inspected by Lieutenant P.G. Von Donop on 19th December 1906. The points to the new siding and associated signals were worked from a 9-lever ground frame with all levers in use. The inspector was of the opinion the connection was *'rather nearer the level crossing than desirable'*, but the company Engineer informed Von Donop the levels of the ground on which the siding was laid made it difficult to avoid. Satisfied with the explanation the inspector sanctioned the use of the siding and connection with the main single line, which were brought into use early in 1907.

On 5th March 1907 the gas prices at Haverhill GE station was reduced by 2½d per thousand cubic feet. In the general trade press there was acclaim for the CV&HR company: *The Locomotive Magazine & Carriage & Wagon Review* for 15th June 1907 reported in the *'past year or two the line has been brought up to standard with Earls Colne station being rebuilt "in a pleasing style" and a new goods depot at White Colne'*. Hawkins had been true to his word and assured local businessmen and farmers that freight facilities were necessary at White Colne in addition to those at Earls Colne.

As the Central Essex Light Railway promoters had made no progress, on 5th June 1907 the Central Essex Light Railway (Extension of Time) Order 1907 was passed granting powers to extend the time for the compulsory purchase of land to nine years and completion of works to nine years. In the meantime the original

Elsenham, Thaxted and Bardfield scheme had been abandoned in 1906 in favour of a more modest plan for a standard gauge line connecting Elsenham and Thaxted, which was submitted to the Light Railway Commissioners on 29th May 1907.

Problems were constantly experienced with the heavily loaded brick trains from Hedingham, where 0-4-2T No. 1 and the three 2-4-2Ts were struggling with all except the lightest load. To resolve the issue an order was placed with Hudswell, Clarke for a new 0-6-2 side tank locomotive to haul the ever increasing loads, but the introduction into traffic of locomotive No. 5 in 1908 highlighted a problem with the bridges on the railway. Hawkins had specified that the new locomotive was to be of equal weight to the 2-4-2 tank engines but in fact it scaled at 5 tons 11 cwt heavier. Fenn, the Civil Engineer, was dubious of allowing the engine to pass over White's Bridges No's 1 and 2 (No's 6 and 7) respectively between Earls Colne and Halstead. After correspondence with Hudswell, Clarke, a short term compromise was agreed to reduce the coal and water capacity whilst in traffic pending a full investigation and report to the board. Some doubted if a full inspection of all the bridges on the line would

serve any purpose but ultimately, and after some persuasion, the directors agreed to an independent examination of all structures. As W. Bailey Hawkins, the Chairman, was also Chairman of the Cambrian Railways and Elyot Hawkins had come from that line, the assistance of the Chief Civil Engineer of that company was sought. The survey was ultimately conducted by James Willlamson, the principal assistant, who found the structures were substandard to take the weight of locomotive No. 5 but also with the 2-4-2 tank locomotives which left little margin for safety. As a result of the alarming findings of the report, Hawkins was instructed to arrange for a bridge rebuilding and strengthening programme and this initially commenced with White's No. 1 bridge in 1908 and White's No. 2 bridge the following year. As well as commencing work on civil engineering infrastructure, Hawkins had persuaded the directors that passenger facilities again be brought into use at White Colne.

Lieutenant Colonel P.G. Von Donop inspected the new passenger station at White Colne on 5th May 1908. The platform was 145 feet in length and 3 feet in height with ample width. It was provided with a booking office, nameboard, lamps and *very slight accommodation*. Being an intermediate station in an Electric Staff section between Chappel and Halstead, the station was not provided with signals except for home signals each side of the station for the protection of the level crossing. The only point calling for attention was the lack of overhang on the front of the platform. The company officials explained that none of the platforms on their line were so constructed and under these circumstances Von Donop was satisfied but required the provision of an overhang on any future platform construction on the railway. The lack of passenger accommodation was discussed and the company had already undertaken in a letter of 23rd March 1908 to provide further accommodation in the form of a carriage body. Von Donop duly sanctioned the use of the platform for trains, providing the combined carriage length did not exceed 145 feet.

The GER Solicitor reported on 2nd June 1908 that the Central Essex Light Railway had made application for a further extension of time for the purchase of lands and completion of works to 1910 and 1912 respectively.

On 30th November 1908, Frederick Gilder, the signalman at Yeldham, went to the platform to uncouple a horsebox from the 4.50pm train. Jumping down between the vehicles he lifted the coupling but in doing so his foot slipped and he overbalanced, falling against the Westinghouse brake pipe and sustaining a broken rib. By 1908 W. Bailey Hawkins of Stagenhoe Park, Welwyn, Hertfordshire was Chairman of the CV&HR, with Stephenson Robert Clarke, Charles Bridger Orme Clarke, William Clarke, Robert E. Vaizey and Arthur Clement Tweedy as fellow directors. The Secretary and General Manager was Elyot S. Hawkins and the Resident Engineer A.G. Fenn, whilst S. Rayner was Accountant, John Wade, Auditor and Blyth, Dutton, Hartley & Blyth, Solicitors. The offices of the company were now based at Halstead.

Permanent way and signalling alterations were completed at Haverhill GER station at the end of 1910. The work included the removal of the scissor crossover between the Halstead and Sudbury single lines and the substitution of separate connections. The crossover road between the Up and Down lines of the station loop was also removed and slips substituted on the previously existing through connection. The existing pointwork was also relaid and in consequence was slightly altered in position. On the Up side of the station the connections were relaid and slightly repositioned. The

LIGHT RAILWAYS ACT, 1896.

CENTRAL ESSEX LIGHT RAILWAY (EXTENSION OF TIME) ORDER, 1907.

ORDER

MADE BY THE

LIGHT RAILWAY COMMISSIONERS,

AND CONFIRMED BY THE

BOARD OF TRADE,

REVIVING THE

POWERS GRANTED AND EXTENDING THE PERIODS LIMITED BY THE CENTRAL ESSEX LIGHT RAILWAY ORDERS 1901 TO 1905 FOR THE COMPULSORY PURCHASE OF LANDS AND EXTENDING THE PERIODS LIMITED BY THOSE ORDERS FOR THE COMPLETION OF THE RAILWAYS AND WORKS THEREBY AUTHORISED.

Presented to both Houses of Parliament by Command of His Majesty.

LONDON:
PRINTED FOR HIS MAJESTY'S STATIONERY OFFICE,
By DARLING & SON, LTD., 34-40, BACON STREET, E.

And to be purchased, either directly or through any Bookseller, from
WYMAN AND SONS, LTD., FETTER LANE, E.C.,
and 32, ABINGDON STREET, WESTMINSTER, S.W.;
or OLIVER & BOYD, TWEEDDALE COURT, EDINBURGH;
or E. PONSONBY, 116, GRAFTON STREET, DUBLIN.

1907.

Central Essex Light Railway (Extension of Time) Order 1907 front page.

In 1908 the CV&HR ordered a strong 0-6-2 tank locomotive from Hudswell, Clarke to haul freight traffic, especially the increasing brick traffic from Hedingham, which was severely overtaxing the 2-4-2T and 0-4-2T engines. Here No. 5 stands at the head of a freight train which includes in its formation a Great Northern Railway 4-plank open wagon and one of the CV&HR ex-Great Western Railway goods brake vans.

Author's collection

existing Haverhill Junction signal box was abolished and replaced by a new structure containing the same frame. Lieutenant Colonel P.G. Von Donop inspected the new works on 20th January 1911 and observed no alterations had been made to the working of the points and signals on the Up side, whereas on the Down side the frame in the previously existing Haverhill Junction signal box was relocated, although the new structure still contained a 42-lever frame with 36 working and 6 spare levers. The interlocking was correct and arrangements satisfactory, and Von Donop sanctioned their immediate use.

At the GER board meeting on 7th July 1911, Charles Bridger Orme Clarke, a director of the CV&HR, made an informal proposal to the GER to purchase his company. In a presentation Clarke advised the CV&HR capital as at 31st December 1910 was formed of:

	£	
'A' debenture stock	61,845	paying a 5 per cent dividend
'B' debenture stock	367,365	dividend payment ceased in 1892
Preference shares	25,590	no dividend
Ordinary shares	61,200	no dividend
Total	516,000	

The gross earnings for 1910 were £18,629 and the net earnings £3,409, with 82 per cent of gross earnings being expended on working expenses. Clarke proposed the takeover on the following terms: CV&HR 'A' debentures to be exchanged for GER 4 per

cent debentures, totalling £61,845; CV&HR 'B' debentures to be exchanged for GER 4 per cent preference stock equal to 1 per cent on £367,365 and totalling £91,841; preference shares, £12 10s 0d to be paid for every £100 nominal holding – totalling £3,199; ordinary shares, £6 1s 0d to be paid for every £100 nominal holding totalling £3,978; the gross total equating to £160,683. Clarke also opined that the equivalent of 4 per cent of the total equaling £6,434 but rounded up to £6,500 could be paid to CV&HR officers as compensation. He also thought the GER could work the line for 60 per cent of the gross receipts, thus increasing the net receipts from £3,409 to £7,500 leaving a safety margin of £1,000.

After carefully listening to the proposals the GER General Manager reported to his Directors that in 1899 the GER Engineer had reported the CV&HR line was not up to GER standards and to improve to the same level would incur costs of £61,500. Clarke claimed some work had been carried out but a complete investigation would have to be carried out to ascertain if costs could be reduced. As to the working arrangements, the *'signalling was primitive and the line gradients were so steep that the working of goods trains would prove difficult'*. Staff rates of pay and conditions were, however, almost the same as the GER and some management staff savings were possible. Thus extra costs would be incurred taking over the line only partially offset by staff savings. These costs would incur an additional estimated £1,500 capital expenditure per annum as well as increased wages to clerical staff. It was estimated there would be loss of earnings by having a mileage division, not the fixed *'little line'* allowance of £1,350 at present claimed by the

CV&HR 2-4-2T *Hedingham* was specially decorated by Halstead staff with flags and bunting for the Coronation of King George V and Queen Mary in 1910.

M. Root collection

CV&HR. There would also be a loss of £275 per annum earnings calculated on the shorter route, if the company owned two parallel routes as stipulated under Railway Clearing House regulation rule 44. After deliberation, the GER Directors were of the opinion the net earnings would be less than at present and as the district was agricultural there was little prospect of commercial development; the only reason to buy the CV&HR was to prevent another railway company gaining access to GER territory. It was therefore resolved the GER Company would decline the offer to purchase the CV&HR on the presented terms.

At the CV&HR board meeting held at 144 Palmerston House London EC on 31st August 1911, chaired by W. Bailey Hawkins, it was agreed to grant one additional day's pay to all staff, including clerical staff, as loyalty pay for not withdrawing their labour during the recent railway strike. At the same meeting the application from Messrs Gurney for provision of a siding to serve their premises was considered but a decision was deferred pending investigation. Then on 17th October 1911 the board learned of the increasing delays to goods traffic brought about by the shortage of wagons, and after due consideration gave authority for tenders to be sought for the provision of twenty open wagons. It was also deemed necessary to purchase a new town delivery lorry for Halstead, whilst progress reports were received regarding the renewal of Blue Bridge and the lengthening of the platform at White Colne. The untidy state of Halstead station carriage yard was raised with the proviso that urgent action be taken to remedy the matter; the Engineer also reported the GER had no second-hand rails available for sale. It was agreed that Gurney's application for a siding would have to be declined owing to the physical and operational difficulties which would be experienced on their chosen site.

A month later, on 14th November 1911, it was announced that Unwin's application to purchase surplus land from the company had fallen through. It was reported the new town delivery lorry had been ordered and tenders invited for the twenty new open wagons. The Engineer advised that the delivery of granite required for making good the approach road to Birdbrook station was expected shortly.

A cow had strayed on to the railway through defective fencing and been killed by a train. The General Manager requested the Secretary to negotiate settlement with the farmer on the best possible terms. The question of a new carriage shed was also discussed and the Chairman and Charles Clarke were delegated to investigate, subject to only one shed being ordered.

At the meeting on 12th December 1911 it was reported another heifer had been killed on the line and it was agreed the order for new fencing be pursued as a matter of urgency because of the two recent incidents. As a result of the Board of Trade Preventions of Accidents Act of 1911, the General Manager reported to the gathering the plan he proposed be adopted to enable the company to carry out the new rules.

W. Bailey Hawkins was re-elected Chairman of the company at the board meeting on 19th February 1912. A.G. Fenn had reported in a letter dated 9th February of the additional work incurred on the repair and reconstruction of bridges on the line, and after discussion it was resolved that a £50 bonus be awarded to Fenn because of this extra responsibility. It was also noted the heavy workload had affected the contractor who was reported to be ill. At the conclusion of the meeting it was agreed to increase the salary of the General Manager by £25 per annum with effect from 1st January 1912.

The satisfactory completion of the rebuilding of Blue Bridge was reported on 12th March 1912, whilst a report on the traffic during the coal strike was submitted. The poor state of Earls Colne station yard had necessitated urgent action to obtain new material to make good the surface and the Engineer advised that 50 tons of granite had been obtained from the Enderby & Stone Stanton Granite Company at the price of 12s 4d per ton delivered to Earls Colne and remedial work was in progress.

Dogged by ailing health, A.G. Fenn, the Resident Engineer, tendered his resignation from 15th April 1912 and it was with regret the directors accepted the letter the following day. Because of the critical position of the company finances, Elyot Hawkins then assumed the title of Company Engineer in additions to his roles as General Manager and Company Secretary.

The application from Sir Peile Thompson to plant trees at Yeldham station was agreed at the meeting on 16th April, although the General Manager and Vaizey were to negotiate with the landowner to ascertain they would not interfere in any way with railway operation. Somewhat belatedly, Ripper's letter of 8th December 1911, seeking permission to erect offices over his loading shed at Sible and Castle Hedingham, received attention and the Secretary was instructed to reply that the company had no objection to the proposal. At the conclusion of the meeting the General Manager reported his concern about the poor receipts from passenger traffic at White Colne and tabled the earnings accrued during the previous twelve months. It was agreed to monitor the situation and seek ways to increase traffic at the station. Bumpstead Rural District Council wrote on 26th April complaining of the condition of the bridge near Birdbrook station; the Engineer was asked to investigate the allegation and report back as a matter of urgency. In the meantime, the GER repair and repainting of stations programme came round again and on 18th April 1912 A. Coe of Ipswich was awarded the contract in respect of Haverhill station at a cost of £149 10s 0d.

The CV&HR board meeting on 17th May 1912 decided the appointment of a new Locomotive Department Foreman be deferred as no suitable applicant had come forward. It was also reported the new open wagons were ready for delivery; to avoid unnecessary empty and unremunerative transit, the General Manager was asked to arrange with Stephenson Clark to have the wagons loaded with coal from Shipley Colliery before the journey south. The matter of the Locomotive Foreman was again raised at the meeting on 19th June, when the General Manager was instructed to look out for a suitable locomotive fitter to fill the post. The gathering were also informed that the sale of a haystack on railway land at Earls Colne containing 25¼ tons of hay had realised £84, equating to approximately £3 7s 0d per ton. Because of financial constraints the revised lighting scheme at Sible and Castle Hedingham was deferred, as was the new shed for carts at Halstead, although the directors agreed to revue the latter in three months. At the conclusion of the gathering the General Manager reported that the twenty new wagons had been delivered from Harrison & Camm.

The draft agreement with Ripper's for the extension of the buildings at Sible and Castle Hedingham was agreed at the board meeting on 25th July 1912, whilst £10 was paid to Jabez Gurteen in compensation for the loss of his bullock which was killed after straying on to the railway through broken down fencing. It was agreed the General Manager would be appointed the Resident Engineer of the Company in place of Fenn, although the post would in fact incorporate both positions. To ease the burden on Elliot Hawkins, J. Williamson was appointed as Consultant and Inspecting Engineer for an annual remuneration of 20 guineas. Williamson attended the meeting on 29th August 1912 and agreed to conduct a survey of the line on 6th September. The board was asked to note the Colne Valley line had escaped the serious flooding which had devastated East Anglia earlier in the month. It was noted the retimbering of Halstead level crossing was in progress and the General Manager was authorised to sanction the reslating of the roof at Halstead station.

Construction of the new cart shed at Halstead was authorised on 17th September 1912, providing the cost did not exceed £60. On the same day the Consultant Engineer reported on the condition of structures on the railway, including Bridge No. 8 Blue Bridge (Road), Hedingham River Bridge, Nunnery Street River Bridge No. 16 and Bridge No. 18 known as 'Apple Dumpling'. After due discussion the Engineer was asked to prepare estimates for the repair of the latter three. With regard to Hepworth Hall Water Bridge No. 11, it was agreed the cross bracings receive attention as a matter of urgency. The last structure to be scrutinised was Bridge No. 26 at Birdbrook. The Engineer was asked to provide estimates for providing a new bridge and repairs to the existing structure. On the same day, the General Manager received an increase in annual salary of £25 in recognition of his additional responsibilities as Engineer.

The General Manager reported on 22nd October 1912 that a Mr French was excavating ballast from a pit on his land which abutted up to the railway near New England and was of the opinion the depth of the pit was such that it might cause the adjacent railway land to subside and thus cause misalignment of the trackbed. The Secretary was instructed to write immediately to French asking him not to excavate to a great depth alongside the railway. Progress reports were also presented on the repairs to Nunnery Street Pile Bridge, 'Apple Dumpling' and Hedingham River bridges. The river bridges were cause for concern and the original estimates were

2-4-2T No. 4 *Hedingham*, running bunker first, heads a train formed of the three ex-Metropolitan District line coaches, near Birdbrook on 29th July 1911. As the CV&HR had no turntables, locomotives had to run bunker first in one direction.
LCGB/Ken Nunn

GER notice at Chappel and Wakes Colne station requesting passengers not to cross the line except by using the footbridge.

J. Watling

the local brickyard and it was resolved on 14th February 1913 there would be no alteration made to the present haulage charges. At the same meeting it was agreed to increase the salary of Mr Coppin, the Halstead station master, to £2 2s 6d per week. It was also agreed to review the age profile of staff over the age of 70 years who were still gainfully employed by the company. Any proposal to dispense with their services was deferred pending further enquiries. Eleven days later it was decided the General Manager should take the responsibility for any action. At the meeting on 25th February it was agreed to take urgent action to renew fencing and crossing gates on a rolling programme of renewals in view of the reported increase of trespass by animals and humans.

On 11th March 1913 the General Manager advised the board meeting that Ganger Eves and Driver Bartholomew, who were both over 70 years of age and with fifty years service, had been retired. He was also negotiating with various parties over the accident to Fireman P. Goulden. A report on the ongoing saga of the three underbridges revealed the General Manager had obtained tenders for the provision of steel sectioning. Encouraging news came from Essex County Council who offered £500 towards the cost of reconstructing Birdbrook underbridge (Hunwick Lane No. 28) and it was agreed to accept the offer and arrange to start the work immediately. The General Manager concluded the meeting by reporting that in the recent high winds a signal post had blown across the line at Parsonage Lane causing slight delays to services. The signal had no stay wires and it was agreed the Engineer be asked to review all signals along the line to ascertain if they required additional support by staying. In the meantime Tyer & Company received the contract to replaced the signal post complete with wires and fittings for £11 6s 2d; the work was completed in early April.

On Good Friday 21st March 1913 a nine-year-old boy, Preston Irons, was killed when he fell from a moving train. At the board meeting held on 8th April 1913, the General Manager was instructed to '*repudiate any liability*'. It was reported that trial bores made for the foundation of Hedingham Pile Bridge had proved satisfactory and that the £500 offered by Essex County Council had included the proviso that the width of the structure at Birdbrook was to be 20 feet from abutment to abutment. Under the new criteria, the Engineer was requested to obtain tenders for the girders. These were received within the month and on 5th May the various replies were scrutinised. By 10th June, Messrs Butterley & Company were awarded the contract for supplying the steel work for the bridges at Hedingham and 'Apple Dumpling' for £278 12s 6d, whilst Birdbrook steel was awarded to Messrs Keays. In mid-June it was agreed to sell the company's black horse-van and purchase a new one. The reapportionment of the rental charged for Colne Green Farm adjoining Earls Colne station was agreed.

For some years the CV&HR wagon examiner had inspected vehicles on goods trains transferring from GER to the CV&HR metals at Chappel. The examination was time consuming and often caused delays, and Charles Clarke suggested the suspension of the inspection procedure for a period of three months. The proposal was agreed at the meeting on 8th July subject to a review at the end of the period. At the same meeting the Accountant advised the company was still overdrawn at the bank. Throughout August the Accountant negotiated a new arrangement and by 9th September he reported he had succeeded in obtaining agreement to a £2,000 limit on overdraft for a period of six months and thereafter a reduction to £1,000 for the next six months, after which there was to be another review.

considered far too low in view of the extensive repairs required. Because of their poor condition, the Engineer was asked to prepare estimates for the renewal of both structures in brick and steel. The appointment of Frank Potter Junior as Permanent Way Inspector was agreed at £1 5s 0d per week subject to three months probation.

On 26th November 1912 it was announced repairs to Nunnery Street Pile Bridge were completed and only remedial work was being carried out on 'Apple Dumpling' and Hedingham Pile bridges pending the reassessment of rebuilding costs. The reslating of Halstead station was also completed. Halstead Gas Company advised the company in early December 1912 that they required to lay a gas main under the railway and after a meeting it was agreed the work would only entail excavating under the footpath section of the station level crossing. Also on 26th November the CV&HR concluded their agreement with Ripper's for construction of sidings at Sible and Castle Hedingham (other preliminary agreements had been signed on 26th January 1904 and 1st May 1905). On 17th December, Marsh's claim for compensation in respect of a cow killed on the line after it gained access through broken down fencing was considered. The Solicitor advised the company was fully liable and the General Manager was requested to settle with the farmer on the best terms possible. At the same meeting the directors recommended adoption of the terms contained in the updated Rates of Pay and Conditions of Service proposals with the exception of the increase in Mr Coppin's salary and payment for Sunday duty to booking clerks, which were deferred for further investigation.

The New Year did not get off to a good start, for Locomotive Fireman P. Goulden received injuries which necessitated the professional services of a doctor. On 14th January 1913 Mr Stainbank duly received a fee of 15 guineas for services rendered. The following month the General Manager reported on the proposed construction of a siding at Purls Hill, Hedingham to serve

View from a passing train on the Haverhill to Long Melford route of the connection to the CV&HR curving away to Colne Valley Junction in August 1911. Occupational overbridge No. 2168 on the GER route is to the left whilst agricultural workers are in the fields.

GER/Windwood 108

The liability over the death of 9-year-old Preston Irons was still being pursued against the CV&HR Company when a letter was received from the solicitors Bates & Ellison and the correspondence was passed to the General Manager for action. It was announced at the same meeting that the new horse-van had been purchased from Goodchild at a cost of 50 guineas and a horse had been hired from G. Monk at a cost of £8 1s 0d. Halstead Rural District Council had written regarding the water supply at Earls Colne and after investigation the General Manager reported the company should accept a supply of drinking water through a metered supply, thereby obviating any dubiety on future charges. He lastly advised that Halstead Council wished to make improvements to the corner of King's Road and Trinity Street but required a small portion of railway land. It was agreed to sell the required portion for £15 provided the council erected and maintained the new boundary fence. The General Manager reported that Bradridge had advised the company he proposed to erect a granary at Yeldham and that he was negotiating with the company whilst the Engineer was of the opinion a wagon weighbridge was required at Halstead. The board agreed to consider the asset but deferred a decision because of the high cost.

Whilst the Central Essex Light Railway scheme was foundering, the Elsenham & Thaxted Light Railway Order had been granted on 19th April 1911 and with the project adopted by the GER the line was opened to passenger and goods traffic on and from 1st April 1913, with traffic worked by the main line company.

On 14th October 1913 the CV&HR Engineer requested the provision of a chaff cutter and agreement was given to purchase subject to it be steam driven. At the same meeting Williamson was granted a fee of £15 15s 0d for preparing the drawings for the new bridges. On 11th November the Secretary reported the company had received a County Court summons for the payment of £100 to Mrs Irons in respect of loss of her son and that counsel had been briefed to settle on those terms and payment was made early in December. The question of improved lighting at Halstead

station and the adjacent workshops was raised at a meeting on 9th December and it was agreed new gas fittings should be ordered by the General Manager. The gathering also heard that Miss Coutauld had given notice to the company to give up possession of Langley Mill gatehouse and Vaizey was asked to negotiate its purchase. Goodchild had offered to buy a section of land called Bubleys near Stambourne cutting and the General Manager was asked to investigate. It was also announced that the bridge reconstruction programme started in 1908 was completed with the reconstruction of Birdbrook Bridge in 1913.

The routine day-to-day operation of the railway continued as storm clouds of conflict threatened Europe. On Saturday 3rd January 1914 an engine failure caused considerable disruption to services whilst some of the delays occurring at Chappel during the exchange of goods traffic had been eliminated by the withdrawal of the wagon examiner; it was agreed on 10th February 1914 to continue the experiment for a further three months. In 1914 the monopoly on passenger traffic enjoyed by the CV&HR was challenged when the National Steam Car Company commenced road motor competition against the company, operating a direct service from Halstead to Colchester.

As the general unrest in Europe gathered momentum, the threat of military action against Britain was constantly under review. As early as 1st April 1908 the Territorial Force had become a volunteer reserve component of the British Army, formed by the Secretary of War Richard Burden Haldane following the passing of The Territorial and Reserve Forces Act of 1907 (7 Edward 7 Cap 9). This combined and reorganised the old Volunteer Army with the Yeomanry, whilst the remaining units of militia were renamed the Special Reserve. The Territorial Force was considered the new home defence for service during wartime; units were liable for service anywhere within the United Kingdom but could not be compelled to serve outside the country although any member or unit could volunteer to be liable for overseas service. Thus for several years small military exercises had been held in the rural landscape of the Essex/Suffolk border, with the CV&HR conveying small detachments to various locations. Vast areas of Suffolk and Norfolk around Thetford, as well as the New Forest in Hampshire, saw huge gatherings of men and horses on full military manoeuvres, and men were sent by train from all the CV&HR stations to join the contingents.

Fully aware of the possible future conflict and the changes it would bring, the CV&HR made another desperate plea to the GER to take over the line under the terms of the GER Amalgamation Act of 1862. The GER board were advised at their meeting on 3rd April that legal opinion taken in 1866 admitted the company might have had to take over the line and work it for 50 per cent of the gross receipts, but concluded the clauses were no longer binding and originally applied to the first opening of the line to Haverhill and not to the date the CV&HR had started to work the line. The board decided not to seek further legal advice and once again declined the application.

The Halstead company directors were undeterred and on 9th June 1914 the GER Directors received an ultimatum from the CV&HR to the effect that, by the provision of section 274 of the Great Eastern Railway Act of 1862, the CV&HR was requiring the GER company to take the plant and stores of the CV company at valuation and to permanently work the railway from Chappel station to Haverhill station. The petition signed by William Clarke and J. Bailey Hawkins, Directors of the CV&HR, and Elyot Hawkins, Secretary, was brought before the Traffic Committee on 18th June and was then placed in the hands of the Solicitor. In a reply dated 3rd July the GER denied the validity of the official notice and the CV&HR board resolved to apply to the Railway & Canal Commission to act as arbiter. Before any action could be taken the outbreak of war resulted in such trivial matters being quickly forgotten.

After Germany declared war on France and Belgium, Britain declared war on Germany on 4th August 1914 and within days initial volunteers for the armed forces were departing from all CV&HR stations. The departures by train were proud but sad occasions as some of the men were not to return. On the outbreak of World War One, the CV&HR and GER, with other British railway companies, came under Government control from the same date, under the powers of section 16 of the Regulation of the Forces Act 1871, with the Railway Executive Committee taking charge under the chairmanship of Herbert Walker, later Sir Herbert Walker, of the London & South Western Railway. At the outset the train services continued to run to pre-war timetables but soon after the commencement of hostilities the competitive bus service operated by the National Steam Car company was withdrawn from the road, whilst the *Halstead Gazette* of 7th August 1914 advised the CV&HR were announcing that henceforth until further notice men in uniform, whether in possession of free passes issued by the War Office or not, would be granted free travel on all the company's trains.

As with other parts of East Anglia, the recruitment of men to join the armed forces became the immediate priority and all the stations on the CV&HR continued to be crowded at times as men departed for training grounds and then for the front, watched by their loved ones. Several of these training establishments were set up locally and in the autumn of 1914 five troop trains departed Earls Colne for the channel ports, each train conveying no fewer than 200 men as well as horses and equipment. Special trains were often organised at short notice, with the GER providing engines and coaching stock as the local company was ill-prepared for such eventualities. The GER

enginemen worked the trains with a CV&HR pilotman whilst on Colne Valley metals.

The accounts for the CV&HR for the year ending 31st December 1914 revealed the authorised capital of the company was £516,305.

YEAR ENDING 31ST DECEMBER	1914			1913		
	£	s	d	£	s	d
Gross receipts	18,177	9	11	18,762	9	7
Expenditure	15,845	6	11	15,612	12	3
Total	2,332	3	0			
Other income						
Rents	348	7	4			
Transfer	1	2	6			
Total	2,681	3	10	3,119	17	4

These amounts included the estimated total received under Government agreement in respect of control of the railway, due to the European War for the period 5th August to 31st December 1914. As a result of the railway being under Government control the Board of Trade authorised the omission of certain statistics and therefore comparisons with previous years were not available for public circulation. However, other statistics were published: the company possessed twelve passenger carriages with seating for 42 First Class and 482 Third Class passengers. The total number of wagons was 177, whilst the railway was 19 miles in length with 6 miles of sidings if reduced to single track mileage. The total mileage of loaded trains were: passenger 56,745, goods 29,010, and the total mileage including empty train miles amounted to 86,968. Shunting miles for goods trains totalled 29,488.

Compensation claims against the railway company were usually dealt with in an efficient manner but after the early morning goods train ran into and killed three foals and a yearling belonging to Katherine Mina Courtauld, which had strayed on to the line after gates were left open, the situation was serious. At that time in World War One, horses were highly valued and threatened with adverse publicity the railway company compensated the claimant to prevent lengthy legal ramifications. As the months of hostilities progressed so the strain of war effort resulted in a further reduction of receipts; in an effort to save costs a bricklayer and a labourer were discharged in July 1915. Despite the hostilities the regular programme of repairing and painting of GER stations continued and on 1st June 1916 the contract for remedial work at Chappel was awarded to B.B. & M. Barrell at a cost of £195. In 1917, 80-year-old Charles Coe, a *'hawker and rabbit skin dealer'* was beheaded by a train near Langley Mill crossing as he was collecting skins from the lineside. Yet again the management had to advise the public of the dangers of trespassing on the railway.

During the war years it was the practice for some of the railway staff at Chappel and Wakes Colne station to play football on the nearby playing field on Saturday afternoons, whilst officially on duty. Because of the arrival of the CV&HR service at 3.34pm and the departure of the Sudbury to Colchester GER train at 3.36pm, the unofficial rule was laid down that when the home signal was lowered, 'half time' was taken. Football gear was quickly removed or hidden and replaced by railway uniform before the staff attended to the trains. As soon as the train had departed for Marks Tey the players returned to the pitch and, once changed into football strip, started the second half. The field was ploughed up in World War Two for the growing of crops.

About forty men, or a fifth of the eligible young men, employed by the CV&HR enlisted in the colours, including General Manager, Secretary and Engineer Elyot S. Hawkins. Many received severe injuries fighting at the front, some were invalided out with lost limbs and five were killed in action. After the hostilities a brass plaque commemorating the five staff of the Colne Valley & Halstead Railway Company who died in active service was mounted in the waiting hall at Halstead station until the railway closed in 1962.

Lance Corporal Walter Coe	Essex Regiment
Private William Barber	Worcestershire Regiment
Private Percy Brown	Grenadier Guards
Private Charles Rulton	Training Reserve
Private Frederick Taylor	Essex Regiment

The Roll of Honour then quoted Tennyson: *'When shall their glory fade'*.

The end of hostilities in November 1918 was greeted with great relief and the stations were decorated with flags to celebrate the armistice, then the line settled down to renewed peacetime activities. The complacency was rudely shattered when a general railway strike lasting from 27th September to 5th October 1919 was called following the Government's proposal to reduce the pay of all railwaymen. No trains ran on the CV&HR for the first four days but on the fifth day Elyot S. Hawkins had amassed enough volunteers to run a goods train with the object of clearing all local traffic awaiting delivery. The engine driver was 80-year-old Charles Evans, long since retired, with locomotive foreman Charles Bartholomew as his fireman. The Company Accountant was appointed guard and Halstead station master Frederick Coppin travelled with the train and operated the signalling with the assistance of local butcher Harold Doe. Guard Herbert Ellis, who refused to join the strike, also travelled and attempted to disguise himself by wearing a straw hat instead of his uniform cap. The journey from Halstead to Haverhill, then return to Chappel and back to Halstead, met with no physical resistance but many strikers and their supporters jeered the passing train.

Despite the industrial action, the financial returns for the year ending 31st December 1919 showed a healthy increase in receipts compared with 1916:

YEAR ENDING 31ST DECEMBER	1916			1919		
	£	s	d	£	s	d
Gross Receipts	20,744	17	7	36,656	5	1
Expenditure	18,586	12	5	33,892	12	5
Net receipts	2,158	5	2	2,763	12	8
Misc receipts B/F	338	4	2	485	10	8
Operating profit	2,496	9	4	3,249	3	4

In 1919 the following number of passengers were conveyed: First Class 2,442, Third Class 134,520, workmen 1,902 and season tickets 141; whilst goods tonnages carried were: merchandise 30,471, coal and fuel 414, other minerals 3,621; livestock was 5,546 animals. The total engine miles for the year amounted to 105,113.

The capital of the company to 31st December 1920 amounted to £516,245; receipts of ordinary shares were £61,200 and preference shares £25,590; 'A' debentures issued amounted to £61,845 and 'B' debentures £367,365, with a miscellaneous balance of £245. No dividend was paid on preference or ordinary shares but full interest

CV&HR cast notice advising road users of weight restrictions applicable under the Motor Car Acts of 1896 and 1903.   *R. Powell*

had been paid on class 'A' debentures up to 30th June 1903. For its half year ending 31st December 1903 2½ per cent was paid leaving 1¾ per cent in arrears. Full interest was paid for every subsequent half year and in February 1907 a further ¾ per cent arrears was paid off. Interest after that was regularly paid. The last dividend on 'B' debentures was 2s 6d per cent for the year ending 31st December 1892. The balance in credit on the revenue account at 31st December 1920 was £506.

Under the provisions of the 1921 Railways Bill, the Minister of Transport advised that he would consider favourably any proposal by a constituent company to acquire a subsidiary company by mutual agreement and not by compulsion if a case was made out. On 8th July 1921 the GER board confirmed that it did not want the CV&HR to be excluded from the list of companies to be absorbed by the future London & North Eastern Railway. On the same date, the General Manager reported on the case submitted to the MOT and the reasons for so doing. The CV&HR was 19 miles standard gauge line worked by the CV&HR from the start and who several times had asked the GER to take over the undertaking. The capital was £516,245 but no dividends had been paid except £3,092 per annum on 'A' stock. In 1913 the gross receipts were £18,762 against working expenses of £15,642, or 83 per cent of the gross receipts. The administrative expenses for the same period were £1,100. Working expenses in 1920 were £55,048. Absorption by the GER would save administrative expenses and other savings were possible with the closure of the locomotive shops. The Engineer reported the line was in fairly satisfactory physical condition but the rail was only suitable for light engines. With sharp gradients, maximum of 1 in 66, and curves, minimum 12 chains, the line could not accommodate heavy goods traffic. There was sufficient land to lay double track for most of the route. As the GER had already agreed not to oppose the Mid Suffolk Light Railway's request to be placed in the schedule the GER could but do the same for the CV&HR. The GER General Manager reminded the board that, remembering the acquisition by competitors of independent lines in Norfolk and the Tilbury line, there was a remote possibility that the MR or L&NWR could still use the CV&HR to reach Colchester.

When No. 13 Up goods train, the 10.15am ex Haverhill, called at Yeldham to detach some wagons on 16th October 1922 for T. Bradridge & Company. William Hardy, an employee of Bradridge was killed when he was crushed between the buffers of two wagons during the shunting operation at the coal wharf. The resultant BOT inquiry was conducted by J.A.A. Pickard who ascertained that Hardy, who was only 17 years of age, employed as a yardman in the employ of Bradridge & Company, had at 11.40am on the day in question been hit by some wagons which were being loose shunted in to the coal road and sustained fatal injuries. The four wagons were being gently lowered by gravity on to three other vehicles which were standing in the middle of the coal road. Before making the shunt, Guard Reynolds gave warning to the only man who was working in the three stationary wagons and on receiving acknowledgement released the brake on the four wagons under his control. The accident was not witnessed and Pickard concluded that as Hardy had no concern with the three wagons already in the siding he must have been going to see whether any of the incoming wagons were consigned to his firm. He evidently failed to keep clear of the moving vehicles with unfortunate consequences.

Although peace had been declared the Government retained the control of the railways until 15th August 1921 as the war effort had debilitated the companies with little or minimal maintenance of infrastructure and rolling stock. In 1918 the Coalition Government had hinted at support for nationalisation, a thought that had been festering since the formation of the Railway Nationalisation League in 1895, with the later support of the railway unions and the formation of the Railway Nationalisation Society in 1908. A number of industrialists and traders were sympathetic, saying the railways should be a public corporation rather than a profit-making concern. In the event the Government fell short of full nationalisation and formed the companies into four groups. It was thus hoped the impending grouping of the railways would engender an increase in receipts as more people took advantage to travel in East Anglia for leisure and recreation. However, all was not favourable for staff costs had increased and the CV&HR company was finding increasing difficulty paying wages from one week to another. The Board had to decide to either reduce the number of staff or reduce wages. In response to a personal appeal from the manager, the men elected to take a 10 per cent reduction in pay with no threat of redundancy in 1920, but after some soul searching and the withdrawal of unremunerative Sunday services enough money had been saved to revert the pay back to the original standing in 1921.

In this post-war period, bus competition against the railway strengthened with the National Omnibus & Transport Company commencing a service in 1920 and later in association with Blackwell's of Earls Colne operating up to ten buses each way between Halstead and Colchester on weekdays and nine each way on Sundays. By offering an almost door-to-door service the number of railway passenger diminished. Chambers & Sons of Bures then operated a service to Haverhill via Sudbury and Halstead every Friday for market day travellers.

In 1922, the last full year of independence, the CV&HR Chairman was Charles Bridges Orme Clarke of 4 St Dunstan's Alley, London EC, with fellow directors, William Clarke of 64 Victoria Street, London SW, W. Bailey Hawkins of Stagenhoe Park, Welwyn, Hertfordshire, J.B. Bailey Hawkins of 144 Palmerston House, London EC, Arthur Clement Tweedy of the The Priory House, Monmouth, and Robert E. Vaisey JP of Attwoods, Halstead, Essex. The General Manager and Locomotive Superintendent and

Engineer was Elyot S. Hawkins; the Accountant S.C. Scillitoe; the Auditor G.E. Shotter of 144 Palmerston Buildings, Bishopsgate Street, London EC, and the Solicitors Blyth, Dutton, Hartley & Blyth of 112 Gresham House, London EC. The capital to 31st December 1920 totalled £516,245, consisting of £61,200 of ordinary shares, £25,590 preference shares, £61,845 of 'A' debenture stock, £367,365 of 'B' debenture stock, leaving a balance on hand of £245.

On 21st December 1922 the GER General Manager submitted to his board a report on the CV&HR covering the history, capital, rolling stock, road vehicles, housing, way and works, and passenger and goods traffic, together with future income prospects. It was agreed the paper be taken forward to the consultation stage with the CV&HR General Manager for amalgamation in to the new company.

The capital of the CV&HR company on 31st December 1922 stood at £516,000:

	£
Ordinary shares	61,200
Preference shares	25,590
Loans and debentures	429,210

The gross receipts for the year were £27,625, together with miscellaneous earnings of £1,961, offset by £25,655 working expenses, leaving a net income of £3,221.

The full standing of the company as at 31st December 1922:

	£
Preference shares	25,590
Ordinary shares	61,200
Loans and debentures	429,210
Gross receipts	27,625
Miscellaneous receipts	1,961
Expenditure	25,655
Total net income	3,221

Other statistics
Locomotives	5
Passenger vehicles	13
Wagons	174
Service vehicles	1
Road vehicles including horses	11

Passenger conveyed in 1922
First Class	1,372
Third Class	159,826
Workmen	203
Season tickets	80

Goods conveyed in 1922
Merchandise	47,278 tons
Coal, coke and minerals	50,327 tons
Heads of livestock	10.271

Staff employed	119

The forthcoming grouping of the railways was an unknown factor and a source of concern to all CV&HR managers and staff as to their future employment. Interesting times were ahead.

6

Grouping Under the L&NER

AS A RESULT OF THE 1921 RAILWAYS ACT, on 1st January 1923 the GER amalgamated with the Great Northern, Great Central, North Eastern, North British and several smaller companies to form the London & North Eastern Railway. Although the CV&HR should have been included and absorbed via the GER into the new company, the Halstead board were far from happy with the terms offered.

On 2nd January 1923 the newly formed L&NER Finance Committee discussing the takeover of smaller companies confirmed the CV&HR was entirely independent from the former GER, being free from any financial obligations. On 24th January, S.A. Parnell, the Divisional General Manager at Liverpool Street, wrote to J. McLaren at Marylebone regarding the finance committee letter of offer to the CV&HR. The company could not agree to exchange L&NER debentures with CV&HR 'A' debentures, neither would they offer four per cent L&NER preference stock for CV&HR

'B' debentures. However, with a view to a quick settlement the company was prepared for each CV&HR 'A' debentures to accept one hundred L&NER second guaranteed stock, whilst for the 'B' debentures, which had not received any return after 1892, the interest offered would be £15 deferred ordinary shares, which on a five per cent basis would produce 15s 0d per annum, comparing favourably with the 2s 6d paid in 1892. With regard to the preference and ordinary shares the L&NER was prepared to give what was requested, namely 3s 0d cash for every £10 CV&HR preference share and 2s 6d cash for every £10 ordinary share. The CV&HR board were notified of the revised terms by letter on 26th January but on 1st February the company declined the offer and notified they would progress the case through the Railways Amalgamation Tribunal asking for 'A' debenture stockholders to be revised as the offer amounted to a twenty per cent deduction in earnings.

CV&HR 0-4-2T No. 1 awaiting cutting up at Stratford in 1923. It had seen very occasional use prior to grouping but the locomotive on inspection was found to be in a derelict condition and was of no use to the L&NER.
Author's collection

On 12th February 1923 the L&NER case was placed in the hands of Lord Farringdon and C.B.O. Clarke, who were asked to mediate, and four days later, after a meeting with the CV&HR Chairman, the L&NER terms were placed before the tribunal. The document stated the L&NER had taken over the CV&HR and associated assets from 1st January 1923 and in return CV&HR five per cent 'A' debenture stockholders were to receive in respect of each £100 holding L&NER first preference stock to the value of £125. CV&HR 'B' debenture holders would receive in respect of each £100 holding L&NER preference ordinary stock to the value of £10. Holders of £10 CV&HR preference shares were to receive 3s 0d cash and £10 ordinary shareholders 2s 6d cash. The CV&HR directors were to receive in addition to their current fees a compensation payment of four years' fees equal to £200 per annum to be divided amongst the board. The General Manager was to receive a one-off payment of £500, with £225 to the company accountant and £20 to the Auditor.

On 16th February the Railway Clerks Association, National Union of Railwaymen and Associated Society of Locomotive Engineers & Fireman each wrote to the retiring CV&HR board thanking them for restoring the ten per cent pay in lieu of the voluntary reductions made in 1921.

By 19th February the L&NER representatives were unsure as to whether the matter should be placed before the tribunal for the CV&HR directors were showing signs of acceptance. Four days later the terms were duly settled. The serviceable rolling stock taken over by the L&NER included:

			£	£
3	Locomotives	valued at	3,300	
2	Coaches	valued at	750	
125	Merchandise and Mineral Wagons	valued at	5,690	
1	Service vehicle		150	
7	Road vehicles		143	
		Total	10,033	10,033
59	vehicles were condemned as unserviceable as scrap	valued at	2,288	2,288
	Stores and materials			
	Civil engineering materials	valued at	1,000	
	Mechanical materials	valued at	1,462	
	Traffic and general stores	valued at	196	
		Total	2,658	2,658
		Accumulative Total		14,979

At the same time it was announced the Government compensation payable to the CV&HR amounted to the grand total of £23.

At an extraordinary general meeting held on Monday 26th March 1923, the CV&HR directors were advised they would be paid a combined total of £800 0s 0d as compensation for loss of office. The question of a loan of £90 made to Reuben Hunt in respect of Earls Colne station was raised at the following board meeting and it was resolved that Hunt be given notice to pay off his loan as a matter of urgency.

The London & North Eastern Railway Absorption (No. 1) 1923 document was published on 29th June 1923 under the signature of H.A. Steward, Clerk to the Tribunal, and witnessed by three members of the Railways Amalgamation Tribunal, H. Babington Smith, W. Plender and G.J. Talbot. Under section 20 paragraph 2 it

was agreed the L&NER would pay to the directors of the CV&HR the sum of £800 0s 0d compensation for the loss of office. The First Schedule of the document enumerated the final exchange rates of stocks and shares:

- Holders of £100 CV&HR 5 per cent 'A' debentures received £125 of L&NER 4 per cent first preference stock.
- Holders of £100 CV&HR 4 per cent 'B' debentures received £10 L&NER 5 per cent preferred ordinary stock.
- Holders of £100 CV&HR preference shares received £1 10s 0d.
- Holders of £100 CV&HR ordinary shares received £1 5s 0d.

Most ordinary share certificates, being worthless, were kept as souvenirs.

The Second Schedule permitted the CV&HR to retain a sum of £767 to settle outstanding affairs, whilst the Third Schedule advised that CV&HR five per cent 'A' Debenture stock to the value of £500 was cancelled.

The final board meeting of the CV&HR directors was held on Wednesday 4th July 1923, when the Secretary reported the scheme permitting the L&NER to absorb the CV&HR had been sealed by the Amalgamation Tribunal on Friday 29th June and the General Manager reported he was waiting instructions from the Chief General Manager with regard to the L&NER Company taking over day-to-day control of the line.

Once L&NER locomotives and men worked across the Colne Valley branch, as it was to become, footplate staff were shocked by the condition of the permanent way on some sections of the line. Cambridge men working an excursion from Cambridge to Clacton with an 'E4' Class 2-4-0 tender locomotive accompanied by a Haverhill pilotman were alarmed to note that between Birdbrook and Yeldham the rails disappeared under a carpet of undergrowth as weeds and foliage had grown through the clinker ballast. The CV&HR man duly advised that it had been sometime since a weedkilling train had been employed. Not all of the line was in such condition, but reports were submitted, with an urgent request for the early attendance of the weedkilling train and an immediate fully detailed inspection of the permanent way by ex-GER staff from the Cambridge Civil Engineering Office.

On 1st February 1924 Engine Driver R. Jennings stepped in front of the engine, which was being moved by his fireman in Yeldham yard, and sustained severe injuries to his leg. From 14th July 1924 the passenger train facilities were withdrawn from Haverhill South (formerly Haverhill CV) and the few services, usually the first Up working and the last Down train, which had previously started or terminated there were transferred to Haverhill North station.

The L&NER management soon instituted changes, for on 27th March 1924 the Divisional General Manager (Southern Area) reported that after investigation the method of working trains on the former Colne Valley & Halstead Railway was unsatisfactory and he submitted a proposal to the Traffic Committee for the installation of Tyers Key Token instruments between Earls Colne and Colne Valley Junction in place of the existing Train Staff and Ticket or Electric Train Tablet method of working. The works, costing £618, included provision of instruments in Earls Colne, Halstead, Sible and Castle Hedingham, Yeldham, Birdbrook and Colne Valley Junction signal boxes, alterations to signal repeater circuits, the provision of locks on intermediate siding points and the alteration in the position of Colne Valley Junction Down home signal. At the same time, Colne Valley Junction to Haverhill Colne

Valley station was to revert to Train Staff only working. The scheme was duly authorised and introduced in 1926.

On 19th April the Engineer submitted a report advising that the agreement made between the CV&HR and the Post Master General on 2nd January 1902 in respect of the fixing and maintaining of the telegraph wires alongside the railway for a period of twenty-one years had terminated on 27th March 1924. Because of the absorption of the company by the L&NER, from that date the L&NER Company staff were to maintain the system. On termination of the agreement the Post Master General was liable for payment to the railway company for wayleaves in respect of any Post Office wires existing on or crossing railway land. It was pointed out the company could legitimately claim the right to maintain the telegraph cable routes for a payment for not exercising such rights. After several meetings, provisional agreement had been reached with the Post Master General:

a) The Post Master General to be allowed to erect and maintain his wire on the Colne Valley line and for the right including joint use of the railway company poles and then pay the L&NER 2s 6d per mile of wire per annum and a proportional part of any expenses incurred by the L&NER if the railway poles require to be strengthened to take additional Post Office wires.

b) The Post Master General to pay the annual sum:
    For single or first wire
    £1 0s 0d per mile of wire per annum.
    For second wire   15s 0d per mile of wire per annum.
    For third wire   10s 0d per mile of wire per annum.
    For fourth or any additional wires
    5s 0d per mile per wire per annum.

c) The Post Master General to pay the railway company an annual sum for wayleaves and wavers of maintenance according to the number and length of Post Office wires on the railway.

As the railway settled down to become another L&NER branch line so the coal strikes of 1926 caused severe problems and to conserve fuel stocks services on many lines in East Anglia were reduced, that on the Colne Valley line, being reduced to three trains each way with one terminating and starting from Sible and Castle Hedingham. Further signalling alterations came when authority was given on 24th March 1927 for the abolition of the ground frame at south end of Chappel station, with the resultant annual saving of £223. The work estimated to cost £222 10s 0d resulted in the saving of one porter's post valued at £132 per annum.

On 19th April 1927 an accident occurred to an employee of Rippers Limited at Sible and Castle Hedingham. At about 11.30am on the day in question a packer, W. Norman, was instructed to proceed to the loading shed with four other men to load woodwork on to a wagon. On arrival they found several empty wagons standing alongside the platform, but none opposite the material waiting to be loaded. One of the men secured a pinch bar and commenced to move the first wagon along the track to the desired position for loading. When he had separated the wagon from the others by a few feet the other four men jumped to the ground to push the vehicle along the track. Unfortunately Norman placed his shoulder against the face of one of the buffers, and while he was in this position, some other wagons were loose shunted into the siding. The wagons between which the men were working closed up, and Norman received injury to his shoulder. The Board of Trade investigation

An Agreement made the fourth day of June one thousand nine hundred and twenty six BETWEEN THE LONDON AND NORTH EASTERN RAILWAY COMPANY (hereinafter called " the Company ") of the one part and THE RIGHT HONOURABLE SIR WILLIAM LOWSON MITCHELL-THOMSON Baronet K.B.E. M.P. His Majesty's Postmaster General (hereinafter called " the Postmaster General ") of the other part WHEREAS by an Indenture dated the sixth day of July one thousand nine hundred and four and made between the Colne Valley and Halstead Railway Company of the one part and the Right Honourable Edward George Villiers Stanley C.B. (commonly called Lord Stanley) then His Late Majesty's Postmaster General of the other part provisions were made as to wayleave and maintenance of telegraphs on the Colne Valley and Halstead Railway AND WHEREAS by a scheme under the Railways Act 1921 dated the twenty ninth day of June one thousand nine hundred and twenty three the said railway was absorbed in the railway of the Company AND WHEREAS the hereinbefore recited Indenture expired by effluxion of time on the second day of January one thousand nine hundred and twenty three and an Agreement between the parties hereto for the temporary continuance of the arrangements under the said Indenture was terminated by the Company giving to the Postmaster General six calendar months' notice expiring on the twenty sixth March one thousand nine hundred and twenty four AND WHEREAS the Company and the Postmaster General have agreed that the following provisions shall have effect with reference to the placing and maintenance of telegraphic lines of the Postmaster General on the section of the Company's railway which was formerly the Colne Valley and Halstead Railway and the lands and buildings held or occupied by the Company in connection therewith (hereinafter referred to as " the said railway ") NOW IT IS HEREBY AGREED as follows (that is to say) :—

1. The Postmaster General shall have full liberty from time to time and at all times during the continuance of this Agreement to keep the telegraphic wires belonging to him and specified in the Schedule hereto together with the insulators and other telegraphic apparatus and appliances connected therewith (all of which telegraphic wires insulators and other telegraphic apparatus and appliances and any additional telegraphic wires insulators telegraphic apparatus and appliances attached or placed by the Postmaster General as hereinafter provided are included in the expression " the telegraphic wires ") attached to the telegraphic posts and other accessory things of the Company on the said railway or any part thereof from time to time used by them as supports for or otherwise in connection with their own telegraphic wires (all which telegraphic posts and other accessory things are

An extract from the agreement between L&NER and the Postmaster General, 6th March 1924.

into the accident was conducted by J.L.M. Moore, who on visiting the site learned that shunting of the siding serving the loading shed was regularly carried out at some time between 11.00am and 12.00 noon, and although Norman and his companions were well aware of this, they showed scant regard for their personal safety by placing themselves between the vehicles without first satisfying themselves that it was safe. The inspector was critical of Samuel Clark, who was in charge of the shunting movement, as he failed to carry out Rule 112A and the only warning of the shunting move was a sound from the engine whistle, which was not heard by the five men. Moore observed: *'Evidence of slackness on the part of the staff at this station in giving proper effect to this rule, and this feature should receive the attention of the Company.'*

During the course of his enquiry Moore noticed that ladders placed against the sides and ends of wagons were being used to facilitate loading; it also transpired that considerable amounts of material, including window and door frames, constructed in a recently acquired workshop on the other side of the line were being carried across the running line to the loading platform. The inspector concluded:

Under such circumstances some special provision appears desirable to safeguard the men against the risk of injury resulting from the movement of wagons while loading was in progress. 'As the portion of the siding' which lies within the shed, is rented and used exclusively by Messrs Rippers, I suggest, for the consideration of the L&NER Company, the provision of a permanent scotch which can be swung across either or both of the rails at the entrance to the building. The scotch should be kept locked across the rails and suitable arrangements made whereby the key will be held by some responsible person employed by Messrs Rippers while their men are at work, and only handed over to enable shunting to take place after due precautions have been taken for the safety of their staff.

The problems encountered by the L&NER management during the early years of grouping saw passenger and parcel receipts fluctuate as the figures below show. Of particular concern were the competitive bus services, which offered direct and almost door-to-door services, especially from Halstead and Hedingham to Colchester.

The average daily number of passengers using the stations reduced dramatically by 30 per cent at Halstead, where weekly travellers reduced from 733 in 1923 to 516 in 1928. White Colne also saw a 28 per cent reduction from 106 passengers per week in 1923 to 76 in 1928. Birdbrook realised a 15 per cent reduction, whilst Sible and Castle Hedingham and Earls Colne suffered a 5 per cent reduction. Yeldham weekly passenger numbers remained almost constant, 336 in 1923 to 332 in 1928.

On 23rd March 1927 the L&NER management authorised the abolition of Colne Valley Junction signal box and associated running

	PASSENGERS	PASSENGER RECEIPTS £	PARCELS RECEIPTS £	SEASON TICKETS RECEIPTS £	TOTAL RECEIPTS £
1923					
Chappel	9,513	846	169	214	1,229
White Colne	5,506	533	64		597
Earls Colne	8,858	822	353		1,175
Halstead	38,161	4,598	802	51	5,451
S & C Hed'm	34,953	2,040	402		2,442
Yeldham	17,509	1,019	270		1,289
Birdbrook	6,381	504	107		611
Haverhill N	32,014	4,715	1,771	116	6,602
Total*	111,368	9,516	1,998	51	11,565
Total+	152,895	15,077	3,938	381	19,396
1924					
Chappel	7,274	739	135	187	1,061
White Colne	4,075	462	64		526
Earls Colne	7,965	712	372	60	1,144
Halstead	29,345	3,965	700	186	4,851
S & C Hed'm	35,546	1,999	367	211	2,577
Yeldham	18,426	1,077	264	10	1,351
Birdbrook	5,939	445	93		538
Haverhill N	34,977	4,665	1,658	68	6,391
Total*	101,296	8,660	1,860	467	10,987
Total+	143,547	14,064	3,653	722	18,439
1925					
Chappel	6,658	699	144	191	1,034
White Colne	3,797	437	52		489
Earls Colne	8,891	738	361	1	1,100
Halstead	31,851	4,034	750	199	4,983
S & C Hed'm	34,406	1,967	3 78	87	2,432
Yeldham	18,478	1,076	355	13	1,444
Birdbrook	6,400	472	95		567
Haverhill N	38,890	4,990	1,790	148	6,928
Total*	103,823	8,724	3,982	300	11,015
Total+	149,371	14,413	5,916	639	18,977

	PASSENGERS	PASSENGER RECEIPTS £	PARCELS RECEIPTS £	SEASON TICKETS RECEIPTS £	TOTAL RECEIPTS £
1926					
Chappel	5,945	662	154	66	882
White Colne	3,328	453	54		507
Earls Colne	7,403	661	343		1,004
Halstead	27,437	3,457	736	139	4,332
S & C Hed'm	31,558	1,834	302	92	2,228
Yeldham	15,162	1,034	217	30	1,281
Birdbrook	4,786	385	81		466
Haverhill N	33,300	4,487	1,846	166	6,499
Total*	89,674	7,824	1,733	261	9,818
Total+	128,919	12,973	3,733	493	17,199
1927					
Chappel	6,829	737	280	39	1,056
White Colne	3,663	477	77		554
Earls Colne	8,138	659	395		1,054
Halstead	29,535	3,579	797	89	4,465
S & C Hed'm	36,393	1,935	281	65	2,281
Yeldham	16,816	1,057	237	31	1,325
Birdbrook	5,031	409	96		505
Haverhill N	37,562	4,796	1,957	111	6,864
Total*	99,576	8,116	1,883	185	10,184
Total+	143,967	13,649	4,120	335	18,104
1928					
Chappel			not available		
White Colne	3,967	488	78		566
Earls Colne	8,578	723	416	8	1,147
Halstead	26,872	3,440	944	107	4,491
S & C Hed'm	32,935	1,677	219	87	1,983
Yeldham	17,272	1,086	259	37	1,382
Birdbrook	5,505	409	91		500
Haverhill N	38,550	4,888	2,068	85	7,041
Total*	91,162	7,823	2,007	239	10,069
Total+	133,679	12,711	4,075	324	17,110

NOTES: *   Total Colne Valley stations only.
         +   Total for all stations including Chappel and Haverhill North.

signals, with an expected annual saving of £223. To compensate for the loss of Colne Valley Junction, Birdbrook signal box was provided with a Key Token instrument although it was not a passing place. The single line sections were then revised Yeldham to Birdbrook and Birdbrook to Haverhill Junction GE. The work was completed on 1st November but it was 17th September 1929 before Lieutenant Colonel E.P. Anderson made the official inspection of the alterations. He found the points were worked by a 2-lever ground frame with full facing point equipment on the line to Haverhill North, whilst the line to Haverhill South was equipped with catch points. The Key Token for the Haverhill North to Birdbrook section of line controlled the ground frame operating the points. Anderson was advised no shunting was conducted at the junction, but in order to permit the passage of another train through the section after the first had reversed to Haverhill South, an awaiting Tyer's Key Token instrument was placed in the hut beside the ground frame, from which there was a telephone connection to Haverhill South. The inspector noted the interlocking was correct.

Over the years the L&NER authorities found that the absorption of the CV&HR had not been finalised, for every so often outstanding issues were brought the their attention. As early as 4th December 1863 the Company had entered into an agreement with E.A.S. Walton and other to rent 8 acres 0 rods and 2 perches of land forming part of the railway between the 16 miles 37 chains and 17 miles 12 chains markers in the Parish of Steeple Bumpstead, instead of purchasing outright, and rental was outstanding from 1st January 1923. After the necessary negotiations the land was purchase from Mrs B.E. Lawrie and others for £1,000 and the L&NER Company was released from their obligation on 22nd November 1924. Another case arose in the Parish of Ridgewell where the CV&HR had agreed on 18th December 1860 to purchase 5 acres, 0 rods and

5 perches of land from St Catherine's College Cambridge at a price of £400. However, the railway company failed to pay the purchase price and were thus beholden to pay a rental charge of £16 per annum. No conveyance was taken and the L&NER paid over the purchase price of £400 to the college on 6th February 1928 and were released from further commitment. Yet another incident arose when the Bursar of St John's College Cambridge alleged the L&NER had encroached on adjoining fields in the Parish of Ridgewell. A site meeting was held and the surveyor on behalf of the college agreed the company had not encroached and the boundary fence was in the correct position.

In November 1928 plans approved in 1927 to rationalise the track layout and signalling at the north end of Chappel and Wakes Colne station – enabling all points and signals to be worked from Chappel signal box and thus allowing the abolition of the ground frame at the south end of the yard – were finalised and the work was completed in August 1929. On the same day that he visited Colne Valley Junction, Lieutenant Colonel E.P. Anderson attended Chappel and Wakes Colne where he inspected the alteration in connection between the Colne Valley line and the Sudbury line to the north of the station, together with the associated signalling. He noted the ground frame at the south end of the yard had been abolished, and that all points which were within the required distance of 350 yards and the signals were worked from Chappel and Wakes Colne signal box, equipped with a 38-lever frame with 37 working and 1 spare lever and the interlocking was correct. The permanent way material was 85 lbs per yard rails. Anderson noted that home signals were provided to admit Up trains from either Halstead or Bures to the Up platform or to the sidings east of the station. Starting signals for corresponding movements on the opposite direction were also provided. A calling on arm mounted

White Colne station, 52 miles 31 chains from Liverpool Street, was opened in 1908 after the original Colne platform and station west of the level crossing gates had been closed in 1889 on the opening of Ford Gate station. Wiser counsels prevailed for the station was centrally situated for the adjoining village and the goods yard was reopened in 1907. View facing west in 1951.

M. Root collection

below the home signal on the Halstead line allowed the signalman to bring a train on to the Down platform line and a disc signal attached to the Down starters controlled shunting into the spur east of the Bures line. The inspector concluded he was satisfied with the alterations.

The L&NER authorities were ever seeking to reduce the operating costs of the line and ongoing investigations were made. On 5th September 1929 the Divisional General Manager (Southern Area) submitted a report to his Traffic Committee advising of the uneconomic working of Parsonage level crossing between Halstead and Earls Colne. Two gate lads working early and late shift performed the opening and closing of the gates but as usage of the crossing was light it was considered the crossing could be operated by a resident gatewoman. It was proposed to erect a gate cottage which would be occupied rent-free by a member of staff, whose wife could attend the gates in his absence. The cost of the cottage was estimated at £550 and the adoption of the scheme would permit the dispensing of the two lad gatekeepers posts at an annual saving of £173. A bonus of 2s 0d per week would be paid to the gatewoman, and including insurance and tax and maintenance costs would amount to £17 per annum, leaving a net saving of £156. The scheme was duly agreed on 26th September 1929 and tenders sought. J.W. Trudgett was subsequently awarded the contract to construct the cottage at a cost of £485 with completion within fourteen weeks.

The last decade had resulted in an influx of road services in competition against the railway, where the time-consuming roundabout route from Halstead to London via Marks Tey was fully exploited by competitive road services; six operators were working services from Halstead to London with two additional routes joining the fray at Braintree. Akers, who owned the 'Bird' coaches at Halstead, and Blackwell from Earls Colne were joined by Chinery who operated Corona Coaches from Acton near Sudbury. As local operators they offered earlier departures to the capital and thus took the monopoly of luxury trade in the area. Later daily returns from the capital and theatre services operated on Saturday nights and a late 10.00pm Sunday services encouraged people to spend weekends away. Seating was luxurious compared with that offered in the motley collection of vehicles owned by the cash-strapped L&NER.

Further signalling alterations were proposed in a memo submitted by the Divisional General Manager (Southern Area) on 4th September 1930, between Bartlow and Clare on the ex-GER Stour Valley line. It was the intention to introduce Electric Key Token working between Bartlow Junction and Haverhill Station signal boxes and abolish Withersfield Siding signal box, whilst the Key Token working was to be installed between Haverhill Junction signal box and Clare signal box, with the abolition of the signal boxes at Sturmer and Stoke. The expenditure of £1,774 was readily agreed when it was realised annual savings of £321 would accrue as the result of the alterations. Colne Valley line trains were unaffected by the changes as their passage between Haverhill Junction and Haverhill Station signal boxes was by the existing double line block.

In August 1930 the Cambridge shed foreman allocated an 'E4' Class 2-4-0 tender locomotive to work an excursion to Clacton via Bartlow and the Colne Valley line. When the engine backed on to the coaching stock the crew were surprised to find the train was formed of nine coaches. Undeterred, they set out and after calling at Shelford were diverted off the main line to pick up passengers at Pampisford, Linton and Bartlow. By this time the train was about half full of passengers and the crew coaxed the Class 'E4' on the climb

of Bartlow bank and were grateful when they arrived at Haverhill to take water. Here over 300 passengers joined the train to enjoy a day by the sea and, on being given 'right away', the crew struggled to get the ancient locomotive to haul the train up the gradient to Colne Valley Junction. Beyond the junction the engine gradually lost speed as the heavy train dragged it back on the short 1 in 87 climb, but after what appeared an interminable time the summit was reached and with the fireman struggling to maintain a good fire and boiler pressure the driver made a concerted effort to increase speed on the falling 1 in 103/76 gradient before tackling the long 1 in 83 away from Birdbrook. The effort was in vain and the engine stalled on the bank beyond the station. The train set back through the station so that pressure could be built up for another try, but yet again the train came to an abrupt halt beyond the platform. After some delay the third attempt was successful and the train limped the rest of the way across the branch, calling at all stations and gathering yet more passengers. The train duly arrived at Clacton at 4.00pm instead of 12.00noon, the long-suffering passengers receiving a full refund of their fares. Recognising the engine was underpowered for the train, arrangements were made for the return to Cambridge to run in two portions. The Class 'E4' returning with a 4-coach train, whilst a Class 'J15' 0-6-0 tender locomotive hauled the second portion formed of the remaining five vehicles.

During shunting operations at Chapel and Wakes Colne on 31st October 1930 an Engineer's Department labourer J. Ling sustained injuries, which necessitated the amputation of his arm. J.L.M. Moore conducted the subsequent BOT enquiry. He learned that Ling, with another man, had been sent to Chappel to unload a wagon of sand. They found the wagon in a suitable position for unloading not far from the buffer stops at the Marks Tey end of the Tranship Road. When they had unloaded some of the sand, Ling happened to glance over the far side of the vehicle and formed the opinion it was too close to the crossover road between the Tranship Road and the Up main line to permit the safe clearance of any vehicle passing over the crossover line. Although he did not realise that shunting was in progress and had no reason to anticipate a movement over the crossover road taking place, he decided to have the wagon of sand moved against the buffer stops as a precaution. Both men alighted from the wagon and were in the process of moving it when a raft of wagons approached from behind and overtook them. Ling's arm, which was across one of the buffers was badly injured. Moore on visiting the site noted the Tranship Road fell sharply towards the dead end where Ling and his colleague were working, and attributed the accident to Shunter William Leatherdale who started a propelling movement in the siding, without first ascertaining whether the vehicles in the raft were coupled together and the whole coupled to the engine. He had placed part of this train himself and coupled it to a raft of wagons left there by a previous train. He omitted to examine the wagons of the previous train and incorrectly concluded that it had been detached in one portion and would therefore be coupled together. Because of this error he had failed to realise two of the wagons were not coupled and thus could not prevent the accident. The inspector concluded the accident was solely due to the want of care on the part of Leatherdale but stated that as the wagon was well clear of the crossover road there was in fact no need for Ling to move the wagon.

In order to rationalise the costs of train working between Marks Tey and Shelford on 14th September 1932 the Divisional General Manager (Southern Area) submitted a memorandum to the Traffic

Hudswell, Clarke 0-6-2T No. 5, hauling a goods train over Trinity Street level crossing, is entering the Down goods loop line at Halstead.

Author's collection

Committee recommending the abolition of Haverhill Station signal box and the concentration of all signalling on Haverhill Junction signal box. The scheme involved the installation of two new ground frames electrically controlled from the Junction signal box to work the Up and Down sidings and crossover road at the west end of the station. The estimated cost was £1,229 but allowing for the £23 value of recovered materials and the £11 net cost of renewals within the next five years, which would be rendered unnecessary, the cost of the scheme was reduced to £1,195. The scheme would also allow for the abolition of two signalmen's posts with a net annual saving of £353. The scheme was duly authorised on 29th September 1932.

Lieutenant Colonel E. Woodhouse later inspected the alterations at Haverhill on 14th November 1934 and found that Haverhill North signal box had been abolished and replaced by a 5-lever ground frame, electrically released from Haverhill Junction signal box which was located at the other end of the yard. The ground frame was installed close to the disused signal box, and from which the connection between the single line and Up and Down platform loops were worked. The connection was protected in the Down direction by a slot on the Down starting signal, which was also worked from the ground frame. An auxiliary Tablet instrument for the Bartlow to Haverhill Junction section was provided close to the ground frame and was worked by station staff.

A second ground frame containing 8 levers, electrically released from Haverhill Junction signal box, was provided to work the connection between the Up and Down sidings and the running lines at the Bartlow end of the station. Haverhill Junction signal box retained its existing 42-lever frame, but now with 37 working and 5 spare levers, whilst two new track circuits were installed in the single line from Bartlow and in the Up platform line with separate indicators. A screw pattern time release was provided in connection

with the track circuit back lock of the Up home signal to enable the 8-lever ground frame to be used for the dispatch of trains arriving from Bartlow. Woodhouse had no objection to the use of the time release – but with the use of the auxiliary Tablet instrument at the station for the disposal of the Tablet received from Bartlow, he ascertained from officials that station staff receiving the Tablet had been instructed to confirm the train had arrived complete before advising the signalman in the Junction box.

Woodhouse found the interlocking and controls of the auxiliary Tablet instrument and ground frames were correct, but he noticed with the 8-lever ground frame that an indicator showing whether the frame was released by the signal was required, as the existing swung out from 'locked' towards 'free' before the release actually took place. The signalling engineer attending the inspection promised immediate attention. The inspector also observed that when the slot on the Down starting signal worked by the 5-lever ground frame was 'off', the mechanical indicator in the Junction signal box was activated. This informed the signalman he was at liberty to lower his distant signal from Long Melford directly the distant signal from Halstead was fixed at caution, but there were no controls to ensure the distant signal was not lowered while the starting signal was at danger. Woodhouse noted that the practice was similar to that adopted elsewhere where signal boxes were close together, since the slot in the distant signal worked from the ground frame would be difficult to open because of the distance of 1,456 yards. He concluded that it was not exceptional in view of the fact every train which passed through the station without stopping had to approach the starting signal slowly in order to collect the Tablet by hand.

During the 1930s many excursions were routed via the Colne Valley line serving the branch stations as more people enjoyed leisure time. However, some excursion trains only used the line as a route to the coast and one such excursion – to Clacton from Ramsey East – deserves mention for on 9th July 1939 'J15' Class 0-6-0 No. 7553 worked a 9-coach train throughout from Ramsey East to the coast and return, travelling via St Ives, Cambridge, Haverhill and outward via the Stour Valley line via Sudbury and Marks Tey to Clacton, returning via the Colne Valley line. Stops were made at Cambridge and Colchester on the outward trip and at Marks Tey, Haverhill and Cambridge on the return run. The late Peter Proud provided the mileage and schedule of the excursion on its marathon trip from Huntingdonshire to the Essex coast, with a 3 hours 40 minutes timing on the outward trip and 3 hours 55 minutes on the return. The highest point-to-point timing on the entire journey was

9TH JULY 1939: 'J15' CLASS 0-6-0 No. 7553 WITH 9 COACHES					
MILEAGE		SCHEDULE			
		OUTWARDS		RETURN	
		MINS	MINS	MINS	MINS
0.0	Ramsey East	—	00		235
3.6	Warboys	06	08	225	227
7.0	Somersham	18	20	213	215
12.5	St Ives	30	38	196	203
15.6	Swavesey	—	45	—	189
17.9	Long Stanton	—	50	—	182
20.4	Oakington	—	55	—	176
22.6	Histon	—	60	—	169
25.2	Cambridge	70	75w	154	159w
28.5	Shelford	—	82	—	147
35.4	Linton	—	94	—	135
37.4	Bartlow	—	99	—	129
43.4	Haverhill North	—	110	—	119w
50.5	Clare	—	123		
53.1	Cavendish	—	129		
56.9	Long Melford	—	136		
60.0	Sudbury	—	142		
64.9	Bures	—	152		
68.2	Chappel	—	160		
71.7	Marks Tey	—	168		
76.8	Colchester	178	183w		
81.3	Wivenhoe	—	191		
90.3	Thorpe-le-Soken	—	205		
92.6	Great Holland	—	213		
95.0	Clacton-on-Sea		220		
					see above
43.4	Haverhill North			114	
47.2	Birdbrook			—	104
51.0	Yaldham			—	94
53.5	Sible & Castle Hedingham			—	88
56.8	Halstead			—	80
59.3	Earls Colne			—	74
62.9	Chappel			—	65
66.4	Marks Tey			52	57w
71.5	Colchester			—	43
76.0	Wivenhoe			—	26
85.0	Thorpe-le-Soken				10
87.3	Great Holland			—	05
89.7	Clacton-on-Sea				00
NOTE:	w water stop.				

on the return run when 40 mph was achieved between Haverhill and Bartlow. Whilst at Clacton the engine was serviced at Clacton shed.

Just prior to the outbreak of World War Two, the L&NER with all other British railway companies came under the control of the Railway Executive Committee. Within weeks of the commencement of hostilities local bus services were reduced and some removed from the roads by petrol rationing. In order to safeguard against air raids, especially at night when station lamps remained dimmed, staff utilised shielded hand lamps to attend to train or shunting duties. Other precautions against enemy ground attacks included the removal of station and signal box name boards, which were stored in lamp rooms or signal boxes but later reinstated. The agricultural nature of the branch was of the utmost importance as vital provisions of home-grown food, grain and vegetables were dispatched and conveyed to markets at Ipswich, Colchester, Chelmsford, Cambridge and London. In addition to an outflow of traffic, the war years brought an influx of tinned foods and dried milk and eggs for distribution in the area under the auspices of the Ministry of Food. As military call-up included some railway personnel there was soon a shortage of suitable staff at Earls Colne, Halstead, Hedingham and Yeldham

In the early evening of 16th August 1940 a number of Luftwaffe Heinkel III bombers, escorted by Messerschmitt 109 and 110 fighters, following the course of the railway from Halstead dropped a considerable number of bombs between Blue Bridge and White Colne. Surprisingly, no bombs fell on the line, although Langley Mill crossing cottage received blast damage, which also affected a short section of track. Several properties in the area suffered, a soldier was killed and a number of people injured at Colne Park. On another occasion a 'J15' Class locomotive on a Down goods service to Cambridge was taking water at Halstead, ready to reverse on to the signal box road to allow the passage of an Up passenger train, when enemy aircraft were spotted through broken cloud. These aircraft had been intercepted by Spitfire fighters and attempted to jettison their bombs around the railway. Fortunately the Up passenger train had arrived, but before it could proceed Ted Amos, a lorry driver based at Earls Colne, and Porter Gordon Bragg from Halstead were delegated to walk towards each other along the line to ascertain if any damage had been sustained. The two met at Blue Bridge and, with no actual damage being registered on the railway, the passenger train was allowed to continue its journey. Large and small craters were noted in fields alongside the line and trains were again halted at 6.30pm for unexploded bombs to be detonated by the Army Bomb Disposal Unit. Later, on 31st August 1940 a Heinkel bomber shot down by a Hurricane fighter skimmed over the railway before crashing at Countess Cross near Colne Engaine. One member of the crew survived.

After Dunkirk in the summer of 1940 it was recognised that heavy bombing of major towns and cities might drive the populous out of their homes before they could be taken away by train. To meet this possibility the Refugee Emergency Scheme was prepared and under this plan, also known as the Crash Evacuation, six trains were to be held in preparation at Chappel and Wakes Colne and Earls Colne to collect people from Colchester. Initially only a rough scheme was drafted; the plans were later improved and held until 1942, by which time invasion became much less probable and they were shelved.

In 1941 First Class facilities were withdrawn from the branch trains and remained so for a decade, whilst cheap day return tickets were also withdrawn. Towards the end of the same year the construction of a new airfield at Earls Colne was in progress and many trainloads of material were delivered to Earls Colne to help with the construction work, including thousands of tons of rubble from the bomb-damaged East London. An additional shunter was employed on a full time basis and as well as airfield traffic he dealt with increasing agricultural machinery traffic from Hunts. About fifty women from a Colchester labour unit, assisted by Irish labourers, unloaded the airfield material on to any available road vehicle for onward conveyance. If the yard at Earls Colne was full, the traffic was diverted to White Colne yard for onward transit. After about three months of preparation, the consignments of construction material gave way to supplies of aircraft fuel, bombs and small armaments. Similar activity took place at Halstead, Hedingham and Yeldham yards as material was conveyed to help with the building of new airfields at Gosfield and Ridgewell. There was also a further shortage of staff at this time, caused by men joining the forces, especially at Earls Colne, Halstead, Castle Hedingham and Yeldham, and junior staff and overtime working were used to overcome the situation.

By May 1943 Earls Colne was registered as the bomb and ammunition offloading and distribution station for up to thirty airfields in East Essex and West Suffolk. Within a short time, delivery was outstripping storage facilities and the United States Air Force established dumps away from the railway at White Colne, Pebmarsh and Bures. Ammunition trains were usually routed in the Down direction on the Colne Valley line to facilitate unloading at Earls Colne, and any loaded wagons diverted to White Colne had to be taken to Earls Colne before being taken in the Up direction as White Colne yard points were trailing in the Up direction. Similarly, empty wagons were taken from White Colne in the Up direction, as propelling was not permitted in the Down direction to Earls Colne because of the 1 in 66 and 1 in 90 steeply falling gradients. Any Up road working over the line was taken through to Marks Tey and reversed before working in the Down direction.

During May and June 1943 the United States Air Force 94th Bomber Group, using B17 Flying Fortress aircraft, operated from Earls Colne airfield. They were superseded by 323rd Bomber Group operating B26B and B26C Marauder aircraft, but only until July 1943. At 3.30am on the morning of 7th September 1943 a high explosive bomb was dropped approximately fifteen yards from the line at Haverhill North. Damage was sustained to adjacent telegraph poles and a signal ladder was buckled. As the wires were brought down, single line working was instituted using a pilotman until linemen could repair the telegraph cable. No track was damaged and normal working resumed at 9.30am. Then on 16th October 1943 a high explosive bomb was dropped adjacent to the railway between Halstead and Sible and Castle Hedingham, causing damage to telegraph cables and putting block instruments out of order. Pilot working was installed at 7.55am until normal working was restored at 10.45am.

It was increasingly necessary to keep the local airfields supplied with bombs, aircraft spare parts, ground stores and oil, and between D Day 6th June and early September 1944, White Colne dealt with 2,971 wagon-loads of American bombs, whilst Earls Colne handled 3,959 wagon-loads and Halstead 288 wagon-loads. All services were routed on to the Colne Valley line via Marks Tey and Chappel as bridges beyond Earls Colne restricted the movement of heavy vehicles. Trains arrived in lengths of up to twenty vehicles and on arrival American personnel worked twenty-four hours a day, seven days a week to unload the wagons and clear the yards so that more trains could arrive. This was in addition to the twenty or so railway staff allocated to Earls Colne, who worked round the clock, liaising with American personnel on unloading priorities. In all, over 100,000 bombs were unloaded in this period. Frequently wagon-loads of bombs were retained at Marks Tey and very occasionally at Chappel, waiting clearance of empty wagons from Earls Colne. Marks Tey acted as a clearing-house for wagons containing bombs and armaments; trains arriving from Whitemoor and other sources had to be split into trains containing fifteen or so vehicles to be within the capability of 'J15' Class locomotives. The situation was eased slightly when 'J17' and 'J19' Class engines were permitted to take heavier loads but only as far as Earls Colne. Bomb dumps were established along the roads in the White Colne to Bures area under camouflage, serving airfields at Earls Colne, Wormingford and Rivenhall as well as Ridgewell.

Many of the special trains conveying armaments and bombs ran under the cover of darkness with open wagons sheeted over to conceal the deadly cargo, although the prominent red flashed labels advised 'SHUNT WITH CARE' and 'PLACE AS FAR AWAY AS POSSIBLE FROM THE ENGINE, BRAKE VAN AND WAGONS LABELLED INFLAMMABLE'. Aviation fuel was conveyed in tank wagons.

In March 1944 the dead-end siding on the Down side of the line at Chappel and Wakes Colne was extended 480 feet in the direction of Marks Tey for the Petroleum Board, to serve as an offloading point for aviation fuel. The facilities included pumping plant and storage tanks and the siding had a capacity for pipes and gantries to offload twenty tank wagons. In the first three months 103 train loads of petrol tanks were offloaded in the siding, some trains arriving via the Colne Valley line. The siding was laid with 85 lbs per yard bullhead rails laid on slag and ash ballast, with trap points at the north end. As the station was on a rising gradient towards Bures a rod-worked derailer was provided between the running line connection and the trap points as a precaution against vehicles on the Down platform road running back and colliding with the petrol tankers standing in the siding. A petrol offloading gantry and associated pumping plant and storage tanks were provided; to save the expense of widening the high embankment, the siding extension was constructed with only a 6 feet clearance from the running line, which was acceptable as all offloading from the tank wagons was executed on the opposite side of the running line. As an added precaution, all pumping ceased with the passage of a passenger train on the adjacent line and an indicator was provided in Chappel signal box to show whether pumping was in progress or not. Minor alterations were made to the signalling and interlocking, including facing point locks and bars; three new sets of points and associated ground signals necessitated the frame in Chappel signal box to be enlarged to hold 42 levers, all levers working with no spares. After just over twelve months' operation the offloading point was mothballed on a care and maintenance basis and it was in that condition when Colonel E. Woodhouse, accompanied by Colonel D. McMullen, carried out the belated BOT inspection on 26th October 1948.

The branch was also of strategic importance during Operation Overlord but congestion and operating contingencies demanded alternative destinations because of the urgency for materials and men. Typical movements to branch destinations on 6th and 7th June 1944 are shown overleaf.

At the height of hostilities on 13th July 1944 a United States Air Force B17 Flying Fortress aircraft based at Ridgewell crashed

Paintings by Malcolm Root

LEFT: In 1861 three new tank engines with outside cylinders were ordered from Manning, Wardle & Company of Leeds but were typical 2-4-0s locomotives common to E.B. Wilson. They were actually purchased by Charles Brewster and delivered over a three-year period. Here the first of the trio to arrive in 1861, *Brewster*, in original green livery, departs from Halstead with a Down service and is passing Colne Valley Ironworks siding. In the background the former London Brighton & South Coast 2-2-2WT is receiving attention at the small shed, which was used for a short period for locomotive maintenance.

BELOW: Sible and Castle Hedingham station on a dark and dismal evening with 'J15' Class 0-6-0 No. 65424, one of five equipped with side window and tender cab especially for working the Colne Valley line, entering with a Down train.

ABOVE: LM '2MT' Class 2-6-0 No. 46467 departing Halstead with a Down train formed of Thompson non-gangway coaching stock as the sun casts long shadows over the snowscape. To the left are the gasworks and the tennis court pavilion, with Portways in the background.

RIGHT: Pride of the CV&HR Hawthorn, Leslie & Company 2-4-2T No. 2 *Halstead* in the black livery adopted from 1906 with the letters C and V located on the side tanks either side of a brass nameplate. The engine had received attention at Stratford Works and been reboilered in 1896 with a two-ring barrel with the dome on the leading ring. The original stove pipe chimney has been replaced by an ornate capped chimney.

Operation Overlord Diverted Traffic			
6th June 1944			
2.00pm	Immingham to White Colne	diverted to Marks Tey	39 wagons
3.00pm	Immingham to White Colne	diverted to Marks Tey	59 wagons
4.00pm	Immingham to White Colne	diverted to Stansted	60 wagons
6.55pm	Immingham to White Colne	diverted to Rayne	60 wagons
2.00pm	Tyne Dock to White Colne	arrived 7th June	60 wagons
3.00pm	Middlesbrough to White Colne	diverted to Stansted	57 wagons
4.00pm	Middlesbrough to White Colne	diverted to Halstead	47 wagons
8.29am	Immingham to White Colne	diverted to Felstead	59 wagons
8.00pm	Middlesbrough to White Colne	arrived 8th June	50 wagons
7th June 1944			
4.00am	Middlesbrough to White Colne	diverted to S & C Hedingham	49 wagons
4.07am	Immingham to White Colne	arrived 8th June	23 wagons*
3.00am	Tyne Dock to White Colne	arrived 7th June	48 wagons+
9.30pm	Middlesbrough to White Colne	arrived 8th June	46 wagons
Notes: * also conveyed 23 wagons for Earsham on the Waveney Valley line.			
+ also conveyed 9 wagons for Bungay on the Waveney Valley line.			

with its full bomb load on the railway near Great Yeldham. Four bombs exploded killing the crew of eight and injuring two others. Fifty yards of railway were destroyed by the blast but the air base ground recovery crew quickly removed the wreckage and assisted railway staff so that the civil engineer had the track replaced and a test train running in less than four hours. A US officer in charge of the recovery remarked it was the *'slickest railroad track relaying and repair job I've ever seen'*. Normal services, however, were not resumed until the next day because of damage to the single line signalling equipment.

As the war progressed the USAAF moved their bases to mainland Europe and so the railway again helped with the transfer of stored ammunition from Earls Colne to East Coast ports for onward transit. On a more personal note, in December 1944 G.L.H. Wilkes, a clerk at Halstead goods and a private in the Essex Regiment, previously reported missing in action, was now in a prisoner-of-war camp.

After the war the railways had resumed peacetime activities with rundown and life-expired equipment and rolling stock in need of maintenance. Questions were raised in Parliament regarding the deteriorating services offered by the L&NER, and the Colne Valley line was no exception. In the spring of 1946 the Down morning goods train from Chappel to Haverhill had almost completed shunting at Yeldham using the siding running parallel to the main single line at the west end of the station. The driver eased the locomotive drawing the wagons out of the siding to place them on to the train stabled on the main single line, but he failed to observe he had not backed the formation of wagons clear of the points. The guard, anxious to continue the journey, also failed to notice the wagons were not clear of the points and walked back to his brake van. The signalman could not alter the points and the driver, thinking his wagons were clear of the connection, opened the regulator and the engine set off with the wagons back along the siding instead of on to the train. The station staff and guard attempted to shout a warning to the driver but it was too late – the wagons demolished the buffer stops and deposited several vehicles on to soft earth. The driver and fireman remained on the footplate and were saved from injury as the tender dropped down the slight embankment with the parcels van which remained intact.

The early months of 1947 can be remembered for continuous snowstorms, which swept across the British Isles causing considerable traffic disruption. The County of Essex was not immune to the chaotic conditions and the Colne Valley line suffered, as did other branch lines in East Anglia. When adverse weather threatened, signalmen and permanent way staff were instructed to come on duty an hour earlier than scheduled, to deal with any eventualities that might occur and to keep the railway open for traffic, but on more than one occasion the elements won the day. On one occasion in early February a blizzard had continued through the night and roads were impassable. It soon became clear that the branch was blocked in several places and staff going on duty were forced to walk through considerable depths of snow. Most men lived relatively locally and all signal boxes eventually opened but on arrival it was found the telephone and single line block had not been affected. It was quickly realised no trains could run between Chappel and Haverhill until the services of a snowplough had been obtained. News came that the main line from Liverpool Street to Colchester and Ipswich had been kept open and the services of a snowplough had only been required at two points. Having cleared the main line the Ipswich-based snow plough was then summoned to the branches and Marks Tey signalman advised the snowplough would be available from 12.00 noon. Chappel signalman, Reg Mathews, then announced the plough would be arriving earlier; the plough, propelled by one 'J15' Class engine, managed to get as far as Earls Colne before the drifts proved impossible for further progress. A second 'J15' Class locomotive was summoned and after valiant efforts the combined motive power cleared the cutting between Blue Bridge and Langley Mill crossing to reach Halstead, from whence they returned to Ipswich. The morning goods train was then allowed to proceed to Halstead, arriving at 3.00pm instead of 5.45am, when the decision was made to abandon the passenger services for the rest of the day until the Cambridge snowplough could clear the rest of the line from the west. As the roads were blocked many people attempted to travel by train but were sent home. With the roads still blocked, many returned the next morning to use the railway until road conditions improved. After the snow melted the railway was flooded in several places with waterlogged sleepers and ballast washed away. When the water subsided permanent way staff had to substitute new sleepers and replace ballast on considerable sections of the line, and whilst this programme was ongoing trains were subject to speed restrictions until the roadbed was settled.

As petrol rationing eased so Eastern National Omnibus Company and several local road operators improved the frequency of services in Essex. The railways were still under Government control and it was the declared intention of the Labour Government to nationalise the majority of public utilities and associated industries, including railways, which they had announced in their 1945 election manifesto. The scene was thus set for further changes to the Suffolk/Essex branch railway.

7

Nationalisation and Closure

THE 1947 TRANSPORT ACT of 6th August brought the amalgamation of the London & North Eastern Railway Company into the nationalised British Railways with effect from 1st January 1948, when the Colne Valley line came under its third ownership – that of British Railways Eastern Region. The new management brought no immediate changes and the line retained its CV&HR/GER/L&NER atmosphere until the withdrawal of steam traction. Most stocks of L&NER tickets initially remained on sale but those in constant demand to popular destinations were soon replaced with tickets bearing the legend Railway Executive or British Railways. Locomotives working the line soon lost their NE or L&NER identity in lieu of the austere BRITISH RAILWAYS on the side tanks or tender, and although varnished teak or brown remained on the older branch coaching stock, some non-gangway vehicles appeared in the corporate crimson livery.

Somewhat belatedly, on 26th October 1948 Colonel E. Woodhouse, accompanied by Lieutenant Colonel D. McMullen conducted the Board of Trade inspection of the petroleum siding at Chappel and Wakes Colne installed in March 1944. They found the siding extension on the Down side of the railway had been laid with 85 lbs per yard rails laid on ballast formed of slag and ash. The siding was properly trapped. As the line though the station was on a rising gradient towards Long Melford a rod-worked derailer was provided between the running line connection and the trap points as a precaution against vehicles on the Down platform running line running back into contact with petrol tank wagons standing in the siding. To save the expense of widening the embankment on

the approach to the viaduct at the south of the station the siding extension was constructed with a minimum clearance of only 6 feet between it and the running line. Woodhouse thought this acceptable as all unloading from the tank cars was carried out on the opposite side to the main line. Arrangements were made to cease the pumping of petrol before the passage of a train on the adjacent line, and an indicator was placed in the signal box to advise when pumping was in progress. The inspectors noted the installation of the siding had required alterations to the facing point locks and bars to three sets of points and the provision of an additional shunt signal. The siding came under the control of Chappel and Wakes Colne signal box, which since the alterations had all 42 levers in the frame working. Woodhouse noted that the siding had not been used for unloading petrol since 1945 but was at the time of inspection retained on a care and maintenance basis.

British Railways management at Liverpool Street were constantly seeking ways to maximise on the value of excess railway land and at the end of 1948 agreement was reached with Rippers Limited at Sible and Castle Hedingham for the sale of 4 acres 1 rod and 14 perches of land west of the goods yard. The conveyance was made on 12th January 1949 in consideration of the sale price of £2,350. In return the purchaser was required to put down boundary plates and, if called upon to do so in future, erect boundary fencing.

After the war years the resumption of excursion traffic was enthusiastically greeted by residents of the Colne Valley, and Sunday special trains to Clacton and Walton were normally sold out as the

'J15' Class 0-6-0 No. 65475 departing Yeldham with a Marks Tey to Haverhill train in April 1949. In the foreground is the goods loop leading to the dock siding. Note the water crane at the end of the platform fed from the water tank to the right. *Author's collection*

LEFT: During World War Two the Colne Valley line was used by munitions trains conveying bombs and armaments to numerous airfields with loads offloaded at White Colne, Earls Colne, Yeldham and Birdbrook. Most traffic was routed from the south where track was strengthened between Chappel and Earls Colne. However, some trains on occasions approached from the north or travelled beyond Earls Colne from the south, and here one of the latter, double headed by two 'J15' Class 0-6-0s led by No. 7872, cross Apple Dumpling underbridge No. 19 spanning the River Colne between Sible and Castle Hedingham and Yeldham as a flying fortress 'B17' aircraft from Ridgewell USAAF base circles overhead. In the distance is Hedingham Castle.

FACING PAGE: A bright but cold winter's evening after a recent snowfall finds several passengers waiting as CV&HR 2-4-2T No. 2 2-4-2T *Halstead* enters Earls Colne station with a Down train from Chappel to Haverhill. The locomotive had acquired a GER smokebox door, for the headlamp is carried at the top of the smokebox.

RIGHT: With blower on and safety valves lifting, 'J15' Class 0-6-0 No. 65440 running tender first darkens the landscape as it approaches Parsonage Lane crossing Down distant signal between Earls Colne and Halstead with a Down freight train en route to Cambridge.

BELOW: LM 2MT 2-6-0 No. 46466 creates a smokescreen as it departs Halstead with a train formed of Gresley and Thompson non-gangway coaches. The signal-man in Halstead signal box is waiting to place the Down starting signal to danger once the train has cleared Trinity Street level crossing.

'J15' Class 0-6-0 No. 65477 waiting to depart Halstead with a Chappel to Haverhill train. The locomotive is not fitted with a side window cab but the tender has a back cab to give enginemen some protection when running tender first.
Author's collection

public headed to the sea for a short break. In view of the debacle of earlier years, 'E4' Class 2-4-0 locomotives were restricted to a tail loading of five coaches but it was soon realised this was insufficient for the patronage. Cambridge shed subsequently rarely rostered an 'E4' Class but relied on initially a single 'J15' Class 0-6-0 tender locomotive and then, after dispensation from the Civil Engineer, booked two Class 'J15' locomotives to haul the trains to the coast.

The new decade brought little change to the Colne Valley line, save that more people enjoyed better leisure time and trains at the weekend were fairly full as passengers travelled to Colchester on shopping expeditions. By the spring of 1952 the newly introduced LM Class '2MT' 2-6-0 tender locomotives were rostered to work most trains across the ex-CV&HR route. The engines were popular with footplate crews, being more powerful than the 'J15' Class 0-6-0s and equipped with tender cabs they were equally at home running engine or tender first.

Despite the almost regular daily routine of branch line operation it was not unknown for the regulations regarding single line working to go awry, especially if staff concerned were not vigilant. On one such occasion signalman Edward Willingham, in the process of crossing the last Down and last Up trains at Halstead, experienced such an event. The confusion was engendered by the fact that the enginemen on the Down working were from Colchester and the crew on the Up train were Haverhill men. In order to ensure they returned to their home depot, the men changed footplates for the continuation of the journey. In the resultant too-ing and fro-ing the key token for the Halstead to Sible and Castle Hedingham section was handed to the crew bound for Earls Colne and the Halstead to Earls Colne token handed to the Haverhill crew bound for Sible and Castle Hedingham. The first intimation of the impeding chaos came when the respective signalmen could not clear the single line sections after the passage of the trains. Charlie Bacon the signalman at Hedingham and Frank Mathias at Earls Colne quickly conferred with Willingham and realised that if officialdom became involved, unwanted inquiries would ensue with no doubt suspension from duty. The two sets of enginemen equally to blame for not checking to see if they were in possession of the correct key token

quickly realised they would be held responsible for the situation. Willingham thus agreed to use his car to exchange the tokens and deposit them at the correct signal box, thus allowing the trains to proceed on their way and for the respective signal boxes to be closed for the night. After two round trips and a couple of pints of ale with Charlie Bacon at Hedingham, Willingham finally closed Halstead signal box two hours later than scheduled.

For the summer timetable of 1954 the working of through coaches from the Colne Valley line to Colchester, which had been introduced after the war, ceased when the vehicles on the 2.20pm ex Haverhill were no longer attached to the 3.16pm Cambridge to Colchester via Sudbury train at Chappel. Equally, the same coaches returning from Colchester at 4.16pm were no longer detached at Chappel at 4.35pm. A correspondent commented it was *'remarkable that this arrangement, which intermittently dated back to the early days of the Colne Valley and Halstead Railway, should have survived so long'*. Yet further savings were made on and from 11th November 1954, when the roadway giving access to Haverhill South goods depot was handed over for adoption to Haverhill UDC, who in turn made the inhabitants of the road responsible for future maintenance.

Almost a decade after the cessation of World War Two the railway was still much involved with military matters and the aftermath of hostilities, for on 9th February 1955 F.G. Carie, Wing Commander, Officer Commanding No. 95 Maintenance Unit of the RAF based at Ridgewell, wrote a letter of thanks to the District Commercial Manager at Ipswich:

Dear Sir

During the last few months we have been working in close co-operation with Halstead station to complete quite a large task in moving explosives from RAF Gosfield.

It has been a pleasure to find such ready assistance and support as was given us by Mr Barrett of Halstead. He kept in constant touch with my working parties and in spite of adverse weather and other difficulties always kept us supplied with empty trucks and arranged instant removal of complete loads. This spirit of cheerful co-operation made a great difference to the morale of my men who were impressed by the fact that British Railways were solidly behind them in seeing a heavy job through as early as possible.

I should be grateful if my warmest appreciation was conveyed to Mr Barrett and his staff.

In 1955 Cambridge crews were authorised to work 10-coach trains over the Colne Valley line with the LM Class '2MT' 2-6-0 tender locomotives. In the same year the ASLEF called a strike of its members and no trains ran on the Colne Valley line for a fortnight. Even when services resumed the first Down freight train of the day was delayed for 20 minutes at Halstead awaiting the signalman to open the box. During the stoppage members of the NUR and TSSA continued to work normally, mostly keeping stations clean and generally tidying up.

On Monday 21st January 1957 the driver of a train from Chappel and Wakes Colne reported on arrival at Halstead that in the darkness as the train crossed Blue Bridge – No. 8 at 55 miles 27 chains spanning the A604 road – the engine had swerved violently almost throwing him off the footplate. The guard, who was standing by the window of his brake van was thrown to the floor sustaining cuts and bruises whilst several passengers registered their alarm at the shaking. 'Obstruction danger' code was sent on the block bell to Earls Colne and the signalman was advised of the circumstances. Station Master C. Barrett was called and he decided to send sub-ganger Sam Barham to investigate with ganger Harry Jarman who was called from Earls Colne. Both men attended the scene and reported back that the bridge span had been forced out of alignment by a lorry hitting the structure. Inspector Chapman of Halstead Police was advised as the vehicle causing the damage was considered to be substantial for the bridge had a 14 feet clearance

above the surface of the road. The line was blocked for traffic and Ipswich breakdown crane asked to attend. The District Civil Engineer also turned out and the bridge was cleared for the passage of trains the following morning. No vehicle was traced but after an account of the incident was published in the *Halstead Gazette* two lads came forward reporting that on the way home from school they had seen a large travelling crane standing under the bridge, probably belonging to the RAF, but nothing was proved.

Some of the branch stations entered the Best Kept Station Competition initiated by the L&NER, which continued after nationalisation. Annually an officers' special train traversed the branch for officials to view and assess the station and associated gardens. The viewing of branch station on Tuesday 9th July 1957 entailed a locomotive and supporting coach propelling Inspection Saloon No. 962451 from Linton, departing 11.48am across the branch to Chappel, arriving 1.37pm, with extended stops at Sible and Castle Hedingham, Earls Colne and White Colne, but as in previous years they all failed to win a prize.

The first signs of modernisation came when timing trials were held with a 2-car diesel multiple unit between Cambridge and Marks Tey via the Colne Valley line on 20th November 1957; but by May 1958 rumours were rife that the line was the subject of possible closure and regular references were made to such possibilities in the *Halstead Gazette*.

On Sunday 10th August 1958, the Railway Correspondence & Travel Society 'Northern and Eastern' rail tour train ran across the branch. The 7-coach special formed of ex-L&NER Gresley corridor stock departed Liverpool Street at 9.57am and was worked from there across the Bishop's Stortford to Braintree and Withem branch by 'J19' Class 0-6-0 tender locomotive No. 64656. The engine

Railway Correspondence & Travel Society 'Northern and Eastern' rail tour train hauled by 'J15' Class 0-6-0 No. 65440 passing Earls Colne on 10th August 1958 and formed of seven L&NER Gresley corridor coaches. The impressive Up starting signal dominates the end of the platform whilst the goods shed is to the left.

Dr I.C. Allen

LEFT: The River Colne follows a meandering course through the Essex meadows as a 'J15' Class 0-6-0 working tender first rattles the timbers of Hepworth Hall underbridge No. 12 with a train formed of a Thompson suburban Composite and a Gresley corridor coach. The cattle are undisturbed.

BELOW: A young girl and boy, complete with bucket and spade, eagerly await the arrival of the Sunday excursion train from Cambridge to Clacton and Walton at Halstead as it approaches hauled by LM '2MT' Class 2-6-0 No. 46469. They will soon join many others in the Gresley ex-L&NER corridor coaches heading for the coast and sea and sand. Halstead signal box stands guardian by Trinity Street level crossing, where an Eastern National omnibus is detained.

ABOVE: The crew of 'J15' Class 0-6-0 No. 65465 working a Down branch goods have halted the train beside Halstead Town football club ground for 5 minutes to watch the game between Halstead Town (in black and white shirts) and Stowmarket Town. Although the railway is fenced, local people have cut through the barrier to take a short cut to the fields. Portways supplied much of the ballast on this section of line, and their premises are behind the football club stand.

RIGHT: A Cambridge to Clacton Sunday excursion formed of Gresley ex-L&NER Corridor stock departing Halstead behind LM '2MT' Class 2-6-0 No. 46466 in plain black livery. Newman & Clark's granary siding is occupied by bulk grain wagons, whilst 16-ton all steel mineral wagons wait unloading in the Down yard.

Railway Correspondence & Travel Society 'Northern and Eastern' rail tour special standing at Haverhill as 'J15' Class 0-6-0 No. 65440 takes water from the column at the end of the Down platform on 10th August 1958. Participants stretch their legs and take photographs during this short stop. *B.D.J. Walsh*

then ran round and hauled the train on to Marks Tey, arriving at 12.50pm. For the onward journey departing at 1.00pm across the Colne Valley line via Halstead and Haverhill, the train was headed by 'J15' Class 0-6-0 tender locomotive No. 65440. A photographic stop was made at Halstead from 1.26pm to 1.35pm and at Haverhill 2.13pm to 2.23pm, where the engine took water, before the train continued to Cambridge. No. 65440 was replaced by BR standard '4MT' Class 2-6-4T No. 80041 for the onward journey on to the London Midland Region before returning to St Pancras.

Following satisfactory trials and the delivery of new stock, the Colne Valley passenger services were ultimately taken over by diesel multiple units and diesel railbuses from 28th September 1958. Unfortunately there was little overall improvement to the services as the railbuses were initially unreliable and trains were cancelled at short notice.

On a brighter note, the fine summer of 1959 generated much traffic for the regular excursion trains which ran from Cambridge to Clacton and Walton-on-the-Naze via Halstead; so great was the crowd one Sunday morning that the signalman at Halstead had to leave his box to help with issuing tickets as the queue stretched out into the station forecourt.

In the spring of 1960, rumours of possible closure of the railway intensified and staff were officially advised in July that the Colne Valley line with several other branches in East Anglia were the subject of detailed investigation as to their viability in the future railway network. The local branch of the National Union of Railwaymen called a special branch meeting and decided to lodge a protest with the Traffic Manager at Cambridge, whilst asking the NUR Headquarters to give urgent consideration to some form of protest. Management made no reply and the NUR were non-committal despite repeated representation. Finally Ted Willingham, the NUR branch secretary, was so desperate that he led a deputation to R.A. Butler, the local Member of Parliament to air their concerns. Following news that a case was being made for closure,

a flurry of correspondence appeared in the *Halstead Gazette* and Ted Willingham urged local residents and organisations to voice their objections to the closure to British Railways and stress the importance the line played in the day-to-day affairs of the towns and villages of the Colne Valley. Objections to closure were made by Halstead Urban and Rural district councils, Haverhill Council and Whitlock's of Yeldham, as well as the NUR and several individuals. The obligatory enquiry by the Transport Users Consultative Committee for East Anglia was established and on 14th February 1961 they conducted a public enquiry in the Co-operative Meeting Hall at Halstead. The inquiry lasted a full two days; the Cambridge Management arguing that the line had never paid its way even under private ownership and including grouping into the L&NER, although this was refuted by Ted Willingham who argued he *'could not find a single year from 1860 when a working surplus could not be shown'* and this was *'always ploughed back into the business'*.

The Committee retired to consider the case and on 14th April 1961 advised they recommended a twelve months reprieve for the line subject to the ratification of the Central Transport Consultative Committee. However, after weighing up the arguments the CTCC announced that the passenger services should be withdrawn from an early date and that the railway would remain open between Chappel and Yeldham for goods traffic. On 14th July the *Halstead Gazette* announced *'The End of the Line for the Colne Valley'*. Several months of uncertainly were to pass before, early in November 1961, the Railway Executive announced the withdrawal of passenger services on and from 1st January 1962, with replacement bus services operated by the Eastern National Omnibus Company. As no Sunday services operated, the last passenger service would run on Saturday 30th December 1961.

A 'rambler's' special train, organised by G.R. Lockie and formed of seven corridor coaches, ran across the branch on Sunday 8th October 1961, hauled by BTH/Paxman type 1 Bo-Bo diesel electric locomotive No. D8236. Starting from Liverpool Street and running

Right: The last steam hauled train headed by Ivatt LM Class '2MT' departing Halstead in September 1958. *Author's collection*

Below: Diesel railbus forming a Marks Tey to Haverhill service standing at Birdbrook in 1958. Note the oil lamp mounted on the extremely low post. *Dr I.C. Allen*

via the Cambridge main line to Audley End, the train ran thence via Bartlow and Haverhill to Halstead. From there the train continued to Chappel and Wakes Colne for the benefit of railway enthusiasts, stopping at the intermediate stations for photographs. Because of engineering work it was not possible to travel between Chappel and Marks Tey. The return was then made to Halstead to pick up the rambling fraternity before the return run following the same route as the outward journey to Liverpool Street.

In the ensuing weeks the Colne Valley passenger numbers were enhanced by railway enthusiasts seeking a last ride on the branch but all too soon the final days approached with little hope of a last minute reprieve. Many local people added to the enthusiasts' numbers on the final day, 30th December 1961, and the last passenger train – the 7.15pm Marks Tey to Cambridge formed of Derby lightweight 2-car diesel multiple unit – arrived at Halstead from Chappel at 7.30pm. The train was crowded and as it departed

LEFT: Parsonage Lane level crossing No. 22, east of Halstead with the redundant 25 feet high signal box towering over the adjacent crossing keeper's cottage. The tall structure was replaced by a 4-lever ground frame which made for ease of working the gates and relevant distant signals. 'J15' Class 0-6-0 No. 5451 of Cambridge shed rouses the echoes whilst making for Chappel with an Up all stations train from Haverhill. The crossing house was provided by the L&NER in 1929 and erected by J.W. Trudgett of Butt Road, Colchester for £485.

BELOW: There are no waiting passengers as 'J15' Class 0-6-0 No. 65458 enters a rain soaked Yeldham station with a 2-coach train for Haverhill. This was to become all too familiar and despite the later introduction of modern diesel trains, passenger services were withdrawn on and from 1st January 1962.

ABOVE: Pedestrians wait patiently at Halstead level crossing as 'J15' Class 0-6-0 No. 65447 enters the station with an Up train. On summer Sundays, excursion trains conveying up to eight coaches would completely block the crossing.

BELOW: BTH/Paxman Bo-Bo diesel electric locomotive, later Class '15', No. D8227 waits in the former Down goods loop at Halstead before departing with an Up goofs service, just prior to the withdrawal of freight facilities. *R. Hutley*

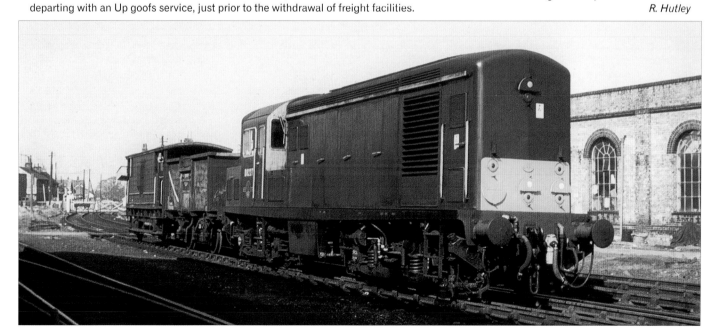

ABOVE: BTH/ Paxman 800 hp diesel electric locomotive No. D8226 standing by the goods yard at White Colne. These diesel locomotives took over the working of freight services in 1959 replacing the 'J15' Class 0-6-0s, which had hauled the services since grouping. *Dr I.C. Allen*

BELOW: BTH/Paxman 800 hp diesel electric No. D8227 passing Birdbrook station with a lengthy freight train. The section of railway west of Yeldham through Birdbrook to Colne Vally Junction was abandoned after the withdrawal of the passenger service on and from 1st January 1962. *Dr I.C. Allen*

SAVE THE COLNE VALLEY RAILWAY

DO YOU KNOW

That, failing sufficient opposition from the Public (and this means YOU), your Railway will be closed in less than three months' time?

DO YOU KNOW

That, with an efficient train service, it would be possible to get from HALSTEAD to COLCHESTER in under 30 minutes? Or from HALSTEAD to LONDON in under 75 minutes?

DO YOU KNOW

That, from HALSTEAD, our new DIESEL TRAINS take only 9 minutes to YELDHAM, 4 minutes to HEDINGHAM, 4 minutes to EARLS COLNE and 7 minutes to WHITE COLNE. And that many of the FARES are CHEAPER than by BUS?

DO YOU KNOW

That, if the RAILWAY is CLOSED, it will be impossible for you to take the kiddies to CLACTON or WALTON next SUMMER? Or do you imagine that some obliging Bus Company will be able to wave a magic wand and produce another 20, or so, coaches at a time when all their available transport is already in heavy demand?

And are you aware that the continued terrifying increase in summer road traffic to the coast ensures that, in future, your only means of reaching the SEASIDE, particularly on BANK HOLIDAYS, will be by TRAIN — even if you own a car?

DO YOU KNOW

That the TRANSPORT USERS' CONSULTATIVE COMMITTEE has been formed for the purpose of hearing YOUR COMPLAINTS and OBJECTIONS, and that if you do not write your protest NOW then the RAILWAY will be CLOSED and will NEVER be RE-OPENED.

DO YOU KNOW

That only **YOU** can prevent the closure of your Railway!

And that your PROTEST must be forwarded to:

F. E. TYLER
Secretary, T.U.C.C.
33, STATION ROAD, CAMBRIDGE

Also, that it must reach him not later than JANUARY 25th.

PLEASE make YOUR PROTEST at this TERRIBLE INJUSTICE to our Community

PLEASE DO IT NOW.

INSIST that British Railways provide an EFFICIENT SERVICE for the COLNE VALLEY with TRAINS run to suit YOUR REQUIREMENTS, and we, the men and women employed on this line, will be able to give you a service SECOND to NONE.

ONLY **YOU** CAN SAVE YOUR RAILWAY

Issued in the PUBLIC INTEREST by local branches of the NATIONAL UNION OF RAILWAYMEN

YOUR RAILWAY IS IN DANGER

It is proposed to withdraw all passenger services to and from Halstead and to close the line from Yeldham to Haverhill altogether.

If this is allowed to happen, a vital link with your near neighbours and connections to main lines to London and all parts of the Country will be lost for ever.

YOU MUST ACT NOW

All organisations, business concerns, and individuals who appreciate the value of a train service, who use the trains, or who would use the trains if the service were improved, are urged to support actively the fight to save the railway

THE COLNE VALLEY RAILWAY WITH GOOD AND ADEQUATE SERVICES IS ESSENTIAL TO US ALL

Efficient transport is vital to the life and prosperity of our area

WHAT YOU CAN DO

The proposals have been submitted for consideration to the Transport Users Consultative Committee for the East Anglian Area. **YOU** can help by writing to the Secretary of the Committee protesting at the injustice and the short-sighted policy behind the proposals. Tell him why you need the railway and how it serves, and could serve even more fully, your area and yourself.

WRITE TO THIS ADDRESS

F. E. Tyler, Esq.,
Secretary to the T.U.C.C.,
33, Station Road,
Cambridge.

BEFORE 25th JANUARY, 1961 OR YOU WILL BE TOO LATE

Issued by the Joint Committee of the Halstead Urban and Rural District Councils.

Consultation on the closure of the railway: a full page advertisement, 30th December 1960 (*above*) and a poster (*right*).

At Birdbrook, two passengers wait to join the morning Chappel to Cambridge train formed of a German-built railbus on a dank 30th December 1961, the last day of passenger train operation.

R. Powell

Left: Halstead station viewed from the train as a few passengers have alighted and make their way to the exit on the last day of passenger services 30th December 1961. The corn exchange, which was used by the railway company as a store, is to the right. *R. Powell*

Below: The final passenger train waiting to depart Halstead for Cambridge on 30th December 1961. As passengers leave the BR/Derby diesel multiple unit, the signalman exchanges the single line token with the driver to the right. *Halstead Gazette*

from the station all available detonators exploded as it passed over the level crossing. Similar scenes were enacted until Haverhill was reached. The weather turned to snow overnight and on Sunday engineering staff commenced dismantling the signalling equipment along the line.

Additional licenses having been issued on and from 1st January 1962, Eastern National Omnibus Company introduced rail replacement services. A brand new route 89 connected Colchester to Earls Colne, Halstead, the Hedinghams and Haverhill on weekdays only, although the return operations offered were far from generous, consisting of two through services and a short Colchester to Halstead working Mondays to Fridays, with five journeys each way on Saturdays plus some short workings. Revised timetables were also offered on route 88 connecting Colchester, Aldham, Earls Colne and Halstead, and route 320 from Halstead to Yeldham and Haverhill, both also operating on a Sunday. To add insult to injury, the same timetable offered a daily express road service between Halstead and London Euston.

Contracts were awarded in late January and early February for the removal of the permanent way and fixed assets, but the work took some time to progress. Demolition trains were worked by BTH/Paxman 800hp diesel electric locomotives, which had to remain with the wagons being loaded with scrap material because of the steep gradients on the line. Rails were cut into 12-foot to 20-foot lengths whilst some point work was recovered for use elsewhere; the material was taken to Haverhill South yard each day for onward disposal. By August 1962 all track had been removed over the closed section from Colne Valley Junction to Yeldham exclusive, a distance of 7 miles 40 chains. The intermediate station at Birdbrook was intact but all signalling and other equipment was dismantled. From Chappel to Yeldham a daily freight service continued to operate Mondays to Saturdays, hauled by BTH type 1 diesel electric locomotives or North British 1,100 hp (later Class '21') diesel electric locomotives.

Coincidental with the signalling alterations came the withdrawal of the Key Token working between Chappel and Yeldham, to be replaced with 'one train only' working over the single line. As months passed, weeds grew through the ballast and where trees overgrew the railway the vegetation was so thick that only the rails

showed through. The freight traffic was sporadic – it mainly ran to fulfil contractual commitments – and the journey across the branch was slower as trainmen had to open and close the level crossing gates for each journey. Although booked to run each weekday, as the weeks progressed and traffic reduced the trip was cancelled if there were no wagons to deliver or collect. Freight facilities were withdrawn from Sible and Castle Hedingham on and from 13th July 1964 and from Earls Colne, White Colne and Yeldham on and from 28th December 1964. British Railways announced withdrawal of freight facilities at Halstead on and from 19th April 1965, but because the Easter weekend intervened the final train ran on Maundy Thursday. The grey afternoon added to the foreboding and the last train departed from Halstead behind the usual BTH/Paxman 800 hp diesel electric locomotive, hauling two covered vans and five empty coal wagons en route to Colchester. Unlike the passenger train closure, only three people turned out to watch the event. On the same day freight facilities were withdrawn from Haverhill South and thus the erstwhile CV&HR route was obliterated from the railway map.

Once again contracts were placed for removal of the track, when BTH 800 hp locomotives again propelled wagons to Yeldham for the demolition contractors men to load with scrap material. The

BTH/Paxman Class '15' Bo-Bo 800hp diesel electric locomotive standing in the cutting just south of Yeldham with a permanent way recovery train on 20th June 1965. The rails were cut into short lengths, loaded on to wagons and conveyed direct to scrap merchants. *M. Root collection*

ABOVE: The former tank house adjacent to Halstead station is devoid of the water tank in this 1965 view just before full closure of the line. *J. Watling*

RIGHT: View from the footbridge at Halstead showing a derelict site with the goods shed and station just before the track-lifting programme commenced. *Author's collection*

rails, mostly second-hand from the main line, were cut into 12-foot to 20-foot lengths but some point work and crossing were recovered for use elsewhere. Some sleepers were sold locally for firewood and those not taken were burnt on site. The operation gradually progressed towards Chappel and opportunity was taken to use the loops at the intermediate stations to store wagons until required and to enable the contractors to remove some material by road. Similar recovery of materials took place between Haverhill South and Haverhill North.

As the years progressed after closure, much of the former trackbed and railway property was sold (see below) and Halstead station site was transformed into a car showroom where the signal box was located, whilst the station forecourt was transformed into a bus station which itself was replaced by a block of flats. Later at Wakes Colne the parish council and local residents who wished to preserve the bridge carrying Lane Road over the former Colne Valley line were given until September 1999 to raise £21,000 by the BR Property Board to cover the costs of urgent repairs to the structure, which would otherwise be demolished and replaced by an embankment to carry the road. BRPB were granted planning permission from Colchester Borough Council for the demolition to go ahead in July 1999.

LAND SALES				
COMPLETION DATE	**LOCATION**	**LAND AREA**	**PURCHASER**	**SALE PRICE**
26th November 1964	Yeldham	0.8 acres	R. Wilson	£64
22nd March 1965	Yeldham	2.85 acres	Garrod Brothers	£108
24th March 1965	Yeldham	9.05 acres	Grays Trustees	£362
9th December 1965	Halstead goods yard	3 acres 2,938 sq yds	Newman Clark Ltd	£16,500
4th March 1966	S & C Hedingham station & coal yard	6 acres 4,550 sq yds	Rippers Limited	£13,000
21st September 1966	Earls Colne	4¾ acres	Colne House Ltd	£1,275
20th October 1966	Drawwell Bridge S & C Hedingham	1,838 sq yds	Essex County Council	£10
2nd December 1966	Earls Colne station and land	4 acres 3,872 sq yds	G.H. Berger	£7,000
14th December 1966	White Colne station and yard	2 acres 1,379 sq yds	Earls Colne Co-op Industrial Society	£3,750
29th December 1966	Birdbrook	2,229 sq yds	J.W. Shard	£217
24th January 1967	Parsonage gatehouse	629 sq yds	Mrs W.T. Benham	£950
30th March 1967	S & C Hedingham	340 sq yds	Essex County Council	£5
22nd May 1967	Birdbrook	2 acres 823 sq yds 6 acres 534 sq yds	St John's College Cambridge	£200
19th July 1967	Earls Colne	1 acre 1,936 sq yds	Halstead RDC	£175
5th August 1967	Halstead goods yard	1 acre 4,186 sq yds	J.W. Horwood	£20,000
29th September 1967	Halstead	823 sq yds	A.H. Rea	£3,750
1st November 1967	Halstead	4 acres 968 sq yds	Executors of the late Mrs Butler	£959
3rd July 1968	White Colne	4 acres 4,085 sq yds	Essex County Council	£1,070
11th September 1968	White Colne	2 acres 4,646 sq yds	Trustees of R.B. Brownley	£240
1st January 1969	White Colne	3 acres 581 sq yds	J.J. Poole	£150
28th March 1969	Earls Colne	5 acres 4,695 sq yds	G. Courtauld	£355
8th May 1969	Wakes Colne	5 acres 2,371 sq yds	Percival & Co	£450
6th June 1969	Halstead	1 acre 3,098 sq yds	Messrs W. & I. Steel	£130
10th November 1969	Halstead	12 acres 1,592 sq yds	J. Courtauld	£2170
7th July 1970	Haverhill	1,540 sq yds	West Suffolk CC	£75
29th May 1971	Halstead	653 sq yds	J.W. Horwood	£5,000
30th September 1971	Haverhill goods station	3 acres 4,743 sq yds	Haverhill UDC	£20,000
7th January 1972	Yeldham	15 acres 1,452 sq yds	Essex County Council	£5,000
7th July 1972	Halstead	2,623 sq yds	Halstead UDC	£6,500
13th November 1974	Halstead	1 acre 315 sq yds	Link House Investments	£136,100
14th December 1974	S & C Hedingham	7 acres 4,102 sq yds	Mrs B.M. Crawsher	£1,650
23rd April 1975	S & C Hedingham	3,500 sq yds	A.R. Clarke Builders Ltd	£3,000
30th June 1976	S & C Hedingham	2 acres 4,114 sq yds	G. Page	£200
20th October 1976	S & C Hedingham	2 acres 484 sq yds	F. Powell	£160
1st December 1976	Great Yeldham	227 sq yds	Mrs Humm	£175
18th February 1980	Nunnery Street	2,285 sq yds	A.R. Clarke Builders Ltd	£16,050
5th September 1980	S & C Hedingham	1 acre 3,750 sq yds	Essex County Council	£350
23rd January 1981	S & C Hedingham	15 sq yds	Essex County Council	£100

8

The Route Described

BEFORE EMBARKING ON THIS CHAPTER, the reader must be made aware that compared with neighbouring GER lines, where mileages and distances were fairly uniform between civil and signalling engineering documents and working timetable information, no such uniformity existed for the CV&HR. The author has consulted over ninety documents issued by the CV&HR, GER, L&NER and BR operating, civil engineering and signalling departments and gross errors are evident. The problem appears to stem from the fact that once the L&NER conducted a detailed survey in 1923, and following on from a GER survey of 1910, a zero point was established at Liverpool Street and the CV&HR zero mileages from Chappel Junction were abandoned. This sufficed until 1939, when a route plan was produced adding on average 8 chains to each mileage for bridges, stations and level crossings, which appears to have been accepted by some but not all departments. Then in 1945 revised documents reverted to the 1923 mileages, which continued in a 1952 survey, only to be aborted by an engineering document which reverted to the 1939 mileages in connection with the conversion of the line to one train only working in 1962. Further investigation revealed there was a difference of opinion between certain civil engineering functions as to the original zero point at Liverpool Street, which was not resolved. A further document even added two chains to the original CV&HR bridge list! In the following description of the route the zero point and subsequent mileages shown in the 1910, 1923, 1945 and 1952 documents have been used, and allowing for minor discrepancies of a quarter chain a fairly accurate record has been achieved. The information will therefore differ from those shown in previous published works, however; for clarification, and for those wishing to while away their leisure time comparing the figures, the 1939 mileages for bridges and level crossings are given as an appendix at the end of the book.

Although at times over the years CV&HR trains worked to and from **Marks Tey** station, 46 miles 50 chains from Liverpool Street on the Norwich main line – encountering in the Down direction an initial climb of 1 in 117 to a level section before descending at 1 in 129/631 and then 1 in 120 rising crossing the famed Chappel Viaduct – the official commencement of journeys on the railway was at Chappel and Wakes Colne where the Great Eastern station

Gradient post on the minor summit east of Chappel and Wakes Colne on 4th April 1952.   *G. Powell*

Gradient Chart.

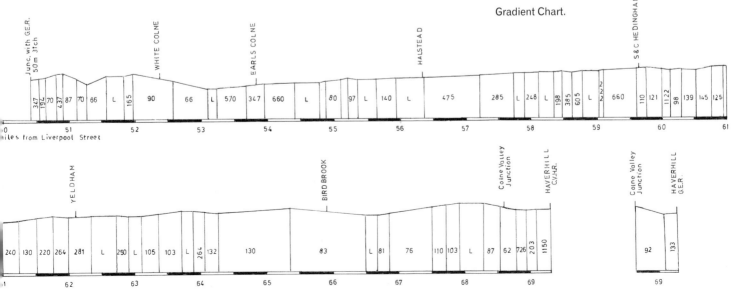

ABOVE: Marks Tey station 46 miles 50 chains from Liverpool Street facing towards London circa 1920, with the Up and Down main line to the left and Stour Valley branch curving away to the right. Colne Valley services, in the form of through coaches and then through trains, also used the bay platform. *Author's collection*

LEFT: Marks Tey branch platform with 'J15' Class 0-6-0 on the Colne Valley branch train. *Author's collection*

Stour Valley and Colne Valley line trains waiting to depart from the curving branch platform at Marks Tey. 'E4' Class 2-4-0 No. 62797 on the Stour Valley train formed of ex-GER corridor coach, a Gresley suburban Brake Third and a Gresley corridor Third will set off for the roundabout journey via Sudbury and Long Melford to Cambridge, to be followed a few minutes later by the LMR '2MT' Class 2-6-0 with the Colne Valley service formed of Gresley corridor stock. Because of the circuitous route with its greater mileage, the 'E4' will not reach Haverhill North until after the Colne Valley train has arrived and been shunted out of the path of the Cambridge train. *Author's collection*

A busy scene at Marks Tey on 19th February 1949 with 'J15' Class 0-6-0 No. 65473 standing on a Colne Valley branch train formed of three coaches including a clerestory Brake Third. The locomotive is stood at the rear of a Stour Valley branch train which would depart ahead of the Colne Valley train but reach Haverhill later.
J.H. Meredith

'J15' Class 0-6-0 No. 65477 crossing the Colne Valley viaduct south of Chappel and Wakes Colne with a Colne Valley branch train. The structure was built for double track but only a single line was installed.
Dr I.C. Allen

KEY TO TRACK DIAGRAMS

BO	BOOKING OFFICE	GS	GOODS SHED	RR	REFRESHMENT ROOM	WBO	WEIGHBRIDGE OFFICE
CD	CATTLE DOCK	LC	LEVEL CROSSING	SB	STATION BUILDINGS	WC	WATER COLUMN
CP	CATTLE PENS	LD	LOADING DOCK	SC	SIGNAL BOX	WPH	WATER PUMPHOUSE
CS	COAL STAGE	LG	LOADING GAUGE	SMH	STATION MASTER'S HOUSE	WR	WAITING ROOM
FB	FOOTBRIDGE	MP	MILE POST	SMO	STATION MASTER'S OFFICE	WT	WATER TANK
FP	FOOTPATH	OB	OVERBRIDGE	SP	SIGNAL POST		
GKC	GATE KEEPER'S COTTAGE	OC	OCCUPATION CROSSING	UB	UNDERBRIDGE		
GO	GOODS OFFICE	PWH	PERMANENT WAY HUT	WB	WEIGHBRIDGE		

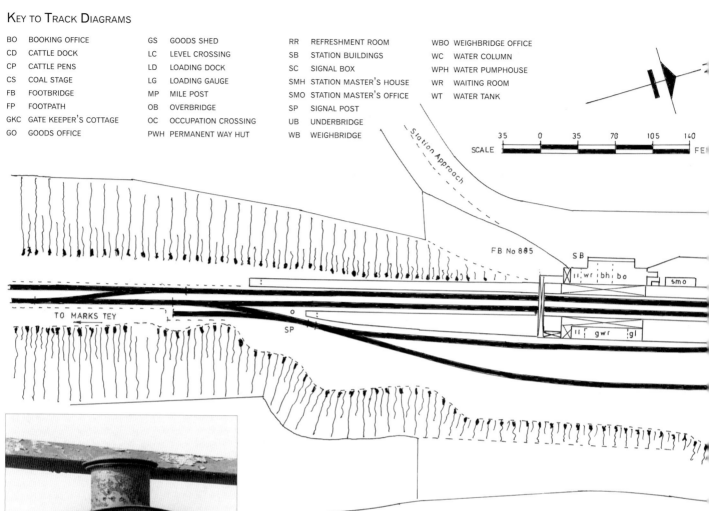

Ornate platform oil lamp at Chappel and Wakes
Colne station in March 1961.   *J. Watling*

Chappel and Wakes Colne

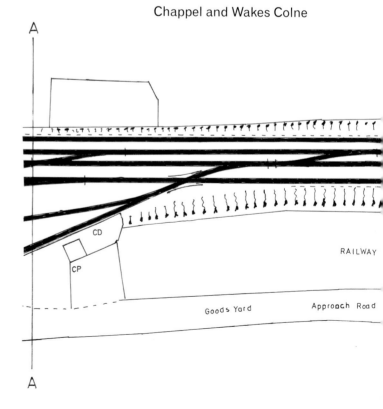

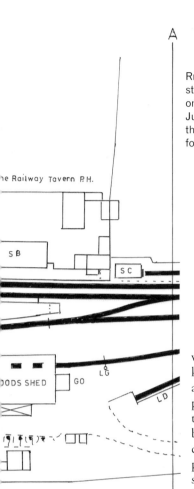

RIGHT: Chappel and Wakes Colne station name or running-in board on the Down platform on 26th July 1948, advising passengers that the station was the junction for the Colne Valley line.

G. Powell

was used for all traffic. The description of the route will thus commence at **Chappel and Wakes Colne**, known as Chappel until 1st October 1914, located 50 miles 18 chains from Liverpool Street and having a single platform on the Down side of the railway until the station was rebuilt and resignalled as a passing loop in 1892. The Down and Up loop lines served the 490 feet Down platform, which was host to the main station buildings and station master's house, and the 470 feet Up platform on which a brick building containing waiting rooms and toilets were located. Station footbridge No. 885, at 50 miles 19 chains, connected the platforms. Runaway points were provided in the Down loop line 80 yards after passing the home signal on account of a 1 in 80 rising gradient. The goods yard on the Up or eastern side of the station was served by a 450 feet loop which ran from the Up platform loop line along the back of the Up platform and at the north end a 220 feet siding led to the 300 feet Up reception road. From this line the 430 feet shed loop siding served the goods shed leading at the southern end back to

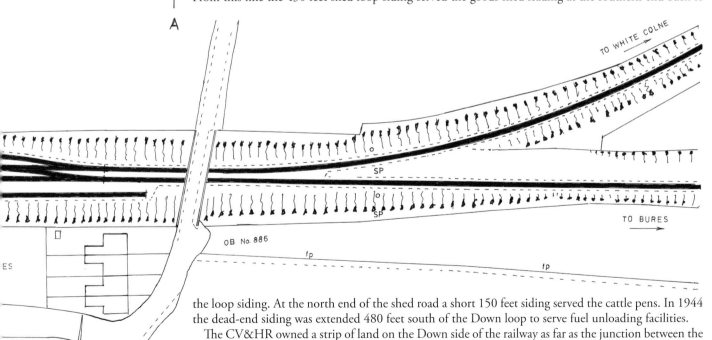

the loop siding. At the north end of the shed road a short 150 feet siding served the cattle pens. In 1944 the dead-end siding was extended 480 feet south of the Down loop to serve fuel unloading facilities.

The CV&HR owned a strip of land on the Down side of the railway as far as the junction between the two lines and installed a 370 feet siding thereon, terminating north of the level crossing which gave road users access to the GER goods yard. When the station was rebuilt by the GER the siding was reduced in length, the crossing abolished and the land nearer the station occupied by the new Station signal box and a platelayers hut, a factor which was contested by the Halstead Company. Thirteen chains north

The GER station at Chappel and Wakes Colne, which for many years was the eastern terminus of CV&HR trains from Haverhill. This view facing north from the Down platform shows the main station buildings at the back of the Down platform and waiting room on the Up platform. Covered footbridge No. 885 connects the platforms. *Author's collection*

Chappel and Wakes Colne station, 50 miles 18 chains from Liverpool Street, viewed from the Up platform facing north on 16th April 1947. The main station buildings are on the Down platform with the signal box beyond, then the Down and Up loop line and waiting rooms and staff rooms on the Up side; to the right is the goods shed. Footbridge No. 885 connecting the platforms is devoid of its overall roof. *L&NER*

View from the Down platform at Chappel and Wakes Colne looking south towards Marks Tey on 16th April 1947 showing the Up platform and associated building containing waiting rooms and staff accommodation. The Up and Down loop lines converge to cross Chappel viaduct.

L&NER

Chappel and Wakes Colne station approach with the stepped entry to the booking office and platform on 16th April 1947. A separate gated entry was available on the level at the end of the building. *L&NER*

ABOVE: 'E4' Class 2-4-0 No. 2794 waiting to depart Chappel and Wakes Colne with a Colchester to Cambridge train via the Stour Valley line on 26th July 1948. The post to the left carries the collecting arm for the loop of the single line Train Staff. *G. Powell*

RIGHT: Looking north towards the junction between the CV&HR and GER lines at Chappel and Wakes Colne. To the left is the former CV siding, then the Down and Up loop lines with the connection from the latter to the goods yard in the foreground. The Sudbury line Down starting signal is cleared for a train whilst the CV starting signal is at danger. *G. Powell*

of Chappel and Wakes Colne station, at 50 miles 31 chains, the Colne Valley route commenced climbing at 1 in 117 to pass under Chappel overbridge No. 886 at 50 miles 32 chains, and sharply to the left away from the GER Sudbury line. The speed of trains approaching or leaving Chappel on the Colne Valley curve was not to exceed 10 mph.

The CV&HR line continued curving away from the GER Sudbury line on a 30-chains left-hand bend, climbing at 1 in 347/194 to pass under Old House Farm overbridge No. 1 at 50 miles 49 chains before climbing at 1 in 70 and a short 1 in 437 following a straight course past the 50¾ milepost with Acorn Wood on the Down side, after which it fell at 1 in 87 passing under Lane

Farm overbridge No. 2 at 51 miles 02 chains. The line then followed a 50-chains radius left-hand curve and just before 51½ milepost the gradient eased to 1 in 924 falling before encountering a short 1 in 66 climb passing Alder Carr Wood on the Down side as the railway curved gently to the right to bisect Fox and Pheasant level crossing No. 1 at 51 miles 64 chains. Also known as Boley Road, this was equipped with a 3-lever ground frame to operate the gate distant signals and gate lock. A cottage was provided on the Up side of the line west of the gates for the resident crossing keeper; in the later years Percy Polston lived rent free in return for his wife and family opening and closing the gates for all trains. The cottage was not supplied with water so a supply was originally obtained from a

LEFT: Unkempt LM Class '2MT' 2-6-0 No. 46467 departing Chappel with a Colne Valley train to Haverhill, whilst a 'J15' Class 0-6-0 stands on the Up loop line. *Dr I.C. Allen*

BELOW: LM Class '2MT' 2-6-0 No. 46469 rounds the curve approaching Chappel on 14th April 1952 with a Colne Valley train. The raised arm of the subsidiary signal authorised the train to terminate at the Down side platform, there to provide a connection with the Sudbury line service. The Sudbury line and associated Up home and subsidiary signals are to the right. *G. Powell*

RIGHT: Southbound Colne Valley line train approaching Chappel Junction, 50 miles 31 chains from Liverpool Street, where the Stour Valley line was joined north of Chappel and Wakes Colne station. *H.C. Casserley*

'J15' Class 0-6-0 No. 65432 fitted with side window cab works the 12.01pm Marks Tey to Haverhill train after passing Lane Farm bridge No. 2 at 51 miles 02 chains on 2nd October 1957.
G.R. Mortimer

Fox and Pheasant level crossing No. 1 at 51 miles 64 chains from Liverpool Street – where the minor road from Bart Hall, White Colne, to Wakes Hall bisected the railway – viewed facing towards Haverhill. *Author's collection*

White Colne

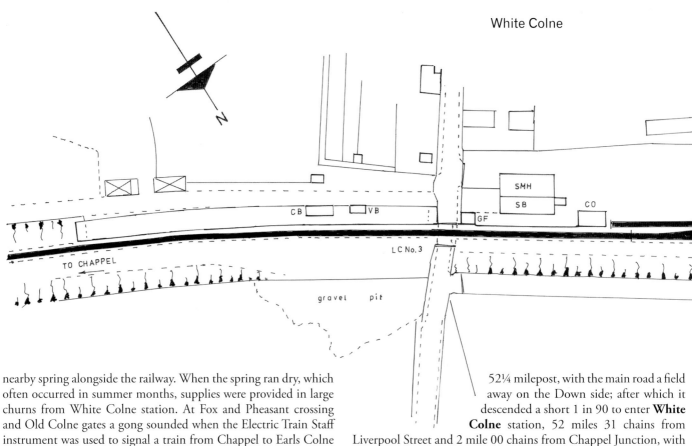

nearby spring alongside the railway. When the spring ran dry, which often occurred in summer months, supplies were provided in large churns from White Colne station. At Fox and Pheasant crossing and Old Colne gates a gong sounded when the Electric Train Staff instrument was used to signal a train from Chappel to Earls Colne signal box or vice versa.

From Fox and Pheasant crossing the single track railway followed a short level section before climbing at 1 in 165 on a shallow right-hand curve over level crossing No. 2 at 52 miles 04 chains to the

52¼ milepost, with the main road a field away on the Down side; after which it descended a short 1 in 90 to enter **White Colne** station, 52 miles 31 chains from Liverpool Street and 2 mile 00 chains from Chappel Junction, with its single 320 feet long platform located on the Down or south side of the line, east of the level crossing. At the formal opening on 18th April 1860 the station was the only intermediate stopping place and remained the smallest on the line. It was originally called Colne but

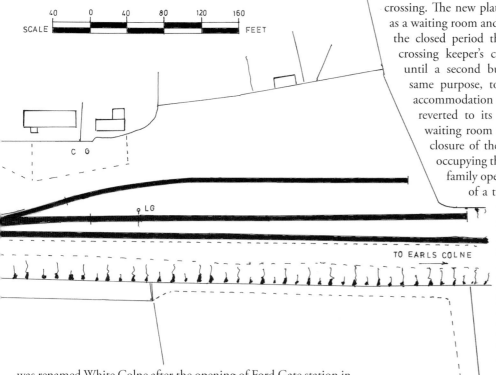

40   0   40   80   120   160   FEET

C G

LG

TO EARLS COLNE

crossing. The new platform hosted an old 4-wheel coach body as a waiting room and a wagon body for parcel storage. During the closed period the original station building became the crossing keeper's cottage and the arrangement continued until a second building was provided alongside for the same purpose, together with a small brick hut for the accommodation of the ground frame. The station building reverted to its former status with booking office and waiting room and served as such after reopening until closure of the line. Ernest Root was ganger in 1924, occupying the cottage rent free in return for he and his family opening and closing the gates for the passage of a train. This main building now serves as a village hall and the later brick-built lamp room is preserved by the Colne Valley Railway Preservation Group at their Castle Hedingham station. The station was very convenient for the community living south of the railway. In 1908 a 9-lever ground frame was provided to work the signals and gate release but later reduced to 4 levers for working the distant signals and wicket and level crossing gate locks.

was renamed White Colne after the opening of Ford Gate station in 1882, and the station buildings and low platform were then located west of the level crossing – the single storey structure containing booking office, parcels office and goods office. The station closed on 1st May 1889 when the name was confusingly transferred to Ford Gate station. The station reopened for goods traffic in 1907 as Colne until it reopened for passenger traffic as White Colne on 1st April 1908. The former station buildings remained in use after the rebuilding of the platform to a greater height east of the

The goods yard located west of the level crossing was quite spacious, with two goods sheds at the west end of the yard served by the 320-feet yard siding entered by facing points in the Down direction controlled by a 2-lever ground frame released and locked by Annett's key attached to the Electric Train Staff, the siding running parallel to the running line, with a 110 feet headshunt at the eastern end. A small building in the middle of the yard served as a coal office and was occupied by Moy's for many years.

ABOVE: Road approach to the original Colne station on 16th April 1947. White Colne station when reopened in 1908 was located out of view to the right. The brick building by the level crossing wicket gate was provided for the resident crossing keeper, the station living accommodation being near left by the entrance to the goods yard. The building beyond, partly obstructed, is the original station.   L&NER

FACING PAGE: The original Colne station building designed by Nathaniel Beardmore, located west of the level crossing together with a brick building provided for the resident crossing keeper. Behind the building an extension was added in 1908 as staff living accommodation. The connection to the goods yard from the main line was added in 1907 when the station reopened for goods traffic.   J. Watling

The original Colne station circa 1880, view facing towards Haverhill with the low and short platform west of the level crossing. The building designed by Beardmore was cloned at Sible and Castle Hedingham. A considerable number of wagons occupy the small goods yard where Moy's coal wharf is prominent. When the station was closed in 1889 on the opening of Ford Gate station the building became the crossing keeper's accommodation, but when the station reopened in 1908 as White Colne with the platform east of the gates the building reverted to its status as a booking office and waiting room. The tall station signal with arms for each direction of travel and operated by levers at ground level is to the right. The main line of flat bottom rail is unusual for this period as the tops of the sleepers are visible above the ballast. The station master, with hands behind his back, stands on the platform surveying the scene.

M. Root collection

Above: White Colne station, 52 miles 31 chains from London Liverpool Street, on 16th April 1947, facing towards Haverhill and showing the coach and van bodies provided for passenger and parcels/goods accommodation. The station buildings and living accommodation provided for the original Colne station in 1860 are beyond the gates. *L&NER*

Left: The 4-wheel coach body providing the passenger waiting accommodation at White Colne in March 1961. *J. Watling*

White Colne station 52 miles 31 chains from Liverpool Street, located on the Down side of the single line east of the level crossing viewed facing towards Haverhill. The original Colne station building is beyond the level crossing. *Author's collection*

White Colne station facing towards Chappel, opened east of the level crossing in 1908 with a 4-wheel coach body providing passenger waiting accommodation and a van body used for the storage of parcels and goods. The station was closed to passenger traffic on and from 1st January 1962 and goods on and from 28th December 1964. *J. Watling*

Views of trains at White Colne station are few and far between but here LM '2MT' Class 2-6-0 No. 46465 waits to depart with a Down train formed of Gresley and Thompson non-gangway stock. With the true branch line malpractice the locomotive carried no headcode. *M. Root collection*

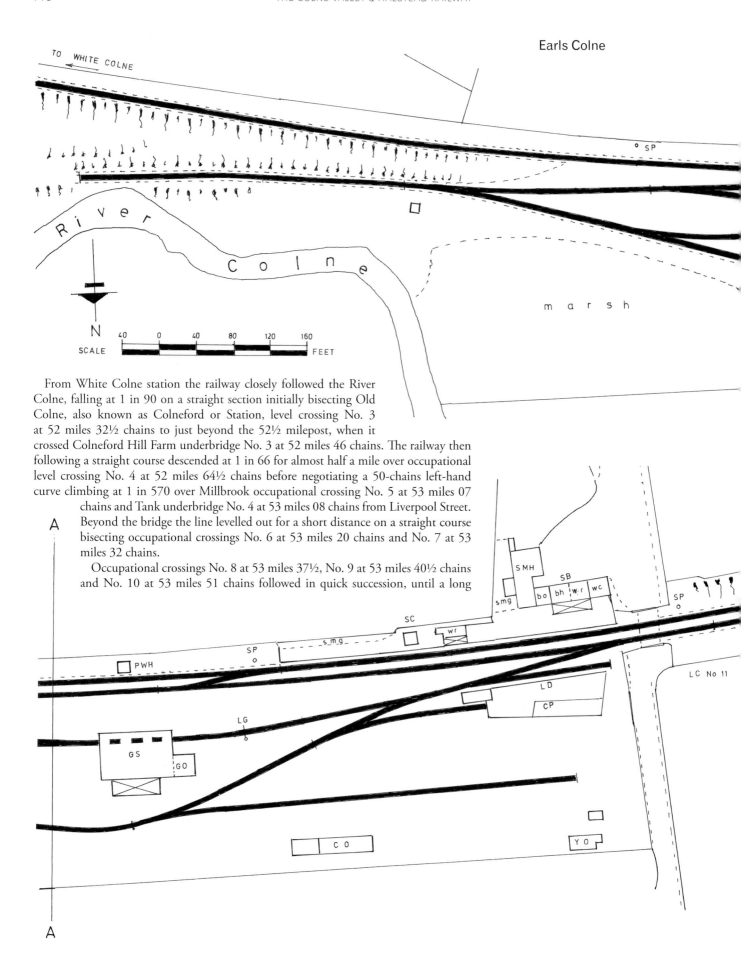

Earls Colne

TO WHITE COLNE

River Colne

N

SCALE 40 0 40 80 120 160 FEET

From White Colne station the railway closely followed the River Colne, falling at 1 in 90 on a straight section initially bisecting Old Colne, also known as Colneford or Station, level crossing No. 3 at 52 miles 32½ chains to just beyond the 52½ milepost, when it crossed Colneford Hill Farm underbridge No. 3 at 52 miles 46 chains. The railway then following a straight course descended at 1 in 66 for almost half a mile over occupational level crossing No. 4 at 52 miles 64½ chains before negotiating a 50-chains left-hand curve climbing at 1 in 570 over Millbrook occupational crossing No. 5 at 53 miles 07 chains and Tank underbridge No. 4 at 53 miles 08 chains from Liverpool Street. Beyond the bridge the line levelled out for a short distance on a straight course bisecting occupational crossings No. 6 at 53 miles 20 chains and No. 7 at 53 miles 32 chains.

Occupational crossings No. 8 at 53 miles 37½, No. 9 at 53 miles 40½ chains and No. 10 at 53 miles 51 chains followed in quick succession, until a long

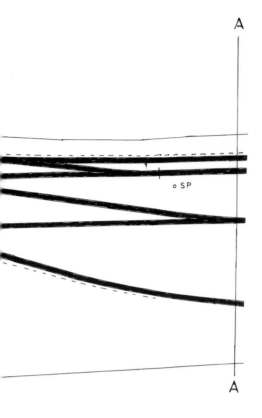

RIGHT: End view of Earls Colne signal box, still supporting its ornate finials, viewed from a Down train on 30th December 1961. Note the canopy overhangs the diesel multiple unit. *R. Powell*

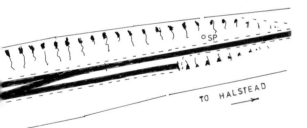

raking left-hand curve culminated in a climb of 1 in 347 to Earls Colne station, with entry points to sidings on the Up side of the line. **Earls Colne** station – 53 miles 67 chains from Liverpool Street and 3 miles 36 chains from Chappel Junction with its 360 feet long platform on the Down side of the line east of the level crossing – was originally opened as Ford Gate in 1882 but was then renamed Colne in 1889. The original buildings were constructed of timber and consisted solely of a shed containing the booking office and waiting room. A timber building near the signal box served as a ladies' waiting room. Later a new structure containing the ladies' waiting room and fronted by a canopy over the platform was located at the east end of the platform adjacent to the signal box. In 1903 Reuben Hunt of Earls Colne, who provided much traffic to the railway from his nearby engineering works, was dismayed at the unkempt structure that presented itself to clients arriving by train. He offered the CV&HR the necessary land for an enlarged station and advanced an amount of money at 4½ per cent interest to enable the rebuilding. The new brick structure of modern design was duly provided and in 1905 the station was renamed Earls Colne to avoid

confusion with Colne in Lancashire, Calne in Wiltshire and other stations. When Elyot Hawkins was asked why Colne station was renamed Earls Colne, he responded '*it was time for this to be done after we had received, amongst other things, a cab intended for Colne in Lancashire together with boxes of bullion for the same town and a truck load of pigs for Calne in Wiltshire on the Great Western Railway*'. Earls Colne station house was occupied by Station Master George Evans and his family in 1924, for which he paid £17 5s 4d annual rental. He gave up residency on 29th February 1924 when the rental was taken up by Christopher Sparrow who was forced to pay an increased rental of £26 0s 0d from 8th November 1924.

The goods yard on the Up side of the railway was extensive and consisted of an 800 feet loop line running parallel with the main single line. At the Halstead end of the loop and west of the level crossing was a 100 feet headshunt and from the loop the 500 feet long shed road served the 60 feet by 40 feet goods shed. From the shed loop a 420 feet connection led to the back road loop 320 feet in length which in turn accessed the 300 feet reception siding at the east end of the yard. At the west end of the back road loop was the 320 feet long coal road. Road vehicle entrance to the yard was from the lane crossing the railway. Points and signals were controlled from Ford Gate, later Earls Colne, signal box, initially from 1882 containing an 11-lever frame but enlarged with a new 26-lever frame in 1889 to cater for the increasing size of the goods yard.

Away from Earls Colne the railway bisected the Station level crossing No. 11 at 53 miles 69 chains and continued on a slight left-hand curve climbing at 1 in 660 to cross the River Colne by White's No. 1 underbridge No. 6 at 53 miles 79 chains, White's (Continued on p. 125)

Ford Gate station, later Colne, and from 1905 Earls Colne; constructed in 1880 but not opened until 1882, showing the relatively short platform on the Down side of the main single line with a simple timber booking office and waiting shelter. The signal box, provided by MeKenzie & Holland, originally containing an 11-lever frame, stands beyond the end of the platform. Beyond the signal box is the Down home signal and on the opposite side of the line the small goods yard entered by trailing points in the Down direction. An equestrian waits patiently at the very narrow level crossing gates guarding the country lane. Three oil lamps provide illumination during the hours of darkness.

M. Root collection

The level crossing at Ford Gate station circa 1880 with the unmade track connecting Colne Engaine, ½ mile north of the railway, to Earls Colne, ¾ mile to the south of the line. The station is to the right of the rudimentary gates. Poor drainage caused the CV&HR constant problems in the early years until ballasting was improved.   *M. Root collection*

The original Ford Gate station buildings prior to demolition in 1903 as the end of the newly completed Colne station building can be seen top left. The sign above the door reads 'George Evans – Collector'. Evans, standing on the edge of the platform, became a clerk on the CV&HR after leaving school. He was station master at Colne before it closed in 1889, when he transferred to Ford Gate. He retired in 1926 at the age of 70 having completed fifty years as station master.   *Author's collection*

A Down train hauled by one of the CV&HR 2-4-2Ts entering Earls Colne station. The ornate station master's house backs on to the platform, which still accommodates the original wooden building advertising Sutton's Seeds. The level crossing in the foreground was later repositioned further from the signal box to permit the extension of the platform. *Author's collection*

Earls Colne station 3 miles 36 chains from Chappel Junction looking towards Chappel circa 1908, with the goods yard and goods shed to the left. The platform of sub-standard height is in the foreground and the extension containing the new waiting area fronted by an awning is next the signal box. *Author's collection*

Earls Colne station with the 360 feet long platform on the Down side of the line with **L&NER** notice boards in situ. To the right are the station offices and in the background the station master's house. Beyond the canopy fronting the waiting room is the signal box, and at the end of the platform the lower quadrant Up starting signal. The gates of level crossing No. 11 span the main single line and the goods loop, the latter with access points to the goods yard.

L&NER

Earls Colne 53 miles 67 chains from Liverpool Street, facing Haverhill showing the wide level crossing gates built to accommodate the goods loop. The station was closed to passenger on and from 1st January 1962 and to goods traffic on and from 28th December 1964.

Author's collection

RIGHT: The new Earls Colne station, of modern appearance, was built in 1905 after Reuben Hunt, a local entrepreneur, offered land to the railway company to improve facilities. This view shows the road frontage with booking hall and booking office to the left and station master's house to the right. *Author's collection*

ABOVE: Road approach to Earls Colne station on 16th April 1947 with station master's house to the right and station buildings to the left. The rural setting is evident as the village of Earls Colne was located a mile to the south and Colne Engaine, three-quarters of the mile to the north of the railway. Note the L&NER delivery lorry on the left. *L&NER*

RIGHT: Earls Colne station buildings to the left and station master's house to the right. *J. Watling*

Earls Colne goods shed located in the goods yard on the Up side of the line was constructed of timber and corrugated iron with a brick goods office alongside. A selection of open wagons awaits unloading on the 500 feet shed road.   *M. Root collection*

Earls Colne goods yard with two open wagons occupying the 500 feet shed road with another open wagon in the goods shed. The main single line to the right is paralleled by the 800 feet goods loop.   *J. Watling*

View from Earls Colne station looking towards Chappel with the main single line serving the platform and the goods loop running parallel. The connection on the left from the goods loop leads to the shed road. The waiting room with ornate canopy shields the signal box from view.   *J. Watling*

Facing west from Earls Colne station platform with the level crossing gates spanning the main single line and the parallel goods loop. The lower quadrant Down starting signal is at the end of the platform and beyond the gates the Up home signal.   *J. Watling*

Langley Mill level crossing No. 16, at 54 miles 53¾ chains circa 1880 with the basic timber cottage provided for the resident crossing keeper by the CV&HR. This view facing south shows the adjacent River Colne has burst its banks and flooded the surrounding land.   *M. Root collection*

Parsonage Lane level crossing No. 22 at 55 miles 78 chains from Liverpool Street with the attendant crossing keeper's cottage and signal box in this 1947 view facing towards Haverhill. This was the second signal box provided, the original having been destroyed by a locomotive in 1899. Four signals were operated from the signal box, which was later replaced by a ground frame located near the gates, the barriers being hand operated. The crossing cottage was provided by the L&NER in 1929 and built by J.W. Trudgett for £485.

Author's collection

(Continued from p. 117)

footpath crossing No. 12 at 54 miles 03 chains and White's No. 2 underbridge No. 7 at 54 miles 04 chains in quick succession. The railway then negotiated a 40-chain right-hand curve over occupation crossing No. 13 at 54 miles 07½ chains before bisecting Munn's occupational crossing No. 14 at 54 miles 21 chains as the line continued on the curve. Towards the top of the rise the line then followed a short straight section bisecting Elms Hall occupational crossing No. 15 at 54 miles 40 chains, after which the railway levelled out with Elms Hall on the Up side, where the cutting of the first sod of earth was enacted to inaugurate the railway. A short 1 in 85 climb followed, taking the railway over Langley Mill public level crossing No. 16 at 54 miles 53¾ chains, equipped with a 3-lever ground frame. The crossing cottage on the Down side of the railway was leased by the CV&HR company from the Courtauld family and in 1924 was occupied by platelayer Charles Copping rent free in return for he and his wife opening and closing the gates for the passage of trains.

From Langley Mill crossing the line continued climbing at 1 in 80 on a slight left-hand curve with the River Colne on the Up side until just before occupational crossing No. 17 at 54 miles 71 chains, where the gradient eased to 1 in 1,352 which continued as the railway bisected two occupational and footpath crossings in quick succession – No. 18 at 55 miles 08¾ chains and No. 19 at 55 miles 12

chains. Beyond the crossings the line climbed at 1 in 72 to cross Blue Bridge No. 8 at 55 miles 27 chains; it then descended at 1 in 97 over the River Colne by Blue Bridge Water No. 9 at 55 miles 37 chains to a short level section before curving to the right, bisecting occupational crossings No's 20 and 21 at 55 miles 46½ chains and 55 miles 67 chains respectively. A short level section brought the railway to Parsons or Parsonage Lane level crossing No. 22 at 55 miles 78 chains on the eastern extremity of the town of Halstead, guarded for many years by a 25 feet high signal box with a 4-lever frame controlling only the signals, the gates being hand operated. To enable the crossing keeper at Parsonage Lane level crossing to open his gates for the passage of a train, the signalman at Halstead sent the following bell signals when services were due:

Train leaving Colne	2 beats consecutively
Train arriving at Halstead from Hedingham	3 beats consecutively
Train leaving Halstead for Colne	4 beats consecutively

Whilst the cancelling signal was 8 beats, sent as 3 pause 5. The signalman at Parsons Lane was required to repeat the beats to show they were correctly received.

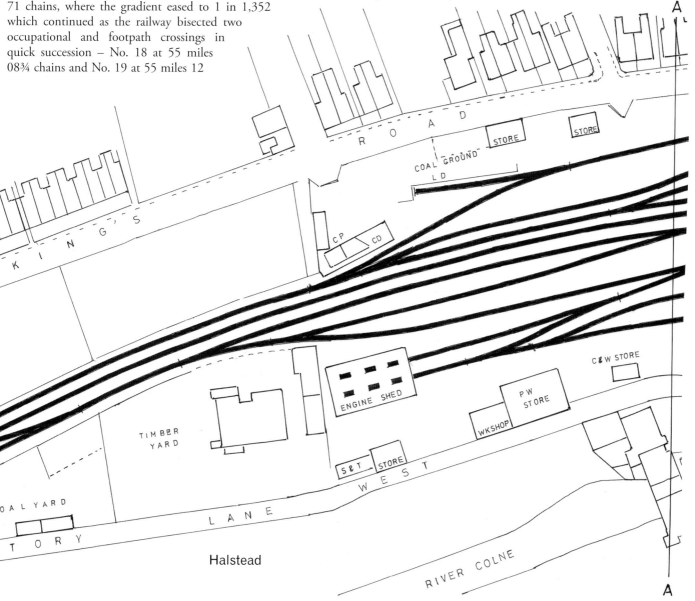

Halstead

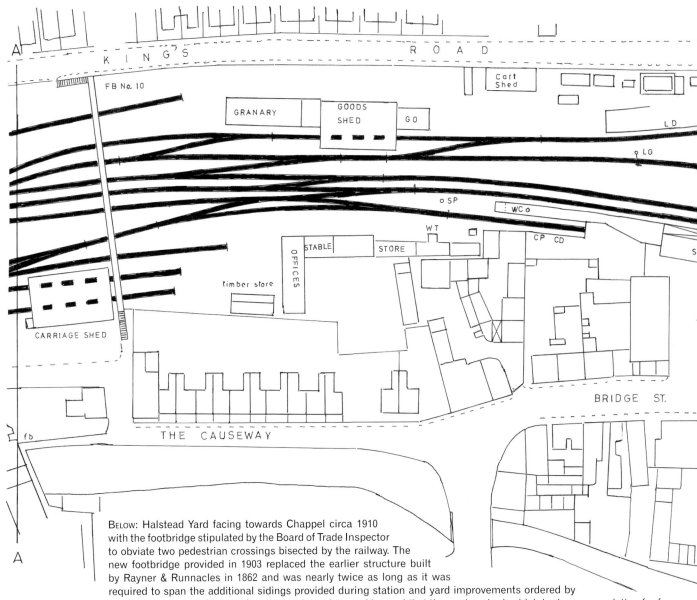

KING'S ROAD

FB No. 10

GRANARY

GOODS SHED

GO

Cart Shed

LD

LG

CARRIAGE SHED

timber store

OFFICES

STABLE

STORE

WT

WC

SP

CP CD

THE CAUSEWAY

BRIDGE ST.

fb

A

A

BELOW: Halstead Yard facing towards Chappel circa 1910 with the footbridge stipulated by the Board of Trade Inspector to obviate two pedestrian crossings bisected by the railway. The new footbridge provided in 1903 replaced the earlier structure built by Rayner & Runnacles in 1862 and was nearly twice as long as it was required to span the additional sidings provided during station and yard improvements ordered by George Copus and completed in 1905/6. On the left is the carriage shop and beyond that the engine shed, which had accommodation for four locomotives. To the right are the coal wharf sidings tenanted by Moy's of Colchester, occupied by a row of private owner wagons. The signal beyond the bridge has Parsonage Lane Up distant and Halstead Down home signals sharing the same post. *Author's collection*

From Parsonage Lane level crossing the line climbed at 1 in 1,959, curving to the right on a 55 chains curve through the plethora of sidings on each side of the railway to pass under the impressive public footbridge No. 10 at 56 miles 17 chains and into **Halstead** station, 56 miles 26 chains from Liverpool Street and 5 miles 75 chains from Chappel Junction, where the permanent structure was constructed soon after the opening of the line. Halstead was described in the GER guide of 1865 as having *'the spirit to carry on its own railway'*.

As befitted the headquarters of the CV&HR, the track layout was extensive with the main single line threading the tracks and serving the 340 feet single platform on the Up side of the single main line south of the Trinity Street level crossing. The canopy fronting the station buildings and providing protection for waiting passengers on the platform was reconstructed in 1914. The station building was constructed of fine red brick with slate roof, erected during station reconstruction when Copus was in office. The former general offices, built in red brick with slate roof, were constructed on the Up side of the line immediately east of the station at the same time. Opposite the station platform and alongside Trinity Street crossing on the Down side of the line was Halstead signal box, which contained a 36-lever frame for operating the signals and points at the station as well as a wheel controlling the crossing gates.

The large number of sidings, enhanced in the early 1900s when Copus was General Manager, were necessary for the railway dealt with traffic from Coutauld's silk mills, Portway's foundry, Clover Limited millers, Hugh Brown & Company tannery and Newman & Clarke's granary. On the Down side the front yard road and back yard road serving the loading dock near the Trinity Street yard entrance were 400 and 330 feet in length respectively. The latter led to the 240 feet shed road entering the 80 feet by 50 feet goods shed built in red brick in 1892 as a replacement for an earlier corrugated iron structure. Alongside the shed was the 100 feet by 40 feet granary and stables for the three horses employed for cartage and shunting. The shed road continued to connect with the Down loop which ran parallel to the main single line running from just west of Parsonage Lane crossing to bisect Trinity Street crossing before it reconnected to the main single line. From this loop east of the goods shed a connection led to the 460 feet back road siding, which ran parallel to the adjacent King's Road, where there was a public entrance to the goods yard near Moy's coal yard. At the Chappel end of back road a connection served the 110 feet cattle dock road. A 10-lever ground frame was provided to control certain points at the east end of the yard, released by Annett's key from the signal box. The L&NER later reduced this to 3 levers released by the Electric Train Staff.

On the Up side west of Trinity Street level crossing was the Tortoise Works siding, 180 feet in length with the 200 feet connection from the main single line. Behind the station platform was the water or tank road, 130 feet in length, used for vehicles providing supplies to the water tank. From here a 580 feet loop siding ran parallel to the main line and off

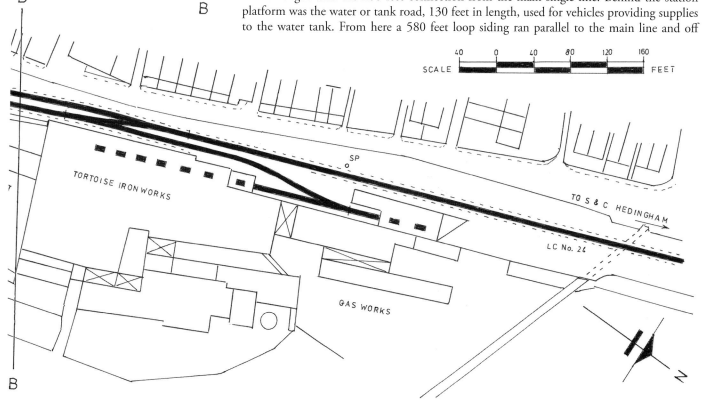

MAIN PICTURE: Halstead station, 5 miles 75 chains from Chappel Junction and 56 miles 26 chains ex Liverpool Street, circa 1880, facing northwest with the original goods shed to the left and cattle wagons occupying the dock road near the Trinity Street goods yard entrance. The signalling is primitive and stop signals for both directions of travel are mounted on the same post by the level crossing. To the right is the tank house with water tank aloft to provide supplies to the water columns located at each end of the platform. The poor condition of the permanent way is much in evidence with short length rails and sub-standard ballast.

M. Root collection

INSET: Panoramic view of Halstead with the goods shed to the left served by the 240 feet shed road. CV&HR 0-6-2T No. 5 is taking the spur to the Down loop. In the background is the station with the platform on the Up side of the railway. To the right are tank sidings and beyond that the railway general offices.

Author's collection

An aerial view of Halstead station with the goods shed and goods office to the left and the granary in the foreground. The company general offices are in the right background and beyond that the stables, joiner's shop and stores. Kings Road is running alongside the railway with Trinity Street beyond the signal box. The loading dock is in the background.

The CV&HR general offices and headquarters on the Up side of the railway on 16th April 1947. In the foreground from left to right are the Down goods loop, main single line and the Up goods loop. The Lassen & Hjort water softener still stands beside the water tank. Note the close proximity of Parsonage Lane crossing Up distant signal (just in view). *L&NER*

this were connections to the carriage and wagon repair shops where sidings 1 and 2 were 245 and 280 feet in length respectively. Directly opposite, two sidings, 260 feet and 155 feet, served the 110 feet by 60 feet engine shed and locomotive repair shop. The engine shed closed in 1928 when locomotives were transferred to Haverhill shed, although the building existed until 1951. At the east end of the loop was the 120 feet coal siding used by Halstead Co-operative Society. The points of Halstead coal yard siding were locked by Annett's key attached to the Train Staff.

Water supplies for locomotives was drawn from a deep well located in front of the station master's office, and was the company's own water supply. Hardness of water playing havoc with locomotive boilers forced the company to invest in a water softener from Lassen

& Hjort, erected and completed in 1916, but the facility was only used for just over a decade for the locomotive shed closed in 1928.

Leaving Halstead, the single track railway passed over Trinity Street by level crossing No. 23 at 56 miles 28 chains and the Tortoise Iron Works and its attendant siding on the Up side before bisecting occupational crossing No. 24 at 56 miles 38 chains, where a 10 mph speed limit was imposed. The line then climbed at 1 in 475, curving to the right following a north/north-westerly direction over level crossings No. 25 at 56 miles 55 chains and No. 26 at 56 miles 59¼ chains in quick succession. Beyond the 56¾ mile post the climb continued on a slight left-hand curve over occupational crossing No. 27 at 56 miles 77 chains before passing under Hepworth No. 1

(Continued on p. 139)

ABOVE: Halstead station, 5 miles 75 chains from Chappel Junction, facing towards Haverhill with the signal box guarding Trinity Street level crossing located opposite the platform. The tall Down starting signal protecting the level crossing towers above the Up starting signal in the foreground. *Author's collection*

RIGHT: Halstead station with the single 340 feet long platform on the Up side of the railway and beyond that Trinity Street level crossing and Halstead signal box. The CV&HR proposed a second platform alongside the goods loop on the left and opposite the established platform so as to create a passing place for passenger trains but traffic density did not justify the outlay and the scheme was aborted.
Author's collection

Halstead station 56 miles 26 chains from Liverpool Street from the level crossing facing towards Chappel with the main single line serving the 340 feet long platform, and the Down goods loop running parallel. At the time this view was taken in 1953 the Up starting signal at the end of the platform had been shortened and an upper quadrant arm fitted. *J. Watling*

Road approach to Halstead station on 16th April 1947. The building was constructed by Rayner & Runnacles at a cost of £2,730 in 1862 as a replacement for the temporary accommodation provided when the station first opened to traffic. *L&NER*

ABOVE: Halstead station, 56 miles 26 chains from Liverpool Street, on 16th April 1947 facing towards Haverhill with the signal box and Trinity Street level crossing to the left. The platform had been rebuilt to a standard level incorporating the original canopy fronting the station building. To the right the station still possesses its original CV&HR nameboard, whilst the Down starting signal stands sentinel at the far end of the platform. *L&NER*

LEFT: Close up of the door to the booking office at Halstead station in 1965, with the elliptical arches over the windows more akin to that of a church building.
J. Watling

BELOW: Halstead station facing towards Sible and Castle Hedingham, with Down goods loop in the foreground.
Author's collection

Halstead station facing towards Chappel from Trinity Street level crossing seen in BR days. This view shows the very narrow upright columns supporting the canopy.

J. Watling

The tank house complete with water tank aloft at Halstead together with the associated workshop. The tank supplied locomotive water columns located at each end of the station platform.

J. Watling

RIGHT: The granary and goods shed at Halstead located on the Down or west side of the railway. During World War Two, items of galvanised equipment intended for the Liverpool Street to Shenfield electrification were stored in both buildings; the smaller items being delivered by road and larger artefacts by rail. It was as a result of the equipment being stored that the electrification programme was completed soon after hostilities in 1947. *M. Root collection*

LEFT: The original Halstead goods shed dating from 1860 viewed from the yard with the small timber office, already connected to the telegraph circuit, added at a later date. The long building alongside was a corn store. The entrance to the yard is rutted and littered with the remnants of discarded agricultural debris.

RIGHT: The new Halstead goods shed circa 1900 with goods office, which contained an attic and basement alongside. A new brick granary is in the course of construction to the left. In the foreground is the Up starting signal together with a subsidiary arm for authorising movements into the Up side yard. Note the support wheels for overhead signal wires to obviate groundwork under points and crossings. This system was quickly replaced by the L&NER at Grouping. *Author's collection*

The deserted yard at Halstead in 1965 with the goods shed and goods office to the right with the houses in King's Road beyond. Footbridge No. 10 spans the tracks.
J. Wading

The construction of Newman's grain silo at Halstead in 1949. The building work required the blockage of two sidings on the Up side of the railway but in recompense the firm provided much incoming and out going traffic which continued until the withdrawal of freight facilities in 1965. *M. Root collection*

LEFT: Halstead signal box and the entrance to the goods yard from Trinity Street on 30th December 1961. The structure has a worn down condition and was subsequently abolished in October 1962. *R. Powell*

BELOW: Halstead station from the east early in 1965 just before closure to all traffic on and from 19th April 1965. To the right are the former CV&HR company offices. At this period all points were hand operated. *J. Warling*

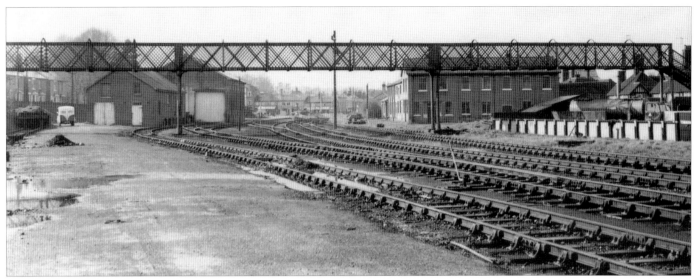

ABOVE: Devoid of all traffic, Halstead goods yard facing towards Haverhill in 1965 shows the footbridge spanning all lines. To the left are the goods shed and granary and on the right the former CV&HR general offices.
J. Wading

LEFT: Halstead station in a forlorn condition early in 1965 with the former Down goods loop now truncated at buffer stops. In the distance footbridge No. 10 still spans the yard whilst the goods shed is to the right. *J. Watling*

BELOW: Halstead station having lost its passenger service on and from 1st January 1962 has a forlorn look on 12th April 1964. The ornate loading gauge, which would continue to serve a purpose for another year, partially blocks the view of the Corn Exchange. *R. Powell*

The remains of the 2-road engine shed at Halstead after demolition of the building, looking towards the station. The shed was noted for the deep inspection pits between the tracks which were prone to flooding after heavy rain.
The late W.A. Camwell

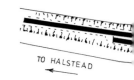

TO HALSTEAD

LEFT: Halstead goods yard looking from the footbridge towards Parsonage Lane crossing on 12th April 1964. To the left is Newman & Clark's granary whilst a rake of 16-ton all-steel mineral wagons stand in the Down yard waiting for the coal to be unloaded.
R. Powell

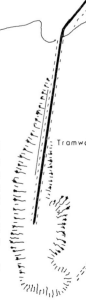

LEFT: A lone 16-ton all-steel mineral wagon stands astride the points leading from the Up goods loop to the main single line a few days before closure of the line to all traffic. The Down goods loop in the foreground has a connection leading to Newman & Clark's granary.
J. Wading

(Continued from p. 131)

overbridge at 57 miles 23 chains. The gradient then altered to 1 in 285 rising as the single line, following a 35 chains right-hand curve, ran close to the waterway before crossing the River Colne and the attendant occupational path by Hepworth No. 2 underbridge No. 12 at 57 miles 41 chains and attendant level crossings No's 28 and 29. A quarter of a mile beyond the structure the gradient levelled out on a straight section to cross occupational crossing No. 30 at 57 miles 60¾ chains; soon after the 58 mile post the line climbed a short 1 in 248 over Wallace occupational crossing No. 31 at 58 miles 06¼ chains. The line curved slightly to the left before a level section took the railway over occupational crossing No. 32 at 58 miles 30 chains and then under the Halstead to Hedingham road by Purlshill overbridge No. 13 at 58 miles 35 chains. After the half mile post the line climbed a short 1 in 198 on a straight section before falling at 1 in 385 curving to the left and then rising at 1 in 605 to the junction points for **Brickworks** siding at 58 miles 72 chains. These trailing points for trains in the Down direction were locked and released from a 5-lever covered ground frame by Annett's key on the Train Staff, later 2 levers released by Electric Key Token, and connected with a 1,200 feet siding which ran parallel on the Up side of the main single line.

The 500 feet siding serving **Purls Hill** and **Hedingham brickworks** was located on the Up side of the line with connections curving away before entering the brickyards. At Hedingham

Brickyard siding engines were prohibited from passing the notice board on the approach to the yard. A 750 feet narrow gauge tramway was also used to convey bricks to a loading dock by the siding.

Just before the 59 mile post the railway straightened out and bisected occupational crossing No. 33 before passing under Alderford overbridge No. 14 at 59 miles 03 chains on a straight and level section. The line then climbed on an embankment at 1 in 222 over the River Colne on Hedingham bridge No. 15 at the 59¼ mile post before negotiating a 42 chains right-hand curve and passing over Hedingham station level crossing No. 34 at 59 miles 40 chains and on a 1 in 660 falling gradient entered **Sible and Castle Hedingham** station, 59 miles 50 chains from Liverpool Street and 9 miles 19 chains from Chappel Junction. The station was known simply as Castle Hedingham until September 1867 when it received the full title.

The 440 feet long platform at Sible and Castle Hedingham was located on the Down side of the line and was host to the simple brick building containing booking office, waiting room and staff room. At the back of the platform was the goods shed and signal box containing a 25-lever frame controlling points and signals at the station, although the points of the station yard were locked by Annett's key attached to the Train Staff. An 800 feet run-round loop was located on the Up side and ran parallel to the main single line, with a 205 feet headshunt at the Haverhill end. From this loop road a 430 feet siding entered by facing points in the Down direction

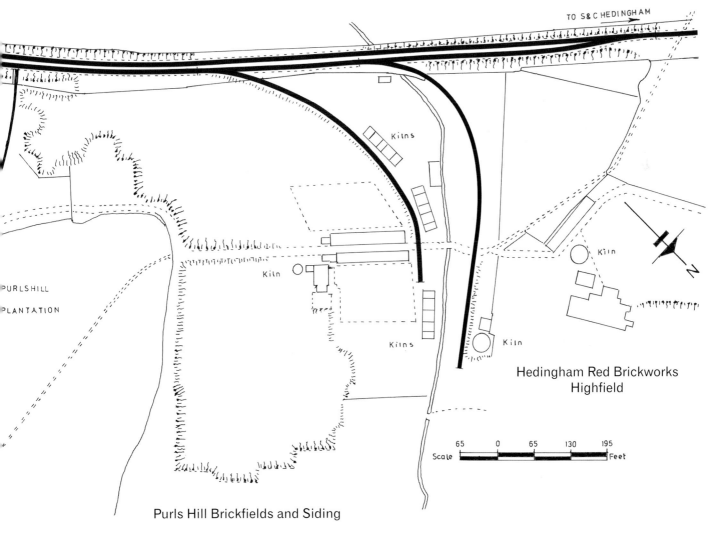

Purls Hill Brickfields and Siding

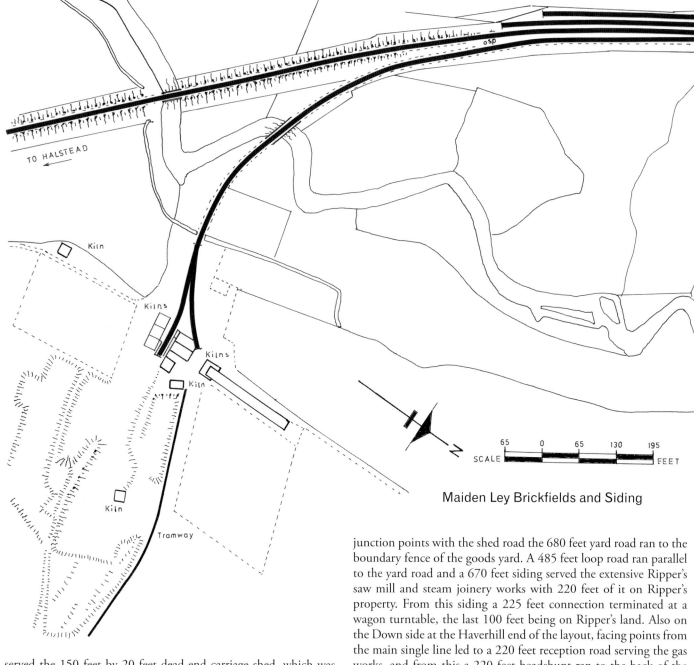

Maiden Ley Brickfields and Siding

served the 150 feet by 20 feet dead-end carriage shed, which was later removed. **Maiden Ley brickworks** was also served by facing points in the Up direction, diverging from the 450 feet long siding beside the loop road. The brickworks main siding 540 feet in length curved to the north east of the railway and had a 130 feet spur serving the kilns. No engine was permitted beyond the boundary gate at the limit of the property siding. The siding was disused by the late 1940s and a track over the river bridge in a dilapidated condition. At one time it was the intention of making the station a passing place on the single line but traffic density was so light that the plan was abandoned. The remains of an intended platform on the Up side of the loop road then became the site of cattle pens and cattle loading dock.

On the Down side the 380 feet shed road served the 65 feet by 30 feet goods shed located at the back of the platform whilst from the

junction points with the shed road the 680 feet yard road ran to the boundary fence of the goods yard. A 485 feet loop road ran parallel to the yard road and a 670 feet siding served the extensive Ripper's saw mill and steam joinery works with 220 feet of it on Ripper's property. From this siding a 225 feet connection terminated at a wagon turntable, the last 100 feet being on Ripper's land. Also on the Down side at the Haverhill end of the layout, facing points from the main single line led to a 220 feet reception road serving the gas works, and from this a 220 feet headshunt ran to the back of the passenger platform. Sible and Castle Hedingham yard possessed a wagon turntable for some years but it was later removed.

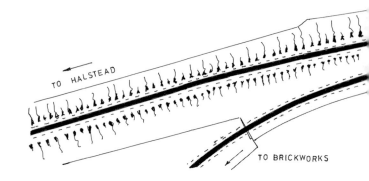

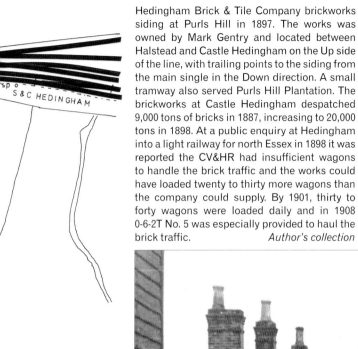

Hedingham Brick & Tile Company brickworks siding at Purls Hill in 1897. The works was owned by Mark Gentry and located between Halstead and Castle Hedingham on the Up side of the line, with trailing points to the siding from the main single in the Down direction. A small tramway also served Purls Hill Plantation. The brickworks at Castle Hedingham despatched 9,000 tons of bricks in 1887, increasing to 20,000 tons in 1898. At a public enquiry at Hedingham into a light railway for north Essex in 1898 it was reported the CV&HR had insufficient wagons to handle the brick traffic and the works could have loaded twenty to thirty more wagons than the company could supply. By 1901, thirty to forty wagons were loaded daily and in 1908 0-6-2T No. 5 was especially provided to haul the brick traffic. *Author's collection*

Sible and Castle Hedingham station from the 440 feet long platform facing towards Haverhill.
Author's collection

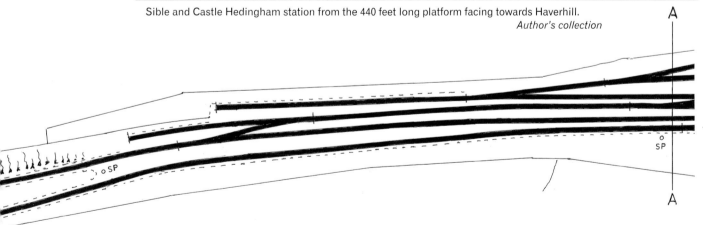

On leaving Sible and Castle Hedingham the line gently curved to the left over Gas Works occupation crossing No. 35 at 59 miles 52¾ chains and climbed a short 1 in 110 to the 59¾ milepost before falling at 1 in 121 over Castle underbridge No. 16 at 59 miles 62 chains where the Sible Hedingham to Castle Hedingham road passed under the railway. The line continued climbing at 1 in

1,122 past the 60 milepost before bisecting Nunnery occupational and towpath crossing No. 36 at 60 miles 03½ chains and Nunnery Bridge No. 1, No. 17 across the River Colne at 60 mile 04 chains. Short inclines of 1 in 99 and 1 in 330 on a left-hand curve brought the line over Nunnery Bridge No. 2, No. 18 at 60 miles 16 chains *(Continued on p. 149)*

Sible and Castle Hedingham

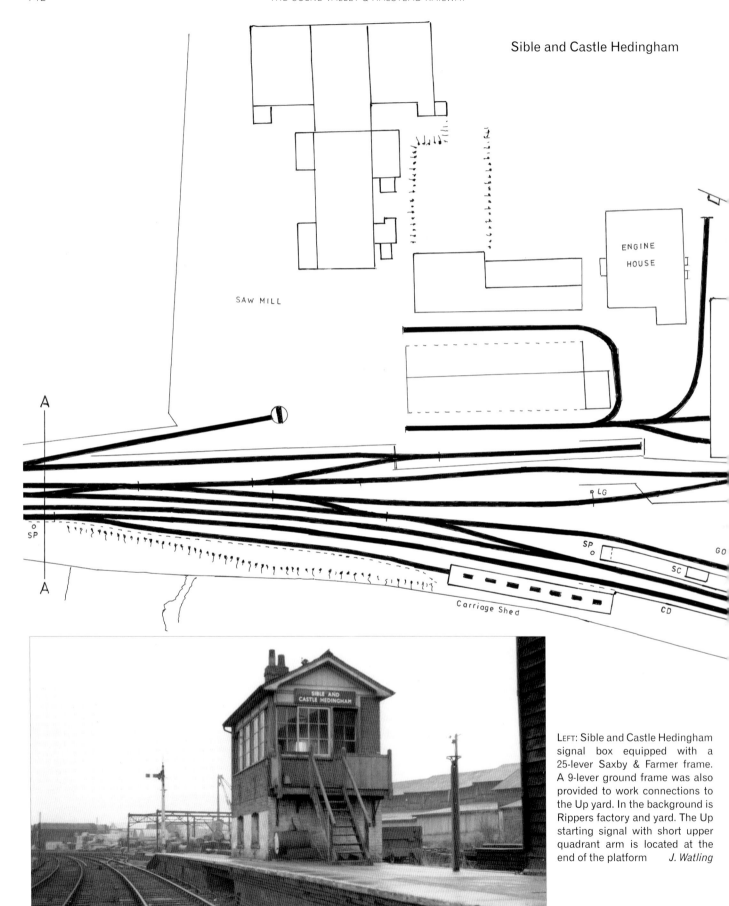

SAW MILL

ENGINE HOUSE

A

A

Carriage Shed

LEFT: Sible and Castle Hedingham signal box equipped with a 25-lever Saxby & Farmer frame. A 9-lever ground frame was also provided to work connections to the Up yard. In the background is Rippers factory and yard. The Up starting signal with short upper quadrant arm is located at the end of the platform   *J. Watling*

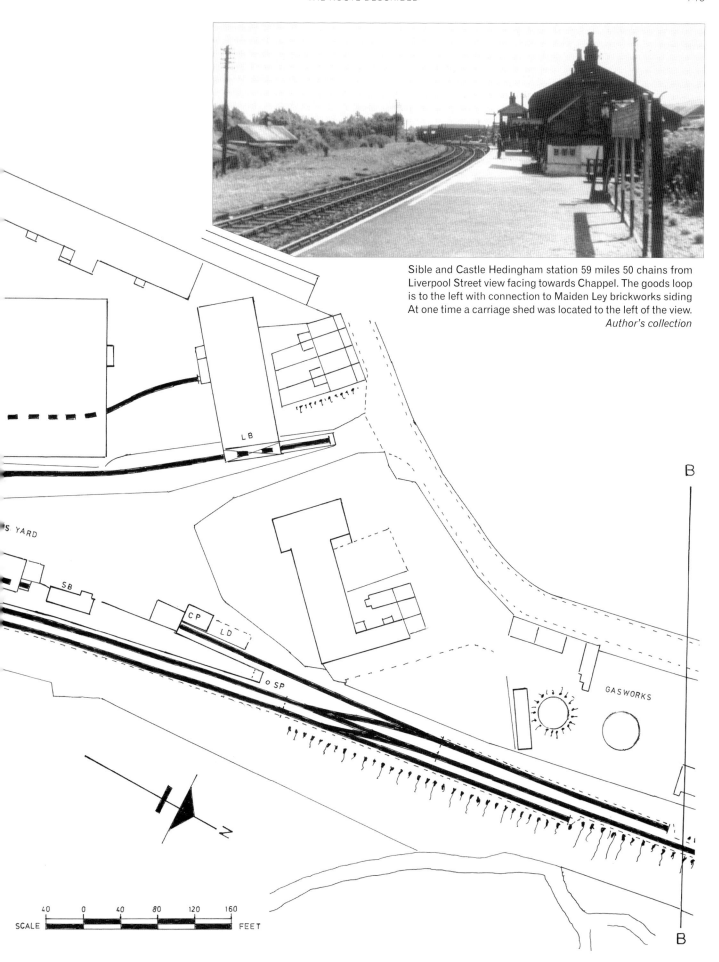

Sible and Castle Hedingham station 59 miles 50 chains from Liverpool Street view facing towards Chappel. The goods loop is to the left with connection to Maiden Ley brickworks siding At one time a carriage shed was located to the left of the view.
Author's collection

LB

S YARD

SB

CP

LD

o SP

GASWORKS

B

B

N

SCALE   40   0   40   80   120   160   FEET

Castle Hedingham station, 9 miles 19 chains from Chappel Junction, circa 1880 facing towards Haverhill with the main line rising at 1 in 110 to clear Castle underbridge No. 16. To the left is the goods shed displaying the advertisement for Hedingham Brick, Tile and Terra Cotta Works, then the station building containing booking office, waiting and staff rooms. The low platform on the Down side of the railway is extremely short and was later raised and lengthened to 440 feet. The parallel goods loop serves the remains of a platform for it was planned to provide a crossing loop to permit passengers trains to pass but work was not fully completed and the idea abandoned. The slotted stop signals with arms for each direction of travel mounted on the same post were operated by windlass from the platform; the spectacles at a lower level displaying three aspects, red for danger, green for caution and white for line clear. The short siding beyond the platform occupied by a wagon was later extended to form a headshunt to serve the gas works siding at the back of the platform. The Hedingham Brick, Tile and Terra Cotta Works as well as Maiden Ley and Purls Hill brickworks were served by sidings on the Up side of the line whilst Rayner's Joinery works occupying the land west of the station provided much traffic for the railway.

M. Root collection

RIGHT: Castle underbridge No. 16 at 59 miles 62 chains spanning the Sudbury to Sible Hedingham road just north of Sible and Castle Hedingham station.
J. Watling

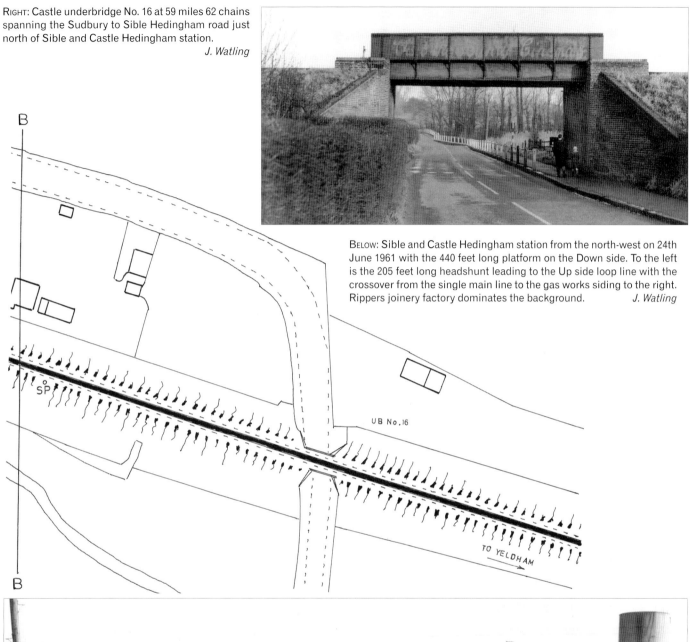

B

BELOW: Sible and Castle Hedingham station from the north-west on 24th June 1961 with the 440 feet long platform on the Down side. To the left is the 205 feet long headshunt leading to the Up side loop line with the crossover from the single main line to the gas works siding to the right. Rippers joinery factory dominates the background.
J. Watling

SP

UB No.16

TO YELDHAM

B

Sible and Castle Hedingham station, 9 miles 19 chains from Chappel Junction, viewed facing Haverhill with the goods shed at the rear of the 440 feet long platform. The goods loop line is to the right and Rippers Joinery Works in the left background. The station was originally called Castle Hedingham but was renamed in October 1907.   *Author's collection*

A close up view of Sible and Castle Hedingham station building in the 1920s. It was identical to the building at White Colne until it was extended in 1908. Both were built of off-white Suffolk stock blocks manufactured in Sudbury, which were larger than the standard bricks, with red brick dressings and tile roof. A selection of enamelled advertisements for Foster Clark's Cream Custard, K Shoes, Venn's Cough Cure and Bryant & May's matches (*'Support Home Industries, Employ British Labour'*) adorn the station. A reminder of the company's desire to expand is evident by the L&NWR signboard. Platform seats exhibit the station name.   *M. Root collection*

Exterior of Sible and Castle Hedingham station on 16th April 1947; unusually it had no access from the road, prospective passengers having to go on to the platform to enter the booking office. The building has now been relocated and re-erected at the nearby Colne Valley Railway preservation site.   *L&NER*

Sible and Castle Hedingham station, 59 miles 50 chains from Liverpool Street, looking towards Haverhill on 16th April 1947. The station was originally called Hedingham, then Castle Hedingham, but was renamed with is full title in September 1867. The station building, similar to that provided at Colne, with small canopy over the main entrance, contained booking office, waiting rooms and toilets, and staff rooms The platform on the Down side was served by the main single line with the goods loop running parallel on the Up side.   *L&NER*

Sible and Castle Hedingham station on 16th April 1947 with a Down train hauled by a 'J15' Class 0-6-0 entering the 440 feet long platform. Beyond the station building is the goods shed and to the left the signal box. The company planned at one stage to provide a crossing loop with a platform on the Up side but the scheme was deferred and only a goods loop installed. Ripper's premises overshadow the station.   *L&NER*

Sible and Castle Hedingham station building with small canopy over the exit from the booking hall. View facing towards Haverhill on 30th December 1961.
J. Watling

LEFT: Sible and Castle Hedingham station located on the Down side of the main single line facing Halstead with Rippers Joinery prominent in the background.
Author's collection

ABOVE: Road frontage to Sible and Castle Hedingham station, complete with tall chimneys on 24th June 1961. The building has since been removed and reconstructed at the Colne Valley Railway preservation site just north of the former station site.
J. Wading

LEFT: Road frontage of Sible and Castle Hedingham goods shed.
J. Watling

(Continued from p. 141)

over Nunnery Street, before a short descent of 1 in 139 for a quarter mile past the 60¼ milepost and occupation crossing No. 37 led to a climb of 1 in 145 as the line negotiated a 38 chains left-hand curve. This took the railway over occupational crossing No. 38 at 60 miles 44 chains on a straight section and then over Apple Dumpling underbridge No. 19 at 60 miles 47 chains. After the bridge a short rise of 1 in 88/125 on straight track took the line past Newmans'

Hill on the Down side and over occupational crossing No. 39 at 60 miles 59 chains as the railway swung on a 30 chains left-hand curve; the climb then eased to a rising 1 in 330 over Yeldham Road underbridge No. 20 at 60 miles 78 chains. The climb continued at 1 in 240/130 round a 35 chains right-hand curve to Duckett's Hill occupational crossing No. 40 at 61 miles 23½ chains, after which the gradient eased to 1 in 269 passing the half mile post and over a short level section. Swinging right on a 38 chains radius

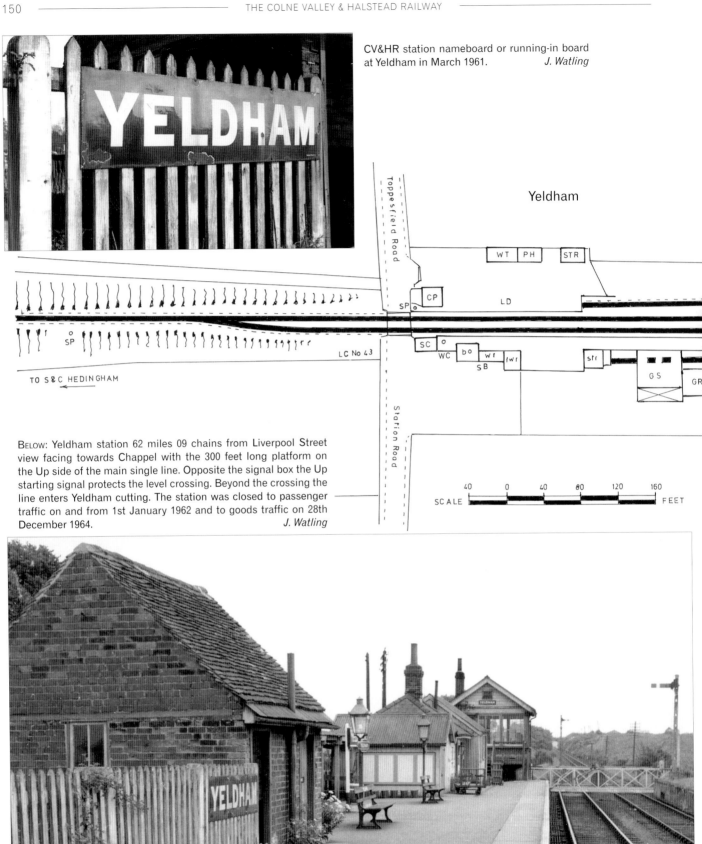

CV&HR station nameboard or running-in board at Yeldham in March 1961. *J. Watling*

BELOW: Yeldham station 62 miles 09 chains from Liverpool Street view facing towards Chappel with the 300 feet long platform on the Up side of the main single line. Opposite the signal box the Up starting signal protects the level crossing. Beyond the crossing the line enters Yeldham cutting. The station was closed to passenger traffic on and from 1st January 1962 and to goods traffic on 28th December 1964. *J. Watling*

Yeldham station, 11 miles 58 chains from Chappel Junction, facing towards Haverhill in 1875. The through main line serving the platform on the Up side is to the right. The station was originally planned as a crossing place with a passing loop for passenger trains but this was never installed. Note the water columns at each end of the platform and the cattle pens alongside the siding to the left. The cattle wagon has gates in position having just been loaded. Toppesfield Road, which bisected the railway at the level crossing, is but a country lane.

Author's collection

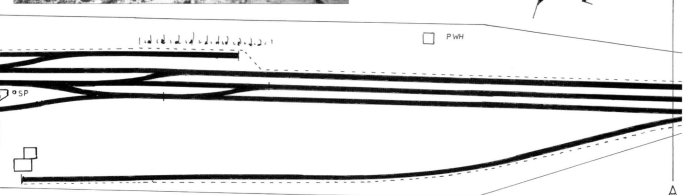

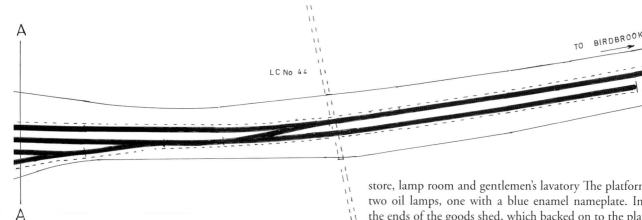

curve the railway bisected occupational level crossing No. 41 at 61 miles 44 chains at Pool Street and then entered a cutting to pass under Yeldham Cutting overbridge No. 21 at 61 miles 59 chains on a rising 1 in 220 gradient. The line then descended at 1 in 264, passing over White Hart Culvert underbridge No. 22 at 61 miles 79 chains and a rising 1 in 281 brought the line over occupational and river towpath crossing No. 42 at 62 miles 01 chains, then Yeldham station level crossing No. 43 at 62 miles 07 chains, before entering **Yeldham** station at 62 miles 09 chains from Liverpool Street and 11 miles 58 chains from Chappel Junction, where the 300 feet long platform was located on the Up side of the line.

The main station building at Yeldham – accommodating booking office, waiting room and ladies' waiting room – was of all-timber construction dating from 1907, replacing the original meagre structure. Passenger access to the platform was by a short flight of steps with handrails backing on the platform. A second brick building at the Haverhill end of the platform contained a parcels

store, lamp room and gentlemen's lavatory The platform was lit by two oil lamps, one with a blue enamel nameplate. In later years the ends of the goods shed, which backed on to the platform, were reconstructed in brick; a modest corrugated office was added to the side of the booking office and at the other end a small store, and the properly surfaced platform extended alongside the goods shed. A CV&HR sign and solitary lamp case made by Lamp Manufacturing Company, which illuminated the ladies' waiting room, was sold for 10s 0d after closure of the line. Signals and points at the station were worked from Yeldham signal box, located on the Up side of the line between the end of the platform and the level crossing gates, containing a 26-lever frame.

Approaching Yeldham the main single line swung to the right as the straight continuation formed the 1,330 feet goods loop, which ran parallel to the main single line on the Down side. From this loop trailing points led to a 320 feet dock siding serving the cattle and loading dock and its attendant 70 feet headshunt. The main goods yard was located on the Up side, served by a 510 feet loop siding off the main single line. From this siding a 160 feet shed road served the 45 feet by 35 feet timber goods shed similar to

Yeldham station, 11 miles 58 chains from Chappel Junction, facing towards Haverhill circa 1880. The main single line serves the platform with the Down side goods loop and loading dock to the left. The single timber building with tile roof and ornate chimney is the only passenger facility provided, containing booking office and waiting rooms with access by a short flight of steps, the handrails of which can be seen beyond the gentleman on the platform. The brick structure at the end of the platform housed the store, lamp room and gentlemen's toilet. The timber goods shed standing in the goods yard was similar to those provided at Hedingham and Haverhill, whilst part of the station signal is to the extreme right. The permanent way is formed of 70 lbs per yard flat bottom rail in 21 feet and 30 feet lengths spiked directly to the sleepers.

M. Root collection

Yeldham station, 62 miles 09 chains from Liverpool Street, facing towards Haverhill on 16th April 1947 with the goods loop serving the loading dock in the foreground. The main single line serves the 300 feet long platform on the Up side of the line and beyond the station buildings is the goods shed. The signal box at the end of the platform controlled signals and points at the station with a wheel operating the level crossing gates. The water crane for replenishing locomotives is located near the signal box with another at the other end of the platform. *L&NER*

Yeldham station in a derelict condition on 7th September 1964. Oil lamps are still extant in the platform over 3½ years after the withdrawal of passenger services. *J. Watling*

LEFT: An elderly lady seeing a passenger off on a Down train at Yeldham, where the station buildings are overshadowed by the signal box. The ornate oil lamps providing meagre illumination during the hours of darkness were of typical GER design and were supplied to the CV&HR in the 1890s.   *G. Powell*

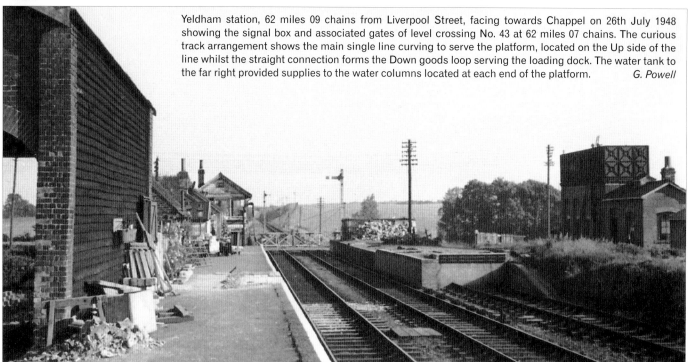

Yeldham station, 62 miles 09 chains from Liverpool Street, facing towards Chappel on 26th July 1948 showing the signal box and associated gates of level crossing No. 43 at 62 miles 07 chains. The curious track arrangement shows the main single line curving to serve the platform, located on the Up side of the line whilst the straight connection forms the Down goods loop serving the loading dock. The water tank to the far right provided supplies to the water columns located at each end of the platform.   *G. Powell*

those at Haverhill and Castle Hedingham, located at the back of the passenger platform. The yard facilities were completed by the 610 feet back road used by coal merchants. Whitlock Brothers' premises adjoined the railway yard; the firm, manufacturing agricultural machinery and carts, made extensive use of the railway to despatch their products. The points to the Haverhill end of the Yeldham goods yard and goods loop were worked from a 10-lever ground frame locked and released by Annett's key attached to the Train Staff. Water cranes were located at each end of the platform to replenish locomotives and were fed from a water tower and brick-built pump house housing a wind-driven, later petrol-driven pump located on the Down side of the railway opposite the platform.

Beyond Yeldham the line continued following a 55 chains left-hand curve climbing at 1 in 281, and just after the 62¼ mile post bisected footpath level crossing No. 44 at 62 miles 26½ chains. The gradient then eased to 1 in 220, then level as the branch crossed Farm Road underbridge No. 23 at 62 miles 42 chains, where there were views of Great Yeldham village and St Andrew's church on the Up or eastern side of the line. From the 62¾ milepost the railway followed a straight course with the infant River Colne to the north and descended at 1 in 250 over Man's Cross footpath crossing No. 45 at 62 miles 63¾ chains, followed by a short half-mile section on level track past the 63 mile post. The railway then climbed in a north-westerly direction at 1 in 105/103 for nearly a mile, passing over Culvert underbridge No. 23A at 63 miles 19 chains and within a few yards Stambourne Road underbridge No. 24 at 63 miles 23 chains. Near the top of the incline the line bisected occupational level crossing No. 46 at 63 miles 59¾ chains and occupational crossing No. 47 at 63 miles 64 chains before approaching the 64 milepost on a shallow right-hand curve on a level section. The line then crossed

ABOVE: The 'Stop and Await Instructions' board on the southern approach to Yeldham level crossing on 27th January 1965. Freight facilities were withdrawn a month earlier on 28th December 1964. *J. Watling*

RIGHT: Yeldham goods yard viewed from the train on 30th December 1961 showing the Up side goods loop and extensive yard. *R. Powell*

BELOW: Road approach to the spartan station buildings at Yeldham on 16th April 1947. To the right is the goods shed and in the foreground a road mobile crane provided to lift heavy loads into and out of wagons in the goods yard. *L&NER*

Birdbrook

TO YELDHAM

SP

CP   LD   LG

BELOW: GER style platform oil lamp on a very short post at Birdbrook in March 1961.   *J. Watling*

BIRDBROOK

Pettyfield occupation and footpath crossing No. 48 at 64 miles 04¼ chains and over the adjacent Pettyfield Lane underbridge No. 25 at 64 miles 07 chains, with Pettyfield Wood on the Down side where the railway fell at 1 in 264. A shorter 1 in 132 descent followed as the railway passed over Roman Villa footpath crossing No. 49 at 64 miles 21 chains, after which the line climbed at 1 in 130 for nearly half a mile passing over Culvert bridge No. 26 at 64 miles 34 chains and Ridgewell Wash underbridge No. 27 at 64 miles 58 chains. Beyond the three-quarter mile post the gradient continued at 1 in 130, and soon after the 65 milepost a right-hand 45 chains curve took the line over occupational footpath crossing No. 50 at 65 miles 11 chains and footpath crossing No. 51 at 65 miles 20 chains. The railway then passed under Whitley's overbridge No. 28 at 65 miles 37 chains to a summit at 65½ miles where the line curved to the left. From here the railway descended at 1 in 83 through a deep cutting to **Birdbrook** station, 65 miles 75 chains from Liverpool Street and 15 miles 44 chains from Chappel Junction, on a straight section of track. On Birdbrook bank drivers were instructed to run their engine or train round the curve with caution whilst guards of goods trains were required to assist by steadying the speed of the train with the astute use of the hand brake in their van.

At Birdbrook the 290 feet platform was on the Up side of the line; the station, opened in 1863 to serve the village a mile distant to the south-west and Wixoe to the north, was of all timber construction. A later corrugated structure provided in 1907 contained a staff room and parcels store. Birdbrook was the

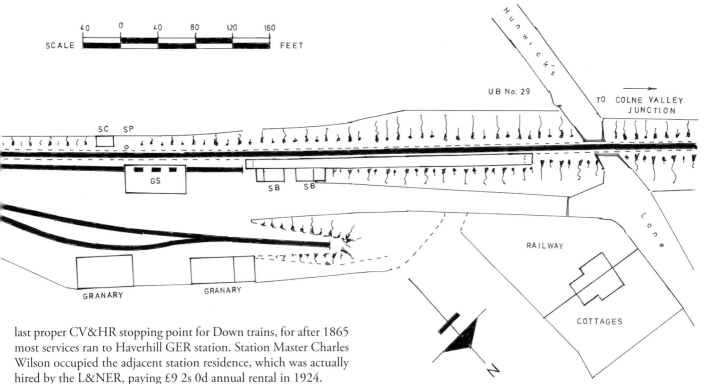

SCALE 40 0 40 80 120 160 FEET

UB No. 29

TO COLNE VALLEY JUNCTION

SC SP

GS

SB SB

RAILWAY

GRANARY   GRANARY

COTTAGES

N

last proper CV&HR stopping point for Down trains, for after 1865 most services ran to Haverhill GER station. Station Master Charles Wilson occupied the adjacent station residence, which was actually hired by the L&NER, paying £9 2s 0d annual rental in 1924.

The goods yard at Birdbrook was located on the Up side of the railway behind the platform, where facing points in the Down direction led to the 440 feet shed road running behind the platform serving the 60 feet by 28 feet goods shed. From this a single yard siding of 520 feet provided accommodation to the goods yard, and from this a 220 feet loop served the coal ground. Facilities were completed by a small granary. Points and signals were controlled from Birdbrook signal box, equipped with an 11-lever frame and located on the Down side of the line south of the entry points to the goods yard.

From Birdbrook station, located on a high embankment, the railway continued descending on a straight course at 1 in 83 over

BELOW: The very rural Birdbrook station, 15 miles 44 chains from Chappel Junction, circa 1880 with the meagre accommodation and the stop signal for each direction of travel mounted on the same post and operated from the platform. A Midland Railway open wagon occupies the shed road which runs at a higher level than the main single line serving the platform, whilst a CVR wagon is at the far right. At this period the roof of the corrugated iron goods shed is arched and the building was later rebuilt with a conventional roof. Birdbrook station opened in June 1863 a few weeks later than the line between Yeldham and Haverhill and served the villages of Wixoe and Birdbrook, a mile north and south of the railway respectively. *M. Root collection*

Birdbrook station, 65 miles 75 chains from Liverpool Street, with a train headed by a 'J15' Class 0-6-0 running tender first approaching the 290 feet long platform. The original building fronted by a small canopy contained the booking office whilst the nearer corrugated building was a later addition. To the right, buffer stops at the end of shed road serving the goods shed terminate at a higher level than the main single line. *L&NER*

ABOVE: Birdbrook station platform shelter with its attendant oil lamp of GER vintage on a cut-down post. The view along the 290 feet platform facing towards Haverhill shows the Down starting and Up home signals, both with upper quadrant arms, sharing the same post. *M. Root collection*

RIGHT: Birdbrook station building in the 1920s with its modest canopy and waiting area. Note the platform edging is of concrete with no overhang and permanent way is still formed of lightweight rail. *M. Root collection*

FACING PAGE: Road approach to Birdbrook station in April 1947, with the main station building to the right and later corrugated building near the entrance gate. *L&NER*

The restricted situation of Birdbrook station, located on the edge of an embankment with the 290 feet long platform on the Up side of the single line. The primitive station building and goods shed are to the left and the signal box to the right. *Author's collection*

Derby Lightweight 2-car diesel multiple unit forming a Marks Tey to Haverhill train departing the elevated platform at Birdbrook on a damp day in 1959. The train is about to cross Hunwick Lane underbridge No. 29. *Dr I.C. Allen*

RIGHT: The timber and corrugated goods shed at Birdbrook with the main single line in the foreground. The 440 feet shed road serving the building is running at a higher level and any vehicles placed into the structure had to be shunted with care and the handbrake immediately applied to prevent a runaway. To the immediate left is the platform ramp whilst inside the shed can be seen the unloading platform.
M. Root collection

ABOVE: The remains of Birdbrook station from across the fields on 12th April 1964. *R. Powell*

RIGHT: A derelict and vandalised Birdbrook signal box on 12th April 1964. *R. Powell*

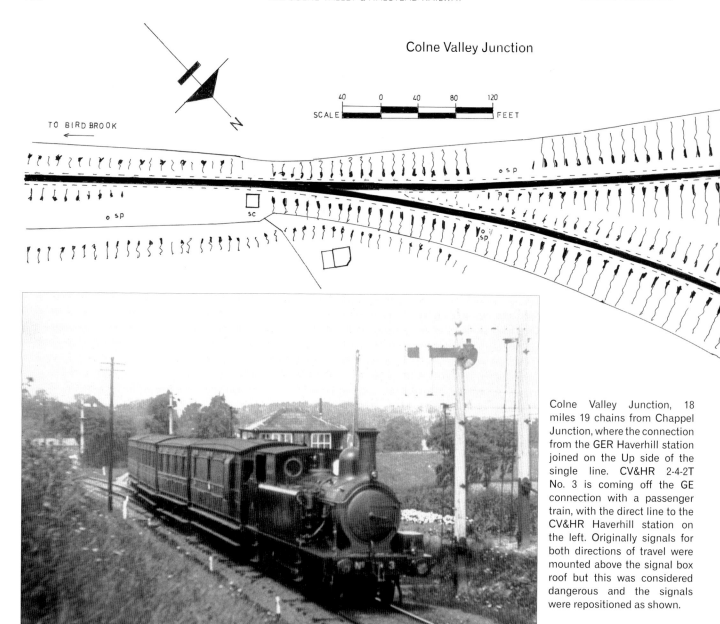

Colne Valley Junction

TO BIRD BROOK

SCALE 40 0 40 80 120 FEET

o sp

sc

o sp

o sp

Colne Valley Junction, 18 miles 19 chains from Chappel Junction, where the connection from the GER Haverhill station joined on the Up side of the single line. CV&HR 2-4-2T No. 3 is coming off the GE connection with a passenger train, with the direct line to the CV&HR Haverhill station on the left. Originally signals for both directions of travel were mounted above the signal box roof but this was considered dangerous and the signals were repositioned as shown.

Hunwick Lane underbridge No. 29 at 65 miles 77 chains and then Hunwick's occupational and footpath crossing No. 41 at 66 miles 06 chains, followed by New England underbridge No. 30 at 66 miles 38 chains, with the hamlet of New England on the Up side. The north-westerly route continued, and beyond the 66½ milepost a short level section took the railway over Watsoe New Culvert underbridge No. 31 at 66 miles 55 chains, after which the line curved at 33 chains radius to the left and climbed again at 1 in 76 from the 66¾ milepost. This unrelenting climb continued for just over a mile as the railway crossed Great Walton's Farm Cattle Creep underbridge No. 32 at 66 miles 77 chains and, two chains beyond, Walton Occupation and footpath crossing No. 53. The line was straight from the 67 mile post entering a shallow cutting with open land on either side. The climb continued on a 32 chains right-hand curve under Sturmer Road overbridge No. 33 at 67 miles 32 chains and then negotiated a 40 chains right-hand curve until at the summit the railway bisected occupational crossing No. 54 at 67 miles 64 chains. A level section then took the railway over Sturmer Hall arch underbridge No. 34 at 68 miles 01 chains, with views

of Sturmer Hall and the attendant St Mary's Church on the Up side. A straight course in a shallow cutting followed before a 1 in 87 descent followed by a steeper 1 in 66 brought the railway to **Colne Valley Junction**, 68 miles 50 chains from Liverpool Street and 18 miles 19 chains from Chappel Junction, where the GER connection to Haverhill veered away on the Up side. The junction was from the opening of the line controlled by Colne Valley Junction signal box containing an 11-lever frame. With the abolition of the signal box in 1929 the junction points were worked from a 2-lever ground frame.

The CV&HR line curved slightly to the left on an embankment and the gradient then eased to 1 in 726 over the Bumpstead Road underbridge No. 35 at 68 miles 64 chains before a shallow right-hand curve and a short rise at 1 in 203 took the line over Brick Works Occupational and Footpath crossing at 68 miles 78 chains with the works on the Up side. The line then descended at 1 in 1,500 to **Haverhill Colne Valley** station, 69 miles 24 chains from London Liverpool Street, with the buffer stops located two chains further on at 69 miles 26 chains and 18 miles 75 chains from

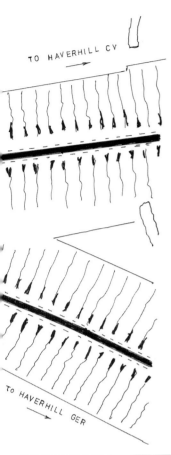

TO HAVERHILL CV

TO HAVERHILL GER

Colne Valley Junction 68 miles 50 chains ex Liverpool Street in later years with the ex GER connecting line to the right and the CV&HR direct route to Haverhill South to the left. *Dr I.C. Allen*

A Colne Valley train hauled by LM '2MT' Class 2-6-0 No. 46468 climbing away from the ex-GE Stour Valley line on 1 in 66 gradient towards Hamlet Road viaduct which carried the railway over the Sturmer Road. *Dr I.C. Allen*

Haverhill Colne Valley

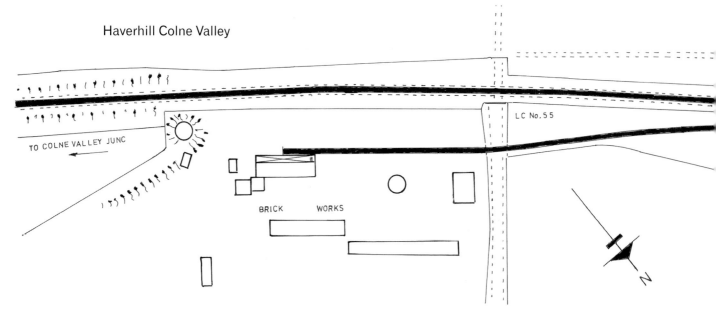

TO COLNE VALLEY JUNC

BRICK WORKS

LC No.55

Chappel Junction, located at the south-west corner of the town and hard against the boundary fence with Duddery Hill.

The terminal was built as a through station with a curved platform 210 feet in length on the Up side of the line, which allowed provision for an extension of the railway, although this was never built. The goods yard was located on the Up or north side of the main single line. Facing points led to the 600 feet reception siding with a connection to the 480 feet shed road serving the 60 feet by

28 feet goods shed. At the south end a long 720 feet siding served the brickworks. On the Down side was a 400 feet run-round loop from which points led to a 200 feet siding and the 330 feet shed road serving the engine shed. The building dating from 1915 was constructed of timber and corrugated iron with a roof of asbestos sheeting, to replace the structure built in 1862 before the opening of the line. The passenger train service was withdrawn from Haverhill South on 14th July 1924, although a few had finished on 1st

The original Haverhill CV&HR station, 18 miles 75 chains from Chappel Junction, together with the goods shed. The main single line served the curved platform and its basic station building, with the possibility of extension to Audley End or Cambridge and a hopeful link with the London & North Western Railway. A straight section also led to buffer stops beside the carriage shed. To the left of the carriage shed are cattle pens and a loading dock. In this 1880s view, track rationalisation has taken place for the siding on the Down side has been truncated by a simple earth bank and some sleepers and points laid from the main line to the carriage shed. To the right a wagon is being unloaded at the timber goods shed stage whilst the siding alongside the main line has a rudimentary stop block of sleepers instead of a set of buffer stops. The passenger station lost its importance after the opening of the connection to the GER from Colne Valley Junction from 1865, when most trains terminated at the GER station. Some services, notably the first Up train in the morning and the last Down service at night, continued to use the station until grouping and passenger facilities were fully withdrawn on and from 14th July 1924.

Author's collection

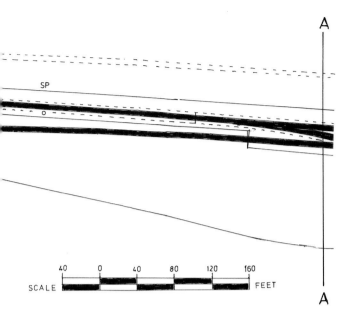

Locomotive water tower and tank at Haverhill South on 10th April 1965. The stand-alone structure was originally attached to the single road engine shed. *J. Watling*

February 1924, after which all services terminated and started back from Haverhill North. Drivers and guards of trains terminating at Haverhill CV station were instructed to approach at such a speed to enable the engine or train to be pulled up by the use of the hand brake only. Officially the CV&HR consisted of 19 miles of single line, 25 miles of single track including sidings.

From Colne Valley Junction, the GE connecting line to Haverhill, later Haverhill North, descended for most of the 70

The former CV&HR passenger station, later Haverhill South goods depot, with line now following a straight course on 16th April 1947. To the right is the former granary. Post-war housing development on the opposite side of Duddery Hill has blocked any hope of extension. *L&NER*

The former CV&HR engine shed at Haverhill continued to be used by the L&NER and this view shows 'J15' Class 0-6-0 No. 7532 fitted with side window cab awaiting its next turn of duty on 27 Match 1937. *W.A. Camwell*

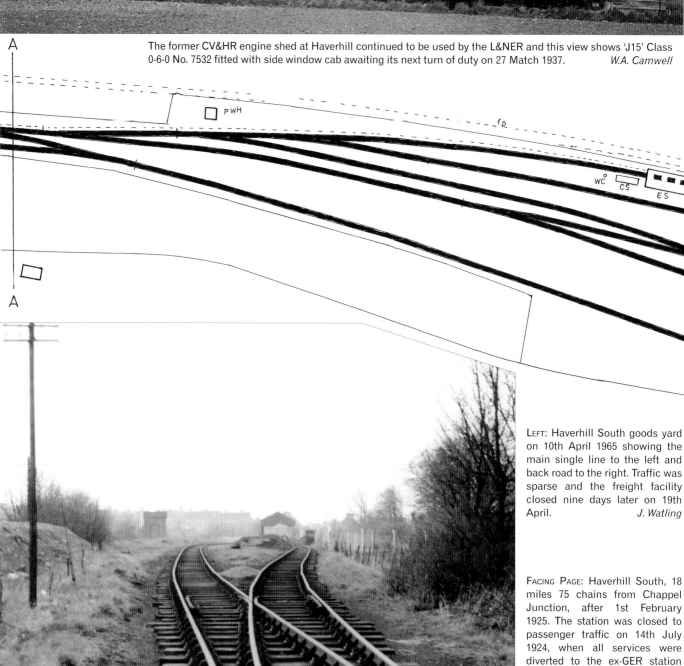

LEFT: Haverhill South goods yard on 10th April 1965 showing the main single line to the left and back road to the right. Traffic was sparse and the freight facility closed nine days later on 19th April. *J. Watling*

FACING PAGE: Haverhill South, 18 miles 75 chains from Chappel Junction, after 1st February 1925. The station was closed to passenger traffic on 14th July 1924, when all services were diverted to the ex-GER station Haverhill North. For many years the sidings were worked by a shuttle goods train from Haverhill GER but were closed on and from 19th April 1965. Note the water tank to the left centre.
Author's collection

ABOVE: The road approach to Haverhill CV&HR, later Haverhill South, station in 1949 with the granary directly ahead and the goods shed to the left. *B.D.J. Walsh*

Haverhill **GER** approach looking east from the Junction signal box on 26th August 1911. Beyond the crossover the single line to Long Melford is to the left whilst the right-hand line leads to Colne Valley Junction and the CV&HR. The lengthy head shunt to Haverhill goods and coal yard on the right in occupied by miscellaneous wagons near the Down home signal. The Up refuge siding is to the left.   *GERS/Windwood 105*

chains to Haverhill Junction where it again joined the cross-country line from Marks Tey to Cambridge. On this section was located the 3-arch Hamlet Road viaduct, No. 2170 at 15 miles 59 chains from Shelford Junction, which carried the line over Sturmer Road, the crown of the central arch being 25 feet above the surface of the thoroughfare. When building the approach embankments the GER contractors had insufficient spoil to make up the banks and had to acquire adjacent land in Haverhill specifically for the purpose. The excavation was known locally as the 'Junction Hole'. The junction with the GER cross-country route was controlled by Haverhill Junction signal box and Up and Down lines were maintained through to Haverhill station, the latter being controlled from Haverhill Station signal box until 1932 when rationalization resulted in the Station box being abolished and the Junction signal box taking overall control. From Haverhill Junction signal box the Colne Valley trains used the double track section falling at 1 in 108 to **Haverhill GER** station, 69 miles 43 chains from Liverpool Street via Halstead and 19 miles 12 chains from Chappel Junction. Runaway points were located 11 yards after passing the Up starting signal facing Up trains on account of the 1 in 110 gradient but this was later amended to 85 yards.

Curiously, Haverhill GER station was located in Suffolk whilst the CV&HR station was in Essex. Up and Down side platforms at the GER station were both 300 feet in length and connected by station footbridge No. 2165 at 14 miles 70 chains from Shelford Junction The main station buildings were on the Down platform whilst the Up side contained a brick structure containing waiting rooms and toilets.

All goods facilities were located on the Down side of the railway, although an 800 feet reception siding was located parallel with the Up line. On the Down side was a 670 feet reception siding entered by trailing points from the Down main line, whilst beyond that facing points led to a 220 feet siding running parallel to the Down

TO COLNE VALLEY JUNCTION

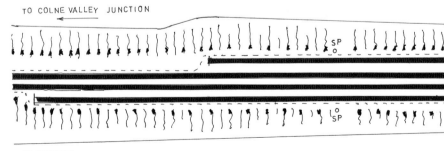

TO STURMER

The east end of Haverhill GER goods yard in August 1911 viewed from Haverhill Junction signal box, with a considerable number of wagons stabled in the headshunt. Opposite the signal box is 19 feet 3 inch vacuum fitted covered van No. 31168 dating from 1903, with the adjoining vehicle 16 feet 0 inch covered van No. 20634 built in 1900; a ventilated large cattle wagon and another 16 feet 0 inches covered van are beyond. Note the ballast has been built up near the point blades.

GERS/Windwood 83

main line; alongside that was a 410 feet siding, then the 440 feet dock road and 280 feet back road, from where a 530 feet siding ran at the back of the goods yard.

The speed limit for trains on the Colne Valley line were limited to 40 mph later 50 mph, except approaching Chappel or Haverhill where 10 mph was stipulated and 30 mph when passing over Yeldham Road underbridge No. 20 at 60 miles 78 chains. Although the CV&HR never issued such instructions, after grouping the L&NER enforced the rule because of the poor condition of the permanent way and bridges, and because of the severe and short gradients encountered on the route.

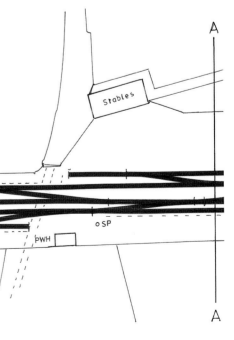

Haverhill GER

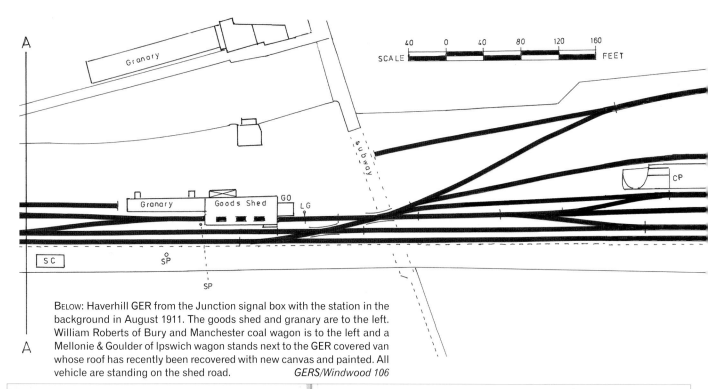

BELOW: Haverhill GER from the Junction signal box with the station in the background in August 1911. The goods shed and granary are to the left. William Roberts of Bury and Manchester coal wagon is to the left and a Mellonie & Goulder of Ipswich wagon stands next to the GER covered van whose roof has recently been recovered with new canvas and painted. All vehicle are standing on the shed road. *GERS/Windwood 106*

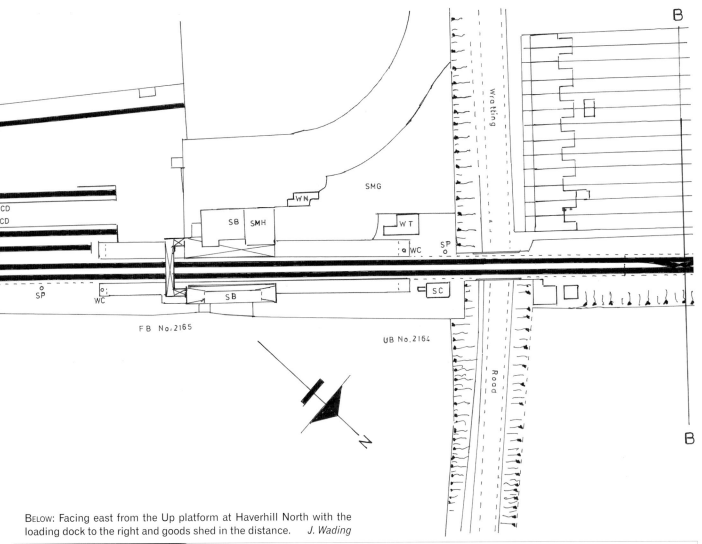

CD
CD

SMG

WN

SB SMH

WT

SP

WC

SP
WC

SB

SC

FB No. 2165

UB No. 2164

Wrating

Road

B

B

N

BELOW: Facing east from the Up platform at Haverhill North with the loading dock to the right and goods shed in the distance. *J. Wading*

ABOVE: Haverhill North station viewed from the east with the cattle dock on the left. *J. Watling*

LEFT: Haverhill GER station was located in the county of Suffolk, whilst the CV&HR terminus was in Essex. This exterior view from the approach road shows the building was constructed under the development of the GER Engineer's 'New Lines Department' under the direction of Robert Sinclair and became known as the' 1865 type'. Altogether twenty-seven were built on new lines in Essex and Suffolk and all had the identical two-storey hipped roof station master's house with the station offices being either large, medium or small depending on the importance of the station. Haverhill, designated in the medium category, had a single-storey central section fronted by a canopy linked to a single-storey hipped pavilion at the far end. *Author's collection*

TO WITHERSFIELD SIDING & BARTLOW →

Top: The exterior of Haverhill North station on 16th April 1947. It opened with the line from Shelford Junction south of Cambridge on 1st June 1865 with the connection to the CV&HR at Colne Valley Junction opening on 30th June 1865. *L&NER*

Above: A Colne Valley line train headed by LM '2MT' Class 2-6-0 working tender first departing Haverhill with the signal set for the Colne Valley line. The Ivatt 2MT locomotives were ideal for working the line as they were equipped with and enclosed cab and tender cab, offering much protection for enginemen. *H.C. Casserley*

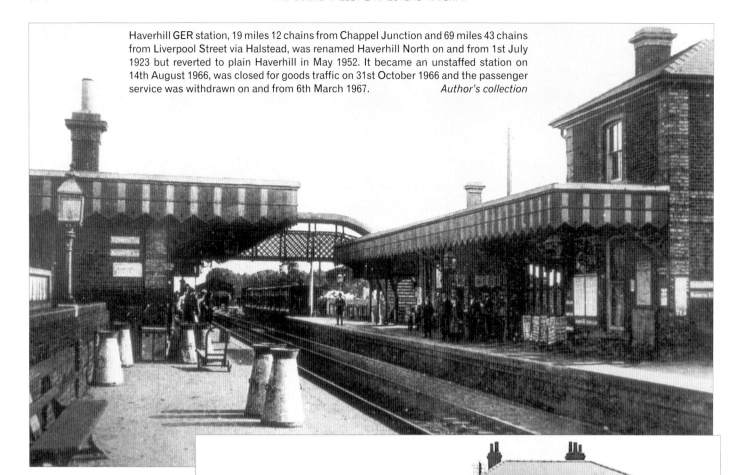

Haverhill GER station, 19 miles 12 chains from Chappel Junction and 69 miles 43 chains from Liverpool Street via Halstead, was renamed Haverhill North on and from 1st July 1923 but reverted to plain Haverhill in May 1952. It became an unstaffed station on 14th August 1966, was closed for goods traffic on 31st October 1966 and the passenger service was withdrawn on and from 6th March 1967. *Author's collection*

RIGHT: Haverhill North station 69 miles 43 chains from Liverpool Street via Halstead on 16th April 1947 with Up line to the left and Down line to the right serving the respective platforms each 300 feet in length, the Down platform playing host to the main station building. The ornate water column at the end of the platform for replenishing locomotives had an equal at the end of the Up platform both being provided with the braziers for heating the facility in frosty and icy weather. *L&NER*

LEFT: The Up platform at Haverhill North with the running in board advising passengers the station was the junction for the Colne Valley line. By the time this photograph was taken the roof had been removed from the footbridge. *Author's collection*

ABOVE: Haverhill GER station circa 1900 view facing towards Cambridge from the Up platform. The alternate light and dark shading on the canopy on the Down platform is prominent. Haverhill Station signal box is located at the end of the Up platform. *J. Wading collection*

LEFT: Haverhill former GE station later North Down platform viewed from the Up platform looking towards Cambridge on 7th September 1960. By this date the footbridge No. 2165 connecting the platforms had lost its canopy. *J. Watling*

RIGHT: Haverhill North station facing west towards Cambridge on 16th April 1947 with Down line and platform to the left and Up line and platform to the right. Footbridge No. 2165 devoid of roof connects the platforms. *L&NER*

LEFT: Haverhill North station on 7th September 1964 with footbridge No. 2165 connecting the platforms. *J. Watling*

ABOVE: Haverhill North looking west towards Bartlow and Cambridge from the footbridge connecting the platforms, each 300 feet in length. *J. Watling*

Water tower at the Cambridge end of Haverhill Down platform. The tank supplied water to the columns at the Down end of the Down platform and Up end of the Up platform, both removed by the 7th September 1964 when the view was taken. *J. Watling*

9

Permanent Way and Signalling

PERMANENT WAY

The initial permanent way of the Colne Valley & Halstead Railway was formed of flat bottom or contractors rail weighing 65 lbs per yard or 70 lbs per yard in the Halstead station area, in lengths varying from 15 feet to 21 feet, ninety per cent being in the longer length. The rails were joined by fishplates with 4-inch by ¼-inch bolts through each fishplate and rail end. The rails were laid on transverse sleepers varying in size from 8 feet by 9 inches by 4½ inches to 8 feet 10 inches by 11½ inches by 5½ inches, placed 3 feet to 3 feet 3 inches apart but only 2 feet 6 inches apart at the rail joints. On the curve on the approach to Chappel Junction an extra sleeper was laid under each section of 21 feet rail. The sleepers were notched out to secure the rails, the surface of the notch being finished off to a cant of 1 in 20 inwards, whilst the rails were secured

to sleepers by dog spikes measuring 4½ inches by ¾ inch by ½ inch, two to each rail or four in every sleeper. The track was laid on ballast of drift gravel stated to be a full average depth of 2 feet below the sleepers. At the inspection, Colonel Yolland, the inspecting officer, required the rails to be secured to the sleepers next to the joints by fang bolts.

On the second section of the line, from Halstead to Hedingham, the flat bottom rails were to a standard weight of 70 lbs per yard, in 20 feet lengths, with a small proportion in 17 feet and 14 feet lengths. The sleepers were creosoted larch measuring 8 feet 10 inches by 10 inches by 5 inches, half rounded in shape with the flat side down and placed 3 feet apart from centre to centre. The rails were fastened to intermediate sleepers by dog spikes each side of each rail and at the joints by chairs 1¾ inches long by 4 inches wide weighing 18½ lbs fastened to the sleepers by Ransomes & Sims

Permanent way gang for the Halstead section stand with their hand trolley alongside the Hepworth Hall No. 1 Halstead to Hedingham road overbridge No. 10 at 7 miles 00 chains, circa 1880. The gang also had use of a velocipede, but after 1935 maintenance was rationalised and the gang responsible for the complete Colne Valley line were provided with a motor trolley and trailer for routine maintenance and inspections.

M. Root collection

Ornate brick-built permanent way
hut at Chappel and Wakes Colne.
J. Watling

compressed oak trenails. The rails were held in the chairs by means of a lip cast in the chair on one side and on the other side by a cast iron shaped washer secured to the chair by means of a ¾-inch bolt and nut. The ballast on this section was only to a depth of one foot below the sleepers.

The permanent way on the third section, between Hedingham and Great Yeldham, was identical except that the sleepers were placed 3 feet 7 inches apart. Another variation was that points were jointed to the rails by two fishplates, each with two holes on what was termed the *'suspended fish joint'* principle. Colonel Yolland considered the rationalisation of sleepers was tantamount to a dangerous practice and required a reversion to 3 feet spacing. After an accident at Faversham on the London, Chatham & Dover Railway, the inspecting officer also required the removal of the oak trenails as fastenings for the chairs at the rail joints and the substitution of iron spikes.

On the last section of line, from Yeldham to Haverhill, the initial permanent way consisted of 70 lbs per yard flat bottom rails in lengths of 14, 17 and 21 feet, fished at the joints and secured to the sleepers by dog spikes at the intermediate points and chairs similar to the LC&DR design near the joints. Sleepers measuring 8 feet 10 inches by 10 inches by 5 inches were half-rounded, laid in some cases flat side up and in other cases the rounded side up.

The permanent way on the GER section of line from Haverhill to Colne Valley Junction was formed of 65 lbs per yard single headed rails in 21 feet lengths fixed in chairs weighing 27 lbs each by compressed timber keys. The chairs were secured to transverse creosoted fir sleepers measuring 9 feet by 10 inches by 5 inches by two Ransomes patented hollow wooden trenails and iron spikes, the latter measuring 4½ inches by 9/16 inch diameter passing through the trenails for each chair. The joints of the rails were connected with pairs of fishplates, together weighing 23 lbs, by four ¾-inch diameter bolts with nuts and washers. The ballast was gravel laid to a depth of one foot below the sleepers.

The permanent way received little enhancement during the next decade until the curve away from Chappel was relaid in the late 1870s with bullhead rails 80 to 85 lbs per yard, as were the points,

crossings and running lines in the stations on a rolling programme until the late 1880s, most being second-hand GER material. The GER officers, when inspecting the railway on the various occasions when possible takeover was suggested, were highly critical of the condition of the track and infrastructure. Because of financial constraints it was to be the turn of the century before serious remedial action was taken. When Hawkins and Fenn became Manager and Engineer respectively in 1903, further second-hand GER 85 lbs per yard rails were purchased and in 1904 these were used for relaying between Chappel and White Colne, replacing 70 lbs per yard rail.

On 31st August 1911 the directors requested the Engineer to seek tenders for the provision of materials for the permanent way relaying programme. It was thought some track might be obtained from the GER but on 17th October it was reported that the company had no second-hand rails available, so the General Manager was asked to arrange the purchase of new rails. In the meantime, 500 new sleepers had been obtained from Messrs Christie at the cost of 4s 3d each delivered to Halstead. No progress had been made on the new rails by 14th November 1911 and little else was obtained save a quantity of old but usable chairs at a cost of £1 1s 4d from R. Hunt in February 1912. On 19th February it was reported an order had been placed for 130 tons of 80 lbs per yard bull head rails at a price of £6 7s 6d per ton from Shelton Iron & Steel Company so that a start could be made on the relaying. A further order of 500 sleepers was made in March at a cost of 4s 1d each from Burt, Boulton & Company delivered free on rail to Silvertown. By 17th May 1912, 2,000 sleepers were ordered from the same firm at the slightly increased price of 4s 1½d each, delivered free on rail to Silvertown. This final delivery permitted the company to commence relaying between Halstead and Sible and Castle Hedingham. The Engineer was, however, still short of chairs and by 19th June 1912 it was reported that an order had been placed for cast iron chairs with Pease & Partners at a price of £70 per ton.

The relaying was well underway when in mid-July it was revealed some of the new rails had been damaged in transit and work was delayed. This gave the Engineer opportunity to order a quantity of ballast from the Endersby & Stoney Stanton Granite Company at a cost of £30 16s 8d and this was delivered in early August to supplement the ash and clinker formation. In the meantime the General Manager had written to the Shelton Iron, Steel & Coal Company regarding the damaged rails seeking replacements and compensation. When no reply was received the Solicitor was requested on 22nd October 1912 to take proceedings against the company.

Mr French commenced excavating ballast from a pit beside the railway at New England in early October 1912 and the company showed an interest in purchasing some of the material for relaying and packing. On inspection it was found not to be suitable and so an alternative supplier was sought. On 26th November 1912 the offer of 300 tons of ballast at 2s 0d per ton was accepted from Mr Cornish who was willing to deliver direct to the railway boundary at Purls Hill. On the same date the company paid £4 to the Cambrian Railways for the supply of a chairing gauge. Early in the new year a quantity of chairs were obtained from the GER for a knock-down price of £13 15s 10d and the bill was settled on 14th January 1913.

As the rolling programme of relaying progressed it became necessary to order further quantities of material. Sleepers and timbers were obtained from Burt, Boulton & Company at a price of £134 17s 5d and the account was settled on 25th February 1913. At the same time it was thought the supplies of ballast were of too high quality and was costly to purchase; to reduce costs the General Manager was asked to investigate the possible use of broken slag and stone as an alternative. On 5th May 1913 the directors sanctioned that tenders be obtained for the supply of sleepers and ballast to complete one mile of relaying, and by early June the offer from Burt, Boulton & Company for 1,500 sleepers at a price of 4s 7½d each was accepted. These were laid under second-hand 85 lbs per yard bull-head rails between Halstead and Hedingham in 1913.

With a view to reducing the cost of the relaying of the line the General Manager was asked on 10th February 1914 to prepare estimates for excavating ballast at the company's White Colne pit and the provision of a siding to serve the facility. The costs were acceptable and on 24th March instructions were issued to install the siding as a priority and commence the removal of ballast. At the same time it was agreed to re-sleeper the curve on the approach

to Chappel after engine drivers had complained of rough riding and undulating track. Of more serious concern was the discovery of a broken rail in the main single line near Earls Colne and the Engineer was asked to arrange for a closer inspection of the track and furnish a full report on the incident. Fortunately no further fractures were found.

With a view to maintaining the rolling renewal programme a supply of fishplates was obtained from Ransome & Rapier of Ipswich in early July at a cost of £55 11s 6d, whilst another 1,000 sleepers were supplied by Burt, Boulton & Company at a cost of 4s 5d each delivered to Silvertown at the end of the month. A further 150 tons of rails were obtained from Shelton in November, the company paying an extra £2 per ton as they were fitted with fishplates. Burt, Boulton also supplied a quantity of sleepers at a cost of £110 8s 4d in November whilst the following months an order was placed with the company for another 1,000. These were delivered in January 1915, as were 85 tons of chairs from Pease & Partner.

On 9th February 1915 the outstanding bill for £110 3s 11d was paid to Burt, Boulton whilst the Engineer submitted his detailed report on the broken rail at Earls Colne. Three months later an order for another 150 tons of new rails was placed with Shelton & Company but the firm replied they could not supply to order and would not begin rolling until the end of the month. There were obviously more pressing and urgent claims for rails as the firm advised in August they were still unable to supply. The rising price of material caused by war shortages was reflected in an order placed with Burt, Boulton for new sleepers. Previously they were supplied 1,000 at a time but when the company advised a price of 8s 8d each in September the order was reduced to 700. By the end of November no rails were forthcoming from Shelton and the relaying programme ceased. To ensure an adequate supply the firm was requested on 7th December to add another 75 tons of rails to the outstanding order but on receipt of the increased order they advised they were still unable to supply because of Government demands.

The New Year was but a few days old when three broken rails were discovered in the main line near Halstead and once again the Engineer was asked to report on the defects. Stung by the huge increase in prices of sleepers the company sought other suppliers and after negotiating with the GER accepted the offer of a supply

Track relaying in progress on the CV&HR with an 18-man gang replacing the original 70 lbs per yard flat bottom track with 85 lbs per yard bull head rails. The new sections of rail delivered earlier to site are laid alongside the sleeper ends. Scattered around the area are various gangers' tools including pickaxes, shovels, spanners, keying and sledge-hammers. *Author's collection*

at a cost of 8s 0d each on 11th February 1916. Surprisingly, no work had been executed to improve the curve at Chappel and the Consultant Engineer, having inspected the section of line, strongly recommended early attention when he attended the directors meeting on 25th February. On the same date it was announced that 400 sleepers had been obtained from the GER at the price of 8s 0d each.

By 3rd April 1916 the remedial work on the Chappel curve was completed with the installation of ten lengths of 85 lbs per yard bullhead rail on new sleepers and ballast, although it was realised this was only a temporary measure. Unfortunately, as one section of line was brought up to the improved standard, so another showed deterioration when another broken rail was discovered at Tank Bridge, Earls Colne. On 1st May 1916 the Engineer submitted a further report on the broken rail at White Colne and explained that a total of thirty-six rails should have been supplied by the GER to relay the Chappel curve some years previously as a quid pro quo for being allowed to shunt on to the CV&HR line. The GER Engineer had *positively* denied any such arrangement and the matter had been allowed to lapse. In the meantime, another crack had been found in a crossover in Halstead yard and was replaced, whilst permanent way staff still awaiting new rails had been delegated to make good the goods yard and approach road at Birdbrook with granite chippings originally intended for track relaying work.

The deterioration in supplies, especially of new rails because of the war effort, had resulted in the General Manager writing to the Railway Executive Committee and he reported his actions to the directors on 1st May 1916. Despite the shortfall the company had succeeded in obtaining a quantity of fang bolts from Guest, Keen. By 5th June 1916 the Railway Executive had arranged for the GER to offer supplies of rails and chairs to the company, whilst some second-hand rails were supplied enabling Parsonage Lane crossing to be relaid with 80 lbs bullhead track on new sleepers. At Halstead

part of the main line and the yard had been re-sleepered and ballasted, and another new crossover installed. A month later the GER had supplied thirty-six 85 lbs per yard bullhead rails complete with fishplates and chairs, whilst 60 tons of 80 lbs per yard bullhead rails complete with fishplates had at last been received from Shelton Iron Company.

On 14th August 1916 the board were advised that relaying had commenced on the Chappel curve using the 85 lbs per yard bullhead rail received from the GER. On the same day authority was given for 500 new sleepers to be ordered from Burt, Boulton & Company at the vastly increased cost of 12s 0d each, with the proviso that a further 500 would be required in 1917. Finally, on 25th September it was reported that work on Chappel curve had been completed using 640 yards of 80 lbs per yard and 280 yards 85 lbs per yard bullhead track with new ballast installed under the new rails.

Another source of supply of ballast was from the pits owned by Broyd's executors when the company obtained 600 cubic yards of packed stones at a price of 7s 0d per yard delivered to Halstead station in November 1916. At the same time the company took steps to obviate the past difficulties they had experienced obtaining new rails. They approached A.J. Hill, the GER Locomotive Superintendent, to negotiate with the Ministry of Munitions for further supplies of rails. The shortage of rails forced the company to relay Hedingham carriage shed road with second-hand flat bottom track in January 1917. Notwithstanding the problems encountered in keeping the permanent way in good order, difficulties were experienced from other sources, namely local landowners. In February 1917 the culvert at Colne Ford Hill was pushed over a distance of nearly 2 feet and on 26th of the month the Secretary was instructed to urgently visit Mr Botterell, owner of the adjacent property, for permission to place stays on his land to prevent further movement. Despite negotiations nothing had been done

Platelayer's hut at Haverhill South on 27th November 1965.
J. Wading

by 2nd April and the Consultant Engineer was asked to visit the site and ascertain what action was necessary. At the same time the GER was asked if they could supply 500 sleepers. Of more serious consequence was the discovery of two broken rails at White Colne; the Engineer was asked to report the matter to the Board of Trade. In the meantime the Consultant Engineer had visited Colne Ford culvert, with the result the Assistant Secretary subsequently met Mr Botterell in early May. As a consequence of the meeting, the landowner agreed to the culvert being extended by 10 feet to ease the situation.

The material situation improved by the early summer and on 4th June 1917 authority was given for relaying between the 7th and 8th mileposts with 80 lbs per yard bullhead rail. Work was done on an as-and-when-required basis and by 2nd July twenty lengths of rail had been installed, although there was still a shortage of sleepers. This shortage was rectified when 250 sleepers were received from the GER in August. Broken rails continued to plague the CV&HR, for another defect was found at White Colne in November 1917. The rash of breakages turned into an epidemic in the New Year, for in January two broken rails were discovered in Halstead yard, one on the 1 in 90 bank between Fox and Pheasant level crossing at White Colne, and one on Colne bank between White Colne and Tank Bridge.

On 3rd April 1918 the Secretary reported he had attended a meeting with A.J. Hill of the GER who was doubtful if any new rails could be obtained. He had seen the Railway Executive Committee, who had suggested that good second-hand rails should be used for portions of line requiring immediate attention. The CV&HR had no objection to the use of such rails and Hill had ascertained the GER would shortly have second-hand rails available. By May the situation appeared desperate for three further instances of broken rails were found at Brewster's cutting, between Blue Bridge and Parson's Lane, and on the level crossing at Halstead. On 1st May 1918 the GER advised they had 150 second-hand bullhead rails available for CV&HR use and the Assistant Secretary was asked to seek prices for the supply of 1,000 sleepers.

To ensure an adequate supply of rails the Assistant Secretary was instructed on 5th June 1918 to seek a meeting with the Secretary of the Railway Executive Committee to press for a supply of steel rails in the event of the GER being unable to supply. At the same time an application was made to the Controller of Timber for a supply of 1,500 sleepers and six sets of crossing timbers. By 3rd July the Assistant Secretary was able to report that the Railway Executive Committee representative had informed him there was likelihood of some new rails being allocated to the CV&HR. The depressed position of permanent way equipment was alleviated in August when the GER offered 50 tons of second-hand rails complete with fastenings. The company was, however, unable to supply a quantity of second-hand sleepers and the Assistant Secretary reported he had ordered a further 500 from the Government supply in addition to the 1,500 on order. During August and September a further three rails in the main line were found to be fractured, two on Cat's bank near the Fox and Pheasant level crossing and one near the 4 mile post. The rails were immediately replaced and the BOT advised. The situation was not eased, for on 25th September 1918 the Secretary read a letter from the Railway Executive Committee advising it was 'most improbable' they would be able to supply the new steel rails and suggested the company use second-hand rails from the GER. Despite the gloomy forecast on rails, the outlook on sleepers was brighter, for 140 new sleepers were received from

the Controller of Timber supplies in September with the promise of more to follow.

The receipt of second-hand bullhead rails from the GER and the new sleepers permitted the company to relay 30 chains of line between Parsons Lane crossing at Halstead and Blue Bridge during October, whilst the following month a further 4 chains received attention. The Engineer reported the average weight of rails installed over the 34 chains was 80 lbs per yard. In November a further supply of sleepers was received, bringing the total to 325, and the Controller of Timber advised that arrangements had been made for the remaining 1,175 to be supplied by Burt, Boulton & Company who would creosote them at an additional cost of 2s 0d per sleeper.

In January and February 1919 two further fractures were discovered in old rails on the main line; renewed instructions were given to permanent way staff to keep a careful watch as on one of the incidents a section of metal had dropped out the rail. At the board meeting held on 12th February 1919 the Consulting Engineer was asked to advise on the matter. On 26th February the Company paid £234 11s 4d for second-hand rails and the following month £91 15s 6d to the BOT for sleepers. In the same month a bank slip occurred at Purls Hill causing minor delays to train services. Further payments were made in May: £96 to the BOT for sleepers and £39 to Burt, Boulton & Company for creosoting of sleepers. Another payment of £122 12s 0d was made to the BOT for sleepers in July. In the same month the position regarding permanent way materials had improved and an order was placed with Shelton & Company for 170 tons of steel rails at a price of £22 5s 0d per ton, together with an order for 3,000 sleepers at a price of 10s 0d each.

Burt, Boulton & Company were paid a further £74 4s 0d for creosoting of sleepers in January 1920 and at the board meeting held on 26th February the Secretary was asked to obtain prices for a further 80 tons of rails and 1,000 sleepers. This was later increased to 250 tons of rails and Shelton Iron Company duly delivered the material at the end of March 1920 at a cost of £20 per ton. On 7th April a further 1,000 sleepers were ordered through the Controller of Timber at a price of 10s 0d each creosoted.

The CV&HR was now in a position to properly plan a relaying programme, although the work executed in April and early May, relaying 300 yards of track near Fox and Pheasant level crossing, utilised second-hand bullhead rails and chairs obtained from the GER laid on new sleepers. The next section to be tackled was that between Sible and Castle Hedingham and Halstead, and the rolling programme continued through the remainder of the year and into January 1921. Although plain track renewal was progressing, no material for points and crossings had been obtained and the Secretary was asked to obtain prices on 6th January. On 10th February 1921, J. Williamson the Consultant Inspecting Engineer resigned and it was agreed to pay his salary to the end of June.

After completing the Castle Hedingham to Halstead section, relaying work was transferred to the Chappel to White Colne section of line and continued through May and June 1921; the work at Chappel and Wakes Colne in association with the GER incorporating 85 lbs per yard bullhead rails. No additional material was ordered until 1922, when 500 sleepers were obtained from Messrs Calders at 8s 6d per sleeper delivered to Halstead. The relaying programme, which had continued sporadically, produced scrap flat bottom rails and quantities were sold to T.W. Ward of Sheffield at £3 2s 6d per ton in October 1922 and £3 5s 0d per ton in December. With the impending grouping, the company was still ordering sleepers, 200 being obtained for immediate use from

Local civil engineering staff carried out an extensive bridge replacement programme between 1908 and 1913 sometimes with the assistance of the GER and with ironwork provided by a number of manufacturers including Butterley Iron & Steel Company and Messrs Keays. Here a gang celebrate the near completion of another span across the River Colne. The heavier work was assisted by the company mobile crane in the left whilst alongside is a CV&HR goods brake van. In most cases train services were not cancelled when possession of the line was taken. Trains operated to each side of the blockage and passengers then walked between the two to continue their journey. *M. Root collection*

Burt, Boulton & Heywood at a price of 7s 0d each delivered to Silvertown, which after conveyance charges equated to a price of 7s 5¾d at Halstead. Whilst the takeover was being negotiated a further 200 sleepers were ordered from the same firm.

From 1923 the L&NER commenced replacing 24 feet length rails with 30 and 45 feet rails, initially weighing 85 to 97 lbs per yard, but in the mid-1930s the weight was increased to 90 and 95 lbs per yard track. Much of the bullhead equipment was second-hand after use on the main line and sufficed for the next decade, worn rails being replaced or turned as and when required. A certain amount of renewal was necessary after the outbreak of World War Two, especially between Chappel and Earls Colne to permit the use of heavier locomotives and rolling stock on military traffic. Much renewal of the permanent way, which continued after the heavy usage during the hostilities, was accomplished using second-hand rails recovered from the main line and work was usually carried out on Sundays. Not all went to plan, however, for the passage of the early morning goods train approaching Langley Mill crossing, the locomotive and following wagons caused such a lurch that the driver halted the train and with the guard walked back to where the incident had occurred. It was discovered that relaying gang had used 60 feet rails but nearer the crossing 30 feet rails had been inserted to obviate the use of rail ends in the middle of the level crossing, and by chance the departing permanent way staff had not completed the task and overlooked the installation of necessary fishplates and bolts. After due discussion the train continued to Parsonage Lane crossing where the services of sub-ganger Samuel Benham were obtained and he walked back along the line to Langley Mill to effect the necessary repairs.

The original bridges between Chappel and Halstead were constructed of wrought iron girders on wooden piles whilst the underbridges between Halstead and Haverhill were cast iron girders on brick abutments. These survived in various states of repair until 1908 when 0-6-2 tank locomotive No. 5 was delivered and proved too heavy for the infrastructure. Problems were initially met with White's Bridge No. 1 and White's Bridge No. 2 near Earls Colne, and as a temporary compromise a full and independent survey was authorised. W. Bailey Hawkins, Chairman of the company, was also Chairman of the Cambrian Railways and he asked the Civil Engineer of that company if James Williamson, his principal assistant, could conduct a detailed survey; Williamson upheld Fenn's opinion that the safety margin on all structure was too small even for the 2-4-2Ts.

Reconstruction of the bridges commenced in 1908 with White's Bridge No. 1, followed by White's Bridge No. 2 in 1909 and thereafter all bridges received attention until completion in 1913. When the entire bridge span was removed CV&HR engineering staff constructed new brickwork and masonry after demolishing the old structure, whilst the Butterley Steel Company supplied and erected the new steelwork. Where girders only were replaced CV&HR engineering staff executed the work, the steel being supplied by Dorman Long & Company Limited.

During the rebuilding programme, the line was closed after the passage of the last Down train on the Saturday evening and the Train Staff for the relevant single line section was handed to the supervisor of the engineering gang who retained it until it was required for the passage of the final train on Sunday evening. The Up and Down trains on Sunday morning were worked as normal but when approaching the works site the trains were brought as close as possible to the obstruction by pilot working to allow passengers to walk by specially laid walkways to connect between the services. The dismantling and replacement of the bridges in less than 22 hours required careful planning.

To assist with permanent way maintenance the CV&HR possessed two rail cycles for inspection purposes as well as for travel between stations when no train or light engine was available. The vehicles each had two pairs of pressed steel wheels and axles similar to permanent way vehicles. They were fitted with a light tubular

The eastern approach to Earls Colne station with the tall Down home signal standing gaunt against the skyline. To the right is the goods yard and goods shed.   *J. Watling*

ABOVE LEFT: The western approach to Earls Colne station with CV&HR lower quadrant Up home signal protecting the level crossing gates, beyond which is the lower quadrant Down home signal at the end of the platform.   *J. Watling*

ABOVE RIGHT: Officially passenger trains were not permitted to cross at Halstead because of the lack of a platform on the Down side. In exceptional circumstances passenger trains were crossed to prevent delays and here on 31st July 1951 an Up train hauled by a '115' Class 0-6-0 running tender first enters the platform, whilst a Down train stands in the Down loop line. The Down train had already served the platform and been shunted into the Down loop to permit the Up train to enter the station. After departure of the Up train the Down train, in possession of the single line token, would continue its journey to Haverhill.   *G. Powell*

frame fitted with handlebars and saddle for the rider. These survived until reorganisation of the branch maintenance from 28th October 1935, when the entire line was included within one maintenance section with staff utilizing a motorised trolley.

PERMANENT WAY STAFF

The maintenance of the permanent way on the CV&HR was divided into two sections: the Halstead gang covering the section from Chappel (exclusive) to Sible and Castle Hedingham (exclusive), and the Yeldham gang covering Sible and Castle Hedingham (inclusive) to Haverhill Colne Valley station and yard. Members of the Halstead gang in the early years included Ganger Harry Jarman and Sub-ganger Sam Benham, later staff included ganger Arthur Mead, sub-ganger Harry Diggins, platelayers Ted Moss, Herbert Sargeant, Ernest Norfolk, Charles Rideout, Charles Coppin, Albert Parker, Frederick Arnold, Jack Sizer, Bert Heavingham, Alfred Corder and father and son Root. The Yeldham gang included Ganger Jack Brown, sub-ganger Francis Dowsett, Charles Wilkins, Charles Turner, Horace Clark, Reg Wallace and Horace Goody. The short section from Haverhill Colne Valley Junction to Haverhill North was shared between the Yeldham gang and the GER Haverhill gang including Ganger Jesse Draine, sub-ganger Sid Peck, and Horace Eves (senior and junior). When the line opened to traffic the pay for permanent way men ranged from 12s 0d per week for a ganger to 9s 0d for a platelayer.

The proposed reorganisation of the CV&HR permanent way department was discussed at the board meeting held on 14th January 1913. On 11th March 1913 it was agreed to retire Ganger Eves as he was over 70 years of age and had spent fifty years in the service of the company. On 9th September 1913 it was agreed to award a 1s 0d per week increase in pay to foreman platelayers, second men and platelayers. The board then approved the appointment of Harry Warren to ganger on No. 2 length on 25th September 1916.

Platelayer Edward Potter resigned after 59 years service with the company in April 1920 and was awarded £15 towards his retirement. Platelayer William Gibbs retired at the same time but his award was deferred. Further members of staff were discharged in April 1921 on reaching 70 years of age. Sub-ganger T. Potter was awarded £15 retirement gratuity, Ganger J. Dowsett £10 and Ganger W. Clayden £5. In 1924 Ernest Roost was ganger living rent free at Fox and Pheasant crossing cottage whilst platelayer Charles Copping resided rent free in a cottage hired by the company at Langley Mill crossing. The free accommodation was provided in recompense for the wives of staff opening and closing the crossing gates.

Of the GER permanent way staff, A.J. Drane, ganger at Haverhill North, retired on 31st August 1928. He commenced his railway career at Marks Tey in July 1883 and transferred to Haverhill in 1885. A few years later he was appointed ganger at Sturmer but returned to Haverhill in 1899 where some of his duties included work on the connecting line to the Colne Valley route. Walter Plumb, foreman platelayer at Haverhill, was forced to retire through illness brought about by an accident. He had spent the whole of his 43 years at Haverhill and in the latter years had covered the northern section of the old Colne Valley line on his inspections. At a ceremony held at Haverhill in January, Station Master W.E. Ellis made a small presentation on behalf of his colleagues. The maintenance of the permanent way from Haverhill station to Colne Valley Junction was under the jurisdiction of the District Engineer Cambridge.

SIGNALLING

The initial signalling on the Colne Valley line was formed of semaphore signals with coloured aspect glasses rotating by the action of a connecting rod attached to bell crank levers and operated from station platforms or from the lineside. Each station and Chappel Junction, Colne Valley Junction and Haverhill Junction had a stop signal for each direction of travel mounted on the same post and ancillary or distant signals located 800 yards in the rear of the stop signal. Haverhill CV&HR station had an auxiliary signal and stop signal in the Down direction but only a stop signal for Up services At the outset there were no specific instructions regarding auxiliary signals, but within a few years and despite having less traffic the CV&HR followed the GER by introducing specific instructions in the event of an ancillary signal being at danger. The driver of an approaching train, having brought the train to a stand, was immediately to move his train forward with great care making sure the line ahead was clear, so as to bring his train well within the protection of the signal. Drivers were especially cautioned as their failure to carry out this regulation could cause an accident, which would otherwise have been averted. If it was not practicable to draw the train far enough within the signal to afford sufficient protection from a following train, the guard was required to go back at once with hand and percussion (sic) signals to protect his train. In 1882

View from a Down train approaching Halstead on 28th July 1950 and passing Halstead Down home signal and Parsonage Lane Up distant signal mounted on the same post. Note the small shunt signal in the Up yard. *G. Powell*

Ford Gate was provided with auxiliary, home and starting signals in each direction and from thereon conventional signals were gradually installed at all stations.

Around the turn of the century modifications were made to some but not all distant signals on the line, probably as a result of recommendations made by GER engineers, where distant signals at the time were painted the same red as stop signals and showed the same red and green aspects to drivers at night. To avoid confusion with home signals the GER fitted their distant signals with Coligny-Welch lamps, which showed an additional white > at night and the CV&HR followed suit. When the L&NER assumed responsibility for the line the distant signal arms were gradually repainted the familiar yellow with black chevron >, the Coligny Welch lamps were removed or modified to serve as ordinary lamps, and yellow and green aspects were displayed at night. As the years progressed several timber signal posts rotted and were replaced by posts of tubular steel or concrete, whilst wooden lower quadrant arms were replaced by L&NER and BR upper quadrant arms on the same post. However, at Birdbrook the Up home and Down starter lower quadrant arms were still displayed on a lattice post until closure; Sible and Castle Hedingham Down starter was also mounted on a lattice post.

As a result of the Regulation of Railways Act 1889, the company was forced to make available £12,000 to finance the improvements to the signalling of the railway. This was obtained by a £12,150 increase in the loans and debentures issue, authorised by a BOT Order under powers conferred by the Act of Parliament. Work was carried out between 1888 and 1894, and included the provision of signal boxes at all stations except Ford Gate (Colne) where a signal box was already provided, together with full interlocking of points and signals. The contract was awarded to Saxby & Farmer Limited although the signal boxes were of local design of timber construction but with brick bases and chimneys. New signal boxes were provided at Parsonage Lane (Halstead), Trinity Street (Halstead), Sible and Castle Hedingham, Yeldham and Birdbrook. Ground frames were also provided at Fox and Pheasant level crossing between Chappel and White Colne, White Colne station level crossing and yard, Halstead Coal Yard, Purls Hill siding, Hedingham brickyard siding, Sible and Castle Hedingham station yard, and Yeldham shunting yard – either the Annett's Key on the respective section Train Staff being used to release the ground frames, or released by the adjacent controlling signal box. The section of line from Colne Valley Junction to Haverhill Junction on the GER line was operated by the GE using Train Staff and Ticket.

When the single line section from Chappel to Halstead was opened to traffic in 1860 it was worked by the Train Staff method of single line working, with One Engine in Steam or two or more

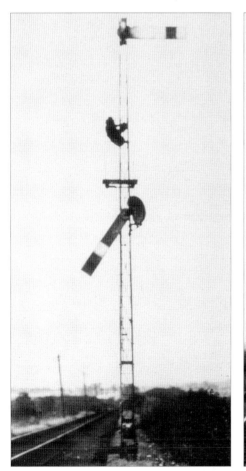

ABOVE LEFT: Down starter and Up home lower quadrant semaphore signals sharing the same post at Birdbrook, with the spectacle of the upper arm set at a lower level. Initially there was no interlocking but after the 1889 Regulation of Railways Act all points and signals on the main line were interlocked.

ABOVE CENTRE: Up distant lower quadrant semaphore signal at Birdbrook with spectacle set at a lower level than the arm. *Both author's collection*

ABOVE: Up starting signal at the end of Sible and Castle Hedingham platform. The post and finial are ornate CV&HR but an upper quadrant arm has replaced the former lower quadrant arm. *J. Watling*

coupled together, and from 1863 in conjunction with the single needle electric telegraph. As the line was extended, so the Train Staff system was introduced with sections from Halstead to Sible Hedingham, Sible Hedingham to Yeldham, Yeldham to Colne Valley Junction, Haverhill and Colne Valley Junction to Haverhill CV station. A further single line section was added in 1882 with the opening of Ford Gate station, which split the Chappel to Halstead section into two new sections: Chappel to Ford Gate and Ford Gate to Halstead.

In 1894, as a result of the signalling improvements and the growth in traffic, the company introduced Train Staff and Ticket working, the single line sections being Chappel and Wakes Colne to Colne (Earls Colne), Colne to Halstead, Halstead to Hedingham, Hedingham to Yeldham, Yeldham to Colne Valley Junction and Colne Valley Junction to Haverhill CV. When Hawkins assumed control of the railway he found the old Train Staff formerly in use on the Chappel to Earls Colne section with its markings for Chappel illegally in use between Earls Colne and Halstead, and pilot working was instituted until the ticket box could be repaired. He then discovered a complete set of Train Staffs and Ticket boxes still in the manufacturer's wrapping in the stores at Halstead, where they had lain since the rearrangement of the single line sections.

Following pressure from the GER the section of line from Chappel to Colne (Earls Colne) was converted to the Electric Train

Staff method of operation. The Railway Signal Company provided the equipment and an Annett's key was fitted to one end of each Staff to release the ground frame controlling the points to White Colne yard. The remaining sections of the line continued to be worked by Train Staff and Ticket principle. The Train Staff for the Colne to Halstead section was wooden, round in shape and yellow in colour. Halstead to Castle Hedingham was wooden, round in shape with an Annett's key attached and dark terracotta in colour. Castle Hedingham to Yeldham had a wood and brass Train Staff, round in shape and painted green, whilst the Yeldham to Haverhill Colne Valley Junction Train Staff was made of brass, square in shape and pink in colour. The section thence to Haverhill Colne Valley station had an iron diamond shaped staff painted red with white tickets. The Haverhill, Colne Valley Junction to Haverhill GE Junction single line section was controlled Train Staff and Ticket, with block telegraph; the Train Staff being iron, diamond in shape and light terracotta in colour. Except for the Haverhill CV Junction to Haverhill CV station section, the colour of all paper tickets corresponded with the colour of the Train Staff. After World War One the CV&HR introduced Electric Train Tablet working in place of Train Staff and Ticket.

The L&NER authorities quickly made alterations to the signalling at Chappel, for in 1927 the ground frame at the south end of the station was abolished and control of the points was transferred to

Three views of the CV&HR Sible and Castle Hedingham lower quadrant Up home signal (clear for the passage of a train, *right*) with the Up goods loop signal at a lower level on a wooden post complete with ornate finial; (*left*) with the station in the background. *All J. Watling*

the signal box. The work, costing an estimated £222 10s 0d, saved the cost of one porter with an annual saving of £132. After further investigation into the signalling of the former CV&HR Company, the Divisional General Manager (Southern Area) reported on the unsatisfactory method of working using the Train Staff and Ticket and/or Electric Train Tablet working between Earls Colne and Colne Valley Junction, south of Haverhill. He recommended replacement of the Train Staff and Ticket or Tablet with Tyer's Key Token instruments, with the locking of the intermediate sidings, and alteration in positioning of the Down home signal at Colne Valley Junction. The work, costing an estimated £618, was accepted and authorised on 27th March 1924 and introduced in 1926. Thereafter until the withdrawal of passenger services the Electric Key Token was used across the entire line, except between Colne Valley Junction and Haverhill South which reverted to Train Staff only, the new Train Staff being inscribed 'Haverhill Colne Valley Junction—Haverhill Colne Valley Station'. After the closure of the section between Colne Valley Junction and Yeldham the single line from Chappel to Yeldham was operated by One Train Only regulations using the single line Train Staff.

SIGNAL BOXES

The GER provided a signal box at **Chappel** in 1875 on the Up side of the line, but when a second platform and crossing loop were installed in 1892 a new signal box was provided on the Down side measuring 27 feet by 11 feet 6 inches with operating floor 6 feet above rail level. The new structure had a 38-lever Saxby & Farmer Duplex frame with 4-inch centres with 31 working and 7 spare levers, and also a 12-lever ground frame, the latter removed in 1927 (see above). Plans were drawn up in November 1928 for the rearrangement of the connection between the former CV&HR and GER single lines north of Chappel and Wakes Colne station together with associated signalling. The works, completed in August 1929, permitted the abolition of a ground frame at the south end of the yard and provided for all points and signals to be within the required 350 yards from the signal box. Home signals were provided to admit Up trains from either Halstead or Bures to the Up platform line or to the sidings east of the Up platform. Starting signals for corresponding movements in the opposite direction were also provided. A calling-on arm located below the home signal for

Chappel and Wakes Colne station 50 miles 18 chains from Liverpool Street facing south towards Marks Tey on 26th July 1948. The station signal box containing a 42-lever Saxby & Farmer Duplex frame with 4-inch centres stands at the end of the Down platform, whilst the truncated former CV&HR siding running at a higher level than the Down loop terminates short of the structure. *G. Powell*

Chappel signalling 1875

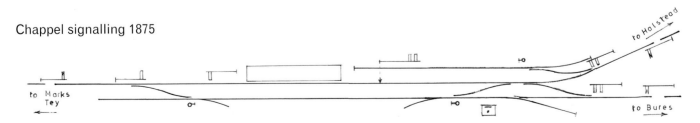

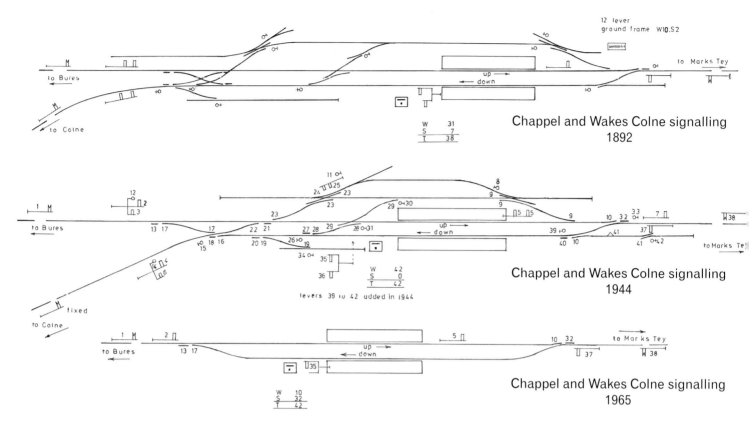

Chappel and Wakes Colne signalling
1892

Chappel and Wakes Colne signalling
1944

Chappel and Wakes Colne signalling
1965

the Halstead line was also provided to permit a Colne Valley train to approach the Down side platform. A disc signal on a bracket attached to the Down starting signals controlled shunting movements into the spur on the east side of the Bures line. All points and signals were operated from Chappel signal box containing a 38-lever frame with 37 working and 1 spare lever. In 1942 the frame was enlarged

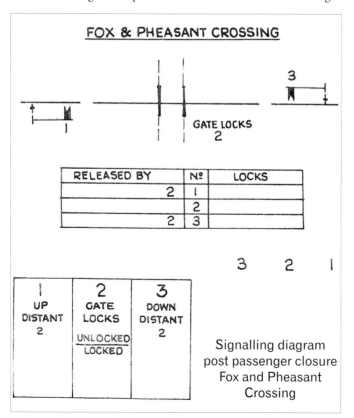

Signalling diagram
post passenger closure
Fox and Pheasant
Crossing

to 42 levers to encompass the new siding on the Down side south of the station for petroleum supplies.

Fox and Pheasant crossing was controlled by a 3-lever Saxby & Farmer gridiron ground frame with 5-inch centres controlling distant signals for each direction of travel and the gate lock, all operated by a resident gatekeeper. In latter years a gong was provided in connection with the Electric Train Staff operation to warn the gatekeeper of an approaching train.

Colne station was provided with station signals until closure on 1st May 1889 but gate distants were still operable worked from a ground frame. The station reopened as **White Colne** in 1907 for goods traffic, and for passengers on 1st April 1908, when a 9-lever Saxby & Farmer ground frame was provided in a brick hut close to the level crossing for operating distant and home signals for each direction of travel and points to the goods yard. With rationalisation in the 1920s the ground frame was reduced to 4 levers to operate the gate distant signals and wicket gates and gate locks when control of the points to the goods yard was transferred to a 2-lever ground frame released and locked by Annett's key on the single line Electric Train Staff. As at Fox and Pheasant crossing, a gong was provided to warn staff of approaching trains. The station was not a block post.

Along the line, when **Ford Gate** station was inspected in September 1880 the station had no signals or sidings other than a station signal protecting the level crossing and worked by the gatekeeper. The station subsequently opened to traffic in 1882 when a new timber signal box was provided containing an 11-lever McKenzie & Holland frame operating auxiliary, home and starting signals for each direction of travel. The station was renamed **Colne** on and from 1st May 1889, and when the goods yard layout was remodelled the signal box was equipped with a new 26-lever Saxby & Farmer Duplex frame with 4-inch centres, with 23 working and 3 spare levers operating Down and Up distant, home and starting signals as well as points to the sidings. The station was renamed

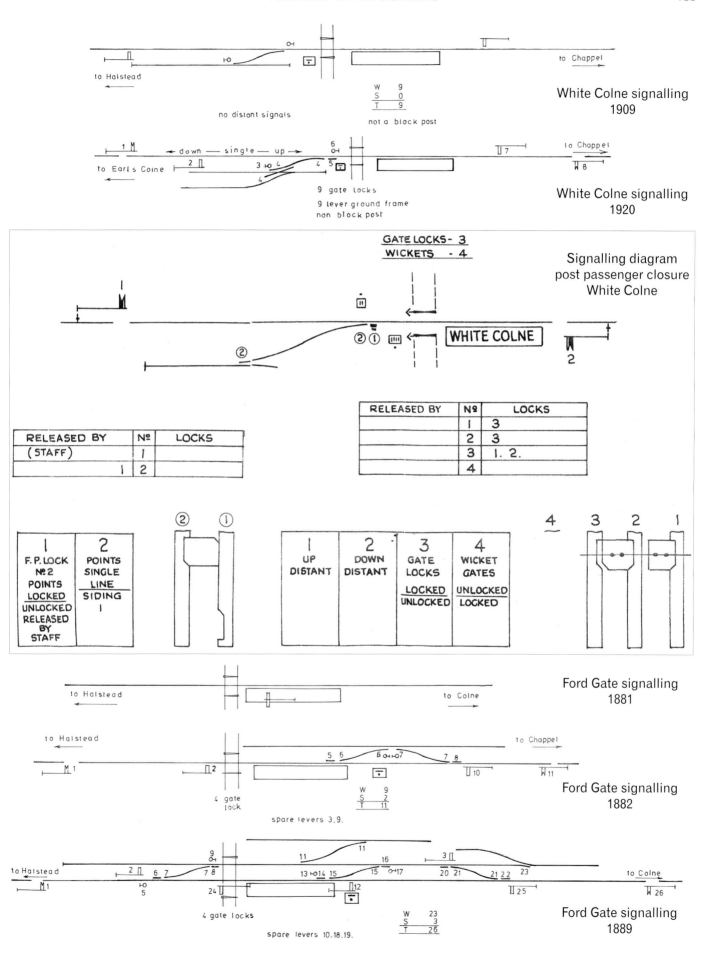

to Halstead

no distant signals

W 9
S 0
T 9

not a block post

**White Colne signalling
1909**

1 M

← down — single — up →

6

to Earls Colne

to Chappel

7

8

3 4

4 5

4

9 gate locks
9 lever ground frame
non block post

**White Colne signalling
1920**

GATE LOCKS - 3
WICKETS - 4

WHITE COLNE

2

**Signalling diagram
post passenger closure
White Colne**

RELEASED BY	№	LOCKS
(STAFF)	1	
	2	

RELEASED BY	№	LOCKS
	1	3
	2	3
	3	1. 2.
	4	

1	2			1	2	3	4
F. P. LOCK №2 POINTS LOCKED UNLOCKED RELEASED BY STAFF	POINTS SINGLE LINE SIDING 1	②	①	UP DISTANT	DOWN DISTANT	GATE LOCKS LOCKED UNLOCKED	WICKET GATES UNLOCKED LOCKED

4 3 2 1

to Halstead

to Colne

**Ford Gate signalling
1881**

to Halstead

to Chappel

M 1

2

5 6 6 7 7 8

10

11

9

W 9
S 2
T 11

4 gate lock

spare levers 3.9.

**Ford Gate signalling
1882**

to Halstead

to Colne

M 1

2 6 7 7 8

5

9

11 11

13 14 15   15 17   16

3

20 21   21 22 23

24   12   25   26

4 gate locks

W 23
S 3
T 26

spare levers 10.18.19.

**Ford Gate signalling
1889**

Earls Colne signal box, of timber and brick construction with ornate finials and located on the platform, was built in 1882 and equipped with an 11-lever McKenzie & Holland frame. With the enlargement of the goods yard the box was re-equipped with a new 26-lever Saxby & Farmer Duplex frame with 4-inch centres; the original frame was subsequently transferred to Birdbrook. *J. Watling*

Earls Colne signalling 1944

cattle pens

goods shed

to Chappel

to Halstead

gate locks 4

286 yards from level crossing

spare levers 8. 10. 16. 18. 19. 20.

W	20
S	6
T	26

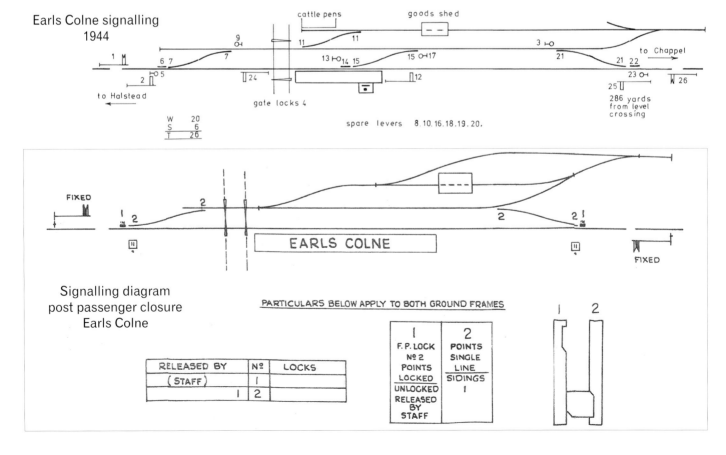

FIXED

EARLS COLNE

FIXED

Signalling diagram post passenger closure Earls Colne

<u>PARTICULARS BELOW APPLY TO BOTH GROUND FRAMES</u>

RELEASED BY	Nº	LOCKS
(STAFF)	1	
	1 2	

1	2
F. P. LOCK Nº 2 POINTS LOCKED UNLOCKED RELEASED BY STAFF	POINTS SINGLE LINE SIDINGS 1

on 1st May 1905 to **Earls Colne** and the signal box survived until abolished on 31st December 1961.

Langley Mill level crossing was provided with a Saxby & Farmer gridiron 3-lever ground frame with 5-inch centres to control the distant signals for each direction of travel and the associated gate locks; the ground frame being released and locked by Annett's Key on the Train Staff. In the latter years the Down distant signal was replaced by a home or stop signal.

A runaway engine and train destroyed the original **Parsonage Lane** signal box located on the Down side of the line in 1899. The brick debris was used in the reconstruction of the replacement on the Up side, which was some 25 feet in height, but some years later the Saxby & Farmer gridiron frame with 5-inch centres which contained only 4 levers was removed from the lofty operating floor to the lower locking room so that an invalid crossing keeper could operate the distant signals protecting the adjacent level crossing. The box was subsequently demolished and the 4-lever ground frame

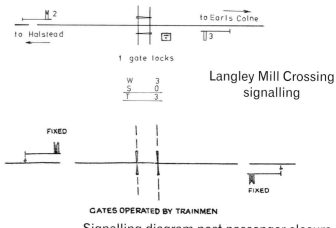

Langley Mill Crossing signalling

Signalling diagram post passenger closure
Langley Mill Crossing

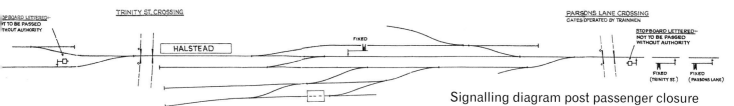

Signalling diagram post passenger closure
Parsonage Lane Crossing and Halstead

was released by Annett's key on the Train Staff. A series of bell codes was sent by the signalman at Halstead to advise the crossing keeper of approaching trains.

Halstead station was provided with a new signal box in May 1892. Of brick and timber construction it contained a 36-lever Saxby & Farmer Duplex frame with 4-inch centres, with 27 working and 9 spare levers together with a key to work an associated 7-lever

ground frame which had 5 working and 2 spare levers to operate points to neighbouring sidings. The signal box also had a gate wheel to work the Trinity Street level crossing. By 1902 additional sidings had been laid east of the station and a 16-lever ground frame was installed to operate the connection with the existing Down loop line as well as some of the sidings. The ground frame was released by Annett's key from Halstead signal box. The ground frame was

Halstead signal box located on the Down side of the railway soon after nationalisation with nameboard on the side of the building. Note the absence of wagons on sidings in the background. *M. Root collection*

Halstead signal box of brick and timber construction located on the Down side of the railway adjacent to Trinity Street level crossing on 31st July 1955. The northern entrance to the Down side goods yard is to the left.

G. Powell

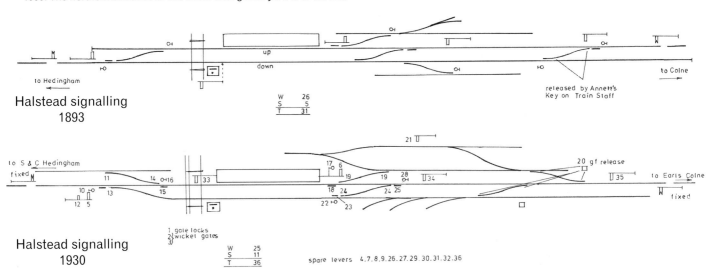

**Halstead signalling
1893**

**Halstead signalling
1930**

later reduced to 3 levers in L&NER days with electric release from Halstead signal box and by 1924 the signal box had 25 working and 11 spare levers to operate distant, home and starting signals for each direction of travel and to reflect other amendments. The signal box was abolished on 4th October 1962.

At **Purls Hill** the siding connections to Highfield brickworks, installed in the spring of 1893, were worked from a 5-lever Saxby & Farmer gridiron covered ground frame with 5-inch centres, released by Annett's key attached to the single line Train Staff. The frame was reduced to 2 levers by the L&NER in 1925/6 and released by the Electric Train Tablet (later Electric Key Token) for the Halstead to Sible and Castle Hedingham single line section.

Sible and Castle Hedingham signal box, of local design and constructed of brick and timber, was opened in November 1892 and contained a 25-lever Saxby & Farmer Duplex frame with 4-inch centres, with 21 working and 4 spare levers working distant, home and starting signals for each direction of travel. A ground frame with 9 levers was also provided, with all levers in use for working connections in the Up yard. To obviate enlarging the frame the points leading to the station yard on the Down side were operated from a 2-lever ground frame released by Annett's key, later by Key Token in the 1950s, and at the last just before closure by the 'One Engine in Steam' single line Train Staff. The signal box was abolished on 31st December 1961 and demolished the following

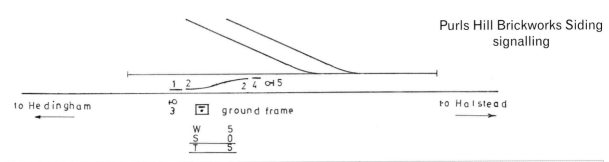

Purls Hill Brickworks Siding
signalling

Sible and Castle Hedingham signal box, located on the platform at the east end of the station in CV&HR days. Of brick and timber construction it opened in November 1892 and was provided with a 25-lever Saxby & Farmer Duplex frame with 4-inch centres, with 21 working and 4 spare levers. In later years a 9-lever ground frame was released from the signal box to operate points in the goods yard. *M. Root collection*

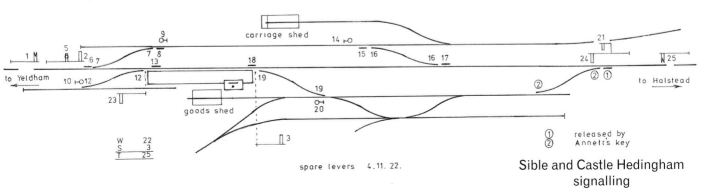

Sible and Castle Hedingham
signalling

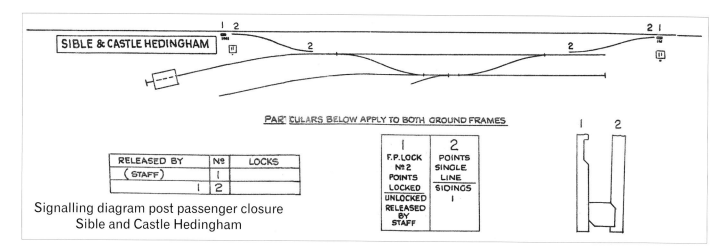

SIBLE & CASTLE HEDINGHAM

PAR' CULARS BELOW APPLY TO BOTH GROUND FRAMES

RELEASED BY	Nº	LOCKS
(STAFF)	1	
	1 2	

1	2
F.P. LOCK Nº 2 POINTS LOCKED UNLOCKED RELEASED BY STAFF	POINTS SINGLE LINE SIDINGS 1

Signalling diagram post passenger closure
Sible and Castle Hedingham

October. After this date the yard ground frame was released by the 'One Engine in Steam' single line Train Staff.

Yeldham station signal box, of local design and constructed of brick and timber, was opened in 1894 and contained a 26-lever Saxby & Farmer Duplex frame with 4-inch centres, with 23 working and 3 spare levers operating distant, home and starting signals for Up and Down road, together with a wheel to operate the level crossing gates. A 10-lever ground frame was also provided to work the points to the goods yard at the Haverhill end of the layout and was released by Annett's key on the Train Staff. The number of levers in the signal box was reduced by the L&NER in 1929 to 21 working and 5 spares. Yeldham signal box was abolished in October 1962.

Along the line at **Birdbrook** no signal box was provided until 1892 when a new brick and timber structure was erected and equipped with the 11-lever McKenzie & Holland frame resurrected from Ford Gate with 10 working and 1 spare lever. Although the signal box was provided to control the Down and Up road distant, home and starting signals, as well as points leading to the goods yard, it was not elevated to the status of a block post until November 1927 when an Electric Train Tablet instrument was installed to cover for the loss of Colne Valley Junction signal box although it was not a passing place. The signal box was abolished on 1st January 1962.

A new signal box was provided at **Colne Valley Junction**, Haverhill by Saxby & Farmer Limited in 1865. This was one of their

Yeldham signal box and level crossing with gates being worked by a wheel, in L&NER days. The structure – of local design, constructed of brick and timber with slate roof and located on the Up side of the line – was provided in 1894 and was equipped with a 26-lever Saxby & Farmer Duplex frame with 4-inch centres, with 23 working and 3 spare levers. Note the close proximity of the Up starting signal to the gates. *M. Root collection*

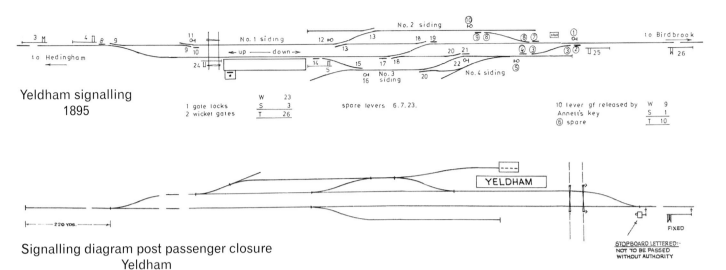

Yeldham signalling 1895

1 gate locks
2 wicket gates

	W	23
	S	3
	T	26

spare levers 6.7.23.

10 lever gf released by Annett's key
⑥ spare

	W	9
	S	1
	T	10

Signalling diagram post passenger closure Yeldham

STOPBOARD LETTERED:-
NOT TO BE PASSED
WITHOUT AUTHORITY

Birdbrook signal box of brick and timber construction was provided in 1892 and was located on the Down side of the single line opposite the platform. It was provided with an 11-lever McKenzie & Holland frame with 10 working and 1 spare levers, which was originally provided in Ford Gate signal box in 1882 and removed when a replacement 26-lever frame was installed in 1889. *M. Root collection*

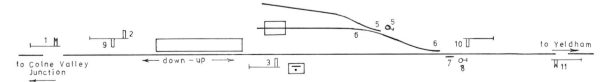

Birdbrook signalling 1930

	W	10
	S	1
	T	11

spare lever 4

type 1 designs and was unusual in that the signals were mounted on posts on the roof of the building. The signal box was actually the property of the GER but was manned by CV&HR signalmen. The building was almost square and had a pavilion roof; the actual signal posts protruded above the eaves, the two uprights being jointed by a verandah spanning the roof, each post bearing two signal arms one on each side of the post with a common lamp for each direction of travel. The signals controlling the junction were placed almost level with the points. There was no protection for trains approaching from Haverhill CV&HR station or Haverhill GER station at the same time, for as they converged there was danger of collision. To avoid this an instruction was issued that engines were not to foul the junction points unless the relevant signal was in the clear position. A further possibility was that trains working Up road from either Haverhill CV&HR or GER stations could meet a Down train from Chappel and Halstead almost 'head on' and almost touch without passing the relevant signal. Certainly until the replacement of

the signal box, and in the absence of block instruments, the only warning a signalman received of an approaching train was by single needle telegraph. An 11-lever Steven's frame with 5¼-inch centres, with 9 working and 2 spare levers replaced the original frame in 1893, and later in 1911 the signals were removed from the roof of the building and separate home signals mounted on individual posts were installed, together with distant signals on each approach to the junction. Each home arm was provided with a backboard to make signal sighting easier and to prevent drivers of approaching trains from misreading the signals.

As part of the rationalisation of the line the L&NER authorities abolished the old Colne Valley Junction signal box and associated signalling on 1st November 1927 and substituted a 2-lever ground frame to work the points at the junction. Facing point locking was provided whilst trap points were installed in the single line approaching the junction from Haverhill South. The ground frame was released and locked by a key token for the new single line section

The original signal box at Colne Valley Junction looking towards Birdbrook showing the connection from the GER station to the left and the CV&HR route nearest the camera. The unusual feature of the structure was the stop signals mounted each side of a single post for both routes but situated above the building. The platform to enable the signalman to deliver and collect the single line Train Staff fronts the signal box.   *Author's collection*

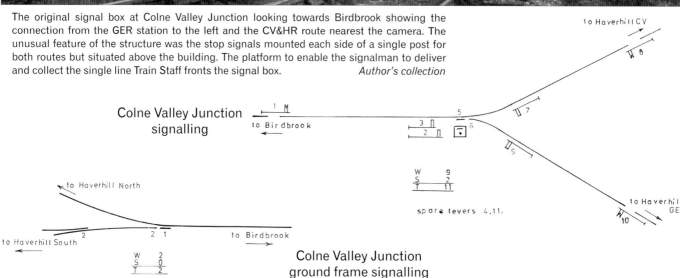

from Haverhill North Junction to Birdbrook. No shunting was permitted at the junction, but to allow the passage of another train through the single line section after the first had been locked into the section between the Junction and Haverhill South an auxiliary Tyers key token was placed in the hut beside the ground frame. Once the goods train or engine was locked away on the Haverhill South single line, the key was inserted in the machine enabling a second key to be released either from Birdbrook or Haverhill North signal boxes to enable a train to run through the single line section. A telephone connection was also provided between the hut at the junction and Haverhill South goods yard. Lieutenant Colonel E.P. Anderson inspected the new arrangements on 17th September 1929.

The subsequent notice in working documents advised that an:

Auxiliary Key Token instrument was provided at the ground frame and the lever working the points to and from Haverhill South was controlled by the Key Token for the Birdbrook and Haverhill North Junction section so that access to the Haverhill South single line could not be obtained unless the Key Token was at the Colne Valley Junction ground frame.

Haverhill CV&HR, later Haverhill South, was never provided with a signal box, initially being protected by auxiliary and stop signals in the Down direction and a stop signal for Up departures. As a result of the opening of the GER connection from Colne Valley Junction

to Haverhill GER station most passenger trains were diverted and the expense of providing full signalling for freight trains was dispensed with.

In October 1891 the GER provided a new timber signal box at **Haverhill Junction** controlling the junction between the Sudbury and Colne Valley line, replacing an earlier structure of 1865. Measuring 28 feet by 11 feet 6 inches with operating floor 10 feet above rail level the signal box was provided with a 42-lever Saxby & Farmer Duplex frame with 4-inch centres with 36 working and 6 spare levers. For Colne Valley services Haverhill Junction signal box had in the Down direction distant, home and starting signals, the latter co-acting with the Station signal box, whilst in the Up direction a distant and then junction home signals gave access to the Long Melford line or the CV&HR route. Haverhill Junction signal box was abolished on 6th March 1967. Also in October 1891 a new signal box was provided at Haverhill Station; measuring 22 feet by 11 feet 6 inches with operating floor 8 feet above rail level, the structure contained a 25-lever Saxby & Farmer Duplex frame with 4-inch centres with 17 working and 8 spare levers. Haverhill Station box was provided with distant home and starting signals on the Down road and distant home and starting signals in the Up road, the latter co-acting with the Junction signal box. The signal box was abolished on 18th July 1933 as part of a modernisation programme when control of signals and points were taken over by Haverhill Junction signal box.

Haverhill GER looking north-west in August 1911, with the granary and goods shed on the left and Haverhill Junction signal box – equipped with a 42-lever Saxby & Farmer Duplex frame with 4-inch centres, with 36 working and 6 spare levers – in the foreground. The short siding in front of the granary was shunted by tow-rope or horse. Allen & Boggis of Sudbury coal depot is on the left whilst the tall signal by the goods shed has the Junction Down starter and Station box distant on the same post. *GERS/Windwood 84*

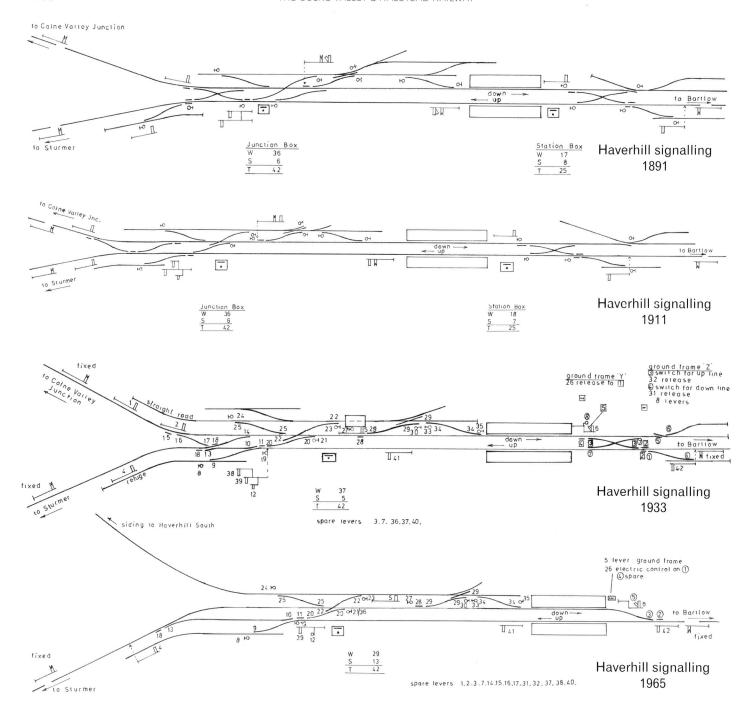

Junction Box	
W	36
S	6
T	42

Station Box	
W	17
S	8
T	25

Haverhill signalling
1891

Junction Box	
W	36
S	6
T	42

Station Box	
W	18
S	7
T	25

Haverhill signalling
1911

W	37
S	5
T	42

spare levers   3. 7. 36, 37, 40,

ground frame 'Y'
26 release to ⑪

ground frame 'Z'
① switch for up line
32 release
④ switch for down line
31 release
8 levers

Haverhill signalling
1933

5 lever ground frame
26 electric control on ①
④ spare

W	29
S	13
T	42

spare levers 1.2.3.7.14.15.16.17.31.32.37.38.40.

Haverhill signalling
1965

OPERATION

The failure of the electric telegraph and signalling equipment on the CV&HR was frequent and in such circumstances the manager assumed responsibility of sending trains forward, often without ensuring the line was clear; but when Elyot Hawkins arrived it was one of his priorities to introduce pilot working with a trained member of the operating staff acting as pilotman. The need for this became all too evident when on one occasion he realised two trains were in the single line section, one without the single line Train Staff as permission to proceed. As a result of the misdemeanour the footplate staff on the locomotive without the Train Staff were suspended from duty without pay for a week, the guards of both trains suspended for three days, whilst the itinerant signalman and manager received the threat of instant dismissal with fourteen

days suspension without pay. Regular travellers, unaware of *'slight'* failures of this kind, complained bitterly stating that *'failures had never caused delays under the old regime'*.

Typical of the routine followed by the CV&HR signalling department came in November 1911 when Saxby & Farmer provided some signal fittings at a cost of £8 4s 11d and further items were delivered in August 1912 at a cost of £9 15s 0d. Then early in March 1913 a signal post was blown across the line near Parsonage Lane level crossing during a heavy gale. The post was soon replaced but the company was short of signal wire and fittings, and ordered a quantity from Tyer's & Company at a cost of £11 6s 2d.

During the independent years Colne Valley signal boxes were open for the running of booked timetabled trains and for those specially advised. In 1891 Haverhill Station and Junction GER signal boxes were closed at night and on Sundays, although the

CHAPPEL, HALSTEAD AND HAVERHILL NORTH.

Stations.	Signal Boxes.	Telephones shewn thus: ●—●	Description of Block System in operation.	Distance from Signal Box next above. Miles.	Chains.	Open. Week-days.	Sundays.	Refuge Sidings. Down.	Up.	Wether Switch provided.	Remarks.
Chappel	Junction			...	...	For running of trains shewn in Working Time Tables, and for trains specially advised.	For running of trains shewn in Working Time Tables, and for trains specially advised.	...	...	...	
White Colne	Station		Electric Staff.	2	6	do.	do.	...	...	...	Not a Block Signal Station.
Earls Colne	do.			1	37	do.	do.	...	...	...	
Halstead	do.		Electric Key Token.	2	41	do.	do.	...	...	...	
Sible and Castle Hedingham	do.			3	20	do.	do.	...	...	...	
Yeldham	do.			2	41	do.	do.]	...	...	...	Not a Block Signal Station
Birdbrook	do.			3	63	do.	do.	...	...	...	
Haverhill North	Colne Valley Junction		S.L. Blck.	2	59	do.	do.	...	...	...	
do.	Junction		D.L. Block.	...	76	do.	do.	...	...	...	
do.	Station			...	16	do.	do.	...	...	...	

COLNE VALLEY JUNCTION TO HAVERHILL SOUTH.

Haverhill North	Colne Valley Junction		Staff only.	...	...	For running of trains shewn in Working Time Tables, and for trains specially advised.	For running of trains shewn in Working Time Tables, and for trains specially advised.	...	...	...	
do.	South			...	33	do.	do.	...	...	...	

ABOVE: Opening and closing of signal boxes 1927. BELOW: Opening and closing of signal boxes 1939.

CHAPPEL, HALSTEAD AND HAVERHILL NORTH.

				Miles.	Chains.	Week-days.	Sundays.	Down.	Up.		Remarks.
Chappel	Junction			...	...	For running of trains shewn in Working Time Tables, and for trains specially advised.	For running of trains shewn in Working Time Tables, and for trains specially advised.	...	...		
White Colne				...	6	...		...	...		Not a Block Signal Station.
Earls Colne	Station		Electric Token.	1	37	do.	do.	...	...		Earl's Colne and Yeldham.—A passenger train must not be arranged to cross another passenger train at these stations.
Halstead	do.			2	41	do.	do.	...	...		
Sible and Castle Hedingham	do.			3	20	do.	do.	...	...		
Yeldham	do			2	41	do.	do.	...	...		
Birdbrook	do.			3	63	do.	do.	...	...		
Haverhill North	§ Colne Valley Junction	●—●		2	59	do.	do.	...	...		§ No signal box. Auxiliary Token instrument provided. Ground frame controlled by Token for the Birdbrook and Haverhill North Junction section, so that access to the Haverhill South single line cannot be obtained unless Token is at ground frame.
do.	Junction			...	7	do.	do.	...	...		

COLNE VALLEY JUNCTION TO HAVERHILL SOUTH.

Haverhill North	§ Colne Valley Junction	●—●	§	...	...	For running of trains shewn in Working Time Tables, and for trains specially advised.	do.	...	...		
do.	South		§	...	33			...	...		

CHAPPEL, HALSTEAD AND HAVERHILL NORTH.

			For running of trains shewn in Working Time Tables, and for trains specially advised.	
Chappel	Junction			
White Colne				
Earls Colne	Station			Not a Token Block Station.
Halstead	do.		do.	Earl's Colne and Yeldham.—A passenger train must not be arranged to cross another passenger train at these stations.
Sible and Castle Hedingham	do.		do.	
Yeldham	do		do.	
Birdbrook	do.		do.	
Haverhill North	§ Colne Valley Junction			§ No signal box. Auxiliary Token instrument provided. Ground frame giving access to the Haverhill South single line controlled by Token for the Birdbrook and Haverhill North Junction section
do.	Junction		do.	

COLNE VALLEY JUNCTION TO HAVERHILL SOUTH.

Haverhill North	§ Colne Valley Junction	
do. South		

ABOVE: Opening and closing of signal boxes 1942.

CHAPPEL, HALSTEAD AND HAVERHILL NORTH.

			For running of trains shewn in Working Time Tables, and for trains specially advised.	
Chappel	Junction			
White Colne				
Earls Colne	Station			No Signal Box.
Halstead	do.		do.	Earl's Colne and Yeldham.—A passenger train must not be arranged to cross another passenger train at these stations.
Sible and Castle Hedingham	do.		do.	
Yeldham	do		do.	
Birdbrook	do.		do.	
Haverhill North	§ Colne Valley Junction			§ No signal box. Auxiliary Token instrument provided. Ground frame giving access to the Haverhill South single line controlled by Token for the Birdbrook and Haverhill North Junction section
do.	Junction		do.	

COLNE VALLEY JUNCTION TO HAVERHILL SOUTH.

Haverhill North	§ Colne Valley Junction	
do. South		

BELOW: Opening and closing of signal boxes 1945.

former opened specifically for the running of booked CV&HR Sunday trains. Chappel Station signal box was also closed at nights and on Sundays between the running of booked trains shown in the working timetable. The CV&HR signal box at Colne Valley Junction was closed at night. These timings continued until grouping.

By 1927 the signal boxes at Chappel, Earls Colne, Halstead, Sible and Castle Hedingham, Yeldham, Birdbrook, Colne Valley Junction, Haverhill Junction and Haverhill Station were open for the running of trains shown in the working timetable and for trains specially advised, and these timings were unaltered until the 1950s except for the closure of Haverhill Station and Colne Valley Junction signal boxes.

Local instructions in independent days required that when an ordinary or special train was run over any portion of the CV&HR between Halstead and Haverhill after 8.00pm, the Halstead station master was required to arrange for a telegraph clerk and porter to remain on duty at the station until the train had reached Haverhill in one direction or Halstead in the other. Every passenger and goods brake van was provided with a red tail board, which was used by day to signal to all concerned that there was a *special train to follow*. During the hours of darkness an extra red tail light was used for the same purpose. When a special train was required to run the station master or other person in charge at the starting station was responsible for seeing that the tail board or tail light was attached to the last vehicle of the next preceding ordinary or special train. The guard was responsible for seeing that the tail board or extra tail light was fully exhibited during the journey and for its removal at the destination station and subsequent replacement in his brakevan. Any failure to carry out such duties rendered the guard subject to disciplinary action. The tail boards were cleaned regularly at stations where the cleaning of coaching stock was executed by the coaching department.

On 19th February 1912 the company granted a wayleave to HM Postmaster General for the maintenance of the telegraph route along the line and in April 1920 and 1921 the company settled a bills for £21 4s 3d in respect of the annual charge for periodic maintenance. As a result of the impending grouping of the railways, the Secretary wrote to the Postmaster General in August advising the CV&HR wished to terminate the agreement for the maintenance of the telegraph on and from 2nd January 1923. The Secretary of the General Post Office duly replied, noting the request but advised under the agreement date 6th July 1904 the period of termination was one year. At the board meeting held on 20th September 1922 it was agreed the present arrangements would continue until the absorption of the company was completed.

CHAPPEL STATION.
Shunting Operations.

Whenever it is necessary to shunt Trucks on to the Colne Valley Single Line at Chappel Station, care must be taken that the Trucks are not pushed beyond the Up Home Signal, and that in every case a Break Van is at the Haverhill end of the Wagons.

"Calling on" Signal.

When the "Calling on" Signal (fixed on the C. V. Branch Up Home Signal Post) is lowered it will be the authority for the Driver of a Colne Valley Passenger train to draw his train slowly past the Home Signal, as far as the Points leading to the Colne Valley Siding, or as far as the Points (near the Signal Box) leading from the Down to the Up Line, as may be most convenient. The lowering of this Signal will also be the authority for the Driver of a Colne Valley Goods train to draw his train slowly past the Home Signal, either for the purpose of going direct into the Goods Yard, or of stopping short of the Points leading to the Goods Yard, as may be most convenient.

Chappel station local instructions 1910.

Specific operating instructions were issued regarding the movement of trains between the CV&HR and GER lines at Chappel. When it was necessary to a shunt a freight train on to the Colne Valley single line care had to be taken to ensure the wagons were not pushed beyond the Up home signal and that in every case a brake van was to be provided at the Haverhill end of the wagons. When the calling-on arm on the signal post on the Colne Valley branch Up home signal was lowered it was the authority for the driver of a Colne Valley passenger train to draw his train slowly past the home signal as far as the points leading to the Colne Valley siding or as far as the points near Chappel signal box leading to the Down to Up line 'as may be convenient'. The lowering of the same signal was also the authority for the driver of a Colne Valley goods train to draw his train slowly past the home signal, either for the purpose of going directly into the goods yard or of stopping short of the points leading to the goods yard, 'as may be convenient'.

Special instructions, which became operative on and from Monday 28th October 1935, were issued regarding the working of Engineer's Rail Motors between Chappel and Haverhill over the Colne Valley branch. Telephonic communication was provided between the signal boxes at Chappel, Earls Colne, Halstead, Hedingham, Yeldham, Birdbrook and Haverhill (North) Junction, and also at a number of plug posts situated by the lineside between these signal boxes. The motor when occupying the line under these arrangements did not required to be protected in accordance with Rule 215 except if stopped by accident or failure of telephonic equipment or failure of apparatus. The motor was to be accompanied by two men and carry a white head and red tail lamp, which had to be lighted during darkness or fog or falling snow, a set of hand signals, not less than 12 detonators and a klaxon horn. The motor was not to exceed a speed of 25 mph and had to be kept in gear when running down gradients. When running out of gear great care was to be taken to keep the vehicle under proper control. The driver of the motor had to observe all fixed signals and not pass any stop signal at danger unless authorised to do so by the signalman. After being authorised to pass the stop signal at danger the driver was responsible for seeing that any points were in the proper position and he was only to proceed as far as the line was clear. The possession of the Occupation Token was the authority to pass at danger the starting signal or advance starting signal controlling the entrance to the section ahead. Public level crossings not protected by fixed stop signals and occupation crossings were to be approached with caution. If the motor was stopped by accident, failure or other exceptional circumstance, which prevented its removal from the running line,

the person in charge of the motor had to immediately arrange for its protection in accordance with Rule 215 and advise the signalman of the circumstances.

The authority for the motor to occupy the line was the Occupation Token, which consisted of a box containing a portable telephone and an electric lock. When not in use the Token was locked in position either in a signal box or at one of the plug points. The Token was inscribed with the name of the section of line to which it applied. Before the motor was placed on the running line at a signal box, the person-in-charge had to obtain the consent of the signalman who had to be informed of the place to which the motor was to run and of what work was to be done. The signalman was not to give his consent until he had consulted the signalman at the other end of the single line section and obtained his permission and that he was satisfied the line could be occupied without interfering with the working of ordinary traffic. When the motor was to be placed on the line at an intermediate plug post, the man in charge had to connect the portable telephone to the plug post and obtain the attention of the signalmen at each end of the single line section and explain exactly what he required to do. The signalmen were then to confer and ascertain whether permission could be given to place the motor on the line. When the motor was removed from the line at a signal box or plug post the person in charge was responsible for checking the line was clear and advise the signalmen accordingly; the signalmen then had to record in the Train Register Book the times which the motor was placed on or removed from the running line.

If the telephonic communication failed or Occupation Token failed to be released when the motor required to be placed on the running line at a plug post, the motor had to be protected in accordance with Rule 215. If due to the failure of the apparatus or other exceptional cause, the Occupation Token could not be obtained at a signal box when the motor required to occupy the line, the motor was to be protected by a flag in accordance with Rule 215, or if the motor was required to run from one signal box to another it had to signalled as a train; the special 'Is Line Clear' bell signal 'Engineer's Rail Motor Running Through Section' (3-3-4) being used. The signal had to be accepted under Regulation 5 and a single line Train Token handed to the driver of the motor. If owing to the failure of the electrical apparatus, the Occupation Token could not be restored at the signal box or a plug post and thus normal working not resumed, working by pilotman had to be introduced after the signalmen had obtained a definite assurance that the motor had been removed from the running line. In all cases of failure of

Sible and Castle Hedingham signal box located on the platform at the Chappel end of the station. The building was of local design and had a 25-lever Saxby & Farmer frame. *J. Watling*

the electrical apparatus the lineman was required to attend and rectify the fault. The Occupation Token was not to be used when pilot working was in operation. The 'Blocking Back Outside Home Signal' bell signal was not to be sent or acknowledged whilst the Occupation Token was released.

It was permissible to attach a trailer to a motor, or two motors could be coupled together with or without a trailer attached. In such cases the leading motor was required to carry the white head lamp and the rearmost motor or trailer the red tail lamp. At least one man was to travel on each motor with another man on the trailer to operate the hand brake. A set of hand signals and not less than twelve detonators were to be carried on the trailer. When occupation of the line was required at a plug post or other place where telephonic communication was available, the line was not to be occupied by any vehicle until permission was obtained from the signalman.

In connection with the working of the Occupation Token, Train Token Locking Switches, fitted with 'Train Token Locking Switch Release', and 'Occupation Token Release' plungers were provided in the signal boxes at Chappel, Halstead, Yeldham and Haverhill North Junction. After the signalman at each end of the single line section concerned had agreed to the release of the Occupation Token and the starting or advance starting signals at each end of the single line section were locked at danger the signalman at the box where the Train Token locking switch for the section was provided had to request the signalman at the other end of the section to hold in the plunger on his token instrument to allow the release of the Train Token. He then had to depress the 'Train Token Locking Switch Release' plunger to enable him to turn the switch to the 'Trolley on Line' position. The 'Occupation Token Release' plunger was then depressed when the Occupation Token could be released. To restore normal working after the motor had been removed from the line, the Occupation Token had either to be locked up by the man in charge of the motor at one of the intermediate plug posts and a release sent to the signalman at the signal box where the Train Token locking switch for the section was provided, or handed to the signalman at the end of the single line section concerned.

The method of locking up the Occupation Token at a plug post, or at the signal box at the opposite end of the single line section to which the Train Token Locking Switch was provided, was by inserting the telephone plug in the cupboard when the release key on the Occupation Token had to be turned to the position marked 'Ring' and the signalman at the box where the Train Token Locking Switch for the section was provided informed that the motor had been removed from the line. The chained key then had to be placed in the lock on the Occupation Token and turned in a counter-clockwise direction, when it became locked. The release key was then turned to the position marked 'Release' after which the signalman turned the Train Token Locking Switch to the normal position. After the Occupation Token had been locked up the signalmen at each end of the Key Token sections had to depress the Key Token instrument plunger to restore the Key Token indicator to normal. The Occupation Token then remained locked up and ordinary train working was resumed. The same process was adhered to when the Occupation Token required to be locked up at a signal box where the Train Token Locking Switch was provided except it was not necessary for the Release Key to be moved to the 'Ring' position.

When the man in charge of the motor required to occupy a portion of one section and subsequently entered the next section he was required on arrival at the signal box to take the Occupation Token to the signalman, who then had to use the Token to release the section that was occupied, and if the next section could be occupied by the motor, obtain the Occupation Token for that section and hand it to the man in charge of the motor. It was important that the signalman had a clear understanding with the platelayer when the Occupation Token was taken from the signal box, as to which section of single line the motor required to proceed, and if placed on the line at a plug post in which direction it was to proceed.

In independent days Halstead staff covered signalling maintenance with bespoke parts manufactured in the company's workshops, although much help came from the GER staff based at Colchester, Sudbury and Haverhill. In later years signal fitters, including William Bettis, based at Sudbury, conducted day-to-day maintenance and repairs.

10

Officers and Railway Staff

OFFICERS

The initial company Chairman was Edward Horner of the Howe, Halstead, a leading advocate for the railway through the Colne Valley. In 1860 Horner was succeeded by James Brewster, who retained the role of Chairman, except for a short period, until 1885. An outspoken man, *'he would offer sharp and swift criticism uttered without fear or favour'*. He disliked Horatio Love, Chairman of the ECR and later GER, particularly because of his wanton dislike of the upstart CV&HR. In a directors' dispute of 1863 Brewster severely criticised fellow director R.E. Greenwood whom he accused, among other things, of arranging the dismissal of the locomotive foreman for refusing to engage Greenwood's son as an engine driver. He was guilty of interfering with the affairs of Robert Watt who was not as straightforward and upright a character, for he submitted in his numerous expenses a gas bill for £7 10s 0d when the total the previous year was only £2 10s 0d. It was asserted Greenwood had accepted commissions on loans raised on the behalf of the Company but no evidence was proven. Greenwood was proprietor of the local gas works and also Manager of the Halstead branch of the London & County Joint Stock Bank.

Yet another skirmish occurred in December 1885 when Brewster circulated a document, which he claimed gave a *few facts regarding the affairs of the Company'*. This infuriated Robert Tweedy, one of the directors. Tweedy, who together with his father owned a considerable shareholding in the CV&HR, observed *'they were the subject of his indignation'*. Tweedy remarked in a blatant retaliatory letter that Brewster was correct in asserting his paper contained a few facts, but added the facts were remarkably *'few indeed'*. Brewster also served as a Justice of the Peace.

W. Bailey Hawkins, who also had an abrupt manner, succeeded Brewster. At a half yearly meeting in August 1888, Jackson, a solicitor from Haverhill, stood up to address the director on the subject of outstanding professional fees owed him by the Company. Bailey Hawkins interrupted him by declaring the matter should be referred to the Company's solicitor and immediately declared the meeting closed. Dumbfounded, Jackson departed and the directors dispersed. Bailey Hawkins, despite his manner, was popular and on 25th February 1914 was unanimously re-elected Chairman for the ensuing year and succeeding years until 1919, when he became ill. Charles B.O. Clarke was elected as temporary Chairman of the Company for the ensuing years. On 23rd February 1922 the death of W. Bailey Hawkins was reported; he had held the position of Chairman of the company for nine annual general meetings, being involved with railway for 34 years. Charles B.O. Clarke was re-elected Chairman of the Company, staying in office until the grouping in 1923.

Nathaniel Beardmore served as the first Engineer of the Company and was succeeded by Joseph Cubitt, son of Sir William Cubitt. His appointment as Engineer to the CV&HR appears purely to have been a consultative post for he had been Engineer to the Great Northern Railway and London, Chatham & Dover Railway. Cubitt handled the decision-making whilst C.B. Sperling oversaw site work and construction. When the railway was completed Cubitt departed and Sperling became the Company Engineer except for the short period when the railway was leased to Daniel Gooch. The new incumbent appointed one of his own men, Rogers, to manage the undertaking and also for a shorter period when Sperling was the lessee. Sperling's successor as Engineer was A.G. Fenn, who joined the CV&HR in 1868 and became Engineer in 1871. He retained the post for a decade until he departed in 1881 to join the Heberlein Brake Company as Consulting Engineer, from whence he returned to the Colne Valley in 1903. A.G. Fenn retired in July 1912 due to ill health but unfortunately passed away in April 1913.

Four secretaries served the railway in its independent days. Initially Alfred Edward Williams served for four years before being replaced by Edmund Harvey in 1860. He reigned for twelve years until December 1872, when after allegedly misappropriating funds he was suspended and subsequently resigned. He died shortly afterwards before charges could be brought in a court of law. William G. Bailey took over as Secretary, remaining with the Company until 1904, when as a result of rationalisation the secretaryship was merged with other posts and taken over by Elyot Hawkins.

Robert Johnson Watt was the initial General Manager, having served on the ECR as a District Inspector at Ely with charge of ten stations, but he was far from popular. 'Wattbaiting' was a recognised pastime in Halstead in the early 1860s. He was so unpopular that on his reappointment after the resignation of Cooper in 1864, shareholders and railway users protested against his return. He once had the misfortune of being sued by a Mr Goodbody of Ely concerning a donkey. The population of Halstead seized the opportunity and to his enemies and detractors he was known as 'Donkey Watts'. A woodcut of a small lop-eared donkey chewing on thistles was considered a representation of Watts in allegorical form. Typical of the evidence from various detractors, and known as 'Warttania', each showed the same picture at the head of the page.

A typical verse showed:

Who when a maid in the train he spied,
Forthwith himself sat by her side?
MY DONKEY!

Who when he caused a great hubbub,
His name did quickly give as 'Tubb'?
MY DONKEY!

What up and down the streets did walk,
And on the walls did 'Cooper' chalk?
MY DONKEY!

Who when the Gas Manager a note did bring,
Disdainfully his head did fling!
MY DONKEY!

Who when the gallant Mac Appeared,
Called Evans out because he feared?
MY DONKEY!

Who when had up before 'the beak'
Displayed a great amount of cheek?
MY DONKEY!

Who now looks quite off his feed,
His mane and tail all gone to seed?
MY DONKEY!

Whose time is up? Whose race is o'er?
Who SHALL go, as he's gone before?
MY DONKEY!

The third and last verse referred to the brief period in 1863 and 1864 when Cooper was General Manager. J.B. Cooper, as manager for this short period, did not distinguish himself for in June 1864 he was asked to account to the CV&HR board for alleged misconduct. He failed to answer but instead tendered his resignation, which was immediately accepted.

Watt departed for pastures new in 1865 when the railway was leased to Daniel Gooch; the *Halstead Times* made brief reference to the departure. *'Many of our readers will be gratified to learn that Mr R.J. Watt, manager of the Colne Valley Railway, has obtained a lucrative appointment as Manager of the Government Railway in the island of Ceylon'*. The *Halstead Gazette* added:

> the appointment was competitive and is proof of Mr Watt's well known abilities and the high character of his credentials; he was unanimously elected by the government from a large number of candidates. We should like to be assured, as one result of the change of management that the long-standing accounts of the tradesmen will be discharged at an early date and without the partiality of which we have heard some rumours.

However, on termination of the lease Watt returned to the CV&HR as General Manager and finally departed in 1877, still unpopular and to the last in dispute with the directors as to the remuneration due to him.

The next General Manager was John Crabtree, formerly Outdoor Goods Agent for the Great Northern Railway at Halifax, but his tenure was short for he departed in 1882 to become General Manager of the Great Northern & Great Eastern Joint Line at Lincoln. His successor was George Copus who retained the position until 1903 when the post was taken over by Elyot S. Hawkins.

Elyot S. Hawkins joined the CV&HR in 1903 as General Manager and subsequently incorporated the post of Engineer and Secretary. He was educated at Shrewsbury School and then spent five years as a pupil in the Cambrian Railways' Locomotive Shops at Oswestry, graduating to the drawing office and ultimately as an inspector in the materials department. He departed from the service with the Cambrian Railways to join the CV&HR. Whilst at Oswestry he joined the Shropshire Rifle Volunteers, which subsequently under Lord Haldane's Territorial scheme became the 4th Battalion King's Shropshire Light Infantry. On the outbreak of World War One he was immediately called for service and spent two and a half years in the Far East, Burma, Singapore and Hong Kong. In 1917 he was transferred to the Western Front where he remained until April 1918, when he sustained serious wounds which necessitated

his repatriation. He left the Army in February 1919 with the rank of Major and returned to the CV&HR, which he continued to manage until the company was absorbed into the L&NER.

Because of the war effort the salary of the General Manager had been reduced to two-thirds of the pre-war level on 10th November 1914. On 26th February 1915 it was agreed to maintain the salary at the same level for a further three months, when it would be subject to review. In the meantime W. Bailey Hawkins had approached the Government for assistance with his salary and it was agreed they would make up the difference between his original salary and the two-thirds paid by the CV&HR, the arrangement being ratified at the board meeting on 10th August 1915. On 3rd June 1920 it was agreed to increase the salary of the Secretary and General Manager to £900 per annum, although the latter would be required to pay his own income tax.

E.D. Cattaway served as CV&HR Locomotive Superintendent from 1861, based at offices at 1 New Broad Street, London EC, but in 1866 Peter Goulden joined the CV&HR as Locomotive Foreman, having served on the Great Western Railway at Wolverhampton. He had initially served his apprenticeship with the L&NWR at Crewe Works and as well as gaining his skills in fitting also gained skill as a blacksmith, boilermaker and coppersmith. He was Locomotive Superintendent in 1901 and retired after 45 years' service with the CV&HR in 1913, being succeeded by Charles Bartholomew who had come from the GER Locomotive Superintendent's department at Stratford Works in 1901, and to which he returned when the company was absorbed.

Accountancy was part of the General Manager's duties but when Elyot Hawkins came to Halstead he found work had been satisfactorily carried out by Samuel Rayner, who had joined the company as boy clerk and in the course of promotion had served for a short while as a station master. Hawkins suggested to the directors, and received agreement, to appoint Rayner as the Company Accountant and he filled this post from 1904 until 7th April 1914 when he was appointed assistant secretary, and from 1st August his salary was increased by £50 per annum. He died in 1919 and was succeeded as Company Accountant by S. Scillitoe on 7th April 1920, at an annual salary of £450. Scillitoe had joined the railway as a boy and acted as Rayner's assistant during the war years while Rayner deputised for the absent Hawkins. James Williamson, the Assistant Engineer of the Cambrian Railways, acted at Consulting Engineer to the CV&HR between 1912 and 1919; he paid frequent visits to Essex to supervise work on permanent way and bridges due to Rayner's lack of technical knowledge. The death occurred on 5th March 1948 of S.T. Scillitoe the retired District Auditor who had been based at Halstead.

STATION MASTERS

CV&HR station masters were:

> responsible for good housekeeping on their stations especially on the consumption of coal, gas water and oil. Oil lights were to be monitored so that none burned unnecessarily during daylight hours, whilst at stations where gas was used the lights were to be kept low except for an interval before and after the arrival and departure of a train and turned down thereafter.

George William Grand was GER station master at Chappel in the 1880s and 1890s, having previously been employed at Colne.

W.H. Wilkes, station master at Chappel from 1906, was transferred to take charge of Woodbridge on the East Suffolk line in August 1913. At a gathering of GER staff and CV&HR personnel he was presented with a silver mounted ebony walking stick by Signalman W. Gosling. Wilkes' successor was A.M. Jarvis who gained promotion from Hatfield Peverel and served at the station until retirement on 30th September 1930; he enjoyed thirteen years of retirement and died on 4th November 1943. C.H. Read took over at the junction which also included the neighbouring station of Bures, serving until his retirement on 5th December 1938 after forty-six years' service. He was presented with a table lighter in the form of L&NER Class 'A4' 'pacific' locomotive No. 4498 *Dominion of Canada* at a ceremony by Mr Lummins the relief station master and attended by local staff. In April 1939, R. Marriott, station master at Morton Road on the former Great Northern Railway Bourne to Sleaford branch was promoted to the resultant vacancy at Bures, whilst N. Timm was transferred from Kimberley on the Wymondham to Wells line to take charge at Chappel. Timms had a short tenure at the station for in September 1942 E.H. Handley from Lincoln District Superintendent's Office was appointed acting station master at Chappel. At the end of hostilities he was promoted in May 1946 to take charge at Waleswood on the former Great Central line between Retford and Sheffield, and S.T. Smith, formerly a Clerk at Woodbridge on the East Suffolk main line, succeeded Handley. C.H. Read, formerly of Chappel and Wakes Colne, died on 15th March 1949.

At Colne, Charles Cork was the initial station master in 1860 but on transfer to Hedingham in 1862 was replaced by Thomas McKay. George Evans then took charge until the station closed in 1889, when he transferred to Ford Gate and retired from railway service at the age of 70 in 1926, having started his railway career as a clerk after leaving school. When the station reopened in 1907, Thomas Taylor became station master having originally served as a senior porter at Earls Colne. He was still in charge when the L&NER took over in 1923 but then the post of station master was abolished and Taylor, not wishing to move, was reduced to a grade one porter, a post which he held until his death in 1937.

John Bennett was station master at Ford Gate when the station opened 1882, serving seven years in the post until replaced by George Evans in 1889. He remained in charge until 1926, overseeing the change of name to Colne and then Earls Colne. On 29th February 1924 he gave up renting part of the station house, for which he had paid £17 5s 4d annually. In September 1924 C. Sparrow, formerly station master at Isleham on the Cambridge to Mildenhall line, was transferred to take charge of Earls Colne including White Colne, but from 8th November 1924 his rent of the station house was increased to £26 per annum. In comparison, along the line at Birdbrook, Station Master Charles Wilson was only paying £9 2s 0d per annum in a residence hired by the company. In December 1927 C. Sparrow, station master at Earls Colne, was transferred to take charge of Mildenhall including Isleham, from where he subsequently retired in August 1933 after 42½ years service. P.E. Pryke, who gained promotion from relief clerk on Colne Valley and Stour Valley line stations, then took over at Earls Colne but gained promotion to Kennett in 1934. C.B. Reeves, who had previously served eighteen months as station master at Standon on the Buntingford branch, later took charge but he died on 11th July 1947.

George R. Hitchcock was appointed the first station master at Halstead and remained in the post for a decade until succeeded by John T. Titman, who was later dismissed in disgrace. Titman was replaced by Samuel Rayner, who on being succeeded by John Willoughby Lee on promotion to Yeldham in 1892, became the Company Accountant, serving the company for over 50 years. T. Blackmore then served as station master for short period after Lee's departure until 1902, when Frederick Coppin was promoted from Birdbrook. Whilst in residence, Coppin lived at 163 King's Road and he retired on 30th September 1931. He had started his career with the CV&HR on 1st July 1882 as a porter at Birdbrook and later served for short periods at Earls Colne and Sible and Castle Hedingham before returning to Birdbrook as station master, aged 23. In June 1902 he was promoted to station master Halstead and served the whole of his career on the Colne Valley. At a presentation he received a leather suitcase, and a pipe from staff at Halstead. As a result of Coppin's departure, further rationalisation took place and E. Herbert, station master at Sible and Castle Hedingham, assumed joint control of Halstead and his own station. During World War Two the post was reinstated, however, and T.J. Rattee was appointed, serving until October 1946 when he was promoted to take charge at Wells on the North Norfolk coast. The new incumbent was E. Theobald.

Along the line at Sible and Castle Hedingham, Charles Cork was station master in 1862 when the station opened for traffic until he was succeeded by George Evans in 1876. Evans transferred to Colne in 1880 and was replaced at Hedingham by Charles Willett. By 1886 Joseph Pittock was in charge before transferring to Yeldham in 1889. Joseph John Vale was then appointed station master and remained in the post for forty years until his retirement on 30th June 1928 aged 70 years. He commenced his career with the GER at Blackwall, Pepper Warehouse in 1875 and twelve years later joined the CV&HR. Shortly after his arrival he was appointed station master at Yeldham before moving on to Sible and Castle Hedingham a few months later. Vale's successor was E.W. Herbert, formerly a clerk at Cambridge.

John Willoughby Lee was recorded as station master at Yeldham from 1880 until he was promoted to take charge at Halstead. He was replaced by Joseph John Vale in 1887, but two years later Joseph Pittock was in charge and there he remained until retirement age 75 on 6th April 1922. For devotion to duty he was awarded a pension of £1 per week. The new incumbent was L. Stribling, but his tenure was short for after a long and painful illness he died on 27th November 1927 at the age of 37. He started on the CV&HR at Yeldham in 1903 and later transferred to Sible and Castle Hedingham as goods clerk before promotion to station master Yeldham in 1922. After much deliberation the vacant station master's post at Yeldham was abolished and C. Mitson, station master at Birdbrook, also assumed charge of Yeldham from January 1928. Evidently this arrangement was unsatisfactory for N.G. Ruggles was then appointed station master at Yeldham. In the intervening period and before his appointment in July 1930, Ruggles was presented with a case of fish knives and forks by Station Master Mitson at Yeldham as a gift for his impending wedding. His stay was short, for in December 1936 Ruggles gained promotion to Felstead on the Bishop's Stortford to Braintree branch. In January 1943 G.A. Kemp, station master at Stainby, was promoted to take charge at Yeldham followed by H.M. Parker, but in June 1947 L. Thompson, a clerk at Sudbury, was promoted to station master at Yeldham.

Frederick Coppin was station master at Birdbrook in the 1880s and he served at the station until 1902, when he was promoted to take charge at Halstead. He was replaced by S. Scillitoe, who served until just before grouping, when C. Mitson was promoted. As mentioned above, Mitson also assumed control of Yeldham for a short period but in June 1932 he gained promotion from Birdbrook to take charge at Haddenham on the Ely to St Ives branch. S. Scilliroe later became district auditor.

Just before grouping, R. Blackmore was CV&HR station master at Haverhill but was retired in view of the impending changes and received a weekly pension of £1. In May 1922 the GER altered the responsibilities of the station master at Haverhill, when R.C. Horsepool took over the control of Sturmer station in addition to Haverhill and Withersfield Siding. His tenure was short for in August 1923 E. Day was promoted from Soham to take charge of Haverhill including Withersfield siding and Sturmer, before retiring on 31st January 1929. He had served as station master at Linton from 1904 to 1912 and Soham from 1912 to 1923 before taking charge of Haverhill North and South. Then in April 1929, W.E. Ellis, also promoted from Soham, took charge at Haverhill North and South including Sturmer until his retirement on 31st March 1934. W. Tabbitt was subsequently transferred from the post of station master Kennett on the Bury St Edmunds to Cambridge line to take charge at the junction station. Tabbitt's position at Kennett was taken over by Station Master P.B. Pryke, who relinquished command at Earls Colne including White Colne. In May 1942 W. Tabbitt gained promotion to Huntingdon North including Huntingdon East and Godmanchester. G.W. Newell, formerly in charge at Haverhill, died in August 1928. Another retired Station Master, R.C. Horsepool who had served at Haverhill, passed away on 28th October 1948, whilst retired Station Master E. Day, who had also served at Haverhill North, died on 8th April 1949.

TRAFFIC STAFF

In the mists of time, details of clerical staff serving on the CV&HR and at the junction stations are sketchy, but on 7th January 1920 the death of Mr Seymour, chief goods clerk at Halstead, was announced. Then on 27th July 1927 the presentation of wedding gifts were made to two members of staff at Haverhill North, Signalman William Morris and Goods Clerk Thomas Fox. Goods Clerk D. Meade retired on 25th April 1928 after fifty years' service. He had commenced his railway career at Haverhill before serving for short periods at Walton-on-the-Naze, Diss, Bury St Edmunds and Kennett. He then returned to Haverhill where he remained for the next forty years. At a gathering of work colleagues he was presented with an eight-day clock by Station Master E. Day. Many serving at the station used their stay as a stepping stone to promotion, for in June 1930 G.B. Tassell, a Clerk at Haverhill North, gained promotion as station master at Wilburton on the Ely to St Ives branch. Alan H. Buck, the chief booking clerk at Haverhill, was promoted to chief parcels clerk at March in August 1930 and at a ceremony attended by L. Clarke the chief goods clerk, J.M. Clow booking clerk and Driver H. Curtis he was presented with

Two members of the carriage shed staff pose for the camera outside the building at Halstead. *M. Root collection*

a shaving outfit by Station Master W.E. Ellis. In January 1938 W. Cresswell, a clerk at Halstead, gained promotion to station master Pye Hill and Somercoates on the former Great Northern Railway Pinxton branch. On 23rd October 1946 the death was announced of H.M. Harrington, a retired clerk who served at Halstead for many years, but on a happier note in the summer of 1948 Shirley Clift, employed as a goods clerk at Halstead, married B. French, the chief goods clerk in the same office; at a presentation attended by colleagues, Station Master E. Theobald wished them well and handed over gifts. In the final years, Halstead staff included Albert French, chief clerk, who commenced his railway career on the CV&HR in 1902 aged 13 and completed fifty-two years' service; Peter Brett and Vera Rogers were the goods clerks, in the passenger office were Molly French, Freda Aldred, Shirley Clift and Iris Goodey.

Porters were the front line staff, having daily contact with passengers. Of the early staff, Percy Willingham, employed as junior porter at Earls Colne and also covered White Colne as required, started his career in 1910. By 1924 Thomas Walter Taylor was porter-in-charge at White Colne station where he resided in part of the station building at an annual rent of £11 14s 0d. He died on 9th January 1937 age 62 years having commenced his railway career at Yeldham in November 1892, and after a time at Earls Colne was transferred to White Colne as porter-in-charge when the station reopened in 1907. He was an avid rose grower and won several prizes for his station in the annual station garden competition. Porter J.N.M. Saunders of Earls Colne gained promotion to motor driver at Clare in March 1938; Clerk Moss and Signalman Mathews made a small presentation to Saunders on behalf of local staff. The following month Porter W.C. Stearn was transferred from Sudbury to fill the vacant position. To cover for staff recruited for the armed services, women were employed during World War Two, including at Earls Colne Eileen Reeves, the daughter of the Earls Colne station master, as well as lad porter Harry Egg. Porters at Halstead in the later years included Alec Arnold, Joe Yoxall, Len Hood, John Walker, Wallace Lovesey, Frank Mathias later signalman Earls Colne, Joe Cornerford, Victor Wilkin and Philip Hewitt.

In the autumn of 1912 the passenger and goods guards employed by the CV&HR applied for an increase in pay and when no response was made by management industrial action was threatened. The matter was raised at the board meeting on 26th November when it was agreed to discuss the matter at a special board meeting to start at 12.30pm on Tuesday 17th December 1912. At the reconvened gathering and after much discussion it was recommended the company adopt the revised Rates of Pay and Conditions of Service, which covered the guards' problems. Only the payment for Sunday duty to booking clerks was declined, subject to further discussion. On 9th December 1913 the application from the goods guards for an increase in pay was deferred. Then on 12th March 1930 Herbert Ellis, a passenger guard at Haverhill

Four members of the CV&HR head office clerical staff stand outside the building on this undated occasion.

M Root collection

North, retired; he joined the CV&HR in 1893 as a porter and was promoted to Porter/Guard and soon after became a passenger guard. At a small ceremony on his retirement his colleagues presented him with a tobacco pipe and pouch. Once the L&NER took over the line in 1923 the ex-CV&HR guards at Haverhill were transferred to the ex-GER station complement and thereafter the line was worked by guards based at Haverhill North or Sudbury, these included Ernest Fox, Bob Canbrook, 'Dickie' Bird (because he wore a 'dickie' tie) and William Brooks.

Signalmen were usually the longest serving of all staff, remaining at their home station for many years. One such member was Signalman T. Benham of Halstead who retired on 3rd June 1933 after forty-six years' service with the CV&HR and L&NER. He was presented with a gift of an inscribed cigarette case and cigarettes on behalf of his colleagues at the station and locomotive depot by Station Master Herbert. In October 1933 Signalman W. Hindes transferred from Haverhill to Halstead to cover the vacancy. A member of staff to die at the relatively young age of 56 was Percy Gibbs, signalman at Earls Colne, who passed away on 18th October 1937; he had commenced with the CV&HR in July 1901 as a platelayer and eventually gained promotion to signalman at Earls Colne. W. Gosling, a retired signalman who had served at Chappel for many years, passed away on 8th February 1942. In the final years before the line closed the Halstead signalmen were David Succamore and Frederick Suckling, with Robert Willingham signalman at Earls Colne. Relief signalmen covering sickness and rest day duties in the final years on the Colne Valley were Charles Chase, Frederick Brooks and Frank Saines.

The working staff of the CV&HR over the years were a close knit community, and as early as Saturday 28th December 1861 held their annual dinner at the Bell Inn, Castle Hedingham, when William Munro occupied the chair. Mr Knight provided the meal and amidst an aura of convivial geniality toasts were offered to James Brewster, the company Chairman and his fellow directors, to Munro and many others. The local press reporting the gathering concluded: *'it was fortunate no service ran on Sunday for many suffered hangovers!'* These convivialities continued over the years and in 1913 the annual CV&HR staff dinner was held at the Eight Bells at Bures on 6th March 1913, with Elyot S. Hawkins presiding in the absence of Station Master C.A. Wadley who was indisposed.

Changes instituted by Elyot Hawkins to improved methods of working were initially unpopular, as many preferred the lackadaisical old days when almost anything was tolerated. However, when they realised much was being done for their benefit they enthusiastically accepted the new conditions. All traffic staff, including guards, shunters and station personnel had been employed on the basis of a seven-day week with no enhancements for Sunday duty. Increase in wages had brought about petty squabbling between grades but in 1907 the board were persuaded to institute a six-day week with overtime paid for Sunday duty; the standard rates of pay used by the GER on adjoining lines were introduced, which many found to their advantage.

Prior to World War One the staff were non-unionists but during the hostilities those not joining the armed forces were persuaded to join the trade union. The introduction of revised rates of pay in 1920 and 1921 by agreement between the railway companies and the unions imposed a burden on the slender financial resources of the CV&HR so that it was ultimately necessary to reduce the number of staff or lower wages. In response to an appeal by the manager, most accepted a 10 per cent reduction in wages. The rigorous campaign to reduce costs was put into operation, including the withdrawal of Sunday trains, but fortunately matters improved and the pay cut was reversed for all staff in 1921. On 7th April 1921 it was agreed to discharge staff over 70 years of age, including Gatekeeper A. Chaplin.

On 19th February 1912 a sum of £1 12s 0d was paid to the Haverhill Co-operative Society in respect of clothing supplies, whilst later in the year on 29th August £6 6s 3d was paid to R.L. Bloomfield for a supply of uniform caps. Another payment of £8 1s 0d was made to the Haverhill Co-operative Society on 17th September 1912 in respect of uniform clothing.

The aftermath of World War One found the railway companies in a parlous financial state and economies were constantly sought. The L&NER continued to seek economies and an example of improvements and the effect on local staff is provided here. The abolition of Haverhill Station signal box and the concentration of all work on Haverhill Junction signal box resulted in an upheaval in staff at the station. On 7th September 1933 five past and present staff received gifts on their retirement: L. Clarke, chief goods clerk, J.W. Clow, chief booking clerk, Signalman W.F. Marks, Foreman Platelayer W. Norfolk and Shunter B. Jacobs; whilst Signalman C. Fox was transferred to Long Melford and Signalman W. Hindes to Halstead. At the ceremony, T. Mizen, the contractor's carman who was displaced by the L&NER taking over the collection and delivery service in the town, also received a suitcase, and Motor Driver H.J. Hall was presented with an eight-day clock as a wedding gift. Station Master W.E. Ellis made all the presentations on behalf of the staff at Haverhill and adjacent stations. Unfortunately Fox, who had served at Haverhill for forty years, was soon found to have defective vision and he was transferred to Cambridge as cloak room attendant in 1935 before retiring on 22nd August 1936. Lorry drivers employed at Halstead in the final years included Edgar Winch, Stanley Maltwood and Wilfred Leatherdale; Peter Willingham later transferred to McGregor of Hedingham as a bus driver.

The outbreak of World War Two also caused staff upheaval and resulted in many of the railmen being called to serve in the forces. For some it resulted in the ultimate sacrifice and others severe hardship, including G.L.H. Wilkes, a clerk in Halstead goods office, who whilst serving as a Private in the Essex Regiment was reported missing during the summer of 1944, before being confirmed as a prisoner of war.

It is now hard to realise that even a small line like the Colne Valley was heavily reliant on staff; as an example, personnel employed at Earls Cole in 1943, when considerable freight and military traffic was handled, included Jack Payne goods porter, Henry Egg lad porter, Joe Marks goods porter, Percy Polston foreman, Albert Wass porter, Henry Gilbert signalman, Ted Willingham lad porter, Eileen Reeves porteress, Joan Willingham clerk, Jack Moss clerk, C.B. Reeves station master, Percy Willingham clerk, Vera Rogers clerk, Ernie Watts signalman, and Dorothy Willingham crossing keeper Langley Mill crossing.

Halstead station staff 1908 Back row left to right: T. Benham, J. Pafflin, E. Dixey, A. Eves, D. Amos, A. Cansell and F. Hart, whilst in the front row left to right are: C. Pavely, F. Cook, H. Wiffen, Station Master F. Coppin, J. Miller, A. Harringron and S. Norfolk.　　　　*Author's collection*

11

Timetables and Traffic

THE COLNE VALLEY AND HALSTEAD RAILWAY was created essentially as a transport feeder to the town of Halstead after the Colchester, Stour Valley & Halstead Railway abandoned their projected branch to the Essex manufacturing centre. Like many other rural East Anglian routes, the area served formed part of large agricultural estates and – except for pockets of industry at Halstead, Earls Colne and Sible and Castle Hedingham – the majority of the populace were employed on the land. Local industry certainly made use of the railway for the conveyance of goods but few used the line to get to and from work. Passenger traffic was therefore spasmodic and long distance, with the only regular traffic conveyed on Thursday, Halstead market day, and the lesser forays to Colchester and Haverhill markets on Saturdays and Fridays respectively. It is therefore of no surprise that the GER refused to take over the railway for they had enough ailing rural branches of their own. The CV&HR company soldiered on, maintaining a service of between four and seven weekday trains to serve the villages and towns in the Colne Valley, but did little to attract an increase in trade and populace in the independent years – a factor which continued into grouping and nationalisation. As the figures below show, the population of the catchment area served remained almost constant for the century the railway served the community.

Before the advent of the railway, Halstead inhabitants wishing to travel further afield were totally reliant on horse drawn coaches or carrier's waggons for conveyance to distant parts. In 1855 'The Eagle' coach ran to Braintree station each morning and afternoon on weekdays only, from the White Hart in the High Street. Haverhill had a coach from the Bell Inn to Saffron Walden and on to Audley End railway station, running daily except Sundays and departing at 8.00am from the Bell Inn and returning at 3.30pm from Audley End station. With the impending arrival of the railway the Braintree omnibus operated by William Smith ran on Wednesdays only from the High Street.

The CV&HR timetable offered from **January 1861** showed the following service of four trains each way on weekdays and two in each direction on Sundays.

TIMETABLE FROM JANUARY 1861							
DOWN		**WEEKDAYS**				**SUNDAYS**	
		am	pm	pm	pm	am	pm
Chappel	dep	10.15	1.40	6.05	7.50	10.00	6.55
Colne	dep	10.20	1.45	*	8.00	10.10	7.05
Halstead	arr	10.40	2.00	6.20	8.10	10.25	7.20
* Calls if required.							

UP		**WEEKDAYS**				**SUNDAYS**	
		am	pm	pm	pm	am	pm
Halstead	dep	8.25	12.35	4.05	6.25	8.50	4.55
Colne	dep	8.35	*	*	*	9.03	5.08
Chappel	arr	8.43	12.55	4.25	6.40	9.10	5.15
* Calls if required.							

After several complaints were received from the residents of Sudbury and Halstead concerning the lack of a late afternoon train to Colchester, the ECR agreed on 27th March 1861 for the 4.15pm Sudbury to Marks Tey train to be extended to Colchester, returning at 5.30pm. Connections to and from Colne Valley stations were maintained at Chappel.

POPULATION FIGURES												
YEAR	**1851**	**1861**	**1871**	**1881**	**1891**	**1901**	**1911**	**1921**	**1931**	**1951**	**1961**	**1971**
Chappel or Pondisbright	452	370	392	363	353	371	390	357	383	422	373	342
Wakes Colne	499	535	524	499	515	482	501	446	470	485	435	442
Colne Engaine	670	627	561	520	510	487	583	578	624	607	581	888
White Colne	459	400	406	374	358	326	385	348	364	369	272	277
Earls Colne	1,518	1,540	1481	1,594	1,720	1,762	1,871	1,806	1,655	1,801	2,106	2,389
Halstead	6,982	6,917	6,904	6,701	6,959	6,900	7,040	6,648	6,619	6,874	7,120	8,448
Sible Hedingham	2,346	2,123	2,097	1,926	1,785	1,701	1,789	1,762	2,149	2,251	2,377	3,326
Castle Hedingham	1,394	1,203	1,235	1,040	1,028	1,097	988	961	873	914	936	995
Great Yeldham	716	696	683	599	619	595	600	581	492	659	738	1,290
Little Yeldham	306	307	313	289	264	263	279	214	230	338	265	264
Birdbrook	616	643	682	581	573	461	432	428	417	356	340	309
Haverhill	2,792	2,695	3,388	4,073	5,048	5,224	4,748	4,083	3,828	4,096	5,445	12,360
Total*	15,506	14,991	14,886	14,123	14,331	14,074	14,468	13,772	13,893	14,654	15,170	18,628
Total+	18,750	18,056	18,666	18,559	19,732	19,669	19,606	18,212	18,104	19,172	20,988	31,330
NOTES: * Excluding Chappel and Haverhill.												
+ Including Chappel and Haverhill.												

When the CV&HR was extended to Castle Hedingham in **July 1861** the company operated the same timetable as in January with trains allowed 15 minutes running time for the additional journey between Halstead and Castle Hedingham in both directions. The last train in the Up direction from Castle Hedingham ran 35 minutes later, whilst the first Down train on Sundays departed Chappel at 10.05am and ran 5 minutes later throughout. Then in September the following additional trains ran: on weekdays departing Halstead at 7.40am, arriving at Castle Hedingham at 7.55am and returning at 8.35am with arrival at Halstead at 8.50am; on Sundays two additional services operated between Halstead and Castle Hedingham in the Down direction, departing Halstead at 8.00am and 2.30pm with a 15 minutes timing to Castle Hedingham; in the Up directions the additional trains departed Castle Hedingham at 11.00am and 8.00pm, with arrival at Halstead at 11.15am and 8.15pm respectively.

The timetable from **1st January 1862** showed a service of five trains in each direction on weekdays and three each way on Sundays, although not all travelled the full length of the line. Connections between Down trains at Chappel were good, but in the Up directions passengers on the first CV&HR service had 37 minutes wait for the forwarding ECR train.

By **August 1862**, when the line had been extended to Yeldham and during the first month of the formation of the GER, the CV&HR timetable again included Sunday services.

On the opening of the final section of the railway to Haverhill in **June 1863** the timetable shown opposite was introduced.

An increase in the service had pre-empted the introduction of the above, for the *Halstead Gazette* was euphoric in their issue of 16th April 1863 that:

Our readers will be pleased to hear that the company will on 10th May put on a second morning train from Chappel for the convenience of Parliamentary passengers, who have hitherto been obliged to go by express to Chappel, thus leaving Yeldham, Hedingham and Halstead half an hour earlier than was necessary and having to wait that half hour by the way at Chappel. This was unavoidable perhaps for a time but we are glad that it is soon to come to an end. The new arrangement will also be a great advantage to all travellers by the Down morning train.

The GER opening of their line from Shelford Junction to Haverhill on 1st June 1865 and the connection to Colne Valley Junction on 25th June 1865 resulted in three passenger services in each direction on weekdays and one on Sundays, which continued when the line was opened throughout to Sudbury on 9th August of the same year. A freight service ran from Cambridge to Wivenhoe via Haverhill and the Colne Valley line to Chappel and this continued until 1867, even after the GER had opened their route via Sudbury. The GER freight train timings in **1866** were as shown opposite top right.

The CV&HR passenger timetable for **1869** (*facing page*) showed services with connections from London and Colchester.

By **1882** the passenger timetable showed the following weekday services in the Down direction: departing Chappel at 9.35am all stations to Haverhill;

TIMETABLE FROM JANUARY 1862

Down			WEEKDAYS						SUNDAYS		
			123	Parl	12	12	123				
			am	am	pm	pm	pm		am	am	pm
Marks Tey	+	dep		10.00	1.25	5.53	7.35			9.50	6.40
Chappel	+	arr		10.10	1.35	6.03	7.45			10.00	6.50
		dep		10.15	1.40	6.05	7.50			10.05	6.55
Colne		dep		10.23	1.45	*	7.55			10.13	7.03
Halstead		dep	7.40	10.40	2.00	6.23	8.10		8.00	10.30	7.20
Castle Hedingham		arr	7.55	10.55	2.15	6.35	8.25		8.15	10.45	7.35

Up			WEEKDAYS						SUNDAYS		
				ThSO	ThSX						
			Parl	123	12	123	123	123	am	pm	pm
			am	am	pm	pm	pm	pm	am	pm	pm
Castle Hedingham		dep	8.10	11.45	12.20	3.50	6.45	8.35	8.35	4.40	8.00
Halstead		dep	8.25	12.00	12.35	4.05	7.00	8.50	8.50	4.55	8.15
Colne		dep	8.35	12.10	*	*	7.15		9.03	5.08	
Chappel		arr	8.43	12.18	12.53	4.23	7.23		9.10	5.15	
	+	dep	9.20	T	1.00	4.32			9.17	5.22	
Marks Tey	+	arr	9.30		1.10	4.42			9.28	5.35	

* Calls if required.
T Through train to Colchester arrive 1.00pm.
+ ECR connecting train service.

TIMETABLE FROM AUGUST 1862

Down		WEEKDAYS					SUNDAYS		
		am	am	pm	pm	pm	am	am	pm
Marks Tey	dep+		10.00	1.25	5.53	7.35		9.50	6.40
Chappel	arr+		10.10	1.35	6.02	7.45		10.00	6.50
	dep		10.15	1.40	6.05	7.50		10.05	6.55
Colne	dep		10.23	1.45	6.10	7.55		10.13	7.03
Halstead	dep	7.30	10.40	2.00	6.23	8.10	7.55	10.30	7.20
Castle Hedingham	dep	7.40	10.50	2.10	6.30	8.20	8.05	10.40	7.30
Yeldham	arr	7.50	11.05	2.20	6.40	8.30	8.15	10.50	7.40

Up		WEEKDAYS					SUNDAYS		
		am	pm	pm	pm	pm	am	pm	pm
Yeldham	dep	8.00	12.10	3.40	6.50	8.40	8.25	4.30	8.00
Castle Hedingham	dep	8.10	12.20	3.50	7.00	8.50	8.35	4.40	8.10
Halstead	dep	8.25	12.35	4.05	7.15	9.00	8.50	4.55	8.25
Colne	dep	8.35	*	*	7.30		9.03	5.08	
Chappel	arr	8.43	12.55	4.25	7.38		9.10	5.15	
	dep+	8.48	1.00	4.32			9.12	5.22	
Marks Tey	arr+	8.57	1.10	4.42			9.28	5.35	

* Calls if required.
+ GER connecting train service.

TIMETABLE FROM JUNE 1863

DOWN

DOWN		WEEKDAYS					SUNDAYS	
		am	am	pm	pm	pm	am	pm
Marks Tey	dep		10.00	1.25	5.52	7.35	9.50	6.40
Chappel	dep	9.30	10.15	1.40	6.05	7.50	10.05	6.55
Colne	dep	9.40	10.23	1.45	6.10	7.55	10.13	7.03
Halstead	dep	10.00	10.40	2.00	6.13	8.10	10.30	7.20
Castle Hedingham	dep	10.15	10.50	2.10	6.30	8.20	10.40	7.30
Yeldham	dep	10.30	10.57	2.20	6.40	8.30	10.50	7.40
Birdbrook	dep	10.48	11.10	2.38	6.58	8.48	11.10	8.00
Haverhill	arr	10.55	11.17	2.45	7.05	8.55	11.17	8.07

UP

UP		WEEKDAYS					SUNDAYS	
		am	am	am	pm	pm	am	pm
Haverhill	dep	7.45	8.15	11.55	3.15	5.25	8.00	4.05
Birdbrook	dep	7.50	8.22	12.00	3.25	5.32	8.05	4.10
Yeldham	dep	8.05	8.35	12.13	3.40	5.50	8.25	4.30
Castle Hedingham	dep	8.12	8.42	12.20	3.50	6.00	8.35	4.40
Halstead	dep	8.25	8.55	12.35	4.05	6.23	8.50	4.55
Colne	dep	8.37	9.07	*	*	6.36	9.03	5.08
Chappel	arr	8.43	9.15	12.55	4.25	6.43	9.10	5.15
Marks Tey	arr	8.57	9.30	1.10	4.42	6.55	9.28	5.35

* Calls when required.

TIMETABLE FOR 1869

DOWN

DOWN		WEEKDAYS			MO		SUNDAYS	
		am	am/pm	pm	pm		am	pm
Bishopsgate	dep	7.15	11.42	3.10*	5.30		7.15	2.45
Colchester	dep	9.25	1.00	5.25	6.52		9.35	4.45
Marks Tey	dep	10.00	1.25	5.55	7.30		9.50	5.05
Chappel	dep	10.20	1.45	6.10	8.30		10.07	5.25
Colne	dep	10.27	1.52	6.16	8.37		10.14	5.32
Halstead	arr	10.40	2.05	6.28	8.50		10.27	5.45
	dep	10.45	2.10	6.31	8.55		10.32	5.50
SC Hedingham	dep	10.55	2.20	6.41	9.05		10.42	6.00
Yeldham	dep	11.03	2.28	6.49	9.13		10.50	6.08
Birdbrook	dep	11.15	2.40	7.01	9.25		11.02	6.20
Haverhill	arr	11.23	2.48	7.09	9.33		11.10	6.28

* Also depart Bishopsgate 4.25pm.

UP

UP			WEEKDAYS	FX	FO	MO	SUNDAYS	
				pm	pm	pm		
		am	am	pm	pm	pm	am	pm
Haverhill	dep	7.40	10.45	3.15	5.00	5.40	8.10	3.20
Birdbrook	dep	7.48	10.53	3.23	5.08	5.48	8.18	3.28
Yeldham	dep	8.00	11.05	3.35	5.20	6.00	8.30	3.40
SC Hedingham	dep	8.08	11.15	3.45	5.28	6.08	8.38	3.48
Halstead	arr	8.18	11.25	3.55	5.36	6.20	8.48	4.00
	dep	8.23	11.30	4.05	5.40	6.28	8.52	4.05
Colne	dep	8.36	11.45	4.18	5.52	6.40	9.05	4.17
Chappel	arr	8.43	11.55	4.25	6.00	6.46	9.12	4.25
Marks Tey	arr	8.57	12.15	4.43	7.00	7.00	9.28	4.45
Colchester	arr	10.04	12.30	4.55	7.35	7.35	9.50	5.03
Bishopsgate	arr	10.40+	1.45	6.35	8.55	8.55	12.15	7.15

+ Also arrive Bishopsgate 12.10pm.

GER FREIGHT TRAIN TIMINGS 1866

		am/pm
Cambridge	dep	6.10
Haverhill	arr	7.50
	dep	8.30
Halstead	arr	9.25
	dep	9.40
Chappel	arr	10.05
	dep	10.30
Colchester	arr	11.25
	dep	12.25
Wivenhoe	arr	12.55

		pm
Wivenhoe	dep	1.15
Colchester	arr	2.10
	dep	2.25
Chappel	arr	3.05
	dep	3.15
Halstead	arr	3.40
	dep	4.05
Haverhill	arr	5.00
	dep	5.35
Cambridge	arr	7.00

11.30am all stations to Halstead; 1.27pm all stations to Haverhill; 4.05pm Colne and Halstead only; 6.07pm all stations to Haverhill, and 8.15pm Fridays only all stations to Haverhill. On Sundays there were two departures from Chappel serving all stations to Haverhill at 10.38am and 5.34pm. In the Up direction, weekday trains departed 7.35am Haverhill and all stations to Chappel, 10.05am Halstead to Chappel, 11.30am and 2.55pm Haverhill and all stations to Chappel, 5.15pm Halstead to Chappel and 5.15pmFO Haverhill and all stations to Chappel. On Sundays trains departed Haverhill at 8.20am and 3.20pm, calling all stations to Chappel.

LYNN, SWAFFHAM, WATTON, THETFORD, BURY, SUDBURY, HALSTEAD, & MARK'S TEY.

FROM	WEEK DAYS.					Mrkt Mxd.	Mrkt Mxd.		Mrkt	Mrkt						SUNDAYS.			
	morn	morn	morn		morn	morn	even.	even.	even.	even.	even.	even.		even.	even.	even.	morn	even.		
LYNN ....dep.	6 55	...	...		8 10	9 0	12 30	...	...	...	...	...	...	...	3 5	5 43	...	...	...	...
SWAFFHAM ....arr.	7 28	...	...		8 41	9 33	1 7	...	...	...	...	...	...	...	3 42	6 19	...	...	...	...
SWAFFHAM........dep.	7 29	...	...		8 44	10 50	1 20	...	...	...	...	...	...	...	4 30	6 40	...	...	...	...
Holme Hale	7 39	...	...		8 54	11 0	1 40	...	...	...	...	...	...	...	4 40	6 50	...	...	...	...
Watton	7 51	...	...		9 7	11 13	1 55	...	...	...	...	...	...	...	4 53	7 3	...	...	...	...
Stow Bedon	7 59	...	...		9 15	11 21		...	...	...	...	...	...	...	5 1	7 11	...	...	...	...
Wretham	8 8	...	...		9 24	11 30		...	...	...	...	...	...	...	5 10	7 20	...	...	...	...
Roudham Junction arr.	...	...	...		...	...		...	...	...	...	...	...	...	5 17	...	...	...	...	...
Roudham Junction ....dep.	...	...	...		...	...		...	...	...	...	...	...	...	5 43	...	...	...	...	...
NORWICH ....arr.	...	...	...		...	...		...	...	...	...	...	...	...	6 40	...	...	...	...	...
Roudham Junction ......dep.	...	...	...		...	...		...	...	...	...	...	...	...	5 18	...	...	...	...	...
Thetford ....arr.	8 22	...	...		9 38	11 45		...	...	...	...	...	...	...	5 28	7 34	...	...	...	...
Thetford ....dep.	8 31	...	...		9 49	12 11		...	...	...	...	...	...	...	5 50	...	...	...	...	...
ELY ....arr.	9 7	...	...		10 36	12 47		...	...	...	...	...	...	...	6 26	...	...	...	...	...
Thetford ....dep.	...	...	...		9 41	11 54		...	...	...	...	...	...	...	G	7 46	...	...	...	...
NORWICH ....arr.	...	...	...		10 48	1 0		...	...	...	...	...	...	...	6 40	8 48	...	...	...	...
NORWICH ....dep.	...	...	...		8 32	11 8		...	...	...	...	...	...	...	4 40	...	...	...	...	...
Thetford ....arr.	...	...	...		9 49	12 11		...	...	...	...	...	...	...	5 50	...	...	...	...	...
ELY ....dep.	...	...	...		8 57	11 13		...	...	...	...	...	...	...	4 42	7 9	...	...	...	...
Thetford ....arr.	...	...	...		9 41	11 54		...	...	...	...	...	...	...	5 33	7 46	...	...	...	...
Thetford ....dep.	...	...	...		9 55	12 15		...	...	...	...	...	...	...	5 53	7 49	...	...	...	...
Thetford Bridge	...	...	...		10 0	12 19		...	...	...	...	...	...	...	5 57	7 53	...	...	...	...
Barnham	...	...	...		10 7	12 26		...	...	...	...	...	...	...	6 4	8 0	...	...	...	...
Ingham	...	...	...		10 20	12 38		...	...	...	...	...	...	...	6 16	8 12	...	...	...	...
BURY ST. EDMDS arr.	...	...	...		10 30	12 48		...	...	...	...	...	...	...	6 26	8 22	...	...	...	...
Bury ....dep.	...	...	...		10 38	2 10		...	...	...	...	...	...	...	6 53	...	...	...	...	...
HAUGHLEY ....arr.	...	...	...		11 6	2 40		...	...	...	...	...	...	...	7 23	...	...	...	...	...
IPSWICH ....arr.	...	...	...		11 53	4 5		...	...	...	...	...	...	...	8 35	...	...	...	...	...
Bury ....dep.	...	...	...		11 22	3 20		...	...	...	...	...	...	...	...	...	...	...	...	...
ELY ....arr.	...	...	...		12 35	4 24		...	...	...	...	...	...	...	...	...	...	...	...	...
CAMBRIDGE ......arr.	...	...	...		1 5	4 33		...	...	...	...	...	...	...	...	...	...	...	...	...
BURY ST. EDMDS dep.	...	7 30	...		11 13	2 37		...	...	4 0	...	5 45	...	...	...	...	...	...	...	...
Bury (East Gate)	...	7 33	...		11 17	2 41		...	...	4 3	...	5 45	...	...	...	...	...	...	...	...
Welnetham	...	7 41	...		11 26	2 50		...	...	4 12	...	5 54	...	...	...	...	...	...	...	...
Cockfield	...	7 46	...		11 32	2 56		...	...	4 18	...	6 0	...	...	...	...	...	...	...	...
Lavenham	...	7 53	...		11 39	3 3		...	...	4 26	...	6 7	...	...	...	...	...	...	...	...
Long Melford ....arr.	...	8 3	...		11 50	3 14		...	...	4 36	...	6 18	...	...	...	...	...	...	...	...
CAMBRIDGE ......dep.	...	...	8 54		10 45	1 51		...	...	...	...	...	...	...	7 10	...	...	...	...	...
LONDON (L'pool St) dep.	...	...	6 0		9 10	11 55		...	...	...	...	...	...	...	5 15	...	...	...	...	...
Shelford	...	...	9 1		10 53	1 59		...	...	...	...	...	...	...	7 18	...	...	...	...	...
Pampisford	...	...	9 8		11 0	2 7		...	...	...	...	...	...	...	7 26	...	...	...	...	...
Linton	...	...	9 15		11 7	2 14		...	...	...	...	...	...	...	7 34	...	...	...	...	...
LONDON (L'pl St) dp.	...	...	6 0		...	...		...	...	...	...	...	...	...	5 15	...	...	...	...	...
Audley End ......dep.	...	...	7 50		...	...		...	...	...	...	...	...	...	6 39	...	...	...	...	...
Saffron Walden	...	...	8 2		...	...		...	...	...	...	...	...	...	6 47	...	...	...	...	...
Bartlow ....arr.	...	...	8 14		...	...		...	...	...	...	...	...	...	7 0	...	...	...	...	...
Bartlow	...	...	9 21		11 13	2 20		...	...	...	...	...	...	...	7 40	...	...	...	...	...
Haverhill	...	...	9 34		11 27	2 35		...	...	5 33	...	...	...	...	7 54	...	...	...	...	...
Sturmer	...	...	9 39		11 32	2 40		...	...	5 38	...	...	...	...	7 59	...	...	...	...	...
Stoke	...	...	9 45		11 38	2 46		...	...	5 44	...	...	...	...	8 5	...	...	...	...	...
Clare	...	...	9 51		11 44	2 52		...	...	5 50	...	...	...	...	8 13	...	...	...	...	...
Cavendish	...	...	9 57		11 50	2 58		...	...	5 56	...	...	...	...	8 19	...	...	...	...	...
Glemsford	...	...	10 1		11 54	3 2		...	...	6 0	...	...	...	...	8 24	...	...	...	...	...
Long Melford ......arr.	...	...	10 6		11 59	3 8		...	...	6 8	...	...	...	...	8 28	...	...	...	...	...
Long Melford ....dep.	...	8 5	10 9		12 1	3 16		...	...	...	4 47	6 20	...	8 30	...	...	...	...	...	...
Sudbury {arr. {dep.	...	8 11 / 8 13	10 15 / 10 17		12 7 / 12 10	3 23 / 3 25		... / 4 35	...	...	4 55	6 26 / 6 29	...	8 37 / 8 39	...	...	8 55	4 5	...	...
Bures	...	8 22	10 26		12 19	3 34		4 49	...	...	...	6 38	...	8 48	...	...	9 8	4 17	...	...
Chappel ....arr.	...	8 30	10 34		12 27	3 42		5 2	...	...	...	6 46	...	8 56	...	...	9 18	4 28	...	...
Haverhill ....dep.	...	7 35	...		11 30	2 43		...	...	...	5 30	...	...	...	...	...	8 20	3 20	...	...
Birdbrook	...	7 44	...		11 38	2 52		...	...	...	5 39	...	...	...	...	...	8 28	3 28	...	...
Yeldham	...	7 50	...		11 48	3 2		...	...	...	5 48	...	...	...	...	...	8 38	3 40	...	...
Castle Hedingham ...	...	7 58	...		11 56	3 9		...	...	...	5 58	...	...	...	...	...	8 46	3 48	...	...
Halstead	...	8 10	10 5		12 10	3 20		...	...	...	5 10 / 6 20	...	...	...	...	...	9 0	4 0	...	...
Ford Gate	...	8 15	10 12		12 16	3 26		...	...	...	5 20 / 6 31	...	...	...	...	...	9 10	4 10	...	...
Colne	...	8 19	10 17		12 20	3 31		...	...	...	5 30	...	...	...	...	...	9 18	4 18	...	...
Chappel ....arr.	...	8 25	10 26		12 26	3 38		...	...	...	5 35	...	...	...	...	...			...	...
Chappel ....dep.	...	8 34	10 36		12 31	3 44		5 7	...	...	...	6 49	...	8 57	...	...	9 23	4 34	...	...
MARK'S TEY ....arr.	...	8 42	10 44		12 39	3 52		5 17	...	...	...	6 57	...	9 5	...	...	9 34	4 45	...	...
COLCHESTER ....arr.	...	9 18	10 55		2 0	4 43		5 31	...	...	...	7 25	...	9 20	...	...	10 46	5 55	...	...
IPSWICH	...	10 6	11 50		...	...		6 18	...	...	...	9 50	...	11 25	...	...	10 46	5 55	...	...
LONDON (L'pool St.) ,,	...	10 10	12 15		2 10	5 50		...	...	...	...	8 53	...	...	...	...	12 25	7 5	...	...

G Passengers from Swaffham and Watton for Norwich change at Roudham Junction.

& Will call only when required to take up or set down Passengers. Passengers wishing to alight at these Stations must intimate the same to the Guard at the preceding stopping Station.

GER public timetable 1884, Up direction.

Two years later, in **1884** the passenger timetable showed a service of six trains in each direction. On the Down road the 9.32am, 1.27pm and 6.07pm ex Chappel ran through to Haverhill, whilst the 11.30am, 4.16pm and 8.15pm terminated at Halstead. On the Up road Haverhill departures were 7.35am, 11.30am, 2.43pm and 5.30pm. The 5.30pm only ran between Haverhill and Halstead on Fridays and on other days departed Halstead at 6.20pm. On Sundays two trains operated in each direction, departing Haverhill at 8.20am and 3.20pm, returning from Chappel at 10.38am and 5.34pm. All trains called at all stations except the 5.30pm ex Haverhill/6.20pm ex Halstead which omitted calling at Colne. All trains were allowed between 52 and 55 minutes for the full journey or 20 minutes for the run between Chappel and Halstead.

By **1886** the service shown right was operative with an extra train on Sunday.

The passenger service for **1889** is shown below.

The working timetable for **1897** provided a weekday service of five MO, four TFO, three WThO and six SO passenger trains, three goods trains and one set of cars in the Up direction. The 9.55am, 2.45pm and 5.50pm ex Haverhill ran each weekday whilst other departures were 7.40amMTFO, 11.30amSO and 8.00pmMSO, all taking 48 to 50 minutes for the run to Chappel. The early morning goods was a short working from Halstead to Chappel, arriving 5.45am, whilst an afternoon 1.00pm ex Haverhill only ran as far as Halstead. The last Up goods train of the day arrived at Chappel at 8.15pm. The ECS departing Haverhill at 7.50pm for Halstead was formed of the stock of the

Timetable for 1886

DOWN

		WEEKDAYS						SUNDAYS		
		am	am	pm	pm	pm	pm	am	pm	pm
Chappel	dep	9.32	11.30	1.27	4.15	6.07	8.15	10.38	5.18	6.45
Colne	dep	9.40	11.40	1.32	4.21	6.13	8.23	10.45	5.23	6.50
Ford Gate	dep	9.43			4.26	6.18	8.26	10.48	5.28	6.55
Halstead	dep	9.52	11a50	1.45	4a35	6.25	8.35	10.55	5a36	7.05
SC Hedingham	dep	10.03		1.54		6.33	8g42	11.05		7.15
Yeldham	dep	10.10		2.02		6.40	8g52	11.15		7.25
Birdbrook	dep	10.19		2.12		6.50	9g02	11.25		7.35
Haverhill	arr	10.27		2.22		6.59	9g12	11.33		7.45

UP

		WEEKDAYS						SUNDAYS		
		am	am	am	pm	pm	pm	am	pm	pm
Haverhill	dep	7.35		11.30	2.45		5f30	8.20	3.30	
Birdbrook	dep	7.44		11.39	2.54		5f39	8.28	3.38	
Yeldham	dep	7.50		11.49	3.04		5f48	8.38	3.50	
SC Hedingham	dep	7.58	9k55	11.57	3.12		5f58t	8.46	3.59	
Halstead	dep	8.08	10.10	12.06	3.22	5.10	6.10	9.00	4.10	5.42
Ford Gate	dep	8.15	10.17			5.20	6.18	9.05	4.15	5.47
Colne	dep	8.19	10.22	12.15	3.31	5.30	6.18	9.10	4.25	5.52
Chappel	arr	8.25	10.31	12.21	3.38	5.35	6.35	9.18	4.31	5.59

a arrival time
f Fridays only; ran as a goods train the other days
g Mondays and Saturdays only; ran as a goods train the other days
k departs SC Hedingham SO
t departs SC Hedingham 5.46pmFX

Timetable for 1889

DOWN

		WEEKDAYS		MSO					MSO	SUNDAYS		
		am	am	am	pm	pm	pm	pm	pm	am	pm	pm
Chappel	dep	9.32	11.30		1.27	4.15	6.10	8.25		10.41	5.18	6.50
Colne	dep	9.45	11.40		1.39	4.25	6.21	8.34		10.52	5.23	7.01
Halstead	dep	9.56	11.45	11.45	1.45	4.35	6.28	8.40	8.40	11.02	5.36	7.09
SC Hedingham	dep	10.05		11.55	1.52	4.42	6.35		8.47	11.10		7.16
Yeldham	dep	10.12		12.05	2.00		6.42		8.55	11.18		7.24
Birdbrook	dep	10.20		12.15	2.10		6.50		9.05	11.26		7.36
Haverhill	arr	10.30		12.25	2.20		6.59		9.15	11.35		7.45

UP

		WEEKDAYS					FX	FO	MSO	SUNDAYS		
		am	am	am	pm	pm	pm	pm	pm	am	pm	pm
Haverhill	dep	7.40		11.30	2.50			5.15	8.00	8.25	3.30	
Birdbrook	dep	7.49		11.39	2.59			5.24	8.09	8.33	3.40	
Yeldham	dep	7.57		11.49	3.08			5.31	8.18	8.43	3.50	
SC Hedingham	dep	8.03		11.56	3.14	4.55	5.46	5.42	8.27	8.51	3.59	
Halstead	dep	8.12	10.10	12.06	3.22	5.10	6.05	6.05	8.35	9.05	4.10	5.45
Colne	dep	8.17	10.17	12.11	3.27	5.25	6.22	6.22		9.10	4.15	5.50
Chappel	arr	8.28	10.31	12.21	3.37	5.35	6.35	6.35		9.20	4.28	6.00

COLNE VALLEY TRAINS DEPARTING FROM CHAPPEL (G. E.) & ARRIVING AT HAVERHILL (G. E.) STATIONS.

Week Days.   **Sundays.**

FROM	1	2	3	4	5	6	7	8	9	10	11	12	13	14	15	16	17	18
	Gds.	A Cars.	Cars.	B Pass.	Pass.	C Pass.	Gds.	Pass.	D Pass.	Pass.	Pass.			Mxd.	Mxd.	Mxd.		
	a.m.	a.m.	a.m.	a.m.	a.m.	p.m.	p.m.	p.m.	p.m.	p.m.	p.m.			a.m.	p.m.	p.m.		
Chappel ....dep.	6 20	...	...	9 30	11 24	1 18	...	4 11	6 10	6 55	9 9	...	...	10 45	3 30	7 42	....	...
Haverhill ....arr.	......	7 20	9 25	10 30	12 16	2 8	2 45	5 5	6 59	7 40	......	......	...	11 35	4 20	....	....	....

A No. 2. Mondays, Tuesdays, Fridays, and Saturdays.   B No. 4. Mondays, Tuesdays, and Saturdays only.
C No. 6. Fridays and Saturdays only.   D No. 9. Saturdays only.

COLNE VALLEY TRAINS DEPARTING FROM HAVERHILL (G. E.) AND ARRIVING AT CHAPPEL (G. E.) STATIONS.

Week Days.   **Sundays.**

FROM	1	2	3	4	5	6	7	8	9	10	11	12	13	14	15	16	17	18
	Gds.	A Pass.	Pass.	B Pass.	Gds.	Pass.		Pass.	Cars.	Gds.	C Pass.			Mxd.	Mxd.	Mxd.		
	a.m.	a.m.	a.m.	a.m.	p.m.	p.m.		p.m.	p.m.	p.m.	p.m.			a.m.	p.m.	p.m.		
Haverhill ....dep.	......	7 40	9 55	11 30	1 0	2 45	......	5 50	7 50	...	8 0	...	...	9 5	2 30	6 10	...	...
Chappel ....arr	5 45	8 28	10 45	12 20	...	3 34	...	6 40	...	8 15	8 50	...	...	9 55	3 23	7 0	...	....

A No. 2. Mondays, Tuesdays, Fridays, and Saturdays only.   B No. 4. Saturdays only.
C No. 11. Mondays and Saturdays only.

ABOVE: GER working timetable 1897.

TIMETABLE FOR 1903

DOWN		WEEKDAYS							SUNDAYS	
		am	am	SO pm	pm	SO pm	pm	pm	am	pm
Chappel	dep	9.25	11.35	1.18	4.15	6.05	6.57	9.18	10.53	7.45
Colne	dep	9.33	11.43	1.28	4.25	6.16	7.05	9.27	11.01	7.53
Halstead	dep	9.41	11.50	1.35	4.32	6.26	7.12	9.35	11.10	8.00
Hedingham	dep	9.50	12.00	1.43	4.42	6.34	7.19	9.42	11.17	8.07
Yeldham	dep	10.05*	12.05	1.50	4.49	6.41	7.26	9.49	11.24	8.14
Birdbrook	dep	10.15*	12.15	2.00	4.59	6.51	7.35	9.59	11.33	8.24
Haverhill	arr	10.25*	12.25	2.08	5.10	7.00	7.45	10.09	11.43	8.33

UP		WEEKDAYS							SUNDAYS	
		am	am	SO am	pm	pm	SO pm		am	pm
Haverhill	dep	7.40*	9.47	11.25	2.45	5.50	8.00		9.10	6.05
Birdbrook	dep	7.49*	9.55	11.34	2.54	5.59	8.09		9.19	6.14
Yeldham	dep	7.57*	10.05	11.44	3.03	6.09	8.19		9.29	6.25
Hedingham	dep	8.03	10.12	11.52	3.09	6.17	8.27		9.37	6.33
Halstead	dep	8.12	10.22	12.03	3.19	6.26	8.37		9.46	6.44
Colne	dep	8.17	10.27	12.08	3.24	6.31	8.43		9.51	6.51
Chapel	arr	8.28	10.37	12.20	3.32	6.40	8.51		10.00	7.00

* MSO

incoming 7.40pm arrival. In the Down direction five MTFO, four WThO and seven SO passenger services were operated together with two goods trains and two ECS. The 11.02am, 4.11pm and 6.55pm ex Chappel ran each weekday whilst the 9.30amMTSO, 1.18pmFSO and 6.10pmSO from Chappel formed the other services. The 9.09pm ex Chappel was a short working to Halstead. All trains called at all stations. Of the goods services, the 6.20am ex Chappel was the return working of the first Up goods whilst the 2.45pm arrival at Haverhill provided connections to GER destinations to Cambridge and the north. The ECS arriving at Haverhill at 7.20amMTFSO provided the stock for the 7.40am Up departure, with the 9.25am arrival forming the 9.55am Up passenger service from Haverhill. On Sundays three mixed trains ran in each direction, departing Haverhill at 9.05am, 2.30pm and 6.10pm, and returning from Chappel at 10.45am, 3.30pm and 7.42pm. These trains provided a connection into and out of the GER Marks Tey to Sudbury services and were permitted 50 minutes running time on the Colne Valley line.

By **1903** the passenger train timetable shown left was in operation.

The timetable for **1905** showed weekday trains departing Chappel at 9.25amMSX all stations to S&C Hedingham, 9.25am MSO all stations to Haverhill, 11.33am all stations to Haverhill, 1.18pmSO all stations to Haverhill, 4.15pm all stations to Haverhill, 6.05pmSO all stations to Haverhill, 6.57pm all stations to Haverhill and 9.18pmSO all stations to Haverhill. On Sundays trains departed Chappel at 10.53am and 7.45pm calling all stations to Haverhill. In the Up direction the weekday train service was 7.40amMSX Haverhill and all stations to Chappel, 8.03MSO S&C Hedingham and all stations to Chappel and the 11.30amSO, 2.45pm, 5.50pm and 8.00pmSO Haverhill to Chappel calling all stations. On Sundays Up trains departed Haverhill at 9.10am and 6.02pm calling all stations to Chappel.

The working timetable for **1907** was more convoluted, with seven MO, four MSX and eight SO passenger services in the Down direction, augmented by four MO, five MSX and six SO goods services and one set of cars; and six MO, four MSX and seven SO passenger services, four MO, six MSX and seven SO

COLNE VALLEY TRAINS DEPARTING FROM HAVERHILL (G. E.) AND ARRIVING AT CHAPPEL (G. E.) STATIONS.

Week Days.   **Sundays.**

FROM	1	2	3	4	5	6	7	8	9	10	11	12	13	14	15	16	17	18	19	20	21	22	23	24
		A			A	C	B		C		B	A	C	B		C	C		D	A	A			
	Gd	Ps	Pas	Pas	Gds	Pas	Gds	Gds	Gds	Gds	Pas	Gds	Gds	Gds	Pas	Cr	Gds	Car	Gds	Pas	Pass	En.	Mx.	
	am	am	a.m.	a.m.	a.m.	a.m.	a.m.	p.m.	p.m.	p.m.	p.m.	p.m.	p.m.	p.m.	p.m.	pm	p.m.	p.m.	p.m.	p.m.	a.m.	a.m.	p.m.	
Haverhill dep.	...	740	...	9 47	11 0	1125	1140	1245	2 30	...	3 36	4 50	...	5 15	6 50	7 0	...	7 52	...	8 0	8 50	1145	5 27	...
Chappel arr.	545	...	8 30	1039	1 45	1220	...	...	...	3 35	3 26	...	5 45	...	6 40	...	7 45	...	8 20	8 50	9 40	...	6 17	...

A Mondays and Saturdays only.   **B** Not Mondays and Saturdays.   **C** Saturdays only.   **D** Not Saturdays.

ABOVE: GER working timetable 1907 in the Up direction.

goods services together with one SX and two SO ECS workings in the Up direction. Passenger services departed Chappel at 9.25am to S&C Hedingham, 11.28am, 1.18pmSO, 4.18pm, 6.05pmSO, 7.01pm and 9.52pmMSO calling all stations to Haverhill GE on the Down road, returning from Haverhill GE at 7.40am all stations to Halstead, then 9.47am, 11.25amSO, 2.36pm, 4.30pm and 8.00pmMSO working through to Chappel. ECS workings included the 6.55am ex S&C Hedingham arriving Haverhill GE at 7.30am in the Down direction, and 7.00pmSO and 7.52pm ex Haverhill. Through goods services calling all stations to Haverhill GE in the Down direction departed 2.20pmMSO and 2.45pmMSX ex Chappel whilst in the Up direction all stations were served by the 11.00amMSO and 11.40amMSX from Haverhill GE. All other services were short trip workings from Chappel or Haverhill, including movements from Haverhill GE to Haverhill CV and return, On Sundays two passenger trains ran in each direction: the 8.35am ex Haverhill GE due Chappel at 9.40am and returning at 10.53am arriving Haverhill GE at 11.43am; the afternoon departure from Haverhill GE left at 5.27pm due Chappel at 6.17pm, returning on the Down road at 7.45pm and terminating at Haverhill CV station. Of the goods services the 5.45am arrival at Chappel and 12.45pm from Haverhill ran each weekday whilst the 11.00amMSX, 11.25amSO, 2.30pmSO ex Haverhill, 4.50pmMSX and 5.15pmMSX ex Haverhill provided the balancing Up services.

The passenger timetable for the **summer of 1909** (*right*), valid from 16th July until 30th September, showed the CV&HR services with GER connections.

TIMETABLE FOR SUMMER 1909

DOWN		WEEKDAYS							SUNDAYS	
		A		SO		SO		B		
		am	am	pm	pm	pm	pm	pm	am	pm
Marks Tey	dep*	9.15	11.12	1.05	4.04	5.52	6.48	8.47	10.41	7.33
Chappel	arr*	9.23	11.21	1.12	4.14	5.59	6.55	8.54	10.49	7.41
	dep	9.25	11.28	1.18	4.18	6.05	7.01	9.02	10.53	7.45
White Colne	dep	9.30	11.33	1.23	4.23	6.10	7.06	9.07	10.58	7.50
Earls Colne	dep	9.33	11.36	1.26	4.28	6.13	7.09	9.10	11.01	7.53
Halstead	dep	9.41	11.42	1.34	4.33	6.23	7.15	9.18	11.09	8.01
S & C Hedingham	dep	9.49	11.50	1.42	4.42	6.31	7.23	9.26	11.17	8.09
Yeldham	dep	10.07	11.58	1.49	4.49	6.38	7.30	9.33	11.24	8.16
Birdbrook	dep	10.18	12.08	2.00	4.59	6.49	7.39	9.44	11.35	8.27
Haverhill	arr	10.25	12.16	2.08	5.10	6.57	7.49	9.52	11.43	8.35
Cambridge	dep*	10.30	12.29		5.28	7.13				
Cambridge	arr*	11.11	1.10		6.10	7.58				

* GER connecting train service.
A Monday and Saturdays only.
   On other weekdays runs in the same timings but terminates at S&C Hedingham.
B Mondays and Saturdays only.
   On other weekdays runs in the same timings but terminates at Halstead.

UP		WEEKDAYS							SUNDAYS	
		C	D		SO			D		
		am	am	am	am	pm	pm	pm	am	pm
Cambridge	dep*			8.58	10.40	1.52	4.47	7.10		
Haverhill	arr*			9.40	11.20	2.33	5.28	7.55		
	dep		7.38	9.45	11.25	2.36	5.48	7.58	8.48	5.18
Birdbrook	dep		7.47	9.54	11.34	2.45	5.57	8.07	8.57	5.28
Yeldham	dep		7.56	10.05	11.44	2.52	6.06	8.16	9.06	5.38
S & C Hedingham	dep	8.03	8.03	10.12	11.52	3.00	6.13	8.23	9.13	5.46
Halstead	dep	8.12	8.12	10.21	12.03	3.08	6.22	8.32	9.22	5.56
Earls Colne	dep	8.20	8.20	10.29	12.08	3.16	6.30	8.40	9.30	6.06
White Colne	dep	8.24	8.24	10.33	12.12	3.20	6.34	8.44	9.34	6.11
Chappel	arr	8.30	8.30	10.39	12.20	3.27	6.40	8.50	9.40	6.18
Marks Tey	dep*	8.34	8.34	10.48	12.27	3.31	7.01	8.57	9.44	6.25
Marks Tey	arr*	8.43	8.43	10.55	12.35	3.38	7.08	9.04	9.53	6.32

* GER connecting train service.
C Mondays and Saturdays excepted.
D Mondays and Saturdays only.

Week Days. Sundays.

FROM	1	2	3	4	5	6	7	8	9	10	11	12	13	14	15	16	17	18	19	20	21	22
	Gds	A Car	Pas	Car	B Gds	A Pas	D Gds	Pas	B Pas	Gds	A Gds	D Gds	Pas	B Pass	Pass	B Gds			Mxd	Car	Pas	Eng Pas
	a.m.	a.m.	a.m.	a.m.	a.m.	a.m.	a.m	a.m.	p.m.	p.m.	p.m.	p.m.	p.m.	p.m.	p.m.	p.m.			a.m.	a.m	a.m	p.m p.m
Chappel ......dep.	6 20	...	9 25	..	...	...	...	...	1132	1 18	...	2 20	2 45	4 15	6 5	6 58	8 0	...	9 2	...	1653	... 7 45
Haverhill ...arr.	...	7 30	...	9 40	10 0	1025	1130	1222	2 8	2 30	4 30	4 55	5 5	6 57	7 48	...	...	...	8 45	1143	5 12	...

A Mondays and Saturdays only.   B Saturdays only.   D Not Mondays and Saturdays.

FROM	1	2	3	4	5	6	7	8	9	10	11	12	13	14	15	16	17	18	19	20	21	22	23	24
	Gd	A Ps	Pas	Pas	A Gds	C Pas	B Gds	Gds	C Gds	B Gds	Pas	A Gds	C Gds	B Gds	Pas	C Gr	Gds	C Car	C Gds	D Pas	C Pass	En.	Mx. Oct. only.	E Mx
	am	am	a.m.	a.m.	a.m.	a.m.	a.m.	p.m.	p.m.	p.m.	p.m.	p.m.	p.m.	p.m.	p.m.	pm	p.m.	p.m.	p.m.	p.m.	a.m.	a.m.	p.m.	p.m.
Haverhill dep.	...	738	...	9 45	11 0	1125	1140	1245	2 30	...	2 40	4 50	...	5 15	5 48	7 0	...	7 52	...	7 58	8 48	1145	5 18	5 58
Chappel .. arr.	545	...	8 30	1039	1 54	1230	...	...	...	2 33	3 32	...	5 48	...	6 46	...	7 48	...	8 20	8 50	9 40	...	6 18	7 0

A Mondays and Saturdays only.   B Not Mondays and Saturdays.   C Saturdays only.   D Not Saturdays.
E *Commences running 6th November.*

ABOVE: GER working timetable 1910 for Colne Valley trains between Chappel (GE) and Haverhill (GE).

TIMETABLE FOR SPRING 1912

		WEEKDAYS							SUNDAYS	
				SO		SO				
		am	am	pm	pm	pm	pm	pm	am	pm
Liverpool Street+	dep	6.40	10.00	11.45	2.22	4.18	5.30	7.12	9.10	4.20
Marks Tey+	dep	9.15	11.17	1.05	3.58	5.52	6.47	8.47	10.41	7.33
Chappel	dep	9.25	11.32	1.18	4.15	6.05	6.58	9.01	10.53	7.45
White Colne	dep	9.30	11.37	1.23	4.20	6.10	7.03	9.07	10.58	7.56
Earls Colne	dep	9.33	11.40	1.26	4.23	6.13	7.06	9.10	11.01	7.53
Halstead	dep	9.41	11.48	1.34	4.31	6.23	7.14	9.18	11.09	8.01
S & C Hedingham	dep	9.49	11.56	1.42	4.39	6.31	7.22	9.26s	11.17	8.09
Yeldham	dep	10.07c	12.03	1.49	4.46	6,38	7.29	9.33s	11.24	8.16
Birdbrook	dep	10.18c	12.14	2.00	4.57	6.49	7.40	9.44s	11.35	8.27
Haverhill	arr	10.25c	12.22	2.08	5.05	6.57	7.48	9.52s	11.43	8.35
Haverhill+	dep	10.30	12.32		5.28					

		WEEKDAYS						SUNDAYS	
				SO			SO		
		am	am	am	pm	pm	pm	am	pm
Haverhill+	arr		9.40	11.20	2.24	5.28	7.55		
Haverhill	dep	7.38c	9.45	11.25	2.40	5.48	7.58	8.48	5.58
Birdbrook	dep	7.47c	9.54	11.34	2.49	5.57	8.07	8.57	6.09
Yeldham	dep	7.56c	10.05	11.44	2.58	6.06	8.16	9.06	6.19
S & C Hedingham	dep	8.03	10.12	11.52	3.05	6.13	8.23	9.13	6.27
Halstead	dep	8.12	10.21	12.03	3.14	6.22	8.32	9.22	6.37
Earls Colne	dep	8.20	10.29	12.08	3.22	6.30	8.40	9.30	6.48
White Colne	dep	8.24	10.33	12.10	3.26	6.34	8.44	9.34	6.53
Chappel	arr	8.30	10.39	12.20	3.32	6.40	8.50	9.40	7.00
Marks Tey+	arr	8.43	10.55	12.32	3.45	7.02	9.04	9.55	7.12
Liverpool Street+	arr	10.10	12.27	2.25	5.48	9.03	0.00	12.30	8.52

c   Mondays and Saturdays only
s   Saturdays only
+   GER connecting service

The passenger train timetable for the **spring of 1912** (*facing page*) showed an increased service.

The **late summer working timetable for 1912** showed six MO, four MX and seven SO passenger trains in the Up direction, augmented by five SX and eight SO goods trains and two SO ECS workings. The 6.00am Halstead to Chappel, 9.45am, 2.40pm and 5.48pm ex Haverhill passenger trains ran each weekday whilst the 7.38amMSX Haverhill to Halstead and the 7.58pm Haverhill to Chappel services formed the other services. The first Up goods train of the day, arriving at Chappel 5.48am, ran each weekday, as did the 11.00am ex Haverhill with a 2 hours 54 minutes timing to Chappel. The 12.45pm goods ex Haverhill, a short working to Halstead, also ran daily. Saturdays saw a proliferation of goods trains departing Haverhill at 11.40am, 2.30pm and short trip workings to Chappel arriving 2.38pm, 5.48pm and 7.48pm. Two sets of empty coaching stock departed Haverhill at 7.00pmSO and 7.52pm, removing the stock of the 6.58pmSO and 7.48pm arrivals. In the Down direction the working timetable showed a weekday service of five MO, four MX and seven SO passenger services, together with four SX and seven SO goods trains. These were augmented by a mixed train which ran daily and two ECS MSO and one ECS MX. On Sundays the Halstead-based engine worked empty stock to Haverhill, arriving at 8.45am to form the 8.48am Up departure to Chappel. On arrival at 9.40am the engine and stock then formed the 10.55am departure back to Haverhill arriving at 11.46am, whence the engine retired to shed arriving at 11.55am. For the afternoon service the engine

arrived at Haverhill station to haul the 5.18pm Up mixed train with a 62 minutes run to Chappel. The engine and stock then returned with the 7.47pm train from Chappel to Halstead, from where the engine ran light to shed.

Just after the outbreak of World War One, in **August 1914** the CV&HR was operating the relatively extensive passenger service shown below.

On 10th November 1914 the CV&HR board considered the possible reduction of services to conserve coal stocks and it was agreed that, from 1st December, the 9.31pm Down train from Chappel would be withdrawn on Saturdays excepted. Later, by February 1915 there was concern over the poor patronage on some trains and at the board meeting on 11th March it was agreed the 9.55pm Halstead to Haverhill train would be discontinued until further notice. The withdrawal of the evening services resulted in many complaints and on 13th July 1915, the Assistant Secretary reported that in response to numerous petitions from the public asking for the reintroduction of the late train to Haverhill on Saturdays, the company had relented and reinstated the train with effect from 1st July.

The working timetable for **1916** showed few alterations to weekday services from previous years but on Sundays the Halstead engine was diagrammed to work a set of cars to Haverhill to form the 8.45am Up passenger train to Chappel, arriving there at 9.37am. The train returned, departing Chappel at 10.55am and arriving back at Haverhill at 11.46am, from whence the engine worked

TIMETABLE FOR AUGUST 1914											
DOWN		WEEKDAYS								SUNDAYS	
		am	am	SO pm	pm	SO pm	pm	SX pm	SO pm	am	pm
Marks Tey+	dep	8.58	11.18	1.55	4.01	5.49	6.55	9.19	9.25	10.41	7.33
Chappel	dep	9.09	11.32	2.08	4.15	6.02	7.07	9.31	9.38	10.55	7.56
Whitte Colne	dep	9.14	11.37	2.13	4.20	6.07	7.12	9.36	9.43	11.00	8.01
Earls Colne	dep	9.18	11.40	2.17	4.24	6.11	6.16	9.40	9.47	11.04	8.04
Halstead	dep	9.25	11.48	2.25	4.32	6.19	7.24	9.48a	9.55	11.12	8.12
S & C Hedingham	dep	9.33	11.56	2.33	4.40	6.27	7.32		10.03	11.20	8.20
Yeldham	dep	9.41*	12.03	2.40	4.47	6.34	7.39		10.10	11.27	8.27
Birdbrook	dep	9.52*	12.14	2.51	4.57	6.45	7.50		10.21	11.38	8.38
Haverhill	arr	10.00*	12.22	2.58	4.55	6.53	7.58		10.29	11.46	8.46
Haverhill+	dep	10.03	12.27	3.01	5.12	6.56				11.53	10.08
a arrival time.											

UP		WEEKDAYS								SUNDAYS	
		am	am	SO am	pm	pm	pm			am	pm
Haverhill+	arr		9.25	11.14	2.13	5.46	8.38			8.39	5.49
Haverhill	dep	7.36*	9.28	11.19	2.16	5.58	8.41			8.45	5.54
Birdbrook	dep	7.45*	9.37	11.28	2.25	6,07	8.49			8.54	6.05
Yeldham	dep	7.54*	9.48	11.39	2.34	6.07	8.49			9.03	6.16
S & C Hedingham	dep	8.01	9.55	11.46	2.41	6.23	9.05			9.10	6.24
Halstead	dep	8.10	10.04	11.55	2.50	6.33	9.14			9.19	6.34
Earls Colne	dep	8.18	10.12	12.03	2.58	6.40	9.22			9.27	6.42
White Colne	dep	8.22	10.16	12.07	2.31	6.44	8.25			9.31	6.46
Chappel	arr	8.28	10.16	12.07	3.01	6.50	9.31			9.37	6.54
Marks Tey+	arr	8.40	10.32	12.24	3.19	7.11	9.43			9.52	8.00
* Mondays and Saturdays only.											
+ GER connecting service.											

TIMETABLE FOR 1917

DOWN		WEEKDAYS					SUNDAYS	
		am	am	pm	pm	pm	am	pm
Marks Tey	dep	9.13	11.21	2.02	3.53	7.00	10.41	7.52
Chappel	dep	9.26	11.21	2.15	4.07	7.12	10.55	8.00
White Colne	dep	9.31	11.38	2.20	4.12	7.17	10.55	8.06
Earls Colne	dep	9.35	11.42	2.24	4.16	7.21	11.04	8.11
Halstead	dep	9.43	11.50	2.36	4.24	7.29	11.12	8.22
S & C Hedingham	dep	9.53	11.57	2.44	4.32	7.37	11.20	8.30
Yeldham	dep	10.00*	12.03	3.51	4.39	7.44	11.27	8.37
Birdbrook	dep	10.12*	12.14	3.02	4.50	7.55	11.38	8.48
Haverhill	arr	10.21*	12.22	3.10	4.58	8.03	11.46	8.56

UP		WEEKDAYS					SUNDAYS	
		am	am	am	pm	pm	am	pm
Haverhill	dep	7.38*	9.25	11.22	2.00	5.48	8.45	5.52
Birdbrook	dep	7.45*	9.34	11.31	2.09	5.57	8.54	6.03
Yeldham	dep	7.54*	9.45	11.42	2.19	6.08	9.03	6.14
S & C Hedingham	dep	8.01	9.52	11.49	2.26	6.15	9.10	6.22
Halstead	dep	8.10	10.01	11.58	2.35	6.25	9.19	6.32
Earls Colne	dep	8.18	10.09	12.06	2.43	6.33	9.27	6.40
White Colne	dep	8.22	10.13	12.10	2.47	6.37	9.31	6.44
Chappel	arr	8.28	10.20	12.16	2.52	6.44	9.37	6.52
Marks Tey	arr	8.40	10.32	12.31	3.04	7.16	9.52	7.06

* Mondays and Saturdays only.

TIMETABLE FOR MAY 1918

DOWN		WEEKDAYS				SUNDAYS	
		am	pm	pm	pm	am	pm
Marks Tey	dep*	10.12	1.49	3.53	7.00	11.00	7.52
Chappel	arr*	10.25	1.58	4.03	7.09	11.10	8.02
	dep	10.27	2.15	4.07	7.12	11.12	8.06
White Colne	dep	10.32	2.20	4.12	7.17	11.17	8.11
Earls Colne	dep	10.36	2.24	4.16	7.21	11.21	8.14
Halstead	dep	10.44	2.36	4.24	7.29	11.29	8.22
Hedingham	dep	10.54	2.44	4.32	7.37	11.37	8.30
Yeldham	dep	11.01	2.51	4.39	7.44	11.44	8.37
Birdbrook	dep	11.12	3.02	4.50	7.55	11.55	8.48
Haverhill	arr	11.20	3.10	4.58	8.03	12.03	8.56
	dep*	11.24		5.07			
Cambridge	arr*	12.06		5.44			

UP		WEEKDAYS				SUNDAYS	
		am	am	pm	pm	am	pm
Cambridge	dep*		8.40	1.12	5.00		
Haverhill	arr*		9.20	1.53	5.44		
	dep	7.38	9.25	2.00	5.48	9.00	5.52
Birdbrook	dep	7.45	9.33	2.09	5.57	9.09	6.03
Yeldham	dep	7.54	9.43	2.19	6.08	9.18	6.14
Hedingham	dep	8.01	9.50	2.26	6.15	9.25	6.22
Halstead	dep	8.11	10.00	2.35	6.25	9.34	6.32
Earls Colne	dep	8.21	10.06	2.43	6.33	9.42	6.40
White Colne	dep	8.24	10.12	2.47	6.37	9.46	6.44
Chappel	arr	8.30	10.19	2.52	6.44	9.52	6.52
	dep*	8.35	10.25	3.00	7.09	10.06	6.59
Marks Tey	arr*	8.42	10.33	3.07	7.16	10.13	7.06

* GER connecting train service.

light to shed. For the afternoon service the engine ran light to Haverhill station, arriving at 5.49pm to work the 5.56pm Up mixed train to Chappel arriving at 6.56pm. After shunting duties, the Down train departed the junction at 7.56pm, arriving at Haverhill at 8.46pm. The engine then worked the empty stock back to Halstead, departing at 9.00pm. All passenger and mixed trains called at all stations and connected at Chappel with GER Sudbury branch services.

The timetable for **1917** (*left*) shows a reduction of services brought about by the requirement to conserve coal supplies.

The passenger timetable for **May 1918** (*below left*) showed a further reduction in services.

Because of the poor state of the company, both financially and physically, the General Manager was given authority in September 1918 to seek ways of reducing the services without recourse to the board.

The public passenger train timetable for the summer of **1920** (*below*) reflected the difficult post-war period when services had not improved.

The passenger train service offered in **1921** consisted of four trains each way, with two in each direction on Sundays. At the board meeting on 2nd November 1921 the General Manager reported the continuing and increasing loss sustained in running the Sunday services and notified they would be discontinued on and after 30th November until further notice.

TIMETABLE FOR SUMMER 1920

DOWN		WEEKDAYS				SUNDAYS	
		am	am	pm	pm	am	pm
Marks Tey+	dep	9.13	11.22	3.53	7.04	10.41	7.52
Chappel	dep	9.26	11.32	4.07	7.15	10.55	8.06
White Colne	dep	9.31	11.37	4.12	7.20	11.00	8.12
Earls Colne	dep	9.35	11.41	4.16	4.24	11.04	8.15
Halstead	dep	9.43	11.49	4.24	7.40	11.12	8.22
S & C Hedingham	dep	9.50	11.56	4.32	7.40	11.20	8.30
Yeldham	dep		12.02	4.39	7.47	11.27	8.37
Birdbrook	dep		12.13	4.50	7.58	11.38	8.48
Haverhill	arr		12.21	4.58	8.06	11.46	8.56
Haverhill+	dep		12.32	5.08			

UP		WEEKDAYS				SUNDAYS	
		am	am	pm	pm	am	pm
Haverhill+	arr		9.20	1.44	5.45		
Haverhill	dep	7.38*	9.25	2.00	6.00	8.45	5.52
Birdbrook	dep	7.46*	9.33	2.09	6.10	8.54	6.03
Yeldham	dep	7.55*	9.43	2.19	6.21	9.03	6.14
S & C Hedingham	dep	8.03	9.50	2.26	6.28	9.10	6.22
Halstead	dep	8.11	10.00	2.35	6.37	9.19	6.32
Earls Colne	dep	8.21	10.06	2.43	6.45	9.27	6.40
White Colne	dep	8.24	10.12	2.47	6.49	9.31	6.44
Chappel	arr	8.30	10.19	2.52	6.56	9.37	6.52
Marks Tey+	arr	8.42	10.33	2.34	7.19	9.53	7.06

* Mondays and Saturdays only.
+ GER connecting service.

The working timetable for **1922** showed a basic service of four passenger and three goods trains in the Down direction weekdays only, augmented by one light engine movement each day and a set of cars MO. On the Up road five passenger and three goods trains operated on weekdays only. No Sunday services were provided. On the Down road the 6.45am LE ran from Halstead to S&C Hedingham to work a set of cars through to Haverhill MO to form the 7.38am Up passenger train from Haverhill GE. On MX the train commenced the Up working, departing S&C Hedingham at 8.03am arriving Chappel at 8.30am. The engine and stock worked back at 9.26am, calling all stations to S&C Hedingham. In the meantime the Haverhill based engine worked ECS from Haverhill CV at 9.05am to Haverhill GE to form the 9.27am Up passenger

train calling all stations to Chappel arriving at 10.21am; it worked back with the 11.33am Down passenger service arriving Haverhill GE at 12.23pm. The next Up passenger train departed Haverhill GE at 2.00pm with a 52 minutes timing to Chappel from where the engine and stock returned with the Down train at 4.05pm. After arrival at 4.56pm the last Up passenger train departed Haverhill GE at 6.04pm, where after arrival at Chappel at 7.00pm a short turn-round time found the last Down service depart the junction at 7.17pm, calling all stations and terminating at Haverhill CV station, before the engine retired to shed. The daily goods service commenced with the 5.30am Halstead to Chappel arriving at 6.03am, from where after shunting the engine departed at 6.20am calling all stations to Haverhill CV arriving at 9.00am. A transfer

DOWN TRAINS.

		Week Days.															Sundays.				
Miles from Chappel.	FROM	2	4	6	8	10	12	14	16	18	20	22	24	26	28	2	4	6	8	10
		L.E.	Cars.	Gds.	Cars.	Gds.	Pass.	Pass.	Gds.	Gds	Gds.	Gds.	Pass.	Pass.	Gds.	Cars.	Pass.	L.E.	L.E.	Pass
			a.m.	a.m.	a.m.	a.m.	a.m.	a.m.	a.m.	p.m.	p.m.	p.m.	p.m.	p.m.	p.m.	a.m.	a.m.	a.m.	p.m.	p.m.
	CHAPPEL dep.			6 20			9 26	11 33			2 5		4 5	7 17	8 0					
2¼	WHITE COLNE ar.			6 25			9 30	11 37			2 12		4 9	7 21	8 5					
	" dep.			6 30			9 31	11 38			2 17		4 10	7 22	8 8					
3¼	EARLS COLNE ar.			6 35			9 34	11 41			2 22		4 13	7 25	8 12					
	" dep.			6 50			9 35	11 42			2 45		4 14	7 26	8 25					
6	HALSTEAD ar.			6 56			9 41	11 48			2 50		4 20	7 32	8 30					
	" dep.	6 45		7 30			9 43	11 50			3 20		4 22	7 34	stop					
9	HEDINGHAM ar.	6 53		7 38			9 50	11 54			3 30		4 29	7 41						
	" dep.		6 55	8 10				11 57			3 40		4 30	7 42						
12	YELDHAM ar.		pass	8 18				12 2			3 48		4 36	7 48						
	" dep.			8 30				12 3			4 0		4 37	7 49						
15¼	BIRDBROOK ar.		pass	8 40				12 12			4 10		4 46	7 58						
	" dep.			8 52				12 14			4 20		4 48	8 0						
18	COLNE VALLEY Jct.		7 20	8 58	9 8	9 35		12 19	12 40	1 44	4 25	4 50	4 53	8 5					
	HAVERHILL G.E. ar.		7 25		9 10	9 40		12 22		1 48	4 30		4 56							
	HAVERHILL C.V. ar.		M.	9 0					12 42			4 55		8 8						

UP TRAINS.

		Week Days.													Sundays.				
Miles from Haverhill.	FROM	1	3	5	7	9	11	13	15	17	19	21	23	25	1	3	5	7	9
		Gds.	Pass.	Pass.	Cars.	Pass.	Gds	Gds.	Gds.	Gds.	Pass.	Gds.	Gds.	Pass.	Cars.	Pass.	L.E.	L.E.	Pass
		a.m.	a.m.	a.m.	a.m.	a.m.	a.m.	a.m.	am	p.m.	p.m.	p.m.	p.m.	p.m.	a.m.	a.m.	a.m.	p.m.	p.m.
	HAVERHILL C.V. dep.				9 5		9 30			1 40			5 15						
	HAVERHILL G.E. dep.			7 38		9 27		10 15	12 31		2 0	4 45		6 4					
1	COLNE VALLEY Jct. ar.			7 40	9 7	9 29	9 34	10 20	12 35	1 43	2 2	4 49	5 18	6 6					
3⅞	BIRDBROOK ar.			7 45		9 33		10 27			2 8		5 25	6 13					
	" dep.			7 46		9 35		10 35			2 9		5 35	6 14					
7	YELDHAM ar.			7 51		9 43		10 55			2 18		5 43	6 24					
	" dep.			7 55		9 45		11 20			2 19		5 53	6 25					
9½	HEDINGHAM ar.			8 1		9 50		11 28			2 25		6 0	6 31					
	" dep		8 3	8 3		9 52		12 0			2 26		6 10	6 32					
13	HALSTEAD ar.		8 10	8 10		10 0		12 10			2 33		6 20	6 40					
	" dep.	5 30	8 11	8 11		10 2		1 0			2 35		6 56	6 41					
15⅞	EARLS COLNE ar.	5 38	8 18	8 18		10 6		1 10			2 41		7 0	6 47					
	" dep.	5 45	8 21	8 21		10 8		1 25			2 43		7 25	6 49					
17¼	WHITE COLNE ar.	5 49	8 23	8 23		10 12		1 30			2 46		7 30	6 52					
	" dep.	5 55	8 24	8 24		10 14		1 40			2 47		7 35	6 53					
19	CHAPPEL ar.	6 3	8 30	8 30		10 21		1 48			2 52		7 43	7 0					
			N.M.	M.															

Week Day Trains.——Notes.

The figures under which a bar (thus——) is placed show where Trains from opposite directions are appointed to cross each other, or allow following trains to pass.

Trains between Chappel and Earls Colne will be worked under the Electric Train Staff Block Telegraph
[Regulations.

M.—Mondays only.

N.M.—Not Mondays.

CV&HR working timetable March 1922.

to the GE yard departed at 9.30am reaching the Haverhill GE 10 minutes later. The engine then formed the 10.15am Up goods working to Chappel arriving at 1.48pm, thence forming the 2.05pm Down working through to Haverhill GE arriving at 4.30pm. A short trip working to Haverhill CV departed at 4.45pm. With little respite, the engine worked the 5.15pm Up goods to Chappel before returning with the 8.00pm Down goods train which terminated at Halstead.

Despite being included within the L&NER umbrella, as a result of grouping the CV&HR issued their final working timetable with effect from 9th April **1923** and then again on 9th July. These was almost identical to the 1922 timetable save that in the Down direction the 6.45am LE from Halstead to Hedingham departed at the later time of 7.40am Tuesdays to Saturdays, and that the 2.45pm SX goods train was replaced SO by the 1.40pm goods from Halstead which ran to Haverhill GE arriving at 2.45pm, each entailing a trip working from Haverhill GE to Haverhill CV and back. The 8.00pm Down goods train from Chappel ran SX and was replaced SO by the 6.15pm goods, which terminated at Halstead at 6.30pm. On the Up road the 10.15am goods ex Haverhill GE operated through to Chappel SX but terminated at Halstead SO at 12.10pm. The 5.15pmSX goods ex Haverhill CV was replaced SO by the 3.30pm departure arriving at Chappel at 5.48pm. The associated trip workings from Heverhill GE and Haverhill CV were altered accordingly. From 3rd June 1923 the company operated a Sunday service using the Haverhill-based locomotive, which departed Haverhill CV with ECS at 8.29am arriving Haverhill GE 8.35am to work the 8.41am Up passenger train calling all stations to Chappel arriving at 9.36am. The engine and stock then returned as the 11.00am ex Chappel arriving Haverhill GE at 11.51am; the stock was then stabled and the engine returned light to shed at 12.05pm, arriving 6 minutes later. For the afternoon service the LE departed Haverhill CV at 5.46pm with a 5 minutes timing to Haverhill GE. The last Up working departed at 5.58pm calling

DOWN TRAINS.

Miles from Chappel.	FROM		2	4	6	8	10	12	14	16	18	20	22	24	26	28	30	32	34	2	4	6	8	10	11
																				Week Days.													**Sundays.**					
			L.E.	Cars.	Gds.	Cars.	Gds.	Pass.	Pass.	Gds.	Gds.	Gds.	Gds.	Gds.	Gds.	Pass.	Pass.	Gds.	Gds.	Cars.	Pass.	L.E.	L.E.	Pass.	Pass.
			a.m.	a.m.	a.m.	a.m.	a.m.	a.m.	a.m.	a.m.	p.m.	p.m.	p.m	p.m.	p.m.	p.m.	p.m.	p.m	p.m.	a.m.	a.m.	a.m.	p.m.	p.m.	p.m.
	CHAPPEL dep.			6 20				9 26	11 33			2 5				4 5	7 17	6 5	8 0		11 0			8 45	8 22
2¼	WHITE COLNE ar.			6 25				9 30	11 37			2 12				4 9	7 21	6 10	8 5		11 4			8 50	8 26
"	" dep.			6 30				9 31	11 38			2 17				4 10	7 22	6 13	8 8		11 5			8 51	8 28
3¼	EARLS COLNE ar.			6 35				9 34	11 41			2 22				4 13	7 25	6 17	8 12		11 8			8 53	8 30
"	" dep.			6 50				9 35	11 42			2 45				4 14	7 26	6 22	8 25		11 9			8 54	8 31
6	HALSTEAD ar.			6 56				9 41	11 48			2 50				4 20	7 32	6 30	8 30		11 15			8 59	8 36
"	" dep.	6 45		7 30				9 43	11 50			3 20	1 40			4 22	7 34	stop	stop		11 17			9 1	8 38
9	HEDINGHAM ar.	6 53		7 38				9 50	11 56			3 30	1 48			4 29	7 41				11 24			9 8	8 45
"	" dep.		6 55	8 10					11 57			3 40	2 0			4 30	7 42				11 25			9 9	8 46
12	YELDHAM ar.		pass	8 18					12 2			3 4	2 9			4 36	7 48				11 31			9 15	8 52
"	" dep.			8 30					12 3			4 0	2 19			4 37	7 49				11 32			9 16	8 53
15¼	BIRDBROOK ar.		pass	8 40					12 12			4 10	2 30			4 46	7 58				11 41			9 25	9 2
"	" dep.			8 52					12 14			4 20	2 35			4 48	8 0				11 43			9 27	9 4
18	COLNE VALLEY Jct.		7 20	8 58	9 10	9 35			12 19	12 36	1 44	4 25	2 40	3 5	4 50	4 53	8 5			8 3	11 48	12 8	5 51	9 32	9 9
	HAVERHILL G.E. ar.		7 25	9 0	9 12	9 40			12 22		1 48	4 30	2 45			4 56				8 30	11 51		5 53		
	HAVERHILL C.V. ar.									12 58				3 7	4 55		8 8			5		12 11		9 35	9 12
			M.S.	M.											N.S.	S.	S.	N.S.		S.	N.S.				

UP TRAINS.

Miles from Haverhill.	FROM	1	3	5	7	9	11	13	15	17	19	21	23	25	27	29	1	3	5	7	9
								Week Days.											**Sundays.**			
		Gds.	Pass.	Pass.	Cars.	Pass.	Gds	Gds	Gds.	Gds.	Pass.	Gds.	Gds.	Gds.	Gds.	Pass.	Cars.	Pass.	L.E.	L.E.	Pass.
		a.m.	a.m.	a.m.	a.m.	a.m.	a.m.	a.m.	a.m	p.m.	p.m.	p.m.	p.m	p.m.	p.m	p m	a.m.	a.m.	a.m.	p.m.	p.m.
	HAVERHILL C.V. dep.					9 7					1 40		5 15		3 30		8 29			5 48	
1	HAVERHILL G.E. dep.			7 38		9 29		10 15	12 31			2 0	4 45					8 44	12 5		6 0
3¾	COLNE VALLEY Jct. ar.			7 40	9 9	9 31	9 34	10 20	12 35	1 43		2 2	4 49	5 18	3 5	2 34	6 8	8 31	8 46	12 7	5 50	6 2
	BIRDBROOK ar.			7 45		9 36		10 27				2 8		5 25		3 40	6 14		8 49			6 7
	" dep.			7 47		9 38		10 35				2 9		5 33		3 48	6 15		8 53			6 9
7	YELDHAM ar.			7 55		9 46		10 55				2 17		5 43		3 58	6 2		9 0			6 16
"	" dep.			7 56		9 47		11 28				2 18		5 53		4 12	6 24		9 2			6 18
9¾	HEDINGHAM ar.			8 2		9 53		11 28				2 24		6 0		4 20	6 30		9 7			6 23
"	" dep.		8 3	8 3		9 54		12 0				2 25		6 10		4 35	6 31		9 9			6 25
13	HALSTEAD ar.		8 10	8 10		10 1		12 10				2 32		6 20		4 45	6 38		9 16			6 32
"	" dep.	5 30	8 12	8 12		10 3		1 0				2 34		6 50		5 5	6 40		9 18			6 34
15¾	EARLS COLNE ar.	5 38	8 18	8 16		10 10		1 10				2 40		7 0		5 15	6 48		9 24			6 40
"	" dep.	5 45	8 20	8 20		10 11		1 25				2 42		7 25		5 30	6 48		9 26			6 42
17¼	WHITE COLNE ar.	5 49	8 23	8 23		10 13		1 30				2 46		7 30		5 35	6 51		9 28			6 45
"	" dep.	5 55	8 25	8 25		10 16		1 40				2 47		7 35		5 40	6 52		9 31			6 47
19	CHAPPEL ar.	6 3	8 30	8 30		10 21		1 48				2 52		7 43		5 48	6 58		9 36			6 52
			N.M.	M.									N.S.	N.S.	S.	S.					

Week Day Trains.——Notes.

The figures under which a bar (thus ——) is placed show where Trains from opposite directions are appointed to cross each other, or allow following trains to pass.

Trains between Chappel and Earls Colne will be worked under the Electric Train Staff Block Telegraph [Regulations.

M.—Mondays only.   **N.S.**—Not Saturdays.

N.M.—Not Mondays.   **S.**—Saturdays only.

M.S.—Tuesday to Saturday inclusive, leave Halstead 7.40 a.m., arrive Hedingham 7.48.

CV&HR working timetable July 1923.

all stations, arriving at Chappel at 6.50m before returning at 8.06pm and terminating at Haverhill CV at 8.57pm.

The initial service arranged by the L&NER in **1923** showed the new Colne Valley branch was served by three trains in each direction together with a short trip from Chappel to S&C Hedingham and return, leaving S&C Hedingham at 8.08amMX, 7.38am Haverhill to Chappel MO, and returning from Chappel at 8.26am. A set of old 6-wheel stock was used on these services but all other trains were formed of bogie stock. Two trains ran each way on Sundays in the summer months only in subsequent years, whilst goods traffic was worked by two trains each way on weekdays only, supplemented at busy times by special trains arranged at short notice.

The coal miners' strikes of **1926** caused problems on the railways and to conserve coal stocks, services on most lines were reduced. The Colne Valley line was no exception and from 31st May Down trains departed Chappel at 9.26am to Sible and Castle Hedingham, and 4.06pm and 7.18pm to Haverhill North. In the Up direction services departed 7.38amMO Haverhill North to Chappel, 7.55amMX Yeldham to Chappel and then 9.29am and 6.06pm Haverhill North to Chappel.

By **1928** the working timetable showed four passenger trains in each direction on weekdays and two each way on Sundays. In the Up direction the 7.55amMX ex Yeldham started back MO at Haverhill North departing at 7.38am, whilst the 2.00pm ex Haverhill North was not to work horsebox traffic for stations beyond Chappel on Saturdays. On the Down road the 9.36am ex Chappel terminated at Sible and Castle Hedingham at 9.50am whilst all other services worked through to Haverhill North; the 4.06pm and 7.18pm ex Chappel being allowed 2 minutes recovery time between Birdbrook and Haverhill North. All trains called at all stations. On Sundays the two services in each direction were the 8.45am ex Haverhill North, which returned from Chappel at 11.10am, and the afternoon 6.00pm ex Haverhill North, which departed Chappel at 8.05pm. Both Down trains were allowed 2 minutes recovery time between Birdbrook and Haverhill North. Three goods services worked in each direction on weekdays and on the Up road the 5.15am was a short working from Halstead to Chappel; the 10.15am ex Haverhill North on SX worked through to Chappel, calling at all stations but SO terminated at Halstead. On SX the engine was changed at Sible and Castle Hedingham, the fresh engine working forward and the relieved

ABOVE AND BELOW: L&NER public timetable 1923.

See page				WEEK DAYS.									SUNDAYS.		
			morn	morn	morn	morn		even.		even.			morn	even.	even.
18– 20	**LIVERPOOL STREET** dep.		...	6 50	...	10 0	...	2 15	...	5 42	...	...	9 20	...	4A40
	Chelmsford "		—	8 10	—	9A48	—	3 3	—	6L34	—	—	10 14	—	—
	Mark's Tey arr.		—	8 50	—	11 9 11A18	—	3 39	—	6L59	—	—	10 43	—	8A 0
21– 23	Ipswich dep.		7 55	—	—	10 27	—	2 5	—	5 58	—	—	9 44	6 24	—
	Colchester "		—	8 44	—	11 5	—	3 30	—	6 46	—	—	10 24	—	7 50
	Mark's Tey arr.		8 45	8 56	—	11 18	—	3 40	—	6 56	—	—	10 38	7 23	8 0
34	Mark's Tey dep.		...	9 13	...	11 22	—	3 52	—	7 4	—	...	10 47	...	8 7
	Chappel & Wakes Colne arr.		—	9 22	—	11 30	—	4 2	—	7 13	—	—	10 56	—	8 16
	CHAPPEL & WAKES COLNE dep.		—	9 26	—	11 33	—	4 5	—	7 17	—	—	11 0	—	8045
	White Colne arr.		—	9 31	—	11 38	—	4 10	—	7 22	—	—	11 5	—	8051
	Earls Colne "		—	9 35	—	11 42	—	4 14	—	7 26	—	—	11 9	—	8054
	Halstead "		—	9 43	—	11 50	—	4 22	—	7 34	—	—	11 17	—	9 1
	Sible & Castle Hedingham "		—	9 50	—	11 57	—	4 30	—	7 42	—	—	11 25	—	9 9
	Yeldham "		—	—	—	12 3	—	4 37	—	7 49	—	—	11 32	—	9016
	Birdbrook "		—	—	—	12 14	—	4 48	—	8 0	—	—	11 43	—	9027
	HAVERHILL "		—	—	—	12 22	—	4 56	—	8 8	—	—	11 51	—	9035
34	Haverhill dep.		...	...	...	12 32	—	5 5	—	...	—	...	...	...	...
	Bartlow arr.		...	...	...	12 43	—	5 16	—	...	—	...	...	...	...
56	Bartlow dep.		...	...	...	1 38	—	5 37	—	...	—	...	...	...	...
	Saffron Walden arr.		...	...	...	1 52	—	5 51	—	...	—	...	...	...	...
	LIVERPOOL ST. "		...	...	...	—	—	7 58	—	...	—	...	...	...	...
34	Bartlow dep.		...	...	...	12 44	—	5 17	—	...	—	...	...	...	...
	Linton arr.		...	...	...	12 49	—	5 22	—	...	—	...	...	...	...
	Pampisford "		...	...	...	12 55	—	5 28	—	...	—	...	...	...	...
	Shelford "		...	...	...	1 3	—	5 36	—	...	—	...	...	...	...
34	**LIVERPOOL ST.** arr.		...	...	...	5B9	—	7 58	—	...	—	...	...	...	...
34	Cambridge arr.		...	...	...	1 9	—	5 42	—	...	—	...	...	...	...

A Via Colchester.
B On Saturdays arrives Liverpool Street 3.18 p.m. **From 23rd July to 15th September inclusive** passengers can arrive St. Pancras station 4.2 p.m.

See page			WEEK DAYS.										SUNDAYS.	
			morn	morn		morn	morn		even.	even.		even.		morn	even.
35	Cambridge dep.		...	...	...	8 40	...	—	1 5	...	...	4 57	...	—	—
35	**LIVERPOOL ST.**— dep.		—	...	—	5 50	—	—	—	—	—	2 48	—	—	—
35	Shelford dep.		...	...	...	8 47	...	—	1 12	...	...	5 5	—	—	—
	Pampisford "		...	...	...	8 55	...	—	1 20	...	...	5 14	—	—	—
	Linton "		...	...	...	9 1	...	—	1 26	...	...	5 23	—	—	—
	Bartlow arr.		...	...	...	9 5	...	—	1 30	...	...	5 27	—	—	—
56	**LIVERPOOL ST.**— dep.		—	...	—	5 50	—	11 50	—	—	—	2 48	—	—	—
	Saffron Walden "		—	...	—	8 42	—	1 10	—	—	—	4H44	—	—	—
	Bartlow arr.		—	...	—	8 56	—	1 24	—	—	—	4L58	—	—	—
35	Bartlow dep.		...	...	—	9 6	—	1 32	—	—	—	5 29	—	—	—
	Haverhill arr.		...	...	—	9 20	—	1 45	—	—	—	5 42	—	—	—
	HAVERHILL dep.		7M038	...	...	9 29	...	2 0	...	—	6 6	—	8 44	...	6 0
	Birdbrook "		7M047	...	...	9 38	...	2 9	...	—	6 15	—	8 53	...	6 9
	Yeldham "		7M056	...	...	9 47	...	2 18	...	—	6 24	—	9 2	...	6 18
	Sible & Castle Hedingham "		8 3	...	...	9 54	...	2 25	...	—	6 31	—	9 9	...	6 25
	Halstead "		8 12	...	...	10 3	...	2 34	...	—	6 40	—	9 18	...	6 34
	Earls Colne "		8 20	...	...	10 11	...	2 42	...	—	6 48	—	9 26	...	6 42
	White Colne "		8 25	...	...	10 16	...	2 47	...	—	6 52	—	9 31	...	6 47
	CHAPPEL & WAKES COLNE arr.		8 30	—	—	10 21	—	2 52	—	—	6 58	—	9 36	—	6 52
35	Chappel & Wakes Colne dep.		8 35	...	—	10 26	—	2 57	—	—	7 12	—	9 42	—	7 0
	Mark's Tey arr.		8 42	...	—	10 33	—	3 4	—	—	7 19	—	9 49	—	7 7
18– 20	Mark's Tey dep.		8 50	...	—	10 35 11 9	—	3 6	—	—	7 28	—	9 57	—	7 11
	Colchester arr.		8 59	...	—	10 44	—	3 15	—	—	7 38	—	10 6	—	7 20
	Ipswich "		9 41	...	...	11 40	—	4K30	—	—	8K39	—	10 49	...	9 46
21– 23	Mark's Tey dep.		8 56	9 2	—	10 45 11 18	—	3A6 4 23	—	—	7 24	—	10 38	—	7 23
	Chelmsford arr.		—	9 39	—	11 57	—	5 4	—	—	8 7	—	11 20	—	8 1
	LIVERPOOL STREET "		9 54	—	11 43	—	—	5A 5	—	—	9 17	—	12 40	—	8 58

D On 23rd and 30th September runs 23 minutes earlier.
E On Saturdays arrives Ipswich 4.4 p.m.
H On Tuesdays leaves Saffron Waldon 4.55 & arrives Bartlow 5.9 p.m.
K On Saturdays arrives Ipswich 9.45 p.m.
L On Saturdays runs 4 minutes earlier.
MO Mondays only.
NS Not Saturdays.
SO Saturdays only.

engine running light to Halstead shed. The final Up goods train departed Haverhill South at 3.25pmSO but ran at the later time of 5.25pmSX. On the Down road the 6.20am ex Chappel called at all stations to Haverhill South arriving at 9.05am, but when conveying cattle traffic for Haverhill was diverted to the North station arriving at 9.00am with the station master Yeldham advising accordingly. If the 6.20am Down train ran direct to Haverhill North the 10.15amSX Up goods was to start at 9.25am and call at Haverhill South departing Colne Valley Junction at 10.21am instead of 10.27am. The 2.05pmSX ex Chappel omitted calling at White Colne and Birdbrook, terminating at Haverhill North at 4.15pm, with the trainmen being relieved en route at Halstead. On SO the return working of the 10.15am ex Haverhill North train returned from Halstead at 1.40pm serving all stations to Haverhill North arriving at 2.45pm. The final Down goods workings of the day were the 6.05pm ex Chappel, the return of the 3.25pm Up service from Haverhill South and the 8.00pm ex Chappel, the return working of the 5.20pm Up train from Haverhill South, which terminated at Halstead at 6.30pm and 8.20pm respectively. The 6.05pm called at all stations but the 8.00pm only served White Colne and Earls Colne when required for cattle traffic.

In **1937** the working timetable provided a service of four passenger trains SX and five SO in each direction on weekdays. Of the Down services the 9.26am ex Chappel was allowed 6 minutes stand time at Sible and Castle Hedingham for pathing purposes, while the 9.33pmSO ex Chappel from 4th May ran WSO. On the Up road the 7.41am ex Haverhill North was permitted 2 additional minutes running time between White Colne and Chappel for exceptional circumstances and the 2.02pm from Haverhill North on Saturdays was not to work horsebox traffic for stations beyond Chappel. The last train of the day, 8.35pmSO ex Haverhill North, from 4th May ran WSO. All passenger trains called at all stations. Goods services commenced with the arrival of the 4.40am ex Colchester, which departed Chappel at 5.47am and called at all stations to Haverhill North arriving at 8.35am. Ten minutes later the 6.20am Up goods train from Cambridge departed Haverhill North running SX to Earls Colne arriving 1.21pm but continuing SO through to Chappel arriving 1.28pm serving White Colne only if required. The working returned to Cambridge departing Chappel 2.05pmSO and Earls Colne 2.22pmSX calling all stations and reaching Haverhill North at 5.30pm. In the intervening period the engine ran light to Chappel departing Earls Colne at 1.33pmSX, returning at 2.05pm to take up the Down working. The 9.58amSX goods train from Colchester terminated at Earls Colne at 12.07pm and, after shunting and outsorting of wagons, returned at 1.00pm to Chappel and then continued to Sudbury. The final goods train of the day departed Haverhill North at 3.30pm, calling at all branch stations and reaching Chappel at 7.47pm before continuing to Colchester. Specific instructions were issued on the formation of this train leaving Halstead. While at Haverhill the engine had worked booked trips between Haverhill North and Haverhill South. A Q 'as and when required' path was also available for an engine to run light from Chappel departing 3.00pmSX to Halstead to perform yard shunting before returning at 3.45pm to Chappel. The station master Halstead was to advise Chappel when the engine was required and when operated the engine had to promptly return to Chappel as it was booked to work the 4.05pm passenger service to Haverhill North. Two passenger trains were provided on Sundays in 1937. The light engine departed Haverhill South shed at 8.00am to work the 8.40am Up passenger service calling all stations to

Chappel arriving at 9.23am. The return Down working departed Chappel at 11.10am, reaching Haverhill North at 11.54am after which the engine retired to shed arriving at 12.11pm. For the afternoon departure the engine departed shed at 5.25pm to work the 6.07pm Haverhill North to Chappel, arriving 6.53pm, the train conveying Sainsbury's meat traffic for London. When this traffic was conveyed it was to be attached in front of the passenger stock with an additional brake van and Haverhill were to advise Chappel so that arrangements could be made for the vehicles to be worked through to Marks Tey by the locomotive. The return working departed Chappel at 8.12pm until 1st May and 8.29pm from 8th May, arriving Haverhill North at 8.58pm or 9.13pm respectively, after whence the engine ran light to shed.

In later L&NER days and during the period of steam operation by BR the following start to stop timings for passenger trains were generally adhered to when compiling the Colne Valley line timetable:

	Minutes
Marks Tey to Chappel	7
Chappel to White Colne	4
White Colne to Earls Colne	3
Earls Colne to Halstead	5
Halstead to S & C Hedingham	6
S & C Hedingham to Yeldham	5
Yeldham to Birdbrook	7
Birdbrook to Haverhill	8
Haverhill to Birdbrook	8
Birdbrook to Yeldham	7
Yeldham to S & C Hedingham	5
S & C Hedingham to Halstead	6
Halstead to Earls Colne	5
Earls Colne to White Colne	4
White Colne to Chappel	4
Chappel to Marks Tey	7

The summer working timetable for **1939** showed a basic weekday service of five passenger and three goods trains in each direction, with all passenger services calling at all stations. These trains were interspersed with several goods and light engine movements between Haverhill North and Haverhill South and return. Of the Down passenger trains, the 4.05pm ex Chappel started back at Marks Tey on Saturdays at 4.00pm, it then departed Chappel at 4.08pm and ran three minutes later throughout, while the 9.33pm ex Chappel after 9th September ran WSO. On the Up road the 7.41am ex Haverhill North was permitted 2 minutes extra running time between White Colne and Chappel for exceptional circumstances, whilst the 1.55pm from Haverhill North was not permitted to work horsebox traffic for stations beyond Chappel. The final Up train of the day, 8.35pm ex Haverhill North, ran WSO after 10th September. The first Down goods service 4.50am ex Colchester conveyed brake goods for White Colne through to Earls Colne and then called at all other stations arriving Haverhill North at 8.35am, after which the engine worked the 9.31am passenger train from Haverhill North to Chappel. The next Down goods, 9.58am ex Colchester, only ran as far as Earls Colne, arriving at 12.07pm and returning from there at 1.00pm to Sudbury, reversing at Chappel. The 3.05pm ex Chappel, a return working of the 6.30am ex Cambridge, called at all sidings except for White Colne and arrived Haverhill North 5.30pm before continuing to Cambridge. On SX this train was preceded by an

CHAPPEL, HALSTEAD AND HAVERHILL NORTH. Single Line.

The Haverhill South Single line connection at Colne Valley Junction is controlled by the Key token. The Haverhill South Single line connection at Colne Valley Junction is controlled by the Key token for the Birdbrook and Haverhill North Junction section.

DOWN — WEEK DAYS.

Miles from Chappel.			1 Eng.	2 Gds.	3	4 Pass.	5	6 Gds. S X	7	8 WSX	9 Gds. WSX	10 Gds.	11 Gds.	12	13 Gds.	14 Gds. E & B	15 Pass. S X	16 Pass.	17	18 Eng. WSX	19	20 Pass.	21 Eng.
M. C.	Chappel	dep.	a.m. —	a.m. 5 47		a.m. 9 26		a.m. 11 57				p.m.	p.m.		p.m. 2 5	p.m.	p.m. 3 04½	p.m. 7 20		p.m.		p.m. 9 33	p.m.
2 10	White Colne	dep.	—	5 53		9 30½											4 9½	7 24½				9 37½	
3 48	Earls Colne	arr. / dep.	—	5 57 / 6 12		9 31 / 9 35		12 2							2 12 / 2 45		Q / 4 10 4 13	7 25 / 7 28				9 38 / 9 41	
6 6	Halstead	arr. / dep.	—	6 18 / 7 2		9 40 / 9 43		11 44 / 11 45							2 57 / 3 35		4 14 / 4 19	7 29 / 7 34				9 42 / 9 47	
9 30	Sible and Castle Hedingham	arr. / dep.	—	7 10 / 7 35		9 49 / 9 55		11 50 / 11 52							3 45		4 21 / 4 27	7 36 / 7 43				9 49 / 9 55	
11 72	Yeldham	arr. / dep.	—	7 43 / 7 8		9 59½ / 10 0		11 58 / 11 59							4 36		4 28 / 4 32½	7 47½ / 7 48				9 56 / 10 0½	
15 56	Birdbrook	arr. / dep.	—	8 15 / 8 25		10 7 / 10 8		12 3½ / 12 4							4 44 / 5 0		4 33	7 55				10 1 / 10 8	
18 31	Colne Valley Jc A	arr.	¶ 7 21					12 11			12 54	1 44	3 9		5 10		4 40½	7 56		8 16		10 9	10 31
19 41	Haverhill South	arr.	7 23	8 35		10 16		12 12			12 57	1 47			5 20		4 41			8 19			10 34
	Haverhill North	arr.	7 41					12 20			1 48		3 13		5 30		4 49	8 4				10 17	

Notes (Down):
2 4.50 a.m. extra White Colne to Colchester. 2 Allowed 2 mins. extra White Colne to Chappel. Brake goods for White Colne to be taken through to Earls Colne. Engine to work 7 up. 4 Advertised S. and C. Hedingham dep. 9.50 a.m. 7 9.58 a.m. ex Colchester. 10 & 11 Runs WSO after 9th Sept. 13 To Cambridge. 14 To perform yard shunting. The S.M. Halstead to advise Chappel when engine is required, and when operated, engine to return sharp to time. 15 On Sats. from Mark's Tey at 4.0, Chappel arr. 4.7, dep. 4.8 and thence three mins. later. =20 & 21 After 9th September runs Weds. and Sats. only.

UP — WEEK DAYS.

Miles from H'rhill Nth			1 Eng.	2 Pass.	3	4 Gds. SO	5 Gds. S X	6 Pass.	7	8 Pass. WSX	9 Gds. S X	10	11 Gds. WSX	12 Pass.	13 Gds.	14 Gds.	15 Eng. S X	16 Gds. WSX	17 Gds.	18 Pass.	19 Eng. WSX	20 Pass.	21 Eng.
M. C.	Haverhill North	dep.	a.m. 7 15	a.m. 7 41		a.m. 8 45	a.m. 8 45	a.m. 9 31		a.m. 12 45			p.m.	p.m. 1 55	p.m. 2 15	p.m.	p.m.	p.m. 3 30	p.m.	p.m. 3 45	p.m. 8 108	p.m. 8 35	p.m. 10 25
	Haverhill South	dep.	7 15																				
1 10	Colne Valley Junc. A	arr. / dep.	7 21	7 17		8 57	8 57	9 38½		12 49 / 12 54			1 35 / 1 39		2 19 / 2 24			Q	3 41	4 / 4		8 12 / 8 16	8 43	10 27 / 10 31
3 66	Birdbrook	arr. / dep.	¶	7 48½ / 7 49		9 10 / 9 10	9 10	9 39 / 9 45½					1 44						4 5 / 4 10	3 56 / 4 56	19½ / 20		8 42½ / 8 43	
7 50	Yeldham	arr. / dep.	¶	7 55½ / 7 56		9 20 / 10 10	9 20	9 46					¶	2 2 / 2 3					4 50	4 15 / 4 50	26½ / 28	8 48 / 8 49	
10 12	Sible and Castle Hedingham	arr. / dep.	¶	8 1 / 8 3		10 18 / 10 30	10 18	9 52 / 9 54						2 9½ / 2 10					5 0 / 5 50	4 58 / 5 0	35	8 54 / 8 55	
13 36	Halstead	arr. / dep.	¶	8 8 / 8 11		11 30 / 11 40	11 30	10 0 / 10 2						2 15 / 2 22					6 10 / 6 55	6 6 / 6 10	41 / 44	9 2 / 9 4	
15 74	Earls Colne	arr. / dep.	8 16 / 8 17			1 7 / 1 21	1 21	10 7				1 0		2 24 / 2 29					7 0 / 7 34	7 0 / 7 6	49	9 8 / 9 9	
17 32	White Colne	dep.	8 20			*	1 40	10 8				1 15		2 30					7 39	7 46	49	9 12	
19 41	Chappel	arr.	8 27			1 28 / 1 55	1 55	10 16				1 21		2 38					7 53	7 52 / 7 26	53 / 58	9 17	

Notes (Up):
4 & 5 6.30 a.m. ex Camb. 9 To Sudbury. =12 On Sat. not to work H.B., &c., traffic for beyond Chappel. 15 To work 15 down. 16 Commences 11th Sept. 17 After 9th Sept. runs WSO. 16 & 17 To Colchester. 18 To leave Halstead marshalled eng., traffic to be weighed at Mark's T., traffic for via Bury, Up'rd. and Down Road. Traffic attached at Earls Colne, White Colne and Chappel to be marshalled accordingly. Traffic for and via Bury, Whitemoor and Peterboro' to be worked through to Mark's Tey for the 4.18 a.m. ex Colchester next morning. =20 & 21 After 10th Sept. runs Weds. and Sats. only. =26 To work from Haverhill N. fitted vans of Sainsbury's meat traffic for London. Haverhill to attach in front with an add'n'l b'ke and advise Chappel, latter to arr'ge special w'k'g to Mark's T. A. Auxiliary Key Token instrument provided for w'k'g connection to H'rhill St. ¶ To or from H'rhill S. The distance from Colne Valley Jc. to H'rhill S. is 55 chains. Earls Colne and Yeldham. A pass'r train must not be arr'g'd to cross another pass'r train at these stations.

SUNDAYS (DOWN)

			22 Eng.	23 Pass.	24 Eng.	25 Eng.	26 Pass.	27 Eng.
Chappel	dep.		a.m. —	a.m. 1110	p.m. —	p.m. —	p.m. 8 52	p.m. —
White Colne	dep.		—	1114½	—	—	8 57	—
Earls Colne	arr. / dep.		—	1115 / 1118	—	—	8 58 / 9 1	—
Halstead	arr. / dep.		—	1119 / 1124	—	—	9 2 / 9 7	—
Sible and Castle Hedingham	arr. / dep.		—	1126 / 1132	—	—	9 9 / 9 15	—
Yeldham	arr. / dep.		—	1133 / 1137½	—	—	9 16 / 9 21	—
Birdbrook	arr. / dep.		—	1138 / 1145	—	—	9 22 / 9 29	—
Colne Valley Jc A	arr.		¶ 7 56	1146	12 8	¶ 5 26	9 30	¶ 9 51
Haverhill South	arr.		7 58	1154	12 11	5 28	9 38	9 54
Haverhill North	arr.		1017					

SUNDAYS (UP)

			22 Eng.	23 Pass.	24 Pass.	25 Eng.	26 Pass.	27 Eng.
Haverhill North	dep.		a.m. 7 50	a.m. 8 32	p.m. 2	p.m. —	p.m. 6 7	p.m. 9 45
Haverhill South	dep.		7 52			5 20		9 47
Colne Valley Junc. A	arr. / dep.		7 56	8 40	12 4	5 22	6 14½ / 6 15	9 51
Birdbrook	arr. / dep.		¶	8 41 / 8 48	12 8	5 26	6 21¼ / 6 22	¶
Yeldham	arr. / dep.		¶	8 49 / 8 54			6 27 / 6 29	¶
Sible and Castle Hedingham	arr. / dep.		¶	8 55 / 9 2			6 35 / 6 37	¶
Halstead	arr. / dep.		¶	9 4 / 9 9			6 42 / 6 44	¶
Earls Colne	arr. / dep.		¶	9 10				¶
White Colne	dep.		¶	9 13			6 48	¶
Chappel	arr.		¶	9 18			6 53	¶

Commences 11th Sept. WSX. Q Commences 11th Sept. WSO after 9th Sept.

L&NER working timetable July 1939.

engine and brake van running in a Q path 'as and when required' to Halstead to perform yard shunting, the engine then returning light to Chappel at 3.45pm. In the Up direction the 6.30am goods ex Cambridge on SX called at all stations but SO called at White Colne only if required. The 3.30pm goods ex Haverhill North ran WSX commencing 11th September and as a result the 3.45pm all stations to Chappel ran WSO after 9th September, both trains working through to Colchester. Two passenger trains were provided in each direction on Sundays. The light engine departed Haverhill South to work the 8.22am ex Haverhill North to Chappel arriving 9.18am and returned with the 11.10am Down train. On arrival at Haverhill North the engine worked light to shed at Haverhill South, arriving 12.17pm. The engine again departed shed at 5.20pm to work the 6.07pm Up train from Haverhill North arriving Chappel at 6.53pm before returning with the 8.52pm Down train due Haverhill North at 9.38pm. The engine then ran light to shed arriving 9.54pm. All four trains called at all stations and provided connections at Chappel with Stour Valley services. The 6.07pm ex Haverhill North was permitted to convey fitted vans of Sainsbury's meat traffic for London. The Haverhill North station master was to arrange for the vehicle or vehicles to be attached to the front of the train with an additional brake vehicle and advise Chappel so the latter could arrange for a special working to Marks Tey, which the locomotive could accommodate with a two hours standover at Chappel.

Soon after the outbreak of hostilities the L&NER authorities introduced an emergency timetable on and from **2nd October 1939** and the service on the Colne Valley line was reduced to three passenger trains in each direction on weekdays and two each way on Sundays. Weekday trains departed Haverhill North at 7.53am, 11.58pm and 4.58pm, returning from Chappel at 10.28am, 2.43pm and 6.48pm. On Sundays trains departed Haverhill North at 8.43am and 4.58pm, returning from Chappel at 11.15am and 6.48pm.

After the initial scare of the 'phoney war' the L&NER introduced a service of four passenger trains in each direction on weekdays and two each way on Sundays, and the timings of 1940 (*right*) continued with minor adjustments throughout the war years.

Although a basic freight service of two trains in each direction serving all stations was maintained throughout the war years, with few short workings, the timetable was often abandoned when military traffic dictated. Of the highest importance was the conveyance of bombs and armaments to Earls Colne, White Colne, Yeldham and Birdbrook to service the RAF and USAAF airfields served by the branch.

The working timetable for passenger trains in **1945** showed a service of four trains in each direction on weekdays and two each way on Sundays. On weekdays the 7.35am ex Haverhill North terminated at Chappel returning at 9.45am, whilst the 9.33am from Haverhill North was a through train to Marks Tey returning from the junction at 11.48am. In the afternoon the 2.13pm Up service from Haverhill North also terminated at Chappel, the engine and stock forming the 4.33pm Down train. The final service of the day was the 6.00pm ex Haverhill North, which was a through train to Colchester. The final Down service departed Marks Tey at 6.44pm and Chappel 10 minutes later. All trains called at all stations. On Sundays the Up services departing Haverhill North at 8.43am and 4.40pm ran through to

Marks Tey, returning at 10.36am and 6.41pm respectively. From 20th May until 9th September the 8.43am ex Haverhill North ran as a through train to Clacton to give Colne Valley residents the opportunity of a few hours by the sea. The return service from the coast departed Clacton at 5.36pm and left Marks Tey for Haverhill North at 6.43pm, running two minutes later throughout. All trains called at all stations. The timetable also showed relevant light engine movements from the engine shed at Haverhill South to and from Haverhill North station.

The working timetable for **1949** showed a weekday service of four passenger and two goods trains in each direction. On the Down service three trains departed from Marks Tey at 9.32am, 11.47am and 6.42pm, whilst the 4.45pm commenced its journey at Chappel. The first train of the day on the Up road was the 6.28am ex Cambridge which arrived at Haverhill North 7.08am and departed at 7.30am calling all stations to Marks Tey, arriving at 8.34am. The 9.20am ex Haverhill North terminated at Marks Tey at 10.28am but the 2.07pm from Haverhill North terminated at Chappel. The final Up service, 5.58pm ex Haverhill North, terminated SX at Marks Tey at 6.56pm but SO ran through to Colchester arriving at 7.12pm. The Down goods service commenced with the 4.50am from Colchester which had mandatory calls at all stations except White Colne, where it only shunted if required, before terminating at Haverhill North at 8.25am. On the Up road the 6.35am Class 'B' goods ex Coldham Lane, after shunting at Haverhill North, departed at 9.00am serving Yeldham and all stations to Earls Colne arriving at 1.08pm; the train then returned departing 2.30pm serving all stations to Haverhill North arriving at 4.57pm before continuing to Cambridge where arrival was scheduled at 6.14pm.

TIMETABLE FOR **1940**							
DOWN		WEEKDAYS				SUNDAYS	
		am	pm	pm	pm	am	pm
Liverpool Street	dep	8.15	1.00	2.15	4a54	8.15	5.00
Chappel & Wakes Colne	dep	10.29	2.43	5.00	6.48	11.15	6.46
White Colne	dep	10.34	2.48	5.05	6.53	11.20	6.51
Earls Colne	dep	10.29	2.53	5.10	6.58	11.25	6.36
Halstead	dep	10.47	3.02	5b25	7.07	11.34	7.05
S & C Hedingham	dep	10.55	3.10	5.37	7.15	11.42	7.13
Yeldham	dep	11.02	3.17	5.43	7.22	11.49	7.20
Bordbrook	dep	11.12	3.27	5.52	7.32	11.59	7.20
Haverhill North	arr	11.20	3.35	6.00	7.40	12.07	7.23
NOTES: a depart 4.18pm SO. b arrive 5.15pm.							

UP		WEEKDAYS				SUNDAYS	
		am	am	pm	pm	am	pm
Haverhill North	dep	7.53	9.22	12.00	4.58	8.43	4.58
Birdbrook	dep	8.03	9.31	12.09	5.07	8.53	5.07
Yeldham	dep	8.13	9.39	12.17	5.16	9.03	5.16
S & C Hedingham	dep	8.20	9.45	12.24	5.23	9.10	5.23
Halstead	dep	8.30	9.53	12.33	5.33	9.20	5.33
Earls Colne	dep	8.36	10.01	12.39	5.39	9.26	5.39
White Colne	dep	8.41	10.05	12.44	5.44	9.31	5.44
Chappel & Wakes Colne	arr	8.45	10.11	12.48	5.48	9.35	5.48
Liverpool Street	arr	10f26	12.04	3.47	7.47	11.31	7.30
NOTE: f arrive 10.36am SO.							

CHAPPEL, HALSTEAD AND HAVERHILL NORTH.

SINGLE LINE.

The Haverhill South Single Line connection at Colne Valley Junction is controlled by the Key token for the Birdbrook and Haverhill North Junction section.

Miles from Chappel	DOWN WEEK DAYS.		1	2	3	4	5	6	7	8	9	10		11	12	13	14
				G							G			G			
			Gds.	Gds.	Gds.	Gds.	Gds		Gds.		Gds.			Gds.	Gds.	Gds.	
M. C.			a.m.	a.m.	a.m.	a.m	p.m.		p.m.		p.m.			a.m.	a.m.	a.m.	
	Chappel .... Ⓔ dep.		5 45	6 30	8 40	11 0	—		—		—			6 30	8 40	11 0	.....
2 10	White Colne .... {arr		—	—	—	—	—		—		—			—	—	—	
	{dep		—	—	—	—	—		—		—			—	—	—	
3 48	Earls Colne ...... Ⓔ {arr.		5 53	6 50	9 0	11 20	—		—		—			6 50	9 0	11 20	
	Ⓚ {dep.		5 58	.....	.....	..								.....	.....	.....	
6 6	Halstead ...... Ⓚ {arr.		6 4	—			—		—		—			—	—	—	
	{dep.		7 2	.....	.....	.....	—		—		3 5			—	—	—	
9 30	Sible and Castle Hedingham Ⓚ {arr.		7 10	.....			—		—		3 15			—	—	—	
	{dep.		7 35	.....			—		—		5 6			—	—	—	
11 72	Yeldham .... Ⓚ {arr.		7 43	.....			—		—		5 14			—	—	—	
	{dep.		0 35	.....			—		—		5 28			—	—	—	
15 56	Birdbrook ...... ◇ {arr.		10 45	—			¶		¶		5 38			—	—	—	
	{dep.		11 0	.....							5 48			—	—	—	
18 31	Colne Valley Jc. A „		—	—			2 31		3 9		—			—	—	—	
	Haverhill Sth. ...... arr.		—				2 31		—		—			—	—	—	
19 41	Haverhill Nth. Ⓚ arr.		11 10	—	—		.....		3 13		5 58			—	—	—	

SUNDAYS

1   4.50 a.m. ex Colchester.

2   6.0 a.m. ex Mark's Tey.

9   To Cambridge. To leave Haverhill with traffic for Cambridge and via Cambridge only.

11   6.0 a.m. ex Mark's Tey.

Miles from Haverhill South	UP WEEK DAYS.		1	2	3	4	5	6	7	8	9	10		11	12	13	14
					Eng. & Bk.										Eng. & Brk		
			Gds.		Gds.	Gds.	Gds.			Gds.	Gds			Gds.		Gds.	
M. C.			a.m.	a.m.	a.m	p.m.	p.m.		p.m.	p.m.	p.m.			a.m.	a.m.	noon	
—	Haverhill North Ⓚ dep.		.....	.....		7 50	.....	9 22		—	3 45			.....	.....	.....	....
—	Haverhill South ... „		.....	.....		—	.....	—		3 0	—			.....	..	.....	
1 10	Colne Valley Jc. A {arr.		—	—		—		2 26		3 4	—			—	—	—	
	{dep.		—	—		—		2 31		3 9	—			—	—	—	
3 66	Birdbrook ...... ◇ {arr.		.....	.....		8 2		¶		¶	3 56			—	—	—	
	{dep.		—	—		8 15					4 5			—	—	—	
7 50	Yeldham .... Ⓚ {arr		—	—		8 25		—		—	4 15			—	—	—	
	{dep.		—	—		8 45		—		—	5 20			—	—	—	
10 12	Sible and Castle Hedingham Ⓚ {arr.		—	—		8 53		—		—	5 28			—	—	—	
	{dep.		—	—		12 25		—		—	5 50			—	—	—	
13 36	Halstead ...... Ⓚ {arr.		—	—		12 35		—		—	6 0			—	—	—	
	{dep.		—	—		—		—		—	6 50			—	—	—	
15 74	Earls Colne ...... Ⓚ {arr.		—	—		—		—		—	6 55			—	—	—	
	Ⓔ {dep.		7 5	10 32		—	12 10	—		—	7 50			7 5	10 25	12 0	
17 32	White Colne .... {arr		7 10	—		—	12 15	—		—	7 55			7 10	—	12 5	
	{dep		7 10	—		—	12 55	—		—	8 0			7 40	—	12 45	
19 41	Chappel .... Ⓔ arr		.....	7 46	10 45	.....	1 10	.....		—	8 8			7 46	10 40	1 0	.....

SUNDAYS

4   5.40 a.m. ex Cambridge.   5   To Mark's Tey. To work empty C.U. wagons.

9   To Colchester.   To leave Halstead marshalled—Engine, traffic to be weighed at Mark's Tey, traffic for via Bury, Up road and Down road. Traffic attached at Earls Colne, White Colne and Chappel to be marshalled accordingly. Traffic for and via Bury, Whitemoor and Peterboro' to be worked through to Mark's Tey for 4.18 a.m. ex Colchester next day.

13   To Mark's Tey. To work empty C.U. wagons.

¶ To or from Haverhill South.

A.   Auxiliary Key Token instrument provided for working connection to Haverhill South.

Distance from Colne Valley Junction to Haverhill South is 55 chains.

L&NER working timetable passenger 1945.

M 14

CHAPPEL, HALSTEAD AND HAVERHILL NORTH
Single Line
The Haverhill South Single Line connection at Colne Valley Junction is controlled by the Key Token for the Birdbrook and Haverhill North Junction Section.

DOWN									WEEKDAYS									SUNDAYS					
No.		1	2‡	3	4	5	6	7	8	9	10	11	12	13	14	15	16	17	18	19	20	21	22
Class			K		B		K		B	K			J			B			B				B
Description																							
Departs from		Colchester 4.45 a.m.	Mark's Tey 9.26 a.m.		Haverhill N. 11.30 a.m.		Mark's Tey 11.41 a.m.	Haverhill S. 12.40 p.m.							Clacton 5.50 p.m.			Mark's Tey 10.36 a.m.				Clacton 5.22 p.m.	
Previous Times on Page		8	8		15		8	15							9			10				10	

M. C.			am	am	am			am	PM		PM		PM			PM		am			PM		
— —	Chappel		5 45	9 33		11 48								6 47		10 43			6 35				
— —	Chappel (S)		5 47	9 34		11 49		4 45						6 49		10 44			6 37				
2 10	White Colne			9 38		11 53		4 49						6 53		10 48			6 41				
— —	White Colne		✳	9 39		11 54		4 50						6 54		10 49			6 42				
3 48	Earls Colne } See Note (S)		5 58	9 43		11 57		4 53						6 57		10 53			6 46				
— —	Earls Colne (T)		6 8	9 44		11 58		4 55		2 30				6 58		10 54			6 47				
6 6	Halstead (T)		6 16	9 49		12⌃3		5 0		2 36				7 3		10 59			6 52				
— —	Halstead		6 40	9 52		12 5		5 4		3 10				7 5		11 3			6 56				
9 30	Sible and Castle H. (T)		6 50	9 58		12 11		5 10		3 20				7 11		11 9			7 2				
— —	Sible and Castle H.		7 15	9 59		12 12		5 12		3 45				7 13		11 11			7 4				
11 72	Yeldham } See Note (T)		7 25	10 4		12 17		5 17		3⌄55				7 18		11 16			7 9				
— —	Yeldham		7 50	10 5		12 18		5 18		4 25				7 19		11 18			7 11				
15 56	Birdbrook } See Note (T)		8 0	10 13		12 25		5 26		4 35				7 26		11 26			7 19				
— —	Birdbrook		8 10	10 14		12 26		5 27		4 45				7 27		11 28			7 21				
18 31	Colne Valley Junction A					11 39				12 49													
— —	Haverhill South					11 43																	
19 41	Haverhill North (T)		8 25	10 22		12 34	12 53	5 35		4 57				7 35		11 36			7 29				
— —	Haverhill North						5 15									11 40			7 32				

Arrives at										Cambridge 6.14 p.m.								Cambridge 12.17 p.m.			Cambridge 8.10 p.m.		
Forward Times on Page										9								10			10		

M 15

HAVERHILL NORTH, HALSTEAD AND CHAPPEL
Single Line
The Haverhill South Single Line connection at Colne Valley Junction is controlled by the Key Token for the Haverhill North Junction and Birdbrook Section.

UP									WEEKDAYS									SUNDAYS					
No.		1	2	3	4	5	6	7	8	9	10	11	12	13‡	14	15	16	17	18	19	20	21	22
Class		B		K		B		K	K	K	B		J			B	J		B				B
Description																							
Departs from		Cambridge 6.28 a.m.		Cambridge 6.45 a.m.				Cambridge 6.45 a.m.								Haverhill N. 3.15 p.m.			Cambridge 8.0 a.m.			Cambridge 3.50 p.m.	
Previous Times on Page		11		11															13			13	

M. C.			am	am	am		am	PM	PM		PM		PM	PM		am			PM		
— —	Haverhill North		7 8	8 7		See		2 7			5 58				8 40			4 30			
— —	Haverhill North (T)		7 20	8 40	9 20	Col. 4	11 30	2 7	3 15		5 58				8 43			4 37			
— —	Haverhill South							12 40													
— —	Colne Valley Junction A						11 34	12 44													
— —	Colne Valley Junction						11 39	12 49													
3 66	Birdbrook } See Note (T)		7 28		9 28			2 15	3 26		6 6				8 51			4 45			
— —	Birdbrook		7 30	8 51	9 29			2 16	3 35		6 7	See			8 53			4 46			
7 50	Yeldham } See Note (T)		7 37	9 0	9 36	9 0		2 23	3⌄45		6 14	Col.			9 1			4 54			
— —	Yeldham		7 39	9 45	9 37	9 45		2 24	4 20		6 15	13			9 3			4 55			
10 12	Sible and Castle H.		7 44		9 42	9 53		2 29	4 28		6 20				9 10			5 0			
— —	Sible and Castle H. (T)		7 46	See	9 44	10 43		2 32	5 13		6 22				9 16			5 2			
13 36	Halstead (T)		7 52	Col.	9 50	10⌄53		2 38	5 23		6 28				9 16			5 8			
— —	Halstead		7 57	8	9 58	12 50		2 41	6 0		6 30				9 20			5 12			
15 74	Earls Colne } See Note (T)		8 2	10 3		12 58		2 46	6 8		6 35	6 8			9 25			5 17			
— —	Earls Colne (S)		8 4	10 5				2 48	7 8		6 36	7 8			9 26			5 18			
17 32	White Colne		8 8	10 9				2 52			6 40				9 30			5 22			
— —	White Colne		8 10	10 10				2 53	See		6 41	✳			9 31			5 23			
19 41	Chappel (S)		8 14	10 14				2 57	Col.		6 46	7 20			9 35			5 27			
— —	Chappel		8 17	10 16					16		6 50	7 30			9 37			5 28			

Arrives at			Mark's Tey 8.24 a.m.	Earls Colne 12.58 p.m.		Mark's Tey 10.23 a.m.		Haverhill 11.43 p.m.	Haverhill 12.53 p.m.		Mark's Tey 7.45 p.m.	Mark's Tey 6.57 p.m. Colchester SX 7.11 p.m. SO	Mark's Tey 7.45 p.m.		Clacton 10.40 a.m.			Mark's Tey 5.35 p.m.		
Forward Times on Page			11	11		11		14	14		13	13	13		13			13		

Side notes (DOWN table)

Distance from Colne Valley Junction to Haverhill South is 55 chains.

A—Auxiliary Key Token instrument provided for working connection at Haverhill South.

Earls Colne and Yeldham
A passenger train must not cross another passenger train at these stations.

Birdbrook
Electric Token Station but not a crossing place.

11   To leave Haverhill, with traffic for Cambridge and via Cambridge only.

Side notes (UP table)

Distance from Haverhill South to Colne Valley Junction is 55 chains.

A—Auxiliary Key Token instrument provided for working connection from Haverhill South.

Birdbrook
Electric Token Station but not a crossing place.

Yeldham and Earls Colne.
A passenger train must not cross another passenger train at these stations.

2   From 3rd July to 9th September extended to Clacton.

BR (ER) working timetable 1950.

After a round trip between Haverhill North and Haverhill South the afternoon Up goods departed at 3.15pm, calling all stations to Marks Tey with arrival at 7.45pm, White Colne was, however, only served if required. Two passenger trains ran in each direction on Sundays during the summer of 1949. The first departed Cambridge at 8.00am and Haverhill at 8.43am serving all stations to Marks Tey arriving at 9.44am, before returning on the Down road at 10.43am, again calling all stations to Haverhill North arriving at 11.36am and ultimately terminating at Cambridge at 12.17pm. The second train departed Cambridge at 3.50pm and Haverhill North at 4.37pm, working all stations through to Marks Tey arriving 5.35pm. The last Down road working departed Marks Tey at 6.28pm and entered the branch at Chappel, departing 6.35pm, calling all stations to Haverhill North arriving 7.29pm and continuing to Cambridge arriving at 8.10pm.

The working timetable for **June 1950** was almost identical with only minor timing alterations and goods trains ran as Class 'K' instead of Class 'B'. The notable exception was the weekdays 6.28am ex Cambridge passenger service which from 3rd July until 9th September was extended to Clacton. On Sundays the 8.00am ex Cambridge was also extended beyond Marks Tey to Clacton, arriving at 10.40am, and in consequence the 6.28pm ex Marks Tey started back at Clacton departing at 5.22pm, entering the branch at Chappel at 6.37pm and arriving at Cambridge at 8.10pm.

In **1952** the working timetable showed a service of four passenger trains in each direction on weekdays augmented by two goods services each way. Of the passenger services the 9.06am, 11.59am and 6.40pm Down trains commenced their journey at Marks Tey, whilst the 4.45pm started at Chappel. In the Up direction the first train of the day started from Cambridge at 6.28am and

entered the branch departing Haverhill at 7.16am and ran through the Marks Tey arriving at 8.17am. Two other trains, the 9.20am and 6.00pm ex Haverhill, terminated at Marks Tey, the latter SX but on SO ran through to Colchester arriving at 7.12pm. The afternoon 2.29pm ex Haverhill terminated at Chappel at 3.06pm. All passenger services called at all stations. The weekdays-only goods services commenced with the arrival of the 4.40am ex Colchester, which departed Chappel at 5.47am and called at all stations except White Colne, which was shunted only if required, with Haverhill reached at 8.30am. On the Up road the 6.45am Class 'H' goods ex Cambridge departed Haverhill at 8.40am and served all stations to Earls Colne, from whence it returned at 2.30pm calling all stations to Haverhill, arriving at 5.13pm before departing conveying Cambridge and destinations via Cambridge traffic only and terminating at the university city at 6.44pm. After trip workings between Haverhill South and Haverhill North, the other Class 'H' goods train departed Haverhill at 3.45pm and called all stations to Chappel with termination 7.45pmSO at Marks Tey and 9.35pmSX at Colchester. On Sundays the Colne Valley was served by two passenger trains on the Up road: departing Cambridge 8.00am and Haverhill at 8.45am as a through train to Clacton arriving at 10.40am, and the 3.53pm ex Cambridge which after departing Haverhill at 4.37pm terminated at Marks Tey at 5.35pm. On the Down road only one train was provided, departing Marks Tey at 6.28pm to Haverhill arriving at 7.28pm and continuing to Cambridge arriving 8.10pm. Day excursionists returning from Clacton thus had to catch a London-bound train from the coast and change at Marks Tey.

In **May 1953** a relic of the past disappeared, for the working of through coaches from the Colne Valley line to Colchester were

HAVERHILL, HALSTEAD AND CHAPPEL
Single Line
The Haverhill South Single Line connection at Colne Valley Junction is controlled by the Key Token for the Haverhill Junction and Birdbrook Section.

			1	2	3	4	5	6	7	8	9	10	11	12	13‡	14	15	16‡	17	18	19	20	21	22	
UP		**WEEKDAYS**																	**SUNDAYS**							
	No.																									
	Class		B		K		B			K	K	K	B		H		B	H					B		
	Description																									
	Departs from		Cambridge 6.28 a.m.		Cambridge 6.48 a.m.					Cambridge 6.48 a.m.						Haverhill 3.45 p.m.							Cambridge 3.53 p.m.		
	Previous Times on Page		11		11																		13		

Miles from Haverhill

M. C.			am 7 9	am 8▽8		am				am See Col. 4	am	PM	PM	PM		PM	PM						PM 4 33		
— —	Haverhill		7 9	8▽8							11 30												4 33		
— —	**Haverhill** .... (T)		7 16	8 40		9 20				See	11 30	1 0	2 19		3 45		6 0						4 37		
— —	Haverhill South									Col.	11 34	1 4													
— —	Colne Valley Junction .. A									4	11 39	1 9													
— —	Colne Valley Junction																								
3 66	Birdbrook .... (T)		7 24			9 28							2 27		3 59		6 8						4 45		
— —	Birdbrook } See Note		7 25		8 52	9 29							2 28		4 8		6 9 See						4 46		
7 50	Yeldham } (T)		7 32		9 2	9 36			9 55				2 35		4 12		6 16 Col.						4 53		
— —	Yeldham } See Note		7 33		9 55	9 37			9 55				2 36		4 55		6 17 · 13						4 54		
10 12	Sible and Castle H. .. (T)		7 38			9 42			10 6				2 41		5 6		6 22						4 59		
— —	Sible and Castle H.		7 40	See		9 50			10 43				2 43		5 21		6 24						5 1		
13 36	Halstead .... (T)		7 46	Col.		9 56			10 55				2 49		5 33		6 30						5 7		
— —	Halstead		7 52	8		9 58			12 40				2 51		6 5		6 33						5 11		
15 74	Earls Colne } See Note (T)		7 57			10 3			12 50				2 56		6 15		6 38 6 15						5 16		
— —	Earls Colne } (S)		7 59			10 5							2 57		7 10		6 40 7 10						5 17		
17 32	White Colne ..		8 3			10 9							3 1				6 44						5 21		
— —	White Colne		8 4			10 10							3 2		See		6 45 ✱						5 22		
19 41	**Chappel** .. .. (S)		8 8			10 14							3 6		Col.		6 49 7 22						5 26		
— —	Chappel		8 10			10 15									16		6 51 7 36						5 28		
	Arrives at		Mark's Tey 8.17 a.m.	Earl's Colne 12.50 p.m.		Mark's Tey 10.22 a.m.				Haverhill S. 11.43 a.m.	Haverhill 1.13 p.m.				Mark's Tey 7.50 p.m. SO / Colchester 9.35 p.m. SX		Mark's Tey 6.59p.m. SO / Colchester 7.12 p.m. SX / Colchester 9.35 p.m. SX						Mark's Tey 5.35 p.m.		
	Forward Times on Page		11		11				14	14					12		13						13		

Distance from Haverhill South to Colne Valley Junction is 55 chains.

A—Auxiliary Key Token instrument provided for working connection from Haverhill South.

Birdbrook
Electric Token Station but not a crossing place.

Yeldham and Earls Colne.
Passenger trains must not cross at these Stations.

16—Saturdays excepted Chappel dep. 8.25 p.m.

BR (ER) working timetable 1952, Up direction.

withdrawn. The stock of the 2.55pm Up train from Haverhill was attached at Chappel to the 3.16pm Cambridge to Colchester train. The coaches returned from Colchester at 4.13pm and were detached at Chappel at 4.35pm.

The working timetable for **1959** showed a weekdays only service of five passenger and one goods train in the Down direction, and four passenger and one goods service on the Up road, augmented by a few trip workings between Haverhill South and Haverhill North. The passenger services were operated by a mixture of 4-wheel diesel railbuses and 2-car diesel multiple units. The 6.35am ex Cambridge diesel railbus called at all stations between Shelford and Haverhill, arriving 7.11am before forming the 7.24½am service to Marks Tey via Halstead calling at all stations except White Colne. After arriving at 8.10½am the railbus returned at 8.21am for a fast run to Haverhill calling at Halstead only and arriving at the junction at 8.59½am. Six minutes later it returned forming an all-stations train to Chappel arriving 9.43½am. The railbus connected at Chappel with the 9.32am Cambridge to Colchester via Sudbury

diesel multiple unit. Departing Chappel at 9.58½am the railbus called at all stations on the Colne Valley line arriving at Haverhill at 10.39½am to connect with a Cambridge service. The railbus then ran light to Marks Tey via Long Melford before working the 12.40pm Marks Tey to Cambridge service via Halstead. A diesel multiple unit then took over the Colne Valley workings. Two 2-car diesel multiple units forming the 2.52pm Cambridge to Colchester service ran as far as Haverhill where the train was split, the first portion departing at 3.12½pm for the journey via Long Melford whilst the second unit formed the 3.18pm to Chappel via Halstead arriving at 3.56½pm to provide a connection with the Colchester service. The Colne Valley unit departed Chappel at 4.51pm calling all stations to Haverhill, arriving at 5.32pm with connections at both Chappel and Haverhill with the Colchester to Cambridge service. The final Up passenger train of the day departed Haverhill at 6.15pm calling all stations except for White Colne to Marks Tey arriving 6.59½pm. The unit then formed the last Down train departing Marks Tey at 7.06½pm calling all stations except White

TIMETABLE FROM 12TH JUNE TO 10TH SEPTEMBER 1961										
DOWN		Weekdays								Sundays
			3					1	2	TD
					SO	SX	SO	SX	SO	
		am	am	am	pm	pm	pm	pm	pm	pm
Liverpool Street	dep	6.54	8.30	11.30				5.45		4.45
Marks Tey	dep	8.19	9.54	12.56		4.45		7.07	7.17	6.23
Chappel & Wakes Colne	dep		10.09	1.03		4.55	5.14	7.13	7.32	6.31
White Colne	dep		10.13	1.08		5.01	5.19	7.19	7.37	
Earls Colne	dep		10.17	1.12		5.04	5.23	7.25	7.42	6.37
Halstead	dep	8.36	10.22	1.17	4.25	5.10	5.28	7.30	7.48	6.44
S & C Hedingham	dep		10.29	1.24	4.42	5.16	5.35	7.37	7.54	6.51
Yeltdham	dep		10.34	1.29	4.48	5.22	5.40	7.42	8.00	6.57
Birdbrook	dep		10.40	1.37	4.56	5.29	5.48	5.48	7.50	8.07
Haverhill	arr	9.00	10.50	1.44	5.04	5.36	5.35	7.57	8.15	7.13
Cambridge	arr		11.36		5.36	6.25	6.44	8.36	8.54	7.49

UP		Weekdays						Sundays	
				2				TU	
				SX	SO				
		am	am	am	pm	pm	pm	am	
Cambridge	dep		8.22		1.20	2.33	5.26	8.40	
Haverhill	dep	7.20	9.10	9.50	2.03	3.17	6.13	9.19	
Birdbrook	dep	7.28	9.18	9.58	2.10	3.24	6.20	9.28	
Yeldham	dep	7.36	9.26	10.06	2.17	3.31	6.27	9.36	
S & C Hedingham	dep	7.42	9.31	10.11	2.22	3.36	6.32	9.43	
Halstead	dep	7.49	9.38	10.18	2.29	3.43	6.39	9.51	
Earls Colne	dep	7.54	9.43	10.29	2.34	3.48	6.44	9.57	
White Colne	dep		9.48	10.34	2.37	3.51	6.47		
Chappel & Wakes Colne	arr	8.02	9.52	10.38	2.42	3.58	6.54	10.05	
Marks Tey	arr	8.09	10.10		2.48		7.01	10.12	
Liverpool Street	arr	9.59	11.38		4.20		8.56	11.30	

NOTES: 1 does not run after 7th July.
2 commences 10th July.
3 runs one minute earlier SO.
TD through train Walton-on-the-Naze dep 5.27pm/Clacton-on-Sea dep 5.33pm to Cambridge.
TU through train Cambridge to Clacton-on-Sea arr 11.09am/Walton-on-the-Naze arr 11.15am.
Italic timings are connecting Stour Valley services between Chappel and Marks Tey.

Colne and Pampisford to Cambridge arriving 8.35½pm. On the freight side the Colne Valley was served by the 4.48am Class 'K' goods train from Colchester calling at White Colne only if required then all stations but omitting Birdbrook, arriving at Haverhill at 8.32am. After a return trip working to Haverhill South the return Class 'K' Up train departed Haverhill at 3.01pm and called all stations to Chappel except White Colne, which was shunted only if required. After arrival at Chappel at 6.22pm wagons requiring forwarding were shunted and then attached to the 4.30pm Bury St Edmunds to Colchester Class 'H' goods train whilst the engine off the Colne Valley goods worked light to Marks Tey, departing at 7.22pm.

The final summer timetable operative from **12th June to 10th September 1961** (*facing page*) included the note that *'These stations may be closed during the currency of this timetable and in this event appropriate notices will be given.'* Some services were through workings to and from Cambridge with diesel units splitting at Haverhill for onward journey to or from Stour Valley or Colne Valley lines.

Right and Below: Two pages from an Eastern National Bus Timetable from 1st January 1962 for Halstead area including rail replacement services.

LEAFLET No. 8035

EASTERN NATIONAL

CLOSURE OF COLNE VALLEY RAILWAY LINE

In consequence of the above, commencing Monday, 1st January, 1962 a new Service 89 will be introduced between Colchester—Halstead—Haverhill together with revised timetables for Services 88 and 320 as shown herein.

SERVICE 88 — **COLCHESTER — ALDHAM — EARL'S COLNE — HALSTEAD** — SERVICE 88

(Including also Service 89 between Colchester and Halstead)

Light figures denote A.M. times — Dark figures denote P.M. times

Weekdays

Service No.		88 NS	88 X NS	88	88 NS	88†	88	88 S	88	88 S	89	88†	88	88	88 SCH
Colchester, Omnibus Station	dep	6 35	7 15	7 40	8 10	9 0	10 0	1030	11 0	1155	1220	1 0	2 0	3 0	......
Lexden, Halstead Road Corner	,,	6 45	7 25	7 50	8 20	9 10	1010	1040	1110	12 5	1230	1 10	2 10	3 10	......
Eight Ash Green, Brick & Tile	,,	6 51	7 31	7 56	8 26	9 16	1016	1046	1116	1211	1236	1 16	2 16	3 16	......
Aldham, Queens Head	,,	6 58	7 38	8 3	8 33	9 23	1023	1053	1123	1218	1243	1 23	2 23	3 23	......
Wakes Colne, Church	,,	7 6	7 46	8 11	8 41	9 31	1031	11 1	1131	1226	1251	1 31	2 31	3 31	*
Earls Colne, The Lion	,,	7 13	7 53	8 18	8 48	9 38	1038	11 8	1138	1233	1258	1 38	2 38	3 38	3 40
Greenstead Turn, Blue Bridge	,,	7 19	......	8 24	8 54	9 44	1044	1114	1144	1239	1 4	1 44	2 44	3 44	3 46
Halstead, Railway Station	arr	7 25	......	8 30	9 0	9 50	1050	1120	1150	1245	1 10	1 50	2 50	3 50	3 52

Service No.		89 S	88 NS	88 NS	88 S	88 S	88 NS	88 S	89	88 S	88	88 S	88 NS	88	
Colchester, Omnibus Station	dep	3 30	4 0	4 25	4 45	5 30	5 40	6 0	6 30	7 0	8 0	8 30	9 0	1030	......
Lexden, Halstead Road Corner	,,	3 40	4 10	4 35	4 55	5 40	5 50	6 10	6 40	7 10	8 10	8 40	9 10	1040	......
Eight Ash Green, Brick & Tile	,,	3 46	4 16	4 41	5 1	5 46	5 56	6 16	6 46	7 16	8 16	8 46	9 16	1046	......
Aldham, Queens Head	,,	3 53	4 23	4 48	5 8	5 53	6 3	6 23	6 53	7 23	8 23	8 53	9 23	1053	......
Wakes Colne, Church	,,	4 1	4 31	4 56	5 16	6 1	6 11	6 31	7 1	7 31	8 31	9 1	9 31	11 1	......
Earls Colne, The Lion	,,	4 8	4 38	5 3	5 23	6 8	6 18	6 38	7 8	7 38	8 38	9 8	9 38	11 8	......
Greenstead Turn, Blue Bridge	,,	4 14	4 44	5 9	5 29	6 14	6 24	6 44	7 14	7 44	8 44	9 14	9 44	1114	......
Halstead, Railway Station	arr	4 20	4 50	5 15	5 35	6 20	6 30	6 50	7 20	7 50	8 50	9 20	9 50	1120	......

Service No.		88	88†	88 NS	88 S	88	88	88†	88 S	88 WS	88	88 S	89 NS	89 S	88 SCH
Halstead, Railway Station	dep	6 45	8 0	8 35	9 0	9 30	11 0	12 0	1255	1 45	2 0	2 30	3 0	3 30	......
Greenstead Turn, Blue Bridge	,,	6 51	8 6	8 41	9 6	9 36	11 6	12 6	1 1	1 51	2 6	2 36	3 6	3 36	*
Earls Colne, The Lion	,,	6 57	8 12	8 47	9 12	9 42	1112	1212	1 7	1 57	2 12	2 42	3 12	3 42	3 45
Wakes Colne Church	,,	7 4	8 19	8 54	9 19	9 49	1119	1219	1 14	2 4	2 19	2 49	3 19	3 49	3 52
Aldham, Queens Head	,,	7 12	8 27	9 2	9 27	9 57	1127	1227	1 22	2 12	2 27	2 57	3 27	3 57	4 0
Eight Ash Green, Brick & Tile	,,	7 19	8 34	9 9	9 34	10 4	1134	1234	1 29	2 19	2 34	3 4	3 34	4 4	4 7
Lexden, Halstead Road Corner	,,	7 25	8 40	9 15	9 40	1010	1140	1240	1 35	2 25	2 40	3 10	3 40	4 10	4 13
Colchester, Omnibus Station	arr	7 35	8 50	9 25	9 50	1020	1150	1250	1 45	2 35	2 50	3 20	3 50	4 20	4 23

Service No.		88	88	88 NS	89 S	88 S	89 NS	89 S	88	89					
Halstead, Railway Station	dep	4 0	5 5	5 35	6 0	6 30	7 7	7 30	8 0	9 30	......	......	......	......	......
Greenstead Turn, Blue Bridge	,,	4 6	5 11	5 41	6 6	6 36	7 13	7 36	8 6	9 36	......	......	......	......	......
Earls Colne, The Lion	,,	4 12	5 17	5 47	6 12	6 42	7 19	7 42	8 12	9 42	......	......	......	......	......
Wakes Colne Church	,,	4 19	5 24	5 54	6 19	6 49	7 26	7 49	8 19	9 49	......	......	......	......	......
Aldham, Queens Head	,,	4 27	5 32	6 2	6 27	6 57	7 34	7 57	8 27	9 57	......	......	......	......	......
Eight Ash Green, Brick & Tile	,,	4 34	5 39	6 9	6 34	7 4	7 41	8 4	8 34	10 4	......	......	......	......	......

SERVICE 320 — **HALSTEAD — MAPLESTEADS — HEDINGHAMS — YELDHAMS — RIDGEWELL** — SERVICE 320

(Including also Service 89 between Halstead and Haverhill and through journeys and connections by Service 88 to and from Colchester)

Light figures denote A.M. times — Dark figures denote P.M. times

Mondays to Fridays

Colchester, Omnibus Station	dep	......	......	......	6 35	8 10	10 0	11 0	11 0	1220	3 0	3 0	3 0	3 0	4 0	4 0	4 25	6 30	8 0	9 0	9 0
Halstead, Railway Station	arr	......	......	......	7 25	9 0	10 50	1150	1150	1 10	3 50	3 50	3 50	3 50	4 50	4 50	5 15	7 20	8 50	9 50	9 50
Service No.		320	320	320	89	320 TWF	320	320 TF	320	89	320 TWF	320 MTh	320 NF	320 F	320	320 X	320	89	320	320 W	320 Th
Halstead, Railway Station	dep	6 16	7D 7	7 7	8 5	9 0	11*10	1210	1247	1 10	4 0	4 0	4*20	4*20	4 50	5 5	5 35	7 20	9*35	1040	1040
Does Corner	,,	......	7 12	......	......	......	......	......	......	......	......	......	......	......	......	......	......	......	......	......	......
Little Maplestead, Church	,,	......	......	......	......	......	......	1218	......	......	4 8	......	......	......	......	......	......	......	......	1048	......
Great Maplestead, Church	,,	......	......	......	......	......	......	1222	......	......	4 12	......	......	......	......	......	......	......	......	1052	......
Gosfield Corner	,,	6 23	......	7 14	8 12	9 7	11 17	......	1254	1 17	......	4 7	4 27	4 27	4 57	5 12	5 42	7 27	9 42	......	1047
Sible Hedingham, Sugar Loaves	,,	6 32	7 20	7 23	8 21	9 16	11 26	......	1 3	1 26	......	4 16	4 36	4 36	5 6	5 21	5 51	7 36	9 51	......	1056
Castle Hedingham, The Bell	,,	6 35	7 23	7 26	8 24	9 19	11 29	1229	1 6	1 29	4 19	4 19	4 39	4 39	5 9	5 24	5 54	7 39	9 54	1059	1059
Castle Hedingham, Eleven Elms	,,	6 38	......	7 29	8 27	9 22	11 32	1232	1 9	1 32	4 22	4 22	4 42	4 42	5 12	5 27	5 57	7 42	9 57	11 2	11 2
Great Yeldham, The Green	,,	6 45	......	7 36	8†34	9 29	......	......	1 16	1†39	4 29	4 29	......	4 49	5 19	5 34	6 4	7†49	10 4	11 9	11 9
Little Yeldham, Church	,,	6 50	......	......	......	9 34	......	......	1 21	......	......	......	......	......	......	5 39	6 9	......	......	......	......
Ridgewell, Memorial	,,	......	......	......	8 40	......	......	......	......	1‡45	......	......	......	......	......	......	......	7 55	......	......	......
Baythorne End, The Swan	,,	......	......	......	8 45	......	......	......	......	1‡50	......	......	......	......	......	......	......	8 0	......	......	......
Sturmer, Railway Station Turn	,,	......	......	......	8 51	......	......	......	......	1‡56	......	......	......	......	......	......	......	8 6	......	......	......
Haverhill, Railway Station	arr	......	......	......	8 58	......	......	......	......	2‡ 3	......	......	......	......	......	......	......	8 13	......	......	......

Service No.		320	320	320	89	320 TWF	320	320 TF	320 TF	320 NTF	89	320	320 NF	320 F	320	320 X	320 NW	320 W	89	89	320	320 WTh
Haverhill, Railway Station	dep	......	......	......	9 0	......	......	......	......	......	2 5	......	......	......	......	......	......	......	6 12	8 15	......	......
Sturmer, Railway Station Turn	,,	......	......	......	9 7	......	......	......	......	......	2 12	......	......	......	......	......	......	......	6 19	8 22	......	......
Baythorne End, The Swan	,,	......	......	......	9 13	......	......	......	......	......	2 18	......	......	......	......	......	......	......	6 25	8 28	......	......
Ridgewell, Memorial	,,	......	......	......	9 18	......	......	......	......	......	2 23	......	......	......	......	......	......	......	6 30	8 33	......	......
Little Yeldham, Church	,,	6 53	......	......	......	9 40	......	......	1 24	1 24	......	......	......	......	......	5 40	6 14	6 14	......	......	......	......
Great Yeldham, The Green	,,	6 58	7 38	......	9†24	9 45	......	......	1 29	1 29	2†29	4 30	......	4 52	5 22	5 45	6 19	6 19	6†36	8†39	10 7	1110
Castle Hedingham, Eleven Elms	,,	7 5	7 45	......	9 31	9 52	1135	1 12	1 36	1 36	2 36	4 36	4 59	4 59	5 29	......	6 26	6 26	6 43	8 46	1014	1117
Castle Hedingham, The Bell	,,	7 8	7 48	8 0	9 34	9 55	1138	1 15	1 39	1 39	2 39	4 40	5 2	5 2	5 32	......	6 29	6 29	6 46	8 49	1017	1120
Sible Hedingham, Sugar Loaves	,,	7 11	7 51	8 3	9 37	......	1141	1 18	......	1 42	2 42	4 43	5 5	5 5	5 35	......	6 32	......	6 49	8 52	1020	1123
Gosfield Corner	,,	7 20	8 0	8 12	9 46	......	1150	1 27	......	1 51	2 51	4 52	5 14	5 14	5 44	......	6 41	......	6 58	9 1	1029	1132
Great Maplestead, Church	,,	......	......	......	......	10 2	......	......	1 46	......	......	......	......	......	......	......	......	6 36	......	......	......	......
Little Maplestead, Church	,,	......	......	......	......	10 6	......	......	1 50	......	......	......	......	......	......	......	......	6 40	......	......	......	......
Does Corner	,,	......	......	......	......	......	......	......	......	......	......	......	......	......	......	......	......	......	......	......	......	......
Halstead, Railway Station	arr	7 27	8 7	8*19	9 53	1014	1157	1 34	1*58	1*58	2 58	4*59	5 21	5 21	5 51	......	6*48	6*48	7 5	9 8	1036	1139
Halstead, Railway Station	dep	8 0	8 35	8 35	10 0	11 0	12 0	2 0	2 0	2 0	3 0	5 5	5 35	5 35	......	......	......	......	7 7	9 30	......	......
Colchester, Omnibus Station	arr	8 50	9 25	9 25	B	1150	1250	2 50	2 50	2 50	3 50	5 55	6 25	6 25	......	......	......	......	7 57	1020	......	......

B–Messrs. Blackwells' service. **D**–Operates from Eastern National Depot, Halstead, only. **F**–Fridays only. **MTh**–Mondays and Thursdays only. **NF**–Not Fridays. **NTF**–Not Tuesdays and Fridays. **NW**–Not Wednesdays. **TF**–Tuesdays and Fridays only. **Th**–Thursdays only. **TWF**–Tuesdays. Wednesdays and Fridays only. **W**–Wednesdays only. **WTh**–Wednesdays and Thursdays only. **X**–Oderates only when works open. *–In connection at Halstead with Express Service X14 from or to London (Euston) on days operating. †–Timing at Gt.Yeldham, " Waggon & Horses." ‡–No passengers are picked up on Fridays between Ridgewell and Haverhill.

FARES

The initial fares charged for CV&HR passengers travelling between Chappel and Colchester were considered exorbitant and after complaints they were revised in mid-August 1860, when it was agreed the road distance would act as a guide for the new charges. Halstead to Sudbury was also included in the structure.

In order to encourage rail travel during the summer of 1861, return fares were offered for the price of a single ticket between all Colne Valley stations but not to Chappel or any stations on the ECR. However, on Sundays return fares for the price of a single journey were offered between all CV&HR stations as well as to Sudbury, Bures, Colchester and intermediate stations to Ipswich and Harwich, departing Harwich at 4.23pm and Ipswich at 4.45pm. Again by arrangement with the ECR, cheap day excursion fares were offered from and to London. The Down train departed Shoreditch at 12.30pm on Wednesdays and the Up service returned from Castle Hedingham at 8.10am on the following Friday. The respective fares offered were 10s 0d First Class, 7s 6d Second Class and 5s 3d Third Class.

After the opening of the line to Haverhill on 10th May 1863 the CV&HR fare structure was as follows:

HAVERHILL To	SINGLE			
	FIRST s d	SECOND s d	THIRD s d	PARLIAMENTARY s d
Birdbrook	0 9	0 5	0 4	0 3
Yeldham	1 9	1 2	0 10	0 7
Castle Hedingham	2 3	1 8	1 2	0 9½
Halstead	3 3	2 2	1 6	1 1
Colne	4 3	2 10	2 0	1 5
Chappel	4 9	3 2	2 4	1 7
Marks Tey	5 7	3 10	2 10	1 10½
London	13 9	10 8	8 1	5 0

HAVERHILL To	RETURN		
	FIRST s d	SECOND s d	THIRD s d
Birdbrook	1 2	0 8	0 6
Yeldham	2 7	1 9	1 3
Castle Hedingham	3 5	2 6	1 9
Halstead	4 6	3 2	2 3
Colne	6 0	4 3	3 0
Chappel	7 2	4 9	3 6
Marks Tey	8 3	5 9	
London	20 7	16 0	

Bona fide men in charge of livestock travelling to or from shows were conveyed free of charge on the same train as the animals, on the basis of one man for each consignment, except where the consignment required more than one vehicle, when one man for each vehicle was sent free. No pass was given unless the revenue from the consignment amounted to the equivalent charge of one horse. When two or more horses forming one consignment were sent in the same horsebox and each animal was attended by a separate person, those persons could travel free provided each horse was charged at the single horse rate. For men in charge of horses or other livestock forwarded by passenger train no separate pass was

issued as the booking clerk made an endorsement across the horse ticket. This document was surrendered in the normal way at the destination.

The single fare tariff from Halstead in 1869 was as follows:

HALSTEAD To	FIRST CLASS s d	SECOND CLASS s d	THIRD CLASS s d
Colne	1 0	0 8	0 6
Chappel	1 6	1 0	0 9
Sible & Castle Hedingham	0 9	0 6	0 5
Yeldham	1 4	1 0	0 9
Birdbrook	2 8	1 9	1 4
Haverhill	3 3	2 2	1 6
Marks Tey	2 4	1 8	1 2
Colchester	3 0	2 2	1 6
Bishopsgate	11 9	9 3	6 11

The table of fares from Liverpool Street and Cambridge to CV&HR stations in 1909 was:

LIVERPOOL STREET To	SINGLE		RETURN		HORSE	CARR'GE
	FIRST s d	THIRD s d	FIRST s d	THIRD s d	s d	s d
Chappel	9 6	4 2½	14 2	8 5	12 6	18 9
White Colne	9 11	4 5	14 10	8 10	—	—
Earls Colne	10 1	4 6	15 1	9 0	15 0	22 6
Halstead	10 6	4 8½	15 8	9 5	15 0	22 6
S&C Heding'm	11 0	4 11½	16 5	9 11	15 0	22 6
Yeldham	11 6	5 2½	17 2	10 5	15 0	33 3
Birdbrook	11 6	4 11	16 9	9 10	14 6	22 0
Haver'll CV/GE	11 0	4 8	16 0	9 4	13 9	20 9
CAMBRIDGE To						
Chappel	8 2	3 7½	12 2	7 3	11 0	18 6
White Colne	6 4	2 11	9 7	5 10	—	—
Earls Colne	6 1	2 10	9 2	5 8	8 3	12 0
Halstead	5 8	2 7½	8 6	5 8	8 0	12 0
S&C Heding'm	5 2	2 4½	7 9	4 9	7 8	11 0
Yeldham	4 8	2 1½	7 0	4 3	7 3	11 0
Birdbrook	4 0	1 9½	6 0	3 7	7 3	11 0
Haver'll CV/GE	3 6	1 6	5 3	3 0	5 0	7 6

Local fares from Chappel:

CHAPPEL To	SINGLE		RETURN	
	FIRST s d	THIRD s d	FIRST s d	THIRD s d
White Colne	5	2½	8	5
Earls Colne	7	3½	11	7
Halstead	1 0	6	1 6	1 0
S & C Hedingham	1 6	9	2 3	1 6
Yeldham	2 0	1 0	3 0	2 0
Birdbrook	2 6	1 3½	3 9	2 7
Haverhill CV or GE	3 2	1 7½	4 9	3 3

Third Class cheap day return tickets to Colchester were offered at the following fares in February 1953:

Chappel and Wakes Colne	2s 0d
White Colne	2s 6d
Earls Colne	3s 0d
Halstead	3s 6d
Sible and Castle Hedingham	4s 0d
Yeldham	4s 9d

Birdbrook and Haverhill stations were omitted from the offer.

The fare structure to branch stations from Liverpool Street in 1955 was:

LIVERPOOL STREET To	FIRST				THIRD			
	SINGLE		RETURN		SINGLE		RETURN	
	£ s	d	£ s	d	£ s	d	£ s	d
Chappel & Wakes Colne	12	0	1 4	0	8	0	16	0
White Colne	12	6	1 5	0	8	4	16	8
Earls Colne	12	9	1 5	6	8	6	17	0
Halstead	13	6	1 7	0	9	0	18	0
S & C Hedingham	14	2	1 8	4	9	5	18	10
Yeldham*	14	11	1 9	10	9	11	19	10
Birdbrook	15	8	1 11	4	10	5	1 0	10
Haverhill	16	6	1 13	0	11	0	1 2	0

Fares were also available from Liverpool Street via Bishop's Stortford and Saffron Walden

Halstead	16	3	1 12	6	10 10		1 1	8
S & C Hedingham	15	8	1 11	4	10 5		1 0	10
Yeldham*	14	11	1 9	10	9 11		19	10
Birdbrook	13	11	1 7	10	9 2		18	6
Haverhill	13	3	1 6	6	8 10		17	8
* Yeldham fare identical by both routes.								

EXCURSIONS

The ECR arranged from mid-August 1860 for Halstead and Colne stations to be included on the weekly excursion listing from London and Harwich at fares similar to those charged to Bures and Sudbury. By the summer of 1861 excursion fares were offered to Ipswich and Harwich every Sunday from Castle Hedingham and all CV&HR stations at the rate of 5s 0d First Class, 3s 6d Second Class and 2s 6d Third Class. The return ECR train departed Harwich and Ipswich at the uniform time of 4.45pm. At the same time return fares for the price of a single ticket were offered from all stations to Sudbury, Bures, Colchester and intermediate stations to Ipswich and Harwich. On Saturdays, return fares for the price of a single ticket were available to all CV&HR stations but not Chappel or any ECR station.

In 1861 cheap fares were available to and from London in association with the ECR, the train departing London at 12.30pm on Wednesdays, the return fare being 10s 0d First Class, 7s 6d Second Class and 5s 3d for Third Class. The Up train departed Sible and Castle Hedingham at 8.10am on Friday and the return half of the ticket was available for travel either the following Friday or a fortnight later.

In 1862 the CV&HR organised a number of excursions in connection with an exhibition held at Kensington. This was an inferior copy of the Great Exhibition on 1851 and was open from 1st May to 1st November. One such train organised by Halstead Mechanics Institute ran on 10th July when most shops in the town were closed for the day. The train departed Yeldham at 5.45am and the return service departed Shoreditch at 7.30pm. Return fares were 7s 6d First Class and 3s 9d Third Class from Yeldham and Hedingham, and 7s 0d and 3s 6d respectively from Halstead and Colne. Children under 12 years of age paid half fare and under three year were free. The outing according to the *Halstead Gazette* was a resounding success with many groups including Sunday Schools, church choirs and congregations travelling on party tickets. The *'very long'* train supplied by the ECR arrived in London at 9.30am, where many took the horse-drawn omnibus to the exhibition whilst others walked. The excursion was such a success that another was arranged for 7th September with a tour of the City of London as the one of the many attractions. Halstead station was inundated for the event when over 1,400 people turned up to travel. This time two trains were provided, again by the newly formed GER. The temporary Halstead station could hardly cope with such a throng and complaints were many.

On 3rd June 1862 the Essex Show was held at Halstead and in preparation a special 'Railway Committee' was established by the Essex Agricultural Society to organise the travel arrangements – the Committee including Robert Watt, the General Manager of the railway. The event was considered a major success with many of the thousands attending travelling by rail. The local press published acknowledgements of the event and included thanks to James Brewster, the CV&HR Chairman, who *'was on the spot nearly all day – not departing until after the last train had left the station at 10.00pm'*.

On a more parochial note an excursion in conjunction with the GER ran to the Agricultural Show at Brentwood on 2nd March 1865, whilst over 400 passengers from Colne Valley line stations took advantage of a cheap trip to London on 15th August 1865, when an excursion was again run in conjunction with the GER. The train returned to Halstead at 10pm.

Another outlet for cheap fares with return tickets issued at single fares was the Halstead Fair, held on fixed dates of 6th May and 29th October each year, where cattle, poultry and even horses were exhibited and sold. Later, on 6th September 1865 another excursion was operated to Shoreditch with single fares charged for the return journey. A total of 619 passengers travelled with individual station loadings: Haverhill 42, Birdbrook 15, Yeldham 46, Hedingham 54, Halstead 372 and Colne 90. Fares were unaltered from those charged in 1862 save that Haverhill and Birdbrook passengers were charged 8s 0d First Class and 4s 0d Third Class.

Once the connecting line was open at Haverhill, the CV&HR organised the first of a series of excursions to Cambridge on 28th September 1865. The local press reported *'the long expected and eagerly awaited excursion'* received an unusual degree of attention for Halstead declared the day a public holiday, as most of the shops closed for the occasion. Even some of the shops were decorated overall with streamers, bunting and flags. As 28th was a Thursday, the staff of the *Halstead Gazette* might have had to stay behind to produce the newspaper but the editor arranged for the paper to be issued on the Wednesday so staff could participate. *'Complete satisfaction'* was expressed by the returning excursionists at the visit to *'the great seat of learning'*. For the record, the train departed Colne

For many years Halstead Co-operative Society ran annual excursions to Clacton and in August 1957 the numbers travelling required three trains, two of ten coaches and one with eight coaches, each hauled by two 'J15' Class 0-6-0 locomotives. Here the final of the trio formed of ten coaches is approaching Chappel headed by 'J15' Class 0-6-0s No's 65440 and 65477. The locomotives were serviced at Clacton shed before the return journey. *Dr I.C. Allen*

at 8.00am, Halstead 8.25am, Castle Hedigham 8.40am, Yeldham 9.00am, Birdbrook 9.12am and Haverhill GE at 9.20am, with arrival at Cambridge at 10.00am The return special train departed the university city at 6.15pm and fares were Colne, Halstead, Castle Hedingham, Yeldham and Birdbrook 5s 0d First Class, 2s 6d Third Class, and from Haverhill 4s 0d First Class and 2s 0d Third Class. Further London excursions operated on 22nd September and 10th October 1865.

From thereon excursions were regularly offered to the local populace and typical of the local excursions was one on 18th August 1899 when Courtaulds arranged a Saturday half-day excursion for their workers to Clacton. The overseers acted as a committee and the train departed Halstead at 2.15pm with over 500 passengers crammed in to the eleven coaches provided by the GER. Thirty to forty passengers joining at Colne station had to be squeezed in to the guard's van. The popularity of such outings meant that some travellers were doomed to disappointment for over one hundred girls who had not pre-booked, on attempting to board the train were turned away! The train arrived at Clacton at 4.00pm and the return service departed the coast at 9.00pm, arriving back at Halstead at 11.00pm with the majority of travellers singing *'popular songs of the time'*.

As the years progressed the company organised three or four half-day excursions to Clacton, the CV&HR arranging if possible to run at times corresponding to a full moon so that passengers could after

disembarking on the return journey find their way home along the unlit streets of villages and towns served by the railway. However, the final excursion operated in independent days ran on Christmas Eve 1922 to Colchester, and although the train was full there were no reported celebrations.

For many years Clacton and Walton were regular destinations with summer Sundays through-trains continuing after grouping and into nationalisation. For some trips the train split at Thorpe-le-Soken, with half if the formation proceeding to Frinton and Walton-on-the-Naze and the other half continuing to Clacton. Other destinations included occasional forays to Felixstowe, Aldeburgh and very occasionally to Lowestoft and Great Yarmouth.

GOODS TRAFFIC

The carriers' carts or waggons were the main source of transportation of goods to and from the towns and villages of the Colne valley before the coming of the railway. In 1855 Smith & Milner, working from Halstead en route to Colchester, served Earls Colne on Tuesdays and Saturday mornings collecting from the White Lion at 11.00am and returning the same evening at 7.00pm. James Pudney also journeyed from Earls Colne to London on Mondays and Fridays, returning on Tuesdays and Saturdays. From Halstead the carrier to London was William Howard whose waggon left Bridgefoot on Mondays, Tuesdays, Thursdays and Fridays for the Bull, Aldgate. Francis Mansfield served Colchester from his home in Trinity Street on Tuesdays, Thursdays and Saturdays, returning the same day. Henry Creswell also journeyed to Braintree from Halstead every day, serving the ECR station with a through journey to London on Fridays returning the next day. Joseph Byford's waggons also served three villages in the Colne valley. Starting at Cavendish en route to the King's Arms, Leadenhall Street in the City, the carrier served Castle Hedingham on Tuesdays and Friday mornings, returning on Monday and Friday afternoons. The same waggon called at the Three Sugar Loaves on Monday night and Friday morning, returning on Monday and Friday mornings. Yeldham was a passing point for Byford's waggons, calling at the White Hart daily en route to Braintree ECR station and on Tuesdays and Fridays for London. John Bowyer ran a daily carrier service from Castle Hedingham to Braintree station whilst William Andrew travelled from the village to Sudbury on Tuesdays, Thursdays and Saturdays, returning the same day. By 1862 the London carrier from Halstead was William Cressall whose waggon ran from Bridgefoot on Mondays only to the Saracen's Head at Aldgate, returning on Wednesdays.

Haverhill in 1855 could boast an excellent service of carriers' waggons to destinations as far afield as London, Cambridge and Ipswich. William Chalk, en route from Linton to the Vine Inn Bishopsgate, called at the Queen's Head on Mondays, Wednesdays and Thursdays. Reginald Ewen journeyed from his own house to Bury St Edmunds and Cambridge every Saturday whilst James Bradman travelled to Ipswich every Monday returning to Haverhill on Tuesday. Local services of John Golding ran to Clare from the Greyhound every Monday and Thursday, whilst William Elmer ran his waggons in competition from the Bell to the same destinations on the same days. Royal Mail carts also served the town, the vehicle for Halstead leaving the Greyhound with parcels and letter bags after 4pm each day. A cart also ran to Newmarket from the Bell at 6pm, offering forward connections for letters and parcels the same day to London, Norwich, Ipswich, Cambridge, Brandon, Lynn and Bury St Edmunds.

Once the railway had opened to traffic a plethora of instructions and agreements were introduced. On 25th January 1860 it was agreed that a junctionman be appointed at Chappel to check the numbers of individual wagons passing between the CV&HR and ECR lines and the Railway Clearing House was duly advised of the arrangement.

Early in April 1860 the CV&HR company requested from the ECR charge rates for the conveyance of cattle, coal and parcels traffic sent from stations on their line to Bures, Sudbury, Marks Tey, Witham, Maldon, Chelmsford, Romford, Stratford, Brick Lane, Blackwall, Colchester, Ipswich, Mistley, Hythe and Peterborough. On 11th April the CV&HR was advised the ECR rates were to be added to their own rates Chappel to Halstead. The Railway Clearing House was duly advised to divide the rates on the agreed terms. Three months later it was agreed that charges of consignments of meats from Halstead to London would remain at £1 0s 0d per ton.

At the end of August 1860 it was reported that Mr Cressall, a private carrier of Halstead, had ceased sending his goods to London via Braintree goods yard and was sending consignments by road because of difficulties with the CV&HR and ECR arrangements. As the client was a valued customer Moseley, the ECR General Manager, was requested on the 29th of the month to negotiate with the CV&HR goods agent to ensure the traffic was returned to rail. After investigating it was found that Cressall was conveying his meat traffic by road because of the high rates charged by the ECR. In an endeavour to regain the traffic it was agreed to reduce the charges from Halstead from £1 10s 0d per ton to £1 2s 6d per ton on and from 7th November 1860. On 21st November the question of terminal charges was raised, with the CV&HR proposing instead of a 4d terminal charge on coal from ECR ports, a 6d terminal charge to each company, with coal via Peterborough raising a terminal charge of 9d invoiced to Chappel only. It was also reported that Colne Valley wagons were being sent to Hythe from Halstead for loading with coal and the ECR proposed a charge of a halfpenny per mile or 6d per truck ton hire charges.

The coming of the railway to Halstead generated entrepreneurship amongst many individuals, for The Angel posting house opposite the station was renamed The Railway Hotel with the proprietor James Milne advertising *'horses and carriages in constant readiness upon the arrival of every train'*. Equally, a former alehouse became The

Immediately after grouping, from July 1923 the L&NER introduced S.D. Holden's GER 'Y65', later 'F7', Class 2-4-2Ts to work Colne Valley services alongside the local 'F9' Class 2-4-2T engines. Here No. 8300 stands outside Halstead shed in 1925 when only one locomotive was diagrammed to work from the depot. Haverhill shed covered the remaining passenger diagrams whilst Cambridge and Colchester sheds worked the freight services. In this distant view the carriage shed is to the left and fronting the scene several private owner open wagons occupy the goods yard sidings, including those of Moy's, John Brown & Company, Bolsover and W.R. Davis & Sons Limited. A heap of clean ballast is stored in the yard for permanent way staff. *M. Root collection*

Locomotive and another establishment The Railway Bell. A local dealer, Mr Clements, advertised he had purchased a large quantity of Peruvian Guano, an important and prized manure delivered by rail, and was selling it in £10 consignments *'at the railway station'*, whilst stressing his office and warehouse were nearby.

The early months of operation found the Halstead and Bishopsgate companies establishing interchange rates and charges for commodities. In December 1860 the ECR advised that an allowance of 9d per ton on inland coal traffic or 6d per ton on sea-borne traffic would be allowed. The CV&HR requested 6d per ton on meat traffic from Halstead to London but this was disputed and a reduced rate of 4d per ton was agreed on 19th December 1860. Then on 2nd January 1861 the Halstead Company was asking for parcels terminals charges of 2d per item but after enquiry the rate of 1d was upheld. A fortnight later the CV&HR was requesting the 9d per ton coal terminal charges for fuel routed via Peterborough to be backdated to 16th April 1860 but the ECR goods manager refused the request. On the same day, the rates for goods traffic between Colchester and Halstead were reduced to First, Second and Third Class 5s 0d per ton, Fourth Class 7s 6d per ton and Fifth Class 10s 0d per ton, inclusive of costs for Halstead cartage. In March the CV&HR Company requested the waiving of wagon hire to the coal merchants rate and this was agreed with the ECR authorities on 27th of the month. For the period May 1860 to March 1861 the wagon hire allowance paid to the CV&HR was £56.

With the impending opening of the Halstead to Hedingham section of line the ECR goods manager advised the CV&HR directors that through rates for minerals and merchandise would remain unaltered but coal traffic would be charged on a mileage basis. The following month it was confirmed that Castle Hedingham would be allocated in District 8 charges for fuel routed via Peterborough. Early in July 1861 the CV&HR Company requested the ECR to provide details of full train rates for coal traffic in small quantities routed via Peterborough, but on the 17th of the month the main line company refused to quote. At the same meeting of the ECR directors it was noted that goods being despatched to London from Haverhill routed via road to Castle Hedingham CV&HR and thence by rail was charged at 12s 0d per ton whereas that travelling by road to Audley End and thence by rail to London varied from 10s 0d to £1 per ton. It was agreed the matter be reviewed from time to time to ensure there was no traffic lost via Audley End which was the more popular routing.

In September 1861 the CV&HR agreed to contribute half the costs of the Railway Clearing House administrative charges for the recording of through bookings, but on the 25th of the month the ECR was advised costs could not be estimated as the CV&HR had not rendered returns for through bookings. An urgent note was forwarded to Halstead requesting the directors to furnish the required details and then to continue forwarding the returns weekly thereafter.

In addition to the BTH/Paxman 800hp diesel electric locomotives, between 1959 and 1960 North British type 2 1,100hp diesel electric locomotives were employed on freight workings. Here No. D6123 is shunting covered vans on the Down loop at Halstead exactly 100 years to the day after the opening of the line. The leading vehicle is a BY parcels van. To the left are a number of bulk grain wagons, which supplied produce to Newman & Clark's granary. In the background is the Down side coal yard.

M. Root collection

Chappel and Wakes Colne was provided with a large goods shed with ornate round topped windows in the Up side yard. The structure had capacity for the storage of 100 quarters of grain.
J. Watling

On 11th May 1863 higher rates for through coal traffic were agreed.

| | THROUGH | APPORTIONMENT | |
STATION	RATES	GER	CV&HR
Colne	5s 6d	4s 9d	0s 9d
Halstead	5s 7d	4s 7d	1s 0d
Castle Hedingham	5s 11d	4s 6d	1s 5d
Yeldham	6s 4d	4s 10d	1s 6d
Haverhill	7s 4d	5s 3d	2s 1d

After the establishment of the GER and with improving relationships between the two companies, the question of charges for goods traffic appeared to be resolved without any major dispute although some issues came to the fore. On Friday 23rd June 1876 a deputation of Halstead traders attended the GER directors meeting to air their grievances over a number of issues, including the charges raised by the railway company for the collection and delivery of goods except from Brick Lane, the charges for the booking and forwarding of small parcels, the delay in the settlement of claims for the loss and damage of goods, irregular charges for the carriage of commodities and the lack of staff to assist with the unloading of goods at stations. The grievances continued, for as late as 1878 Mrs Rebecca Cressall was still operating her carrier's waggon in competition against the railway, connecting Bridge Street Halstead to the Saracens Head at Aldgate on Monday, returning on Wednesday.

From the early years, wheat, hay and straw traffic was conveyed in increasing quantities and these basic commodities were augmented by vegetables, including potatoes, swedes, turnips, parsnips, carrots, mangold wurzels and other root crops, which were forwarded on a regular basis by rail until the early 1960s to the markets at Halstead, Haverhill, Colchester, Cambridge and Chelmsford. Barley grown in small quantities was sent further afield – to Bury St Edmunds, Romford, Godmanchester and destinations in Scotland. From the latter part of the 19th century until the end of World War One, truck loads of hay and straw were loaded at the stations and sent to

London, Cambridge, Ipswich and Colchester for use in the many stables in those towns and cities, a greater need being required during World War One when the commodity was required for military stables.

Milk was regularly dispatched from all stations to dairies at Halstead, Sible and Castle Hedingham, Haverhill and occasionally Colchester in the familiar 17-gallon churns. Two loads were forwarded daily during the summer months by an early morning train and then again in the late afternoon. During the winter months it was despatched by the early morning train only. This area of Essex was not noted for its dairy farming and the relatively small amount of traffic conveyed was quickly lost to road transport in the late 1930s.

Eggs became another significant commodity conveyed by rail from CV&HR stations and during World War One the GER even exhibited an Egg and Poultry train at various stations in East Anglia to promote higher yields. However, from the early 1930s most of the conveyance of eggs was transferred to road haulage and the railway saw little if any traffic thereafter. Mention must be made of the conveyance of manure for local farms, a much-maligned commodity detested by railway staff because of the pungent smell, which took some time to clear from wagons and required the thorough cleaning of rolling stock.

Before the coming of the railway, drovers herded animals along the roads to and from markets and prices fluctuated according to the condition of the beasts. The arrival of the railway meant animals could be conveyed relatively quickly to local and London markets, arriving in much fresher condition and therefore gaining a higher price.

Livestock handled at the stations was two-way traffic from the early years. The potential of the railway was quickly realised and horses were regularly conveyed in wagons or horseboxes attached to passenger trains until World War Two. Hunting horses were conveyed to or from local hunt meetings on 24 hours' notice being given to the forwarding station. Ordinary horse traffic declined after World War One with the advent of the internal combustion engine but cattle wagons were a feature on the railway until the early 1950s for the conveyance of livestock to Braintree market held on a Wednesday, Halstead market held on Thursday, Haverhill and Chelmsford on Friday, and Cambridge and Colchester on Saturday. Certain passenger trains were permitted to convey cattle wagons, especially useful on market days. The conveyance of cattle traffic required the cattle wagons as well as the pens at stations to be limewashed to prevent disease. The pens, constructed of timber, were originally painted white but the continuing white finish as depicted in photographs was usually limewash.

Coal and coke traffic was handled at all stations as early as 1861, with consignments for local fuel merchants received from Sherwood, Newstead, Kirkby, Bestwood, Hucknall, Sheepbridge, Stanton, Shirebrook, Clipstone, Worksop, Blidworth and other collieries. The wagons usually travelled via Peterborough where the Stanground sidings acted as a clearing house for empty wagons en route to the collieries and loaded ones travelling to the CV&HR stations. Later some coal traffic was routed by the Great Northern & Great Eastern Joint line for outsorting at Whitemoor marshalling yard. The majority of wagon-loads were then routed via March, Ely and Cambridge for the Stour Valley line to Haverhill, although some took the roundabout route via Bury St Edmunds, Ipswich and Colchester. In the 1920s and 1930s coke was conveyed for horticultural purposes but after World War Two this commodity was conveyed by road. Coal merchants with depots or coal grounds at stations included Moy's at White Colne, Halstead and Sible and Castle Hedingham, the Halstead Co-operative Society at Halstead, Cole at Birdbrook and Hunts at Earls Colne.

In the late 1920s and early 1930s many of the roads in Essex and Suffolk remained unmetalled – dust tracks in summer and quagmires in winter. Both county councils undertook a rolling programme of road improvements, which involved levelling the surface before covering it in granite chippings and tarmacadam. Much of this material was delivered by rail to station goods yards in the Colne valley, from where the material was offloaded and taken to site by horse and waggon. The granite and tarmacadam was then levelled by steamroller.

Several traders and businessmen benefited from and supplied much traffic to the railway before the advent of the internal combustion engine, which to some provided a better service. R. & R. Hunt at their Atlas Foundry Works in Earls Colne employed over 300 people at their zenith with an output of agricultural machines and farming implements including chaff cutters, root cutters, root pulpers, cake mills and oat crushers, furrow hoes, horse hoes and sheep hurdles. They also produced animal feed in small quantities. Before the coming of the railway Courtaulds Textile Mills of Halstead boasted about 240 looms, but expansion as a result of railway activity increased to over a thousand looms by the last decade of the nineteenth century. The workforce also expanded and with over 1,500 workers the establishment was one of the largest employers in Essex. Rippers Joinery Works, with a large establishment beside the station at Sible and Castle Hedingham, were woodworkers and timber contractors, receiving consignments of tree trunks by rail, whilst Whitlocks of Yeldham built carts and agricultural machinery. Charles Portway JP founded Portway's Tortoise Works and produced patent lamps, which were dispatched by rail from Halstead. Along the line at Birdbrook, Unwin's had a thriving seed and fertilizer business dispatching regular consignments by rail.

By far the largest of exports by rail were bricks produced for the burgeoning housing development in north and east London. As early as 1864 brickworks were established at Sible Hedingham but it was not until brickfields were opened at Maiden Ley, Castle Hedingham in 1893 by William Rayner & Son, with a standard gauge siding adjacent to the CV&HR, that traffic mushroomed. The works also had a narrow gauge tramway to the clay pit, which connected the six up-draught Scotch kilns to the main line siding. Mark Gentry and the Corder and Cornish families also established brickfields in the area. Gentry was the proprietor of the Hedingham Brick & Tile Works, making bricks at Langthorne brickworks, Wethersfield Road, and Highfields adjacent to Purls Hill, Sible Hedingham; whilst Corder had brickworks at Southey Green, Sible Hedingham, Potters Hall, Great Yeldham and Gosfield – all remote from the railway.

At Purls Hill was the Hedingham Brick Company – initially owned by the Rayner family – which later became the Sible Hedingham Red Brick Company registered in December 1919, then effectively owned by Rippers Limited who had purchased the former Highfield, Purls Hill and Sidings brickworks, and all conveyed to the Sible Hedingham Red Brick Limited in 1920. Purls Hill brickworks had a standard gauge siding and narrow gauge tramway from sand pit at adjacent Purls Hill plantation to a tipping dock alongside the CV&HR. Initial directors of the new company were Reuben Hunt, Eli Cornish (who had previously owned the Siding works and managed the Hedingham Brickworks), Harry Ticker Ripper and William Charlton Ripper.

In 1887, 5,000 tons of bricks were dispatched by rail from Hedingham, increasing to 20,000 tons in 1898, but all was not well. At a public enquiry held at Hedingham into the proposed new Light Railways for North Essex, Mark Gentry stated the CV&HR *'did not have sufficient resources to meet his requirements'*. He *'could have loaded 20 and sometimes 30 more trucks of bricks a week than the railway could give'*. The GER came to the rescue in the short term and these additional wagons improved the situation so that by 1901 between thirty and forty wagons of bricks were loaded daily from an industry employing some 500 men. By the turn of the century the various brickworks in the area were producing almost 10 million bricks, half of that total at Hedingham alone. The bricks were dispatched to GER suburban stations where the material was used on the construction of late-Victorian and Edwardian terrace houses which were mushrooming in the outer suburbs. One Hedingham brickmaker alone provided the bricks for the construction of sixteen churches in North London. The CV&HR invested in a considerable number of new wagons and acquired the 0-6-2T locomotive No. 5 essentially to maintain regular haulage, often requiring at times a seven-day-a-week service.

However, by the end of the first decade of the twentieth century the general depression of the building trade and the slump in brick manufacturing had a huge effect on CV&HR finances, where receipts reduced. Trade never fully recovered and the sidings at Maiden Ley were derelict by 1951; the river bridge, built partly of wood and partly cast iron girders, was then in a precarious state and the works finally closed in 1952 having provided little traffic to the railway post World War Two. The Sible Hedingham Red Brick Company Limited ceased production in 1954, having dispatched bricks by road for many years, lorries having the advantage of direct delivery to customers.

At the zenith of production numerous cases were reported of bricks being broken in transit and also of wagons conveying bricks being damaged by rough shunting when fully loaded. Guards, shunters and engine drivers were instructed to take caution when shunting brick traffic, whilst station masters were required to report all cases of rough shunting to the General Manager so that appropriate disciplinary action could be taken against the culprits. Goods guards were also instructed that trucks containing hay or straw traffic were not to be attached next to the engine. When hay and straw traffic was despatched to destinations south of the River Thames in GER or other company wagons, GER tarpaulin sheets were to be used to protect the goods. Only when CV&HR wagons were utilised were CV&HR wagon sheets to be used.

During World War Two the Ministry of Food established cold storage depots local to the branch and considerable tonnages of meat, dried egg powder, dried milk, orange juice and other foodstuffs were conveyed to the depots by rail both during and after hostilities. There has already been mention of the considerable contribution made by the CV&HR and L&NER in the conveyance of military equipment and armaments to airfields, initially in World War One and later during World War Two, and it is not repeated here.

The CV&HR Company used six, latterly eight, dray horses for local delivery of goods and parcels in the Halstead area as well as one horse for shunting the yard. At one time grass cut from the embankments and cuttings was used as fodder for the horses. The hay was collected by special train before being taken to Earls Colne station yard and stacked for future use. On the waterlogged ground adjacent to Earls Colne goods yard beds of osiers were grown and collected for the making of baskets. Henry Pooley & Sons of Birmingham were responsible for the maintenance of all scales and weighing machines on the railway.

The wagon capacity of sidings at stations on the Colne Valley line were as under:

CHAPPEL

GOODS YARD		PRIVATE SIDING		REFUGE	
Back Platform	28	Petroleum Board	22	North End	13
North End	11				
Dock	5				
Shed Road	22				
South End Spur	1				

WHITE COLNE

GOODS YARD	
New Road	17
Loop	3
Old Road	16

EARLS COLNE

GOODS YARD	
Side Dock	2
End on Dock	4
Shed Road	19
Coal Road	16
Back Road	26
Loop Road	9

HALSTEAD

GOODS YARD		PRIVATE SIDINGS	
New Road	17	Ravin's	8
Dock Road	12	Moy's	6
Front Coal	20	Norman's	3
Back Coal	17	Co-op siding	6
Storage	5	Co-op Road No. 1	14
		Co-op Road No. 2	11
		Loco Road No. 1	25
		Loco Road No. 2	5
		Tortoise	11

SIBLE & CASTLE HEDINGHAM

GOODS YARD		PRIVATE SIDINGS		REFUGE	
Coal Road	16	Ripper's Gantry Road	10	Siding	9
Front Road	9	Ripper's Timber	18		
Ripper's	8	Red Brick Company			
Carriage	20	Purls Hill	40		
Gas Works	9				
Rayner's	30				
Shed Road	6				

Yeldham goods yard and station view facing towards Chappel. A road mobile crane provides lifting facilities whilst coal and fuel stage grounds are at the back of the yard. From the left is the goods loop siding, main single line and then the Down loop with trailing access to the loading dock. *J. Watling*

YELDHAM

GOODS YARD			REFUGE	
Coal Road	20		Up (in rear)	23
Dock siding	16			
Shunt Spur	14			

BIRDBROOK

GOODS YARD	
Back Road	10
Coal Road	15
Shed Road	15

HAVERHILL CV

GOODS YARD	
Down 4 roads	103

HAVERHILL GER

GOODS YARD		SORTING		REFUGE	
Yard 7x Down	101	2 x Down	64	Junction Down	26
Cattle pen	6			Station Up	27
Up Loop	44			Down	50
Down Loop	39			Up	50

The following facilities were available at the stations.

CHAPPEL

Loading gauge
Loading dock
Fixed crane, 1 ton 10 cwt capacity
Goods shed with storage for 100 qtrs of grain
Weighing machine, 10 cwt
Weighing machine, 5 cwt
Lock up for small parcels
Cattle pen, paved
Water supply for animals in transit
Facilities for loading furniture and vans on wheels
Facilities for lifting vans
Latest time for receipt of goods requiring
                delivery the following day   5pm SX
                                       3pm SO

COLNE, LATER WHITE COLNE

Loading gauge
Fixed crane, 1 ton capacity
Goods shed
Lock up for small parcels

FORD GATE, LATER COLNE, THEN EARLS COLNE

Loading gauge
Loading dock
Goods shed
Fixed crane, 1 ton
Cattle pens
Watering facilities for animals in transit
Lock up for small parcels

HALSTEAD

Loading gauges
Loading dock
Goods shed
Granary
Fixed crane, 5 ton capacity
Lock up for small parcels
Coal wharf

CASTLE HEDINGHAM, LATER SIBLE AND CASTLE HEDINGHAM

Loading gauges
Loading dock
Goods shed
Fixed crane, 1 ton capacity
Cattle pens
Watering facilities for animals in transit
Lock up for small parcels
Wagon turntable (later removed)

YELDHAM

Loading gauge
Loading dock
Goods shed
Granary
Fixed crane, 1 ton capacity
Cattle pens
Watering facilities for animals in transit
Lock up for small parcels

BIRDBROOK

Loading gauge
Loading dock
Goods shed
Granary (private)
Fixed crane, 15 cwt capacity
Cattle pens
Watering facilities for animals in transit
Lock up for small parcels

HAVERHILL CV&HR, LATER HAVERHILL SOUTH

Loading gauge
Loading dock
Goods shed
Fixed crane, 15 cwt capacity
Cattle pens
Watering facilities for animals in transit
Lock up for small parcels

HAVERHILL GER, LATER HAVERHILL NORTH

Loading gauge
Loading dock
Fixed crane, 1 ton, later 1 ton 10 cwt capacity
Weighing machine, 1 ton, later 1 ton 1 cwt capacity
Goods shed } combined storage 300
Granary   } quarters of grain
Cattle pens, 2
Watering facilities for livestock in transit
Facilities for loading furniture vans on wheels
Facilities for lifting vans
Latest time for goods to be forwarded for
                    next day delivery   3pm via Marks Tey
                                   5pm via Shelford

The timing allowance for freight trains between Chappel and Haverhill in L&NER and BR days was as follows for Class 'F', 'H', 'J' and 'K' trains.

	STARTING ALLOWANCE (MINUTES)	STOPPING ALLOWANCE (MINUTES)	PASSING ALLOWANCE (MINUTES)
Chappel to White Colne	3	2	5
White Colne to Earls Colne	2	2	3
Earls Colne to Halstead	3	2	5
Halstead to S & C Hedingham	3	2	7
S & C Hedingham to Yeldham	3	2	6
Yeldham to Birdbrook	3	2	8
Birdbrook to Haverhill	3	2	9
Haverhill to Birdbrook	3	2	9
Birdbrook to Yeldham	3	2	8
Yeldham to S & C Hedingham	3	2	6
S & C Hedingham to Halstead	3	2	7
Halstead to Earls Colne	3	2	5
Earls Colne to White Colne	3	2	3
White Colne to Chappel	3	2	5

The maximum number of wagons to be worked by any train on any section of the line in CV&HR days was originally limited to thirty wagons but was increased to forty wagons with the delivery of locomotive No. 5. The load was reduced by one-eighth during unfavourable weather conditions. The ordinary loads permitted were:

DOWN	NO. 1 0-4-2T	'HALSTEAD' CLASS 2-4-2T	NO. 5 0-6-2T
Chappel to Colne	16	28	35
Colne to Halstead	16	28	35
Halstead to Castle Hedingham	17	30	40
Castle Hedingham to Yeldham	17	30	40
Yeldham to Birdbrook	14	24	40
Birdbrook to Haverhill CV Junction or Haverhill GE station	14	24	36
Haverhill CV station to Haverhill GE station	10	18	25
UP			
Haverhill GE station to Haverhill CV station or Birdbrook	10	18	25
Birdbrook to Yeldham	10	18	25
Yeldham to Castle Hedingham	17	30	40
Castle Hedingham to Halstead	17	30	40
Halstead to Colne	17	30	40
Colne to Chappel	15	26	32

A misty last day of passenger train operation, 30th December 1961, at Birdbrook with enthusiasts waiting on the lineside for a Down train. The shabby condition of the timber building is evidence that little remedial maintenance was carried on the infrastructure in the last few years. Two wagons occupy the shed road waiting unloading in the open-ended goods shed, for freight facilities were to close on and from 2nd January 1962. The Up starting signal stays firmly at danger beside the signal box. *R. Powell*

In calculating the loads, three wagons of minerals were equal to four wagons of goods, whilst three empty goods, cattle or mineral wagons were equal to two loaded goods wagons.

In the event of a train being overloaded and the guard finding it necessary to reduce the load, direction and judgement was to be used in deciding which wagons to detach. Wagons containing perishable traffic were not to be left behind and as a general rule guards were instructed initially to detach wagons containing locomotive coal to reduce the load, and then wagons of coal, stores, timber and non-perishable traffic. Trains were not to be delayed whilst the choice of wagons was made and guards were required to do their best in the time at their disposal. When it was desired to get urgent traffic away by any train which was up to maximum limit, the guard was to consult with the driver to ascertain whether he could, under the circumstances, take the traffic or a portion of it. In these circumstances the driver's decision was final. No vehicles were to be conveyed behind the rear brake van of a goods train, except cripple wagons labelled by examiners to be sent for repair behind the van.

After grouping the L&NER authorised the following loads for freight trains:

	MINERAL	GOODS	EMPTIES
CLASS OF ENGINE: No. 1			
Chappel to Halstead	16	24	32
Halstead to Yeldham	28	39	52
Yeldham to Haverhill	18	27	36
Haverhill to Yeldham	18	27	34
Yeldham to Halstead	26	39	52
Halstead to Chappel	16	24	32
CLASS OF ENGINE: No. 2			
Chappel to Halstead	17	25	34
Halstead to Yeldham	29	43	56
Yeldham to Haverhill	20	30	40
Haverhill to Yeldham	20	30	34
Yeldham to Halstead	29	43	56
Halstead to Chappel	17	25	34
CLASS OF ENGINE: No. 3			
Chappel to Halstead	19	28	38
Halstead to Yeldham	32	48	56
Yeldham to Haverhill	22	33	40
Haverhill to Yeldham	22	33	34
Yeldham to Halstead	32	48	56
Halstead to Chappel	19	28	38

Trains were not to convey more than twenty-five wagons into Haverhill South, no more than sixteen wagons from Haverhill South.

By 1950 the authorised loadings of freight trains had been amended:

	HEAVY	GOODS	EMPTIES
No. 1 ENGINE			
Chappel to Halstead	13	23	26
Halstead to Yeldham	23	41	46
Yeldham to Haverhill	16	28	32
Haverhill to Yeldham	16	28	32
Yeldham to Earls Colne	23	41	46
Earls Colne to Chappel	13	23	26
No. 2 ENGINE			
Chappel to Halstead	16	28	32
Halstead to Yeldham	26	46	52
Yeldham to Haverhill	18	32	36
Haverhill to Yeldham	18	32	34
Yeldham to Earls Colne	26	46	52
Earls Colne to Chappel	16	28	32
No. 3 ENGINE			
Chappel to Earls Colne only	17	30	34
Earls Colne to Chappel	17	30	34

A 'No. 1' Class engine was an 'E4' Class 2-4-0, and a Class '2' a 'J15' Class 0-6-0.

In addition, a 'J17' Class 0-6-0 locomotive could work twenty-two heavy wagons between Chappel and Earls Colne and return, and a 'J19' Class 0-6-0, twenty-seven heavy wagons over the same section of line, but these locomotives were only authorised in an emergency.

After dieselisation freight services were hauled by BTH/Paxman 800 hp or North British 1,100 hp diesel electric locomotives which were permitted to haul the following wagon-loads:

CLASS OF TRAIN	4, 5 OR 6	7	8 OR 9
Chappel to Halstead	20	27	36
Halstead to Yeldham	27	37	44
Yeldham to Earls Colne	27	37	44
Earls Colne to Chappel	20	27	36

Trains were not to convey more than 25 wagons from Haverhill North to Haverhill South or more than 14 wagons from Haverhill South to Haverhill North.

RIGHT: Haverhill South ex-CV&HR goods shed on 16th April 1947 with the 480 feet shed road entering and the former main single line beyond the structure.   *L&NER*

12

Locomotives

FROM GROUPING AND AFTER THE WITHDRAWAL of the surviving CV&HR tank locomotives the L&NER only permitted the following classes of locomotive to work between Chappel and Haverhill: 'E4' Class 2-4-0 and 'J15' Class 0-6-0 tender locomotives, together with 'J17' and 'J19' Class 0-6-0s between Chappel and Earls Colne, the latter subject to a speed restriction of 30 mph and also restricted from entering Earls Colne goods yard; tank engines permitted included 'F7' Class 2-4-2Ts and 'J65' to 'J70' Class 0-6-0Ts, plus 'Y1', 'Y3', 'Y5', 'Y6' and 'Y10' Class shunting locomotives, although there is no evidence of any of the 'Y' classes working between Chappel and Haverhill. Later the L&NER and BR designated the line to RA (Route Availability) 2, with Class 'J17' of RA4 and Class 'J19' of RA5 0-6-0 tender locomotives permitted between Chappel and Earls Colne subject to a 30 mph speed limit. From Earls Colne to Haverhill the RA2 classification continued, subject to a maximum axle loading of 14¼ tons. Excursion trains could be double headed by two 'J15' Class locomotives subject to a 20 mph speed limit.

From the foregoing it would appear the regulations regarding motive power had been standardised for a number of years but nothing could be further from the truth, for until 1903 the CV&HR had no official register of locomotives or rolling stock.

However, from 1897 to 1907 inclusive, four engines were registered – increasing to five from 1908 until 1922 – in the annual returns to the Board of Trade.

THE GEORGE ENGLAND ENGINES

There was difficulty in the early years raising capital for rolling stock so the company hired the two small 2-4-0 side tank locomotives from William Munro, the contractor. These were standard George England light tank engines built in 1854 at Hatcham Ironworks, and were named *Cam* and *Colne* whilst working on the CV&HR. Both had outside cylinders, with feed pumps driven from the crossheads and the England form of inside framing with openings in them that permitted the knocking out of the spring hanger pins. The coal bunker had very limited capacity and a travelling jack was carried. With such small cylinders the engines were underpowered as the weights of trains increased, especially on the 1 in 60 gradient on White Colne bank. Their traffic days were numbered when Munro wanted them on the extension of the railway to Haverhill. The locomotives were painted in a red livery whilst on the construction work. In 1861 the engines were removed from the line to assist with the construction of the Wivenhoe &

Two 2-4-0 tank locomotives built in 1854 by George England & Company of Hatcham Ironworks, later named *Cam* and *Colne*, were employed by William Munro on the construction of the CV&HR, after which the pair were used for a short period on the initial train services, operating in a red livery. The engines were then used on the building of the Wivenhoe & Brightlingsea Railway before being re-gauged for employment on railway construction in Ireland.

Author's collection

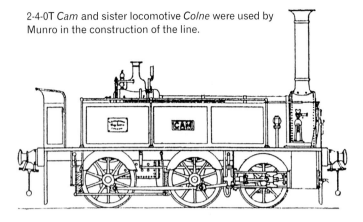

2-4-0T *Cam* and sister locomotive *Colne* were used by Munro in the construction of the line.

Brightlingsea Railway, where Munro was also contractor, but before transfer *Cam* was damaged in a fire at Haverhill shed. Later they were transferred to Ireland and re-gauged to haul works trains during construction of the Athenry to Ennis line, which opened to traffic in 1869.

The leading dimensions of *Cam* and *Colne* were:

Cylinders 2 outside	11 inches x 13 inches
Heating surface Total	700 sq feet
Grate area	8.5 sq feet
Boiler pressure	120 psi
Leading wheels	3 feet 0 ins
Coupled wheels	3 feet 8 ins
Wheelbase	10 feet 0 ins
Weight in working order	17 tons 0 cwt

ECR 2-4-0 Tender Locomotive

To cover for the absence of *Cam* and *Colne* two locomotives were purchased, one from the ECR being a 2-4-0 tender engine built in 1845 by Kitson, Thompson & Hewitson of Leeds (Maker's No. 35), the forerunner of Kitson & Company of Leeds, which when new was supplied to the Midland Railway. The engine was one of eight acquired by the Eastern Counties Railway in 1847, where it was initially numbered 140. It was later renumbered 217 and at the time of purchase by the CV&HR No. 95. The locomotive had bar frames with axle guards bolted thereto, a form of construction used before the introduction of the plate frame. A large manhole was located in front of the Gothic firebox casing and the feed pumps were driven from the crosshead. The locomotive was painted green and had a 4-wheel tender.

The leading dimensions of the long boiler 2-4-0 tender locomotive were:

Cylinders	2 inside	14 ins x 18 ins
Boiler	Barrel length	11 feet 9½ ins
	Diameter	3 feet 1½ ins
	Tubes	145 x 1¼ ins
	Firebox	3 feet 8½ ins
Heating surface		
	Tubes	797.0 sq feet
	Firebox	63.0 sq feet
	Total	860.0 sq feet
Leading wheels		3 feet 0 ins
Coupled wheels		4 feet 6 ins
Wheelbase		11 feet 0¼ ins

LB&SCR 2-2-2 Well Tank

The second of the replacement locomotives was a 2-2-2 well tank locomotive which had seen considerable service with the London, Brighton & South Coast Railway. It was built by Sharp Brothers of Manchester in January 1849 (Maker's No. 275) as tender locomotive No. 50 and was then renumbered 45 by the LB&SCR before being rebuilt as a 2-2-2 well tank in February 1851. On Wednesday 10th October 1855 the engine was bringing a train of empty coaches from New Cross to London Bridge, when near Spa Road it was diverted by error into a siding. Driver C. Taunton and his fireman jumped off the footplate before the engine ran through the buffer stops at the end of the siding and demolished a wall, falling into the adjacent College Street with a crash *'resembling the discharge of a park of artillery'*. The coaches followed on top of the locomotive, causing considerable damage to the machine. Curiously, Driver Taunton transferred with the rebuilt locomotive to the CV&HR when it was bought for £500 in July 1860, and worked for the company until his death a few years later. When the engine was constructed it was the intention to have smaller driving wheels than those actually fitted. A small tank was fixed under the cylinders in front of the leading wheels, and another under the footplate behind the trailing wheels. The brake arrangement was also unusual, for it was fitted to one side of the engine only and operated one brake block on the driving wheel and another on the trailing wheel. On the CV&HR the framing on this engine was painted a dark brown and the boiler and side sheets green. The locomotive was reputedly worn out and was ultimately advertised for sale in the *Railway Times* of 16th January 1861.

The leading dimensions of the engine were:

Cylinders 2 inside	15 ins x 22 ins
Leading wheels	3 feet 8 ins
Driving wheels	5 feet 6 ins
Trailing wheels	3 feet 8 ins

L&NWR Locomotive

On 18th July 1860 the ECR directors agreed to a CV&HR locomotive being hauled to Stratford for repairs and return at the usual commercial rates with no reductions allowed, but on 7th November 1860 Sinclair was advising against acceptance

ECR 2-4-0 tender locomotive.

of any repair work on Colne Valley locomotives. In desperation the company reportedly hired for a short period in August 1861 a locomotive from the London & North Western Railway at the behest of a request from Major Vereker but there are no records of the transfer of the engine.

Brewster's 2-4-0 Well Tanks

In 1861 the CV&HR company ordered three new tank locomotives with outside cylinders from Manning, Wardle & Company of Leeds, ready for completion the line to Haverhill. In actual fact the trio were purchased by Charles Brewster of Little Maplestead near Halstead, who hired them to the CV&HR. They were typical 2-4-0 tank engines of a type common to Manning, Wardle's predecessors, E.B. Wilson. Because of financial difficulties they were delivered over a three-year period, the first Maker's No. 34 in 1861, the second Maker's No. 59 in 1862, and the last Maker's No. 61 the following year. They were named soon after arrival on the CV&HR, No. 34 being *Brewster*, No. 59 *Colne* and No. 61 *Halstead*. *Colne* and *Halstead* were both fitted with light cab sheets by the maker but *Brewster* only had a simple weatherboard, although all were later equipped with a cab. They were painted dark green and had the maker's characteristic fittings, but in the latter years of service were painted brown. The locomotives worked regularly until 1887, when they were underpowered for hauling the longer and heavier trains. *Brewster* and *Halstead* were scrapped at Haverhill in 1888 but *Colne* after being retained as spare engine was sold for service in a colliery near Wigan in 1890.

The principal dimensions of the trio were:

Cylinders 2 outside	14 ins x 18 ins
Heating surface	
Tubes	654.0 sq feet
Firebox	66.0 sq feet
Total	720.0 sq feet
Grate area	9.50 sq feet
Leading wheels	3 feet 9 ins
Coupled wheels	5 feet 0 ins
Wheelbase	14 feet 0 ins
Water capacity	490 gallons

Former CMR 0-6-0 Side Tank

In 1874 the railway was being worked under contract by R.J. Watt but in 1877 John Crabtree of the Great Northern Railway was appointed General Manager; to strengthen the motive power available to the CV&HR, in 1879 he purchased second-hand from Sharp, Stewart & Company of Manchester, one of the 0-6-0 side tank engines with outside cylinders built in 1873 (Maker's No. 2358) for the Cornwall Minerals Railway. Eighteen were constructed by Sharp, Stewart of Manchester to the design of F. Trevithick and delivered in 1873 and 1874. They were arranged so they could work in pairs, coupled together footplate to footplate. Nine of the engines were taken over by the Great Western Railway when the line was absorbed in October 1877, and nine taken back by the maker. Because of the decline in traffic the GWR sold the remaining nine engines back to the maker, who later sold three to the Lynn & Fakenham Railway, five to their successor the Eastern & Midlands Railway (forerunner of the Midland & Great Northern Joint Railway) and one to the CV&HR. As the diminutive tank engines normally worked in pairs, no bunker was provided and only rear sheets were fitted, so the coal was carried on the tops of the side tanks. On the CV&HR the 0-6-0 carried the Cornwall Minerals Railway No. 10, although this was removed when the engine was named *Haverhill*. It also received an iron and wooden weatherboard to the cab and was painted in a green livery. In 1889 the engine was sold to South Hetton Coal Company where it ran for many years as their No. 21 with the brass nameplate on the side tanks. It was finally withdrawn in 1948.

The principal dimensions of No. 10 were:

Cylinders	16¼ ins x 20 ins	
Motion	Allan straight link	
Heating surface		
Tubes	195 x 1¾ ins	752.8 sq feet
Firebox		70.7 sq feet
Total		853.5 sq feet
Coupled wheels	3 feet 6 ins	
Wheelbase	12 feet 0 ins	
Weight in working order	30 tons 15 cwt	
Water capacity	780 gallons	

Three 2-4-0 well tank locomotives were built between 1861 and 1863 by Manning, Wardle to an order placed by James Brewster and loaned to the CV&HR worked on the railway until 1887. The trio were named *Brewster*, *Colne* and *Halstead*, and the first is shown at Halstead. After withdrawal *Colne* saw further service on colliery lines whilst the others two were broken up at Halstead.

Author's collection

Former CV&HR 0-6-0T *Haverhill* ex-Cornwall Minerals Railway, as modified and working at South Hetton Colliery.

Author's collection

NEILSON 0-4-2 TANK

To obviate the hiring of locomotives from the GER, Fenn the locomotive superintendent ordered an 0-4-2 tank locomotive from the firm of Neilson & Company of Glasgow, receiving order No. E464. The new locomotive bore a marked resemblance to Samuel Johnson's '81' or 'T7' Class 0-4-2 tank locomotives built by the GER and introduced into service between 1871 and 1875. These fifteen engines were built without cabs and the original specification for the CV&HR locomotive was the same – but before construction commenced the order was amended to include the provision of a cab. The new locomotive (Works No. 2204) was subsequently delivered early in 1877 and became CV&HR No. 1. The locomotive, always known as No. 1 and never named, when delivered was painted dark green and had the following dimensions:

Cylinders	2 inside	15 ins x 22 ins	
Motion		Stephenson with slide valves	
Boiler	Max diameter outside	3 feet 9¾ ins	
	Barrel length	9 feet 1 inch	
	Firebox outside length	4 feet 4¾ ins	
Heating surface			
	Tubes	158 x 1¾ ins	680.34 sq feet
	Firebox		72.81 sq feet
	Total		753.15 sq feet
Grate area		12.7 sq feet	
Boiler pressure		140 psi	
Coupled wheels		5 feet 3 ins	
Trailing wheels		3 feet 7 ins	
Tractive effort		9,350 lbs	
Length over buffers		27 feet 1 inch	
Wheelbase		13 feet 6 ins	
Weight in working order		36 tons 0 cwt	
Coal capacity		1 ton 5 cwt	
Water capacity		850 gallons	

No. 1 was repaired by the GER at Stratford Works between 4th November and 9th December 1878 and returned to the CV line the following day. It was again at Stratford from 3rd April until 4th August 1882 when, in addition to receiving general overhaul, the cylinders were rebored (Stratford order D&P 709). Evidently the

company was experiencing trouble with the engine, for No. 1 was back at Stratford from 22nd January until 19th April 1883, and again between 4th October to 14th November 1884 (D&P 1146) when it was recorded as weighing 34 tons 18 cwt, with a maximum axle loading of 13 tons 1 cwt. In the same year the engine, together with two coaches, was equipped with the Heberlein continuous automatic friction brake at Haverhill shed and subsequently carried out trials. The Heberlein brake gear was worked by a light rope which ran along the tops of the vehicles, supported by guides, and kept in tension while the train was running, by hand reels fitted in the brake van and on the engine, thus keeping the brake off. On one axle of each carriage, as well as on the engine, a cast iron drum was fitted, being put on in halves and bolted round the axle. A wrought iron frame carried friction rollers, which were put in and out of contact with the iron drum on the axle by means of levers and rods operated by the brake rope worked from the guards van or the engine. As the rollers were in contact with the drums on the axles, the friction force obtainable from the revolving axles and the momentum of the train were efficiently used in working the brakes. At speeds of 30 to 35 mph the train could be halted in under twenty seconds. No. 1 was back at Stratford for unspecified repairs in March 1885 (D&P 1236). Despite the experiment the engine was later equipped with the Westinghouse air brake with the pump being mounted in front of the right-hand side tank

Hawthorn, Leslie & Company of Newcastle-upon-Tyne rebuilt the locomotive in 1888, when two supplementary water tanks were added over the front splashers and the cab modified with a flatter roof of low pitch, fitted with eaves. At the same time the engine was painted in deep red livery before re-entering traffic. The next visit to Stratford was in October 1890 when unspecified repairs were made to the locomotive (D&P 1208). Then in 1892 the engine arrived in the Stratford works yard on 24th May but did not enter the shops until 17th June. As well as more repairs the cylinders were rebored and the engine emerged from the shops on 25th August before departing for Halstead two days later. The engine was back at Stratford on 10th May 1894 and entered the works the following day. Over four months was spent receiving attention as No. 1 was fitted with a new boiler, a new smokebox on the old footings and a stovepipe chimney under Stratford D&P 2547. It was also repainted raven black. The new boiler was accounted separately under D&P No. 2601 dated 2nd July 1894.

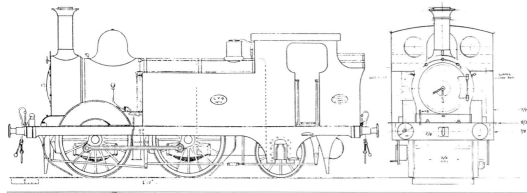

LEFT: Neilson 0-4-2T CV&HR No. 1 side and front elevation.

LOWER LEFT: In 1877 a 0-4-2 tank locomotive was ordered from Neilson & Company of Glasgow to work passenger services and it became No. 1 in the company's fleet. It was very similar to the GER 'T7' Class 0-4-2Ts. Here the locomotive is fitted with the auxiliary side water tanks by the smokebox, added by Hawthorn, Leslie & Company during a visit for overhaul in 1888. The cab was also modified from rounded corners to square corners and an almost flat top, and painted deep red. *Author's collection*

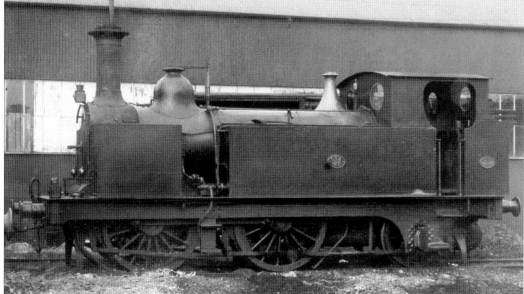

BELOW: CV&HR 0-4-2T No. 1, fitted with bell-top chimney with polished dome and auxiliary side tanks standing at Halstead on 3rd August 1909. The locomotive survived until 1923 but had been in a derelict condition for some time. It was considered life expired by the L&NER and withdrawn from traffic in the same year. Had the engine been taken into stock it would have been the sole member of L&NER Class 'Z6'. *LCGB/Ken Nunn*

No. 1 again visited Stratford Works in the last days of the nineteenth century, arriving in the yard on 18th December 1899 before entering the shops on 15th January 1900. The engine was not released until 10th May, after having the cylinders bored under Stratford D&P 5157. It spent two weeks in the Stratford area before departing for home territory on 24th May 1900. The engine received another new boiler after it entered Stratford shops on 22nd January 1903. It had in fact arrived in the yard on 13th December of the previous year but because of the Christmas holiday immediate transfer to the works was delayed. During this visit the engine was also equipped with Ramsbottom safety valves over the firebox in a GER style casing in place of the Salter spring balance valves on the dome and a single safety valve encased in a brass trumpet on the firebox (D&P 6749 of 4th March 1903). The work took longer than expected as the cylinders were again bored (D&P 6685) and No. 1 did not emerge from the shops until 15th July 1903. After running in and testing the engine departed for the CV&HR on 25th July.

By 1909 the locomotive was again running with a built-up chimney and in 1911 another rebuilding took place at Halstead works when the supplementary side tanks were removed and a bell top chimney refitted, the work being completed in early December. At the end of April 1913 No. 1 sustained a broken axle whilst working a passenger train, and although it was replaced the subject was still being investigated in July 1914. No. 1 was stopped for repairs in July 1915 and, as No. 5 was also needing attention, the Assistant Secretary negotiated with the GER for the hire of an

engine. The 0-4-2 tank locomotive subsequently received attention at Halstead whilst the 0-6-2 tank engine was sent to Stratford.

In the final years No. 1 was treated as spare engine on the CV&HR, covering as required the 2-4-2 tank locomotives on passenger work or the 0-6-2 tank engine on freight turns. At grouping the L&NER took the locomotive into stock but found the engine derelict and had no use for the diminutive machine. It was taken to Stratford and condemned on 23rd August 1923 without being allocated a new number or class, although had the locomotive survived No. 1 would have been the sole member of the 'Z6' Class. It was noted in a neglected state in the scrap lines at Stratford in January 1924, having outlasted the last of the GER '81' or 'T7' Class by thirty years!

To overcome a shortage of motive power in 1883 the CV&HR purchased from the Whitehaven Colliery Company a Beyer, Peacock 0-4-2 saddle rank locomotive dating from 1860 (Works No. 190), which had seen previous service with the North London Railway as their No. 42. Prior to transfer the engine was overhauled by Fletcher, Jennings of Parton, Whitehaven who fitted a cab and an ugly stove pipe chimney. The locomotive worked Colne Valley services until 1894 when it was sold to the South Hetton Coal Company. This photograph, believed to have been taken when the locomotive was offered for sale, shows the builders plate on the wheel arch. Having no bunker, coal was conveyed in bags in the cab and then placed in a fuel locker, which made for uncomfortable conditions for the footplate crew. *M. Root collection*

FORMER NLR 0-4-2 SADDLE TANK

During the intervening period, in 1883 the CV&HR purchased from the Whitehaven Colliery Company the former North London Railway 0-4-2 saddle tank goods locomotive No. 42. The engine dated from 1860 and was built by Beyer, Peacock & Company (Works No. 190). Five locomotives were originally constructed and prior to transfer to the CV&HR the engine was overhauled by Fletcher, Jennings of Parton, Whitehaven. It was recognised as number 2 in the Colne Valley fleet but never carried the number or a name. The engine had screw reversing gear with the wheel on the left-hand side of the cab, and radial axleboxes. On the NLR it had run without a cab but arrived on the CV with a cab, probably fitted by Fletcher, Jennings, and also sported an ugly stovepipe chimney in place of the Beyer, Peacock copper capped pattern. No. 2 only remained on the Essex line for eleven years before being sold to the South Hetton Coal Company in 1894. It survived until 1902 when it was withdrawn. The sale of this locomotive and the 2-4-0 tank

locomotive *Haverhill* was probably due to the association the Bailey Hawkins family had with both the railway and the coal company.

The leading dimensions of No. 2 were:

Cylinders 2 inside	16 ins x 24 ins
Heating surface	
Tubes	857.0 sq feet
Firebox	72.0 sq feet
Total	929.0 sq feet
Grate area	13.0 sq feet
Boiler pressure	120 psi
Coupled wheels	5 feet 0 ins
Trailing wheels	3 feet 6 ins
Wheelbase	14 feet 2 ins
Length over buffers	27 feet 6 ins
Water capacity	800 gallons
Coal capacity	15 cwt
Weight in working order	32 tons 10 cwt

HAWTHORN, LESLIE 2-4-2 SIDE TANKS

As the Manning, Wardle locomotives were becoming life expired and unable to work the increasingly heavy trains, George Copus, the General Manager, prepared specifications for a 2-4-2 tank locomotive class to work the passenger services; in 1887 two engines were built by Hawthorn, Leslie & Company (Works No's 2079 and 2080). Such was the success of the pair that a third was added in 1894 (Hawthorn, Leslie Works No. 2283). When delivered they carried no company running number but only the maker's number on the buffer beams. For identification they were

Former North London Railway 0-4-2ST.

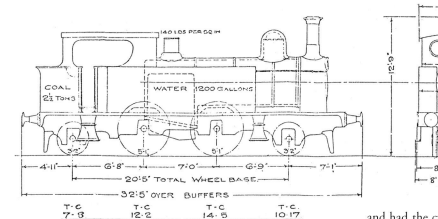

ABOVE: Hawthorn, Leslie 2-4-2T *Hedingham* in original condition with stovepipe chimney and dome on the second ring of the boiler soon after delivery in 1894. The locomotive is standing at Halstead and displays the dark crimson livery with black edging to the panels, lined out in black with incurved corners.

Author's collection

LEFT: Hawthorn, Leslie 2-4-2T, later L&NER Class 'F9'.

also named *Halstead*, *Colne* and *Hedingham* respectively, the name being displayed on straight brass nameplates attached centrally on the side tanks. When built the original boilers were constructed with barrels formed of three rings, with the dome positioned on the centre ring, giving the following heating surfaces: tubes 849.0 sq feet, firebox 70.0 sq feet, total 919.0 sq feet, grate area 15.3 square feet. The side tanks could take 1,200 gallons of water and the bunker capacity was 106 cubic feet. Stovepipe chimneys were fitted when new but were later replaced by copper capped chimneys. They had inside bearings on the leading and trailing wheels and solid ends to the coupling rods. The engines were painted red, the weight in working order was 43 tons 0 cwt, and they were fitted with the Westinghouse brake, with the pump attached in front of the right-hand side tank. *Colne* being fitted during a visit to Stratford Works in October 1889 (D&P 893) which authorised the fitting of Westinghouse brakework.

In 1892 *Colne* again received works attention at Stratford, arriving in the yard on 29th August before entering the shops on 5th September. The visit was fairly short with the cylinders being re-bored and the engine emerged on 19th November and returned to the Colne Valley two days later. Sister engine *Halstead* received works attention at Stratford the following year, arriving in the yard on 24th January 1893 before entering the shops on 16th February. Here it received light repairs (D&P 2107 of 1st February 1893)

and had the cylinders re-bored before emerging on 8th May. Trial trips showed minor problems and it was 25th May before *Halstead* returned to home territory. *Halstead* was back at Stratford for further repairs in April 1894 (D&P 2535 of 26th April).

Halstead received general repairs at Stratford in 1896 (D&P 3413 of 8th July 1896), which included the fitting of a new boiler (D&P 3490 of 31st August 1896). *Colne* was also sent to the GER works in the same year, arriving on 21st February and entering the shops five days later. The rebuilding of this locomotive was quite extensive for it was fitted with a new boiler (D&P 3301 of 17th April) and new cylinders and did not emerge until 27th February 1897. Trial running and testing continued for over a week and it was not dispatched back to Halstead until 8th March. *Colne* was back at Stratford on 18th May 1898 but it was over a month, on 21st June, before it entered the works for attention (D&P order 4457). After almost three months in the shops, *Colne* was released on 14th September 1898 and returned to the CV&HR a week later. *Halstead* was again at Stratford in 1899, arriving in the works yard on 2nd May and entering the works on 29th May for repairs (D&P 4861). It was released on 11th September 1899 and returned to the Colne Valley the same day. *Hedingham*, by now carrying the number 4, made a first visit to Stratford on 24th August 1901 and entered the shops five days later. An extensive rebuilding was carried out with a new boiler (D&P 6085 of 19th November 1901) and repairs (D&P 5985) so that it was 3rd June 1902 before it was released and returned to Halstead the same day. The following year *Halstead*, now carrying number 2, arrived in

Hawthorn, Leslie 2-4-2T *Hedingham* with large C and V insignia on the side tanks after rebuilding in 1902 with the dome on the leading boiler ring. The nameplates were later removed by which time the locomotive had become No. 4 in the CV&HR fleet. *Author's collection*

Stratford works yard on 11th July 1903 for general repair before entering the shops on 7th August. The engine was in the works for over four months receiving a new firebox and having the cylinders bored (D&P 6960) before emerging on 13th November. It was after Christmas, however, before No. 2 went back to the CV&HR on 28th December. *Colne*, now No. 3, was the last of the 2-4-2 tank engines to receive attention at Stratford, arriving on 8th August 1907 and entering the works twenty days later. It was released after repairs (D&P 9057) on 4th October and returned to Halstead on 14th October.

The new boilers had two-ring barrels with the dome on the front ring; at the same time the engines were equipped with the Westinghouse brake with the pump being attached in front of the right-hand side tank and fluted side rods. They were also repainted in a black livery relieved by a broad vermilion band edged on either side by a fine white line with the initials CV in large gilt letters on either side of the nameplates. The bell top chimney was also fitted, whilst the opening in the cab sides was equipped with sliding shutters for the protection of footplate crews in adverse weather conditions. As a general precaution, Stratford Works was authorised to obtain and keep in stock for *Halstead* two pairs of tyres for the driving wheels and two pairs of tyres for the radial wheels by D&P order dated 20th February 1908. About 1902/3 the works numbers were removed and the engines numbered, *Halstead* becoming No. 2, *Colne* No. 3 and *Hedingham* No. 4.

The trio of engines still carried nameplates in 1911 and in May 1912 negotiations were conducted with Hawthorn, Leslie to provide a new set of cylinders for No. 4 *Hedingham*. Their quote of £128 was accepted but other fittings were included in the price. It was, however, deemed necessary for the locomotive to undergo heavier repairs and an approach was made to Hudswell, Clarke in July 1912 to obtain tenders. The firm replied in August quoting a price of £250 13s 3d. By September work had started on No. 4 at Halstead, including attention to the boiler, and the engine was still under repair on 26th November 1912. In November 1913 Hawthorn, Leslie provided another set of cylinders at a cost of £132 16s 0d. In December 1915 a further set of cylinders were ordered for No. 3, although the price had increased to £156 – but by 14th August 1916, when the account was settled, the price had increased

yet again to £167 10s 4d. In September 1916 the proposed overhaul of No. 3 at Stratford by the GER was deferred and it was decided to tackle the general repairs at Halstead. This was a much slower process and although much material was to hand the company had to procure a crank axle from Hawthorn, Leslie at a cost of £100 0s 1d in November.

The locomotives settled down to regular service and in June 1917 a new blast pipe was ordered from Hawthorn, Leslie at a cost of £6 19s 9d. By August 1918 the firm was supplying a new set of slide bars at a cost of £5 7s 3d. On 14th August 1918 it was reported that the tube plates on 2-4-2 tank locomotives No's 2 and 3 were leaking, as they were on 0-6-2 locomotive No. 5. It was agreed as a matter of urgency to send No. 2 to Stratford Works for overhaul as it was approaching the due date for general overhaul, whilst patch repairs would be made on the other engines. Hawthorn, Leslie provided another set of slide bars in September 1918 at a cost of £7 15s 0d, whilst Westinghouse Brake & Signal Company staff visited Halstead to effect repairs to brake pumps, charging £21 3s 6d for the service. During this period, Hawthorn, Leslie had also provided new sets of tyres for the three engines and the account, valued at £309 13s 6d, was not settled until 16th July 1919. No. 2 failed early in the last week of 1919 after running a low mileage since attention at Stratford and entered Halstead Works for repairs. Engineers from Hudswell, Clarke, who were inspecting 0-6-2T No. 5 for firebox repairs, also examined No. 2. On 26th February 1920 the firm quoted a combined price for cutting part out of the old firebox and refitting the section on No. 5 and the fitting of a new firebox on No. 2 at £706. At the same time the General Manager was instructed to obtain quotes for a set of copper patches for the new firebox on No. 3. By May 1920 a quote for a set of copper plate patches from Messrs Virians had been accepted after the GER Engineer thought the price reasonable.

During overhauls at Stratford No. 3 acquired a GER-type smokebox door and GER-style safety valve casing. Numbers 2 and 4 also received the GER safety valve casing, whilst 2 and 3 acquired GER-pattern dome covers – but No. 4 retained the original dome cover until scrapping.

The standard dimensions of the three locomotives when taken over by the L&NER were:

CV&HR No. 3 formerly *Colne* at Stratford waiting shopping in April 1924. The locomotive still carries the wheel release for the smokebox door.
Author's collection

Cylinders	2 inside	16 ins x 24 ins	
Motion		Stephenson with slide valves	
Boiler	Max diameter outside	4 feet 2 ins	
	Barrel length	9 feet 8 ins	
	Firebox length outside	5 feet 1 ins	
Heating surface			
	Tubes	225 x 1⅝ ins	961.13 sq feet
	Firebox		77.36 sq feet
	Total		1,038. 49 sq feet
Grate area		14.58 sq feet	
Boiler pressure		140 psi	
Leading wheels		3 feet 2 ins	
Coupled wheels		5 feet 1 inch	
Trailing wheels		3 feet 2 ins	
Tractive effort		11,986 lbs	
Length over buffers		32 feet 5 ins	
Wheelbase		20 feet 5 ins	
Weight in working order		44 tons 12 cwt	
Max axle loading		14 tons 5 cwt	
Coal capacity		2 tons 10 cwt	
Water capacity		1,200 gallons	

At grouping the trio was designated to L&NER Class 'F9' but No. 4 was beyond economic repair and was condemned on 20th September 1923. No. 2 was renumbered 8312 in June 1924, whilst No. 3 became 8313 in October of the same year. In 1923 No. 2 was running with its safety valves set at 150 psi but this was reduced to 140 psi in October 1927. No. 8312 was equipped with steam heating equipment at Stratford in December 1924 and received general repairs, entering Stratford Works on 18th June and being released on 21st October 1927. No. 8313 entered Stratford Works for general repairs on 4th April 1924 but was not released until 7th October. The engine was back at Stratford in December 1924 for fitting of steam heating equipment. No. 8313 was condemned and withdrawn from traffic on 3rd December 1927, but No. 8312 soldiered on after general overhaul, working Colne Valley services until January 1930, when it was the last of the CV&HR locomotives to be withdrawn on 13th of the month. Westinghouse brakes were standard on the CV&HR and none of the locomotives absorbed by the L&NER were fitted with steam or vacuum brake equipment.

The three 2-4-2Ts locomotives were absorbed by the L&NER, but only two, No's 2 and 3, were taken into stock – renumbered 8312 and 8313 and included in new Class 'F9'. No. 4 was scrapped without renumbering whilst No. 8313 was subsequently withdrawn from traffic in December 1927 and No. 8312 in January 1930, shown here awaiting scrapping in June of the same year. *Author's collection*

HUDSWELL, CLARKE 0-6-2 SIDE TANK

The rebuilding of bridges and installation of heavier permanent way enabled the company to introduce into service their most powerful locomotive in 1908. Built by Hudswell, Clarke & Company (Works No. 836) specifically to handle the increasing brick traffic between Sible and Castle Hedingham and Chappel, CV&HR No. 5 was a 0-6-2 tank locomotive with high running plate and very deep buffer beams. The rear wheels were carried in radial axleboxes. The engine was painted in the new style of black with the initials CV&HR in gilt on the side tanks, company crest transfer on the side of the cab and brass number plate picked out in vermilion. The *Halstead Gazette* enthused:

> *they have just added to their rolling stock a fine new engine. It is a six wheel couple – a system that is largely used in Wales for hill climbing. It is fitted with all the latest improvements. This addition to the company's engines will enable all repairs to the others to be carried out without any inconvenience.*

After entering traffic little alteration or attention was made to the engine until Hudswell, Clarke fitters carried out repairs at Halstead in September 1911 at a cost of £250. The firm supplied axleboxes for the locomotive in February 1914 at a cost of £45 12s 0d. No. 5 was stopped for overhaul in August 1915 before travelling to the GER Stratford Works, arriving in the yard on 20th September 1915 and entering the shops over two months later on 30th November. The boiler pressure was then recorded at 160 psi but the engine was stripped (D&P 4771) and received general repair (D&P 4772). On 28th February it was reported repairs were nearing completion and the engine finally emerged on 6th March 1916. No. 5 returned to the Colne Valley line on 20th March. In February 1919 a cylinder failure in traffic caused consternation and it was thought it would be necessary to order a new set of cylinders for the locomotive. After examination the damage was found to be superficial and only required new cylinder covers and piston rings, which Hudswell, Clarke supplied in April at a cost of £9 16s 6d and £9 4s 0d respectively. The engine was again in trouble in May 1919 when the firebox required attention. The board was undecided whether to send for the GER to carry out repairs or offer it to Hudswell, Clarke. By November it had been decided the engine required a new copper firebox and steel tubes and arrangements were made to have the work carried out by the GER at Stratford. It was evident the company required Stratford to carry out more than firebox repairs, for a new set of cylinders were also obtained from Hudswell, Clarke at a cost of £221 12s 10d. As recorded earlier, in February Hudswell, Clarke quoted a price of £706 for cutting out the old firebox on No. 5 and fitting a new firebox on 2-4-2T No. 2. In

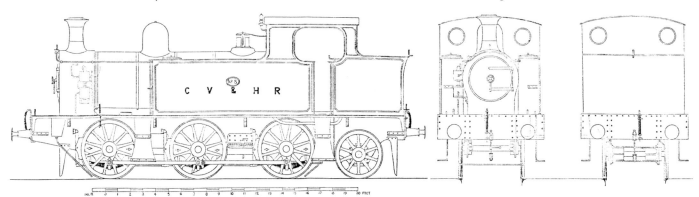

Hudswell, Clarke 0-6-2T CV&HR No. 5 side elevation, front and rear elevations.

Hudswell, Clarke & Company Limited official photograph of 0-6-2T No. 5 in photographic grey livery.

April 1920 work on No. 5 was progressing and by the end of the month was completed. On 6th January and 10th February 1921 the CV&HR settled the account for the repairs costing £300 and £200, which included attention to No. 2. The 0-6-2T received little further attention save the fitting of a blast pipe obtained from Hudswell, Clarke in December 1921 for £5 10s 0d.

The locomotive was never re-boilered although the pressure was reduced to 150 psi, and by grouping the boiler feed arrangement had been amended from delivery via the faceplate to the method favoured by the GER of side feed through the clack box on each side of the boiler near the front end of the barrel. The injectors were then mounted on the footplating in front of the side tanks, with steam being taken from the cocks high up on the boiler. The locomotive was also fitted with the Westinghouse brake with the pump being attached to the right-hand side of the smokebox.

At grouping the 0-6-2 tank locomotive became the sole member of L&NER 'N18' Class but was not renumbered 8314 until March 1924 during a general overhaul at Stratford Works. It never returned to the Colne Valley line and spent much of its remaining years shunting at Colchester. During this period No. 8314 worked for short periods on the Wivenhoe to Brightlingsea branch services but was unpopular with the footplate staff; it was finally withdrawn from traffic on 18th January 1928 and cut up at Stratford in the same month.

The leading dimensions of the Hudswell, Clarke 0-6-2 tank locomotive at grouping were:

Cylinders	2 inside	16 ins x 24 ins	
Motion		Stephenson and slide valves	
Boiler	Max diameter outside	4 feet 3 ins	
	Barrel length	9 feet 8⅜ ins	
	Firebox outside length	4 feet 10¾ ins	
Heating surface			
	Tubes	209 x 1⅝ ins	887.2 sq feet
	Firebox		87.2 sq feet
	Total		974.4 sq feet
Grate area		14.65 sq feet	
Boiler pressure		150 psi	
Coupled wheels		4 feet 6 ins	
Trailing wheels		3 feet 8 ins	
Tractive effort		14,507 lbs	
Length over buffers		32 feet 11½ ins	
Wheelbase		20 feet 0 ins	
Weight in working order		50 tons 3 cwt	
Max axle loading		14 tons 11 cwt	
Coal capacity		2 tons 10 cwt	
Water capacity		1,300 gallons	

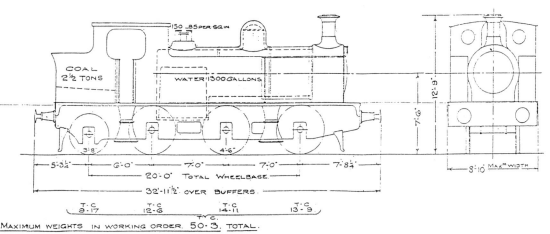

Left: Hudswell, Clarke 0-6-2T No. 8314 L&NER Class 'N18'.

Below: CV&HR 0-6-2T No. 5 built by Hudswell, Clarke and introduced into traffic in 1908 essentially to handle the extensive brick traffic emanating from Sible and Castle Hedingham and the brickfields at Purls Hill.
Author's collection

The sole member of L&NER 'N18' Class 0-6-2T ex CV&HR No. 5, by now renumbered 8314. The locomotive built by Hudswell, Clarke in 1908, shown ex works at Stratford in 1924, was used for a time on the Wivenhoe to Brightlingsea branch and shed shunting at Colchester before withdrawal in January 1928.
Author's collection

In 1906 a new livery was adopted by the CV&HR for their locomotive fleet. The engines were painted a standard black lined out with a broad vermilion band edged on either side by a fine white line. The initials C V were provided in large gilt capitals on the tank sides with brass nameplate, if carried between the letters.

THE GER 'T7' CLASS

The CV&HR motive power situation had little spare capacity and when locomotives were under repair or in works the company was forced to hire engines from the GER. In 1886 and 1887, and again in 1890 to 1892, the main line company provided members of the 'T7' Class and 'K9' Class 0-4-2 tank locomotives to cover as they were very similar in dimensions to the CV&HR No. 1. The 'T7' Class was built especially for light branch traffic

and designed by Samuel W. Johnson, who later gained fame on the Midland Railway. Fifteen locomotives were built between 1871 and 1875. The first three, No's 81 to 83, were actually prototypes of the 'T7's but were included in the total class. No. 15 is recorded hauling CV&HR services but all were withdrawn by 1894, with No. 15 one of the last survivors.

The leading dimensions of the 'T7' Class were:

Cylinders	2 inside	15 ins x 22 ins	
Motion		Stephenson with slide valves	
Boiler	Max diameter	3 feet 10 ins	
	Barrel length	9 feet 1 in	
	Firebox	4 feet 4½ ins	
Heating surface			
	Tubes	204 x 1½ ins	754.0 sq feet
	Firebox		76.0 sq feet
	Total		830.0 sq feet
Grate area		12.75 sq feet	
Boiler pressure		140 psi	
Driving wheels		5 feet 3 ins	
Trailing wheels		3 feet 7 ins	
Length over buffers		23 feet 7 ins	
Wheelbase		14 feet 6 ins	
Weight in working order		33 tons 12 cwt	
		30 tons 19 cwt*	
Water capacity		750 gallons	
		500 gallons*	

NOTE: *   No's 81 to 83

THE GER 'K9' CLASS

The 'K9' Class 0-4-2 tank engines designed by William Adams totalled ten in number and were all built in 1877 and 1878. No's 7, 9, 21, 23 and 24 were recorded working Colne Valley passenger services and the class was withdrawn between 1903 and 1907. No. 7 was withdrawn in 1907, No. 9 in 1903, No. 21 in 1904 and No's 23 and 24 in 1905. Ironically they were the only locomotives built at Stratford while Adams was in office. At first only a hand brake was supplied but the class was later fitted with

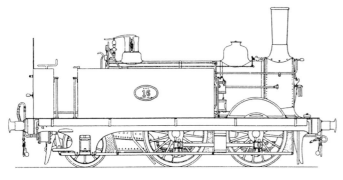

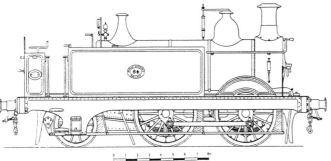

GER 'T7' Class 0-4-2T.

ABOVE: GER 'K9' Class 0-4-2T locomotives were used on Colne Valley services in the event of a shortage of CV&HR engines including No. 23 which is shown at Stratford in 1905. *Ken Nunn*

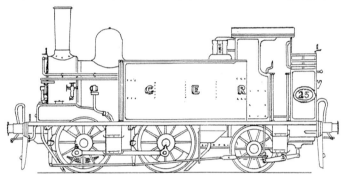

GER 'K9' Class 0-4-2T.

the Westinghouse brake. A half cab was originally provided when the locomotives were built, but after a few years back weather plates were fitted and later the roof was extended to completely cover the footplate.

The principal dimensions of the 'K9' Class were:

Cylinders	2 inside	15 ins x 22 ins
Motion		Stephenson with slide valves
Boiler	Max diameter	4 feet 2 ins
	Barrel length	9 feet 1 in
Heating surface		
	Tubes	203 x 1¾ ins 874.87 sq feet
	Firebox	75.43 sq feet
	Total	950.30 sq feet
Grate area		12.30 sq feet
Boiler pressure		140 psi
Driving wheels		4 feet 10 ins
Trailing wheels		3 feet 8 ins
Wheelbase		14 feet 0 ins
Weight in working order		38 tons 11 cwt
Water capacity		850 gallons
Coal capacity		15 cwt

THE 'M15'/'F4' CLASS

In 1901, with two locomotives out of traffic waiting repairs, the CV&HR was forced to hire a locomotive from the GER. The engine provided was 'M15' Class 2-4-2 tank locomotive No. 240 which was very similar in dimensions to the CV&HR 2-4-2 tank

engines. On another occasion sister locomotive No. 149 was sent to work the services. The initial members of the 'M15' Class entered service between 1884 and 1887 to the design of T.W. Worsdell. Between 1903 and 1909 a further 120 locomotives were built, and from 1911 until 1920 the GER rebuilt thirty engines with higher boiler pressure and designated them 'M15R'. The earliest built locomotives were all condemned by 1929, whilst the L&NER reclassified the 'M15's to Class 'F4' and the rebuilt engines Class 'F5'. They were nicknamed 'Gobblers' because the original locomotives had a voracious appetite for coal, and although improvements were made the name persisted. Ironically, after grouping the 'F4' and 'F5' Class were officially restricted from working on the Colne Valley line.

GER No.	L&NER 1924	L&NER 1946	BR No.	WITHDRAWN
149	7149	—	—	May 1931
240	7240	—	—	June 1937

The leading dimensions of the 'F4' Class were:

Cylinders	2 inside	17½ ins x 24 ins
Motion		Stephenson with slide valves
Boiler	Max diameter	4 feet 2 ins
	Barrel length	10 feet 2½ ins
	Firebox	5 feet 5 ins
Heating surface		
	Tubes	227 x 1⅝ ins 1,018.0 sq feet
	Firebox	98.4 sq feet
	Total	1,116.4 sq feet
Grate area		15.3 sq feet
Boiler pressure		160 psi
Leading wheels		3 feet 9 ins
Coupled wheels		5 feet 4 ins
Trailing wheels		3 feet 9 ins
Tractive effort		15,618 lbs
Length over buffers		34 feet 10 ins
Wheelbase		23 feet 0 ins
Weight in working order		51 tons 11 cwt
Max axle loading		14 tons 18 cwt
Water capacity		1,200 gallons
Coal capacity		3 tons 10 cwt

The hire of a GER engine during the autumn of 1915 cost the CV&HR company £350 including a proportion for locomotive repairs, the bill being settled in January 1916.

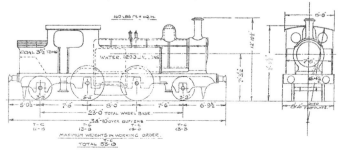

GER 'M15' Class, later L&NER 'F4' Class, 2-4-2T.

ECR Stothert & Slaughter 0-6-0 Tender Engines

The GER freight train service between Cambridge and Wivenhoe via the Colne Valley line operated between 1865 and 1867, and was entrusted to two Stothert & Slaughter 0-6-0 tender locomotives with open cabs numbered 1570 and 1580. They were a pair of five goods locomotives built in March and April 1846 for the ECR, numbered 97 to 101, but soon renumbered 155 to 159, and delivered with 6-wheel tenders. In 1858 the tenders received new tanks giving a greater water capacity and although the first two engines were early casualties for scrapping, No's 157 to 159 were placed on the duplicate list in 1864 becoming No's 1570, 1580 and 1590 respectively. The first two were rebuilt with new boilers in 1866 whilst allocated to Cambridge to work goods trains to Colchester via Sudbury and the CV&HR. No. 1590 was scrapped in April 1873, No. 1580 in August 1880 and 1570 in October 1883. The leading dimensions were:

Cylinders	2 inside	16 ins x 24 ins
Boiler	Outside diameter	3 feet 9 ins
	Length	10 feet 2 ins
	Firebox	4 feet 8 ins
Heating surface		tubes 152 x 1⅞ ins
Driving wheels		5 feet 0 ins
Wheelbase	Locomotive	13 feet 8 ins
Water capacity		1,350 gallons
Weight in working order		24 tons 18 cwt*
Max axle loading		10 tons 3 cwt*
Note: * after rebuilding.		

The 'E22'/'J65' Class

Immediately after grouping, former GER locomotives were drafted on to the Colne Valley line diagrams as replacements for withdrawn CV&HR locomotives. Initially GER 'E22' Class 0-6-0 tank locomotives, reclassified by the L&NER to 'J65', took over some of the services, with usually one of the class outbased at Halstead and later Haverhill. The engines were built to the design of James Holden and ten were introduced in 1889 for light branch duties. Four years later a further ten, built with detailed differences entered service. Many of the class were sent to work on the Fenchurch Street to Blackwall services in East London with the result that they were quickly nicknamed the 'Blackwall Tanks'. Soon after grouping in 1923 No. 7254 was working the line and on 13th June 1929 No's 7248, 7249, 7250 and 7252 were allocated to the Colne Valley workings. By 1934 the 'J65's had been replace by 'J15' Class locomotives No's 7523 and 7888. 'J65' Class locomotives known to have worked Colne Valley services are shown below.

GER No.	L&NER 1924 No.	L&NER 1946 No.	BR No.	Withdrawn
151	7151	—	—	July 1937
152	7152	—	—	October 1935
248	7248	—	—	May 1936
249	7249	—	—	July 1937
250	7250	8214	68214	October 1956
252	7252	—	—	August 1935
254	7254	—	—	June 1937

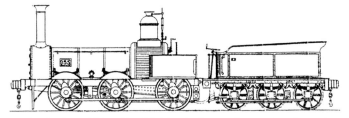

ECR Stothert & Slaughter 0-6-0 tender locomotive used on through ECR freight trains via the CV&HR.

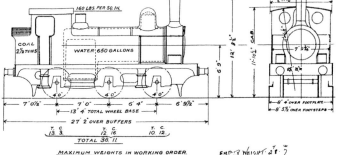

Above: GER 'E22' Class, later L&NER 'J65' Class 0-6-0T.

Left: GER 'E22' Class, later L&NER 'J65' Class, 0-6-0T No. 7249 at Stratford in April 1937. The locomotive was one of several allocated to work the Colne Valley line services after grouping but they were not popular with the enginemen, who frequently found they required topping up with water en route, a factor which occasionally led to late running.

Author's collection

The leading dimensions of the 'J65' Class were:

Cylinders		14 ins x 20 ins	
Motion		Stephenson with slide valves	
Boiler	Max diameter	4 feet 2 ins	
	Barrel length	9 feet 1 in	
	Firebox	4 feet 6 ins	
Heating surface			
	Tubes	227 x 1⅝ ins	909.40 sq feet
	Firebox		78.00 sq feet
	Total		987.40 sq feet
Grate area		12.40 sq feet	
Boiler pressure		160 psi	
Driving wheels		4 feet 0 ins	
Tractive effort		11,106 lbs	
Length over buffers		27 feet 2 ins	
Wheelbase		13 feet 4 ins	
Weight in working order		36 tons 11 cwt	
Max axle loading		13 tons 3 cwt	
Water capacity		650 gallons	
Coal capacity		2 tons 10 cwt	

THE 'Y65'/'F7' CLASS

Another class associated with the line soon after grouping was the former GER 'Y65' Class 2-4-2 tank locomotives designed by S.D. Holden and introduced into service in 1909 and 1910. Built for light passenger branch duties to replace the 'E22' Class they were the least successful of Holden's 2-4-2 tank classes. Twelve locomotives, No's 1300 to 1311, were constructed at Stratford Works and their small boiler and enormous cab soon earned them the nickname of 'Crystal Palaces'. The L&NER reclassified the class to 'F7' and renumbered them 8300 to 8311 inclusive. The Cambridge District

ABOVE: GER 'Y65' Class, later L&NER 'F7' Class 2-4-2T.

RIGHT: 'F7' Class 2-4-2T No. 8300 was employed on Colne Valley services after grouping, working alongside the surviving CV&HR 2-4-2Ts until the advent of the 'J15' Class 0-6-0 tender locomotives. This was the pioneer member of the GER 'Y65' Class, built in 1909/10. With No. 8301, the locomotive differed from other members of the class by having contoured front and rear windows in the cab.   *Author's collection*

occasionally allocated 'F7' Class engines on Colne Valley duties in the late 1920s and No's 8300, 8301 and 8306 were regularly employed for some months but increasing loads found they were seriously underpowered and they were transferred away. The locomotives known to have operated services included:

GER No.	L&NER 1924 No.	L&NER 1942 No.	L&NER 1946 No.	WITHDRAWN
1300	8300	—	—	August 1938
1301	8301	7593	—	April 1943
1302	8302	—	—	May 1931
1306	8306	—	—	April 1931
1308	8308	7597	7093	November 1948
1310	8310	7598	7094	November 1948

The leading dimensions of the 'F7' Class were:

Cylinders		15 ins x 22 ins	
Motion		Stephenson with slide valves	
Boiler	Max diameter	3 feet 11½ ins	
	Barrel	9 feet 1 in	
	Firebox	4 feet 6 ins	
Heating surface			
	Tubes	199 x 1⅝ ins	797.2 sq feet
	Firebox		75.7 sq feet
	Total		872.9 sq feet
Grate area		12.2 sq feet	
Boiler pressure		160 psi	
Leading wheels		3 feet 6 ins	
Coupled wheels		4 feet 10 ins	
Trailing wheels		3 feet 6 ins	
Tractive effort		11,607 lbs	
Length over buffers		30 feet 11 ins	
Wheelbase		19 feet 6 ins	
Weight in working order		45 tons 14 cwt	
Max axle loading		14 tons 3 cwt	
Water capacity		1,000 gallons	
Coal capacity		2 tons 0 cwt	

THE 'T26'/'E4' CLASS

After the closure of Halstead shed it was normal for the line to be worked by tender locomotives and from time to time the services were hauled by the former GER 'T26' Class 2-4-0 tender locomotives nicknamed 'Intermediates'. The class of 100 was built to the design of James Holden at Stratford between 1891 and 1902. Most were assigned for mixed traffic duties, long cross-country routes and slower traffic on the main line. The L&NER reclassified the class to 'E4', but with the absence of turntables they were unpopular with footplate staff, especially when required to work tender first in one direction. Many were withdrawn in the 1920s and early 1930s, after which visits to the line were spasmodic although they were regularly diagrammed on Stour Valley trains. Locomotives which worked on Colne Valley services, included those below.

GER No.	L&NER 1924 No.	L&NER 1946 No.	BR No.	WITHDRAWN
417	7417	—	—	January 1930
427	7427	2780	62780	September 1955
430	7430	—	—	April 1926
432	7432	—	—-	July 1929
433	7433	—	—	April 1927
436	7436	—	—	June 1929
438	7438	—	—	May 1926
454	7454	—	—	June 1928
456	7456	—	—	December 1928
459	7459	—	—	March 1935
460	7460	—	—	April 1929
473	7473	—	—	December 1935
479	7479	—	—	March 1938
500	7500	—	—	June 1936
502	7502	—	—	January 1939
504	7504	—	—	November 1938

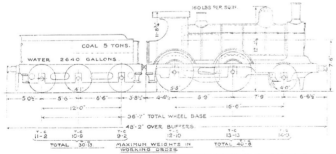

ABOVE: A GER 'T26' Class, later L&NER 'E4' Class 2-4-0.

RIGHT: 'E4' Class 2-4-0 No 62789 heads the 1.22pmSO Cambridge to Colchester train via the Stour Valley at Haverhill on 6th July 1857. Standing behind the train, a 'J15' Class 0-6-0 working tender first is at the head of the connecting Colne Valley service.
Ian L Wright

The principal dimensions of the 'E4' Class were:

Cylinders		17½ ins x 24 ins	
Motion		Stephenson with slide valves	
Boiler	Max diameter outside	4 feet 4 ins	
	Barrel length	10 feet 0 ins	
	Firebox	6 feet 0 ins	
Heating surface			
	Tubes	242 x 1⅝ ins	1,063.8 sq feet
	Firebox		100.9 sq feet
	Total		1,164.7 sq feet
Grate area		18.0 sq feet	
Boiler pressure		160 lbs psi	
Leading wheels		4 feet 0 ins	
Driving wheels		5 feet 8 ins	
Tractive effort		14,700 lbs	
Length over buffers		48 feet 2 ins*	
Wheelbase		16 feet 6 ins	
Weight in working order		40 tons 6 cwt	
Max axle loading		14 tons 3 cwt	
Tender	Wheelbase	12 feet 0 ins	
	Wheel diameter	4 feet 1 in	
	Weight in working order		30 tons 13 cwt
	Water capacity	2,640 gallons	
	Coal capacity	5 tons	

NOTE: * Engine and tender.

THE 'Y14'/'J15' CLASS

From the late 1890s occasional GER goods services again worked across the Colne Valley route by special arrangement and because of the limited capacity of the underbridges the trains were hauled by one of the ubiquitous 'Y14' Class 0-6-0 tender locomotives, originally introduced in 1883 to the design of T.W. Worsdell. The success of the design resulted in a total of 289 entering service by the time construction of the class ceased in 1913. All except nineteen of the class were constructed at Stratford Works, the others being built by Sharp, Stewart & Company. They were later classified 'J15' by the L&NER and their low RA1 route availability made them ideal for working across the branch after grouping. In 1934 and 1935 new side-window cabs were fitted to five 'J15' Class locomotives to provided protection for enginemen, especially when working services on the Colne Valley line and former GER branches where some tender first running was necessary. At the same time the engines were fitted with vacuum ejectors, steam heating pipes and balanced wheels. No's 7523 and 7941 were fitted in July 1934,

No. 7888 in August 1934, No. 7911 in September 1934 and No. 7512 in January 1935, and thereafter these locomotive regularly maintained the passenger services. Other locomotives of the class worked excursion trains from Cambridge to Clacton, as well as the regular goods services and out of course engineering trains.

Usually the class were limited to four of five coach trains but on Sunday 9th July 1939, No. 7553 worked an excursion from Ramsey East to Clacton, a distance of 95 miles, running non-stop from Cambridge to Colchester via Sudbury except for a water stop at Haverhill North, with a tail load of 270 tons. On the return run the locomotive hauled the train via the shorter Colne Valley route.

The following 'J15' Class locomotives shown right are known to have operated on the Colne Valley line.

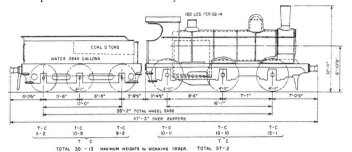

GER 'Y14' Class, later L&NER 'J15' Class 0-6-0.

GER No.	L&NER 1924 No.	L&NER 1946 No.	BR No	Withdrawn
512	7512	5432	65432*	March 1958
523	7523	5438	65438*	June 1958
542	7542	5470	65470	December 1959
545	7545	5473	65473	March 1960
548	7548	5476	65476	September 1962
551	7551	5479	65479	August 1960
553	7553	5451	65451	September 1959
558	7558	5456	65456	September 1958
567	7567	5465	65465	September 1962
570	7570	5468	65468	December 1959
640	7640	5440	65440	October 1960
641	7641	5441	65441	October 1958
643	7643	5443	65443	December 1959
645	7645	5445	65445	August 1962
648	7648	5448	65448	March 1960
888	7888	5391	65391*	December 1958
911	7911	5405	65405*	August 1958
941	7941	5424	65424*	December 1959

NOTE: *   Fitted with side window cab and balanced wheels.

An animated scene at Halstead as railway enthusiasts jostle for the best position to take photographs of 'J15' Class 0-6-0 No. 65440 at the head of the Railway Correspondence & Travel Society 'Northern and Eastern' railtour train on Sunday 10th August 1958.   *J. Spencer Gilks*

The leading dimensions of the class were:

Cylinders　2 inside　　　17½ ins x 24 ins
Motion　　　　　　　　Stephenson with slide valves
Boiler　Max diameter　　4 feet 4 ins
　　　　Barrel length　　10 feet 0 ins
　　　　Firebox outside length　6 feet 0 ins
Heating surface
　　　　Tubes　　242 x 1⅝ ins　1,063.8 sq feet
　　　　Firebox　　　　　　105.5 sq feet
　　　　Total　　　　　　1,169.3 sq feet
Grate area　　　　　　17.9 sq feet
Boiler pressure　　　　160 psi
Coupled wheels　　　　4 feet 11 ins
Tender wheels　　　　　4 feet 1 in
Tractive effort　　　　16,942 lbs
Length over buffers
　　　　Engine and tender 47 feet 3 ins
Wheelbase Engine　　　16 feet 1 in
　　　　Tender　　　　　12 feet 0 ins
　　　　Total　　　　　　35 feet 2 ins
Weight in working order
　　　　Engine　　　　　37 tons 2 cwt
　　　　Tender　　　　　30 tons 13 cwt
　　　　Total　　　　　　67 tons 15 cwt
Max axle load　　　　　13 tons 10 cwt
Water capacity　　　　2,640 gallons
Coal capacity　　　　　5 tons

THE 'G58'/'J17' CLASS

To assist with the movement of heavy armament trains immediately before, during and after World War Two, 0-6-0 tender locomotives of Class 'J17' and 'J19' were permitted to travel across the branch between Chappel and Earls Colne. Their introduction required the Civil Engineer to strengthen the permanent way between the two points but no work was needed strengthening underbridges, and strict instructions were issued prohibiting the classes west of Earls Colne. The introduction of eight-coupled heavy goods locomotives on the Whitemoor to Temple Mills and other freight services gradually released these 0-6-0s for cross-country and branch line freight workings. The sixty Class 'J17's built to the design of James Holden were originally introduced from 1900 as GER Class 'F48' with round topped fireboxes, with a further batch of thirty engines produced with Belpaire fireboxes as Class 'G58' from 1905 to 1911. Thereafter some of the earlier engines were rebuilt with Belpaire fireboxes and reclassified. After grouping the 'F48's became L&NER Class 'J16' and the 'G58's L&NER Class 'J17' but by 1932 all round topped

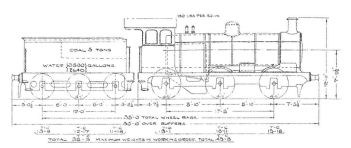
GER 'G58' Class, later L&NER 'J17' Class 0-6-0.

firebox locomotives had been rebuilt with Belpaire fireboxes as Class 'J17' and the Class 'J16' became extinct. Locomotives known to have worked between Chappel and Earls Colne were:

GER No.	L&NER 1924 No.	L&NER 1946 No.	BR No.	WITHDRAWN
1153	8153	5503	65503	August 1960
1163	8163	5513	65513	March 1961
1170	8170	5520	65520	February 1951
1172	8172	5522	65522	September 1958
1181	8181	5531	65531	April 1959
1189	8189	5539	65539	August 1960
1200	8200	—	—	November 1944 +
1214	8214	5564	65564	August 1960

NOTE:　+　No. 8200 was withdrawn as a result of extensive damage sustained in a German V2 rocket explosion at Channelsea, Stratford.

The principal dimensions of the 'J17' Class were:

Cylinders　2 inside　　　19 ins x 26 ins
Motion　　　　　　　　Stephenson with slide valves
Boiler　Max diameter outside　4 feet 9 ins
　　　　Barrel length　　11 feet 9 ins
Firebox outside length　　7 feet 0 ins
Heating surface
　　　　Tubes　156 x 1¾ ins　863.5 sq feet
　　　　Flues　18 x 5 ins　282.7 sq feet
　　　　Firebox　　　　　117.7 sq feet
　　　　Total evaporative　1,263.9 sq feet
　　　　Superheater 18 x 1³⁄₃₂ ins　154.8 sq feet
　　　　Total　　　　　　1,418.7 sq feet
Grate area　　　　　　21.24 sq feet
Boiler pressure　　　　180 psi
Coupled wheels　　　　4 feet 11 ins
Tender wheels　　　　　4 feet 1 in
Tractive effort　　　　24,340 lbs
Length over buffers　　50 feet 6 ins*
Wheelbase
　　　　Engine　　　　　17 feet 8 ins
　　　　Tender　　　　　12 feet 0 ins
　　　　Total　　　　　　38 feet 0 ins
Weight in working order
　　　　Engine　　　　　45 tons 8 cwt
　　　　Tender　　　　　38 tons 5 cwt
　　　　Total　　　　　　83 tons 13 cwt
Max axle loading　　　16 tons 11 cwt
Water capacity　　　　3,500 gallons
　　　　　　　　　　　2,640 gallons
Coal capacity　　　　　5 tons
NOTE: *　Engine and tender.

THE 'J19' CLASS

'J19' Class 0-6-0 tender locomotives were also authorised to work trains between Chappel and Earls Colne but initially excluding Earls Colne goods yard, although during hostilities this instruction was blatantly ignored. A.J. Hill designed ten 'E72' Class 0-6-0 goods locomotives for the GER and introduced them into traffic in 1912, followed by twenty-five 'T77' Class engines between 1916 and 1920. They were used on main line freight workings until displaced by larger and more modern locomotives in the 1930s. Between 1934 and 1939 all thirty-five were rebuilt by the L&NER with larger boilers and round topped fireboxes similar to the rebuilt Claud Hamilton 'D16/3' Class 4-4-0 tender locomotives. Known in the rebuilt form as Class 'J19/2', the suffix /2 was usually ignored. Like the 'J17' Class, they were officially banned from the Colne Valley line but heavy military traffic destined for local airfields, which often overloaded the 'J15' Class locomotives, found the management allowing the class to work the eastern end of the line. Locomotives known to have worked to Earls Colne included:

GER No	L&NER 1924 No.	L&NER 1946 No.	BR No.	WITHDRAWN
1246	8246	4646	64646	October 1961
1147	8147	4657	64657	September 1962

The leading dimensions of the 'J19' Class were:

Cylinders	2 inside	20 ins x 28 ins	
Motion		Stephenson with 10 in piston valves	
Boiler	Max diameter outside	5 feet 1½ ins	
	Barrel length	11 feet 9 ins	
Firebox	Outside length	7 feet 0 ins	
Heating surface			
	Tubes	172 x 1¾ ins	957.1 sq feet
	Flues	21 x 5¼ ins	346.3 sq feet
	Firebox		126.0 sq feet
	Total evaporative		1,429.4 sq feet
	Superheater	21 x 1¼ ins	302.5 sq feet
	Total		1,731.9 sq feet
Grate area		21.4 sq feet	
Boiler pressure		160 psi	
Coupled wheels		4 feet 11 ins	
Tender wheels		4 feet 1 in	
Tractive effort		25,817 lbs	
Length over buffers		52 feet 4 ins*	
Wheelbase			
	Engine	17 feet 8 ins	
	Tender	12 feet 0 ins	
	Total	38 feet 7 ins	
Weight in working order			
	Engine	50 tons 7 cwt	
	Tender	38 tons 5 cwt	
	Total	88 tons 12 cwt	
Max axle loading		18 tons 15 cwt	
Water capacity		3,500 gallons	
Coal capacity		5 tons 0 cwt	

NOTE: * Engine and tender.

THE LONDON MIDLAND REGION '2MT' CLASS

As a result of the redistribution of locomotives between regions after nationalisation, former GER depots on the Eastern Region received an allocation of ex-London Midland Region '2MT' Class 2-6-0 tender engines. Designed by H.G. Ivatt, they were initially introduced in 1946 and building continued after nationalisation. In 1951 five of the class commenced their operational life in East Anglia. No's 46465, 46466 and 46467 at Cambridge and 46468 and 46469 at Colchester. Except for No. 46466 these locomotives had very narrow chimneys and were the first to carry the modification. Introduced as replacements for older engines, the 2MTs were immediately put to work on the Stour and Colne Valley lines as well as the Mildenhall branch. Being slightly superior in power to the 'J15' Class 0-6-0 tender locomotives, the LM '2MT's easily coped with the light train formations, their light axle loading and well-distributed power ratio being suitable for the task. With their tender cabs they were ideal for tender-first working in one direction and were popular with footplate crews who found their power over the 'J15' Class 0-6-0s an advantage on the switchback gradients on the line. They also had the benefit of self-cleaning smokebox and rocking grate, which aided preparation and disposal of the engines on shed. Cambridge depot considered from 1955 they were capable of hauling 10-coach trains across the Colne Valley line and one regular turn was the 8.00am Sundays only, Cambridge to Clacton, returning at 5.27pm, which used the Colne Valley line between Haverhill and Chappel. Cambridge also used the engines on the Kettering services via Huntingdon and as a result in January 1961 No's 46468 and 46469 were transferred to Cambridge, by which time the Colne Valley passenger services were operated by diesel multiple units and diesel railbuses. When hauling the return through Clacton excursion it was not unknown for the driver of an LM '2MT' on a lengthy Down train, after calling at Chappel station, to request permission of the signalman to set the formation back over the viaduct. Instead of a cold start this enabled him to get enough speed and power over the junction beyond the station for the locomotive to negotiate the curve and gain momentum to ascend the switchback gradients en route to White Colne. To some observers and passengers on the train the resultant cacophony of noise and miniature firework display was *a joy to behold!*

No.	BUILT	WITHDRAWN
46465	June 1951	March 1967
46466	June 1951	August 1962
46467	June 1951	July 1964
46468	July 1951	October 1965
46469	July 1951	August 1962

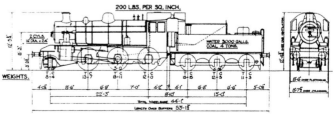

ABOVE: LMR '2MT' Class 2-6-0 tender locomotive.

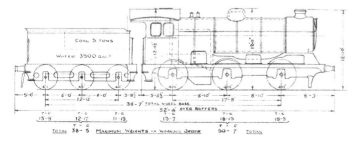

LEFT: GER 'E72'/'T77' Class, later L&NER 'J19' Class 0-6-0.

Newly outshopped LM '2MT' Class 2-6-0 No. 46467 and a 'J15' Class 0-6-0 double head a return Clacton excursion on the Hedingham side of Halstead.
G. Root

The principal dimensions of the Ivatt '2MT' locomotives were:

Cylinders	2 outside	16½ ins x 24 ins	
Motion		Walschaerts valve gear	
Boiler	Diameter	4 feet 3 ins/4 feet 8 ins	
	Barrel length	10 feet 9⅞ ins	
	Firebox outside length	5 feet 11 ins	
Heating surface			
	Firebox		101.0 sq feet
	Tubes	162 x 1⅝ ins	924.5 sq feet
	Total		1,025.5 sq feet
Superheater		12 x 5⅛ ins	134.0 sq feet
Grate area		17.5 sq feet	
Boiler pressure		200 psi	
Leading wheels		3 feet 0 ins	
Coupled wheels		5 feet 0 ins	
Tractive effort		18,510 lbs	
Tender	Coal capacity	4 tons	
	Water capacity	3,000 gallons	
	Wheel diameter	3 feet 6½ ins	
Length over buffers			
	Engine and tender	53 feet 1¾ ins	
Weight in working order			
	Engine	47 tons 2 cwt	
	Tender	37 toms 3 cwt	
Wheelbase			
	Engine	22 feet 3 ins	
	Tender	13 feet 0 ins	
	Total	44 feet 1 in	
Max axle loading		13 tons 15 cwt	

RAILBUSES

In 1957 British Railways placed orders with five manufacturers for the delivery of twenty-two lightweight diesel railbuses with a view to carrying out extensive trials on selected rural services. Five 150 hp 4-wheel diesel railbuses were built by Waggon und Maschinenbau gmbh at Donauworth, Germany to Lot No. 50482 for use on Eastern Region routes. The first two, No's E79960 and E79961, travelled via the Zeebrugge to Harwich train ferry and were delivered to Stratford diesel depot on 31st March 1958. The other three, No's E79962, E79963 and E79964, quickly followed and after trials on the Witham to Maldon East and Witham to Braintree branches they were sent to Cambridge on 19th April to commence trials on the Saffron Walden, Mildenhall and Haverhill lines. Such was their success that they completely replaced steam traction on the Witham to Maldon East, Witham to Braintree and Saffron Walden branches from 7th July 1958.

The bodies of these railbuses were designed to British Railways requirements and the underframe, power equipment, transmission and brake gear was similar to the Uerdingen type of railbuses then running on the German Federal Railway. The underframe consisted of channel-shaped cross beams welded to longitudinal girders whilst the body framing was of light steel structure. The side and roof panels were of light alloy sheets riveted to the body framing. The body of the railbus was suspended elastically and swung from four points of the running frame bogie. The floor, body sides and roof were fitted with insulation materials against heat and sound. The interiors were lined with polished plywood panels whilst ceilings were painted ivory. The upper parts of the side windows were hinged to provide limited ventilation whilst curtains were also fitted.

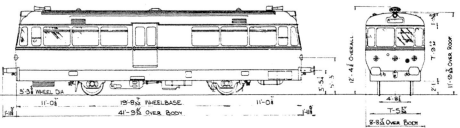

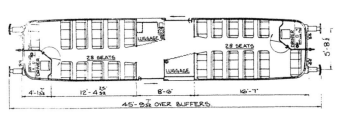

Above: In the latter years of passenger traffic the Waggon und Maschinebau 150hp railbuses were employed on some of the Colne Valley workings as well as the Audley End to Bartlow branch on cyclic diagrams. Here E79962 stands in the Down platform at Haverhill.   *Author*

Left: Waggon und Maschinenbau 150hp 4-wheel railbus.

The centrally situated doors on each side of the body were power operated and under the control of the driver. Push button operation for the guard or passengers was also used. In cases of emergency the doors were opened and closed by hand and once in service this appears to be the method adopted by train crews to open and close doors at stations. Seating was arranged for fifty-six passengers in rows of two seats on one side of the car and three seats on the other in two saloons. Initially the railbuses were unpopular on all the branches, where the limited seating capacity meant overcrowding during morning and evening peak periods. City commuters and others bemoaned the withdrawal of First Class facilities, added to which failure rates were high. The vehicles were withdrawn one at a time for adjustments and after modification the railbuses settled down to work cyclic diagrams before returning to Cambridge, Coldham Lane depot for maintenance. The diagrams included their use on Colne Valley services and were:

Day 1 6.22am Cambridge to Mildenhall, 7.36am Mildenhall to Cambridge thence to Chappel and Wakes Colne via the Colne Valley line, before working the Witham to Braintree branch; stabled overnight at Braintree.

Day 2 Worked the Braintree branch in the morning, then to the Witham to Maldon East branch; stabled overnight at Maldon East.

Day 3 Worked the Maldon East branch in the morning, then empty railbus to Marks Tey to work the 1.22pm to Cambridge via the Colne Valley line. From Cambridge worked the 4.27pm Cambridge to Mildenhall, 5.46pm Mildenhall to Newmarket, 6.37pm Newmarket to Mildenhall, 7.21pm Mildenhall to Cambridge. Thence light diesel railbus to Audley End and Saffron Walden; stabled overnight at Saffrom Walden.

Day 4 Worked the Saffron Walden branch, then light diesel to Cambridge for maintenance.

Day 5 Maintenance at Cambridge.

By the early 1960s traffic had reduced to such degree that the railbuses were adequate for most loadings and in off peak periods they often ran empty across the branch. After the withdrawal of passenger services from the Colne Valley line they continued to serve the branches to Mildenhall and Saffron Walden, but were soon displaced from the Witham to Braintree line and later from the Maldon East branch, where they were replaced by 2-car diesel multiple units. After closure of the Mildenhall line in 1962 and Saffron Walden and Maldon East branches in 1964, all five railbuses were placed in store at Cambridge until June 1965 when No. E79964 was sent north for trials on the Haltwhistle to Alston line on the North Eastern Region. After failing dismally it joined No. E79961, by then prefixed M, at Buxton, and both worked the Buxton branch. No's E79960, E79962 and E79963 were withdrawn from Cambridge in November 1966, No. M79961 was withdrawn from Buxton depot on 29th October 1966, whilst No. M79964 lasted until April 1967, also being withdrawn from Buxton. Four of the five railbuses – No's 79960, 79962, 79963 and 79964 – have survived for further service on preserved railways.

The leading dimensions of the railbuses were:

Type	2-2 (1-A)
Weight in working order	18 tons
Wheelbase	19 feet 8¼ ins
Wheel diameter	3 feet 3½ ins
Length over buffers	45 feet 9¼ ins
Length over body	41 feet 10 ins
Width over body	8 feet 8½ ins
Inside width	8 feet 4 ins
Overall height from rail	11 feet 9 ins
Floor height from rail	4 feet 0 ins
Interior height floor to ceiling	7 feet 8¼ ins
Power weight ratio	10 hp/ton
Maximum speed,	1st gear, 8 mph, 1,800 rpm, 5.54
equivalent engine speed	2nd gear, 14 mph, 1,800 rpm, 2.99
and gear ratio	3rd gear, 24 mph, 1,850 rpm, 1.85
	4th gear, 33 mph, 1,800 rpm, 1.34
	5th gear, 45 mph, 1,850 rpm, 1.00
	6th gear, 55 mph, 1,600 rpm, 0.72
Fuel oil capacity	44 gallons
Fuel oil capacity for pre-heat unit	5½ gallons
Cooling water system	22 gallons
Control system	Pneumatic and electro-pneumatic
Brake	Compressed air – disc brakes
Engine*	One horizontal 6-cylinder diesel 4-stroke engine underfloor Bussing Braunschweig 150 hp at 1,900 rpm
Transmission	Bussing type F K 9-2
Fluid coupling	Oil capacity 17½ to 18½ pints
Heating equipment	Dreiha hot water heating type W604, connected to 6-cylinder engine cooling water system

NOTE: * Three of the railbuses, No's E79961, E79963 and E79964, were later fitted with AEC A220X type engines, which proved more reliable in service.

DERBY DIESEL MULTIPLE UNITS

The remaining Colne Valley passenger workings were covered by a variety of 2-car diesel multiple units including those built by Derby Works and introduced into traffic in 1955. The vehicles were numbered in the series E79021 to E79046 for the Driving Motor Brake Seconds and E79250 to E79262 and E79613 to E79625 for the Driving Composite Trailers, with a combined seating of 109 Second Class and sixteen First Class passengers. The principal dimensions of these units were:

	DMBS	DTC
Engine	2 x BUT (AEC) 6-cylinder horizontal 150 bhp	—
Transmission	Mechanical cardan shaft and freewheel to 4-speed epicyclic gearbox and further cardan shaft to final drive	
Weight	27 tons	21 tons
Length over body	57 feet 6 ins	57 feet 6 ins
Height	12 feet 7 ins	12 feet 7 ins
Width	9 feet 2 ins	9 feet 2 ins
Maximum speed	70 mph	70 mph
Coupling code	Yellow diamond	Yellow diamond
Seating		
First Class	—	16
Second Class	56	53

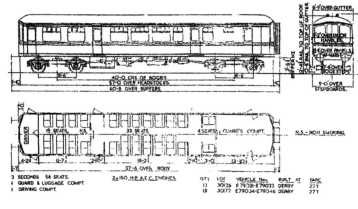

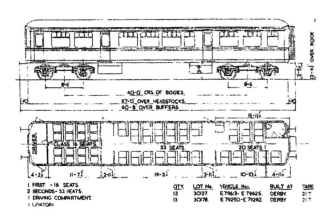

RIGHT: BR/Derby Lightweight Motor Brake Second Open DMU (top) and BR/Derby Lightweight Trailer Lavatory Composite DMU (bottom).

CRAVEN DIESEL MULTIPLE UNITS

Alongside the Derby Lightweight units, Craven 2-car diesel multiple units were introduced on the Colne Valley services. Initially entering service in 1956 they consisted of a Driving Motor Brake Second and Driving Trailer Composite with combined seating for 103 Second Class and twelve First Class passengers. The units were numbered in the series E51254 to E51301 for the Driving Motor Brake Seconds and E56412 to E56461 for the Driving Trailer Composites.

The leading dimensions of these units were:

A Derby lightweight two car diesel multiple unit working a Down service from Marks Tey to Cambridge (incorrectly displaying a Witham destination on the blind) stands at Halstead station platform in 1959. It is passing a steam hauled Up train, which has been looped alongside waiting clearance to proceed to Earls Colne and Chappel.

M. Root collection

	DMBS	DTC
Engine	BUT(AEC) BUT(Leyland) 2 x 150 hp	—
Transmission	Mechanical cardan shaft and free wheel to 4-speed epicyclic gearbox and further cardan shaft to final drive	
Weight	29 tons	23 tons
Length over body	57 feet 6 ins	57 feet 6 ins
Height	12 feet 7 ins	12 feet 7 ins
Width	9 feet 3 ins	9 feet 3 ins
Maximum speed	70 mph	70 mph
Coupling code	Blue square	Blue square
Seating		
First Class	—	12
Second Class	52	51

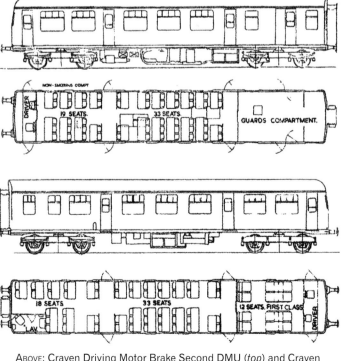

ABOVE: Craven Driving Motor Brake Second DMU (*top*) and Craven Driving Trailer Composite Lavatory DMU (*bottom*).

Craven 2-car diesel multiple unit forming the 10.57am Haverhill to Marks Tey train comes off the Colne Valley line at Chappel Junction on 20th July 1959. The train was running 26 minutes late awaiting a late running Stour Valley service at Haverhill.

G.R. Mortimer

BELOW: BTH/Paxman '8/5' Class, later BR Class '15' 800hp diesel electric locomotive.

BOTTOM: A permanent way recovery train hauled by a BTH/Paxman Class '15' Bo-Bo 800hp diesel electric locomotive standing just east of Yeldham. Because of the relatively steep gradients on the line a locomotive had to remain with the wagons during the removal and loading of scrap rails and sleepers.

M. Root collection

BTH/AEI Bo-Bo Class '15' Diesel

With the demise of steam traction the Colne Valley freight services were handled by the BTH/AEI 800hp Class Bo-Bo diesel electric locomotives, later BR Class '15'. The principal dimensions were:

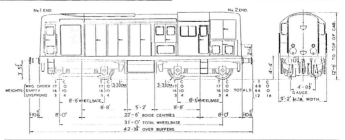

Type	Bo-Bo
Weight in working order	68 tons
Tractive effort – maximum	38,000 lbs
Wheelbase	31 feet 0 ins
Wheel diameter	3 feet 3½ ins
Bogie wheelbase	8 feet 6 ins
Bogie pivot centres	22 feet 6 ins
Width overall	9 feet 2 ins
Length overall	42 feet 3⅜ ins
Height overall	12 feet 6 ins
Minimum curve negotiable	4 chains
Maximum permitted speed	60 mph
Fuel tank capacity	Main tank 400 gallons
Brakes	Oerlikon/Davies & Metcalfe compressed air brake and hand brakes on locomotive. Vacuum brake equipment giving proportional air braking on the locomotive
Power equipment	16-cylinder diesel engine Davey Paxman type 16 YHXL 800 hp at 1,250 rpm
Traction motors – 4	D8200–10 GEC forced ventilated type 137AZ D8211–43 GEC forced ventilated type 137BZ

North British Bo-Bo Class '21' Diesel

Another class used for a short period after introduction in 1959 was the North British Locomotive Company (NBL) 1,100 hp Bo-Bo diesel electric locomotive, later BR Class '21', of which No's D6110 to D6137 were allocated to Stratford and Ipswich depots. After a short period of service in East Anglia, major technical difficulties were experienced and in September 1960 all were reallocated to the Scottish Region, enabling them to be nearer the NBL works for rectification. The leading dimensions of the locomotives were:

Type	Bo-Bo
Weight in working order	72 tons 10 cwt
Tractive effort – maximum	45,000 lbs
Wheelbase	37 feet 0 ins
Wheel diameter	3 feet 7 ins
Bogie wheelbase	8 feet 6 ins
Bogie pivot centres	28 feet 7 ins
Width overall	8 feet 8 ins
Length overall	51 feet 6 ins
Height overall	12 feet 8 ins
Minimum curve negotiable	4½ chains
Maximum permitted speed	75 mph
Fuel tank capacity	460 gallons
Brakes	Vacuum
Power equipment	NBL/MAN 12-cylinder diesel engine

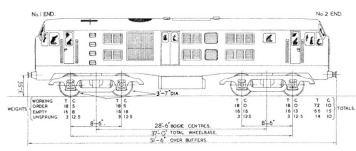

NBL 1,100hp diesel electric locomotive, later BR Class '21'.

Engine Headcodes

The engine headcode for CV&HR trains was one red light at the base of the chimney and one white light on the left-hand buffer beam for ordinary passenger and/or goods trains, whilst special trains carried one red light at the base of the chimney and one white light at each end of the buffer beam; the terms right and left denoting the engineman's right or left hand as viewed from the cab. If the GER was called on to assist, the engine or a breakdown train going to clear the line or light engine going to assist a disabled train carried by day one white disc at each end of the buffer beam and one green disc with white rim in the centre of the buffer beam. By night the discs were replaced by white and green lights. The engine of a breakdown train returning from site carried one white disc at the foot of the chimney and one green disc with white rim in the centre of the buffer beam by day and one white light and green light in the same positions during the hours of darkness. After grouping the L&NER phased out the red and green lamps and discs as a possible source of danger and from 1925 the standard stopping passenger train code of a white light or white disc at the base of the chimney was used on the Colne Valley stopping passenger services and remained so until the withdrawal of steam traction. Freight services then carried the appropriate Railway Clearing House class headcode.

Engine Whistle Codes

The engine whistle codes used by CV&HR enginemen were:

Marks Tey Junction
To or from the Sudbury branch	3 distinct sounds
Engine standing at the branch platform or middle road requiring to use the turntable	4 short pause 4 short

Chappel
To or from the GE line	1 distinct sound
To or from the CV line	3 distinct sounds

Earls Colne
To or from main single line, Up direction to Straight Road	2 long
To or from main single line, Down direction to Straight Road via No. 21 points	2 long
To or from main single line to Shed Road via No. 11 points	3 short
To or from main single line to Straight Road via No. 15 points	4 short

Halstead
To or from No. 1 siding	2 long
To or from No. 24 siding	2 short

Castle Hedingham
From main road to sidings Up or Down road	2 long

Yeldham
From main road to sidings Up or Down road	2 long

Birdbrook
Train requiring to detach trucks on Down journey	2 long
All trains not stopping on approaching the station	2 long, 1 short

Colne Valley Junction
To or from CV line and Haverhill CV station	3 distinct sounds

Haverhill Junction GE
To or from Sudbury	1 distinct sound
To or from CV line	2 distinct sounds
	3 distinct sounds*

NOTE: * by GER drivers.

The L&NER and BR stipulated no specific whistle codes for the line.

Facilities and Footplate Staff

In the early years locomotive repairs were carried out by a firm owned by one of the directors, Robert Ellington Greenwood, who incurred the wrath of his fellow board members by charging exorbitant sums of money for minimal attention at a Halstead foundry. A small workshop was then established at Haverhill. After initial altercations with the ECR in 1860, locomotives were sent to Stratford for heavy repairs and locomotives were hired from the GER to cover. By 1905 costs were expensive and in a rationalisation exercise on the CV&HR Elyot Hawkins closed the locomotive repair shops at Haverhill and transferred all heavy maintenance work to Halstead. The equipment in the shops included an overhead travelling gantry carrying two sets of 12-ton capacity pulley blocks and a second with one set of 2-ton and one set of 3-ton Weston differential pulley blocks. Other machinery included a treadle lathe, hand screwing machine, port facing machine and a hand drilling machine. The smith's shop was equipped with two forges and an outside smith's shop with a pair of hand rolls for rolling plate metal. A wheel lathe was not provided and all wheels were sent away to the GER for tyre turning. These alterations made the CV&HR self-sufficient and only on one occasion was it necessary to hire a replacement locomotive from the GER because the heavy gantry was in use for repairs to another engine. On another occasion a locomotive sheared a coupling rod necessitating the engine to be lifted to accomplish the repair; the locomotive was sent to Stratford Works and a GER locomotive hired for the duration of its absence.

The CV&HR originally based their locomotives at Haverhill where an engine shed was provided in 1862 before the full opening of the line. This structure was replaced in 1915 by a single-road dead-end shed constructed of timber and corrugated iron measuring 55 feet by 20 feet located on the Down side of the railway. A primitive engine shed was also established at Halstead and this was later developed into a two-road structure constructed of timber and corrugated iron measuring 110 feet by 60 feet, served by two sidings, 260 feet and 155 feet in length. This building, on the Up side of the railway, also served as a locomotive repair shop. From the opening and before the expansion of Halstead shed a locomotive was stabled on the Up side of the line west of Trinity Street crossing in an open-ended shed on the premises of the Colne Valley Ironworks. Halstead shed closed in 1928 and the enginemen were transferred to Haverhill and Colchester; thereafter until the abolition of steam traction an engine continued to be based at Haverhill and all running repairs were handled at Cambridge or Colchester. A travelling fitter attended to minor faults. Curiously,

after grouping there were no locomotive facilities at Haverhill North so a locomotive and two sets of men continued to be based at Haverhill South until the demise of steam traction.

In the early years, footplate staff, especially drivers, moved with their locomotives, hence Charles Taunton transferred from the London, Brighton & South Coast Railway when his engine was purchased by the CV&HR in July 1860. Like traffic staff, footplate staff were scheduled on duty for a seven-day week, working Sundays with no enhanced rate of pay. Drivers in the early years earned the handsome sum of £1 10s 0d per week. After persuasion by Elyot Hawkins, the directors agreed in 1907 to introduce a six-day week and adopt the standard rates of pay similar to GER men working on the neighbouring Marks Tey to Cambridge and Bury St Edmunds lines. Before World War One the men did not belong to a trades union but during hostilities those that did not enlist in the colours joined the Associated Society of Locomotive Engineers & Fireman. The introduction of enhanced rates of pay as agreed between the railway companies and trades unions imposed a burden on the company, which was faced with reducing the numbers of staff or reducing wages. In response to a personal appeal by the Manager in 1920 all staff accepted a ten per cent reduction in their rates of pay. However, as noted earlier, a reduction of loss making Sunday services and the resultant savings enabled the pay cut to be made up in 1921. Initially two sets of men were based at both Haverhill and Halstead sheds, later increased to three sets at the former, but by grouping Halstead boasted only one driver and fireman. In 1925 the Halstead men, after signing on duty, worked their engine with ECS to Haverhill MO and to Yeldham MX before working a passenger train to Chappel and return to Sible and Castle Hedingham. After acting as goods and passenger pilot the engine returned to Halstead shed for disposal. The men then relieved a Colchester crew on a goods train to work a round trip to Chappel before signing off duty. The Haverhill-based engine on weekdays worked several round trips from Haverhill North to Chappel, with the first set of men being relieved by the second set at 2.00pm. On

HALSTEAD DEPOT.

WEEK DAYS.

No. 1.

	arr. a.m.		dep. a.m.	
		On Duty	{ 6 5	M O
			6 35	M X
		Loco'	{ 6 50	L M O
			7 20	L M X
		Halstead	{ 6 50	L M O
			7 20	L M X
M O	6 58	{ Sible and	} 7 0	E M O
M X	7 28	Hedingh'm	} 7 35	E M X
M X	7 40	Yeldham	7 55	M X
M O	7 28	Haverhill N.	7 38	M O
	8 29	Chappel	9 26	
	9 50	{ Sible and C. H'dgham	} G P L	
	11 22	Halstead	G P	

After disposal of engine, men to relieve on goods engine and work 1.0 p.m. goods Halstead to Chappel, and 2.5 p.m. return Chappel to Halstead.

HAVERHILL DEPOT.

WEEK DAYS.

No. 1.

arr. a.m.		dep. a.m.	
	On Duty	6 10	
	Loco'	8 45	L
8 50	Haverhill Nth.	9 29	
10 20	Chappel	11 36	
p.m.		p.m.	
12 23	Haverhill N.	12 34	G
12 42	„ C.V.	1 40	G
1 45	„ N.	2 0	
2 51	Chappel	4 0	
4 55	Haverhill N.	6 6	
6 57	Chappel	7 18	
8 7	Haverhill N.	8 15	L
8 24	Loco'		

Second set take charge 2.0 p.m.

SUNDAYS.

No. 1.

arr. a.m.		dep. a.m.		
	On Duty	7 45		
	Loco'	8 30	L	
8 35	Haverhill N.	8 42		
9 35	Chappel	11 0		
		noon		
11 49	Haverhill N.	12 0	L	
p.m.		p.m.		
12 6	Haverhill C.V.	5 48	L	
5 53	„ Nth.	5 58		
		6 51	Chappel	8†45, 8*20
9*9,	Haverhill C.V.	9 34	9 45 L	9*20 L
9*29,	Loco'	9 54		

Second set of men on duty Haverhill, 2.30 p.m.

* September 20th only.

† Not after September 13th.

Locomotive and enginemen's workings for Halstead and Haverhill depot 1925.

Sundays the Haverhill engine worked the morning and afternoon return trips to Chappel with the second set of men relieving the first set at 2.20pm.

Early footplate staff included ex-LB&SCR driver Charles Taunton who testified in a court case against engine cleaner Medhech Nicholls, charged with being drunk and disorderly on 12th January 1863. The case was brought before Halstead Petty Sessions the following day and judged by E. Horner and B. Harvey, both railway company directors. Nicholls was sentenced to 14 days' hard labour and was dismissed from his job. Other footplate staff included Driver J. Creswell, who died in June 1928 at the relatively young age of 42, and Elizah Amey, who retired as a fireman in October 1933 after 50 years service, mostly spent on the CV&HR. Footplate staff based at the ex-Haverhill CV&HR shed in the latter years included drivers Percy Gerachty who was a JP and Walter Underhill, the former as fat as the latter was slim. Gerachty was not averse to stopping a train and collecting mushrooms or vegetable crops from fields adjoining the railway before setting off again. In recompense he would drop a few lumps of coal off at neighbouring signal boxes to appease the respective signalmen for causing the delay. The trio was completed by Albert Warner, who unfortunately suffered from persistent asthma and often could not climb up the steps on the side of the engine to reach the footplate. Albert was fortunate in having a benevolent fireman, John Newman, who, as well as performing his usual duties, often took over the driving of the locomotive, leaving Warner to watch the road ahead. The passed fireman at Haverhill was Bill Redgrave, who was known as 'The Maniac' on account of his regular disregard of speed limits. It was Redgrave who demolished the gates at Langley Mill crossing on one

occasion, and snatched a freight train conveying Bren gun carriers, to such effect that the couplings snapped between four wagons. Colchester, Sudbury and Cambridge men signed route knowledge sheets for the branch in L&NER and BR days.

Locomotive water supplies were available at Halstead, where water columns were provided at each end of the platform and in the goods yard, the supply being fed from a water tank located on the Up side of the line near the station. At Yeldham, water columns were located at each end of the platform fed from a water tank sited in the Down side of the railway. A water column was provided by the engine shed at Haverhill CV station fed from a tank at the back of the building. At Haverhill, Pumper R. Walford was still employed at the age of 70 when he died in April 1929. GER locomotive water supplies at Haverhill were available from the columns located at the west end of the Cambridge-bound platform and east end of the Sudbury-bound platform, both fed from an adjacent water tank. On the GE, water supplies were also available from a Jib crane at Marks Tey, located by the goods shed to serve the branch siding. No engine turntables were available on the CV&HR but in emergencies and after grouping the locomotives had use if required of the ex-GER turntable at Marks Tey, which was originally 45 feet diameter but was later extended to 46 feet 6 inches.

In the event of a breakdown or derailment, initially the Ipswich breakdown train covered Chappel to Haverhill CV and Colne Valley Junction to Haverhill North Junction, but later the Cambridge District breakdown vans covered the GER connection from Haverhill Junction to Colne Valley Junction and the entire CV&HR, although the Ipswich train or Colchester BD vans also covered the southern half of the line.

CV&HR 0-4-2T No. 1 rests between turns at Halstead accompanied by one of the 2-4-2T locomotives. The engine has a builders plate on the bunker and a temporary wooden door had been fitted in the cab for the benefit of enginemen. In the background a CV open wagon awaits repair.

M. Root collection

With blower on, LMR '2MT' Class 2-6-0 No. 46466 approaches Chappel Junction with the Sunday 4.01pm Cambridge to Marks Tey train on 4th May 1958. This locomotive was fitted with the wider chimney than others of the class allocated to Colchester and Cambridge depots.

G.R. Mortimer

13

Coaching Stock

J. Wright & Sons of Saltley, Birmingham, predecessors of the Metropolitan Amalgamated Railway Carriage & Wagon Company, provided the initial coaching stock to the company. These consisted of eight 4-wheel vehicles, four full Thirds, two First/Second Class Composites and two full brake vans, all delivered in 1859. Two additional Composites and one brake van were added in 1863. The coaches were straight sided with low elliptical roofs and two doors on each side, and were originally fitted with seats placed round the internal body sides rather than transverse as normal. The Third Class seats were wooden, whilst the First and Second Class were upholstered. The coaches measured 18 feet 6 inches over the headstock and the last was scrapped in 1903, the body of one of the vehicles at one time serving as waiting accommodation at White Colne station. Curiously, at the date of construction it was not the practice to prepare drawings, instead dimensions were chalked on the workshop wall for engineer's guidance!

When the GER Locomotive Superintendent carried out a survey of the line in 1884 with a view to possible takeover, the company had fourteen coaching vehicles, which were considered to be life expired and of no use to the main line company and therefore carried no value.

In 1887 the CV&HR purchased a 6-wheel 5-compartment Composite coach from an unknown source. This vehicle measured 31 feet 6 inches in length was lit by colza oil lamps but was later converted to acetylene. The next vehicles to be acquired by the company through a dealer were two former Midland Railway 6-wheel coaches: a Brake Third and a 5-compartment Composite. The vehicles measured 31 feet 6 inches in length and lighting was originally by oil but was later converted to acetylene. The Third Class compartments seated ten passengers, whilst the First Class seated six in each compartment.

On 25th March 1897 the company purchased two Third Class 6-wheel coaches from the Lancaster Railway Carriage & Wagon Company Limited. These had five compartments, seating ten passengers in each compartment and had an overall length of 32 feet 0 inches. Originally illuminated by oil lamps they were later provided with acetylene lighting. Two years later, in 1899 the Metropolitan Railway Carriage & Wagon Company provided two 5-compartment 6-wheel Third Class vehicles. The compartments

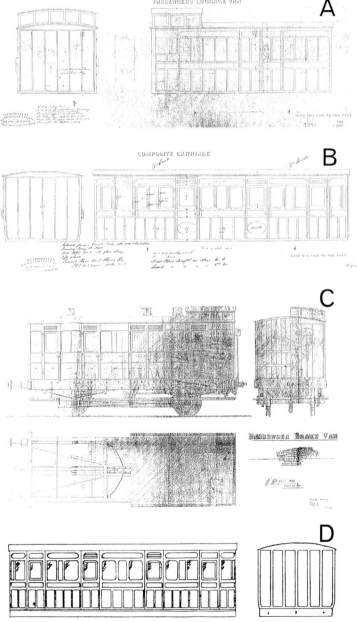

An example of an early coach supplied to the railway by J. Wright & Sons of Saltley, precursor to the Metropolitan Railway Carriage & Wagon Company. Some vehicles remained operational until 1903.
Author's collection

(A) CV&HR passenger luggage van 1862.
(B) CV&HR 4-wheel Composite 1869.
(C) CV&HR 4-wheel Brake Third.
(D) CV&HR 4-wheel coach.

CV&HR *Hedingham* after rebuilding with the dome on the leading boiler ring but still carrying the stovepipe chimney standing at the head of a motley collection of vehicles at Haverhill GE. At the rear of the train are two ancient straight-sided 4-wheel coaches.

Author's collection

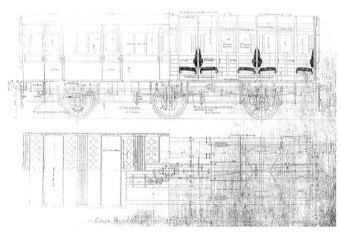

CV&HR 6-wheel 5-compartment Third.

accommodated ten passengers but the body length was only 31 feet 6 inches. Once again the initial lighting was by oil but was later converted to acetylene. The same company also provided a 6-wheel brake van.

From 1897 the company registered twelve passenger vehicles and eight other passenger vehicles in BOT returns but by 1899 the totals were combined when only nineteen vehicles were recorded. A 6-wheel brake van built by the Metropolitan Railway Carriage & Wagon Company was purchased in 1899 and by 1900 the company recorded having three Composite carriages, seven Third Class vehicles, nine brake vans and one horsebox. This total remained until 1902; from 1903 only fifteen passenger vehicles were recorded, reducing to twelve (nine passenger vehicles and three other vehicles) in 1905.

In 1906 a breakthrough came when Elyot Hawkins visited Lillie Bridge depot of the Metropolitan District Railway to inspect old withdrawn 4-wheel coaching stock which had been offered for sale. Although the CV&HR was in need of vehicles he considered those

on offer were totally unsuitable to the company's needs. On leaving the premises Hawkins noted some vehicle stored under dust sheets and on requesting an inspection was shown three coaches of an electric multiple unit which had run an experimental service in 1900 between Earls Court and South Kensington. He was advised that if no further experiments were required the company might consider disposing of the bogie coaches and on returning to Halstead he immediately staked a claim on the vehicles by letter. Surprisingly, he received a reply asking for a definite offer. Without consulting the CV&HR board Hawkins offered £250 stating that because of the special construction one of the trio could only be regarded as scrap. The Metropolitan District authorities ultimately requested £275. Hawkins could make no decision without his board's approval, but as there was no meeting for three weeks he was concerned the deal might fall through. Fortunately the directors agreed the price and the vehicles were subsequently transferred. On receipt, the two trailer coaches, one a 6-compartment Composite and the second a 7-compartment Third were modified and then commissioned for traffic on Monday 22nd October 1906. The third coach of the set, a Motor Brake Composite, required extensive modification as the armatures of the traction motors were wound directly on to the axles of the bogie. The two ends of the main frame had been set to take the larger bogies and it was necessary to remove these bogies and convert the frame with rolled steel joists to take new pressed steel frame bogies supplied by the Metropolitan Railway Carriage & Wagon Company, the original builders of the coaches. This vehicle was subsequently placed into traffic in April 1908. The high price realised for the scrap recovered from the coaches partly offset the expenditure on modifications. Hawkins also persuaded the board to equip all three coaches with electric lighting by Stones generator. The bodies of these coaches were 39 feet 6 inches in length and, as with the 6-wheel vehicles, there was accommodation for ten passengers in each Third Class compartment, whilst seating in the First Class compartments was increased from six to eight passengers. The *Halstead Gazette* lauded the introduction of the vehicles into traffic remarking:

we think the public should warmly appreciate the enterprise and progressive policy of the Colne Valley Company; they are doing their

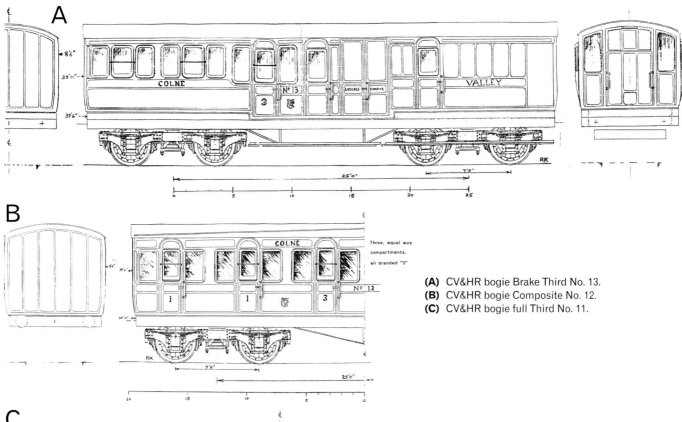

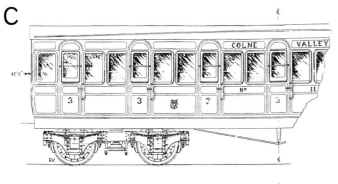

(A) CV&HR bogie Brake Third No. 13.
(B) CV&HR bogie Composite No. 12.
(C) CV&HR bogie full Third No. 11.

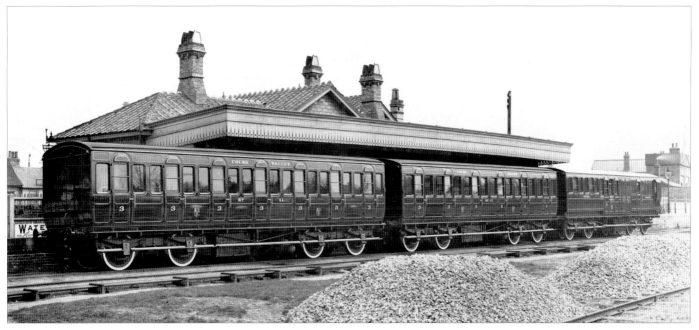

BELOW: Pride of the CV&HR coaching stock: 7-compartment full Third No. 11, 6-compartment Composite No. 12 and Brake Third No. 13 converted from electric motor coach stand at Halstead station. In 1906 Elyot Hawkins visited Lillie Bridge depot of the Metropolitan District Railway to inspect withdrawn 4-wheel coaching stock offered for sale but considered none acceptable for further use. However, he noted three vehicles of an electric multiple unit used on an experimental service in 1900 in store As they were no longer required, Hawkins staked a claim and obtained the three coaches for £275 and the two trailer coaches subsequently entered traffic on the CV&HR on 22nd October 1906. The third vehicle, a motor coach, required considerable alterations and did nor enter traffic until April 1908.

M. Root collection

best to meet the requirements of the public and it must not be forgotten they are hemmed in at both ends of their system.

In 1907 these vehicles were painted in varnished teak livery with gold stripes, with the company coat of arms on the lower panels and the name 'Colne Valley' in bold lettering along the top panels above the windows.

With the purchase of these three coaches the BOT returns showed nine passenger vehicles and six other passenger stock, increasing to sixteen from 1908 to 1910 and reducing yet again to fifteen vehicles (ten passenger and five other passenger) from 1911 through to 1919, although in 1913 the returns were more specific: eight Third Class, four Composite, two Luggage/Brake vans and one horsebox.

Upon withdrawal from service in 1910 one of the 4-wheel Brake Third coaches was purchased by James Meadows of Colne Engaine and the body conveyed over a mile and a half to serve as a garden shed. A similar coach was purchased to act as a sports club pavilion at Portways, Halstead.

The carriage and wagon shops at Halstead could handle most repairs but not all coaching stock maintenance was carried out by the CV&HR and small tasks were sub-contracted to outside firms. Thus on 16th January 1912 payment of £1 13s 11d was made to T. & H. Gibbs for repairs to a coach. Then on 12th March, Stone & Company were paid £2 15s 7d for supplying electric light fittings, whilst W. & J.R. Hunter supplied a quantity of teak and mahogany for carriage repairs and received payment of £67 18s 7d on 16th April 1912. T. & H. Gibbs were again repairing stock in May and June at a cost of £14 3s 9d.

The question of improving lighting in coaching stock was discussed in the autumn of 1913 and as a result of investigations it was agreed on 9th December that one coach would be experimentally fitted with the 'Phos' system of acetylene gas lighting. The trial was evidently successful for on 10th February 1914 the General Manager was authorised to equip additional coaches if necessary. On the same date payment of £3 3s 11d was made to Laycock for the supply of brackets.

The increased passenger traffic brought about by World War One resulted in a shortage of stock and it was agreed on 5th June 1916 for some of the older carriages to receive immediate repairs to enable them to remain in service. On 14th August Messrs Phosphor quoted a cost of £26 9s 10d for the installation of five sets of lighting in carriages, whilst on 6th November G.S. Wood was paid £1 16s 0d for supplying netting for luggage racks. The following year, on 13th August authority was given for two brake vans, one Composite and one Third Class coach to receive immediate repairs. It was also agreed that one passenger brake van and two carriages be equipped with acetylene lighting.

During hostilities carriage maintenance had been minimal but matters then improved, for it was agreed the passenger coaching stock would again be varnished and on 26th February 1919 Nobles & Hoare received payment of £4 18s 10d for the supply of best varnish. From 1920 until 1922 the company registered fourteen passenger stock (eleven coaches and three other passenger vehicles) although this was cast in doubt when the company showed fifteen passenger vehicles in the returns for 31st December 1920 including two brake vans and a horsebox, and in a separate return for 1922: seven Third Class coaches, three Composite plus a mess and tool van. Despite the anomaly, on 24th August 1921 Gibbs received £16 12s 6d for upholstering some of the company's coaching stock. For some considerable time the CV&HR borrowed – it was not

officially shown as hired – a full 6-wheel GER passenger brake van to diagram 518 and quarterly rental was paid but no vehicle number was identified.

The original livery of CV&HR coaching stock was described as drab or khaki green, picked out with narrow black and yellow lining, lettered CVR in small letters on the side panels. The First Class compartment seats were upholstered in blue material, Second Class was brown, whilst Third Class passengers had wooden seating. After the abolition of Second Class the Third Class seats were upholstered in brown. After the introduction of the Metropolitan District bogie coaches all stock was finished in varnished teak livery with gold stripes, the words 'Colne Valley Railway' being painted in large letters along the top panel above the windows and the company coat of arms transferred to the lower panels.

In the last years of the 19th century and early years of the 20th century the CV&HR occasionally hired GER 6-wheel vehicles to cover shortages of passenger carrying stock. The same types of vehicle were also used on through excursion trains to Clacton or London excursions, the latter making main line connections at Marks Tey. These were generally of four types with the addition of full Third to diagram 407, which was almost identical to diagram 404 Thirds. The leading dimensions were:

DIAGRAM	404	422
Type	6-wheel Third	6-wheel Third
Length over buffers	37 ft 4½ ins 37 ft 7½ ins	37 ft 7½
Length over body	34 ft 6 ins	34 ft 6 ins
Height overall	11 ft 3 ins	11 ft 7 ins
Body height	7 ft 0 ins	7 ft 4 ins
Width over body	8 ft 0 ins	8 ft 0 ins
Width over guard's lookout	—	—
Wheelbase	21 ft 0 ins	22 ft 6 ins
Seating Third Class	60	60
Luggage	—	—
Weight empty	13 tons 3 cwt	13 tons 3cwt

DIAGRAM	513	514
Type	6-wheel Brake/Third	6-wheel Brake/Third
Length over buffers	37 ft 7½ ins	37 ft 4½ ins 37 ft 7½ ins
Length over body	34 ft 6 ins	34 ft 6 ins
Height overall	11 ft 7 ins	11 ft 3 ins
Body height	7 ft 4 ins	7 ft 0 ins
Width over body	8 ft 0 ins	8 ft 0 ins
Width over guard's lookout	9 ft 3½ ins	9 ft 3½ ins
Wheelbase	22 ft 6 ins	22 ft 6 ins
Seating Third Class	30	30
Luggage	2 tons	2 tons
Weight empty	12 tons 12 cwt	12 tons 16 cwt

After grouping the older 6-wheel CV&HR coaches were quickly withdrawn but two of the bogie coaches were taken into L&NER stock. CV&HR No. 12, built in 1900 and purchased in 1906,

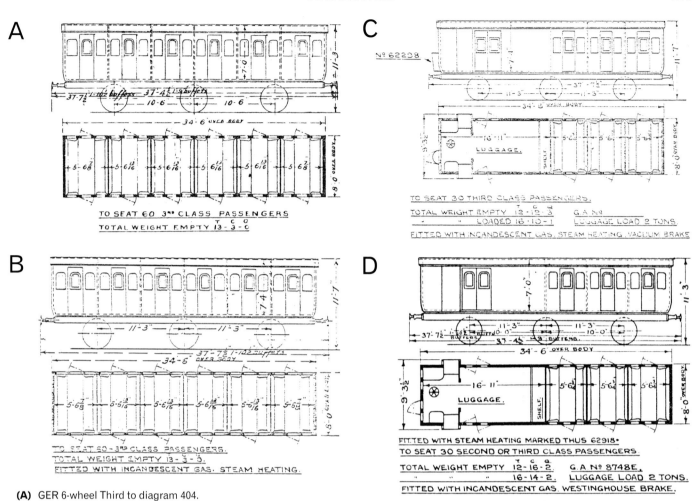

A

TO SEAT 60 3ᴿᴰ CLASS PASSENGERS
TOTAL WEIGHT EMPTY 13-3-0

B

TO SEAT 60 - 3ᴿᴰ CLASS PASSENGERS.
TOTAL WEIGHT EMPTY 13-3-0.
FITTED WITH INCANDESCENT GAS. STEAM HEATING.

C

Nº 62208

TO SEAT 30 THIRD CLASS PASSENGERS.
TOTAL WEIGHT EMPTY 12-12-3   G.A. Nº
          LOADED 16-10-1   LUGGAGE LOAD 2 TONS.
FITTED WITH INCANDESCENT GAS, STEAM HEATING, VACUUM BRAKE

D

FITTED WITH STEAM HEATING MARKED THUS 62918•
TO SEAT 30 SECOND OR THIRD CLASS PASSENGERS.
TOTAL WEIGHT EMPTY 12-16-2   G.A. Nº 8748E.
          "   16-14-2.   LUGGAGE LOAD 2 TONS.
FITTED WITH INCANDESCENT GAS. WESTINGHOUSE BRAKE.

(A) GER 6-wheel Third to diagram 404.
(B) GER 6-wheel Third to diagram 422.
(C) GER 6-wheel Brake/Third to diagram 513.
(D) GER 6-wheel Brake/Third to diagram 514.

CV&HR 2-4-2T No. 3 standing at Halstead station before 1920 with possibly an 8-coach excursion train formed chiefly of GER 6-wheel coaches including, from the engine: a Brake Third to diagram 514 followed by a full Third to diagram 407, then two 6-compartment Thirds to diagram 404 or 422, next is a Brake Third to diagram 513 followed by a full Third to diagram 404 or 422, plus two further vehicles. The engine is taking water so the rear of the train is blocking Trinity Street crossing – a cause of much disagreement between the town authorities and the railway company.

M. Root collection

became L&NER No. 63562 to diagram 252 and was withdrawn on 31st March 1951, whilst CV&HR No. 11, also built in 1900 and purchased in 1906, became L&NER No. 61304 to diagram 452. Both entered L&NER stock in March 1924 and although No. 61304 was operational in the early 1950s the withdrawal date is unknown. On arrival to the GE section both vehicles had electric lighting and steam heating equipment. The leading dimensions of the vehicles and the GER passenger brake van were:

Diagram	252	452	518
Type	Bogie Composite	Bogie Third	6-wheel Brake
Length over buffers	42 ft 6 ins	42 ft 6 ins	35 ft 1½ ins
Length over body	39 ft 6 ins	39 ft 6 ins	32 ft 0 ins
Height overall	11 ft 7 ins	11 ft 7 ins	11 ft 7 ins
Body height	6 ft 11⅝ ins	6 ft 11⅝ ins	7 ft 4 ins
Width over body	8 ft 6¾ ins	8 ft 6¾ ins	8 ft 0 ins
Width over guard's lookout	—	—	9 ft 3½ ins
Wheelbase	32 ft 0¼ ins	32 ft 0 ins	33 ft 6 ins
Bogie wheelbase	7 ft 0 ins	7 ft 0 ins	—
Seating			
First Class	16	—	—
Third Class	40	70	—
Luggage	—	—	4 tons
Weight empty	22 tons 0 cwt	22 tons 0 cwt	12 tons 2 cwt

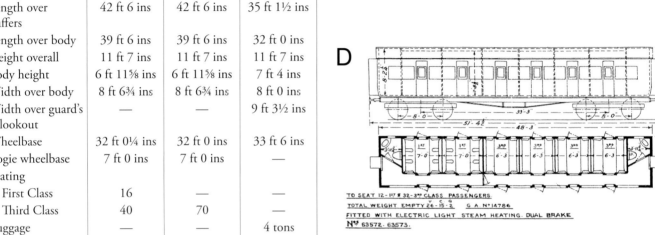

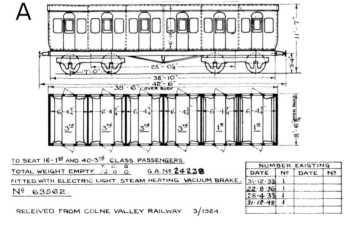

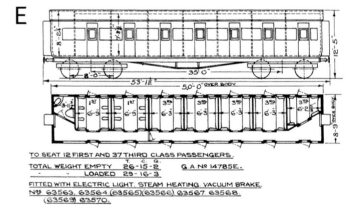

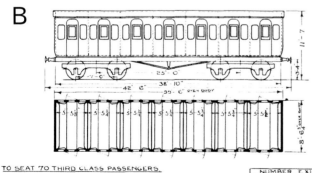

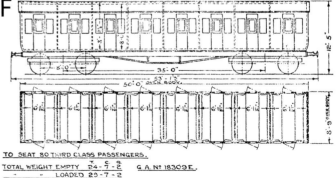

G

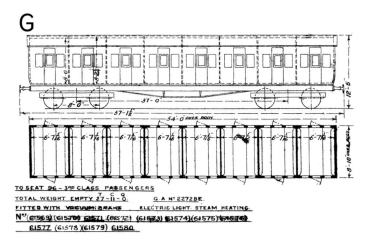

TO SEAT 96 - 3ʳᴰ CLASS PASSENGERS
TOTAL WEIGHT EMPTY 27-11-0.   G A Nº 22728E.
FITTED WITH VACUUM BRAKE   ELECTRIC LIGHT. STEAM HEATING.
Nᵒˢ (61569)(61570) 61571 (61572) (61573)(61574)(61575)(61576)
61577 (61578)(61579) 61580.

H

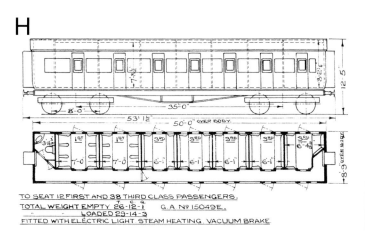

TO SEAT 12 FIRST AND 38 THIRD CLASS PASSENGERS.
TOTAL WEIGHT EMPTY 26-12-1   G A Nº 15049E.
LOADED 29-14-3
FITTED WITH ELECTRIC LIGHT. STEAM HEATING. VACUUM BRAKE.

I

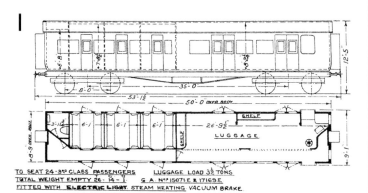

TO SEAT 24 -3ᴿᴰ CLASS PASSENGERS   LUGGAGE LOAD 3½ TONS
TOTAL WEIGHT EMPTY 26-14-1   G A Nº 15071E & 17169E
FITTED WITH ELECTRIC LIGHT. STEAM HEATING VACUUM BRAKE.

(A) L&NER bogie Composite to diagram 252.
(B) L&NER full Third to diagram 452.
(C) GER 6-wheel full brake to diagram 518.
(D) GER corridor Composite to diagram 221.
(E) GER corridor Composite to diagram 222.
(F) GER bogie non-gangway Third to diagram 430.
(G) GER bogie non-gangway Third to diagram 439.
(H) GER bogie corridor Composite to diagram 227.
(I) GER corridor Brake Third to diagram 541.

To cover for the loss of stock some ex-GER bogie vehicles were initially drafted to the line, including bogie Brake Third to diagram 222 and bogie Composite with two First and four Third Class compartments and luggage vestibule to diagram 221 used for a short period then eight compartment Thirds to diagram 430 or 439, Composite to diagram 227 and Brake Third to diagram 541. The leading dimensions were:

Diagram	221	222	430
Type	Bogie Composite	Bogie Composite	Bogie Third
Length over buffers	51 ft 4½ ins	53 ft 1½ ins	53 ft 1½ ins
Length over body	48 ft 3 ins	50 ft 0 ins	50 ft 0 ins
Height overall	12 ft 5 ins	12 ft 5 ins	12 ft 5 ins
Body height	8 ft 2¼ ins	8 ft 2¼ ins	8 ft 2¼ ins
Width over body	8 ft 9 ins	8 ft 9 ins	8 ft 9 ins
Width over guard's lookout	—		—
Wheelbase	41 ft 3 ins	43 ft 0 ins	43 ft 0 ins
Bogie wheelbase	8 ft 0 ins	8 ft 0 ins	8 ft 0 ins
Seating			
First Class	12	12	—
Third Class	32	37	80
Luggage	—	—	—
Weight empty	26 tons 15 cwt	26 tons 15 cwt	24 tons 7 cwt

Diagram	439	227	541
Type	Bogie Third	Bogie Composite	Bogie Brake/ Third
Length over buffers	57 ft 1½ ins	53 ft 1½ ins	53 ft 1½ ins
Length over body	54 ft 0 ins	50 ft 0 ins	50 ft 0 ins
Height overall	12 ft 5 ins	12 ft 5 ins	12 ft 5 ins
Body height	8 ft 2¼ ins	8 ft 2¼ ins	8 ft 2¼ ins
Width over body	8 ft 10 ins	8 ft 9 ins	8 ft 9 ins
Width over guard's lookout	—	—	9 ft 1 in
Wheelbase	43 ft 0 ins	43 ft 0 ins	43 ft 0 ins
Bogie wheel base	8 ft 0 ins	8 ft 0 ins	8 ft 0 ins
Seating			
First Class	—	12	—
Third Class	96	38	24
Luggage	—	—	3½ tons
Weight empty	27 tons 11 cwt	26 rons 12 cwt	26 tons 14 cwt

Varieties of L&NER suburban bogie coaches then appeared on the line, including Gresley panelled non-corridor stock. These were supplemented by Thompson steel panelled non-corridor stock and augmented by ex-GER bogie Composites to diagram 212 and 231 and ex-North Eastern Railway full Thirds to diagram 503 transferred to the GE area from 1936, both before and after hostilities. These survived until the withdrawal of steam hauled passenger services.

Diagram	212	231	503
Type	Bogie Composite	Bogie Composite	Bogie Brake/Thitd
Length over buffers	51 ft 4½ ins	51 ft 4½ ins	55 ft 8 ins
Length over body	48 ft 3 ins	48 ft 3 ins	48 ft 3 ins
Height overall	12 ft 8 ins	12 ft 8 ins	12 ft 7 ins
Body height	8 ft 5 ins	8 ft 5 ins	—
Width over body	8 ft 6 ins	8 ft 6 ins	8 ft 0 ins
Width over guard's lookout	—	—	9 ft 0 ins
Wheelbase	40 ft 3 ins	40 ft 3 ins	44 ft 6 ins / 41 ft 3 ins
Bogie wheelbase	8 ft 0 ins	8 ft 0 ins	8 ft 0 ins
Seating			
First Class	9	9	—
Third Class	33	33	50
Luggage	—	—	2 tons
Weight empty	25 tons 9 cwt	25 tons 9 cwt	23 tons 2 cwt

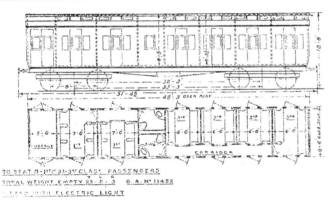

To seat 9-1st 33-3rd class passengers. Total weight empty 25.9.3 G.A. No. 11452. Fitted with electric light.

Above: GER bogie Composite to diagram 212.

Below: Former Metropolitan District line CV&HR full bogie Third L&NER No. 61304 at Harlow on 2nd July 1955. The vehicle was withdrawn from traffic in the late 1950s. *J. Wading*

The L&NER coaching stock used on the services in later years included corridor bogie Brake Third to diagram 37 coded BT, bogie Composites to diagram 215 coded C and non-vestibule bogie Brake Thirds to diagrams 64, 65 and 340 which had the following dimensions.

Diagram	37	64	65
Type	Gresley Bogie Brake/Third Corridor	Gresley Bogie Brake/Third Non-vestibule	Gresley Bogie Brake/Third Non-vestibule
Length over body	61 ft 6 ins	51 ft 1½ ins	51 ft 1½ ins
Width over body	9 ft 3 ins	9 ft 0 ins	9 ft 3 ins
Seating			
First Class	—	—	—
Third Class	40	40	40

Diagram	215	340
Type	Gresley Bogie Composite Non-vestibule	Thompson Bogie Brake/Third Non-vestibule
Length over body	51 ft 1½ ins	52 ft 4 ins
Width over body	9 ft 3 ins	9 ft 3 ins
Seating		
First Class	20	—
Third Class	60	40

In independent days, routine coaching stock repairs and maintenance was undertaken at Halstead, although on some occasions assistance was sought from the specialists at the GER Stratford carriage and wagon department. Ipswich carriage and wagon shops also provided or fabricated parts when required in an emergency, often without charge for the work.

14

Wagons

THE CV&HR HAD FEW WAGONS when the railway opened and as embryonic traffic increased the company had to resort to hiring vehicles from the ECR, which proved an expensive luxury the company could ill afford. Thus, on 27th March 1861 the CV&HR requested the ECR to waive the supplementary charges for wagon hire which were being added to rates paid by coal merchants for deliveries and caused loss of traffic to both companies. After due discussion, and on balancing the loss of wagon hire against loss of traffic, the ECR board recommended the abolition of wagon hire charges. The wagon hire allowance from the CV&HR bill of £56 for the period May 1860 to March 1861 was subsequently agreed on 24th April subject to the Railway Clearing House mileage proportion being transferred.

The company returns for 1868 gave the freight rolling stock owned as twenty-nine vehicles, consisting of twenty-four open wagons, two covered wagons, two timber vans and a travelling crane. By 1884, when the GER Locomotive Superintendent conducted a survey of CV&HR stock, the total had risen to sixty-seven vehicles, which he valued at £1,185 – but many he considered were of doubtful quality and ready for scrapping. Many of these earlier vehicles were fitted with dumb buffers.

As the fleet increased, wagons were built by Harrison & Camm, the Lancaster Carriage & Wagon Company, Metropolitan Wagon Company, Birmingham Wagon Company and Craven Brothers. In addition, the company hired ten open wagons from the Lancaster Carriage & Wagon Company and a further twenty open wagons were later hired from the same source. The Yorkshire Railway Wagon Company also hired twenty wagons to the CV&HR as well as a goods brake van.

In January 1897 the company entered into an agreement with the Lancaster Carriage & Wagon Company for the hire of thirty wagons, and on 25th March 1897 hired a further five box wagons from the same company – by which time the total had increased to 110, although in 1898/1899 the company registered only 109 vehicles. By 1901 the fleet had expanded to 149, the increase due to the requisition of vehicles for brick traffic from Sible and Castle Hedingham, which had developed to such an extent that thirty to forty wagons were required every day. The summary of registered goods vehicles was then:

    118 open
      9 covered vans
      9 timber wagons
     10 cattle wagons
      2 ballast wagons
      1 travelling crane.

Like locomotives and carriages, no official record of wagon stock was maintained until after 1903 and prior to this many vehicles were withdrawn from service without being officially taken off the books. The wagon register was difficult to compile and harder to

maintain; reporting was poor and many vehicles were broken up without the deed being recorded. So dire was the situation that if a wagon failed or became defective on a foreign line, a CV&HR wagon would have to be stopped and cannibalised to permit spare parts to be sent to make the defective one good for onward transit.

Other wagons requiring repair often had to await spare parts removed from other vehicles or have spare parts specially made at Halstead. On other occasions urgent messages were sent to the GER shops at Stratford or Ipswich requesting help. Standardisation of parts such as springs, axleboxes, buffers and couplings helped improve availability. Wagons reaching the end of their useful life were confined to 'internal user' movements on the CV&HR between Chappel and Haverhill, or were used for 'one journey only' and then withdrawn, often being cannibalised and used for storage of scrap. Goods brake vans were second hand, purchased from the GER and Great Western Railway

Despite the establishment of a wagon register, alterations continued and in 1902/3, 152 vehicles were recorded, decreasing to 137 in 1904 and then increasing to 138 for the years 1905 to 1910 inclusive. A considerable increase in stock was then made and in 1911 164 wagons were in the company books. On 17th October 1911 payment of £69 was made to Harrison & Camm for the supply of wagon wheels. On the same day the General Manager reported a shortage of wagons which was having a detrimental effect on goods traffic receipts. After a short debate, the directors duly authorised the officer to seek tenders for the supply of twenty open goods wagons. Delivery was protracted and it was 17th May 1912 before advice was received that the new wagons were ready for delivery from Harrison & Camm. Even then the company was keen not to have the vehicles delivered empty, and arrangements were made for them to be loaded with coal from Shipley Colliery before arrival on the Colne Valley line in mid-June. The cost of the open wagons was £1,410 and two payments of £705 were made: the first on 25th July 1912 and the second on 17th September. Evidently some older vehicles were scrapped during this period, for the total wagon fleet registered at the end of the year was 176, a net gain of twelve. This total included 143 open wagons, three special wagons, six rail/timber trucks, nine 10-ton capacity covered vans, three goods brake vans and two service vehicles, a ballast wagon and a mobile crane.

For several years a CV&HR wagon examiner had inspected vehicles destined for stations on the Colne Valley line at Chappel before their onward transit. The examination, however, caused delays and it was felt that as few wagons were found defective the exercise was not worth continuing. Reporting to the board meeting on 8th July 1913, Charles Clarke suggested the suspension of examination for a period of three months, pending a review. Later in the same year on 9th September 1913 application was made for the provision of a wagon weighbridge at Halstead but because of financial constraints a decision was deferred.

Hawthorn, Leslie 2-4-2T *Hedingham* standing at the head of a freight train in Haverhill CV&HR station yard on 29th July 1911. The locomotive has the large letters CV on the side tanks either side of the nameplate. Although used primarily on passenger work the 2-4-2Ts also worked goods trains.
LCGB/Ken Nunn

No further additions or deletions were made to the wagon fleet in 1913 or 1914 and the total stock remained at 176, consisting of 143 open wagons, nine 10-ton covered vans, three special wagons, ten cattle trucks, six rail/timber trucks, three goods brake vans plus two service vehicles, a ballast wagon and a mobile crane. With wagons now travelling much further afield, the directors were concerned about the cost of repairs incurred whilst away from home territory and on 13th July 1915 required a monthly report of all wagon repairs whether on the Colne Valley or on foreign railways. On the same day it was agreed that S. Stevens should repair a total of eight wagons at a cost of £53 12s 9d each. The work was completed by 9th November, some being repaired at Halstead and some in his own shops. On 28th February 1916, S. Stevens was paid £229 2s 0d and £201 10s 6d in settlement of the wagon repairs. Then on 5th June 1916 the Assistant Secretary approached Thomas Moy & Company to repair three of the company's cattle wagons. By the end of the month Moy agreed to send a wagon examiner to Halstead to inspect and report on the condition of the vehicles and provide an estimate. Moy subsequently provided the estimate for the repair of the three vehicles, priced at £104 each wagon, and the board accepted this tender on 14th August 1916.

For some time the Permanent Way Department had expressed interest in obtaining some tipping wagons to assist with reballasting of the line but because of the financial problems had been reluctant to approach the directors. On 6th November 1916 a submission was made but despite the poor condition of the track and the urgent requirement for the wagons the directors were undecided and deferred a decision. In the meantime, Moy had taken delivery of the three cattle wagons for repairs – but when they had not

been returned by mid-February 1917 urgent enquiries were made to ascertain when the vehicles would be returned. At the directors meeting on 26th February the Secretary read a report from the company saying they could not promise a firm delivery date as they had urgent Government work in hand as higher priority. By May 1917 the directors were again under pressure from the Permanent Way Department and on 7th of the month asked the Secretary to obtain prices from suitable wagon builders. For the entire period from 1912 through World War One until 1919 the company registered 176 wagons.

By the summer of 1918 the company was experiencing another wagon shortage and had to hire vehicles. On 14th August £1 6s 0d was paid to Thomas Moy and £3 19s 0d to Platt Brothers in respect of short-term hire. The problem stemmed from the absence of vehicles which had been sent to destinations far and wide; because of the war effort these wagons became common user and were not returned promptly to their home system. In some instances they suffered failure and required attention, and on 25th September 1918, £7 8s 5d was paid to the Great Western Railway in respect of repairs. The end of hostilities did nothing to ease the situation and further repairs were made away from home territory, for on 12th February 1919 £1 17s 9d was paid to the Lancashire & Yorkshire Railway and £1 11s 8d to the Great Western. Yet further bills were settled on 2nd April, when £2 9s 6d was paid to the GWR, £1 1s 10d to the Cheshire Lines Committee and £1 9s 3d to the Great Northern Railway.

The following month the situation of errant wagons was so desperate that a complaint was made to the Board of Trade regarding the shortage of wagons after no success had been made complaining

Hudswell, Clarke, CV&HR 0-6-2T No. 5 hauling the 11.00am freight train from Haverhill to Chappel, seen near Birdbrook on 29th July 1911. The train of considerable length includes in its formation in the final wagon, a boiler from 0-4-2T No. 1 en route for repair at Stratford. The locomotive was absorbed by the L&NER at Grouping as the sole member of Class 'N18' and was renumbered 8314. It never worked on its home territory and was usually employed on the Wivenhoe to Brightlingsea branch or as shed and station pilot at Colchester before withdrawal from traffic in January 1928. *Author's collection*

to the Railway Clearing House. This had little effect, for wagons, being common user, continued to travel almost the length and breadth of the British Isles. On 16th July 1919 payments were made to the GWR (£1 11s 3d) and Midland Railway (£1 11s 9d) for wagon repairs, whilst in November the Midland received £1 2s 10d and the GWR £2 9s 7d. Then on 7th January settlement was made with the Midland, £2 2s 11d, the North British Railway, £1 5s 0d and the Great Central Railway, a mere 19s 10d. Later in the year, on 3rd June £3 7s 8d was paid to the London & North Western Railway, followed by £3 5s 3d to the Midland, £1 19s 7d to the Caledonian Railway, £1 4s 3d to the North Eastern Railway and £2 0s 3d to the North British on 9th November 1920.

Colne Valley goods wagon No. 75 was destroyed by fire whilst standing at March GER and on 4th July 1921 the General Manager was instructed to purchase a second-hand wagon as a replacement. In the meantime CV&HR wagons continued their wanderings and need for repair and attention. On 11th August settlement was made to several new companies in addition to old favourites: £2 11s 6d was paid to the London & South Western Railway, £1 14s 0d to the

Great Central, £3 11s 4d to the North Eastern, £6 16s 1d to the L&NWR, £1 12s 0d to the GNR, £1 1s 9d to the South Eastern & Chatham, £1 13s 3d to the North British, £1 1s 0d to the London, Brighton & South Coast Railway and £13 3s 3d to the GWR. Then on 12th October 1921 settlement was being made to the SE&CR to the value of £5 5s 10d, GER £52 10s 0d and GWR £14 12s 8d. The following month, on 2nd November payments were made to the L&SWR for £2 7s 11d, the Hull & Barnsley Railway for 18s 6d and Thomas Moy for £235 for routine maintenance and repair of vehicles, followed by £6 5s 0d to the North British on 9th February 1922.

As the year progressed yet more payments were incurred and on 11th May 1922 settlement was made with no fewer than nine companies for repairs made to CV&HR wagons: £1 14s 3d to the L&SWR, 17s 5d to the GER, 18s 5d to the Caledonian, £6 3s 10d to the NER, £8 3s 2d to the Midland, 16s 11d to the North British, £2 5s 3d to the North Staffordshire, £1 10s 1d to the SE&CR and £6 4s 6d to the L&NWR. On 7th November the GCR was paid £2 7s 10d and the Midland £1 17s 8d, whilst on 11th January

A 'J15' Class 0-6-0 is shunting a rake of goods wagons at Haverhill South on a trip working from Haverhill North. *Dr I.C. Allen*

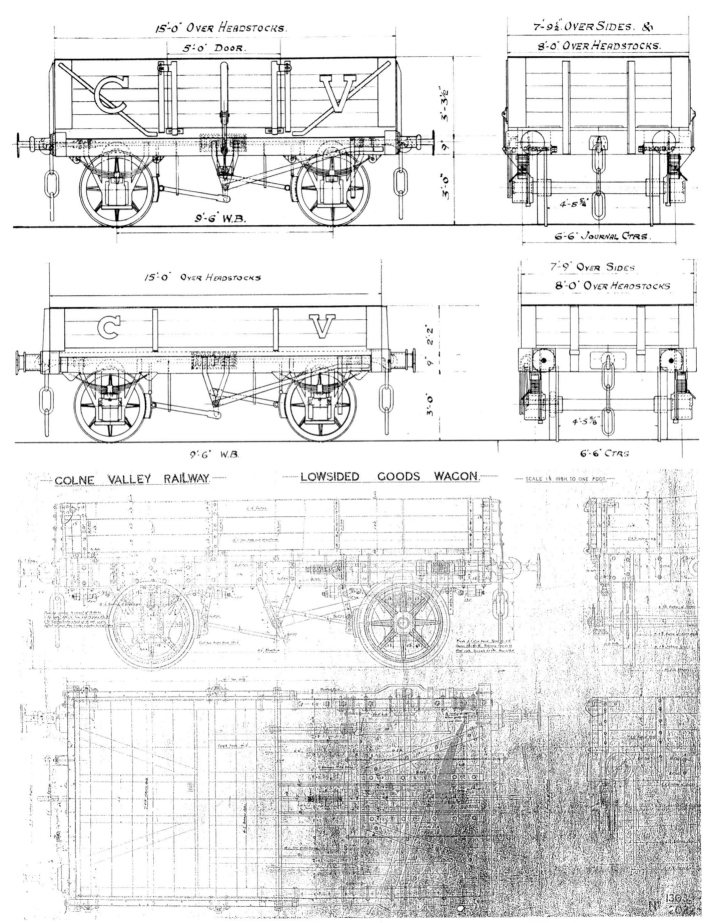

Top: CV&HR 5-plank 10-ton open wagon.   **Centre:** CV&HR 3-plank 8-ton open wagon.   **Above:** CV&HR 3-plank open wagon.

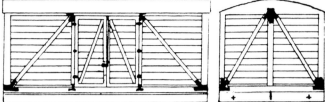

LEFT: Halstead Co-operative Society open wagon.
ABOVE: CV&HR-covered van body.
(A) GER 10-ton high-sided open wagon to diagram 16.
(B) GER 10-ton high-sided open wagon to diagram 17.
(C) GER 10-ton 7-plank high-sided open wagon to diagram 55.
(D) GER 10-ton covered goods van to diagram 15.

1923 outstanding settlements were made to the London Midland & Scottish Railway in respect of repairs made by the Midland (£1 4s 8d) and the Glasgow & South Western Railway (19s 0d), the Southern Railway in respect of £1 0s 6d owing to the LB&SCR, £1 10s 3d to the GWR and £1 2s 4d to the L&NER in respect of work performed by the GER. For the remaining life of the company from 1919 until absorption into the L&NER the company registered 174 vehicles and these included 143 open wagons, three special wagons, nine covered wagons, six timber wagons, ten cattle trucks, and three brake vans. Typical dimensions of a CV&HR 5-plank 10-ton open wagon were: length over headstocks 15 feet 0 inches, wheelbase 9 feet 6 inches; whilst a 3-plank 8-ton open had identical wheelbase measurement and length over headstocks. The cattle wagons with wooden underframes were 19 feet in length, whilst a 10-ton wagon with timber underframe for dealing with equipment from the Tortoise Foundry at Halstead was a 3-plank dropside vehicle with a length of 14 feet 11 inches.

CV&HR goods wagons were painted in a dull grey livery, later recorded as French grey but realistically a standard lead colour, with black below solebar level. White lettering was used for the initials 'C.V.R.' but during the early 20th century the initials 'C V' appeared in large white characters with bold serifs between 12 and 18 inches high, although some covered vans had non-serifed lettering. The fleet number was painted in the lower left of the sides of open wagons in serif style. Brake vans carried the earlier lettering with 'C.V.R.' centrally on the side and running number below, prefixed by 'No' about 6 inches in height. Because of the parlous financial position, as with the coaching stock the carriage and wagon painter mixed various remnants of paint in the bottom of tins to cover minor wagon repairs and the uniform appearance was far from standard. The ironwork below solebar level, buffer guides, buffers, drawbars, drawbar plates and couplings were black.

In addition to the CV&HR and GER fleet, many wagons owned by other railway companies were used to deliver and collect agricultural and livestock traffic, whilst coal and coke supplies came in private owner wagons. These fell into two categories: those belonging to the collieries consigning the coal; and merchants and coal factors wagons, which were loaded at the collieries. Private owner wagons seen daily included those of Thomas Moy and the Halstead Co-operative Society Limited.

In view of the close association the CV&HR had with the ECR and GER it would be remiss not to include brief details of vehicles which would have found regular use on the line. The initial vehicles were wooden open wagons with side doors and fitted with dumb buffers. Where grain, straw or merchandise traffic was susceptible to wet weather a tarpaulin sheet was utilised to cover the contents. If a brake van was included at the tail of the train it would have been a 10-ton vehicle. In the years prior to the turn of the century the GER utilised 4-plank bodied open wagons with wooden frames dating from 1882 for the conveyance of general merchandise and

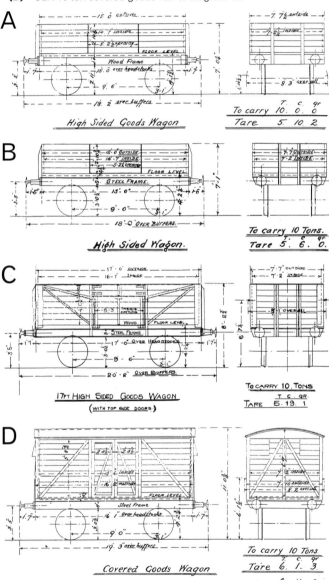

minerals. From 1887, these wagons were gradually superseded by 5-plank, 9-ton capacity, later 10-ton, opens to diagram 16 with 9 feet 6 inch wheelbase and measuring 15 feet 0 inches over headstocks. Later, 10-ton 7-plank open wagons to diagram 17, with a length of 15 feet over headstocks and 9 feet 6 inches wheelbase were also used. Another variation was the use of 10-ton 7-plank opens to diagram 55, measuring 17 feet 6 inches over headstocks and 9 feet 6 inches wheelbase for vegetable and root traffic. For fruit and perishable traffic, 10-ton ventilated vans to diagram 15 were provided, measuring 16 feet 1 inch over headstocks, with 9 feet 0 inches wheelbase and overall height of 11 feet 0¾ inches. Covered goods vans to diagram 47 were later also utilised; they measured 17 feet 3 inches over headstocks, had a wheelbase of 10 feet 6 inches and were 11 feet 2 inches in height. A third variation was the 10-ton capacity covered goods wagon to diagram 72, which measured 19 feet 0 inches over headstocks, whilst maintaining a 10 feet 6 inches wheelbase.

The extensive cattle traffic conveyed to various local markets stretched the CV&HR resources and three types of GER cattle wagons would also have been employed. The first, of 8 tons capacity, was to diagram 5 and was 18 feet 7 inches over headstocks, had a 10 feet 6 inches wheelbase and was 10 feet 10¾ inches in height. The second to diagram 6, was of 9 tons capacity and measured 19 feet 0 inches over headstocks with a 10 feet 6 inches wheelbase

and overall height of 11 feet 2 inches. The third GER variant of cattle wagon, to diagram 7, was of 10 tons capacity, 19 feet 3 inches over headstocks with a 10 feet 6 inches wheelbase and overall height of 11 feet 2 inches. The company also utilised a GER goods brake van at the tail of the train which was usually a 20-ton 4-wheel vehicle to diagram 56, measuring 17 feet 6 inches over headstocks, a 10 feet 3 inches wheelbase and 3 feet 1 inch diameter wheels.

After grouping, the CV&HR wagons continued in use in the short term but gradually L&NER standard wagons made an appearance. The most numerous were probably the 12-ton, 5-plank opens with 8 feet 0 inches wheelbase to code 2, and 12-ton 6-plank opens with 10 feet 0 ins wheelbase to code 91, built after 1932. Later variations included 13-ton 7-plank open wagons to code 162, measuring 16 feet 6 inches over headstocks, and with a 9 feet 0 inches wheelbase. All were used on vegetable and sugar beet traffic and some were even utilised for brick traffic. Fitted and unfitted

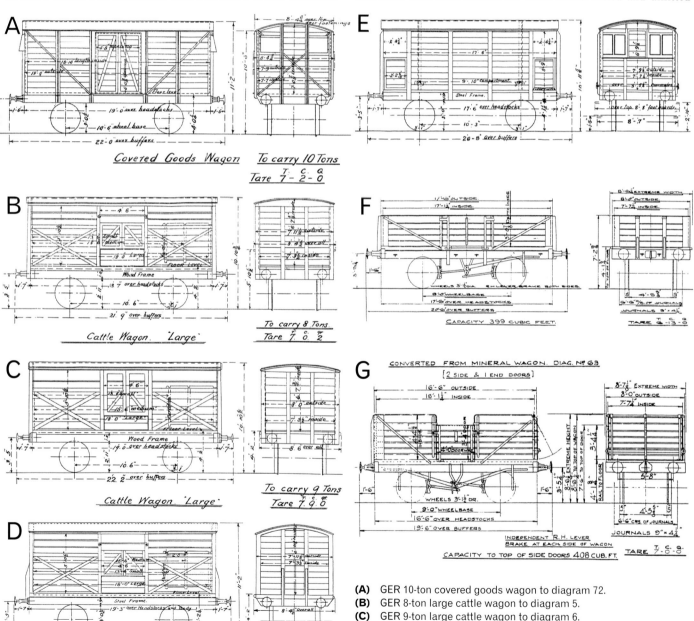

(A) GER 10-ton covered goods wagon to diagram 72.
(B) GER 8-ton large cattle wagon to diagram 5.
(C) GER 9-ton large cattle wagon to diagram 6.
(D) GER 10-ton large cattle wagon to diagram 7.
(E) GER 20-ton goods brake van to diagram 56.
(F) L&NER 12-ton open goods wagon to code 2.
(G) L&NER 13-ton open goods wagon to code 162.

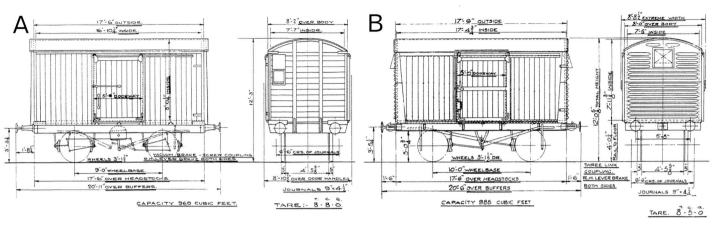

12-ton, 9 feet 0 inches wheelbase covered vans to code 16 conveyed perishable goods, fruit and malt, and later some were designated for fruit traffic only. From 1934, 12 tons capacity vans to code 171 with steel underframes and compressed corrugated steel ends were introduced, whilst at the same time the wheelbase was extended to a length of 10 feet 0 inches. Specific fruit vans with both 9 feet 0 inches and 10 feet 0 inches wheelbase also saw service on the Colne Valley line for malt traffic. Agricultural machinery destined for local farms and exports from Earls Colne used 12-ton 'Lowfit' wagons, with 10 feet 0 inches wheelbase and overall length over headstocks of 17 feet 6 inches. Larger machinery arrived and departed on one of the ex-GER 14-ton, 25 feet 6 inches, 'Mack K2' machinery wagons to diagram 75 and later L&NER builds. L&NER brake vans provided for branch traffic included 20-ton 'Toad B' to code 34 and 'Toad E' to code 64 vehicles, with 10 feet 6 inches wheelbase and measuring 22 feet 5 inches over buffers. 'Toad D' brake vans to code 61 with 16 feet 0 inches wheelbase and measuring 27 feet 5 inches over buffers were also employed. After nationalisation many of the older wooden-bodied wagons were scrapped and much of the traffic conveyed in open wagons was transported in 16-ton all-steel mineral vehicles. In the latter years malt traffic was conveyed in 20-ton bulk grain wagons which became a familiar sight in Halstead yard. The L&NER wagon livery was grey for non-fitted wagons and vans, whilst all vehicles fitted with automatic brakes were painted red oxide, which changed to bauxite around 1940. Similar liveries were carried in BR days.

In CV&HR days wagon stock returns were sent to the company head office at Halstead but after grouping the stock return was submitted to the District Office at Cambridge.

In independent years the CV&HR maintained the wagon fleet at Haverhill and later Halstead. The carriage and wagon shops at Halstead could handle most types of repairs to wagon stock but no wagon building was attempted. Halstead shops also manufactured and repaired tarpaulin wagon sheets and one man was employed full time on the project with assistance as necessary from a second man. Soon after grouping Ipswich and Cambridge wagon repairs shops carried out maintenance of wagon stock used on Colne Valley services. In the event of a failure or defect of a wagon at an intermediate station, a travelling wagon examiner based at Halstead and later Sudbury attended to repairs locally.

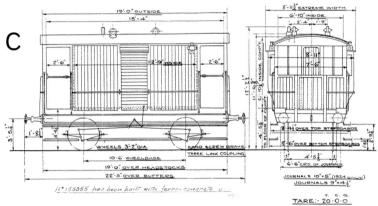

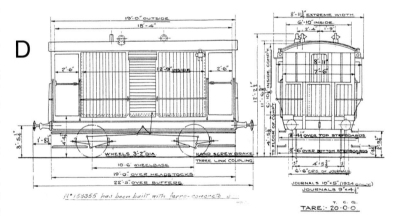

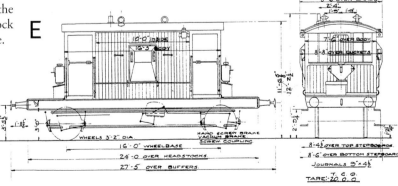

(A) L&NER 12-ton covered goods wagon to code 16.
(B) L&NER 12-ton covered goods wagon with steel ends to code 171.
(C) L&NER 20-ton goods brake van 'Toad B' to code 34.
(D) L&NER 20-ton goods brake van 'Toad E' to code 64.
(E) L&NER 20-ton goods brake van 'Toad D' to code 61.

The corrugated iron carriage shed and repair shop at Halstead standing hard against the original footbridge circa 1880, before improvements to the track layout in the yard. Much of the surrounding area used for permanent way materials, presents an unkempt appearance with heaps of scrap iron interspersed with short lengths of rail. The shed was also used for the making and repair of wagon sheets and maintenance of the eight horse drawn drays.

M. Root collection

Appendix 1

Level Crossings

No.	Location	Mileage from Liverpool Street		Local Name	Status
		M	Ch		
	Chappel & Wakes Colne Station	50	18		
	Junction with CV&HR	50	31		
1	Chappel & White Colne	51	64	Fox & Pheasant	Public
2	Chappel & White Colne	52	04		Occupation
	White Colne Station	52	31		
3	White Colne & Earls Colne	52	32½	White Colne	Public
4	White Colne & Earls Colne	52	64½		Occupation
5	White Colne & Earls Colne	53	07	Millbrook	Occupation
6	White Colne & Earls Colne	53	20		Occupation[1]
7	White Colne & Earls Colne	53	32		Occupation & Footpath[1]
8	White Colne & Earls Colne	53	37½		Occupation
9	White Colne & Earls Colne	53	40½		Occupation
10	White Colne & Earls Colne	53	51		Occupation
	Earls Colne Station	53	67		
11	Earls Colne & Halstead	53	69	Earls Colne Station	Public
12	Earls Colne & Halstead	54	03	White's	Footpath
13	Earls Colne & Halstead	54	07½		Occupation
14	Earls Colne & Halstead	54	21	Munn's	Occupation
15	Earls Colne & Halstead	54	40	Elms Hall	Occupation
16	Earls Colne & Halstead	54	53¾	Langley Mill	Public
17	Earls Colne & Halstead	54	71		Occupation
18	Earls Colne & Halstead	55	08¾		Footpath
19	Earls Colne & Halstead	55	12		Occupation
20	Earls Colne & Halstead	55	46½		Occupation[2]
21	Earls Colne & Halstead	55	67		Occupation[3]
22	Earls Colne & Halstead	55	78	Parsons Lane	Public[4]
	Halstead Station	56	26		
23	Halstead & S & C Hedingham	56	28	Trinity Street	Public
24	Halstead & S & C Hedingham	56	38		Footpath
25	Halstead & S & C Hedingham	56	55		Occupation
26	Halstead & S & C Hedingham	56	59¼		Footpath
27	Halstead & S & C Hedingham	56	77		Occupation
28	Halstead & S & C Hedingham	57	40		Footpath
29	Halstead & S & C Hedingham	57	52½		Occupation
30	Halstead & S & C Hedingham	57	60¼		Occupation
31	Halstead & S & C Hedingham	58	06½	Wallace	Occupation & Footpath
32	Halstead & S & C Hedingham	58	30		Occupation & Footpath
33	Halstead & S & C Hedingham	58	73		Occupation & Footpath
34	Halstead & S & C Hedingham	59	40		Footpath
	Sible & Castle Hedingham Station	59	50		

No.	Location	Mileage from Liverpool Street		Local Name	Status
		M	Ch		
35	S & C Hedingham & Yeldham	59	52¾	Gas Works	Occupation
36	S & C Hedingham & Yeldham	60	03½	Nunnery	Occupation
37	S & C Hedingham & Yeldham	60	24¼		Occupation
38	S & C Hedingham & Yeldham	60	44	Apple Dumpling	Footpath
39	S & C Hedingham & Yeldham	60	59	Newman's Hill	Occupation
40	S & C Hedingham & Yeldham	61	23½	Duckett's Hill	Occupation
41	S & C Hedingham & Yeldham	61	44	Pool Street	Occupation
42	S & C Hedingham & Yeldham	62	01		Footpath
43	S & C Hedingham & Yeldham	62	07	Yeldham Station	Public Road
	Yeldham Station	62	09		
44	Yeldham & Birdbrook	62	26½		Footpath
45	Yeldham & Birdbrook	62	63¾	Man's Cross	Occupation & Footpath
46	Yeldham & Birdbrook	63	59¾		Occupation
47	Yeldham & Birdbrrok	63	64		Occupation
48	Yeldham & Birdbrook	64	04¼	Pettyfield	Occupation & Footpath
49	Yeldham & Birdbrook	64	21	Roman Villa	Footpath
50	Yeldham & Birdbrook	65	11		Occupation
51	Yeldham & Birdbrook	65	20		Footpath
	Birdbrook Station	65	75		
52	Birdbrook & Haverhill CV	66	06	Hunwick's	Occupation
53	Birdbrook & Haverhill CV	66	79	Walton	Occupation
54	Birdbrook & Haverhill CV	67	64		Occupation
	Junction with GER connection	68	50		
55	Birdbrook & Haverhill CV	68	78	Brickworks	Occupation
	Haverhill CV Station	69	26	at buffer stops	
GER Line from Colne Valley Junction to Haverhill Junction					
14	Colne Valley Jnc & Haverhill Jnc	69	13		Occupation & Footpath
13	Colne Valley Jnc & Haverhill Jnc	69	31		Footpath
	Haverhill GER	69	43		

Notes:

1 Closed 17th December 1957.
2 Widened 5th July 1955 on closure of crossing No. 21.
3 Closed 5th July 1955.
4 Also known as Parsonage Lane.

Appendix 2

Bridges

CV&HR Bridge No. & Mileage			L&NER Bridge No. & Mileage			Location	Local Name	Under or Over	Type	Spans	Square Span Between Abutments or Supports		Skew Span Between Abutments or Supports		Depth of Construction		Distance from Road or Surface of Water to Rail		Construction
No.	M	CH	No.	M	CH						FT	IN	FT	IN	FT	IN	FT	IN	
1	0	28	1	50	49	Chappel & White Colne	Old House Farm	Over	Public	1	25	1	28	8	3	3	19	0	Brick abutments, brick arch 5 ring & parapets.
2	0	60	2	51	02	Chappel & White Colne	Lane Farm	Over	Public	1	16	0	—	—	2	6	17	2	Brick abutments, brick arch 3 ring & parapets.
3	2	24	3	52	46	White Colne & Earls Colne	Colneford Hill Farm	Under	Public	1	19	6	28	8	2	3	17	8	Brick abutments, wrought iron girders & trough floor.
4	2	66	4	53	08	White Colne & Earls Colne	Tank	Under	Stream	1	13	2	—	—	2	7	8	5	Brick abutments, No. 4 15 x 5 RSJs per track. Rebuilt 1910.
5	3	11	5	53	33	White Colne & Earls Colne	Burrows	Under	Occup'n & River Colne	1	38	0	—	—	2	8	10	4	Brick abutments, steel girders & RSJ cross girders. Rebuilt 1908.
6	3	57	6	53	79	Earls Colne & Halstead	White's Bridge No. 1	Under	River Colne	1	38	0	—	—	2	7	13	2	Brick abutments, steel girders & RSJ cross girders. Rebuilt 1908.
7	3	61	7	54	04	Earls Colne & Halstead	White's Bridge No. 2	Under	Occupation	1	38	0	—	—	2	7	8 7 path / 11 2 river		Brick abutments, steel girders & RSJ cross girders. Rebuilt 1908.
8	5	05	8	55	27	Earls Colne & Halstead	Blue Bridge	Under	Public Road A604 & Stream	1	35	0	—	—	1	10	16	1	Brick abutments wrought iron girders.
9	5	15	9	55	37	Earls Colne & Halstead	Blue Bridge Water	Under	River	1	17 0 / 16 9		23 0 / 22 7		3 1 / 3 1		14 8 river / 10 2 path		Brick abutments, No. 4 20 x 7½ RSJs per track. Rebuilt 1910 by Dorman Long.
9A	5	74	10	56	17	Earls Colne & Halstead	Footbridge	Over	Public	1 1 1	70 4 / 70 4 / 70 4		—	—	—	6	16	3	Cast iron columns, wrought iron girders. Built 1887.
10	7	00	11	57	23	Halstead & Hedingham	Hepworth No. 1	Over	Public Road A604	1	25	0	—	—	2	8	16	6	Brick abutments, brick jack arches, cast iron girders. Restricted to 5 tons weight limit 1942.

CV&HR Bridge No. & Mileage (M CH)	L&NER Bridge No. & Mileage (M CH)	Location	Local Name	Under or Over	Type	Spans	Square Span between abutments or supports (FT IN)	Skew Span between abutments or supports (FT IN)	Depth of Construction (FT IN)	Distance from road or surface of water to rail (FT IN)	Construction
11 7 17	12 57 41	Halstead & Hedingham	Hepworth No. 2	Under	Occupation & River	1 1 1	12 4 14 2 14 6	— —	2 9 2 9 2 9	11 3 13 0	Timber with steel centre girder, No. 4 15 x 5 RSJs per track.
12 8 11	13 58 35	Halstead & Hedingham	Purls Hill	Over	Public	1	25 0	25 6	3 0	16 7	Brick abutments, brick jack arches, cast iron girders. Restricted to 8 tons weight limit 1942.
13 8 59	14 59 03	Halstead & Hedingham	Alderford	Over	Public	1	25 0	— —	2 8	18 3	Brick abutments, brick arch 4 ring and parapets.
14 8 77	15 59 20	Halstead & Hedingham	Hedingham	Under	River Colne	1	41 0	— —	2 8	9 11	Brick abutments, steel girders, RSJ cross girders. Rebuilt 1913.
15 9 37	16 59 62	Hedingham & Yeldham	Castle	Under	Public	1	29 11	30 9	2 1	16 3	Brick abutments, steel girders & cross troughing, one girder designed as cross girder.
16 9 61	17 60 04	Hedingham & Yeldham	Nunnery Bridge No. 1	Under	Occupation & River Colne	1 1 1	15 2 14 1 14 7	— —	4 2 4 2 4 2	11 10 road 16 2 river	Timber.
17 9 73	18 60 16	Hedingham & Yeldham	Nunnery Bridge No. 2	Under	Public	1	20 0	— —	1 9	15 0	Brick abutments, steel girders & cross troughing.
18 10 24	19 60 47	Hedingham & Yeldham	Apple Dumpling	Under	River Colne	1	33 0	— —	2 8	11 6	Steel girders & RSJ cross girders. Rebuilt 1913.
19 10 54	20 60 78	Hedingham & Yeldham	Yeldham Road	Under	Public Road A604	1	30 0	39 0	2 0 later 2 8	16 11	Brick abutments, wrought iron girders. Reconstruction completed 22 January 1947. All welded steel plate girder RSJ and concrete floor, gas tube handrail.
20 11 37	21 61 59	Hedingham & Yeldham	Yeldham Cutting	Over	Occupation	1	25 2	— —	2 11	18 5	Brick abutments, brick arch 4 ring and parapets.
21 11 56	22 61 79	Hedingham & Yeldham	White Hart Culvert	Under	Stream	1	12 0	— —	28 0	32 3	Brick abutments, brick arch 4 ring & parapets.
22 12 19	23 62 42	Yeldham & Birdbrook	Farm Road	Under	Occupation	1	16 2	— —	4 0	18 2	Brick abutments, brick arch 4 ring & parapet. Rebuilt Down side spandrel & repaired by brick 1949 cost £415.
—	23A 63 19	Yeldham & Birdbrook	Culvert	Under	Stream	1	6 0	— —	— —	— —	Concrete.
23 13 01	24 63 23	Yeldham & Birdbrook	Stambourne Road	Under	Public	1	19 9	21 4	1 11½	16 4	Brick abutments, No. 4 15 x 4 channels per track. Rebuilt 1910.

CV&HR Bridge No. & Mileage (M Ch)	L&NER Bridge No. & Mileage (M Ch)	Location	Local Name	Under or Over	Type	Spans	Square Span between abutments or supports (Ft In)	Skew Span between abutments or supports (Ft In)	Depth of Construction (Ft In)	Distance from road or surface of water to rail (Ft In)	Construction
24 13 64	25 64 07	Yeldham & Birdbrook	Petyfield Lane	Under	Occupation	1	16 0	— —	2 8	14 2	Brick abutments, No. 4 15 x 5 RSJs per track. Rebuilt 1910.
25 14 12	26 64 34	Yeldham & Birdbrook	Culvert	Under	Stream	1	8 6	— —	8 8	14 6	Brick abutments, brick arch 3 ring & parapets.
26 14 36	27 64 58	Yeldham & Birdbrook	Ridgewell Wash	Under	Public	1	19 9	— —	2 0½	15 9½	Brick abutments, No. 4 15 x 4 channels per track. Rebuilt 1910
27 15 15	28 65 37	Yeldham & Birdbrook	Whitley Bridge	Over	Public	1	25 2	— —	4 3	19 5	Brick abutments, brick arch 4 ring & parapets.
28 15 55	29 65 77	Birdbrook & Haverhill	Hunwick Lane	Under	Public	1	20 0	26 0	1 9	15 9	Brick abutments, steel girders & cross troughing. Rebuilt 1913 by EC&JKealy.
29 16 16	30 66 38	Birdbrook & Haverhill	New England	Under	Public	1	20 0	— —	3 1	25 10	Brick abutments. brick arch & parapets.
30 16 33	31 66 55	Birdbrook & Haverhill	New Culvert Watsoe	Under	Stream	1	14 0	— —	28 6	36 6	Brick abutments, brick arch 4 ring and parapets.
31 16 54	32 66 77	Birdbrook & Haverhill	Great Walton's Farm Cattle Creep	Under	Occupation	1	11 9	— —	2 2½	11 5½	Brick abutments, No. 4 12 x 5 RSJs per track. Rebuilt 1910.
32 17 09	33 67 32	Birdbrook & Haverhill	Sturmer Road	Over	Public	1	25 2	— —	3 3	17 9	Brick abutments, brick arch 4 ring & parapets.
33 17 59	34 68 01	Birdbrook & Haverhill	Sturmer Hall Arch	Under	Occupation	1	15 10	— —	4 3½	20 10½	Brick abutments, brick arch 4 ring and parapets.
34 18 42	35 68 64	Birdbrook & Haverhill	Bumpstead Road	Under	Public	1	19 7	19 10	2 7½	19 3	Brick abutments, No. 4 18 x 7 RSJs per track. Rebuilt 1909-10.
Buffer Stops 69 26											

HAVERHILL GER TO COLNE VALLEY JUNCTION

GER Bridge No. (M Ch)	Location	Local Name	Under or Over	Type	Spans	Square Span (Ft In)	Skew Span (Ft In)	Depth of Construction (Ft In)	Distance to rail (Ft In)	Construction
2169 15 57	Haverhill & Colne Valley Jnc	Stream	Under	Stream	1	6 0	— —	36 0	40 0	Brick abutments, brick arch & parapets.
					1	6 0	— —	36 0	40 0	
2170 15 59	Haverhill & Colne Valley Jnc	Sturmer aka Hamlet Road	Under	Public	1	35 0		4 4	38 0	Brick abutments, brick arch & parapets.
					1	35 0		4 4	38 0	
					1	35 0		4 4	38 0	

Appendix 3

L&NER Amended Bridge Mileages, 1939

L&NER BRIDGE No.	AMENDED MILEAGE M	CH	NAME	L&NER BRIDGE No.	AMENDED MILEAGE M	CH	NAME
1	50	57¾	Old House Farm	19	60	55	Apple Dumpling
2	51	10	Lane Farm	20	61	05½	Yeldham Road
3	52	53¾	Colneford Hill Farm	21	61	67½	Yeldham Cutting
4	53	16¾	Tank	22	62	06½	White Hart Culvert
5	53	41½	Burrows	23	62	50	Farm Road
6	54	07	White Bridge No. 1	23A	63	25½	Culvert
7	54	11¾	White Bridge No. 2	24	63	31½	Stambourne Road
8	55	35	Blue Bridge	25	64	15	Pettyfield Lane
9	55	45½	Blue Bridge Water	26	64	66½	Culvert
10	56	24¾	Footbridge	27	64	66½	Ridgewell Wash
11	57	31¼	Hepworth No. 1	28	65	45½	Whiteley Bridge
12	57	49¼	Hepworth No. 2	29	66	05½	Hunwick Lane
13	58	43	Purls Hill	30	66	46½	New England
14	59	10¾	Alderford	31	66	63½	New Culvert Watsoe
15	59	28½	Hedingham	32	67	04¾	Great Walton's Farm Cattle Creep
16	59	70¼	Castle	33	67	40	Sturmer Road
17	60	11¾	Nunnery Bridge No. 1	34	68	08¾	Sturmer Hall Arch
18	60	24	Nunnery Bridge No. 2	35	68	72	Bumpstead Road

Halstead station is a forlorn sight in the spring of 1965, five years after the withdrawal of passenger traffic and days before the passage of the last freight train. The canopy still fronts the building but Trinity Street gates are left open for road users and closed only when necessary by trainmen for the passage of a train over the crossing. *J. Watling*

Appendix 4

L&NER Amended Level Crossing Mileages, 1939

L&NER CROSSING No.	AMENDED MILEAGE M CH		L&NER CROSSING No.	AMENDED MILEAGE M CH		L&NER CROSSING No.	AMENDED MILEAGE M CH		L&NER CROSSING No.	AMENDED MILEAGE M CH	
1	51	72	15	54	47¾	29	not recorded		43	62	15½
2	52	10½	16	54	60¾	30	57	67¼	44	62	34
3	52	39	17	54	78	31	58	14½	45	62	70¾
4	52	72½	18	55	15¾	32	58	38¼	46	63	66¾
5	53	05	19	55	18¾	33	59	00	47	63	72½
6	53	18¾	20	55	53½	34	not recorded		48	64	04¼
7	53	28¾	21	55	74	35	59	59¾	49	64	29¼
8	53	37½	22	56	06	36	60	09¾	50	not recorded	
9	not recorded		23	56	35¾	37	not recorded		51	55	28¼
10	53	47½	24	56	45¾	38	60	43¼	52	66	14
11	53	77	25	56	62½	39	60	67	53	67	06
12	not recorded		26	56	66½	40	61	31½	54	67	73¾
13	54	13	27	57	05	41	61	53¼	55	not recorded	
14	54	27	28	not recorded		42	62	07½			

LM '2MT' Class 2-6-0 No. 46468 rouses the echoes as it heads a return Sunday excursion on Colne Valley line away from Chappel Junction.

Dr I.C. Allen

Appendix 5

CV&HR Appendix to the Working Time Book, 1905

Private and not for Publication.

NO. 1.

Colne Valley & Halstead Railway.

APPENDIX

TO

Working Time Book

FOR THE INFORMATION OF COMPANY'S SERVANTS ONLY.

1st JANUARY, 1905,

AND UNTIL FURTHER NOTICE.

☞ The issue of these Instructions is not intended to relieve Servants of the Company from the obligation to make themselves thoroughly acquainted with the Rules and Regulations approved by the Board of Directors on 26th April, 1904.

ELYOT S. HAWKINS,

Secretary and General Manager

Halstead,

December, 1904.

Printed by W. H. Root, Caxton Works, Halstead.

CONTENTS.

	PAGE.
Advertising on Railway	33
Accidents to Company's Servants and other persons	34
Booking to distant places	24
Continuous Brakes	7
Carriage Windows Damaged	19
Cleansing and Disinfecting of Horse Boxes	20
Ditto Cattle Trucks and Pens	21
Cattle Pens	21
Carriage Trucks	22
Conveyance of Dogs by Railway	23
Cleanliness, Smartness and Civility	25
Carriage Keys	25
Cleaning and Trimming Lamps	26
Cancelling Newspaper Stamps	26
Careless Shunting	26
Cleaning and Oiling Points and Signals	27
Cattle Trucks by Passenger Trains	27
Consumption of Coal, Gas, Water, Oil and other Stores	27
Covering of Gas and Water Meters in Frosty Weather	28
Carriage Labels	30
Correspondence by Train	30
Cleansing of Empty Wagons	32
Defective Road or Works	17
Damaged Waggons	31
Derailment of Rolling Stock	31
Electric Bell Communications	6
Electric Telegraph Instructions	8
Engine Head Lights	13
Engine Whistles	14
Examination of Tickets	23
Emission of Smoke from Engines	30

	PAGE.
Foreign Co's. Vehicles not fitted with Hand Brakes	7
Foreign Ropes and Chains	31
General Instructions	19
Guards Journals	28
Goods Guards' Vans with Stoves in them	29
Goods Trains outside Station Limits	29
Goods Brakes not supplied with required articles	30
Hay and Straw Traffic	16
Ditto to Lines South of Thames	16
Horse Boxes	19
Horse Boxes received at G.E. Stations	21
Hounds on Line	34
Inclines steeper than 1 in 150 and more than a ½ mile long	16
Instructions as to Carriage Cleaning	22
Instructions to be observed in connection with Repairs to Carriages, Wagons and other Vehicles	27
List of Electric Train Tablet, Train Staff and Block Telegraph Sections	28
List of Electrical Apparatus between Signal Cabins, &c.	30
List of Sidings Locked by Annett's Key	32
Locking Gear, Signals and Points	17
Loading of Horse Boxes	31
Line Blocked with Snow	31
Loading of Iron and Round Timber, &c.	27
Lighting of Roof Lamps in Ordinary and Special Trains	28
Live Stock Traffic Received for Conveyance on Saturdays	32
Last Vehicle on Train	33

	PAGE.
Live Stock to and from Shows	34
Missing Parts of Rolling Stock	24
Maintenance of Weighing Machines	27
Notice to Ticket Collectors	22
Ordinary Loads of Goods Engines	18
Orders for Rolling Stock	22
Overcrowding of Live Stock	31
Particulars of Telegraph Circuits	8
Pens (Cattle)	21
Privacy of Booking Office	22
Parcels and Milk Traffic	24
Passenger Fares Boards	25
Private Wagons	32
Parcels Post Baskets	34
Preventing Fire at Stations during night	34
Regulations re Telegraph Instruments	8
Running of Late Passenger Trains	21
Releasing Brakes when Shunting	26
Roadside Vans loaded from other Companies' Lines to C.V. Line	29
Red Tail Signal Notice of running of Special Trains	33
Reporting Accidents	35

	PAGE.
Stamped Newspaper Parcels	26
Station Platforms	26
Shunting Poles	26
Shunting over Points worked from Elevated Boxes	27
Securing Wagon Doors	31
Sheets	31
Scotch Blocks and Safety Points	32
Snow and Frost	32
Signal Notice of Running Special Trains	33
Train Staff and Ticket Boxes	6
Telegraph Circuits	8
Telegraph Apparatus	11
Telegrams	12
Trucks, Cleansing	21
Time Tables and Bills	23
Train Alteration Slips	23
Trespassing on Line	24
Trains entering Stations on Wrong Road	25
Trainmen	29
Trains stopping short of Water Columns, &c.	30
Timber Wagons	32
Tail Board, re Running Special Trains	33
Ventilating Carriages	30
Wagons put off Goods Trains to reduce loads	15
Working of Trains at certain Stations, &c.	15
Working of Brick Traffic	16
Water Columns	18
Warning before moving Wagons, &c.	25
Working of Travelling and Stationary Cranes	28
Working of Engines near Banks of standing Grass, Orchards, Corn, and Plantations	30
Wagon Labels	32

	PAGE.
Sidings locked by Annett's Key	17
Shunting Passenger Trains into Sidings	17
Shunting in Sidings next Main Line	17
Special Events	19
Shackles on Passenger Vehicles	22
Statement of Special Bookings	23
Sanding Rails in Slippery Weather	25

5

List of Electric Train Tablet, Train Staff and Block Telegraph Sections.

Section.	System.	Form of Staff.	Colour of Staff and Ticket.
Chappel and Mark's Tey G.E.R. Section.	Tablet.		
Chappel and Colne	Electric Train Staff.		
Colne and Halstead	Train Staff and Ticket.	Wood Round.	Yellow.
Halstead and Castle Hedingham	Ditto.	Wood Round. (Annett's Key Attached.)	Dark Terra Cotta.
Castle Hedingham and Yeldham	Ditto.	Wood and Brass. Round.	Green.
Yeldham and Haverhill C.V. Junction	Ditto.	Brass. Square	Pink.
Haverhill C.V. Junction and Haverhill, Colne Valley Station.	Ditto.	Iron Diamond Shape.	Ticket, White. Staff, Red.
Haverhill C.V. Junction and Haverhill G.E. Junction.	Block Telegraph and Train Staff and Ticket.	Iron Diamond Shape.	Light Terra Cotta.

4

Extracts from the Rules and Regulations approved by the Board of Directors, on 26th April, 1904.

17.—Every Station Master, Inspector, Engine Driver, Fireman, Guard, Signalman, Policeman, Ganger, Foreman, Shunter, Yardman and Gatekeeper, every Clerk, Porter, and other Servant connected with the working of the Railway, and also every man engaged on the Permanent Way or Works affecting the Running Lines, must be supplied with, and have with him when on duty and produce when required, a copy of these Rules and Regulations.

(b.) Except as shown below, every person above referred to must also be supplied with, and have with him when on duty, a copy of the current Working Time Table Book, or section of the Book, the Appendix thereto, and any Signalling, Permanent-way, or Special Train Notices; a copy of each must also be kept in the Station Master's Office.

Exceptions.   EXCEPTIONS.—(i.) *Where two or more men are employed at one Signal-box, it is not necessary to supply each man with a separate copy of the Working Time Table Book or section of the book, as the case may be, nor of the Appendix or other Notices, but one copy of each must be supplied for the use of all the men employed at the Signal-box.*

(ii.) *At Stations where the Foremen, Porters or other servants connected with the working of the traffic, use, or have ordinary access to, the Station Master's Office, it is not necessary to supply each man with a copy of the Working Time Table Book, or section of the book, nor of the Appendix or other Notices, but a copy of each must be kept in the Station Master's Office, so as to be accessible for reference by those men. At Stations where the men do not use the Station Master's Office, a copy of each must be kept in a convenient place to which all engaged in the working of the traffic have ready access.*

(iii.) *It is not necessary to supply Firemen who have not been passed to act as Engine-drivers with the Working Time Tables or other Notices, but those supplied to an Engine-driver must be accessible to his Fireman.*

(iv.) *It is not necessary to supply the ordinary Labourers working under the Superintendence of Gangers or Foremen, with Working Time Tables*

7

Continuous Brakes.

The following is a description of the Continuous Brakes in use on the various Railways:—

VACUUM AUTOMATIC BRAKE.	WESTINGHOUSE BRAKE.
Barry.	*Caledonian.
Brecon and Merthyr.	Colne Valley and Halstead.
Cambrian.	East and West Junction.
*Cheshire Lines.	*Glasgow and South Western.
*Furness.	*Great Eastern.
*Glasgow and South Western.	*Great North of Scotland.
*Great Northern.	*Hull, Barnsley and West Riding Junction.
*Great Western.	London, Brighton and South Coast.
*Great Central.	*London, Tilbury and Southend.
*Highland.	*North British.
*Hull, Barnsley and West Riding Junction.	*North Eastern.
*Lancashire and Yorkshire.	Portpatrick and Wigtownshire.
*Lancashire, Derbyshire, and East Coast.	Rhymney.
*London and North Western.	*South Eastern and Chatham.
*London and South Western.	West Lancashire.
Manchester and Milford.	West Coast Joint Stock.
Manchester South Junction and Altrincham.	(London and North Western and
Maryport and Carlisle.	Caledonian.)
Mersey.	
*Midland.	
*Midland and Great Northern Joint.	
Midland and South Western Junction.	
Neath and Brecon.	
North London.	
North Staffordshire.	
Rhondda and Swansea Bay.	
*South Eastern and Chatham.	
Taff Vale.	
West Coast Joint Stock.	
(London & North Western & Caledonian.)	
Wirral.	
Wrexham, Mold and Connah's Quay.	

*Note.—These Companies have Stock fitted with both the Vacuum and Westinghouse Brake.

All applications for Coaching Stock to be loaded to stations on above Railways to be marked "Vacuum."

Stations requiring vehicles to load to any line where the Vacuum Automatic Brake is in use must be careful in all cases to order a vehicle fitted with the dual Brake, or if there is not time to procure one, the traffic must be loaded in other vehicles, and a Telegraphic Advice sent to the transfer station on the Foreign Company's line on which the Westinghouse system applies.

Note.—All pipes operating blocks are painted black, and all pipes not operating blocks are painted bright red.

Foreign Companies' Vehicles not fitted with Hand Brakes.

The attention of the Station Staff is specially called to the fact that Horse Boxes, Carriage Trucks, Fruit and Fish Vans, and other similar Vehicles belonging to Foreign Companies, are not, as a rule, fitted with Hand Brakes, nor do such Vehicles (which are fitted for the Vacuum Brake only) when running on this Railway contain any Automatic power for putting on the Brake.

Care must be taken that such vehicles are properly secured by hand scotch, or a man should be ready to control them with a Brake Stick before they are uncoupled from the train at any station where the line is on a falling gradient.

In calling attention to this matter, the Staff are reminded that under the "Continuous Brake" Regulations only one unbraked Vehicle (fitted with continuous pipe) is allowed in the rear of any train.

Station Masters are requested to see that this instruction is properly carried out.

6

Train Staffs and Ticket Boxes to be periodically examined.

Each Station Master who has to deal with two or more Train Staffs at his Station, must test them at least once every three months, by placing each Staff in the wrong Ticket Box to see if it will unlock it; should it do so, a prompt report must be sent to the General Manager and to the Engineer. **No force must be used in the testing, or the Staff may become jammed or the lock damaged.**

The examination must be made on the 1st January, 1st April, 1st July, and 1st October in each year, and the result reported to the General Manager.

Station Masters at *all* Train Staff Stations must carefully watch the working of their Train Staffs in the Boxes, and should a Staff work loosely owing to its being worn, the Engineer must be advised, and he will, if necessary, arrange for the Staff to be sent to Halstead for renewal.

List of Electrical Apparatus between Signal Cabins, Stations, &c.

BETWEEN.	MODE OF COMMUNICATION.
All Sections.	Telegraph.
Chappel C.V. & Fox & Pleasants.	Gong ⎫ In connection with
" " Old Colne Gates.	" ⎬ Electric Train Staff
Colne " Old Colne Gates.	" ⎭ Instrument.
" " Fox & Pleasants.	"
Halstead Station Box and Parsons Lane Crossing.	Electric Bell.
Haverhill G.E. Junction Box and Haverhill C.V. Junction.	Block Telegraph.

Electric Bell Communications between Halstead Station and Parsons Lane.

SIGNAL BOXES.

	Mode of Communication.	How to be Given.
Train leaving Colne	2 Beats.	Consecutively.
Train arriving at Halstead from Hedingham	3 Beats.	"
Train leaving Halstead for Colne	4 Beats.	"
Cancelling Signal	8 Beats.	3 pause—5.

Each signal must be repeated by the signalman in the receiving box to show that it has been correctly received.

9

3rd. Then indicate your own Station in the same way. This will also be repeated by your correspondent. [All these movements must be made *with steadiness and regularity.*]

4th. In transmitting the message, the prefix must first be signalled, denoting the nature of the communication, such as S.P.D.I, &c.

5th. Then follow the name and address of Sender.

6th. Then the name and address of Receiver.

7th. Then the Signal D.Q., showing the completion of the addresses or other words preceding the message.

8th. Then the message itself.

2. Any instructions as regards the delivery of a message are to be prefixed M.M, and sent after the message, before giving R. T.

3. The message (and instructions) being finished, the signal R. T. is to be given, denoting the entire completion of the message.

4. A full stop will be signalled thus ||||| A bar as in 5/6 will be signalled thus |||||

5. The finish of each word or complete signal is denoted by a pause the Receiving Station will return "E," "not understand"; or "T," understand." If the word or signal is not understood the sending, station must at once repeat it.

6. In receiving Signals, should a doubt arise as to the correctness of a word after several of the following words have been taken, stop the communication, then give "After," and send back one or two of the words preceding the one to be repeated.

7. The Receiving Clerk must *write down each word immediately it is received;* when he has no writer to assist him, he must *not return the* "understand" *signal till he has written down the word.*

8. The Clerk by whom each inward message is received must in all cases on its completion carefully read it over to ascertain if it be correct and then sign his name in the space provided for that purpose.

PREFIXES.

9. The following Cypher Prefixes will indicate *the order of precedence* and character of the intelligence they are intended to convey:—

A message once commenced, whatever may be the prefix, is not to be stopped, but it is to be finished before a message bearing a prefix taking precedence (L B excepted) is sent.

1. LB—Line Blocked.

This prefix *takes* precedence of all others and will immediately stop any communication engaging the instrument. It is on no account to be used, except in cases of accident or to prevent the same.

NOTE.—*Messages bearing this prefix are to be most carefully received and repeated back to the forwarding Station so as to ensure accuracy in transmission, and copies sent by next train to the General Manager with a special report as to the necessity for sending same.*

8

Electric Telegraph Instructions.
Telegraph Offices, with Calls and Times of Opening and Closing.

STATION.	CALL.	NUMBER OF CIRCUIT	OPEN FROM
Chappel Signal Box	S.O.	2	} 8 a.m. to 9.30 p.m.
" Station, Passenger	C.Y.	2	
Colne Signal Box	C.O.	1 and 2	} 8 a.m. to 9 p.m.
" Goods	C.G.	1 and 2	
Halstead Station, Passenger	H.A.	1 and 2	} 7.15 a.m. to 9 p.m.
" Goods	H.G.	2	
" Signal Box	J.	1	
Castle Hedingham Station, Pass.	C.H.	1 and 2	} 7.30 a.m. to 7.30 p.m.
" " Signal Box	P.	1	
Yeldham Station, Passenger	Y.L.	1 and 2	} 7.30 a.m to 7.30 p.m.
" Signal Box	Y.A.	1 and 2	
Birdbrook Passenger Station	B.D.	1 and 2	Ditto.
Haverhill, Colne Valley Station	H.V.	2	8 a.m. to 8 p.m.
" G.E. Junction for C.V. Line	H.J.	1 and 2	Ditto
" G.E. Station, Passenger	R.L.	2	7.15 a.m. to 8.15 p.m.

PARTICULARS OF TELEGRAPH CIRCUITS.
STATIONS BETWEEN.

No. 1 Circuit. From Colne Goods Office to Haverhill G.E Junction Box.

No. 2 Circuit. From Chappel Passenger to Haverhill G.E. Station.

NOTE.—No. 1 Circuit is to be used for Train Signals only. Any infringement of this rule will be severely dealt with; in the case of No. 2 Circuit breaking down; urgent messages may be sent with ; on No. 1 Circuit but the numbers must be curtailed as much as possible, cases of No. 1 Circuit being so used must be reported to General Manager.

Regulations to be Strictly observed by Station Masters, Clerks, and others in charge of Telegraph Instruments.

RULES FOR SIGNALLING.

1. The importance of an undeviating, uniform system renders it imperatively necessary that the following Rules be strictly adhered to:—

TO CALL A STATION—

1st. Move the needles backwards and forwards a few seconds, to attract attention.

2nd. Indicate the name of the Station you require, by giving the Code Signal denoting that Station, until it is repeated by the Station you are calling.

2. SP—Special Passenger Train or Light Engine.
3. RO—To be used only for important Railway Messages.
4. DB (or DL for transmitted) Ordinary Railway Messages.
5. DQ—End of Address in Message.
6. ||||| Full Stop.
7. GQ—Fresh Line.
8. FI—Figures.
9. FF—End of Figures.
10. MQ—Engaged, (Wait.)
11. KQ—Call when disengaged.
12. RQ—Repeated message to be used when messages require repetition from Forwarding Station.
13. RT—End of Message and Acknowledgement.
14. GS—General Manager's Message.
   To be used only by the General Manager or his principal assistant.

NOTE—Messages prefixed D.B, D.I, take turn on any Circuit according to *time received.*

Every attention and care *must* be given to the above *prefixes*, and they must not be misapplied, as any disregard to the order of precedence may be productive of serious results. *This is to be particularly noted.*

GENERAL REGULATIONS.

10. *The strictest secrecy* is to be observed by the persons engaged in this department, and *on no account* are any matters relating to the business of the Company or of private individuals to be divulged.

11. No person is to be admitted into the Instrument Office, to examine the apparatus, or for other purposes, unless on business of the Company, which absolutely requires his presence inside.

12. *No railway messages are to be sent by wire when there is time to make communication by other means.* It is most essential that the wires be kept as clear as possible for all unnecessary messages that may tend to block the circuit and delay others of immediate importance. *This is to be particularly noted.*

13. Clerks uselessly occupying the Instrument, **holding conversation with each other,** or in any way impeding the business of the line by sending frivolous or unnecessary messages, are to be reported to the General Manager.

14. Clerks are cautioned against causing interruptions by *moving or holding over the handle of their instrument,* whilst signals are passing, except when a Station is being called; in such case the clerk having a message should give "Wait" by holding the needle over to "T" then give his "prefix" when the prefix of his message entitles him to precedence, possession of the circuit will at once be given up to him; but otherwise the Station first having possession of the Instrument will retain it until the message has been forwarded, except in cases provided for by paragraph 17 All alterations of code will be strictly dealt with.

15. *Quarrelling for possession of Instruments is prohibited,* as more time might be lost in wrangling than the transmission of the message would occupy. Irritable and Irregular sending is also strictly forbidden.

16. No clerk is *on any account* to answer any call but the one opposite the name of his Station in the call list.

17. A Station being unable to obtain the attention of another for fifteen minutes must not continue to call if the Instrument be required for another Station, but must renew the call at intervals—it being better to delay one message than the entire work of the line.

18. Particular care must be taken to see that the Instrument is disengaged before commencing to use it, as very serious delays are frequently caused by one Station interrupting another when in the middle of a message; to make sure of this give E (not understand) two or three times, when, should the Instrument be engaged, clerks will see the last word sent repeated.

19. All Company's messages are to be written on the proper forms, and signed by the officer in charge.

20. When a message is of such paramount importance that an error in it would result in very serious consequences, it should be repeated by the Receiving to the Forwarding Station. The sender of the message desiring its repetition should insert the word "repeat" at the foot thereof. These messages should bear the prefix R.Q.

21. When a message is received requiring a reply, the answer must be returned without delay. Should any investigation or enquiries be necessary, they are to be made with all possible despatch, and the reply send back as early as practicable.

22. All messages must be delivered immediately on their receipt, however long they may have been delayed in the transmission.

23. Any delay or irregularity in the transmission of a message must be noted and written upon the form in **red ink.**

24. When the Electric Telegraph is fixed at a Station the Station Clerks, and Porters there are to learn the same, so as to be enabled to transmit and receive messages.

25. Any Telegraph Clerk not being on duty when his Station is "called," or not answering to the "call" within five minutes from the commencement of it, will be strictly dealt with. If engaged when called he must ascertain what Station requires his attention, and the prefix of the message, then give M.Q (*vide* General Signals). As soon as disengaged the Station must be called and the message taken. If a Station giving the M.Q signal, does not cancel it by calling up and giving R.Q the Station receiving M.Q must again offer his message within 15 minutes.

26. When a clerk is compelled to be absent from duty through illness or other cause, he is without delay to send notice of such absence to the Station Master, who must report to the General Manager.

TELEGRAPH APPARATUS.

27. Instructions are hereby given to all Guards, Porters, Platelayers, and others, to look to the Telegraph Wires on the Line, and that they are *perfectly free from contact with any objects,* such as *boughs of trees, straw, waste, grass, &c.,* and if they observe any of the Wires *lying across or touching each other, or in contact with any post, bridge or other object,* or if any of the Poles, Wires, or Insulators are broken, to make a report of it immediately to the nearest Station, and request the Station Master to forward the same without delay to the Telegraph Lineman.

28. Each Station Agent should do his best to repair temporarily any damage that may arise to the Wires, at or near his station—bearing in mind that the Wires must be kept from touching each other, and from resting on metal, wet wood, or the ground.

(6.) The Chief Clerks to exercise a close supervision over the despatch of Messages, and where necessary report the receipt of Telegrams which have been sent in contravention of these regulations.

(7.) Prompt attention should invariably be given to Telegrams, and a reply, if necessary, sent as quickly as possible, so as to avoid their being repeated.

Stations Masters must arrange that the Telegraph Instruments shall be attended to throughout the whole of the day. In all cases of Accident, a person must remain in attendance upon the Telegraph Instrument at the nearest station from which telegraphic information can be sent, to forward and receive messages without delay, as long as may be necessary.

The transmission of messages must not be interrupted by any other Station on the Circuit, *unless in those cases of extreme urgency* for which provision is made by the regulations.

ENGINE HEADLIGHTS.

The terms "Right Hand Buffer Beam" and "Left Hand Buffer Beam" are to be understood as referring to the Enginemens' "Right" or "Left Hand" as they are running.

COLNE VALLEY.

1. *All ordinary Passenger and Goods Trains* carry one Red Light at foot of chimney, and one White Light on left hand buffer beam.

2. *All Special Trains* carry one Red Light at foot of chimney and one White Light on each buffer beam.

The lamps must be carried in their proper positions whether they are lighted or not.

1. *Break Down Van Train going to clear the line, or Light Engine going to assist disabled train.*

(a.) *By Day.* One White Disc on each buffer beam, and one Green Disc with White Rim in centre of the buffer beam.

(b.) *By Night.* One White Light on each buffer beam and one Green Light in centre of buffer beam.

2. *Break Down Van Train not going to clear line.*

(a.) *By Day.* One White Disc at foot of chimney and one Green Disc with White Rim in centre of buffer beam.

GREAT EASTERN.

(b.) *By Night.* One White Light at foot of chimney and one Green Light in centre of buffer beam.

3. *Mark's Tey, Sudbury and Bury Single Line.*

(a.) *Ordinary Trains. By Day.* Green Disc with White Rim over Right Hand Buffer Beam.

(b.) *By Night.* One Green Light over Right Hand Buffer Beam, and one Red Light at foot of chimney.

(c.) *Special Trains by Day.* Green Disc with White Rim over Right Hand Buffer Beam, and White Disc at foot of chimney.

(d.) *By Night.* One Green Light over Right Hand Buffer Beam, one Red Light at foot of chimney, and one White Light over Left Hand Buffer Beam.

---

29. It is to be borne in mind that if any of the Wires touch each other, even for a moment, the communication is interrupted; no persons must therefore be permitted to hang anything on the Wires or arms of the Telegraph.

30. The Poles or Wires must on no account be interfered with without the permission of the Engineer.

31. No person may touch any of the mechanism of the Instrument, Bell or Wires, *nor disconnect any Wire from a Terminal*, without written or telegraphic authority from the Engineer or Lineman.

32. The *dial* must not be *defaced* by pencil marks, but the instrument kept clean and in good order.

33. *Violent working* is useless and *strictly prohibited*; the violence makes no difference to the signals, but may break a handle or derange the instrument.

34. When the communication is interrupted, the apparatus is to be *carefully* examined; if a wire be lose or broken, replace it. If you cannot move your own needles when others can, or when the instrument is put on short circuit by connecting the line terminals by a piece of wire, it is probable your battery wires are broken, or that a plate is faulty. In the latter case connect the defective battery across by a wire from terminal to terminal without disturbing the other connections. All battery connections should be carefully examined.

35. Report all faults you cannot remedy to the Telegraph Lineman at Halstead, *describing exactly what its appearance or effect is on your own dial*, stating especially whether you can work while others cannot, and *vice versa*. This report should be forwarded *by telegraph if possible*, if not then by *first train*, and if not properly attended to, report the case to the General Manager. (No Clerk must use earth wire unless it is to test for, or overcome a fault existing on such wire.)

36. The Instruments must not be oiled by the clerks and others in charge. It is the duty of the Telegraph Lineman alone to do this.

37. When a needle sticks against the pins, the pins and the sides of the needle must be *carefully* wiped with a piece of clean blotting paper.

38. The greatest care is to be taken that the handles of the Instruments are left *perpendicular*, both when reading off from the Instrument and when it is disengaged.

39. *Each Station must be ready to answer immediately* as to the state of the Instruments when enquired of by Telegraph, by the Telegraph Lineman, at eight o'clock every morning.

In the absence of the lineman, the Telegraph Clerk at Halstead will make the enquiry and report according to the lineman on his arrival.

40. Neglect and disobedience of these regulations and instructions must be reported, and will be *severely dealt with*.

TELEGRAMS.

41. The attention of the Officers and Servants of the Company is called to the necessity of restricting the use of Telegraph Messages to those cases were the business is of such urgency as to justify a resort to this mode of communication, and in which a less expeditious means will not answer for the purpose.

It is difficult to lay down any specific rules as to when and under what circumstances it may be necessary for Telegrams to be despatched, but every servant of the Company is expected to exercise due discretion in the matter, and to observe the following general instructions:—

(1.) Telegrams are not to be sent when a letter by Train will suffice.

(2.) They should be made as short and as concise as possible.

(3.) The Code must be used wherever practicable.

(4.) Complimentary phrases, such as "Mr.," "please," &c., should be omitted.

(5.) References to correspondence are to be left out as far as practicable.

14

Engine Whistles.

Station or Junction.	To or from	Whistles.
Mark's Tey Junction	Sudbury Branch.	3 distinct sounds.
Chappel	G.E. Line.	1 distinct sound.
	Colne Valley Line and G.E. Line	3 distinct sounds.
Colne	Up Main to Straight Road. No. 7	2 long whistles.
	Main Down to Straight Road. No. 21	2 long whistles.
	Main to No. 11 Shed Road. (Shunting)	3 short whistles.
	Main to Straight Road, No. 15	4 short whistles.
Halstead.	No. 1 Siding	2 long whistles.
	No. 24 ,,	2 short whistles.
Castle Hedingham.	From Main Road to Siding up or Down Road	2 long whistles.
Yeldham.	From Main Road to Siding up or Down Road.	2 long whistles.
Birdbrook.	Trucks off on down journey	2 long whistles.
	All Trains not stopping on approaching Station	2 long whistles and 1 short whistle.
Haverhill Junction, G.E.	Sudbury	1 distinct sound.
,, ,, C.V	C.V. Line	2 distinct sounds.
,, ,, C.V	C.V. Line and the old C.V. Station.	3 distinct sounds.

15

Wagons put off Goods Trains to Reduce Loads.

When Guards find it necessary to reduce loads of Goods Trains, they must exercise discretion and judgment in putting off or not picking up; but in no case must Wagons containing perishable traffic be put off or left behind. As a general rule, however, the following order should be observed in putting off Wagons :—

1st. Wagons with Locomotive Coal.

2nd. Wagons of Coal, Stones, Timber, or Non-perishable Traffic.

Trains must not, however, be delayed after due time picking out wagons to reduce loads, and in such circumstances Guards must do the best they can in the time at their disposal.

The maximum number of Wagons to be worked by any train on any Section of the Line is 30. The load to be reduced by one-eighth during unfavourable weather.

Any difficulty that may be experienced in getting traffic worked away must be at once reported to the General Manager, Halstead.

Where it is desirable to get urgent traffic away by any train which has already the load prescribed in the foregoing tables, the Guard must consult the Driver as to whether he can, under the circumstances, take the traffic or a portion of it.

Three empty Goods, Cattle, or Mineral Wagons to average as two loaded Wagons.

No vehicles must be conveyed behind the rear Van of a Goods Train, except Cripples, labled by Examiners to be sent for Repairs behind the Van.

WORKING OF TRAINS.

Special Instructions to be observed in the Working of Trains at certain Stations and over Inclines, Curves, Cuttings, &c.

HAVERHILL C.V. STATION.

This being a Terminal Station care must be taken to run in at such a speed that the train can be pulled up by the Hand Brake. (See *Rule* 113 *Rule Book, pages 69 and 70.*)

BIRDBROOK BANK CURVE.

Drivers to run round this curve with caution. Guards of Goods Trains to assist by steadying train with the Hand Brake.

HEDINGHAM BRICK YARD SIDINGS.

Engines must not under any circumstances travel past the Notice Boards, where such are fixed.

HALSTEAD ; CROSSING NEAR PORTWAY'S FOUNDRY.

Speed of all Trains passing over this Crossing not to exceed 10 miles per hour.

CHAPPEL CURVE.

Speed of all Trains over this Curve not to exceed 10 miles per hour.

17

List of Sidings locked by Annett's Key.

Halstead Coal Yard Sidings.
Castle Hedingham Station Yard.
Pearls Hill Brick Yard Siding.
Yeldham Shunting Yard.

Locking Gear, Signals and Points.

To prevent any alteration of Points during the passage of a train, Signalmen must be specially careful not to alter the Signal which locks the Points until the last vehicle of the train has passed over them; they must also be careful to place the Signal to Danger immediately afterwards.

If, from any exceptional cause, a train is brought to a stand before it has passed through the Facing Points, the Signal must be placed to "Danger," for its protection, but in such cases care must be taken that the Points are not altered until the train has passed over them.

Signalmen must also take care not to open the Points of any Crossover or Connection leading into or across the Line over which a train has been signalled to pass, until the rear of such train has passed well clear of the fouling point.

Signalmen must be careful to secure each lever as they move it by placing the spring catch properly in the notch in the frame, before moving another lever.

Shunting Passenger Trains into Sidings in which are Hand-worked Points.

When it is found necessary to shunt a Passenger train into a Siding in which there are Hand-worked Points, the Station Master must take care that all such Points, which may be Facing to the train when entering or leaving the Siding, are held for the train to pass over them.

Shunting in Sidings next to the Main Line, and on the Main Line, when Passenger trains are approaching.

While Passenger trains are approaching or passing, the following instructions must be strictly carried out by all concerned :—

When shunting trucks into a Siding or Sidings adjacent to the Main Line, or back on to the rear portion of a train standing on the Main Line, the Shunter in charge of the shunting operations (or the Guard if no Shunter is there) must satisfy himself that the trucks so shunted are at rest before he makes another shunt; during rough, windy weather, or where the Sidings or the Main Lines are on a falling gradient, the trucks so shunted must, in all cases, be secured either by Brakes, Sprags, or Hand Scotches, and when shunted back on to the trucks standing on the Main Line they must be coupled on to such trucks before the next shunt is made.

When a Passenger train is approaching or passing on the next Line of rails, no truck must be detached from the engine when making a shunt.

Signalmen must, when practicable, intimate to the Guards and Shunters when a Passenger train is approaching, but this will not relieve the latter of the responsibility of keeping a sharp look out for themselves.

Defective Road or Works.

Referring to Rule No. 191 of the Book of Rules and Regulations.

All matters of a serious character must be reported immediately to the Engineer by wire or letter as the case may be.

16

Working of Brick Traffic.

Numerous cases having occurred of Bricks being broken, and also of Trucks conveying Bricks being damaged, owing to the Trucks being roughly shunted, Guards, Shunters, and others concerned are cautioned that more care must be exercised in dealing with this traffic in future, in order that such breakages and damage may be prevented.

The special attention of Station Masters is also drawn to the matter, and they are requested to watch the working as far as possible and report any case of rough shunting which may come under their notice.

Hay and Straw Traffic.

Notice to Goods Guards. Guards are informed that Trucks containing Hay or Straw must not be attached next the Engine.

Hay and Straw Traffic to Lines South of Thames.

Where Wagons are loaded (other than Colne Valley Stock) with above Traffic consigned to Stations on Lines of Companies South of the Thames, Great Eastern Sheets must be used, arrangements must be made by the staff accordingly.

Colne Valley Sheets to be used only on Colne Valley Wagons for this and similar Traffic to lines of Companies South of the Thames. Agents will be held responsible for this instruction being carried out.

Inclines Steeper than 1 in 150, and more than a ¼ Mile long.

MAIN LINE.

INCLINE BETWEEN.	LENGTH ABOUT.	GRADIENT 1 IN	FALLING TOWARDS.
Chappel and Colne	¼ mile.	70	Chappel
,, ,,	...	60	Chappel
,, ,,	...	60	Colne
Colne and Chappel	...	70-80	Colne
Halstead and Colne	...	70	Halstead
Yeldham and Birdbrook	...	99	Yeldham
Birdbrook and Yeldham	...	90	Birdbrook
Birdbrook and Haverhill	1	70-80	Birdbrook
Haverhill and Birdbrook	...	80-99	Haverhill
,, ,,	...	80	Birdbrook

18

Water Columns.

Halstead	...	3	...	2 on Platform, 1 in Goods Yard.
Yeldham	...	2	...	On Platform.
Haverhill	...	1	...	In Locomotive Shed.
Haverhill, G.E.		2	...	Up and Down Platform.

Ordinary Loads of Goods Engines.

	Halstead Class.	Number of loaded Goods Wagons.	No. 1 Engine.
DOWN TRAINS. FROM			
Chappel to Colne	28	3 5	16
Colne to Halstead	28	3 5	16
Halstead to Castle Hedingham	30	4	17
Castle Hedingham to Yeldham	30		17
Yeldham to Birdbrook	24		14
Birdbrook to Haverhill C.V. Junction or G.E.	24	3 4	14
Haverhill C.V. Station to Haverhill G.E.	18		10
UP TRAINS.			
Haverhill G.E. or C.V. to Birdbrook	18		10
Birdbrook to Yeldham	18		10
Yeldham to Castle Hedingham	30		17
Castle Hedingham to Halstead	30		17
Halstead to Colne	30		17
Colne to Chappel	26		15

NOTE. In calculating the loads for Goods Engines, three wagons of minerals must be computed as equal to four wagons of Goods, and three empty wagons must be reckoned of the same weight as two loaded Goods wagons.

19

GENERAL INSTRUCTIONS.

Notice to Station Masters.

Each Station Master is required to make himself acquainted with all general and special instructions relating to working of that portion of the Line which is within the distance Signals worked from the Cabins under his jurisdiction, and to see that each member of his staff thoroughly understands and rigidly observes all regulations that effect him. He must pay a daily visit to each Signal Cabin, examine and sign the "*Train Register*" *Books, and satisfy himself that the records* required to be posted therein are duly, and correctly made, and that the locking and telegraph apparatus and signals are in proper order. Every defect or irregularly must be promptly reported to the proper officer.

Special Events.

It is important that Station Masters should advise the General Manager, as long beforehand as possible, of all special events about to take place in the neighbourhood of their Stations, such as Agricultural or Horticultural Shows, Bazaars, Fairs, Horse and other Sales, etc.

Carriage Windows, &c., damaged or broken by Passengers.

The following are the amounts to be collected from Passengers accidentally breaking Door lights and Side lights, viz :—

For Door lights. ... ... 7s. 6d. each
For Large Side Lights (Saloons) ... 15s. 0d. ,,
For Ordinary Side Lights ... ... 6s. 6d. ,,

Amounts so collected must be paid in to **the credit of the Carriage and Wagon Department,** and an advice of the same promptly sent to the General Manager.

If the Passenger declines to pay, his name and address must be taken, and the circumstances reported to the General Manager.

Horse Boxes.

The attention of the Station Masters and others concerned is directed to the importance of seeing that all Horse Boxes received are properly supplied with Head Collars, and that they are in good condition.

Horse Boxes are supplied with communication cords fitted on each side. When not in use these cords must be carefully attached to the vehicles.

Station Masters must instruct all concerned as to this, and see that the instructions are carried out.

They must also report to the General Manager any case in which Horse Boxes are received with head Collars missing or defective, or not supplied with communication cords, giving number, train received by, and sending station.

A space has been provided on each side of the horse boxes for the insertion of address cards. These must not in any case be tacked on the side of the Horse Boxes, and the vehicles must be treated with the same care as other Carriage Stock.

Loading of Horse Boxes.

1. In tying up Horses, the length of the upper and lower ropes must be regulated by the height of the Horse, so as to keep its head in its natural position; the top rope should be of sufficient length to allow the animal's nose to reach the manger, but not longer, and the length of the bottom rope should be from twelve to eighteen inches, according to the height of the Horse, but in no case to exceed eighteen inches. A diagram of the proper knot to be used in tying the ropes is shown on page 20, and the men whose duty it is to fasten up Horses must practice tying this until they become proficient.

Horse Boxes received at G.E. Stations.

It is the duty of Guards in charge of Trains when receiving Horse Boxes loaded from Foreign Lines at Junctions with the Colne Valley Line to examine them, and satisfy themselves that the Horses which they contain are in proper order, and that the fastenings are right. If anything is found to be wrong with horses or fastenings the Guard must call the attention of the Station Master thereto, and also make an entry on his report of the result of the examination in every case.

Cleansing and Disinfecting of Cattle Trucks and Pens.

The following are the Privy Council Regulations respecting the Cleansing and Disinfection of Cattle Trucks and Pens, which must be carefully observed by all the members of the staff concerned :

TRUCKS.—(1.) A railway truck, if used for animals on a railway shall, on every occasion after an animal is taken out of it, and before any other animal, or any horse, ass, or mule, or any fodder or litter, or anything intended to be used for or about animals, is placed in it, be cleansed and disinfected as follows :—

(i.) The floor of the truck, and all other parts thereof with which animals or their droppings have come in contact, shall be scraped and swept, and the scrapings and sweepings, and all dung, sawdusts, litter, and other matter shall be effectually removed therefrom; then

(ii.) The same parts of the truck shall be thoroughly washed or scrubbed or scoured with water, then

(iii.) The same parts or the truck shall have applied to them a coating of lime-wash.

(2.) The scraping and sweepings of the truck, and all dung, sawdust, litter, and other matter removed therefrom shall forthwith be well mixed with quicklime, and be effectually removed from contact with animals.

PENS.—(1.) Every pen or other place being in, about, near, or on a station, building, or land of a railway company, and used or intended to be used by or by permission of a railway company, or otherwise, for the reception or keeping of animals before, after, or in course of their transit by railway, shall be cleansed or disinfected, either on each day on which it is used and after it has been used, or at some time not later than twelve o'clock at noon of the next following day and before it is used or such next following day : Provided that where such user is on a Saturday the Monday following shall be considered to be the next following day for such purpose.

(2.) Every such pen or other place shall be cleansed and disinfected as follows :—

(i.) All parts of the pen or other place with which animals or their droppings have come in contact shall be scraped and swept, and the scraping and sweepings, and all dung, sawdust, litter, and other matter shall be effectually moved therefrom; then

(ii.) The same parts of the pen or other place shall be thoroughly washed or scrubbed or scoured with water : then

(iii.) The same parts of the pen or other place shall have applied to them a coating of lime-wash,

(3.) The scraping and sweepings of the pen or other place, and all dung, sawdust, litter, and other matter removed therefrom shall forthwith be well mixed with quicklime, and be effectually removed from contact with animals.

Running of late Passenger Trains.

When any Ordinary or Special train is run over any portion of the line between Halstead and Haverhill after 8 p.m., the Station Master at Halstead is required to arrange for a Telegraph Clerk and Porter to remain on duty at the Station until the train has reached Haverhill in one direction and Halstead in the other.

---

2. No box must be used unless the whole of the fittings, ropes, and headstalls are in sound working order, and great care must be taken that the partitions are properly secured.

3. The head doors opening into the coupe must always be closed and properly secured with the bolts.

4. If the Station Staff at any Station discovers that any injury has occurred to a Horse whilst in transit, care must be taken to note how the animal was tied, and to measure the length of top and bottom ropes from rings to headstall. If the original headstall and the ropes have been broken, or require cutting, they must be retained, and the Horse Box must not again be used until the General Manager has been communicated with, and his instructions received.

Short end.

Halter end and attached to head collar.

The above diagram represents the knot to be used in fastening the ropes to the rings. In tying this knot the end of the rope must be taken in the right hand, then passed through the ring **downwards**, brought out at the left-hand side of that end of the rope attached to the head collar, carried over this rope towards the right, then passed again through the ring **downwards**, and brought out between the ring and the rope loop; the end rope then being pulled tight, completes the knot.

Cleansing and Disinfecting of Horse Boxes, &c.

Station-masters, and others concerned, are requested to give their particular attention to the order issued by the Privy Council with regard to the disinfection of Horse Boxes, Guards' Vans, &c., and the transit of animals by Railway, the contents of which are given below :—

1. A Horse Box used for carrying horses, asses, or mules on a Railway shall, on every occasion immediately after a horse, ass, or mule is taken out of it, and before any other horse, ass, or any animal is placed therein, be cleansed as follows :—

(i.) "The floor of the Horse Box, and all other parts thereof "with which the droppings of horse, ass, or mule have come in "contact, shall be scraped and swept, and the scrapings and sweep-"ings and all dung, sawdust, fodder, litter, and other matter, shall "be effectually removed therefrom; and

(ii.) "The sides of the Horse Box and all other parts thereof "with which the head or any discharge the mouth or nostrils of any "horse, ass, or mule have come in contact, shall be thoroughly "washed with water by means of a sponge, brush, or other "instrument.

2. The scrapings and sweepings of the Horse Box, and all dung, sawdust, fodder, litter, and other matter removed therefrom, shall forthwith be well mixed with quicklime.

NOTE.—*The Station-master must take care that Horse Boxes are cleansed immediately on arrival.*

Carriage Trucks.

The Scotch Bars of Carriage Trucks, (which are all numbered,) and Straps, must be kept in their respective trucks, whether required or not, and any Station receiving one without any of these fittings must report the matter to the General Manager.

Privacy of Booking Office.

No person except the authorized Officers and Servants of the Company must be allowed within the screen or counter of any Booking Office.

Orders for Rolling Stock.

Guards to take Orders for Wagons.

Horse Boxes and Carriage Trucks to be ordered by Station Masters from Chappel, 24 hours notice to be given by the public.

Instructions as to Carriage Cleaning.

Carriages must be thoroughly cleaned as follows every day :—

(a) Loose cushions taken out, backs well beaten and brushed, seat frames and floors brushed clean, all insides including glass, window frames, side and door lights cleaned, cushions to be taken outside of coach and well beaten and brushed, all doors and windows afterwards to be shut, but ventilators left open.

(b) Loose cushions must not be taken out when rain or snow is falling heavily if they would be likely to become damp or sustain damage thereby.

(c) Carriages to be thoroughly washed at sides and ends with clean cold water. Brushes or sponge may be used for this purpose.

(d) All carriage-door handles and hinges to be thoroughly cleaned with ground bath-brick damped with water, after this polished with a clean dry cloth, the hinges to be rubbed with a greasy cloth when finished. Care must be taken that the spaces behind the handles of the coaches are thoroughly cleaned.

(e) The Coaches must occasionally be cleaned with soft soap, when the following instructions must be observed :—Put a quantity of soft soap into a bucket, and place by side of it another bucket containing water (warm, if possible). Dip the brush which is supplied for the purpose of washing carriages, first into the water, then mix it with the soap, and rub the panels until the dirt is removed, and afterwards wash off with clean water. Care must be taken that all soap is thoroughly washed off before leaving the work.

Guards must insert on their Journal particulars of Carriages attached to their trains in a dirty condition.

Shackles on Passenger Vehicles.

Hooks are provided on the Head Stocks of Passenger Vehicles on which Shackles when not in use should be suspended. Guards, Shunters, and others must see that Shackles are suspended on these hooks and not on the Drawbar hooks.

Station Masters will give special attention to this matter and see that this instruction is strictly carried out.

Notice to Ticket Collectors.

Excursion Passengers travelling by Excursion Trains without tickets on the outward journey must be excessed the full return excursion fares and an excess ticket must be given for the amount, bearing the words and "back," in addition to the names of the stations inserted in the usual way, so that the excess ticket may be used on the return journey. Passengers found in such trains without tickets on the return journey must be treated as ordinary passengers without tickets, and required to pay their fare.

Examination of Tickets.

At Stations where tickets have to be examined, every competent member of the staff must be drafted for this duty and the work performed as smartly and efficiently as possible, every care being exercised in seeing that Passengers hold proper tickets for the class of carriage in which they are travelling, and also that such tickets are properly routed, any irregularity in the latter respect to be reported to the Audit Accountant.

The Special attention of the staff engaged in this work is drawn to the necessity of informing Passengers holding Through Tickets at what station, if any, they must change, and thus obviate the risk of their being over-carried in the event of not hearing the change called.

Conveyance of Dogs by Railway.

Dogs must be carried in the Guard's Van and securely chained.

When Dogs are making long journeys or are detained at Stations waiting a forward connection they must be supplied with water, and food if necessary. Which can be bought and the charge debited to the consignee.

Statement of Special Bookings.

Station Masters must send to the General Managers office a return of all special bookings by first possible train upon the day on which such bookings take place. In cases where similar bookings were in force in the preceding year similar information for that year must also be shewn on the return.

Time Tables and Bills.

In order to facilitate reference to the trains at each station, Station Masters are instructed to rule a line in red ink under the name of their station, in all the sheet time tables exhibited thereat, carrying the line across the table under the times of the trains shewn in each column ; taking care that this is done every time the bills are renewed.

Station Masters are to check the times shown against their stations in Foreign Time-Tables, reporting any inaccuracy.

The Time Bill Boards must be cleaned and old Bills carefully removed immediately their contents become obsolete. If Time Bills become soiled or torn they must be promptly renewed.

The attention of Station Masters is particularly directed to the careful and orderly arrangement of all Bills and Notices posted at their stations. As far as is possible they must only be affixed on the Boards provided for the purpose, and not upon the Walls or Windows.

The manner in which Time Bills and other Notices are exhibited at the Stations will be taken into account when the awards are made for the best kept Stations.

The Station Masters attention must be directed to any non-observance of these instructions. Due prominence must in all cases be given to the Company's own Bills and Notices.

Bills and other announcements sent to stations for distribution are to be delivered, immediately on receipt, to Hotels, Inns, Shops, Warehouses, Institutions, and other places where they will most readily come under the Notice of the public.

No bills or announcements made by the public, or other Railway Companies must be exhibited at stations unless they bear the stamp of the General Manager's Office.

Train Alteration Slips.

The monthly Public Slips of Train Alterations must be exhibited as close to the Sheet Time Tables as possible, the Slips for the previous month being removed. Station Masters must give this their personal attention.

25

Warning to be given before moving Wagons, and by Porters Wheeling Barrows on Platforms.

Enginemen must give notice to persons removing goods into or out of Trucks, and to men engaged in repairing Wagons, by whistling once before moving Wagons that are standing in Sidings, or which may be under repair, and Shunters and others before giving the Signal to the Enginemen to move such Wagons *must always walk the whole length of the wagons and must personally caution each individual who is engaged as described, and advise him at what time it will be safe to resume his work.*

Porters and others Wheeling Barrows or moving Articles of Luggage must take precautions to avoid injuring Passengers on Platforms.

Station Masters are required to see that these regulations are strictly observed by the Staff.

Instructions to be observed in connection with the Repairing or Lifting of Carriages, Wagons, or other Vehicles.

Carriages, wagons, or other vehicles must, in all cases where practicable, be repaired or lifted on lines set apart for the purpose.

Men engaged in repairing or lifting a vehicle on any line or siding, except the Repairing Shop sidings, must, before commencing such work, advise the foreman or other person in charge of the shunting operations, what they are about to do. They must also conspicuously exhibit a Red Flag on each side of the vehicle to be repaired or lifted, and the wheels of the vehicle in the front and of the vehicle in the rear of the defective vehicle must be spragged or securely scotched, or the brakes must be pinned tightly down, to prevent the vehicles from moving while the repairs are being proceeded with.

When the repairs have been completed, all scotches and sprags must be cleared away and the brakes liberated, and then the Red Flags must be removed.

Trains entering Stations on the Wrong Road.

In all cases where it is necessary to bring a train into the station on the wrong road for the purpose of crossing other trains, such train must be brought to a dead stop at the inner Home Signal. The Signalman, or Signal Porter, must stand at the facing points and see that they are properly set for the road on which the train is to be run. After satisfying himself on this point he must signal the train on by hand

Cleanliness, Smartness, and Civility.

Station Masters are requested to give special and constant attention to Rules 4, 5, and 92, requiring them to see that persons under their charge are clean, smart, and civil and that the Station premises are kept neat and clean. Water-closets and Urinals must be well cleansed and ventilated daily, and supplied with disinfectants.

Carriage Keys.

Station Masters must see that all members of their Staff who have to deal with Passenger trains are supplied with Carriage Keys, and that they carry them in their possession whilst on duty.

Sanding Rails in Slippery Weather.

Every assistance must in this respect be rendered to the Enginemen by the various servants at the roadside Stations and Junctions in wet weather, or when from any other cause the rails are likely to be slippery. Sand must not be used when passing over Locking Bars, Points, &c.

Passenger Fares Boards.

Station Masters must see that the Fares Boards exhibited at Passenger Stations shew the correct fares, and that new fares are inserted immediately on coming into operation. Where fares have to be *altered*, the

---

24

Parcels and Milk traffic.

Guards must check off in their vans all parcels entered on Way Bills, stamping all Way Bills which pass through their hands, with the Rubber Stamp supplied for that purpose. They must note upon the Way Bills, and in their Memorandum Book any deficiency or other irregularity, and report the same at the next stopping Station in order that enquiry may be made.

When receiving Parcels at Junction Stations accompanied by Through Way Bills, the Guards must in all cases, point out to the Staff at the Junction any deficiency or other irregularity.

A record must be kept of all value Parcels received without a Way Bill, and a receipt obtained for the former when handed over.

Way Bills should always accompany milk and parcels.

Sample bags of Corn and other similar traffic must be so loaded in the vans as to keep them free of fish water or other objectionable matter.

Cases have occured of Milk Cans being loaded up, in the *same van* as Boxes of Fish, and in some cases of the Fish Boxes being placed on the top of Cans. It must be distinctly understood that in no case are Milk Cans (full or empty) to be loaded in the same van as fish or any other commodity likely by their character to effect it injuriously nor are articles of any kind to be placed on the lids of Milk Cans. Guards will be held responsible in seeing that this order is carried out and Station Masters must report any cases of this character which may occur. Station Masters at Stations where carriages are cleaned must see that the Vans are thoroughly washed out and disinfected periodically.

Booking to Distant Places.

When application is made late in the day for Through Tickets to Stations on other companies Lines, with which there is no direct communication until after midnight, the Passenger must invariably be informed that he cannot reach his journey's end until the following day.

Trespassing on the Line.

Attention has frequently been called to which trespassing on the Line is practised by the public and permitted by the employees of the Company. In order to avoid accidents and to maintain the right of the Company it is imperative that Station Masters and all other members of the Staff should do everything in their power to stop this irregularity. Trespassers should be warned that they are committing a breach of the Company's Bye-Laws, and that if their trespass is repeated their names and addresses will be required, and that they render themselves liable to prosecution. All concerned must keep a record of the date and time of such warning, with the names and addresses of the trespassers, and if the trespass is repeated, particulars must be reported, in order that legal proceedings may be instituted.

The Directors have sanctioned the issue of a limited number of permits for persons under special circumstances to walk on certain specified sections of the Line, and as every such case permits have been issued to these parties; and only those holding these permits have permission to walk the Line. All trespassers who do not produce such permits must be reported as instructed above.

If the employees of the Company permit unauthorised persons to trespass, they will be severely dealt with.

Missing Parts of Rolling Stock

Parts of Rolling Stock, such as Screw Shackles, Buffer Plungers, and parts of Brake-work, are frequently missing, and are not sent to the Works when found. The Station Staff and Platelayers are requested to keep a lookout for such articles, and when found they must be sent into the Halstead Shops at once properly addressed, and labelled with the name of the forwarding station.

correction must be neatly done, and when necessary, a piece of paper should be pasted over the old fare, so that the correct fares to every station where bookings are in operation, may by readily ascertained by the public.

Cleaning and Trimming Lamps.

Special attention must be given to the cleaning and trimming of Carriage and other Lamps.

Guards must report in every case where the Lamps in their Trains are not in proper order.

Stamped Newspaper Parcels.

Parcels which do not bear stamps of the proper value must be dealt with in accordance with the Company's Regulations, viz:—To charge the difference between the amount represented by labels and full ordinary parcels rate.

Cancelling Newspaper Stamps.

The sending Station must effectually deface the stamp or label by crossing it with a red chalk pencil or red ink. The receiving Station must also see that this is done. The newsagents' messengers and others must not be allowed to place parcels in Guards' vans. They must in all cases be handed in at the parcels office and the stamps or labels defaced. Guards must examine stamps of parcels in their vans, and cancel any which have not been defaced, reporting specially all such cases.

Station Platforms.

Particular attention is called to the necessity of keeping the Station Platforms clean, and Station Masters are hereby reminded that this is a duty devolving on the Station Staff.

Rubbish must not be swept from the Platforms on to the Permanent Way, but placed on the dust heaps.

Careless Shunting.

Shunters, and other servants of the Company, whose duties are connected with the arranging and sorting of wagons, are cautioned to exercise every care in shunting. Station Masters and Foremen must give the matter their strict attention, and report all cases where carelessness in this respect has been exhibited on the part of the men, in order that they may be suitably dealt with. The effect of rough shunting wagons loaded with timber may be such as to lead to a serious accident in running.

Station Masters, Foremen, and others concerned, are requested to see, when it is necessary to connect carriages together for shunting purposes, that the screw-coupling is invariably used.

Releasing Brakes when Shunting.

Guards, Shunters, and others, must see that the brakes of Carriages, Wagons, &c., are released before being shunted.

Station Masters and Foremen must give this special attention.

Shunting Poles.

Each Station at which Goods Shunting is done must keep on hand a supply of Shunting Poles, which can be obtained from the Stores Department. When any Pole becomes worn out, or breaks, the iron hook must be taken off and placed on the new Pole issued from the Station Stores.

Each Brakesman is required to have his Shunting Pole with him, and to use it on all occasions when coupling or uncoupling wagons. Should it be necessary under exceptional circumstances for him to go between the buffers of wagons, he must be careful not to do so unless the vehicles are at a standstill.

Shunters are warned against riding upon their Brake Sticks or shunting Poles whilst braking wagons during shunting operations, as this is a very objectionable and dangerous practice.

It must be understood that Shunting Poles are not to be used as Brake Sticks or for any other purpose than that for which they are intended.

The Shunting Poles and hooks supplied by the Colne Valley Company must not be exchanged by the men for those supplied by other Companies.

Shunting over Points worked from Elevated Boxes.

When a train is shunting over points situated some distance from the signal cabin, the Guard or Shunter in charge of the shunting train must at all times give a hand signal to the Signalman when the train is clear of the points. Signalmen are warned against turning the points until they have received such Signal.

Cleaning and Oiling Points and Signals.

The duty of cleaning and oiling points devolves upon the Staff of the Traffic Department, unless otherwise specially arranged.

Line blocked with Snow.

Station Masters to arrange for Platelayers to be sent to clear the line.

Cattle Trucks by Passenger Trains.

Cattle Trucks must not be attached to Passenger Trains without special authority from the General Manager, and when this is obtained, the wagons should in all cases where practical, be passed by an Examiner as fit to travel by such trains.

They must under no circumstances be attached in front of the Passenger Vehicles on Passenger or Mixed Trains.

Maintenance of Weighing Machines.

Every Weighing Machine, on Goods Shed or Platform, Luggage Scale, Spring Balance or other description of Weighing Machine, or Scales, must be kept perfectly clean, and the steelyard or indicating plate must be kept bright, and when required, slightly oiled, that the figures and marks may be clean and legible.

Every week-day morning each Machine must be examined before being used, to see that it is in good working order, accurately balanced, and ready for use.

Every Machine which has a lever or other ungearing apparatus, must be kept out of gear, when not in use.

Loose weights belonging to Machines must be carefully preserved, and must not be used for any other than weighing purposes.

Messrs. H. Pooley & Son, of Birmingham, maintain the whole of the Weighing Machines.

Whenever a machine is broken or is in any way out of order, a written advice must at once be sent to the General Manager.

Each Machine bears a number, which must be quoted in all reports respecting the Machine.

Consumption of Coal, Gas, Water, Oil, and other Stores.

The attention of Station Masters is called to the necessity of personally attending to the consumption of Coal, Gas, Water, Oil, and other Stores, and of reporting immediately to the Engineer any leakages of Gas or Water mains or fittings. They must see that no unnecessary burners are lighted and that none are allowed to remain burning during the day in offices or signal boxes, &c. At Stations where Gas is used, the Gas lights on the platforms must be kept low, except for the necessary interval before the arrival or departure of a train, and turned down immediately there-

28

after. In the same manner at Stations which are lighted up with Oil, the lamps must be lighted only during the time at which light is necessary for the work connected with the trains, and every care must be taken to lessen the consumption of Gas and Oil in waiting rooms, urinals, yards and other parts of the Company's premises.

Covering of Gas and Water Meters in Frosty Weather.

During frosty weather, Gas and Water Meters should be covered over with old sacks, straw or sawdust to prevent their being frozen up. Station Masters should have material for this covering, ready to put on, about the middle of October each year.

Loading of Iron, Round Timber, &c.

Station Masters, Foremen, Loaders, Shunters, Guards, and others, are instructed that under no circumstances must long pieces of Iron, Round Timber, or other articles of unusual length, be despatched from stations unless securely bound with either ropes, chains, or iron bands.

Shunters and Guards must carefully examine loads of the description referred to at junctions or other places where the Train may stop, to see whether they have shifted or require adjustment in any way, and if so, the wagons must not be taken on until the loads have been made perfectly secure.

Working of Travelling and Stationary Cranes.

Careless working of the Company's Cranes. The special attention of the Staff concerned is called to Rules Nos. 109 and 188 in the Company's Book of Rules and Regulations, as well as to the following :—

Under no circumstances must the weight to be lifted exceed the registered carrying power painted on the Cranes.

Before lifting any weight, the jib must be raised to the proper working radius, and on no consideration must any weight be lifted with the jib in travelling position.

The lifting handles must, except when dealing with heavy weights, be taken off the shaft before lowering the load by the brake, and securely placed in the bracket for that purpose.

In dealing with the heavy weights, care must be taken not to lower them by the Crane Brake, but by the Lifting Handles.

Before working the Travelling Crane, the four clips affixed near the buffers must be properly fastened to the rails.

Guards Journals.

The attention of Guards is directed to Rule No. 192 of Rules and Regulations which must be strictly carried out.

All Journals must be sent to the General Managers Office not later than 10 a.m. on the day following the entries.

When Porters or others not regularly employed in working Trains are sent out in charge of a train, the Stations Masters from whose Station such men are sent must see that a journal is duly rendered.

The attention of Passenger and Goods Guards is called to the importance of explaining on their Journals every delay to trains fully and accurately, and thus avoid unnecessary correspondence.

In the case of delays waiting "Line Clear," the number of the train occupying the Section must be given. When delayed awaiting a connecting train (other Company's or Branch) the time of arrival of such train must be given.

If a connection is missed the time of departure of the nominal connecting train must be given and the number of passengers left behind, and how sent forward.

29

Any other information with a view to avoid enquiry should also be given.

When a Guard works a Passenger or Goods Train to a point short of its destination he must make out and sign his journal for that portion of the journey worked by him and hand same to the Guard who takes the train forward to be completed and despatched to the General Manager.

Guards of Passenger trains must insert on their Journals the number and owner of all Vehicles attached to their trains, showing where attached and detached, and how labelled.

Guards must especially record on their Journals whenever their trains are stopped at places other than those at which it is timed to stop.

Goods Guards' Vans with Stoves in them.

Goods Guards must make sure that the fire in the stove is entirely extinguished before leaving the Van.

Roadside Vans Loaded from other Companies' Lines to Colne Valley Line.

When practicable Goods Guards should look into the Road Side Vans received from other Companies Lines before taking them forward from the Junction in order to see that the Goods have not been roughly dealt with, and that there are no breakages or leakages apparent. If anything wrong is discovered, the attention of the other Company's Guard or some responsible person must be drawn to same at the time and a report sent to the General Manager.

Goods Trains Outside Station Limits to have Brake Van.

Without the special authority of the General Manager, no Goods train must be run on any Running Line beyond the limits of Stations unless there is a break van in the rear.

Where a train is authorised to run without a break van in the rear, a break van, or other suitable vehicle, for the use of the man in charge of such a train, must be so attached as to be conveniently used by him, and also with due regard to safety in working the train.

A Tail Signal must be carried on the last vehicle.

Trainmen.

Firemen of passenger trains must couple their Engines to and uncouple them from the trains, and are to be held responsible for properly coupling up the Westinghouse brake and other connections.

Enginemen and Guards must see that this is properly done and report any neglect.

Enginemen must whistle when approaching level crossings to warn persons using the same, and must approach cautiously, and keep a sharp look out for Signals or any obstruction upon the crossing.

The movement of vehicles by means of a prop or pole, or by towing with a rope or chain attached to a locomotive or vehicle moving on an adjacent line, is prohibited.

Wagon axle guards are bent and other damage is caused by Sprags being unnecessarily used to stop the wagons during shunting operations, or to secure them when they have been shunted, instead of the wagon brakes being applied for the purpose. Guards, Shunters, and others concerned must take care that Sprags are not so used, in order that the damage complained of may be avoided.

Guards must not attach to their train any loaded wagon unless it is labelled or directed on both sides, nor any empty wagon which requires to be labelled or directed, unless such wagon is labelled or directed on both sides.

In addition to the articles to be carried by Goods Guards in their Vans, as laid down in Rule No. 164, a set of Wagon Links must also be carried, which can be obtained from the Carriage and Wagon Department, Halstead.

Any Guard having occasion to make use of these Links will give full particulars of the case on his Journal, and also report same, so that arrangements may be made for the Links to be replaced.

Overcrowding of Live Stock.

Station Masters, Inspectors, Guards, and all other Servants of the Company are requested to prevent overcrowding in trucks, and to report any cases which come under their notice.

Foreign Ropes and Chains.

Station Masters and others are requested to see that all Foreign Ropes and Chains received, securing Traffic on Wagons, are returned to the Sending Station with as little delay as possible.

Securing Wagon Doors.

The attention of all concerned is drawn to the necessity of properly securing the doors of all wagons, including cattle wagons, with the pins provided for the purpose. In all cases the doors of Wagons whether loaded or empty, must be properly secured on both sides.

Sheets.

Folding of Sheets.—Station Masters will be held responsible for seeing that all Sheets arriving, or on hand at their Stations, are carefully folded and laid aside when not in actual use.

All concerned must see that this instruction is strictly adhered to, and the sheets, after being folded, must be kept on hand until application is made for them, or instructions received from the General Manager as to disposal.

Damaged Sheets.—All Damaged Sheets must at once be returned to the Stores Department, Halstead, properly labelled and accompanied by an invoice, or waybill.

Damaged Wagons.

In the event of Draw-bars breaking, or being pulled out from Wagons, or of Coupling Chains, Hooks, Shackles, &c., breaking (whether the Wagons be the Company's, Foreign, or Private), the Draw-bars, Chains, Brake-work, &c., must in all cases, be placed inside the Wagons, so as to be returned home with the vehicles to which they belong, and the circumstances, with the number and owner of the vehicles, and other particulars, duly recorded in the Goods Guards Journal for reference.

In the case of Foreign Company's Wagons, the Station Master at whose Station a Wagon is put off for repairs, must advise the General Manager time and date when stopped and sent forward, so that exemption from demurrage charges may be claimed in accordance with Railway Clearing House Regulations.

Derailment of Rolling Stock.

In all cases where Rolling Stock is derailed it must not be sent forward until it has been certified by a representative of the Carriage and Wagon Department as fit to travel. At places where no examiner is stationed the nearest one must be sent for.

The Windows of all Carriages, Vans and Horse Boxes, must be closed when not in use.

Carriages are not to run or stand spare with the Covers of Roof Lamp Apertures open. The Covers must be kept closed, and when the Lamps are taken out the Blocks must be inserted. Lampmen, Cleaners, and Guards, must give strict attention to this, and report when the Catches of Covers are out of order.

GUARDS must be careful to see that Empty Carriages are not run with the Windows down, and must see to this at intermediate stations, and in every case when any Carriage or Compartment of a Carriage is empty, to at once put up the Windows. Guards of Passenger Trains must put up the Windows of their Vans before leaving them at destination.

Train stopping Short of Water Columns, &c.

When Drivers of Passenger or Mixed trains have once stopped at platforms, they must not again move their Engines for any purpose unless uncoupled from the train, until they get a signal to do so, all cases where this instruction is infringed must be reported on the Guard's Journal.

Emission of Smoke from Engines.

Complaints have been made of smoke being emitted from Engines when running into or standing at Stations causing considerable annoyance to passengers and others in the vicinity. The special attention of Enginemen is called to the necessity of their preventing occasion for complaint.

Working of Engines near Banks of Grass or Fields of Standing Corn, Plantations, &c.

During dry weather the Enginemen must work their Engines with extra care over portions of the line where there is special danger of setting fire to grass, trees, or standing corn.

Ventilating Carriages.

Station Masters, Foremen, Carriage Cleaners, and others, must in all cases see that the Ventilators of all Coaches standing at their respective Stations are opened and allowed to remain so.

Carriage Labels.

Carriages are frequently disfigured by the careless manner in which paper labels, after having been affixed to the quarter lights to indicate "Smoking," "Engaged," or the destination or the vehicle, are removed. Porters and others engaged in cleaning the carriages must take care that the windows are properly cleaned after the removal of the labels.

Correspondence by Train.

Letters conveyed by train must not be placed under the strings or straps of Portmanteaus, parcels or other packages, but must in all cases be handed by the Parcel Porter at the sending Station to the Guard, and by him delivered to the properly appointed person at the transfer Station or destination.

Lighting of Roof Lamps in Ordinary and Special Trains.

Station Masters must see that all Ordinary and Special trains which require lighting on outward or return journey are supplied with Trimmed Roof Lamps before leaving the Starting Station, and must arrange as to their being lighted up at the point required.

Goods Brakes not Supplied with Required Articles.

Special attention is drawn to Rule No. 164. Every Goods Guard is required to see that this Van is properly equipped.

Station Masters must periodically examine the Goods Brakes and report any case of non-compliance with this rule.

Timber Wagons.

Attention is called to the serious risk of accident arising from the omission to secure chains on empty Timber Wagons, whereby the chains are liable to drag along the line and the hooks may become entangled in point-rods, &c.

Chains must in all cases be twisted round the stanchions, and properly secured before the trucks are despatched, and Station Masters, Foremen, Guards, and others concerned must see that this is strictly carried out. Examiners at Foreign Junctions must see that the chains on returned empty wagons, and on such wagons when acting as check trucks, are properly secured when handed over to the Company.

The floors of Timber Wagons must be cleaned of all refuse before being loaded, and the Bolsters and Chains must not be removed from the Wagons.

Live Stock Traffic Received for Conveyance on Saturdays.

Before accepting Live Stock Traffic for conveyance on Saturdays, Station Masters or others concerned must first ascertain whether or not there is a service by which the Traffic can get through to destination before Monday, otherwise feeding and other charges may be incurred.

Scotch Blocks and Safety Points.

At Stations where Safety Points are provided, care must be taken that they are always in order and properly set to secure safety. Station Masters must see that all the Siding Scotches are in good and sound condition; and Brakesmen and others concerned must exercise the greatest care in the securing of Wagons in Sidings by means of Fixed Scotches, so as to prevent their being blown out, or otherwise passing on to the Main Line, or running foul thereof.

Private Wagons.

Every effort must be made to prevent the detention of Private Wagons at Stations. They must be shunted as quickly as possible into the position required by Coal Merchants and others, and removed and worked away from the Station as soon as possible after being unloaded or loaded.

Wagon Labels.

In cases where Wagons are provided with Clips for holding the Labels, the Labels must be placed under them, and not be tacked on to the Wagons.

CLEANSING OF EMPTY WAGONS.

With a view of preventing Wagons taking fire, the attention of all concerned is directed to the following instructions:—

"All Railway Companies' Trucks after unloading, must be properly swept out, or otherwise cleansed, as may be necessary. All Trucks (whether Railway Companies' or Private Owners, must, after unloading, be cleared of ignitable matter."

SNOW AND FROST.

Wheels and Couplings of Carriages and Wagons.—Special care must be taken by the carriage and wagon examiners to sound the tyres and examine the wheels and couplings of rolling stock during severe frost.

Signals and Points.—Constant attention must be given to the working of Signals, and Points, during snow and severe frost. The machinery must be kept clear of snow and ice, and in thorough working order. When from any temporary defect, a signal is not working correctly, notice must be given by telegraph to the next station or signal box in the rear to inform engine drivers and guards.

Gas and Water Meters must, during severe frost, be well looked to and protected.

Water Cranes, &c.—Special attention must be given to keep these in proper working condition. Fires must be kept up near water-cranes during frost.

Clearing Snow from Station Platforms, Approaches, &c.—Snow must be thoroughly and promptly cleared from Station Platforms, Approaches, Foot-crossings, Staircases, steps, &c., and when necessary, ashes and sand must be sprinkled upon same. The snow so cleared must be removed out of the way, and where it will dissolve with least harm.

Clearing Snow from Carriages and other Vehicles.—Snow must be carefully swept off the roofs, sides, ends, steps, and window frames of carriages, guards' vans, and other vehicles, with as little delay as possible, before it becomes caked and hardened by frost; and this must be done at any station where the opportunity is afforded, as much damage is occasioned to the stock through snow remaining upon it until a thaw takes place. Snow must also be promptly swept out of wagons, and other goods vehicles.

ADVERTISING ON THE RAILWAY.

Messrs. Smith & Sons possess, under certain restrictions, the privilege of placing advertisements on Company's retaining and other walls, fences, under bridges and over bridges, outside and contiguous to stations as well as at stations. If any objectionable advertisement or any announcement in opposition to the interests of this Company is exhibited, or if any notice is placed in an objectionable position, particulars must be sent to the General Manager.

THE LAST VEHICLE ON EVERY TRAIN TO CARRY A TAIL LAMP BY DAY AS WELL AS BY NIGHT.

Referring to Rule 126 of the Book of Rules and Regulations, as to a Tail Lamp being carried on the last vehicle of every train by day as well as by night.

This Lamp must be provided at the Terminal starting Station, and must at all times be properly cleaned and trimmed, so as to be available for lighting when required. The Guard in charge of the train will be responsible for seeing that the Lamp is placed on the hook provided for the purpose before starting from the Terminal Station, and, when vehicles are attached or detached on the journey, that the Lamp is replaced in its proper position on the last vehicle before the train starts again.

NOTE.—The attention of Guards and Enginemen is called to the second paragraph of Clause 20 of the Block Telegraph Regulations.

RED TAIL SIGNAL NOTICE OF THE RUNNING OF SPECIAL TRAINS.—TAIL BOARD BY DAY.—EXTRA TAIL LAMP BY NIGHT.

Every Passenger and Goods Brake Van is to be provided with a Red Tail Board, which is to be used by day for the purpose of Signalling to all concerned "a Special Train to follow",—an extra Red Tail Light being used for the same purpose by night.

When a Special Train is required to be run the Station Master or other in charge of the Station from which, the Special is to start will be responsible for seeing that one of these Tail boards by day, or if by night then an extra Red Light, is attached to the last Vehicle of the next preceding Ordinary or Special Train.

The Guard will be responsible for seeing that the Tail Board by day, or extra Tail Light by night, is under all circumstances, exhibited on the last Vehicle of the Train during its journey, and that it is removed at the proper Station and replaced in his Brake Van.

35

It will be necessary for a register of such accidents (as provided by the Home Office) to be kept at each Station, and all accidents must be entered therein within seven days of the occurrence, and the registers must be open at all times to the inspection of the Factory Inspector and Certifying Surgeon of the district.

REPORTING ACCIDENTS.

The person in charge of the Station nearest to which an accident occurs must immediately telegraph the fullest particulars available to the General Manager and Engineer, and say what steps he is taking to clear the Line, he should also promptly send a full report in writing to the General Manager.

All accidents, whether to Goods or Passenger trains, or during shunting operations, must be reported as above; also any personal injury, whether to Company's Servants or the Public.

This instruction does not set aside the requirements of Rule No. 115 in the Company's Book of Rules and Regulations which must in all cases be observed.

ELYOT S. HAWKINS,

Secretary and General Manager.

December, 1904.

34

Any Guard failing to replace the Tail Board in his Brake Van after it is done with will be strictly dealt with.

These Tail Boards are to be cleaned as often as required, at the Stations where the washing of Carriage Stock is performed by the Coaching Department.

LIVE STOCK TO AND FROM SHOWS.

Men *bonâ fide* in charge of Live stock travelling to and from Shows are conveyed Free in the same Train as the animals as follows:—

One man for each consignment, except when the consignment requires more than one vehicle, when one man for each vehicle may be sent free, but no Pass is given unless the charge for the Consignment amounts to as much as the charge for one horse.

When two or three Horses forming one consignment are sent in the same Horse Box, and a man is required to travel with each animal, the men may be conveyed free, provided each Horse is charged at the Single Horse Rate.

For men in charge of Horses or other Live Stock forwarded by Passenger Train no seperate Pass is issued; the only form of Pass is the endorsement of the Station Clerk written across the Horse Ticket, which must be delivered up on the arrival of the animals at their destination.

PARCELS POST BASKETS.

The Post office authorities having requested that Baskets containing parcels may be so handled and placed that the Lids of the Baskets may always be uppermost, the Staff are requested in all cases of transfer of the Baskets between Road Vehicles and the Railway Vans, and in transhipment from one train to another, to use every care in the handling of the Baskets and to keep the Lids uppermost.

PREVENTING FIRE AT STATIONS DURING THE NIGHT.

The special attention of Station Masters and others is directed to the importance of carefully inspecting all the Rooms and Offices before closing the Station for the night. The person in charge of the Station at the time of closing will be held responsible for locking up the Rooms and satisfying himself that the fires and lights are extinguished.

At Stations where Fire Pails and other appliances for extinguishing Fire are provided, Station Masters must take care that the Pails are kept full of water, and that the man left in charge of the Station is fully acquainted with the water supply, and with the position and working of any appliances provided for extinguishing Fire. The Fire Pails must not be used for any purpose except for the extinguishing of Fire.

HOUNDS ON LINE.

Whenever an Engineman sees that Hounds are on the Line, or appear likely to be coming on, he must immediately shut off steam and be prepared to stop, so has to avoid the slightest risk of accident either to the Huntsmen or Hounds.

Enginemen must specially report every case where such slackening or stopping has occurred.

ACCIDENTS TO COMPANY'S SERVANTS AND OTHER PERSONS IN THE COMPANY'S GOODS SHEDS AND WAREHOUSES.

With reference to the Home Office Circular (No. 710) dated December, 1901, in the event of an accident occuring to a Servant of the Company, or any other Person, in the Goods Sheds, or Warehouses belonging to this Company, a report of the circumstances must be sent immediately to the General Manager.

Bibliography

GENERAL WORKS
Aldrich, C.L., *GER Locomotives*
Allen, C.J., *The Great Eastern Railway*, Ian Allan
Gordon, D.I., *Regional History of the Railways of Great Britain Volume 5*, David & Charles
RCTS, *Locomotives of the L&NER*
Whitehead, R.A. & F.D. Simpson, *The Colne Valley & Halstead Railway*, Francis Ridgway Ltd
Willingham, E., *From Construction to Destruction: An Authentic History of the Colne Valley and Halstead Railway*, Halstead & District Local History Society

PERIODICALS
Bradshaw's Railway Guide
Bradshaw's Railway Manual
British Railways (Eastern Region) Magazine
Buses Illustrated
East Anglian Magazine
Essex Countryside
Great Eastern Railway Magazine
Herepath's Railway Journal
Locomotive, Carriage & Wagon Review
Locomotive Magazine
L&NER Magazine
Railway Magazine
Railway Times
Railway World
Railway Year Book
Trains Illustrated

NEWSPAPERS
Chelmsford Chronicle
Essex Chronicle
Halstead Gazette
Halstead Times

OTHER SOURCES
Minute Books of the Colne Valley & Halstead Railway
Minute Books of the Eastern Counties Railway
Minute Books of the Great Eastern Railway
Minute Books of the London & North Eastern Railway
Minute Books of the London & North Western Railway
Public Timetables
    CV&HR, GER, L&NER, BR (ER)
Working Timetables
    CV&HR, GER, L&NER and BR (ER)
Appendices to the Working Timetables
    CV&HR, GER, L&NER, BR (ER)
Miscellaneous Operating Instructions
    CV&HR, GER, L&NER, BR (ER)

Acknowledgements

The publication of this history would not have been possible without the assistance of many people. In particular I would like to thank:

The late A.R. Cox
The late W. Fenton
The late W. Blois
The late G. Woodcock
The late Dr I.C. Allen
The late Bernard Walsh
The late Canon Charles Bayes
The late Geoff Pember

The late Peter Proud
The late R.C. (Dick) Riley
The late R.H.N. (Dick) Hardy
The late Ted Vaughan
The late Ken Riley
The late Jim Bosley
John Watling
Dave Hoser

John Petrie
Peter Webber
The late H.C. Casserley
The late R.M. Casserley
The late M. Brooks
The late F. Hennessey
The late S. Orrin
The late K. Townend

The late Les Wood
The late G.R. Mortimer
Doug Stephenson
The late P. Townend
Chris Cock for signalling
    matters
The late M. Back
Robert Powell

Special thanks to Malcolm Root, a native of Halstead and a lifelong enthusiast of anything CV&HR, who has kindly allowed me access to his photographic portfolio of the system. As a Fellow of the Group of Railway Artists his interest has resulted in many paintings depicting the railway through various decades, and these are produced in this volume to allow the reader to wallow in nostalgia.

Also thanks to staff of the former Cambridge, Colchester and Stratford motive power depots, Cambridge and Ipswich wagon repair depots and many other staff of the Cambridge and Ipswich districts, some of whom worked on the Colne Valley line.

Grateful thanks are also due to staff the National Archives, British Railways Eastern Region, British Museum Newspaper Library, House of Lords Record Office, Cambridge County Record Office, Essex County Record Office, Suffolk County Record Office and many members of the Great Eastern Railway Society.

Index

absorption of the CV&HR:
    by the GER   30, 35, 37, 70, 71
    by the L&NER   73 *et seq*
accidents and incidents   14, 22, 23, 27, 29, 30,
    31, 33, 34, 38, 39, 40, 41, 43, 50, 52, 57,
    66, 67, 68, 69, 70, 72, 74, 75, 84, 85, 88
Acts of Parliament   12, 15, 22, 29, 31, 46 *et
    seq*, 56
agreement L&NER with the Postmaster
    General   75

Bedford & Cambridge Railway   20
Birdbrook   156-61
Board of Trade inspections   16, 17, 21, 23, 24,
    27, 28, 31, 39, 43, 51, 52, 53, 54, 55, 61,
    63, 71, 79
bomb dumps   81
Braintree   11 *et seq*
breakdown arrangements   267
Brewster, James   13
brickworks development   55, 139-40
bridge reconstruction   51 *et seq*, 67 *et seq*,
    182 *et seq*
bridges and culverts   287-9
British Railways Eastern Region   85 *et seq*
Bury St Edmunds   15 *et seq*
bus services, competitive   78, 84

Census figures population   209
Chappel   14 *et seq*, 23 *et seq*, 104-8
Chappel Junction   108

closures:
    freight traffic   98
    passenger traffic   92 *et seq*
coach connection, Haverhill to Cambridge   30
coaching stock:
    CV&HR   10 *et seq*, 18 *et seq*, 269 *et seq*
    GER   273-6
Colne station, closure   50
Colne Valley Junction   162-3
Colne Valley Viaduct   11
cutting of first sod   18

diesel electric locomotives:
    BTHI AEI 800 hp Class '15'   264
    NBL Bo-Bo Class '21'   265
diesel multiple units:
    BR/Derby lightweight   262
    Craven   263
diesel railbuses   260-62
disposal of land and property   100

Earls Colne   116-23
Eastern Counties Railway   9 *et seq*, 21 *et seq*,
    26
Eastern Union Railway   9 *et seq*
Elsenham & Thaxted Light Railway   63
engine and men's diagrams   266
engine headcodes   265
engine loads (summary)   239-40
engine sheds:
    Halstead   233

    Haverhill   166
Engineer's report to directors   20
excursion traffic   85 *et seq*, 231, 232

fares   230-31
financial dispute   44, 46-8
flooding of the railway   23, 34
footbridge, Halstead   36 *et seq*
footplate staff   51
Ford Gate station   43
freight train loading   240

Gooch, Sir Daniel   31 *et seq*
goods facilities (summary)   237-8
goods traffic   232-7
Government control of the railways   69,
    80
gradient diagram   101
Great Eastern Railway   26 *et seq*
Grouping of the railways   71 *et seq*

Halstead   126-38
Halstead station   23
Haverhill, Colne Valley   162-7
Haverhill, GER   168-76
Hawkins, Elyot S.   62 *et seq*
headcodes, engine   265

industrial action   71, 89
inspection of CV&HR by GER   35, 57, 65
Ipswich & Bury St Edmunds Railway   9 *et seq*

LMR 2MT 2-6-0 No. 46465 is shown soon after departing from Chappel and Wakes Colne, passing Acorn Wood with the 12.15pm train to Haverhill on Easter Monday 14th April 1952.
G.R. Mortimer

Langley Mill crossing   124-5
level crossings   285-6
Light Railways Act 1896   56
Light Railway Order:
    Bardfield and Sible Hedingham   60 *et seq*
    Central Essex   64
locomotives:
    Brewster 2-4-0WT   243
    Cornwall Mineral Railway 0-6-0T   40, 243
    ECR 0-6-0 tender   254
    ECR 2-4-0 tender   242
    Ex-LB&SCR 2-2-2WT   19
    George England 2-4-0T   241-2
    GER 'E22'/L&NER '165' 0-6-0T   254
    GER 'E72'/L&NER '119' 0-6-0   259
    GER 'G58'/L&NER '117' 0-6-0   258
    GER 'K9' 0-4-2T   252-3
    GER 'M15'/L&NER 'F4' 2-4-2T   253
    GER 'T7' 0-4-2T   252
    GER 'T26'/L&NER 'E4' 2-4-0   256
    GER 'Y14'/L&NER 'J15' 0-6-0   256-8
    GER 'Y65'/ L&NER 'F7' 2-4-2T   255
    Hawthorn, Leslie 2-4-2T   246-9
    Hudswell, Clarke 0-6-2T   250-52
    LMR '2MT' 2-6-0   88, 259-60
    L&NWR   22, 242
    Neilson 0-4-2T No. 1   244-5
    North London Railway 0-4-2ST   246
London & North Eastern Railway   71 *et seq*
London & North Western Railway, borrowed
    locomotive   22

Maldon, Witham & Braintree Railway   10
Marks Tey   18, 23, 27, 102-3

military traffic:
    World War One   69 *et seq*
    World War Two   81 *et seq*
motive power staff   51
Munro, William, contractor   14 *et seq*

Nationalisation   85 *et seq*
Northern & Eastern Railway   9

opening of the railway:
    Chappel to Halstead   16
    Halstead to Hedingham   21
    Hedingham to Yeldham   24
    Yeldham to Haverhill CV   29
    Colne Valley Junction to Haverhill GER   32

Parsonage Lane level crossing   125
permanent way   177 *et seq*
    maintenance by motor trolley   184
    staff   184
point to point timings:
    freight trains   239
    passenger trains   222
population figures   209

rail tour trains   89, 90, 92
railway officers   203-4
Railways Act 1921   71, 73
rolling stock returns   27 *et seq*
route availability of locomotives   241

signal box opening and closing times   199-200
signal boxes:
    Birdbrook   195-6

Chappel   187
Colne Valley Junction   196
Earls Colne   190
Halstead   191
Haverhill Junction   197-8
Sible and Castle Hedingham   192-3
Yeldham   194-5
signalling   39, 184 *et seq*
special instructions   198 *et seq*
speed limits   169
spite wall, Halstead   59
station masters   204-6
station receipts   76
strikes   71, 89
Sudbury & Clare Railway   18, 22

telegraph   37
timetables, working and public   209-29
traffic staff   206-9
Train Staff and Ticket working of single
    lines   186

wagon maintenance   293
wagons   277 *et seq*
water supplies, locomotives   267
whistle codes, locomotive   26
White Colne   110-16
working arrangement with Sir Daniel
    Gooch   32
working and public timetables   209-29
World War One   69 *et seq*
World War Two   80 *et seq*

Yeldham   150-55

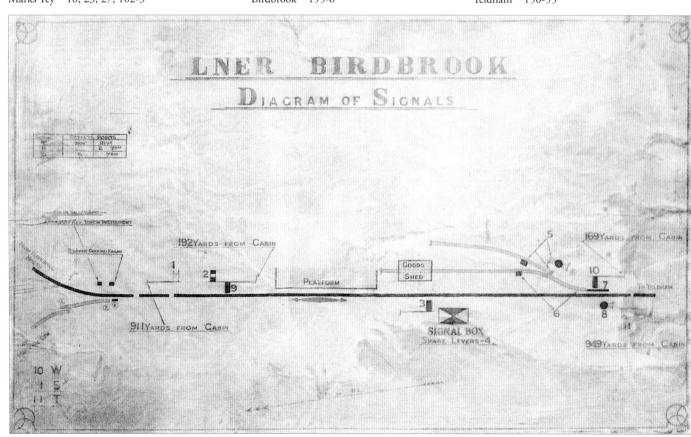